VBScript
Programmer's Reference
Third Edition

(Continued)

VBScript
Programmer's Reference
Third Edition

Adrian Kingsley-Hughes

Kathie Kingsley-Hughes

Daniel Read

Wiley Publishing, Inc.

VBScript Programmer's Reference, Third Edition

Published by
Wiley Publishing, Inc.
10475 Crosspoint Boulevard
Indianapolis, IN 46256
www.wiley.com

Published simultaneously in Canada

ISBN: 978-0-470-16808-0

Manufactured in the United States of America

10 9 8 7 6 5 4 3 2

Library of Congress Cataloging-in-Publication Data

Kingsley-Hughes, Adrian.
 VBScript programmer's reference / Adrian Kingsley-Hughes, Kathie Kingsley-Hughes, Daniel Read.
   p. cm.
 Includes index.
 ISBN 978-0-470-16808-0 (paper/website)
 1. VBScript (Computer program language) 2. HTML (Document markup language) 3. World Wide Web.
I. Kingsley-Hughes, Kathie. II. Read, Daniel, 1969– III. Title. IV. Title: VB Script programmer's reference.
 QA76.73.V27K56 2007
 005.2' 762—dc22

2007028895

About the Authors

Adrian Kingsley-Hughes has made his living as a technology writer for over a decade, with many books and articles to his name. He can also be found teaching classes on the Web, where he has successfully taught technology skills to thousands of learners, with his own special brand of knowledge, experience, wit, and poor spelling. He is also editor of the ZDNet blog Hardware 2.0 (`http://blogs.zdnet.com/hardware`).

Kathie Kingsley-Hughes has worked in IT training for many years. In addition to writing, she now works as a courseware developer and e-trainer, specializing in Internet technologies. She also runs a web development company in the United Kingdom.

Daniel Read is a software developer living and working in Atlanta, GA, USA. He currently works for Connecture Inc., an Atlanta-based software consulting firm specializing in the insurance industry. Daniel also publishes and writes essays for developers at `DeveloperDotStar.com`, a web-based magazine for software professionals.

Credits

Acquisitions Editor
Katie Mohr

Development Editor
Maureen Spears

Technical Editor
Andrew Moore

Copy Editor
Mildred Sanchez

Editorial Manager
Mary Beth Wakefield

Production Manager
Tim Tate

Vice President and Executive Group Publisher
Richard Swadley

Vice President and Executive Publisher
Joseph B. Wikert

Project Coordinator, Cover
Adrienne Martinez

Proofreader
Ian Golder

Indexer
Johnna VanHoose Dinse

Anniversary Logo Design
Richard Pacifico

Acknowledgments

Writing a book is hard work, and writing a third edition is even harder! The process involves a lot more people than just those listed on the cover (although thanks must got to Kathie and Dan for their hard work). My sincerest thanks goes out to everyone who made this book possible, from the initial idea of revamping this title for a second time to getting it onto the shelves.

—Adrian

Many thanks to family, friends, and colleagues, who have been very supportive during the writing of this book. A big thank you to all the editors, tech reviewers, and production staff who worked so hard on this edition.

—Kathie

I thank my fellow authors, Adrian and Kathie, and also the fine editorial staff at Wiley.

—Daniel

Contents

Contents

Contents

Contents

Contents

Contents

Contents

Contents

Contents

Introduction

Imagine having the ability to write code quickly and easily in a text editor without having to worry about complex development environments.

Imagine not having the hassles of compiling code or distributing complex set-up programs.

Imagine being able to deploy your code in a wide variety of ways.

Imagine learning one language that allows you to code for server-side Internet, client-side Internet, and desktop.

Stop imagining. VBScript gives you all this and much more.

VBScript is an absolutely superb language to be able to "speak" in. It's quick and easy to learn, powerful, flexible, and cheap. This makes it a winning language for both experienced programmers and those starting out in their programming careers. If you are an experienced programmer, you can enjoy writing code free from complex development environments and the need for compiling. On the other hand, if you are a beginner, you can get started programming, needing nothing more than a little knowledge and a text editor.

Knowledge and experience in VBScript can open many technology doors, too. Having a good grounding in VBScript can lead you into areas such as Internet development, network administration, server-side coding, and even other programming languages (Visual Basic being the most popular route to take because the languages are so similar in syntax). With VBScript, you can also create applications that look and feel like programs written using complex programming languages, such as C++. Also worth bearing in mind is that support for scripting is now embedded into every installation of the newer Windows operating systems — a dormant power that you can tap into with VBScript know-how. By writing some simple script in a text editor, you can do a variety of tasks, such as copy and move files, create folders and files, modify the Windows registry, and lots more. One easy-to-use scripting language can do it all.

We believe that knowing how to program in VBScript is a skill that many people will find both useful and rewarding, whether they are involved in the IT industry, a SOHO PC user, a student, or simply a home user. Knowing and using VBScript can save you time and, more importantly, money.

Whom This Book Is For

This is the one-stop book for anyone who is interested in learning VBScript. How you use it depends on your previous programming/scripting knowledge and experience:

❑   If you are a complete beginner who has heard about VBScript and have come this far, that's great. You've come to the best possible place. As a beginner, you have a fascinating journey ahead of you. We suggest that you go through this book from cover to cover to get the best from it.

❑ If you already have IT and programming experience and want to learn VBScript (perhaps for Active Server Pages (ASP) or Windows Scripting Host (WSH), then you, too, have come to the right place. Your background in programming means that you will already be familiar with most of the terms and techniques that we cover here. For you, the task of learning another language is made simpler by this. If you know what you plan to be using VBScript for (say ASP or WSH), then you can read with this in mind and skip certain chapters for speed.

❑ Network administrators are likely to find this book not only useful, but also an enormous time-saver because they can use VBScript to write powerful logon scripts or automate boring, repetitive, time-consuming, and error-prone tasks using WSH.

❑ You're already using VBScript and just want to fill in some of the blanks or bought this new edition just to keep up-to-date. You will no doubt find new information and you might want to read certain chapters more than others (such as the Windows Vista–specific chapters of the revamped appendixes).

What This Book Covers

As you'd expect, a book on VBScript covers VBScript. To be precise, this book covers VBScript right up to the latest version (version 5.7). However, VBScript is a tool that can be used in a variety of different ways and by a variety of different applications. Therefore, along with covering VBScript in detail, this book also covers technologies that are linked to and associated with VBScript. These include technologies such as Windows Script Host (WSH). Likewise, if you come from a Visual Basic background, then most of what is covered in the first third of the book (variables, data types, procedures, flow control, and so on) will be familiar to you. This book also shows you how to get deep into the Windows operating system and make changes with just a few lines of code.

How This Book Is Structured

Take a quick look at the table of contents of this edition and you'll see that it's broken up into three broad sections:

❑ The book begins with chapters that are core VBScript — basically how VBScript works as a language.

❑ The book looks at how to make use of VBScript within other technologies (such as WSH or ASP). These chapters look at more advanced examples of VBScript code in action.

❑ The book has a detailed and comprehensive reference section in the form of a series of appendixes. You can use this reference section as a stand-alone section, or to gain greater insight into how the VBScript from earlier chapters works.

How you decide to progress through the book really depends on your current skill level with regards to VBScript or other programming languages and what you want to do. It's your book — use it the way that best suits you!

If you're not sure about the best way to approach this book, we suggest that you read it from beginning to end, so that you benefit fully. Don't worry too much about actually remembering everything you read — that's not the point. The book is a reference, which means you can refer back to it again and again. Make notes in the book as you go. This will help you remember better and aid in your finding key parts you've read before.

What You Need to Use This Book

VBScript is possibly a low-cost solution to many of your scripting/programming needs. The good news is that you (and your end users) use a Microsoft Windows operating system, so you already have everything you need to be able to make full use of this book (or you can go online to download it).

All the code writing can be done using the Windows Notepad application that you already have installed. We will make a few suggestions about other tools you can use that may make life easier for you, but a text editor is all you really need.

The Microsoft Scripting web site contains documentation relating to VBScript that is available for download. You may like to download these, too, to augment your reading here.

If you are not using Windows Vista or XP, you might want to download the latest VBScript engine — point your browser at `www.microsoft.com/scripting`.

Conventions

To help you get the most from the text and keep track of what's happening, we've used a number of conventions throughout the book.

> **Boxes like this one hold important, not-to-be forgotten information that is directly relevant to the surrounding text.**

Tips, hints, tricks, and asides to the current discussion are offset and placed in italics like this.

As for styles in the text:

❑ We *highlight* important words when we introduce them.

❑ We show keyboard strokes like this: Ctrl+A.

❑ We show filenames, URLs, and code within the text like so: `persistence.properties`

❑ We present code in two different ways:

```
In code examples, we highlight new and important code with a gray background.
```

```
The gray highlighting is not used for code that's less important in the present
context, or has been shown before.
```

Source Code

As you work through the examples in this book, you may choose either to type in all the code manually or to use the source code files that accompany this book. All the source code used in this book is available at www.wrox.com. Once at the site, simply locate the book's title by using the Search box. You can then choose what you want to download.

Because many books have similar titles, you may find it easiest to search by ISBN; this book's ISBN is 978-0-470-16808-0.

Errata

We make every effort to ensure that there are no errors in the text or in the code. However, no one is perfect, and mistakes do occur. If you find an error in one of our books, like a spelling mistake or faulty piece of code, we would be very grateful for your feedback. By sending in errata, you may save another reader hours of frustration; at the same time, you will be helping us provide even higher quality information.

To find the errata page for this book, go to www.wrox.com and locate the title using the Search box or one of the title lists. Then, on the book's detail page, click the Book Errata link. On this page, you can view all errata that has been submitted for this book and posted by Wrox editors. A complete book list including links to each book's errata is also available at www.wrox.com/misc-pages/booklist .shtml.

If you don't spot "your" error on the Book Errata page, go to www.wrox.com/contact/techsupport .shtml and complete the form there to send us the error you have found. We'll check the information and, if appropriate, post a message to the book's errata page and fix the problem in subsequent editions of the book.

p2p.wrox.com

For authors and peer discussion, join the P2P forums at p2p.wrox.com. The forums are a Web-based system for you to post messages relating to Wrox books and related technologies and interact with other readers and technology users. The forums offer a subscription feature to email you topics of interest of your choosing when new posts are made to the forums. Wrox authors, editors, other industry experts, and your fellow readers are present on these forums.

At p2p.wrox.com, you will find a number of different forums that will help you not only as you read this book, but also as you develop your own applications. To join forums, just follow these steps:

1. Go to p2p.wrox.com and click the Register link.
2. Read the terms of use and click Agree.

3. Complete the required information to join as well as any optional information you wish to provide and click Submit.

4. You will receive an email with information describing how to verify your account and complete the joining process.

You can read messages in the forums without joining P2P, but in order to post your own messages, you must join.

Once you join, you can post new messages and respond to messages other users post. You can read messages at any time on the Web. If you would like to have new messages from a particular forum emailed to you, click the Subscribe to this Forum icon by the forum name in the forum listing.

For more information about how to use the Wrox P2P, be sure to read the P2P FAQs for answers to questions about how the forum software works as well as many common questions specific to P2P and Wrox books. To read the FAQs, click the FAQ link on any P2P page.

VBScript
Programmer's Reference
Third Edition

A Quick Introduction
to Programming

A chapter covering the basics of VBScript is the best place to begin this book. This is because of the type of language VBScript is and the kind of users the authors see turning to it. In this chapter, you get a crash course in programming basics. You might not need this chapter because you've come to VBScript with programming skills from another language (Visual Basic, Visual Basic .NET, C, C++, Delphi, C#) and are already both familiar with and comfortable using programming terminology. In that case, feel free to skip this chapter and move on to the next one. However, if you come from a non-programming background, then this chapter will give you the firm foundation you need to begin using VBScript confidently.

If you're still reading, chances are you fall into one of three distinct categories:

❑   You're a Network/Systems administrator who probably wants to use VBScript and the Windows Script Host or PowerShell to write logon scripts or to automate administration tasks.

❑   You might be a web designer who feels the need to branch out and increase your skill set, perhaps in order to do some ASP work.

❑   You're interested in programming (possibly Visual Basic or Visual Basic .NET) and want to check it out before getting too deeply involved.

Programming is a massive subject. Over the years countless volumes have been written about it, both in print and on the Internet. In this chapter, in a single paragraph, we might end up introducing several unfamiliar concepts. We'll be moving pretty fast, but if you read along carefully, trying out your hand at the examples along the way, you'll be just fine.

Also, do bear in mind that there will be a lot that we don't cover here, such as:

❑   Architecture

❑   System design

❑   Database design

❏ Documenting code

❏ Advanced testing, debugging, and beta testing

❏ Rollout and support

Think of this chapter as a brief introduction to the important building blocks of programming. It certainly won't make you an expert programmer overnight, but it will hopefully give you the know-how you'll need to get the most out of the rest of the book.

Variables and Data Types

In this section, you'll quickly move through some of the most basic concepts of programming, in particular:

❏ Using variables

❏ Using comments

❏ Using built-in VBScript functions

❏ Understanding syntax issues

Using Variables

Quite simply, a *variable* is a place in the computer memory where your script holds a piece (or pieces) of information, or data. The data stored in a variable can be pretty much anything. It may be something simple, like a small number, like 4, something more complex, like a floating-point number such as 2.3, or a much bigger number like 981.12932134. Or it might not be a number at all and could be a word or a combination of letters and numbers. In fact, a variable can store pretty much anything you want it to store.

Behind the scenes, the variable is a reserved section of the computer's memory for storing data. Memory is temporary — things stored there are not stored permanently like they are when you use the hard drive. Because memory is a temporary storage area, and variables are stored in the computer's memory, they are therefore also temporary. Your script will use variables to store data temporarily that the script needs to keep track of for later use. If your script needs to store that data permanently, it would store it in a file or database on the computer's hard disk.

To make it easier for the computer to keep track of the millions of bits of data that are stored in memory at any given moment, the memory is broken up into chunks. Each chunk is exactly the same size, and is given a unique address. Don't worry about what the memory addresses are or how you use them because you won't need to know any of that to use VBScript, but it is useful to know that a variable is a reserved set of one or more chunks. Also, different types of variables take up different amounts of memory.

In your VBScript program, a variable usually begins its lifecycle by being declared (or dimensioned) before use.

It is not required that you declare all of the variables you use. By default, VBScript allows you to use undeclared variables. However, it's strongly recommended that you get into the good habit of declaring all of the variables you use in your scripts. Declaring variables before use makes code easier to read and to debug later. Just do it!

By declaring variables you also give them a name in the process. Here's an example of a variable declaration in VBScript.

```
Dim YourName
```

By doing this, you are in fact giving the computer an instruction to reserve some memory space for you and to name that chunk `YourName`. From now on, the computer (or, more accurately, the VBScript engine) keeps track of that memory for you, and whenever you use the variable name `YourName`, it will know what you're talking about.

Variables are essential to programming. Without them you have no way to hold all the data that your script will be handling. Every input into the script, output from the script, and process within the script uses variables. They are the computer's equivalent of the sticky notes that you leave all over the place with little bits of information on them. All the notes are important (otherwise why write them?) but they are also temporary. Some might become permanent (so you take a phone number and write it down in your address book or contact list), while others are thrown away after use (say, after reminding you to do something). This is how it works with variables, too. Some hold data that you might later want to keep, while others are just used for general housekeeping and are disposed of as soon as they're used.

In VBScript, whenever you have a piece of information that you need to work with, you declare a variable using the exact same syntax you saw a moment ago. At some point in your script, you'll need to do something with the memory space you've allocated yourself (otherwise, what would be the point of declaring it?). And what you do with a variable is place a value in it. This is called *initializing* the variable. Sometimes you initialize a variable with a default value. Other times, you might ask the user for some information, and initialize the variable with whatever the user enters. Alternatively, you might open a database and use a previously stored value to initialize the variable.

When we say database, *we don't necessarily mean an actual database but any store of data — it might be an Internet browser cookie or a text file that we get the data from. If you are dealing with small amounts of data a cookie or text file will suffice, but if you are dealing with a lot of data you need the performance and structure that a database offers.*

Initializing the variable gives you a starting point. After it has been initialized, you can begin making use of the variable in your script.

Here's a very simple VBScript example.

```
Dim YourName
' Above we dimensioned the variable
YourName = InputBox("Hello! What is your name?")
' Above we ask for the user's name and initialize the variable
MsgBox "Hello " & YourName & "! Pleased to meet you."
' Above we display a greeting containing the user's name
```

Rightly so, you're now probably wondering what all this code means. Last time, you were showed one line and now it's grown to six.

All of the examples in this chapter are designed so that you can run them using the Windows Script Host (WSH). The WSH is a scripting host that allows you to run VBScript programs within Windows. WSH allows you to try out these example programs for yourself. You may already have WSH installed. To find out, type the previous example script into a text editor, save the file as TEST.VBS *(it must have the* .VBS *extension, and not a* .TXT*), and double-click the file in Windows Explorer. If the script runs, then you're all set. If Windows does not recognize the file, then you need to download and install WSH from* http://msdn2.microsoft.com/en-us/library/ms950396.aspx.

Using Comments

You already know what the first line of code in the previous block does. It declares a variable for use called YourName.

The second line in the code is a comment. In VBScript, any text preceded by the single quote character (') is treated as a comment, which means that the VBScript engine completely ignores the text, which begs the question why bother typing it in at all? It doesn't contribute to the execution of the script, right? This is absolutely correct, but don't forget one of the most important principles of programming: It is not just computers that may have to read script. It is equally important to write a script with human readers in mind as it is to write with the computer in mind.

Of course, none of this means you should for one moment forget that when you write scripts, you must do so with the computer (or, more specifically, the script engine) in mind. If you don't type the code correctly (that is, if you don't use the proper syntax), the script engine won't be able to execute the script. However, once you've written some useful scripts, you'll probably need to go back to make some changes to a script you wrote six months or a year ago. If you didn't write that code with human readers, as well as computers, in mind it could be pretty difficult to figure out what you were thinking and how you decided to solve the problems at the time you wrote the script. Things can get worse. What happens when you or one of your coworkers has to make some changes to a script you wrote many months ago? If you did not write that script to be both readable and maintainable, others who use your code will encounter difficulties deciphering it — no matter how well written the actual computer part of the code is.

Adding comments to your code is just one part of making sure code is clear and readable. There are many other things that you can do:

❑   Choose clear, meaningful variable names.

❑   Indent code for clarity.

❑   Make effective use of white space.

❑   Organize the code in a logical manner.

All of these aid human-readability and are covered later, but clear, concise comments are by far the most important. However, too much of a good thing is never good and the same is true for comments. Overburdening code with comments doesn't help. Remember that if you are scripting for the Web that all the code, including the comments, are downloaded to the browser, so unnecessary comments may adversely affect download times.

You learn about some good commenting principles later in this chapter, but for now just be aware of the fact that the comment in line 2 of the script is not really a good comment for everyday use. This is because, to any semi-experienced programmer, it is all too obvious that what you are doing is declaring the `YourName` variable on the code line above. However, throughout this book you'll often see the code commented in a similar way. This is because the point of the code is to instruct the reader in how a particular aspect of VBScript programming works, and the best way to do that is to add comments to the code directly. It removes ambiguity and keeps the code and comments together.

Also worth noting is that comments don't have to be on a separate line. Comments can also follow the code, like so:

```
Dim YourName ' initialize the variable
YourName = InputBox("Hello! What is your name?") ' ask for the user's name
MsgBox "Hello " & YourName & "! Pleased to meet you." ' display a greeting
```

This works in theory but it isn't as clear as keeping the comments on separate lines in the script.

Using Built-in VBScript Functions

OK, back to the script. Take a look at line 3.

```
YourName = InputBox("Hello! What is your name?")
```

Here you are doing two things at once. First, you're initializing the variable. You could do it directly, like this:

```
YourName = "Fred"
```

However, the drawback with this is that you're making the arbitrary decision that everyone is called `Fred`, which is ideal for some applications but not for others. If you wanted to assign a fixed value to a variable, such as a tax rate, this would be fine.

```
Dim TaxRate
TaxRate = 17.5
```

Because you want to do something that gives the user a choice, you should employ the use of a function, called `InputBox`. This function and all the others are discussed in later chapters, but for now all you need to know is that `InputBox` is used to display a message in a dialog box, and it waits for the user to input text or click a button. The `InputBox` generated is displayed in Figure 1-1.

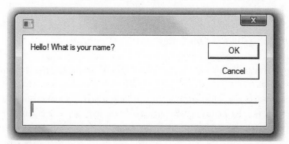

Figure 1-1

The clever bit is what happens to the text that the user types into the input box displayed — it is stored in the variable `YourName`.

Line 4 is another comment. Line 5 is more code. Now that you've initialized this variable, you're going to do something useful with it. MsgBox is another built-in VBScript function that you will probably use a lot during the course of your VBScript programming. Using the MsgBox function is a good way to introduce the programming concept of passing function parameters, also known as *arguments*. Some functions don't require you to pass parameters to them while others do. This is because some functions (take the Date function as an example — this returns the current date based on the system time) do not need any additional information from you in order to do their job. The MsgBox function, on the other hand, displays a piece of information to the user in the form of a dialog box, such as the one shown in Figure 1-2.

Figure 1-2

You have to pass MsgBox a parameter because on its own it doesn't have anything useful to display (in fact, it will just bring up a blank pop-up box). The MsgBox function actually has several parameters, but for now you're just going to look at one. All of the other parameters are optional parameters.

Understanding Syntax Issues

Take another look at line 5 and you'll probably notice the ampersand (&). The ampersand is a VBScript operator, and is used to concatenate (join) pieces of text together. To concatenate simply means to "string together." This text can take the form of either a literal or a variable. A literal is the opposite of a variable. A variable is so named because it is exactly that — a variable — and can change throughout the lifetime of the script (a script's lifetime is the time from when it starts executing, to the time it stops). Unlike a variable, a literal cannot change during the lifetime of the script. Here is line 5 of the script again.

```
MsgBox "Hello "& YourName & "! Pleased to meet you."
```

An operator is a symbol or a word that you use within your code that is usually used to change or test a value. Other operators include the standard mathematical operators (+, -, /, *), and the equals sign (=), which can actually be used in either a comparison or an assignment. So far, you've used the equals sign as an assignment operator. Later in this chapter you'll find out more about operators.

Now take a closer look at variables. Remember how we said that a variable is a piece of reserved memory? One question you might have is, How does the computer know how large to make that piece of memory? Well, again, in VBScript this isn't something that you need to worry about and it is all handled automatically by the VBScript engine. You don't have to worry in advance about how big or small you need to make a variable. You can even change your mind and the VBScript engine will dynamically change and reallocate the actual memory addresses that are used up by a variable. For example, take a quick look at this VBScript program.

```
' First declare the variable
Dim SomeVariable

' Initialize it with a value
SomeVariable = "Hello, World!"
MsgBox SomeVariable

' Change the value of the variable to something larger
SomeVariable = "Let's take up more memory than the previous text"
MsgBox SomeVariable

' Change the value again
SomeVariable = "Bye!"
MsgBox SomeVariable
```

Each time the script engine comes across a variable, the engine assigns it the smallest chunk of memory it needs. Initially the variable contains nothing at all so needs little space but as you initialize it with the string `"Hello, World!"` the VBScript engine asks the computer for more memory to store the text. But again it asks for just what it needs and no more. (Memory is a precious thing and not to be wasted.) Next, when you assign more text to the same variable, the script engine must allocate even more memory, which it again does automatically. Finally, when you assign the shorter string of text, the script engine reduces the size of the variable in memory to conserve memory.

One final note about variables: Once you've assigned a value to a variable, you don't have to throw it away in order to assign something else to the variable as well. Take a look at this example.

```
Dim SomeVariable

SomeVariable = "Hello"
MsgBox SomeVariable

SomeVariable = SomeVariable & ", World!"
MsgBox SomeVariable

SomeVariable = SomeVariable & " Goodbye!"
MsgBox SomeVariable
```

Notice how in this script, you each time keep adding the original value of the variable and adding some additional text to it. You tell the script engine that this is what you want to do by also using the name of the `SomeVariable` variable on the right side of the equals sign, and then concatenating its existing value with an additional value using the ampersand (`&`) operator. Adding onto the original value works with numbers, too (as opposed to numbers in strings) but you have to use the + operator instead of the & operator.

```
Dim SomeNumber

SomeNumber = 999
MsgBox SomeNumber

SomeNumber = SomeNumber + 2
MsgBox SomeNumber

SomeNumber = SomeNumber + 999
MsgBox SomeNumber
```

Here are the resulting message boxes generated by this code. The first is shown in Figure 1-3.

Figure 1-3

The second message box is shown in Figure 1-4.

Figure 1-4

The final message box is shown in Figure 1-5.

Figure 1-5

You can store several different types of data in variables. These are called data types and so far you've seen two:

❑   `String`

❑   `Integer`

You've also seen a single-precision floating-point number in the tax rate example.

We'll be covering all of them later on in the book. For now, just be aware that there are different data types and that they can be stored in variables.

Flow Control

When you run a script that you have written, the code executes in a certain order. This order of execution is also known as *flow*. In simple scripts such as the ones you looked at so far, the statements simply execute from the top down. The script engine starts with the first statement in the script, executes it, moves on to the next one, and then the next one, and so on until the script reaches the end. The execution occurs this way because the simple programs you've written so far do not contain any branching or looping code.

Branching

Take a look at a script that was used earlier.

```
Dim YourName
'Above we initialized the variable
YourName = InputBox("Hello! What is your name?")
'Above we ask for the user's name and initialize the variable
MsgBox "Hello " & YourName & "! Pleased to meet you."
'Above we display a greeting containing the user's name
```

If you save this script in a file with a `.vbs` extension, and then execute it using the Windows Script Host, all of the statements will be executed in order from the first statement to the last.

Note that it was previously mentioned that all of the statements will be executed. However, this isn't what you always want. There is a technique that you can use to cause some statements to be executed, and some not, depending on certain conditions. This technique is called *branching*.

VBScript supports a few different branching constructs, and they are covered in detail in Chapter 5, but here we only cover the simplest and most common one, which is the `If...Else...End If` construct.

Take a look at this modified code example.

```
Dim YourName
Dim Greeting

YourName = InputBox("Hello! What is your name?")
```
```
If YourName = "" Then
    Greeting = "OK. You don't want to tell me your name."
Else
    Greeting = "Hello, "& YourName & ", great to meet you."
End If
```
```
MsgBox Greeting
```

Walking through the code, you do the following:

1. You declare the two variables that you are going to use:

```
Dim YourName
Dim Greeting
```
```
YourName = InputBox("Hello! What is your name?")
```

You ask the user for some input, again using the InputBox function. This function expects one required parameter, the prompt text (the text that appears on the input box). It can also accept several optional parameters. Here, you only use the one required parameter.

Note that the parameter text that you passed "Hello! What is your name?" *is displayed as a prompt for the dialog box. The* InputBox *function returns the value that the user types, if any. If the user does not type anything or clicks the* Cancel *button (both do the same thing), then* InputBox *returns a zero-length string, which is a strange kind of programming concept that basically means that it returns text that doesn't actually contain any text. Your script stores the result of the* InputBox *function in the* YourName *variable.*

2. You come to the actual loop you're going to use:

```
If YourName = "" Then
    Greeting = "OK. You don't want to tell me your name."
Else
    Greeting = "Hello, "& YourName & ", great to meet you."
End If
```

This code presents the VBScript engine with an option that is based on what the user typed (or didn't type) into the input box. The first line tests the input from the user. It tests to see if the input that is stored in the variable YourName is a zero-length string. If it is, the next line of code is run and the variable Greeting is assigned a string. Figure 1-6 shows the message displayed if the user doesn't type his or her name into the InputBox.

Figure 1-6

3. What happens if the user does (as you expect) type something into the input box? Well, this is where the next line comes in.

```
Else
```

You can actually begin to read the code and in fact doing this helps it to make sense. What the whole loop actually means is that if the value of variable YourName is a zero-length string, then assign the variable Greeting with one value; however, if it contains something else, do something else (assign Greeting a different value). This doesn't protect your script from users entering data like numbers of non-alphabet characters into the test box, although you could code for all these conditions if you wanted to.

4. The final line of the code uses the MsgBox function to display the value of the variable Greeting. Notice that both lines of code assign a value to the Greeting variable. However, only one of these lines will actually execute in any one running of the script. This is because the If...Else...End If block makes an either/or decision. Either a given condition is True, or it is False. There's no way it can be neither (not a string that contains text nor a zero-length string) or both (a zero-length string that contains text). If it is True, then the script engine will execute the code between the If and Else statements. If it is False, then it will execute the code between the Else and End If statements.

So, what the complete script does is test the input, and then executes different code, depending on the result of that test, and hence the term branching. Using this technique allows your script to adapt to the unpredictable nature of the input. Compare the intelligent script to the following one, which looks pretty lame.

```
Dim YourName
Dim Greeting
YourName = InputBox("Hello! What is your name?")

Greeting = "Hello, "& YourName & ", great to meet you."

MsgBox Greeting
```

This script is just plain dumb because it does not contain any branching logic to test the input; so when the user does something unpredictable, such as clicking the Cancel button, or not entering any name at all, the script does not have the ability to adapt. Compare this to your intelligent script, which is capable of adapting to the unpredictability of input by testing it with If...Else...End If branching.

Before you move on to looping, you should know a few other things about `If...Else...End If`:

❑ The block of code containing the `If...Else...End If` is known as a block of code. A block is a section of code that has a beginning and an end, and it usually contains keywords or statements at both the beginning and the end. In the case of `If...Else...End If`, the `If` statement marks the beginning of the block, while the `End If` marks the end of the block.

The script engine requires these beginning and ending statements, and if you omit them, the script engine won't understand your code and won't allow your script to execute. Over the course of this book you will encounter many different types of code blocks in VBScript.

To confuse matters, the term "block of code" is often used informally to describe any group of lines of code. As a rule, "block of code" will refer to lines of code that work together to achieve a result.

❑ Notice that the lines of code that are inside the block itself are indented by four spaces. This is an extremely important concept but not for the reason you might think. This indenting has nothing whatsoever to do with the script engine — it doesn't care whether you add four spaces, 44 spaces, or none at all. This indenting is for the benefit of any humans who might be reading your code. For example, the following script is completely legal and will execute just fine:

```
Dim YourName

        Dim Greeting

    YourName = InputBox("Hello! What is your name?")


    If YourName = "" Then

            Greeting = "OK. You don't want to tell me your name."
    Else

  Greeting = "Hello, "& YourName & ", great to meet you."
                                End If

                MsgBox Greeting
```

However, this code is very difficult to read. As a general rule of thumb, you indent code by four spaces whenever a line or series of lines is subordinate to the lines above and below it. For example, the lines after the `If` clause and the `Else` clause belong inside the `If...Else...End If` block, so you indent them to visually suggest the code's logical structure. Presentation, while having no bearing whatsoever on how the computer or script engine handles your code, is very important when it comes to how humans read it. You should be able to look at the code and get a sense for how it is organized and how it works. By seeing the indentations inside the `If...Else...End If` block, you can not only read the code, but also "see" the branching logic at that point in the code. Indenting is only one element of programming style, but learning and following proper style and layout is essential for any programmer who wants to be taken seriously.

❑ The `Else` part of the block is optional. Sometimes you want to test for a certain condition, and if that condition is `True`, execute some code, but if it's `False`, there's no code to execute. For example, you could add another `If...End If` block to your script.

```
Dim YourName
Dim Greeting

YourName = InputBox("Hello! What is your name?")

If YourName = "" Then
    Greeting = "OK. You don't want to tell me your name."
Else
    Greeting = "Hello, " & YourName & ", great to meet you."
End If
```

```
If YourName = "Fred" Then
    Greeting = Greeting & " Nice to see you Fred."
End If
```

```
MsgBox Greeting
```

❑ The If...Else...End If block can be extended through the use of the ElseIf clause, and through nesting. *Nesting* is the technique of placing a block of code inside of another block of code of the same type. The following variation on your script illustrates both concepts:

```
Dim YourName
Dim Greeting

YourName = InputBox("Hello! What is your name?")

If YourName = "" Then
    Greeting = "OK. You don't want to tell me your name."
```

```
ElseIf YourName = "abc" Then
    Greeting = "That's not a real name."
ElseIf YourName = "xxx" Then
    Greeting = "That's not a real name."
Else
    Greeting = "Hello, "& YourName & ", great to meet you."

    If YourName = "Fred" Then
        Greeting = Greeting & " Nice to see you Fred."
    End If

End If
```
```
MsgBox Greeting
```

Once again, seeing how the code has been indented helps you to identify which lines of code are subordinate to the lines above them. As code gets more and more complex, proper indenting of the code becomes vital as it will become harder to follow.

❑ Even though the branching logic you are adding to the code tells the script to execute certain lines of code while not executing others, all the code must still be interpreted by the script engine (including the code that's not executed). If any of the code that's not executed contains any syntax errors, the script engine will still produce an error message to let you know.

Looping

Branching allows you to tell the script to execute some lines of code, but not others. *Looping*, on the other hand, allows you to tell the script to execute some lines of code over and over again. This is particularly useful in two situations:

❑   When you want to repeat a block of code until a condition is `True` or `False`

❑   When you want to repeat a block of code a finite number of times

There are many different looping constructs, but this section focuses on only two of them:

❑   The basic `Do...Loop While` loop

❑   The basic `For...Next` loop

Using the Do...Loop While Loop

This section takes a look at the `Do...Loop While` construct and how it can be used to repeatedly execute a block of code until a certain condition is met. Take a look at the following modification of the example script:

```
Dim Greeting
Dim YourName
Dim TryAgain

Do
    TryAgain = "No"

    YourName = InputBox("Please enter your name:")

    If YourName = "" Then
        MsgBox "You must enter your name to continue."
        TryAgain = "Yes"
    Else
        Greeting = "Hello, "& YourName & ", great to meet you."
    End If

Loop While TryAgain = "Yes"

MsgBox Greeting
```

Notice the block of code that starts with the word Do and ends with the line that starts with the word Loop. The indentation should make this code block easy to identify. This is the definition of the loop. The code inside the loop will keep being executed until at the end of the loop the TryAgain variable equals "No".

The TryAgain variable controls the loop. The loop starts at the word Do. At the end of the loop, if the TryAgain variable equals "Yes", then all the code, starting at the word Do, will execute again.

Notice that the top of the loop initializes the TryAgain variable to "No". It is absolutely essential that this initialization take place inside the loop (that is, between the Do and Loop statements). This way, the variable is reinitialized every time a loop occurs. If you didn't do this, you would end up with what's called an infinite loop. They are always bad. At best, the user is going to have to exit out of the program in an untimely (and inelegant) way because, as the name suggests, the loop is infinite. At worse, it can crash the system. You want neither and you want to try to avoid both in your code.

Take a look at why the `TryAgain = "No"` line is essential to preventing an infinite loop. Going through the script line by line:

1. This first line starts the loop.

```
Do
```

This tells the script engine that you are starting a block of code that will define a loop. The script engine will expect to find a loop statement somewhere further down in the script. This is similar to the `If...End If` code block because the script engine expects the block to be defined with beginning and ending statements. The `Do` statement on a line all by itself means that the loop will execute at least once. Even if the `Loop While` statement at the end of the block does not result in a loop around back to the `Do` line, the code inside this block will be executed at least one time.

2. Moving on to the second line of code, you initialize the "control" variable. It's called the "control" variable because it ultimately controls whether or not the code block loops around again. You want to initialize this variable to `"No"` so that, by default, the loop will not loop around again. Only if a certain condition is met inside the loop will you set `TryAgain` to `"Yes"`. This is yet another strategy in an ever-vigilant desire to expect the unexpected.

```
Do
    TryAgain = "No"
```

3. The next line of code should look familiar. You use the `InputBox` function to ask the user to enter a name. You store the return value from the function in the `YourName` variable. Whatever the user types, unless they type nothing, will be stored in this variable. Put another way, the script receives some external input — and remember that we said input is always unpredictable:

```
Do
    TryAgain = "No"
    YourName = InputBox("Please enter your name:")
```

4. In the next part of the code, you test the input. The line `If YourName = " " Then` tests to see if the user typed in their name (or at least some text). If they typed something in, the code immediately after the `Else` line will execute. If they didn't type in anything (or if they clicked the `Cancel` button), then the `YourName` variable will be empty, and the code after the `If` line will execute instead:

```
Do
    TryAgain = "No"

    YourName = InputBox("Please enter your name:")


    If YourName = "" Then
        MsgBox "You must enter your name to continue."
        TryAgain = "Yes"
    Else
        Greeting = "Hello, "& YourName & ", great to meet you."
    End If
```

If the user didn't type anything into the input box, you will display a message informing them that they have done something you didn't want them to. You then set the `TryAgain` variable (the control variable) to `"Yes"` and send them around the loop once more and ask the users for their name again (wherein this time they will hopefully type something into the input box). If the user did type in his or her name, then you initialize your familiar `Greeting` variable. Note that in this case, you do not change the value of the `TryAgain` variable. This is because there is no need to loop around again because the user has entered a name. The value of `TryAgain` is already equal to `"No"`, so there's no need to change it.

5.   In the next line of code, you encounter the end of the loop block. What this `Loop` line is essentially telling the script engine is "If the `TryAgain` variable equals `"Yes"` at this point, then go back up to the `Do` line and execute all that code over again." If the user entered his or her name, then the `TryAgain` variable will be equal to `"No"`. Therefore, the code will not loop again, and will continue onto the last line:

```
Do
    TryAgain = "No"

    YourName = InputBox("Please enter your name:")

    If YourName = "" Then
        MsgBox "You must enter your name to continue."
        TryAgain = "Yes"
    Else
        Greeting = "Hello, "& YourName & ", great to meet you."
    End If

Loop While TryAgain = "Yes"

MsgBox Greeting
```

If the user did not enter his or her name, then `TryAgain` would be equal to `"Yes"`, which would mean that the code would again jump back to the `Do` line. This is where the reinitialization of the `TryAgain` variable to `"No"` is essential because if it wasn't done then there's no way for `TryAgain` to ever equal anything but `"Yes"`. And if `TryAgain` always equals `"Yes"`, then the loop will keep going around and around forever. This results in total disaster for your script, and for the user.

Using the For...Next Loop

In this kind of loop, you don't need to worry about infinite loops because the loop is predefined to execute only a certain number of times. Here's a simple (if not very useful) example.

```
Dim Counter

MsgBox "Let's count to ten. Ready?"

For Counter = 1 to 10
    MsgBox Counter
Next

MsgBox "Wasn't that fun?"
```

This loop is similar to the previous loop. The beginning loop block is defined by the `For` statement, and the end is defined by the `Next` statement. This loop is different because you can predetermine how many times it will run; in this case, it will go around exactly ten times. The line `For Counter = 1 to 10` essentially tells the script engine, "Execute this block of code as many times as it takes to count from

1 to 10, and use the `Counter` variable to keep track of your counting. When you've gone through this loop ten times, stop looping and move on to the next bit of code."

Notice that every time the loop goes around (including the first time through), the `Counter` variable holds the value of the current count. The first time through, `Counter` equals 1, the second time through it equals 2, and so on up to 10. It's important to note that after the loop is finished, the value of the `Counter` variable will be 11, one number higher than the highest value in your `For` statement. The reason for this is that the `Counter` variable is incremented at the end of the loop, after which the `For` statement tests the value of index to see if it is necessary to loop again.

Giving you a meaningful example of how to make use of the `For...Next` loop isn't easy because you haven't been exposed to much VBScript just yet, but here's an example that shows you don't need to know how many times the loop needs to run before you run it.

```
Dim Counter
Dim WordLength
Dim WordBuilder

WordLength = Len("VBScript is great!")

For Counter = 1 to WordLength
    MsgBox Mid("VBScript is great!", Counter, 1)
    WordBuilder = WordBuilder & Mid("VBScript is great!", Counter, 1)
Next

MsgBox WordBuilder
```

For example, the phrase `"VBScript is great!"` has exactly 18 letter spaces. If you first calculated the number of letters in the phrase, you could use that number to drive a `For...Next` loop. However, this code uses the VBScript `Len()` function to calculate the length of the phrase used. Inside the loop, it uses the `Mid()` function to pull one letter out of the phrase one at a time and display them separately. The position of that letter is controlled by the counter variable, while the number of letters extracted is defined by the `length` argument at the end. It also populates the `WordBuilder` variable with each loop, adding each new letter to the previous letter or letters, rebuilding the phrase.

Here's a variation of the last example: here giving the user the opportunity to type in a word or phrase to use, proving that there's nothing up your sleeve when it comes to knowing how many times to loop the code.

```
Dim Counter
Dim WordLength
Dim InputWord
Dim WordBuilder

InputWord = InputBox ("Type in a word or phrase to use")

WordLength = Len(InputWord)

For Counter = 1 to WordLength
    MsgBox Mid(InputWord, Counter, 1)
    WordBuilder = WordBuilder & Mid(InputWord, Counter, 1)
Next

MsgBox WordBuilder & " contains "& WordLength & " characters."
```

Figure 1-7 shows the final summary message generated by the code. Notice how well the information is integrated.

Figure 1-7

Operators and Operator Precedence

An operator acts on one or more operands when comparing, assigning, concatenating, calculating, and performing logical operations. Say you want to calculate the difference between two variables X and Y and save the result in variable Z. These variables are the operands and to find the difference you use the subtraction operator like this:

```
Z = X - Y
```

Here you use the assignment operator (=) to assign the difference between X and Y, which was found by using the subtraction operator (-).

Operators are one of the single-most important parts of any programming language. Without them, you cannot assign values to variables or perform calculations or comparisons. In fact, you can't do much at all.

There are different types of operators and they each serve a specific purpose, as shown in the following table.

Operator	Purpose
assignment (=)	The most obvious and is simply used for assigning a value to a variable or property.
arithmetic	These are all used to calculate a numeric value, and are normally used in conjunction with the assignment operator and/or one of the comparison operators.
concatenation	These are used to concatenate ("join together") two or more different expressions.
comparison	These are used for comparing variables and expressions against other variables, constants, or expressions.
logical	These are used for performing logical operations on expressions; all logical operators can also be used as bitwise operators.
bitwise	These are used for comparing binary values bit by bit; all bitwise operators can also be used as logical operators.

When you have a situation where more than one operation occurs in an expression, the operations are normally performed from left to right. However, there are several rules.

Operators from the arithmetic group are evaluated first, then concatenation, comparison, and finally logical operators. This is the set order in which operations occur (operators in brackets have the same precedence):

- ❑   ^, −, (*, /), \, Mod, (+, −)
- ❑   &
- ❑   =, <>, <, >, <=, >=, Is
- ❑   Not, And, Or, Xor, Eqv, Imp

This order can be overridden by using parentheses. Operations in parentheses are evaluated before operations outside the parentheses, but inside the parentheses, the normal precedence rules still apply.

Take a look at the following two statements:

```
A = 5 + 6 * 7 + 8
A = (5 + 6) * (7 + 8)
```

They look the same but they're not. According to operator precedence, multiplication is performed before addition, so the top line gives A the value 55 (6 * 7 = 42 + 5 + 8 = 55). By adding parentheses, you force the additions to be evaluated first and A becomes equal to 165.

Organizing and Reusing Code

So far, the scripts you've worked with have been fairly simple in structure. The code has been all together in one unit. You haven't done anything all that complicated, so it's easy to see all the code in just a few lines. The execution of the code is easy to follow because it starts at the top of the file, with the first line, and then continues downward until it reaches the last line. Sometimes, at certain points, choices redirect the code using branching, or sections of code are repeated using loops.

However, when you come to writing a script that actually does something useful, your code is likely to get more complex. As you add more code to the script, it becomes harder to read in one chunk. If you print it on paper, your scripts will undoubtedly stretch across multiple pages. As the code becomes more complex, it's easier for bugs and errors to creep in, and the poor layout of the code will make these harder to find and fix. The most common technique programmers use to manage complexity is called *modularization*. This is a big, fancy word, but the concept behind it is really quite simple.

This section defines some terminology used when organizing and reusing code, and then discusses how to write your own procedures by turning code into a function. You then learn a few advantages of having procedures.

Modularization, Black Boxes, Procedures, and Subprocedures

Modularization is the process of organizing your code into modules, which you can also think of as building blocks. You can apply the principles of modularity to create your own personal set of programming building blocks, which you can then use to build programs that are more powerful, more reliable, easier to debug, and easier for you and your fellow programmers to maintain and reuse. When you take your code and divide it into modules, your ultimate goal is to create what are known as black boxes. A *black box* is any kind of device that has a simple, well-defined interface and that performs some discrete, well-defined function. A black box is so called because you don't need to see what's going on inside it. All you need to know is what it does, what its inputs are, and (sometimes) what its outputs are.

A wristwatch is a good example of a black box. It has inputs (buttons) and outputs (time) and does a simple function well without you worrying about how the innards of the watch work in order to be able to tell the time. The most basic kind of black box programmers use to achieve modularity is the procedure. A *procedure* is a set of code that (ideally) performs a single function. Good examples of procedures are:

- ❑ Code that adds two numbers together
- ❑ Code that processes a string input
- ❑ Code that handles saving to a file

Bad examples include:

- ❑ Code that takes an input, processes it, and also handles saving to a file
- ❑ Code that handles file access and database access

You've been using procedures throughout this chapter, but they have been procedures that VBScript provides for you. Some of these procedures require input, some don't. Some of these procedures return a value, some don't. But all of the procedures you've used so far (MsgBox(), InputBox(), and so on) are black boxes. They perform one single well-defined function, and they perform it without you having to worry about how they perform their respective functions. In just a moment, you'll see how to extend the VBScript language by writing your own procedures.

Before you begin though, it's time to get some of the terminology cleared up. *Procedure* is a generic term that describes either a function or a subprocedure. This chapter touched on some of this confusing terminology earlier, but a *function* is simply a procedure that returns a value. Len() is a function. You pass it some text, and it returns the number of characters in the string (or the number of bytes required to store a variable) back to you. Functions do not always require input, but they often do.

A *subprocedure* is a procedure that does not return a value. You've been using MsgBox() as a subprocedure. You pass it some text, and it displays a message on the screen comprising of that text. It does not return any kind of value to your code. All you need to know is that it did what you asked it to do. Just like functions, procedure may or may not require input.

Turning Code into a Function

Some of the code that follows is from an example you used earlier in the chapter. Here's how to turn code into a function.

```
Function PromptUserName

    ' This Function prompts the user for his or her name.
    ' If the user enters nothing it returns a zero-length string.
    ' It incorporates various greetings depending on input by the user.
    Dim YourName
    Dim Greeting


    YourName = InputBox("Hello! What is your name?")

    If YourName = "" Then
            Greeting = "OK. You don't want to tell me your name."
    ElseIf YourName = "abc" Then
            Greeting = "That's not a real name."
    ElseIf YourName = "xxx" Then
            Greeting = "That's not a real name."
    Else
            Greeting = "Hello, " & YourName & ", great to meet you."

            If YourName = "Fred" Then
                Greeting = Greeting & " Nice to see you Fred."
            End If

    End If

    MsgBox Greeting

    PromptUserName = YourName

End Function
```

The first things to take note of in the code are the first and last lines. While not groundbreaking, these are what define a function. The first line defines the beginning of the function and gives it a name while the last line defines the end of the function. Based on the earlier discussion of code blocks, this should be a familiar convention by now. From this, you should begin to realize that a procedure is nothing but a special kind of code block. The code has to tell the script engine where it begins and where it ends. Notice also that you've given the function a clear, useful name that precisely describes what this function does. Giving your procedures good names is one of the keys to writing programs that are easy to read and maintain.

Notice also how there's a comment to the beginning of the procedure to describe only what it does, not how the function does what it does. The code that uses this function does not care how the function accomplishes its task; it only cares about inputs, outputs, and predictability. It is vitally important that you add clear, informative comments such as this to the beginning of your procedures, because they make it easy to determine what the function does. The comment also performs one other valuable service to you and any other developer who wants to call this function — it says that the function may return a zero-length string if the user does not enter his or her name.

Finally, notice how, in the second to last line, the function name `PromptUserName` is treated as if it were a variable. When you use functions (as opposed to subprocedures, which do not return a value), this is how you give the function its return value. In a sense, the function name itself is a variable within the procedure.

Here is some code that uses the `PromptUserName` function.

```
Dim Greeting
Dim VisitorName

VisitorName = PromptUserName

If VisitorName <> "" Then
    Greeting = "Goodbye, " & VisitorName & ". Nice to have met you."

Else
    Greeting = "I'm glad to have met you, but I wish I knew your name."
End If

MsgBox Greeting
```

If you are using Windows Script Host for this code, bear in mind that this code and the `PromptUserName` function itself must be in the same `.vbs` script file.

```
Dim PartingGreeting
Dim VisitorName

VisitorName = PromptUserName

If VisitorName <> "" Then
    PartingGreeting = "Goodbye, " & VisitorName & ". Nice to have met you."

Else
    PartingGreeting = "I'm glad to have met you, but I wish I knew your name."
End If

MsgBox PartingGreeting

Function PromptUserName

    ' This Function prompts the user for his or her name.
    ' It incorporates various greetings depending on input by the user.
    Dim YourName
    Dim Greeting

    YourName = InputBox("Hello! What is your name?")

    If YourName = "" Then
        Greeting = "OK. You don't want to tell me your name."
    ElseIf YourName = "abc" Then
        Greeting = "That's not a real name."
    ElseIf YourName = "xxx" Then
        Greeting = "That's not a real name."
```

```
    Else
        Greeting = "Hello, " & YourName & ", great to meet you."

        If YourName = "Fred" Then
            Greeting = Greeting & " Nice to see you Fred."
        End If

    End If

    MsgBox Greeting

    PromptUserName = YourName

End Function
```

As you can see, calling the `PromptUserName` function is pretty straightforward. Once you have written a procedure, calling it is no different than calling a built-in VBScript procedure.

Advantages to Using Procedures

Procedures afford several key advantages that are beyond the scope of this discussion. However, here are a few of the most important ones:

❑   Code such as that put in the `PromptUserName` function can be thought of as "generic," meaning that it can be applied to a variety of uses. Once you have created a discreet, well-defined, generic function such as `PromptUserName`, you are free to reuse it any time you want to prompt users for their name. Once you've written a well-tested procedure, you never have to write that code again. Any time you need it, you just call the procedure. This is known as code reuse.

❑   When you call a procedure to perform a task rather than writing the code in-line, it makes that code much easier to read and maintain. Increasing the readability, and therefore the manageability and maintainability, of your code is a good enough reason to break a block of code out into its own procedure.

❑   When code is isolated into its own procedure, it greatly reduces the effects of changes to that code. This goes back to the idea of the black box. As long as the procedure maintains its predictable inputs and outputs, changes to the code inside of a procedure are insulated from harming the code that calls the procedure. You can make significant changes to the procedure, but as long as the inputs and outputs are predictable and remain unchanged, the code will work just fine.

Top-Down versus Event-Driven

Before you leave this introduction to programming, it may be helpful to point out that you will encounter two different *models* of programming in this book: top-down and event-driven programs. The differences between the two have to do with the way you organize your code and how and when that code gets executed at runtime. As you get deeper into programming in general, and VBScript in particular, this will become clearer, so don't be alarmed if it doesn't completely sink in right now.

Understanding Top-Down Programming

So far in this chapter you've written very simple top-down style programs. The process is simple to follow:

- ❏ Write some code.
- ❏ Save the code in a script file.
- ❏ Use Windows Script Host to execute the script.
- ❏ The Script Host starts executing at the first line and continues to the last line.
- ❏ If a script file contains some procedure definitions (such as your `PromptUserName` function), then the Script Host only executes those procedures if some other code calls them.
- ❏ Once the Script Host reaches the last line of code, the lifetime of the script ends.

Top-down programs are very useful for task-oriented scripts. For example, you might write a script to search your hard drive for all the files with the extension `.htm` and copy all the names and file locations to a file, formatted in HTML to act as a sitemap. Or you might write a script that gets executed every time Windows starts and which randomly chooses a different desktop wallpaper bitmap file for that session of Windows. Top-down programming is perfect for these kinds of scripts.

Understanding Event-Driven Programming

Event-driven code is different, and is useful in different contexts. As the name implies, event-driven code only gets executed when a certain *event* occurs. Until the event occurs, the code won't get executed. If a given event does not occur during the lifetime of the script, the code associated with that event won't be executed at all. If an event occurs, and there's no code associated with that event, then the event is essentially ignored.

Event-driven programming is the predominant paradigm in Windows programming. Most of the Windows programs you use every day were written in the event-driven model. This is because of the graphical nature of Windows programs. In a graphical user interface (GUI), you have all sorts of buttons, drop-down lists, fields in which to type text, and so on. For example, the word processor program Microsoft Word is totally jam-packed with these. Every time a user clicks a button, chooses an item in a list, or types some text into a field, an event is "raised" within the code. The person who wrote the program may or may not have decided to write code in response to that event. However, if the program is well written, an item such as a button for saving a file, which the user expects to have code behind it, will indeed have code behind it.

How Top-Down and Event-Driven Work Together

When a GUI-based program starts, there is almost always some top-down style code that executes first. This code might be used to read a setting stored in the registry, prompt the user for a name and password, load a particular file at startup or prompt to take the user through setup if this is the first time the application has been run, and so on. Then a form typically comes up. The form contains all the menus, buttons, lists, and fields that make up the user interface of the program. At that point, the top-down style coding is done, and the program enters what is known as a wait state. No code is executing at this point and the program just waits for the user to do something. From here on, it's pretty much all about events.

When the user begins to do something, the program comes to life again. Suppose the user clicks a button. The program raises the `Click` event for the button that the user clicked. The code attached to that event starts to execute, performs some operations, and when it's finished, the program returns to its wait state.

As far as VBScript is concerned, the event-driven model is used heavily in scripting for the Web. Scripts that run inside of HTML web pages are all based on events. One script may execute when the page is loaded, while another script might execute when the user clicks a link or graphic. These "mini scripts" are embedded in the HTML file, and are blocked out in a syntax very similar to the one you used to define the `PromptUserName` function in the previous section.

An Event-Driven Code Example

As you progress through the second half of this book, the finer points of event-driven programming will become much clearer to you. However, just so you can see an example at this point, type the following code into your text editor, save the file with a .HTM extension, and then load it into Internet Explorer 6 (if you are running Internet Explorer 6/7 and you are running this file off your desktop, you might have to dismiss some security warnings and allow ActiveX).

```
<html>
<head>
<title>Simple VBScript Example</title>
<script language="vbscript">
    Sub ButtonClicked
        window.alert("You clicked on the button!")
    End Sub
</script>
</head>
<body>
  <button name="Button1" type="BUTTON" onclick="ButtonClicked">
  Click Me If You Can!!!
  </button>
</body>
</html>
```

Figure 1-8 shows the result of clicking the button on the page. In this case it's only a message box but it could be much more.

Coding Guidelines

It's a really good idea to get into healthy programming habits right from the beginning. As you continue to hone your programming skills and possibly learn multiple languages, these habits will serve you well. Your programs will be easier for you and your fellow developers to read, understand, and modify, and they will also contain fewer bugs.

When you first start writing code, you have to concentrate so hard on just getting the syntax correct for the computer that it may be easy for you to forget about all the things you need to do in order to make sure your code is human friendly as well. However, attentiveness early on will pay huge dividends in the long run.

Figure 1-8

Expect the Unexpected

Always remember that anything that can happen probably will happen. The idea here is to code defensively — preparing for the unexpected. You don't need to become totally fixated on preparing for all contingencies and remote possibilities, but you can't ignore them either. You especially have to worry about the unexpected when receiving input from the user, from a database, or from a file.

Whenever you're about to perform an action on something, ask yourself questions such as:

❑   What could go wrong here?

❑   What happens if the file is flagged read-only?

❑   What happens if the file isn't there?

❑   What happens if the user doesn't run the program from the right folder?

❑   What happens if the database table doesn't have any records?

❑   What happens if the registry keys I was expecting aren't there?

❑   What happens if the user doesn't have the proper permission to carry out the operation?

If you don't know what might go wrong with a given operation, find out through research or trial and error. Get others to try out your code and get their feedback on how it worked for them, on their system configuration, and on their operating system. Don't leave it up to your users to discover how well (or not) your script reacts to something unexpected. A huge part of properly preparing for the unexpected is the implementation of proper error handling, which is discussed in detail in Chapter 6.

Always Favor the Explicit over the Implicit

When you are writing code, constantly ask yourself: Is my intent clear to someone reading this code? Does the code speak for itself? Is there anything mysterious here? Are there any hidden meanings? Are the variable names too similar to be confusing? Even though something is obvious in your mind at the moment you are typing the code, it doesn't mean it will be obvious to you six months or a year from now — or to someone else tomorrow. Always endeavor to make your code as self-documenting as possible, and where you fall short of that goal (which even the best programmers do — self-documenting code can be an elusive goal), use good comments to make things clearer.

Be wary of using too many generics in code, such as x, y, and z as variable names and Function1, Function2, and Function3 as function names. Instead, make them explicit. Use variable names such as UserName and TaxRate. When naming a variable, use a name that will make it clear what that variable is used for. Be careful using abbreviations. Don't make variable names too short, but don't make them too long either (10–16 characters is a good length, but ideal length is largely a matter of preference). Even though VBScript is not case-sensitive, use mixed case to make it easier to distinguish multiple words within the variable name (for example, UserName is easier to read than username).

When naming procedures, try to choose a name that describes exactly what the procedure does. If the procedure is a function that returns a value, indicate what the return value is in the function name (for example, PromptUserName). Try to use good verb–noun combinations to describe first, what action the procedure performs, and second, what the action is performed on (for example, SearchFolders, MakeUniqueRegistryKey, or LoadSettings).

Good procedure names tend to be longer than good variable names. Don't go out of your way to make them longer, but don't be afraid to either. Fifteen to thirty characters for a procedure name is perfectly acceptable (they can be a bit longer because you generally don't type them nearly as much). If you are having trouble giving your procedure a good name, that might be an indication that the procedure is not narrow enough — a good procedure does one thing, and does it well.

That said, if you are writing scripts for web pages to be downloaded to a user's browser, it is sometimes necessary to use shorter variable and procedure names. Longer names mean larger files to download. Even if you sacrifice some readability to make the file smaller, you can still take time to create descriptive names. With web scripts, however, you may encounter instances where you don't want the code to be clear and easy to understand (at least for others). You'll look at techniques that you can employ to make scripts harder for "script snoopers" to follow while still allowing you to work with them and modify them later (see Chapter 17).

Modularize Your Code into Procedures, Modules, Classes, and Components

As you write code, you should constantly evaluate whether any given code block would be better if you moved it to its own function or subprocedure:

❑   Is the code rather complex? If so, break it into procedures.

❑   Are you using many Ands and Ors in an If...End If statement? Consider moving the evaluation to its own procedure.

❑   Are you writing a block of code that you think you might need again in some other part of the script, or in another script? Move it to its own procedure.

❑   Are you writing some code that you think someone else might find useful? Move it.

This isn't a science and there are no hard and fast rules for code — after all, only you know what you want it to do. Only you know if parts are going to be reused later. Only you know how complex something will turn out. However, always keep an eye out for possible modularization.

Use the "Hungarian" Variable Naming Convention

You might hear programmers (especially C++ programmers) mention this quite a bit. While this is a bit out of scope of this introductory discussion, it is still worth mentioning nonetheless. The Hungarian naming convention involves giving variable names a prefix that indicates what the scope and data type of the variable are intended to be. So as not to confuse matters, the Hungarian convention was not used in this chapter, but you will find that most programmers prefer this convention. Properly used, it makes your programs much clearer and easier to write and read.

See Chapter 3 for more on Hungarian notation variable prefixes. The standard prefixes for scope and data types are in Appendix B.

Don't Use One Variable for More Than One Job

This is a big no-no and a common mistake of both beginner and experienced programmers alike (but the fact that experienced programmers might have a bad habit does not make it any less bad). Each variable in your script should have just one purpose.

It might be very tempting to just declare a bunch of generic variables with fuzzy names at the beginning of your script, and then use them for multiple purposes throughout your script — but don't do it. This is one of the best ways to introduce very strange, hard to track down bugs into your scripts. Giving a variable a good name that clearly defines its purpose will help prevent you from using it for multiple purposes. The moral here is that while reusing variables might seem like a total timesaver, it isn't and can lead to hours of frustration and wasted time looking for the problem.

Always Lay Out Your Code Properly

Always remember that good code layout adds greatly to readability later. Don't be tempted to save time early on by writing messy, hard to follow code because as sure as day turns to night, you will suffer if you do.

Without reading a single word, you should be able to look at the indentations of the lines to see which ones are subordinate to others. Keep related code together by keeping them on consecutive lines. Also, don't be frightened of white space in your code. Separate blocks of unrelated code by putting a blank line between them. Even though the script engine will let you, avoid putting multiple statements on the same line. Also, remember to use the line continuation character (_) to break long lines into multiple shorter lines.

The importance of a clean layout that visually suggests the logic of the underlying code cannot be overemphasized.

Use Comments to Make Your Code More Clear and Readable, but Don't Overuse Them

When writing code, strive to make it as self-documenting as possible. You can do this by following the guidelines set out earlier. However, self-documenting code is hard to achieve and no one is capable of 100% self-documenting code. Everyone writes code that can benefit from a few little scribbles to serve as reminders in the margins. The coding equivalents of these scribbles are comments. But how can you tell a good comment from a bad comment?

Generally speaking, a good comment operates at the level of intent. A good comment answers the questions:

- ❏ Where does this code block fit in with the overall script?
- ❏ Why did the programmer write this code?

The answers to these questions fill in the blanks that can never be filled by even the best, most pedantic self-documenting code. Good comments are also generally "paragraph-level" comments. Your code should be clear enough that you do not need a comment for each and every line of code it contains, but a comment that quickly and clearly describes the purpose for a block of code allows a reader to scan through the comments rather than reading every line of code. The idea is to keep the person who might be reading your code from having to pore over every line to try and figure out why the code exists. Commenting every line (as you probably noticed with the earlier examples) makes the code hard to follow and breaks up the flow too much.

Bad comments are generally redundant comments, meaning they repeat what the code itself already tells you. Try to make your code as clear as possible so that you don't need to repeat yourself with comments. Redundant comments tend to add clutter and do more harm than good. Reading the code tells you the how; reading the comments should tell you the why.

Finally, it's a good idea to get into the habit of adding "tombstone" or "flower box" comments at the top of each script file, module, class, and procedure. These comments typically describe the purpose of the code, the date it was written, the original author, and a log of modifications.

```
' Kathie Kingsley-Hughes
' 22 Feb 2007
' This script prompts the user for his or her name.
' It incorporates various greetings depending on input by the user.
'
' Added alternative greeting
' Changed variable names to make them more readable
```

Summary

In this chapter you took a really fast-paced journey through the basics of programming. The authors tried to distill a whole subject (at least a book) into one chapter. You covered an awful lot of ground but also skimmed over or totally passed by a lot of stuff. However, the information in this chapter gave you the basics you need to get started programming with VBScript and the knowledge and confidence you need to talk about programming with other programmers in a language they understand.

2

What VBScript
Is — and Isn't!

VBScript (or Microsoft's Visual Basic Scripting Edition) is a powerful interpreted scripting language that brings active scripting to a variety of environments, both client and server side. But VBScript is part of a bigger programming world — the world of Visual Basic.

This chapter gives you a peek into this bigger programming world and shows you how VBScript fits in with the bigger picture. As the chapter name suggests, you'll look at what VBScript is and also what it isn't (this, hopefully, will dispel any myths that you might have read about VBScript).

Before you go any further, you should spend a little time clearing up a few points and getting the terminology, not just that of VBScript, but also that of related terminology, clear.

Windows Script

Windows Script is the technology that provides the backbone for scripting on the Windows platform. Windows Script itself has two separate script engines for use in the Windows operating system:

❑   Visual Basic Scripting Edition

❑   Microsoft JScript

Both of these scripting languages can be embedded and used side by side if you want — there is no restriction on using only one language within your project, although this does make for more complex code and we don't recommend that you do this.

Windows Script also provides an array of supporting technologies. These include tools such as debuggers and script encoders (see Chapter 17).

Version Information

The latest version of Windows Script is version 5.7. This is the version that this book uses because it is the latest, most fully featured, and contains all the latest security patches. Code written for Windows Script Engine 5.7 might work for earlier versions but cannot be guaranteed (for example, certain new scripting features designed for Windows Vista won't work on earlier operating systems or with earlier versions of the Windows Script Engine).

Version 5.7 introduces integration with Windows Vista, tighter security controls, and a new object model. Windows Script has gone through many versions, each with a different host application behind it, as shown in the following table.

Version	Host Application
1.0	Microsoft Internet Explorer 3.0
2.0	Microsoft Internet Information Server 3.0
3.0	Microsoft Internet Explorer 4.0 Microsoft Internet Information Server 4.0 Microsoft Windows Scripting Host 1.0 Microsoft Outlook 98
4.0	Microsoft Visual Studio 6.0
5.0	Microsoft Internet Explorer 5.0 Microsoft Internet Information Server 5.0
5.5	Microsoft Internet Explorer 5.5
5.6	Microsoft Visual Studio .NET
5.7	Microsoft Windows Vista

VBScript Is a Subset of VB

VBScript is a subset of Microsoft's Visual Basic (VB). What this means is that if you are already using Visual Basic and begin to use VBScript, you will find similarities in the syntax. The same is true if you make the leap from VBScript to Visual Basic (although you must learn how to use the development environment in Visual Basic). Likewise, if you go to VBScript from VB, don't expect this scripting language to look or feel too much like the full-blown programming environment. Certainly don't expect a VB-like integrated development environment (IDE) when you're working with VBScript.

However, the fact that VBScript is a subset of Visual Basic certainly makes it a compelling language to learn, both as a stand-alone tool to use in day-to-day problem solving and as a language to learn that is simple to pick up, with all the advantages of Visual Basic and without the hassle of an IDE and the cost of purchasing the software.

Reinforcing their commitment to VBScript, Microsoft released a script editor with their Microsoft Office 2003 suite and this is also present in Microsoft Office 2007.

VBScript Is a Scripting Language

VBScript is a scripting language, as opposed to a programming language. The difference can be vague but the key test is what happens to the source code before it becomes the end product — for example, what is actually "run" and thought of as the program or application. The end product for a programming language is usually a compiled binary executable program, while for a scripting language the end product is still the source code. What this means is that VBScript source code and the VBScript end product are basically the same thing — a plain-text file that is readable and editable in any text editor (such as the trustworthy old Windows Notepad application included with all Windows versions). No special development environment is needed and the script in the file is not protected in any way.

VBScript Is Interpreted at Runtime

Interpreted is another fuzzy term. It is vague because any language you care to think about can be either compiled or interpreted. This is because for any computer language, you could write both a compiler and an interpreter. As long as the language itself is properly formed, all the compiler/interpreter does is make it machine-readable.

Now you might begin to see why VBScript is interpreted — because it isn't compiled!

> Compiled *means that the code has been recoded into an executable format that has the* .exe *file extension. Programs written in languages, such as C++, need to be compiled into an executable before they are distributed to the user.*

Instead of building a compiler, an interpreter was written that takes the high-level VBScript "source code" and interprets it as it is processed. The interpreter in this case is the VBScript script engine, which is both very versatile and easily accessible for a variety of applications.

This doesn't mean that VBScript is never compiled. All computer languages are compiled at some point; otherwise the computer wouldn't know what to do with it and how to respond to it. The language the computer uses is the lowest level possible — the 1's and 0's of machine or binary language. Different sequences of 1's and 0's mean different things. One binary sequence may tell the computer to add two numbers together while another sequence tells it to store a value in a particular memory address. It's pretty hard to imagine it, but everything you ask a computer to do is ultimately digested into 1's and 0's.

VBScript has some advantages over compiled code. A long time ago, if you wanted to write a program, the only option available to you was to write it in binary language. As you can imagine, this wasn't easy or convenient. Over time, more advanced programming languages were invented. With each language, higher levels of abstraction were added, which meant that programmers could use syntax that was closer to that of the English language. However, while programming languages have become cleverer, computers still continue to use machine language.

Plain text is easily readable by a human (although he or she might not understand what it means). Here's some VBScript code — even if you know nothing about VBScript, you can still read it and perhaps make some sense out of it. At least you aren't looking at a bunch of 1's and 0's!

```
Dim Counter
Dim WordLength
Dim InputWord
Dim WordBuilder

InputWord = InputBox ("Type in a word or phrase to use")

WordLength = Len(InputWord)
For Counter = 1 to WordLength
    MsgBox Mid(InputWord, Counter, 1)
    WordBuilder = WordBuilder & Mid(InputWord, Counter, 1)
Next

MsgBox WordBuilder & " contains "& WordLength & " characters."
```

When code is compiled, the higher-level language, which the programmer understands and writes, is turned into the binary language that the computer understands. The main difference between "normal" programming languages and interpreted scripting languages is not whether the source code is compiled, but when compilation takes place. Take languages such as C and C++ that are commonly known as compiled languages, not because this distinguishes them from noncompiled languages but because they are compiled to machine code at design time (at the time the program was written). This is where scripting languages differ. They are compiled (or, more accurately, interpreted) when they are executed, and hence runtime. This means that right up until runtime, the script remains as plain text. Even during runtime, the actual file isn't altered; all the work in interpreting it is done in memory and has no effect whatsoever on the actual source file. Compare this to a C++ program, which if you were to look at the compiled code would make no sense at all because it has already been processed into machine language. This means that the edit-debugging cycle for scripting languages is usually shorter than that of compiled code, because you do not have to go through the separate step of compiling the code at design time.

All the runtime interpretation of script is carried out by a script engine. The script engine is a special program that understands how to interpret the text in the script and turn that into machine-understandable commands. In this respect, it is similar to any other design-time compiler, with the single exception that users never get to see runtime compilation errors of C++ executable programs, but if you make a mistake in script and don't test it, they will.

Runtime Compilation — Disadvantages

Compiling a program at runtime does have a few disadvantages that are worth bringing out into the open at the beginning:

❑ It's going to be slower. This has to be said early and there's no disputing it. This is simply because the system has to do more at runtime — it has to interpret the code. And remember that the system has to do this each and every time the code is run. However, because you are not normally dealing with programs that span many thousands of lines of code, this step, albeit adding to the load, is normally quite fast.

Note: Don't try asking which is faster — VBScript or JScript/JavaScript; you'll never get a straight answer because it's so subjective and depends on what the code it trying to accomplish, what the system running the code is like, and myriad other factors. For all intents and purposes you can say that VBScript and JScript are, speed wise, identical. It prevents a lot of argument!

❑ A compiled program, once compiled into binary language, is afforded protection from snooping and change. This protects both the application and the developer or company that owns the code. Curious users or malicious hackers cannot read the code to find out how things work, make changes, or "borrow" code for their own applications. Because a script is plain text, it isn't afforded such protection and anyone who can gain access to the file can read it and make changes.

❑ Some will argue that this transparency of code is what has made script so popular (in the same way the ease in reading and making alterations to web pages made HTML a huge success). Transparent code makes it easier for others to find it, read it, copy it, and ultimately learn from it.

Note: Later on in the book you'll be examining ways that you can protect your intellectual property from unwanted snooping using a variety of techniques. None of these techniques are 100 percent foolproof (or close to it) but they do help protect your code from casual eyes. If you want total protection, you need patents and a team of crack lawyers!

❑ When you compile code at design time, you can catch and debug any syntax errors you come across, whereas syntax errors in script aren't caught until runtime. Remember that even expert programmers make syntax errors occasionally when they write code. It's human nature. The design-time compiler or runtime script engine expects you to write code that follows stringent rules of syntax. You can't misspell variable names or have ambiguity over parameters passed. Everything has to be right. And even if you are an expert, simple typos can creep in and wreak havoc. The more complicated the code, the more likely it is to contain a mistake — accept this and plan accordingly. What that ultimately boils down to is one word — testing. Test all code and never rely on thinking that it looks OK or the fact that it worked last time. When the end user sees script errors, it reflects badly on the programmer.

Runtime Compilation — Advantages

With the downsides come the upsides. Here are the advantages of using script over compiled languages.

One of the main advantages of script code being plain text is that it can be embedded with other types of code, for example:

❑ HTML

❑ XHTML

❑ XML

❑ Other script languages

As you've probably guessed, the classic example of this is web scripting where you are free to mix scripts based on different languages (VBScript and JavaScript for example) with HTML (a markup language that handles the content), and CSS (a style-sheet language handling formatting all in one file).

Here is a simple example of VBScript code incorporated into a simple HTML web page.

```
<html>
<head>
<script language="vbscript">
    Sub ButtonClicked
         window.alert("You clicked on the button!")
    End Sub
</script>
</head>
<body>
  <button name="Button1" type=BUTTON onclick="ButtonClicked">
  Click Me If You Can!!!
  </button>
</body>
</html>
```

Even if you don't know much about VBScript just yet, you can probably understand what this code does (the easiest way for you to figure it out is type the code out into Windows Notepad, save it with a .HTM file extension, and run it in Internet Explorer).

In the same way, you can mix script, HTML, and XML (a markup language that handles data structure) in another file. These files can then be downloaded over the Internet in a web browser where it is executed. If you want the same level of flexibility in a compiled language, it would be very hard (or at least expensive) to achieve.

Scripting is ideally suited for quick, ad hoc solutions. For example, say you want to write a small application to back up certain files stored on a hard drive. This is an ideal job for script. Of course, you could do the same job by hand, but if the task is one that is going to be repeated on a regular basis, then an automatic solution would be faster and more accurate. Creating a simple script to solve such problems can be much faster and easier than doing the same thing in a compiled language. Also, compiled solutions take up greater disk space and are not platform-independent.

Finally, because scripting does not require a complicated IDE, such as those required to program with Visual Basic and Visual C++, scripting languages are easier to learn.

Scripting can be an excellent gateway into the vast, exciting, and lucrative world of programming. Scripting languages are much easier to learn and far more forgiving to mistakes than compiled languages, and they are great for solving simple tasks. Also, because VBScript has its roots firmly in the BASIC programming language, it is especially quick and easy for the nonprogrammer to pick up and begin using.

Advantages of Using VBScript

Other advantages to using VBScript as a programming language are as follows:

❑   Good platform coverage. A powerful aspect of VBScript is that it can be run in many environments. Currently there are VBScript script engines for the 32-bit Windows API, 16-bit Windows API, and the Macintosh. VBScript is also integrated into Microsoft Internet Explorer and the latest Windows operating systems. Over the Internet, VBScript can be run both on the client side (through the browser, for example) or server side (using Microsoft's Internet Information Service).

❑ The ability to implement VBScript in your own applications. Add to all that the fact that VBScript is appearing in a variety of other tools and applications thanks to the fact that you can license the VBScript source implementation from Microsoft, completely free of charge, for use in your products and applications. We'll look at what this means in greater detail later in this chapter.

Is VBScript Right for You?

How do you know if VBScript is right for you? Answering a few simple questions should help you come to the right decision.

❑ Are you new to programming? If yes, VBScript is a good entry choice. It's powerful and has a lot of features for you to use (because it is based on a full-fledged programming language — Visual Basic) while still remaining low cost and easy to learn.

❑ Do you want to learn ASP (Active Server Pages)? If the answer is yes, then VBScript is pretty much a must. While you don't have to use VBScript for ASP, you'll find the learning curve steeper because so much ASP-related material uses VBScript as the language of choice.

❑ Do you want to leverage your existing Visual Basic skills? If the answer is yes, diversifying into VBScript can open up new avenues to you, such as server-side ASP and client-side web development. You can also use VBScript to automate tasks and carry out administrative functions on desktops using Windows Script. In this case, VBScript is superior to VB because you can quickly write and debug small files and deploy them over a network to carry out such tasks.

But how do you know if VBScript is the wrong tool for you to use? Faced with many different programming languages to choose from, it can be hard to come to the right decision, especially if you don't understand the capabilities of each language.

Fortunately, it's easy to find out if VBScript is the right choice for the project you have in mind. For example, VBScript isn't for you if you want to end up with a compiled executable program, if you want to make extensive use of file I/O, or if speed or graphical manipulation is important to you.

This isn't an exhaustive list by far, but it does cover the areas of programming best left to another language. However, this isn't to say that VBScript can't handle graphical manipulation or file I/O — it can do both — it's just that it's not ideally suited to those applications and other languages exist that can do the job much better. This doesn't reflect badly on VBScript in any way, it's just a case of using the right tools for the right job.

For example, VBScript is for you if you want to quickly prototype code, you write code to carry out repetitive processes (such as backing up or deleting files) or administrative functions (such as registry tweaks), you want to use ASP, you are a web developer who builds web pages aimed at Internet Explorer users either on the Internet or intranet, or you are developing an application and want to include scripting support for it.

How VBScript Fits in with the Visual Basic Family

VBScript (sometimes referred to as VBS), Visual Basic for Applications (VBA), Visual Basic (VB) — what's the difference between them all?

Visual Basic

Let's begin by taking a look at Visual Basic. VBScript and VBA are both subsets of Visual Basic itself, which is a stand-alone, hybrid language (that is hybrid between compiled and interpreted), complete with its own IDE. This IDE includes all the things you'd expect of an IDE — language editor, form designer, debugging tools, code project managers, controls to integrate into applications, wizards, and so on, to aid the developer. Visual Basic provides a full set of language features and includes the ability to access the Windows API and, thus key functions of the Windows operating system.

> ### Is VB a Hybrid Language?
>
> It's not accurate to call Visual Basic a compiled language. It is more of a hybrid between a compiled language and an interpreted language. Applications written in VB are indeed compiled, but they rely on a very large "runtime library" to work. This runtime library consists of a set of DLL files (`Asycfilt.dll`, `Comcat.dll`, `Msvbvm60.dll`, `Oleaut32.dll`, `Olepro32.dll`, and `Stdole2.tlb`) that have to be installed on the system that wants to run the VB application. This isn't a big problem because the program that builds the installer includes these files; the problem is just that even the smallest VB application distribution becomes bigger than 1MB when these files are included. This situation is changed in Visual Basic .NET (VB.NET) with the introduction of the Common Language Runtime Framework.

Let's add another bit of confusion. Although VBA is considered a subset to VB based on the functionality that it offers, VB actually uses VBA at its core because the VBA library defines both the VB language itself and allows other applications (such as Microsoft Word) to host Visual Basic capabilities. So you could look at the Visual Basic IDE as just another host.

Visual Basic for Applications

Visual Basic for Applications is an "embedded" version of Visual Basic. VBA gives developers with an existing application a powerful tool to customize and extend the application. The biggest and best example of this is the Microsoft Office suite of applications, Microsoft Word, Microsoft Excel, Microsoft Outlook, and Microsoft Access. These applications all support VBA and come fully equipped with a VBA IDE similar to that provided by VB. Using the VBA IDE, you can write code that goes well beyond the basic features these applications offer and design custom tools to handle pretty much any job you want to carry out. For example, you could write some code that would control how templates function or which populate Excel spreadsheets with data and check that the results are correct so you could test the functions and equations you've used.

VBA is quite fast, but not as fast as Visual Basic. VBA code is compiled by the host application into interpreted P-code in a similar way that VB version 4.0 and earlier were capable of.

The main thing to remember here is that VBA can only live and work, and is therefore, irrevocably bound, within the host applications. You can't write a small application in VBA, distribute it, and expect it to work stand-alone. Neither can you distribute a whole Microsoft application with it! You can, however, distribute VBA to others who have the host application, but you must bear in mind that the hosts must be the same to ensure that all functionality is present. There would be no point, for example, in distributing VBA code that works on a spreadsheet and expect it to work in a word processor.

VBScript

Syntactically, VBScript is similar to both VB and VBA. If you've used either before, the syntax that we use in VBScript code should be pleasantly familiar to you. However, it is quite different in other important respects.

VBScript, like VBA, needs a hosting application. However, VBScript depends on a scripting host that can interpret, compile, and execute plain-text VBScript code at runtime. VBScript began life as a browser scripting language but it's grown from being merely a Microsoft alternative to JavaScript (called LiveScript in the early days), where Microsoft wanted VB developers to be able to embed code into plain-text HTML pages and have it run at runtime into a scripting language that goes way beyond scripting for the Internet Explorer browser and has found many new hosts — including the Windows operating system itself.

Is VBScript a "Real" Programming Language?

Many people worry about this needlessly. They have heard or read that serious C++ or VB developers don't think that VBScript, or any scripting language, is "real" programming, and as such isn't worth learning. This is absolutely wrong. It's just a matter of picking the right tool for the job. If you were going to develop a new word processor, web browser, or accounting system, choosing VBScript as the main tool would be unwise for a variety of reasons. However, including VBScript support in that application, so that the end user might automate repetitive tasks, would be a major bonus.

Also, let's face it; it's not every day that you want to write something major. Sometimes programming skills come into play to solve much smaller problems, which is where VBScript can be useful. Also, try embedding C++ code into an HTML or ASP page — that's not going to work, no matter how "real" you think it is.

The basic fact of the matter is that Microsoft didn't come up with VBScript as a replacement for all other development tools — although a free tool that did that would be cool. VBScript is designed to supplement and augment other languages and to provide a low-impact, easy solution to some tasks while leaving the big stuff to the more powerful languages.

Think of VBScript as an important tool in today's programmer toolkit and you won't go far wrong.

What Can You Do with VBScript?

As the last section illustrated, VBScript is a powerful language, but on its own it can't do anything. In order to make it do something you need a host because the code itself isn't compiled. As already mentioned, a host is an application that can interpret, compile, and execute plain-text VBScript code.

The following is a quick tour of possible hosts for VBScript code.

PowerShell

Windows PowerShell, formerly called Microsoft Shell, MSH, and Monad, is an interactive command-line and task-based script technology that gives administrators a way to automate tasks on a PC. It is based on object-oriented programming and the Microsoft .NET Framework.

PowerShell doesn't make use of VBScript, but the syntax of the language is so similar to VBScript that you'll see the basics of PowerShell here in this book. PowerShell requires .NET Framework 2.0 and is supported on Windows XP, Windows Server 2003, Windows Vista, and Windows Server "Longhorn."

Windows Script Host

The Windows Script Host (WSH — previously called the Windows Scripting Host) is just one host that allows you to run VBScript, in this case directly from within the Windows operating system. The concept of WSH is similar to that of the DOS batch file or Unix Shell scripting. You can also choose how these scripts are run:

❑   From the command line

❑   Within Windows (for example, by double-clicking the script file)

WSH is perfect for a variety of common network and administrative tasks, such as making registry changes and creating network logon scripts.

The great thing about WSH is that you can run script just as simply as you run any other program installed on the system. It looks just like any other compiled application to the user, but under the hood it is powered by script.

WSH also comes complete with a set of objects that allow the programmer access to the Windows file system and environment.

> *You don't have to write WSH scripts in VBScript. In fact, you can use any language that conforms to the ActiveX scripting specification, including Perl, Jscript, and Python.*

WSH is the perfect way to try out many of the code examples that appear in this book. Remember, though, that some scripts depend on certain hosts. For example, client-side web scripts require Microsoft Internet Explorer browser while Active Server Pages (ASP) script needs Microsoft's Internet Information Service (IIS) or Personal Web Server (PWS) or equivalent to run. WSH is supported on all Windows operating systems from Windows 98 to Windows Vista.

Gadgets

Windows Gadgets are small, self-contained mini programs that are designed to give the user at-a-glance information and to offer easy access to frequently used tools. The Windows Sidebar helps users control and organize their gadgets. Gadgets have a number of functions, but three of the most common uses are:

- ❑ Offer access to information on the Web.
- ❑ Perform tasks.
- ❑ Interact with software and applications.

Windows Script Components

A Windows Script Component (WSC) is a COM component that combines XML with script code. These are run server side and can perform a variety of tasks, such as performing middle-tier business logic, accessing and manipulating databases, adding transaction processing to applications (in conjunction with Microsoft Transaction Server), and adding interactive effects to a web page in conjunction with DHTML behaviors. Previously, this level of control and application was only available to C++, Visual Basic, and Delphi developers.

Client-Side Web Scripting

Client-side web scripting is probably the VBScript host that offers you, as the developer, the greatest reach in terms of potential users. Web use is on the increase daily and now even the simplest HTML page often contains script code. The script code in HTML pages is downloaded into the browser with the corresponding HTML code that defines the structure of the page (and any CSS that might be used for formatting). The visitor's browser then interprets this code.

You can use script not only to make web pages look compelling to the visitor to the site, but also to add functional features to a page, help to reduce server load and page load times, and maximize on bandwidth.

Server-Side Web Scripting

Server-side web scripting is done using ASP pages, which are HTML pages that contain specially formatted script code. This, unlike client-side script, is then processed at the server when a request is made for the page and the output is sent to the browser that made the request. Pages created with ASP can, just like ordinary HTML pages, contain script that is processed client side by the browser.

The host for ASP is installed on the server. In order to take advantage of ASP on the Internet you need access to a server running an appropriate host, such as IIS.

Here is a simple ASP example (don't worry about what it means just yet. In fact it is a simple ASP-based counter for a web page).

```
<%
Set FS=Server.CreateObject("Scripting.FileSystemObject")
Set RS=FS.OpenTextFile(Server.MapPath("counter.txt"), 1, False)
fcount=RS.ReadLine()
RS.Close

fcount=fcount+1

Set RS=FS.OpenTextFile(Server.MapPath("counter.txt"), 2, False)
RS.Write fcount
RS.Close

Set RS=Nothing
Set FS=Nothing

%>
<html>
<body>
<p>
This page has been visited <%=fcount%> times.
</p>
</body>
</html>
```

If you don't have access to an ASP capable server, you can always download PWS for Windows 95, Windows 98, and Windows Me or Install IIS on Windows NT, Windows 2000, Windows XP Professional, and Windows Vista Ultimate or Professional. Using this, you can develop your own ASP and view them in any web browser you have installed on your system.

Remote Scripting

Remote scripting is a technology that allows you to treat all ASP pages as if they were COM objects. This allows the client to "call" scripts that are embedded in ASP pages on the server. This means you can allow scripts to be run server side as if they were client side. The advantage of this is that large, complicated code doesn't have to be downloaded to the user's browser, speeding up the process as well as protecting any proprietary code from prying eyes and alteration.

HTML Applications

An HTML Application (HTA) is a web page that runs in its own window outside of the browser window. This offers many advantages over running a script from within the browser itself:

❑ HTAs run outside the browser and as such are considered "trusted" and are subject to different security constraints.

❑ You can use HTAs to build stand-alone graphical applications that may be run without the need for a web server, network, or Internet connection to work.

❑ HTAs are likely to be of great interest to WSH programmers who were previously limited to using pop-up dialog boxes to communicate with the user, instead enabling them to create an effective interface using HTML.

Add VBScript to Your Applications

Imagine giving users of your application the power to automate general functions within that application using a simple-to-learn scripting language. Would that be something you'd be interested in? How much would that be worth to you? Read on if you are interested.

Giving the user the ability to control and customize an application using script is a compelling one. Adding a solution that has been designed in-house is one possibility, but that is likely to be difficult and probably second rate. Now, Visual Basic, C++, Delphi, and other developers can add VBScript support directly to their applications using the free Microsoft Script Control (MSC).

Adding the MSC adds support not only for VBScript, but also for JScript, Perl, and other ActiveX-enabled scripting languages — all by adding a few extra lines of code to the application. The ActiveX control you need (the Microsoft Windows Script Control) is freely available for download from the Microsoft site at `http://www.microsoft.com/` (although you will have to search for it — it's not easy to find at present and the link is too long and complex to include here). And don't think you have to download a massive component — the current file size is just 200KB.

The MSC is supported by Windows 98, Windows Me, Windows 2000, Windows XP, and Windows Vista.

> *The Windows Script Control is currently available only in the English and German languages.*

Tool of the Trade — Tools for VBScript

As already mentioned, VBScript has no development environment; so, what tools should you use for VBScript? Well, if you don't want to spend money on an editor, just use plain old Windows Notepad that comes with every install of Windows. It's fast, easy-to-use, reliable, and does the job just fine. However, it's primitive and not customized for any specific coding or scripting application.

So, if you want more, you might have to spend a little cash (depending on what you choose). Hundreds of text editors are on the market that allow you to edit text and do a lot more. Some come with advanced clipboard control, auto-indenting, color-coded syntax, auto-backup, and many more functions.

Text Editor Listing

The following table shows a selection of editors — some free, some shareware, and some commercial — that exist. Any would be ideal for VBScript writing and the final choice you make will be based on personal preference.

Editor	Share- or Freeware?	Manufacturer	Web Site
UltraEdit-32	Shareware	IDM Computer Solutions, Inc	http://www.ultraedit.com/
TextPad	Shareware	Helios Software Solutions	http://www.textpad.com/
EditPlus Text Editor	Shareware	ES-Computing	http://www.editplus.com/
Jedit	Freeware	Slava Pestov	http://www.jedit.org
Edit Pad	Shareware	Jan Goyvaerts	http://www.just-great-software.com/
Vim	Charityware	Bram Moolenaar	http://www.vim.org/
HomeSite	Commercial	Adobe	http://www.adobe.com/products/homesite/

If you don't like any of these, then fire up your browser, log on to your favorite search engine or shareware site, and start looking! There are literally hundreds out there, so take your pick!

Summary

Now that you read this chapter you should have a pretty good idea of what VBScript is, what it isn't, and how VBScript fits in with the Visual Basic family of languages. This chapter also introduced the VBScript hosts that you can use and touched upon the fact that if you develop applications in another language you can add VBScript support to them for free. Now that you've had a brief introduction to programming and taken a tour of VBScript, it's time to take a look at the detailed nitty-gritty of the language, beginning with variables and data types.

3

Data Types

This chapter introduces VBScript data types, which, jumping ahead a little, is linked to the subject of the next chapter, "Variables and Procedures." The concepts of variables and data types are closely related. A *variable* is a name given to a location in memory where some data used by a program is stored. For example, a program that manages your music collection might have a variable called Artist that might store the value "James Brown". The variable named Artist is a *pointer* to a location in the computer's memory where the value "James Brown" is stored. (Lucky for us, for the most part VBScript keeps us from having to worry about things like pointers and memory.)

Variables can hold different *types* of data: numbers, dates, text, and other more specialized, or complex, categories. These categories into which values can be divided are called *data types*.

A full discussion of programming language design relative to the strengths and weaknesses of, and alternate techniques for, the use of data types is out of the scope of this book. Suffice to say that in VBScript programming, data types help simplify the logic of a programming language compiler and also help ensure proper and correct results during the program's execution. Even if you did not know a lot about how compilers work, you could imagine that the instructions given to your computer for adding numbers together, computing the length of time between two dates, and searching a long string of text for the occurrence of the word "apple" would be much different from each other. Data types help the compiler figure out what you're trying to make your program do.

Here is why this chapter is important, even if you're an experienced programmer in other languages: While your success as a VBScript programmer does not depend on your understanding of low-level details such as compilers and machine instructions, it is critical to understand how VBScript handles data types and variables, including the particulars of VBScript's "universal" data type, the Variant. VBScript has some features and behaviors that are unique and, on the surface, confusing.

Scripting Languages as Loosely Typed

Generally speaking, when it comes to data types programming languages come in two flavors:

❑ A *strongly typed* language forces the programmer to declare, in advance, the data type of every variable so that the compiler knows exactly what kind of value to expect in that variable. A strongly typed language is "strict" on the topic of data types: You must say in advance what type of data you are going to store in a variable, and you have to stick to it in your program's code. If a programmer declares a variable with a numeric data type, the compiler expects that variable to hold a number, and produces an error if the programmer violates that assumption by trying to, for instance, store a date in that variable.

❑ In a *loosely typed* language, the programmer does not have to declare in advance the data type of a variable. The type of data stored in a variable still matters (you can't ask the computer to add 2 + banana), but the language isn't so strict about it. Often, in fact, a loosely typed language does not even provide a way to declare the data type, while a strongly typed language forces you to declare every variable's type.

Scripting languages such as VBScript are often loosely typed. VBScript, like other scripting languages, uses an all-purpose, *universal*, super data type that can hold any type of data. In VBScript, as you will learn, this universal data type is called the *Variant*.

The opposite of a scripting language is a *compiled language*. Scripting languages are often loosely typed, and compiled languages are often strongly typed, but it can and does go both ways. Code written in a compiled language is processed in advance by a compiler, which produces an optimized binary executable file — such as the .EXE files you are no doubt accustomed to seeing on your computer. A scripting language is not compiled in advance, but rather on the fly. The process for a compiled language is:

1. Write the code in plain text.

2. Compile the code to produce an executable file.

3. Run the compiled executable file.

4. The program runs.

Instead of a compiler, most scripting languages, including VBScript, have the concept of a *runtime engine*, which "interprets" the code "at runtime" instead of compiling it in advance. The process for a scripting language goes a bit differently:

1. Write the code in plain text.

2. Execute the script file.

3. The scripting runtime engine compiles the code on the fly.

4. The program runs.

The delayed compilation that comes with a scripting language goes hand in hand with the loose typing of the language. At the risk of oversimplifying, because code is compiled on the fly, the compiler can examine the data being placed into a variable and what kinds of operations are being performed on the variable to arrive at an educated guess for what the data type of that variable should be. It makes a good guess, moves forward based on that guess, and usually everything comes out just fine — but there are ways a VBScript programmer can get into trouble, which you'll learn to avoid in this chapter.

The concepts of loose typing, the universal Variant data type, and the educated data type guessing of the VBScript runtime engine lead to some interesting scenarios and behaviors when you execute the VBScript code you have written. Throughout this chapter, you examine these details to ensure that you do not fall into any programming traps related to VBScript's unique way of working with variables and data types.

Why Data Types Are Important

Consider for a moment the Visual Basic programmer's perspective on data types. It may seem odd to suddenly change the subject to a different programming language, but VBScript and Visual Basic are actually very closely related and often used together. You can think of Visual Basic as a kind of parent of VBScript. VBScript syntax is derived directly from Visual Basic, and in many cases Visual Basic and VBScript syntax are identical.

It may seem counterintuitive, but VBScript data type concepts are simpler to explain and easier to grasp when presented in the context of Visual Basic. After a brief discussion about data types in Visual Basic, the next section connects these concepts directly to VBScript's Variant data type and its peculiarities.

Visual Basic is a strongly typed language, which, as mentioned earlier, means that a Visual Basic programmer must declare a specific data type for each variable used in his or her program. For example, here is a variable declaration in Visual Basic. This line of code means that the programmer is telling the computer to reserve space in memory for a variable called OrderTotal and that the data type that will be stored in that variable is the Currency data type. (The Currency type is used to store numeric values that represent an amount of money.)

```
Dim OrderTotal As Currency
```

By declaring the OrderTotal variable with the Currency data type, the programmer is signaling his or her intention to store *only* numeric amounts of money in this variable. He does not plan to store a date or a customer's name in the OrderTotal variable. And if he did, the Visual Basic compiler would produce an error. Take a look at the next two lines of code, which assign two different values to the OrderTotal variable.

```
OrderTotal = 695.95
OrderTotal = "Bill's Hardware Store"
```

The first line of code works fine, because a numeric value is being stored in the Currency type variable. However, the second line of code will produce an error because the type of data going into the variable does not match the declared data type. A strongly typed language also makes a line of code like the following produce an error.

```
OrderTotal = 695.95 + "Bill's Hardware Store"
```

(Believe it or not, this line of code would not produce an error in VBScript — keep reading to find out why.)

Use of strong typing in a Visual Basic program produces several technical benefits in the compilation and performance of a Visual Basic application. However, because this book is about VBScript, we don't get into that. We *do* discuss benefits that translate directly to VBScript — namely, the predictability and clarity that strong typing brings to programming (once again, in the interest of simplicity we are side-stepping some debates in the programming community on this topic).

Regardless of the languages and tools applied, a programmer always wants to accomplish at least three things:

❑ Fulfill the requirements for the program (in other words, build a program that will do what it is supposed to do).

❑ Produce a program that is free of bugs and mistakes.

❑ Leave behind code that is easy for other people to read and understand.

Code that is clear, readable, and predictable will always be easier for human beings to read, understand, and change. Code that is easy to read, understand, and change is always more likely to fulfill the requirements and more likely to be free of bugs than code that is not.

A Visual Basic programmer must declare a variable for a specific purpose, give the variable a specific name, and declare the intention to store only a specific type of data in that variable. If all of the elements of a program are this neatly segmented, given good specific names like OrderTotal, and used in a very consistent manner, the program is likely to do what it's supposed to do without a lot of bugs. Internal order and elegance often have a correspondence with correctness and quality. Strong typing tends to encourage a certain amount of internal order because the programmer must think in advance about the type of data he intends to store in each variable. If the programmer missteps, the compiler (or the runtime) will smack him on the hand.

Things are a little different, though, for the VBScript programmer. VBScript does not have any syntax for declaring a variable with the Currency data type, or any other specific data type. All VBScript variables have the same "universal" data type, Variant. Here is the OrderTotal variable again in Visual Basic:

```
Dim OrderTotal As Currency
```

And here is the equivalent variable declaration in VBScript:

```
Dim OrderTotal
```

The syntax is almost the same, but VBScript does not support the As keyword for declaring a data type. This means that the VBScript programmer is free to put any kind of data in this variable he or she wants. The following lines of VBScript code are equally valid in VBScript. Unlike in Visual Basic, neither the second or third line of code produces an error in VBScript:

```
OrderTotal = 695.95
OrderTotal = "Bill's Hardware Store"
OrderTotal = 695.95 + "Bill's Hardware Store"
```

That third line of code results in the value "695.95Bill's Hardware Store" stored in the OrderTotal variable.

The reason for these seemingly strange VBScript behaviors will become clear as you delve into the `Variant` data type and its subtypes. Before you get there, however, there is a lesson to take away from this comparison of Visual Basic and VBScript variables and data types: Even though VBScript does not inherently offer the benefits that come with the rigidity of Visual Basic's strong typing and declared data types, VBScript programmers can still realize these benefits. Realizing the benefits takes two things.

❑ You must understand how the `Variant` data type works — in particular, how the `Variant` subtypes correspond almost exactly to the Visual Basic data types. There are specific ways to control the subtype of a `Variant` variable so that your programming techniques won't be that much different than if you were programming in Visual Basic. You'll learn these techniques in this chapter.

❑ When you program in VBScript, you must *pretend* you are programming in Visual Basic. You must pretend that each variable you declare has been declared with a specific data type. Just because the VBScript runtime engine does not care if you store the value `"Bob's Hardware Store"` in the `OrderTotal` variable does not mean that you can't be careful to ensure that your code never does that. In fact, when you get to the section "Hungarian Notation Variable Prefix" later in this chapter you'll see a way that you can declare your intention for each variable to hold a specific data type even though VBScript will not enforce that intention in the way that Visual Basic would.

The Variant: VBScript's Only Data Type

As discussed in the previous sections, the `Variant` is the only data type supported in VBScript. Programmers in other non-scripting languages, who are likely accustomed to a wide range of data types that are enforced by the compiler, might find this disconcerting. However, once you see the full range of the `Variant` "subtypes," and how you can test for and control them, even die-hard strong typing fans will be at least comfortable. Because the `Variant` subtype feature allows you to store many different data types and still keep track of what the data type should be, your scripts can handle just about any kind of data you need: numbers, strings (text), and dates, plus other more complex data types such as objects and arrays.

At this point, please flip back to the end of the book and check out Appendix I, "The Variant Subtypes." This appendix contains two tables that can be of great use to you as you read along with this chapter and as you write VBScript code on your own.

Keep a bookmark in Appendix I, as you'll want to refer to it as you progress through this chapter.

The first table in Appendix I contains a list of all of the possible subtypes of the `Variant` data type. For each subtype, you can see the equivalent Visual Basic data type, followed by some information about some special functions that you can use to test for and control what the subtype is in each of your `Variant` variables. For now, don't worry too much about these function-related columns (we'll get to these very soon). Just take a look at the list of subtypes and how they line up with the Visual Basic data types.

The second table is a list of all of the native Visual Basic data types. As you saw in the first table, all of these data types have an equivalent `Variant` subtype (that is, except for the `Variant` data type itself, which in Visual Basic is pretty much the same as it is in VBScript). Take a few moments and look through this second table. Notice what kinds of values can be stored in each of the data types. The properties of each Visual Basic data type are exactly the same as the equivalent `Variant` subtype.

A *subtype*, as the name suggests, is a type within a type. You can think of the `Variant` itself as the parent data type and the subtype as the child. The "child" subtype can be one of the many types listed in the aforementioned table in Appendix I. Another analogy could be that the Variant is a generic container that can hold many different types of things, and that this container is smart enough to keep track of the type of what it is storing.

A `Variant` variable has exactly one subtype; in other words, the `Variant`'s subtype can only be one type at a time. For example, the subtype cannot be both a `String` and a `Long` at the same time.

The subtype of a variable can change depending on what kind of data your code puts into the variable. That is, not only is the `Variant` "container" smart enough to keep track of the subtype, but it's pretty good at guessing what the subtype should be no matter what kind of data is put in it. As a rule, the subtype and the type of data will always be compatible. For example, it is impossible to have a subtype of `Long` with the value `"Hello"` stored in it. If the value of `"Hello"` was placed into the variable, then the subtype will automatically be changed to `String`. The `Variant` will, like a chameleon, automatically change its subtype based on the type of data placed into it. This process of changing the subtype even has a fancy name: *type coercion*.

Even with this fancy name, the subtype concept may seem simple. However, some real pitfalls are waiting for you, and we haven't even brought up implicit versus explicit type coercion. Starting in the next section, you will dig deep into subtypes and type coercion. The investment in reading time (and perhaps trying out the examples) will be well worth it.

Testing for and Coercing Subtypes

Two built-in VBScript functions allow you to check what the subtype is for any `Variant` variable. These functions are `VarType()` and `TypeName()`. These two functions do pretty much the same thing, but `VarType()` returns a numeric representation of the subtype, and `TypeName()` returns a text representation (the terms "text" and "string" are sometimes used interchangeably). Take a look at the last two columns of the subtypes table in Appendix I, and you'll see the different values that `VarType()` and `TypeName()` will return for each of the subtypes. Notice also that there are *named constant* equivalents for each of the values that `VarType()` returns.

A named constant is similar to a variable, in that it represents a certain value, but constants cannot be changed at runtime as variables can. You can use a named constant in place of an actual value, which improves the understandability of your code. For example, it's much clearer to write:

```
If VarType(MyVariable) = vbString Then
```

rather than

```
If VarType(MyVariable) = 8 Then
```

The constant named `vbString` is the same as saying `8`, but using the constant makes the code easier to understand. VBScript comes with a few built-in named constants, and you can also declare your own. These constants are covered later in this chapter.

As you can see in the third column of the subtypes table, VBScript also provides some functions that you can use to force (or coerce) the Variant to have a specific subtype, assuming that the value stored in the variable is legal for that subtype. Manual coercion (so called because the programmer is explicitly coercing the type in the code) is useful when you want to ensure that the value stored in a Variant variable is treated in a certain way — for example, something of mathematical significance, such as ensuring that the number stored in the OrderTotal variable is treated as Currency and not as a floating point type like Single or Double.

> *The conversion functions are also useful when you need to pass data to a VB/COM object that expects data of a specific data type — but that's jumping ahead to Chapter 7.*

Sometimes the subtype can go different ways. The value 12 can be stored in a Variant variable with either a String subtype or one of the numeric subtypes, such as Long. If you want to make sure that the number 12 is treated as a number, and not text, you can use the CLng() conversion function to force the subtype to be Long and not String.

A Variant variable automatically chooses its subtype whenever you place a new value into it. It does this by examining the value placed into it and making its best guess about what the appropriate subtype is. Sometimes, though, the Variant's best guess is not quite what you expect. You can control this apparent lack of predictability by being careful and explicit in your code. This will all become clearer as you walk through some examples.

Automatic Assignment of String Subtype

Let's look at some code examples that will demonstrate the principles that we have been talking about here.

About the Windows Script Host

All of the examples in this chapter are tailored so that they can be run by the Windows Script Host (WSH). The Windows Script Host is a program that runs within Windows that knows how to interpret script files coded in VBScript. The WSH provides a context within which the script can execute, and also exposes some of the functionality of the Windows operating system to your scripts. (To learn more about the WSH, please see Chapter 15.)

The WSH allows you to try out the examples in this chapter and many of the chapters that follow (some chapters focus on other hosts such as Active Server Pages and PowerShell).

If you are running a newer version of Windows such as Windows 2000, Windows XP, Windows Server 2003, or Windows Vista, you probably already have the WSH installed and running, just waiting to execute a script.

If you are running an older version of Windows, you may or may not have the WSH installed. To find out, follow the example below by attempting to run the script. You can create the .VBS file yourself or download the script files for this chapter from the Wrox web site.

(continued)

> ### About the Windows Script Host *(continued)*
>
> To run a .VBS script file, simply double-click the .VBS file in Windows Explorer. If the script runs, then you're all set. If Windows does not recognize the file, then you'll need to download and install WSH from: http://msdn.microsoft.com/scripting.
>
> Keep in mind that some virus protection programs will be suspicious of .VBS files, because some viruses propagate using WSH scripts. Rest assured that the script files in this book are harmless.

Run the following script using the Windows Script Host. You can type it in yourself, but it's much easier to download the code for this book from the Wrox web site (visit www.wrox.com). All of the scripts in this chapter are available as individual .VBS files. Throughout the book, before each code example, we will identify the filename in which the script is contained. This script can be found in SUBTYPE_STRING.VBS.

```
Dim varTest
varTest = "Hello There"
MsgBox TypeName(varTest)
```

Running this code results in the dialog box shown in Figure 3-1.

Figure 3-1

You placed the text value "Hello There" into the variable called varTest, and VBScript automatically decided that the variable should have the String subtype. VBScript Variant variables are smart this way. VBScript takes an educated guess about what the appropriate subtype should be and sets it accordingly.

Dealing with string values such as "Hello There" is generally straightforward — unless your string value looks like a number, as in the following examples. The script file for the first example is SUBTYPE_STRING2.VBS.

```
Dim varTest
varTest = "12"
MsgBox TypeName(varTest)
```

Running this code results in the exact same dialog box (see Figure 3-2) as in the previous example where you used the string `"Hello There"`.

Figure 3-2

At first glance, it may seem like VBScript's `Variant` is not that smart after all. Why does the `TypeName()` function return `"String"` when you clearly passed it a numeric value of 12? This is because you placed the value 12 in quotes. VBScript is doing only what you told it to do. By placing the number in quotes, you are telling VBScript to treat the value as a string, not a number.

Coercing String to Long

Following are three variations on the previous example that are, in different ways, explicit about the desire to have the value 12 treated as a number, not a string (SUBTYPE_NUMBER.VBS, SUBTYPE_NUMBER2.VBS, and SUBTYPE_NUMBER3.VBS, respectively):

```
Dim varTest
varTest = 12
MsgBox TypeName(varTest)
```

```
Dim varTest
varTest = CInt("12")
MsgBox TypeName(varTest)
```

```
Dim varTest
varTest = "12"
varTest = CInt(varTest)
MsgBox TypeName(varTest)
```

All three scripts have the same result, as illustrated in the dialog box shown in Figure 3-3.

Figure 3-3

These three examples achieve the same result because they are ultimately doing the same thing: *coercing* the varTest variable to have the Integer subtype:

❑ The first example results in the Integer subtype because you did not enclose the value 12 in quotes, as you did previously. Omitting the quotes tells VBScript that you want the number to be treated as a number, not as text. (It just so happens that in this situation VBScript chooses Integer from among the several numeric types — more on that later.)

❑ The second example uses the CInt() conversion function to transform the string value "12" into an integer value *before* placing it in the variable. This tells the VBScript that you want the subtype to be Integer right from the start.

❑ The third example does basically the same thing as the second but uses two lines of code instead of one. All three examples represent valid ways to make sure that the value you are placing in the variable is treated as a numeric Integer value and not text. However, the first example is better for two reasons: one, because it is more straightforward and succinct; and two, because it is theoretically faster as you're not making the extra call to the CInt() function.

Note that this code would be redundant.

```
Dim varTest
varTest = CInt(12)
```

Because you do not have quotes around the 12, the subtype will automatically be Integer, and so the CInt() call is unnecessary. However, this code has a different effect.

```
Dim varTest
varTest = CLng(12)
```

This tells VBScript to make sure that the subtype of the variable is Long. The same numeric value of 12 is stored in the variable, but instead of being classified as an Integer, it is classified as a Long. Generally speaking, in a VBScript program this distinction between Integer and Long is not so important (unless you have some large numbers to work with), but the distinction *would* be significant if you were passing the value to a VB/COM function that required a Long. When passing variables between VBScript and VB/COM, it is more important to be particular about data types. (If you remember from the lists of data types mentioned earlier in this chapter, Integer and Long are distinguished by the fact that the Long type can hold larger values.)

54

By default, the `Variant` subtype will be `Integer` when a whole number within the `Integer` range is placed in the variable. However, if you place a whole number outside of this range into the variable, it will choose the `Long` subtype, which has a much larger range (–2,147,483,648 to 2,147,483,647). You will find that the `Long` data type is used far more often than the `Integer` in VB/COM components and ActiveX controls, so you may need to use the `CLng()` function often to coerce your `Variant` subtypes to match, although this is not always necessary — when you are passing `Variant` variables to a COM/VB function, VBScript often takes care of the type coercion for you implicitly (more on this later in the chapter).

Given that VBScript chooses the `Integer` subtype by default instead of the `Long`, you would also expect it to choose the `Single` by default instead of the `Double` when placing floating-point numbers into a `Variant` variable, because the `Single` takes up less resources than the `Double`. However, this is not the case. When floating-point numbers (that is, numbers with decimal places) are assigned to a `Variant` variable, the default subtype is `Double`.

Also, as you'll see later, in the section "Implicit Type Coercion," when you are placing the result of a mathematical expression into an un-initialized `Variant` variable, VBScript will choose the `Double` subtype.

Hungarian Notation Variable Prefixes

You may have noticed that the variable in the last code examples used the `var` prefix. This might look strange if you have not seen *Hungarian notation* before. Hungarian notation is a convention for naming variables that uses prefixes to convey the data type of the variable (as well as its "scope" — you learn about scope in the next chapter).

A data type prefix can tell you (and other programmers who are reading or modifying your code) what type of data you *intend* for a variable to hold. In other words, `Variant` variables *can* hold any kind of data, but in practice, any given variable *should* generally hold only one kind of data.

In Visual Basic, because it is a strongly typed language, each variable can hold the type of data only for which it is declared. For example, a Visual Basic variable declared with the `Long` data type can hold *only* whole numbers within the lower and upper ranges of the `Long` data type. In VBScript, however, where every variable is a `Variant`, any given variable can hold any kind of data.

Remember earlier it was said that when you code in VBScript, you want to pretend you are programming in Visual Basic? This is one example of this pretending technique. If you use Hungarian prefixes to signal what kind of data you intend for a variable to hold, it makes it a lot easier to avoid accidentally placing the value `"Bill's Hardware Store"` in the `OrderTotal` variable.

Here is a short list of data type prefixes that are commonly used (see Appendix B):

- ❑ var — `Variant`
- ❑ str — `String`
- ❑ int — `Integer`
- ❑ lng — `Long`
- ❑ byt — `Byte`

- ❏   sng — Single
- ❏   dbl — Double
- ❏   cur — Currency
- ❏   obj — Object
- ❏   bool — Boolean

The var prefix is best used when you don't know exactly what type of data might end up in the variable, or when you intend for that variable to hold different kinds of data at different times. This is why you're using the var prefix often in this chapter where you're doing all sorts of playing around with data types. In normal practice, however, you will want your variables to have one of the other more specific prefixes listed previously or in Appendix B.

Automatic Assignment of the Date Subtype

Take a look at a similar example, this time using date/time values (SUBTYPE_DATE.VBS).

```
Dim varTest
varTest = "5/16/99 12:30 PM"
MsgBox TypeName(varTest)
```

Running this code results in the dialog box shown in Figure 3-4.

Figure 3-4

The variable assignment results in a subtype of String, although you might expect it to be Date. You get the String subtype because you put the date/time value in quotes. You saw this principle in action in the examples in the preceding sections when you put the number 12 in quotes in the variable assignment. Once again, there are different ways that you can force the subtype to be Date instead of String (SUBTYPE_DATE2.VBS).

```
Dim varTest
varTest = #5/16/99 12:30 PM#
MsgBox TypeName(varTest)
```

Or (SUBTYPE_DATE3.VBS).

```
Dim varTest
varTest = CDate("5/16/99 12:30 PM")
MsgBox TypeName(varTest)
```

Running either of these examples produces the dialog box shown in Figure 3-5.

Figure 3-5

The first example surrounds the date/time value in # signs instead of quotes. This is the VBScript way of identifying a date literal. A *literal* is any value that's expressed directly in your code, as opposed to being expressed via a variable or named constant. The number 12 and the string "Hello There" that you used in previous examples are also literals. By enclosing the date/time in # signs rather than quotes, you are telling VBScript to treat the value as a Date, not as a String. As a result, when the Date literal gets stored in the Variant variable, the subtype comes out as Date. The second example uses the CDate() conversion function to achieve the same thing. Once again, the first version is theoretically faster because it does not require an extra function call.

The "Is" Functions

Often you are not exactly sure what type of data a variable might hold initially, and you need to be sure of what type of data it is before you try to use a conversion function on it. This is important because using a conversion function on the wrong type of data can cause a runtime error. For example, try this code (SUBTYPE_DATE4_ERROR.VBS).

```
Dim varTest
varTest = "Hello"
varTest = CLng(varTest)
```

This code causes a runtime error on line 3: "Type Mismatch". Not a nice thing to happen when your code is trying to accomplish something. Obviously, this little code sample is pretty silly, because you knew that the variable contained a `String` when you tried to convert it to a `Long`. However, you often do not have control over what value ends up in a variable. This is especially true when you are:

❑   accepting input from the user

❑   reading data from a database

❑   reading data from a file

You can often get around these `"Type Mismatch"` errors by using one of the "Is" functions that are listed in the fourth column of the Variant subtypes table in Appendix I. For example, the following code asks the user his or her age. Because you don't have any control over what the user types in, you need to verify that he or she actually typed in a number (GET_TEST_AGE.VBS).

```
Dim lngAge

lngAge = InputBox("Please enter your age in years.")

If IsNumeric(lngAge) Then
    lngAge = CLng(lngAge)
    lngAge = lngAge + 50
    MsgBox "In 50 years, you will be " & CStr(lngAge) & _
        " years old."
Else
    MsgBox "Sorry, but you did not enter a valid number."
End If
```

Notice how you use the `IsNumeric()` function to test whether or not the user actually entered a valid number. Because the plan is to use the `CLng()` function to coerce the subtype, you want to avoid a `"Type Mismatch"` error. What has not been stated explicitly is that the subtype of the variable does not have to be numeric in order for `IsNumeric()` to return `True`. `IsNumeric()` examines the actual value of the variable, rather than its subtype. The subtype of the variable and the value of the variable are two different things.

This behavior is actually what allows you to use `IsNumeric()` to avoid a `"Type Mismatch"` error. If `IsNumeric()` examined the subtype, it would not be quite so useful. In line 3 of the previous example, the subtype of the `lngAge` variable is `String`, yet `IsNumeric()` returns `True` if the variable has a number in it. That's because `IsNumeric()` is considering the *value* of `lngAge`, not the subtype. You can test the value before trying to convert the variable's subtype to a different subtype to make sure you don't get that `"TypeMismatch"` error. This points to a general principle: Never trust or make assumptions about data that comes from an external source — a database, a file, a web page, and in particular, from user entry.

The function `IsDate()` works the same way as `IsNumeric()` (GET_TEST_BIRTH.VBS).

```
Dim datBirth

datBirth = InputBox("Please enter the date on which " & _
    " you were born.")

If IsDate(datBirth) Then
    datBirth = CDate(datBirth)
    MsgBox "You were born on day " & Day(datBirth) & _
        " of month " & Month(datBirth) & " in the year " & _
        Year(datBirth) & "."
```

```
Else
    MsgBox "Sorry, but you did not enter a valid date."
End If
```

> `Day()`, `Month()`, and `Year()` are built-in VBScript functions that you can use to return the different parts of a date. These functions are covered in detail in Appendix A.

An exception to a previous statement about the "Is" functions: Not all of the "Is" functions work strictly on the value, as `IsNumeric()` and `IsDate()` do. The functions `IsEmpty()`, `IsNull()`, and `IsObject()` examine the subtype of the variable, not the value. These three functions are covered later in the chapter.

Before you move on, here's a brief jump-ahead regarding the use of the `If` statement in the code example shown earlier.

This line of code

```
If IsNumeric(lngAge) Then
```

is functionally equivalent to this line

```
If IsNumeric(lngAge) = True Then
```

And likewise, this line

```
If Not IsNumeric(lngAge) Then
```

is functionally equivalent to this line

```
If IsNumeric(lngAge) = False Then
```

However, when using the `Not` operator, you want to be sure you are using it only in combination with expressions that return the `Boolean` values `True` and `False` (such as the `IsNumeric()` function). This is because the `Not` operator can also be used as a "bitwise" operator (see Appendix A) when used with numeric (non-`Boolean`) values.

Implicit Type Coercion

So far, we have been discussing *explicit* type coercion using conversion functions. We have not yet discussed a phenomenon called *implicit* type coercion. Explicit type coercion refers to when the programmer deliberately changes subtypes using the conversion functions and variable assignment techniques described earlier.

Implicit type coercion is when a `Variant` variable changes its subtype automatically. Sometimes, implicit type coercion can work in your favor, and sometimes it can present a problem. While this material about type coercion may seem like something "theoretical" you can skip over, it is vitally important to understand how this works so that you can avoid hard-to-find bugs in your VBScript programs.

Implicit Type Coercion in Action

Remember the example code that asks the user for his or her age that was used in the previous section (see the section "The 'Is' Functions")? Here it is again (GET_TEST_AGE.VBS).

```
Dim lngAge

lngAge = InputBox("Please enter your age in years.")

If IsNumeric(lngAge) Then
    lngAge = CLng(lngAge)
    lngAge = lngAge + 50
    MsgBox "In 50 years, you will be " & CStr(lngAge) & _
        " years old."
Else
    MsgBox "Sorry, but you did not enter a valid number."
End If
```

Notice how the CLng() and CStr() functions are used to explicitly coerce the subtypes. Actually, in the case of this particular code, these functions are not strictly necessary. The reason is that VBScript's implicit type coercion would have done approximately the same thing for you. Here's the code again, without the conversion functions (GET_TEST_AGE_IMPLICIT.VBS).

```
Dim lngAge

lngAge = InputBox("Please enter your age in years.")

If IsNumeric(lngAge) Then
    lngAge = lngAge + 50
    MsgBox "In 50 years, you will be " & lngAge & _
        " years old."
Else
    MsgBox "Sorry, but you did not enter a valid number."
End If
```

Because of implicit type coercion, this code works exactly the same way as the original code. Take a look at this line (the fourth line in the preceding script).

```
lngAge = lngAge + 50
```

You did not explicitly coerce the subtype to Long, but the math still works as you'd expect. Run this same code, but with some TypeName() functions thrown in so that you can watch the subtypes change (GET_TEST_AGE_TYPENAME.VBS).

```
Dim lngAge

lngAge = InputBox("Please enter your age in years.")

MsgBox "TypeName After InputBox: " & TypeName(lngAge)

If IsNumeric(lngAge) Then
    lngAge = lngAge + 50
```

```
        MsgBox "TypeName After Adding 50: " & TypeName(lngAge)
        MsgBox "In 50 years, you will be " & lngAge & _
            " years old."
    Else
        MsgBox "Sorry, but you did not enter a valid number."
    End If
```

If the user enters, for example, the number 30, this code will result in the dialog boxes, in order, shown in Figures 3-6 to 3-8.

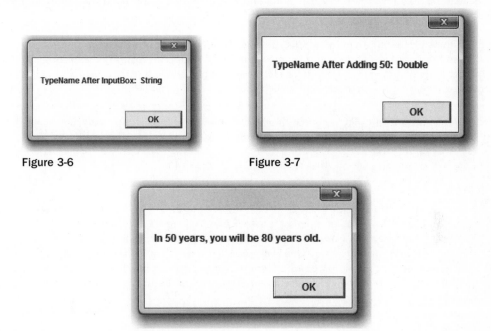

Figure 3-6   Figure 3-7

Figure 3-8

The first call to the `TypeName()` function shows that the subtype is `String`. That's because data coming back from the `InputBox()` function is always treated as `String` data, even when the user types in a number. Remember that the `String` subtype can hold just about any kind of data. However, when numbers and dates (and `Boolean` `True`/`False` values) are stored in a variable with the `String` subtype, they are not treated as numbers or dates (or as `Boolean` values) — they are treated simply as strings of text with no special meaning. This is why when the code tries to do math on the `String` value, VBScript must first coerce the subtype to a numeric one.

It's as if the VBScript compiler behind the scenes is following logic such as this:

1. The code is trying to perform math with the variable.

2. Math requires numeric values. This variable's subtype is `String`, but is the value numeric?

3. It is numeric, so perform some implicit type coercion and change the variable to a numeric subtype.

4. Now that we are sure we are working with a numeric value, do the math the code is asking for.

The second call to the `TypeName()` function comes *after* 50 is added to it, and shows that the subtype is `Double`. Wait a minute — `Double`? Why `Double`? Why not one of the whole number subtypes, such as `Integer` or `Long`? You didn't introduce any decimal places in this math. Why would VBScript implicitly coerce the subtype into `Double`? The possibly less than satisfying answer is because VBScript determined this was the best thing to do; because in this code you're trusting VBScript to do the type coercion for you implicitly, you have to accept its sometimes mysterious ways.

Because you did not use a conversion function to explicitly tell VBScript to change the variable to one subtype or another (explicit coercion), the VBScript compiler evaluated the situation and chose the subtype that it thought was best. VBScript automatically knew that you wanted the value in the variable to be a number. It knew this because the code added 50 to the variable.

Automatic transformation to a numeric subtype before doing math seems pretty straightforward. What isn't so straightforward is that the compiler chose the `Double` subtype, instead of some other numeric subtype like `Long` or `Integer` or `Byte`. This is the reason you have to be careful with implicit type coercion; it can be tricky to predict exactly which subtype VBScript will choose.

> Before you continue, take note that there is one other instance of implicit type coercion in the current example. The coercion is incidental, but useful for discussion; it occurs on this line:
>
> ```
> MsgBox "In 50 years, you will be " & lngAge & " years old."
> ```
>
> At the time this line executes, you have just finished adding the number 50 to your `lngAge` variable, and the subtype is a numeric one. When you use the concatenation operator (&) to insert the value of the variable into the sentence, VBScript implicitly changes the subtype to `String`. This is similar to the way in which the subtype is changed from `String` to `Double` when you performed a mathematical operation on it. However, this coercion is not permanent. Because you did not assign a new value to the variable, the subtype does not change.

Avoiding Trouble with Implicit Type Coercion

While you have to be aware of implicit type coercion, there is no reason to fear it. VBScript is not going to arbitrarily go around changing subtypes. There is a logic to it. Implicit type coercion happens only when you assign a new value to a variable that does not fit the current subtype. Generally, once a `Variant` variable has a subtype (based on the value first placed within it, or based on a subtype that your code explicitly coerced), it will keep that subtype as you place new values in the variable.

One way to be sure that implicit type coercion won't cause you any problems is to be careful about using each variable you declare for exactly one purpose. Don't declare generic, multipurpose variables that you use for different reasons throughout your script. If you are going to ask the user for his or her age and then later ask the user for the birth date, don't declare a single generic variable called `varInput`. Instead, declare *two* variables, one called `lngAge` and another called `datBirthDate`. This makes your code more clear and understandable and ensures that you don't get in trouble with implicit type coercion.

Where you do need to watch out for implicit type coercion is when you're dealing with a mixture of data types. You saw this in the example: When the data came back from the `InputBox()` function, it was a string. Then you did some math on it, which turned it into a number. Give this code a try (`IMPLICIT_COERCION.VBS`).

```
Dim lngTest

lngTest = CLng(100)
MsgBox "TypeName after initialization: " & TypeName(lngTest)

lngTest = lngTest + 1000
MsgBox "TypeName after adding 1000: " & TypeName(lngTest)

lngTest = lngTest * 50
MsgBox "TypeName after multiplying by 50: " & _
    TypeName(lngTest)

lngTest = "Hello"
MsgBox "TypeName after assigning value of 'Hello': " & _

    TypeName(lngTest)
```

If you run this code, you'll see that the first three calls to the TypeName() function reveal that the subtype is Long. Then, after you change the value of the variable to "Hello", the subtype is automatically coerced into String. What this code illustrates is that once the subtype is established as Long, it stays Long as long as you keep changing the value to other numbers. VBScript has no reason to change it, because the values you put in it remain in the range of the Long subtype. However, when you place text in the variable, VBScript sees that the new value is not appropriate for the Long subtype, and so it changes it to String.

That said, these kinds of mixed-type situations should be rare, and you should try to avoid them. The best way to avoid them is to declare specific variables for specific purposes. Don't mix things up with a single, multipurpose variable like the preceding example does.

The preceding example also reinforces the reason that you use the Hungarian subtype prefix in the variable name. By placing that lng prefix on the variable name, you indicate that you intend for this variable to hold Long numeric values only. The code at the end of the example violates this by changing the value to something nonnumeric. VBScript allows this, because it can't read your mind, but that's not the point.

On the contrary, the fact that the VBScript allows you to store any type of data you please in any variable increases the need for subtype prefixes. The point is to protect your code from strange errors creeping in. Six months from now, if you or someone else were modifying this code, the lng prefix would make it clear that the original intent was for the variable to hold Long numeric values.

In the next example, you will look at how implicit type coercion can happen with numeric variables as the size of the number increases. Give this code a try (IMPLICIT_COERCION_NUMBER.VBS).

```
Dim intTest

intTest = CInt(100)
MsgBox "TypeName after initialization to 100: " & _
    TypeName(intTest)

intTest = intTest + 1000000
MsgBox "TypeName after adding 1,000,000: " & _
    TypeName(intTest)

intTest = intTest + 10000000000
MsgBox "TypeName after adding another 10,000,000,000: " & _
    TypeName(intTest)
```

Running this code results in the three dialog boxes shown in Figures 3-9 to 3-11.

Figure 3-9   Figure 3-10

Figure 3-11

Notice that you initialize the variable with a value of 100, and use the CInt() function to coerce the subtype to Integer. The first call to the TypeName() function reflects this. Then you add 1,000,000 to the variable. The next call to the TypeName() function reveals that VBScript coerced the subtype to Long. Why did it do this? Because you exceeded the upper limit of the Integer subtype, which is 32,767. VBScript will promote numeric subtypes when the value exceeds the upper or lower limits of the current numeric subtype. Finally, you add another 10 billion to the variable. This exceeds the upper limit of the Long subtype, so VBScript upgrades the subtype to Double.

Avoiding Trouble with the "&" and "+" Operators

Throughout this chapter you have seen example code that uses the & operator to *concatenate* strings together. This is a very common operation in VBScript code. It is an unfortunate quirk that VBScript also allows you to use the + operator to concatenate strings. However, this usage of the + operator should be avoided. This is because the + operator, when used to concatenate strings, can cause unwanted implicit type coercion. Try this code (PLUS_WITH_STRING.VBS).

```
Dim strFirst
Dim lngSecond

strFirst = CStr(50)
lngSecond = CLng(100)
MsgBox strFirst + lngSecond
```

The resulting dialog box displays the number 150, which means that it added the two numbers mathematically rather than concatenating them. Now, this is admittedly a very silly example, but it illustrates that the + operator has different effects when you are not using it in a strictly mathematical context. The + operator uses the following rules when deciding what to do:

❑ If both variables have the `String` subtype, then VBScript will concatenate them.

❑ If both variables have any of the numeric subtypes, then VBScript will add them.

❑ If one of the variables has a numeric subtype, and the other has the `String` subtype, then VBScript will attempt to add them. If the variable with the `String` subtype does not contain a number, then a `"Type Mismatch"` error will occur.

Your best bet is to not worry about those rules and remember only these:

❑ Use the + operator *only* when you explicitly want to perform math on numeric values.

❑ *Always* use the & operator to concatenate strings.

❑ *Never* use the + operator to concatenate strings.

Empty and Null

You may have noticed that the first two subtypes in the table of subtypes in Appendix I have not been mentioned: `Empty` and `Null`. These two subtypes are special in that they do not have a corresponding specific Visual Basic data type. In fact, it's a bit of a misnomer to call these subtypes, because they are actually special values that a `Variant` variable can hold. When the subtype of a variable is `Empty` or `Null`, its *value* is also either `Empty` or `Null`.

This is different from the other subtypes, which describe only the type of value that the variable holds, not the value itself. For example, when the subtype of a variable is `Long`, the value of the variable can be 0, or 15, or 2,876,456, or one of about 4.3 billion other numbers (–2,147,483,648 to 2,147,483,647). However, when the subtype of a variable is `Empty`, its value is also always a special value called `Empty`. In the same fashion, when the subtype of a variable is `Null`, the value is always a special value called `Null`.

`Empty` is a special value that can only be held in a `Variant` variable. In Visual Basic, variables declared as any of the specific data types cannot hold the value of `Empty`— only variables declared as `Variant` can hold the value. In VBScript of course, all variables are `Variant` variables. A `Variant` variable is "empty," and has the `Empty` subtype, after it has been declared, but before any value has been placed within it. In other words, `Empty` is the equivalent of "not initialized." Once any type of value has been placed into the variable, it will take on one of the other subtypes, depending on what the value is.

Take a look at some examples. First, SUBTYPE_EMPTY.VBS.

```
Dim varTest
MsgBox TypeName(varTest)
```

This simple example results in the dialog box shown in Figure 3-12.

The subtype is `Empty` because you have not yet placed any value in the variable. `Empty` is both the initial subtype and the initial value of the variable. However, `Empty` is not a value that you can really do anything with. You can't display it on the screen or print it on paper. It only exists to represent the condition of the variable not having been initialized yet. Try this code (SUBTYPE_EMPTY_CONVERT.VBS).

Figure 3-12

```
Dim varTest
MsgBox CLng(varTest)
MsgBox CStr(varTest)
```

The code will produce, in succession, the two dialog boxes shown in Figures 3-13 and 3-14.

Figure 3-13   Figure 3-14

The first box displays a 0 because Empty is converted to 0 by the CLng() function. The second box displays nothing because the CStr() function converts Empty to a "zero length" String (often represented in code as two double quote marks next to each other: " ").

Once you place a value in a Variant variable, it is no longer empty. It will take on another subtype, depending on what type of value you place in it. This is also true when you use a conversion function to coerce the subtype. However, if you need to, you can force the variable to become empty again by using the Empty keyword directly.

```
varTest = Empty
```

Sometimes this is useful when you want to make a variable appear to be uninitialized. You can test for whether a variable is empty in either of two ways.

```
If varTest = Empty Then
    MsgBox "The variable is empty."
End If
```

Or

```
If IsEmpty(varTest) Then
    MsgBox "The variable is empty."
End If
```

The `IsEmpty()` function returns a `Variant` value of the `Boolean` subtype with the value of `True` if the variable is empty, and `False` if not.

The value/subtype of `Null`, in a confusing way, is similar to the value/subtype of `Empty`. The distinction may seem esoteric, but `Empty` indicates that a variable is uninitialized, whereas `Null` indicates the absence of valid data. `Empty` means that no value has been placed into a variable, whereas a `Variant` variable can only have the value/subtype of `Null` after the value of `Null` has been placed into it.

In other words, a variable can only be `Null` if the `Null` value has explicitly been placed into it. `Null` is a special value that is most often encountered in database tables. A column in a database is `Null` when there is no data in it, and if your code is going to read data from a database, you have to be ready for `Null` values. Certain functions might also return a `Null` value. The concept of "null" reflects not just that there is an absence of a value, but also that the value is unknown.

Another way to think about it is that `Empty` generally happens by default — it is implicit, because a variable is empty until you place something in it. `Null`, on the other hand, is explicit — a variable can only be `Null` if some code made it that way, or if it came from some external source, like a database table.

The syntax for assigning and testing for `Null` values is similar to the way the `Empty` value/subtype works. Here is some code that assigns a `Null` value to a variable.

```
varTest = Null
```

However, you cannot directly test for the value of `Null` using the equals (=) operator in the same way that you can with `Empty` — you can use only the `IsNull()` function to test for a `Null` value. This is because `Null` represents invalid or unknown data; when you try to make a direct comparison using invalid or unknown data, the result is always more invalid or unknown data — garbage in, garbage out, as the saying goes. Try running this code (NULL_BOOLEAN.VBS).

```
'This code does not work like you might expect
Dim varTest

varTest = Null
If varTest = Null Then
    MsgBox "The variable has a Null value."
End If
```

You did not see any pop-up dialog box here. That's because the expression `If varTest = Null` always returns `False`. If you want to know if a variable contains a `Null` value, you must use the `IsNull()` function (NULL_BOOLEAN_ISNULL.VBS).

```
Dim varTest

varTest = Null
If IsNull(varTest) = True Then
    MsgBox "The variable has a Null value."
End If
```

As mentioned, often your code has to be concerned with receiving Null values from a database or certain functions. The reason we say that you need to be concerned is that, because Null is an indicator of invalid data, Null can cause troubles for you if you pass it to a function that breaks with a null value or try and use the null value to perform mathematical operations. You saw this just a moment ago when you tried to use the expression If varTest = Null. This unpleasantness occurs in many contexts where you try to mix in Null with valid data. For example, try this code (NULL_INVALID_ERROR.VBS).

```
Dim varTest
Dim lngTest
varTest = Null
lngTest = 2 + varTest
MsgBox TypeName(lngTest)
```

Running this code produces an error on line 3: "Invalid Use of Null". This is a common error with many VBScript functions that don't like Null values to be passed into them. Sometimes, though, you can experience silent, unwanted behavior, with no helpful error message to tell you that you did something wrong. Take a look at the odd behavior that results from this code (NULL_IMPLICIT.VBS).

```
Dim varTest
Dim lngTest
varTest = Null
lngTest = 2 + varTest
MsgBox TypeName(lngTest)
```

Running this code results in the dialog box shown in Figure 3-15.

Figure 3-15

Did you see what happened here? When you added the number 2 to the value Null, the result was Null. Once again when you mix invalid data (Null) with valid data (the number 2, in this case), you always end up with invalid data.

The following code uses some ADO (ActiveX Data Objects) syntax that you might not be familiar with (see Chapter 18), but here's an example of the type of thing you want to do when you're concerned that a database column might return a `Null` value.

```
strCustomerName = rsCustomers.Fields("Name").Value
If IsNull(strCustomerName) Then
    strCustomerName = ""
End If
```

Here you are assigning the value of the `Name` column in a database table to the variable `strCustomerName`. If the `Name` column in the database allows `Null` values, then you need to be concerned that you might end up with a `Null` value in your variable. So you use `IsNull()` to test the value. If `IsNull()` returns `True`, then you assign an empty string to the variable instead. Empty strings are much more friendly and easy to work with than `Null`. This kind of defensive programming is an important technique. Here's a handy shortcut that achieves the same exact thing as the preceding code.

```
strCustomerName = "" & rsCustomers.Fields("Name").Value
```

The trick displayed here is one of the most useful that you will ever learn relative to VBScript. This trick harnesses VBScript's implicit type coercion behavior to your advantage, avoiding bugs and error messages because of null values. Notice that you are appending an "empty string" (`""`) to the value coming from the `Name` database column. Concatenating an empty string with a `Null` value transforms that value into an empty string, and concatenating an empty string to a valid string has no effect at all, so it's a win-win situation: If the value is `Null`, it gets fixed, and if it's not `Null`, it's left alone.

> **A caution for Visual Basic programmers:** You may be accustomed to using the `Trim$()` **function to transform** `Null` **database values into empty strings. VBScript does not support the "$" versions of functions such as** `Trim()`, `UCase()`, **and** `Left()`. **As you may know, when you don't use the "$" versions of these functions in Visual Basic, they return a** `Variant` **value. This behavior is the same in VBScript, because all functions return** `Variant` **values. Therefore,** `Trim(Null)` **always returns** `Null`. **If you still want to be able to trim database values as you read them in, you need to both append an empty string and use** `Trim()`, **like so:**
>
> ```
> strName = Trim("" & rsCustomers.Field("Name").Value)
> ```

The Object Subtype

So far, we have not discussed the `Object` subtype from the Appendix I table. As the name suggests, a variable will have the `Object` subtype when it contains a reference to an object. An *object* is a special construct that contains *properties* and *methods*. A property is analogous to a variable, and a method is analogous to a function or procedure. An object is essentially a convenient way of encompassing both data (in the form of properties) and functionality (in the form of methods). Objects are always created at runtime from a *class*, which is a template from which objects are created (or *instantiated*).

For example, you could create a class called Dog. This Dog class could have properties called Color, Breed, and Name, and it could have methods called Bark() and Sit(). The class definition would have code to implement these properties and methods. Objects created at runtime from the Dog class would be able to set and read the properties and call the methods. A class typically exists as part of a *component*. For example, you might have a component called Animals that contains a bunch of different classes like Dog, Elephant, and Rhino. The code to create and use a Dog object would look something like this:

```
Dim objMyDog

Set objMyDog = WScript.CreateObject("Animals.Dog")

objDog.Name = "Buddy"
objDog.Breed = "Poodle"
objDog.Color = "Brown"
objDog.Bark
objDog.Sit
```

Don't worry if this object stuff is a little confusing at this point. Objects and classes are discussed in much greater detail throughout the book, starting in Chapter 8. The point in this section is simply to illustrate how variables with the Object subtype behave. Now take a look at some code that actually uses a real object: in this case the FileSystemObject, which is part of a collection of objects that allow your VBScript code to interact with the Windows file system. (FileSystemObject and its cousins are discussed in detail in Chapter 7.) The script file for this code is OBJECT_SIMPLE.VBS.

```
Dim objFSO
Dim boolExists

Set objFSO = WScript.CreateObject("Scripting.FileSystemObject")

boolExists = objFSO.FileExists("C:\autoexec.bat")
MsgBox boolExists
```

In this code, you create a FileSystemObject object and store it in the variable called objFSO. You then use the object's FileExists() method to test for the existence of the autoexec.bat file in the root of the C: drive. Then you display the result of this test in a dialog box. (Note the use of the Set keyword. When changing the value of an object variable, you must use Set.)

Now that you've seen an object in action, take a look at two concepts that are germane to this chapter: the IsObject() function, and the special value of Nothing. The script file for this code is OBJECT_ISOBJECT.VBS.

```
Dim objFSO
Dim boolExists

Set objFSO = WScript.CreateObject("Scripting.FileSystemObject")

If IsObject(objFSO) Then
    boolExists = objFSO.FileExists("C:\autoexec.bat")
    MsgBox boolExists
End If
```

This illustrates the use of the `IsObject()` function, which is similar to the other "Is" functions that were discussed earlier in the chapter. If the variable holds a reference to an object (in other words, if the subtype is `Object`), then the function will return `True`. Otherwise, it will return `False`.

`Nothing` is a special value that applies only to variables with the `Object` subtype. An object variable is equal to the value `Nothing` when the subtype is `Object`, but the object in the variable either has been destroyed or has not yet been instantiated. The `Nothing` value is similar to the `Null` value. When testing for whether an object variable is equal to the value `Nothing`, you do not use the = operator, as you normally would to test for a specific value. Instead, you have to use the special operator `Is`. However, when you want to destroy an object, you have to use the `Set` keyword in combination with the = operator.

If that sounds confusing, don't feel bad, because it is confusing. Let's look at an example (`OBJECT_SET_ NOTHING.VBS`).

```
Dim objFSO
Dim boolExists

Set objFSO = WScript.CreateObject("Scripting.FileSystemObject")

If IsObject(objFSO) Then
    boolExists = objFSO.FileExists("C:\autoexec.bat")
    MsgBox boolExists
    Set objFSO = Nothing
    If objFSO Is Nothing Then
        MsgBox "The object has been destroyed, which " & _
            "frees up the resources it was using."
    End If
End If
```

Why would you want to destroy an object using the `Set <variable>` = `Nothing` syntax? It's a good idea to do this when you are done with using an object, because destroying the object frees up the memory it was taking up. Objects take up a great deal more memory than do normal variables. Also, for reasons too complex to go into here, keeping object variables around longer than necessary can cause fatal memory errors. It's a good idea to develop a habit of setting all object variables equal to `Nothing` immediately after you are done with them.

The Error Subtype

The `Error` subtype was left for last because it is seldom used. However, there's a remote chance that you might end up coming across a component or function that uses the `Error` subtype to indicate that an error occurred in the function. We are not necessarily endorsing this methodology, but what you might encounter is a function that returns a `Variant` value that will contain either the result of the function or an error number.

Imagine a function called `GetAge()` that returns a person's age in years. This function would take a date as a parameter, and return to you the person's age, based on the computer's current system date. If an error occurred in the function, then the return value would instead contain an error number indicating what went wrong. For example:

```
Dim datBirth
Dim lngAge

datBirth = _
    InputBox("Please enter the date on which you were born.")

If IsDate(datBirth) Then
    lngAge = GetAge(datBirth)
    If Not IsError(lngAge) Then
        MsgBox "You are " & lngAge & " years old."
    Else
        If lngAge = 1000 Then
            'This error means that the date was greater
            'than the current system date.
            MsgBox "That date was greater than the " & _
                "current system date."
        Else
            'An unknown error occurred.
            MsgBox "The error " & lngAge & _
                " occurred in the GetAge() function."
        End If
    End If
Else
    MsgBox "You did not enter a valid date."
End If
```

Keep in mind that GetAge() is a fictitious function, and you cannot actually run this code (unless you wanted to write a GetAge() function yourself using Visual Basic). The point here is only to illustrate how someone might use the Error subtype, and how your code might have to respond to it. We say *might* because the Error subtype and the error-returning technique illustrated previously is unorthodox and seldom used.

You could not easily implement the use of the Error subtype yourself in VBScript because the VBScript does not support the CVErr() conversion function, as Visual Basic does. (The CVErr() function coerces the subtype of a Variant variable to Error.) Therefore, without the aid of Visual Basic, you could never coerce the subtype of a variable to be Error. In other words, VBScript code cannot create a variable with the subtype of Error.

> There is a 99 percent probability that as a VBScript programmer you will never have to worry about the Error subtype. And we do not recommend adopting it for error handling purposes — instead, please see Chapter 6 on error handling in VBScript.

Arrays as Complex Data Types

The discussion so far has focused on variables that hold a single value. However, VBScript can work with two other types of data that are more complex than anything you've looked at so far: objects and arrays. Objects are not discussed in this chapter because they were introduced briefly in the previous section, and because they are covered in various ways throughout the book. However, we *are* going to take a detailed look at arrays.

What Is an Array?

An *array*, as the name suggests, is a matrix of data. While a normal variable has one "compartment" in which to store one piece of information, an array has multiple compartments in which to store multiple pieces of information. As you can imagine, this comes in very handy. Even though you might not know it, you are probably already very familiar, outside the context of VBScript, with all sorts of matrices. A spreadsheet is a matrix. It has rows and columns, usually labeled with numbers and letters; you can identify a single "cell" in the spreadsheet by referring to the row number and column letter where that cell resides. A Bingo game card is also a matrix. It has rows of numbers that span five columns, which are headed by the letters B-I-N-G-O. A database table is also a matrix — once again, rows and columns.

An array can be a very simple matrix, with a single column (an array column is called a *dimension*), or it can be much more complex, with up to 60 dimensions. Arrays are typically used to store repeating instances of the same type of information. For example, suppose your script needs to work with a list of names and phone numbers. An array is well suited for this. Rather than trying to declare separate variables for each of the names and phone numbers in your list (which would be especially challenging if you did not know in advance how many names were going to be in the list), you can store the entire list in one variable.

Arrays Have Dimensions

A VBScript array can have up to 60 *dimensions*. Most arrays have either one or two dimensions. A one-dimensional array is best thought of as a list of rows with only one column. A two-dimensional array is a list with multiple columns (the first dimension) and rows (the second dimension). (Beyond two dimensions, however, the two dimensional, matrix-based, rows-and-columns analogy starts to break down, and the array turns into something much more complex. We're not going to discuss multidimensional arrays much here. Luckily, for the needs of your average script, a two-dimensional array is absolutely sufficient.)

Note that a two-dimensional array does not mean that you are limited to two columns. It only means that the array is limited to an x- and a y-axis. A one-dimensional array really does have two dimensions, but it is limited to a single column. A two-dimensional array can have as many columns and rows as the memory of your computer will allow. For example, here is a graphical representation of a one-dimensional array, in the form of a list of colors.

```
Red
Green
Blue
Yellow
Orange
Black
```

And here is a two-dimensional array, in the form of a list of names and phone numbers.

```
Williams   Tony     404-555-6328
Carter     Ron      305-555-2514
Davis      Miles    212-555-5314
Hancock    Herbie   616-555-6943
Shorter    Wayne    853-555-0060
```

An array with three dimensions is more difficult to represent graphically. Picture a three-dimensional cube, divided up into slices. After three dimensions, it becomes even more difficult to hold a picture of the array's structure in your mind.

Array Bounds and Declaring Arrays

It's important to make a distinction between the number of dimensions that an array has, and the *bounds* that an array has. The phone list array in the previous example has two dimensions, but it has different upper and lower bounds for each dimension. The upper bound of an array determines how many "compartments" that dimension can hold. Each compartment in an array is called an *element*. An element can hold exactly one value, but an array can have as many elements as your computer's memory will allow. Here is the phone list array again, but with each of the elements numbered.

```
        0           1          2
0    Williams    Tony      404-555-6328
1    Carter      Ron       305-555-2514
2    Davis       Miles     212-555-5314
3    Hancock     Herbie    616-555-6943
4    Shorter     Wayne     853-555-0060
```

The lower bound of the first dimension (the columns) is 0, and the upper bound is 2. The lower bound of the second dimension (the rows) is once again 0, and the upper bound is 4. The lower bound of an array in VBScript is always 0 (unlike Visual Basic arrays, which can have any lower bound that you want to declare). Arrays with a lower bound of 0 are said to be zero-based. This can become a bit confusing, because when you are accessing elements in the array, you have to always remember to start counting at 0, which is not always natural for people. So even though there are three columns in the first dimension, the upper bound is expressed as 2 — because you started numbering them at 0. Likewise, even though there are five rows in the second dimension, the upper bound is expressed as 4.

When you declare an array, you can tell VBScript how many dimensions you want, and what the upper bound of each dimension is. There is no need to tell VBScript what you want the lower bound to be because the lower bound is always 0. For example, here is a declaration for an array variable for the list of colors from the previous section.

```
Dim astrColors(5)
```

The list of colors is one-dimensional (that is, it has only one column) and it has six elements. So the upper bound of the array is 5 — remember that you start counting at 0. Notice the Hungarian prefix (see Appendix B) that was used for the variable name: `astr`. For a normal string variable name, you would just use the `str` prefix. You add an extra `a` to convey that this variable is an array. It is very useful for someone reading your code to know that a variable you are using is an array. An additional example: An array of `Long` numbers would have this prefix — `alng`. For more information on subtypes and arrays, see the last section of this chapter, "Using VarType () with Arrays."

Moving on to the declaration of variables with more than one dimension, here is a declaration for an array variable for the two-dimensional phone list.

```
Dim astrPhoneList(2,4)
```

If you want to add another dimension, you add a comma and another upper bound definition to the declaration. Because the phone list has three columns, the upper bound of the first dimension is 2. And because it has five rows, the upper bound of the second dimension is 4.

Starting in the next section, you'll cumulatively build a script that illustrates three things about arrays:

❑   how to declare and populate an array

❑   how to add dimensions and elements to an array dynamically

❑   how to loop through an array and access all of its contents

The variable declaration for `astrPhoneList` is your first building block. However, before you start adding more building blocks, you need to know about array subscripts.

Accessing Arrays with Subscripts

In order to read from or write to an array element, you have to use a subscript. *Subscripts* are a syntax for accessing the data in the array, similar to the column-letter and row-number syntax that you use in a spreadsheet program, or the x,y coordinates you learned about in geometry class. Here's the phone list array again, with the elements numbered for convenience.

```
        0          1          2
0    Williams    Tony      404-555-6328
1    Carter      Ron       305-555-2514
2    Davis       Miles     212-555-5314
3    Hancock     Herbie    616-555-6943
4    Shorter     Wayne     853-555-0060
```

The last name `"Williams"` is stored in subscript 0,0. The first name `"Miles"` is stored in subscript 1,2. The phone number `"305-555-2514"` is stored in subscript 2,1. You get the idea.

So now you can add some code that will populate the `astrPhoneList` array variable with the data for your phone list (`ARRAY_LIST_STATIC.VBS`).

```
Dim astrPhoneList(2,4)
'Add the first row
astrPhoneList(0,0) = "Williams"
astrPhoneList(1,0) = "Tony"
astrPhoneList(2,0) = "404-555-6328"

'Add the second row
astrPhoneList(0,1) = "Carter"
astrPhoneList(1,1) = "Ron"
astrPhoneList(2,1) = "305-555-2514"

'Add the third row
astrPhoneList(0,2) = "Davis"
astrPhoneList(1,2) = "Miles"
astrPhoneList(2,2) = "212-555-5314"

'Add the fourth row
astrPhoneList(0,3) = "Hancock"
astrPhoneList(1,3) = "Herbie"
astrPhoneList(2,3) = "616-555-6943"

'Add the fifth row
astrPhoneList(0,4) = "Shorter"
astrPhoneList(1,4) = "Wayne"
astrPhoneList(2,4) = "853-555-0060"
```

First, this code declares the array variable `astrPhoneList`. Because you know in advance that you want this array to have three columns (one each for last name, first name, and phone number), and five rows (one for each of the names in your list), you declare the array with the dimensions you want: `(2,4)`. (Remember that subscripts are zero-based.) Then, you add the data to the array, one element/subscript at a time.

When you declared the array variable with the upper bounds `(2,4)`, VBScript made space in memory for all of the compartments, and the rest of the code puts data into the empty compartments. You use subscripts to identify the compartment you want for each piece of data. You should be careful to be consistent by making sure that last names, first names, and phone numbers each go into the same column across all five rows.

But what happens when you don't know in advance how many elements you're going to need in your array? This is where the dynamic array comes in. A *dynamic array* is one that is not pre-constrained to have certain upper bounds, or even a certain number of dimensions. You can declare the array variable once at design time, and then change the number of dimensions and the upper bound of those dimensions dynamically at runtime. To declare a variable as a dynamic array, you just use the parentheses without putting any dimensions in them.

```
Dim astrPhoneList()
```

The parentheses after the variable name tell VBScript that you want this variable to be an array, but the omission of the upper bounds signals that you don't know at design time how many elements you're going to need to store in it, which is very common.

If you're going to open a file or database table and feed the contents into an array, you might not know at design time how many items will be in the file or database table. Because the number of columns in a database table is relatively fixed, you can safely hard-code an assumption about the number of columns. However, you would not want to assume how many rows are in the table. The number of rows in a database table can potentially change frequently. Even if you know how many rows there are right at this moment, you would not want to hard-code that assumption. So the dynamic array solves that dilemma by allowing you to resize the array at runtime.

In order to change the number of dimensions in a dynamic array you have to use the `ReDim` statement. You can use the `ReDim` statement anywhere in any code that is in the same scope as the dynamic array variable (for more about scope, see Chapter 4).

However, there is one caveat to keep in mind with `ReDim`: Using `ReDim` all by itself clears out the array at the same time that it resizes it. If you stored some data in the array, and then used `ReDim` to resize it, all the data you previously stored in the array would be lost. Sometimes that's a good thing, sometimes it's not — it depends on the program you're writing. In those cases where you don't want to lose the data in the array as you resize it, use the `Preserve` keyword. Using the `Preserve` keyword ensures that the data you've already stored in the array stays there when you resize it. (However, if you make the array *smaller* than it already was, you will of course lose the data that was in the elements you chopped off, even if you use the `Preserve` keyword.)

Following is the phone list code, this time with two changes. First, the declaration of the array variable is changed so that it is a dynamic array. Second, the code that populates the array is changed so that it uses the `ReDim` statement with the `Preserve` keyword to add rows to the array as you go (ARRAY_LIST_DYNAMIC.VBS).

```
Dim astrPhoneList()

'Add the first row
ReDim Preserve astrPhoneList(2,0)
astrPhoneList(0, 0) = "Williams"
astrPhoneList(1, 0) = "Tony"
astrPhoneList(2, 0) = "404-555-6328"

'Add the second row
ReDim Preserve astrPhoneList(2,1)
astrPhoneList(0, 1) = "Carter"
astrPhoneList(1, 1) = "Ron"
astrPhoneList(2, 1) = "305-555-2514"

'Add the third row
ReDim Preserve astrPhoneList(2,2)
astrPhoneList(0, 2) = "Davis"
astrPhoneList(1, 2) = "Miles"
astrPhoneList(2, 2) = "212-555-5314"

'Add the fourth row
ReDim Preserve astrPhoneList(2,3)
astrPhoneList(0, 3) = "Hancock"
astrPhoneList(1, 3) = "Herbie"
astrPhoneList(2, 3) = "616-555-6943"

'Add the fifth row
ReDim Preserve astrPhoneList(2,4)
astrPhoneList(0, 4) = "Shorter"
astrPhoneList(1, 4) = "Wayne"
astrPhoneList(2, 4) = "853-555-0060"
```

There is one caveat when using the `Preserve` keyword: You can only resize the *last* dimension in the array. If you attempt to resize any dimension other than the last dimension, VBScript will generate a runtime error. That's why, when you work with two-dimensional arrays, it's best to think of the first dimension as the columns, and the second dimension as the rows. You will generally know how many columns you need in an array at design time, so in most situations you won't have to resize the columns dimension.

It's the number of rows that you generally won't be sure about. For example, in your phone list array, you know that you need three columns: one for the last name, one for the first name, and one for the phone number. So you can hard code these at design time and dynamically resize the rows dimension at runtime.

Regardless of whether you use a column-and-row metaphor or some other metaphor (an array is just an abstract concept, after all — it's your code and imagination that gives it meaning), make sure that the dimension you want to resize with `ReDim Preserve` is the *last* dimension in your array.

Note that when you declare a variable with the parentheses at the end of the variable name — for example, `varTest()` — that variable can *only* be used as an array. However, you can declare a variable *without* the parentheses at the end, and still use the `ReDim` statement later to turn it into a dynamic array. (Owing to the universality and versatility of the `Variant` data type.) Then you can assign a normal number to the variable again to stop it from being an array. However, using a variable for multiple purposes in this manner can be confusing and might allow bugs to creep into your code. If you need a variable to be both an array and not an array, you might consider declaring two separate variables instead of using one variable for two purposes.

Looping through Arrays

Now that you've declared an array, sized it appropriately, and filled it up with data, let's do something useful with it. Following is the code, this time with some new additions. A few more variables have been added as well as a block of code at the end that loops through the array and displays the contents of the phone list (ARRAY_LIST_DISPLAY.VBS).

```
Dim astrPhoneList()
Dim strMsg
Dim lngIndex
Dim lngUBound

'Add the first row
ReDim Preserve astrPhoneList(2,0)
astrPhoneList(0, 0) = "Williams"
astrPhoneList(1, 0) = "Tony"
astrPhoneList(2, 0) = "404-555-6328"

'Add the second row
ReDim Preserve astrPhoneList(2,1)
astrPhoneList(0, 1) = "Carter"
astrPhoneList(1, 1) = "Ron"
astrPhoneList(2, 1) = "305-555-2514"

'Add the third row
ReDim Preserve astrPhoneList(2,2)
astrPhoneList(0, 2) = "Davis"
astrPhoneList(1, 2) = "Miles"
astrPhoneList(2, 2) = "212-555-5314"

'Add the fourth row
ReDim Preserve astrPhoneList(2,3)
astrPhoneList(0, 3) = "Hancock"
astrPhoneList(1, 3) = "Herbie"
astrPhoneList(2, 3) = "616-555-6943"

'Add the fifth row
ReDim Preserve astrPhoneList(2,4)
astrPhoneList(0, 4) = "Shorter"
astrPhoneList(1, 4) = "Wayne"
astrPhoneList(2, 4) = "853-555-0060"

'Loop through the array and display its contents
lngUBound = UBound(astrPhoneList, 2)

strMsg = "The phone list is:" & vbNewLine & vbNewLine

For lngIndex = 0 to lngUBound
    strMsg = strMsg & astrPhoneList(0, lngIndex) & ", "
    strMsg = strMsg & astrPhoneList(1, lngIndex) & " - "
    strMsg = strMsg & astrPhoneList(2, lngIndex) & vbNewLine
Next

MsgBox strMsg
```

Running this script results in the dialog box shown in Figure 3-16.

The phone list is:

Williams, Tony - 404-555-6328
Carter, Ron - 305-555-2514
Davis, Miles - 212-555-5314
Hancock, Herbie - 616-555-6943
Shorter, Wayne - 853-555-0060

OK

Figure 3-16

Let's examine the additions to the code. First, three new variables have been added.

```
Dim strMsg
Dim lngIndex
Dim lngUBound
```

You use these in the new block of code at the end of the script. You store the text version of the phone list that you build dynamically as you loop through the array in the `strMsg` variable. You use the `lngIndex` variable to keep track of which row you are on inside the loop. Finally, you use `lngUBound` to store the count of rows in the array.

Turning your attention to the new block of code, first you use the `UBound()` function to read how many rows are in the array.

```
lngUBound = UBound(astrPhoneList, 2)
```

The `UBound()` function is very useful in this type of situation because it keeps you from having to hard-code an assumption about how many rows the array has. For example, if you added a sixth row to the array, the loop-and-display code would not need to change at all because you used the `UBound()` function to keep from assuming the number of rows.

The `UBound()` function takes two arguments. The first argument is the array variable that you want the function to measure. The second argument is the number for the dimension you want to have a count on. In your code, you passed in the number 2, indicating the second dimension — that is, the rows in the phone list array. If you had wanted to count the number of columns, you would have passed the number 1. Notice that this argument is 1 based, not 0 based. This is a little confusing, but that's the way it is.

Next, you initialize the `strMsg` variable.

```
strMsg = "The phone list is:" & vbNewLine & vbNewLine
```

As you go through the loop, you continually append to the end of this variable, until you have a string of text that you can feed to the `MsgBox()` function. You initialize it before you start the loop. vbNewLine is a special named constant that is built into VBScript that you can use whenever you want to add a line break to a string of text. (You can learn more about named constants and why they're so important in Chapter 4.)

Next you have your loop.

```
For lngIndex = 0 to lngUBound
    strMsg = strMsg & astrPhoneList(0, lngIndex) & ", "
    strMsg = strMsg & astrPhoneList(1, lngIndex) & " - "
    strMsg = strMsg & astrPhoneList(2, lngIndex) & vbNewLine
Next
```

We're going to ignore for now the exact syntax of the loop, because loop structure and syntax is covered in detail in Chapter 5. If the syntax is unfamiliar to you, don't worry about that for now. Notice the following, though:

❑ You use the `lngUBound` variable to control how many times you go through the loop.

❑ The `lngIndex` variable automatically increases by 1 each time you go through the loop. It starts out at 0, and then for each row in the array, it increases by 1. This allows you to use `lngIndex` for the row subscript when you read from each element of the array. This illustrates another good thing to know about array subscripts: You don't have to use literal numbers as you did in all of the previous examples; you can use variables as well.

❑ When the loop is done, you display the phone list in the dialog box shown in Figure 3-16.

```
MsgBox strMsg
```

Erasing Arrays

You can totally empty out an array using the `Erase` statement. The `Erase` statement has slightly different effects with fixed size and dynamic arrays. With a fixed size array, the data in the array elements is deleted, but the elements themselves stay there — they're just empty. With a dynamic array, the `Erase` statement completely releases the memory the array was taking up. The data in the array is deleted, and the elements themselves are destroyed. To get them back, you would have to use the `ReDim` statement on the array variable to add elements to it again. Here's an example.

```
Erase astrPhoneList
```

Using VarType() with Arrays

The Microsoft VBScript documentation has an error in its description of the `VarType()` function in regards to arrays. It states that when you use the `VarType()` function to determine the subtype of an array variable, the number returned will be a combination of the number 8192 and the normal `VarType()` return value for the subtype (see the table in Appendix I for a list of all the subtype return values and their named constant equivalents). The named constant equivalent for 8192 is `vbArray`.

According to the documentation, you can subtract 8192 from the `VarType()` return value to determine that actual subtype. This is only partially correct. The `VarType()` function does indeed return 8192 (`vbArray`) plus another subtype number — but that other subtype number will always be 12 (`vbVariant`). The subtype of a VBScript array can *never be anything but* `Variant`.

Give this code a try and you'll see that no matter what types of values you try to place in the array (String, Date, Long, Integer, Boolean, and so on), you'll never get the message box in the Else clause to display (ARRAY_VARTYPE_NOMSG.VBS).

```
Dim strTest(1)
Dim lngSubType

strTest(0) = CLng(12)
strTest(1) = "Hello"

lngSubType = VarType(strTest) - vbArray

If lngSubType = vbVariant Then
  MsgBox "The Subtype is Variant."
Else
  MsgBox "The subtype is: " & lngSubType
End If
```

A final note for Visual Basic developers: Because we are discussing complex data types, keep in mind that *User Defined Types* (UDTs) are not supported in VBScript. You cannot define UDTs with the Type statement, nor can you work with UDT variables exposed by VB components.

Summary

This chapter covered the ins and outs of VBScript data types, including one of the "complex" data types, arrays. VBScript supports only one data type, the Variant, but the Variant data type supports many "subtypes."

A Variant variable always has exactly one subtype. Subtypes are determined either implicitly or explicitly. Implicit setting of the subtype occurs when you assign a value to a variable. Sometimes VBScript will change the subtype of a variable "behind your back" without your realizing it. It is important to understand when and why VBScript implicitly coerces subtypes. Sometimes you can use implicit type coercion to your advantage. In addition, as a VBScript programmer you can explicitly set the subtype of a variable using conversion functions such as CLng().

You can test for the subtype of a Variant variable using functions such as IsNumeric() and IsNull(). In addition, you can obtain the name of a variable's subtype using the VarType() function. Often it is important to test the subtype rather than make assumptions about it. Errors and unwanted behavior can result in certain circumstances if you are not careful with the subtype of your variables.

VBScript also has some "special" subtypes such as Empty, Null, and Object, and it is important for a VBScript programmer to understand these subtypes.

This chapter also covered arrays, which, along with objects, are a form of complex data type. An array is considered "complex" because it can hold many values at the same time. Arrays hold multiple values in a "dimensional" structure, usually a simple two-dimensional matrix (like a spreadsheet). However, arrays can also have more than two dimensions. Data can be placed into and read from arrays using "subscripts," which is a convention for referring to a particular location within the dimensional array structure.

Variables and Procedures

In this chapter, the discussion of VBScript variables continues and also expands to include VBScript procedures and functions. Some important variable-specific topics have not been discussed yet, including rules for naming and declaring variables, the important Option Explicit statement, and the concepts of variable *scope* and *lifetime*. You also learn the syntax for defining procedures and functions, including arguments and return values, and get introduced to some "design strategies" for your scripts.

If you are already an experienced programmer in another language and tempted to skip this chapter, you may try just skimming it instead. Even where the material is rudimentary programming-wise you will pick up some useful information that is particular to VBScript.

Option Explicit

You might not be able to guess it based on the code examples presented so far, but declaring variables in VBScript is optional. That's right. You can just start using a new variable anywhere in your code without having declared it first. There is no absolute requirement that says that you must declare the variable first. As soon as VBScript encounters a new nondeclared variable in your code, it just allocates memory for it and keeps going. Here's an example. (The script file for this code is OPTION_EXPL_NO_DECLARE.VBS; you can download the code examples for each chapter in this book from www.wrox.com.)

```
lngFirst = 1
lngSecond = 2
lngThird = lngFirst + lngSecond
MsgBox lngThird
```

Even though none of these three variables were explicitly declared, VBScript does not care. The code runs as you'd expect, and a dialog box comes up at the end displaying the number 3. This sounds pretty convenient. However, this convenience comes at a very high price. Take a look at this next example (OPTION_EXPL_MISSPELLING.VBS).

```
lngFirst = 1
lngSecond = 2
lngThird = lngFirst + lgnSecond
MsgBox lngThird
```

Isn't this the same code as in the previous example? Look again. Do you notice the misspelling in the third line? This is an easy mistake to make while you're typing in line after line of script code. The trouble is that this misspelling does not cause VBScript any trouble at all. It just thinks the misspelling is yet another new variable, so it allocates memory for it and gives it the initial subtype of Empty. When you ask VBScript to do math on an empty variable, it just treats the variable as a zero. So when this code runs, the dialog box displays the number 1, rather than the number 3 you might be expecting.

Easy enough to find the error and fix it in this simple do-nothing script, but what if this script contained dozens, or even hundreds, of lines of code? What if instead of adding 1 to 2 to get 3, you were to add 78523.6778262 to 2349.25385 and then divide the result by 4.97432? Would you be able to notice a math error by looking at the result? If not, you might not even notice that your script contained this bug. In this very realistic VBScript scenario, you could end up with a math error that you might not notice for weeks — or worse yet, your boss or customer might find the error for you.

So what can you do to prevent this? The answer is a statement called Option Explicit. What you do is place the statement Option Explicit at the top of your script file, before any other statements appear. This tells VBScript that your code requires all variables be explicitly declared before it can use them. Now VBScript will no longer let you introduce a new variable right in the middle of your code without declaring it first. Here's an example (OPTION_EXPL_ERROR.VBS).

```
Option Explicit

Dim lngFirst
Dim lngSecond
Dim lngThird

lngFirst = 1
lngSecond = 2
lngThird = lngFirst + lgnSecond
MsgBox lngThird
```

Notice that the Option Explicit statement has been added to the top of the code. Because you have added Option Explicit, you must now declare all of your variables before you use them, which is what you see on the three lines following Option Explicit. Also, notice that the misspelling is still on the second-to-last line. This is to illustrate what happens when you try to use an undeclared variable. If you try and run this code, VBScript will halt the execution with the following error: Variable is undefined: 'lgnSecond'. This is a good thing, because now you know that you need to go fix this bug. As long as you use Option Explicit, VBScript will catch your variable-related typing errors.

One thing that's very nice about Option Explicit is that it applies to the entire script file in which it resides. We have not discussed this too much so far in this book, but a single script file can contain multiple procedures, functions, and class definitions, and each class definition can itself contain multiple procedures and functions (which is covered in Chapter 8). As long as you place Option Explicit at the top of the script file, all of the code within the file is covered.

Start a good habit today: Every single time you start a new script file, before you do anything else, type the words Option Explicit at the top of the file and hit Enter. This will prevent silly typing errors from seriously messing up your code, and your fellow script developers (and customers) will appreciate it.

Naming Variables

VBScript has a few rules for what names you can give to a variable. The rules are pretty simple, and leave you plenty of room to come up with clear, useful, understandable variable names.

> **Rule Number 1: VBScript variable names must begin with an alpha character.**

An *alpha character* is any character between "a" and "z" (capital or lowercase). Non-alpha characters are pretty much everything else: numbers, punctuation marks, mathematical operators, and other special characters. For example, these are legal variable names:

- ❑   `strName`
- ❑   `Some_Thing`
- ❑   `Fruit`

And these are illegal variable names:

- ❑   `+strName`
- ❑   `99RedBalloons`
- ❑   `@Test`

> **Rule Number 2: Numbers and the underscore (_) character can be used in the variable name, but all other non-alphanumeric characters are illegal.**

VBScript does not like variable names that contain characters that are anything but numbers and letters. The lone exception to this is the underscore (_) character. (Some programmers find the underscore character to be useful for separating distinct words in a variable name (for example, `customer_name`), while other programmers prefer to accomplish this by letting the mixed upper and lower case letters accomplish the same thing (for example, `CustomerName`). For example, these are legal variable names:

- ❑   `lngPosition99`
- ❑   `Word1_Word2_`
- ❑   `bool2ndTime`

And these are illegal variable names:

- ❑   `str&Name`
- ❑   `SomeThing@`
- ❑   `First*Name`

> **Rule Number 3: VBScript variable names cannot exceed 255 characters.**

Hopefully, your variable names will not exceed 20 characters or so, but VBScript allows them to be as long as 255 characters.

These rules for variable naming should be pretty easy to follow, but it is important to make a distinction between coming up with variable names that are legal, and coming up with variable names that are clear, useful, and understandable. The fact that VBScript *allows* you to use a variable name, such as `X99B2F012345`, does not necessarily mean that it's a good idea to do so.

A variable name should make the purpose of the variable clear. If you store the user's name in a variable, a name such as `strUserName` is a good one because it removes any doubt about what the programmer intended the variable to be used for. Good variable names not only decrease the chances of errors creeping into your code, but also make the code itself easier for humans to read and understand.

Another technique that many programmers have found useful is the "Hungarian naming convention," which has been mentioned a couple times before, and which you use throughout this and the preceding chapters. (Even VBScript programmers who don't find it useful tend to use it anyway because in the world of VBScript and Visual Basic, the Hungarian convention is so common as to be almost required.) The Hungarian naming convention simply involves adding a prefix to the variable name to indicate what type of data the programmer intends for that variable to store.

For example, the variable name `strUserName` indicates not only that the variable should hold the user's name, but also that the subtype of the variable should be `String`. Similarly, the variable name `lngFileCount` indicates not only that the variable should hold a count of the number of files, but also that the subtype of the variable should be `Long`.

Appendix B of this book contains additional guidelines for naming variables, including a list of suggested data type prefixes.

Procedures and Functions

At this point, you need to learn about the concept of procedures and functions, which are essential building blocks for more complex scripts. Procedures and functions allow you to *modularize* the code in your script into named blocks that perform specific functions. Modularization allows you to think about a more complex problem in a structured way, increases the readability and understandability of your code, and creates opportunities to reuse the same code multiple times in the same script.

A *function* is a named block of code that returns a value to the calling code, while a *procedure* is a named block of code that does *not* return a value. Let's break down some of the new concepts in that last sentence.

❏ **A named block of code:** This refers to a grouping of lines of code that are related in some logical way, that work together to perform a certain programming task. Procedures and functions are "named" blocks of code because you put an explicit boundary around the code and give it a name. For example, you might separate a block of code that processes a customer's order into a procedure with the name `ProcessCustomerOrder()`.

❏ **Calling code:** This means the code that *calls* a procedure or function. One of the primary purposes of naming a block of code is that other code can invoke that block of code using the name. Programmers often call this invocation a "call." For example, throughout the preceding chapters, you have been looking at code that uses the MsgBox() procedure to display a message in a dialog box. The script code that invokes the MsgBox() procedure is referred to as the *calling code*, and MsgBox() is the procedure being *called*.

❏ **Returning a value:** Some named blocks of code can return a value to the calling code. A procedure does not return a value, whereas a function does. Sometimes you need a block of code to return a value, and sometimes you do not. As you have been using it, the MsgBox() procedure does not return a value (though it can if you ask it to — MsgBox() is interesting because you can use it as either a procedure or a function). You just pass MsgBox() a value to display, it displays the value to the user, and when the user clicks the OK button, the subsequent code continues executing. On the other hand, the CLng() function returns a value to the calling code. For example, in the following code, the CLng() function returns a value of 12 with the Long subtype and that returned value is stored in the lngCount variable.

```
lngCount = CLng("12")
```

Procedure Syntax

A named block of code that is a procedure is identified with the Sub keyword. "Sub" is short for "subprocedure," which is another way of saying "procedure." A procedure is declared with the following syntax:

```
[Public|Private] Sub Name ([Argument1],[ArgumentN])

    [code inside the procedure]

End Sub
```

Sometimes the word procedure *is used in the generic sense to refer to either a procedure or a function, but this chapter does its best to use the term* procedure *in the specific sense.*

Note the following about the syntax:

❏ You can optionally precede the Sub keyword with the keywords of Public or Private, but these keywords are really relevant only within a *class*, in which case you might want some procedures visible outside the class and other procedures not visible (see Chapter 8 for more on classes).

❏ In a Windows Script Host file (which is what all of the book's .VBS file examples are), the keywords Public and Private do not really do anything for you because no procedures, functions, or variables can be visible to any other scripts in other files. A .VBS file is an island unto itself; no other script can access the code inside of it.

❏ In VBScript classes and other contexts where the Public and Private keywords are relevant, if you do not specify one or the other, Public is the default.

❏ The ending boundary of a procedure must be defined with the keywords End Sub. Between the Sub and End Sub boundaries, normal VBScript syntax rules apply.

❏ The rules for naming a procedure are the same as those for naming variables (see the section "Naming Variables" earlier in the chapter). It is a good idea, however, to use clear, purposeful names that make it obvious what the purpose of the procedure is and what the code inside of it does. A good technique is to use verb–noun combinations, such as ProcessOrder or GetName.

Procedures and functions can accept *arguments* (also known as *parameters*), but they often do not. An argument is a value that is "passed into" a procedure or function so that the code inside will have access to the value. Here is a bare-bones procedure that does not use any arguments.

```
Sub SayHelloToBill
    MsgBox "Hello, Bill. Welcome to our script."
End Sub
```

However, a procedure just sits there and does nothing unless there is some other code to call it. So the next example (PROCEDURE_SIMPLE.VBS) not only defines the SayHelloToBill() procedure, but also *calls* it.

```
Option Explicit

SayHelloToBill

Sub SayHelloToBill
    MsgBox "Hello, Bill. Welcome to our script."
End Sub
```

Notice the following about this code:

❏   The first line of code (following the standard Option Explicit declaration) is not part of the procedure definition, but rather is in the "main body" of the script. You may recall that the VBScript runtime first loads and compiles the script as a whole, and then it executes the main body of the script from the top down. In the example, the compiler parses the script, creates a definition for the SayHelloToBill() procedure, and then the runtime executes the main body of the script from top to bottom. The main body of your script has only one line:

```
SayHelloToBill
```

❏   One way to think of it is that the main body of the script is the puppetmaster, and the procedures and functions (and classes) that you create within a script are puppets. Not only do you get to design and build the puppets, but you get to orchestrate the puppetmaster as well. We'll return more to this perspective later in the chapter, when we discuss script design strategies.

❏   The Public/Private keywords are omitted, as explained earlier, because in the assumed Windows Script Host context they don't have any relevance.

❏   Parentheses are not included after the procedure name. It's coded this way because this particular procedure does not take any arguments.

❏   The code inside of the procedure is indented, so that it looks "nested" inside of the lines above and below. This is not required, but is a common convention because it makes the code easier to read and understand. The indentation suggests the hierarchical relationship between the procedure and the code within it. Clear management of the "white space" in your scripts (blank lines and indentations) is one of your primary ways of communicating with yourself and other programmers who might have to look at a script later. If you cram everything together on one unindented line after another, your scripts becomes unreadable, even to you yourself.

Here is another example procedure that takes one argument (PROCEDURE_ARGUMENT.VBS).

```
Option Explicit

GreetUser "Bill"

Sub GreetUser(strUserName)
    MsgBox "Hello, " & strUserName &_
        ". Welcome to our script."
End Sub
```

Notice how the addition of the strUserName argument, along with an adjustment to the procedure name, allows you to make the procedure more generic, which in turn makes it more reusable. The previous example was flawed because it assumed that every user of the script would be named Bill. This example is flawed in the same way, but gets you one step closer to accommodating users who are not named Bill — keep reading to find out how.

Function Syntax

The syntax for a function is identical to that of a procedure, except that you change the keyword Sub to the keyword Function.

```
[Public|Private] Function Name ([Argument1],[ArgumentN])

    [code inside the function]

End Function
```

The rules for naming, the relevance of Public/Private, and the declaration of arguments are the same for functions and procedures. As mentioned before, the distinction between a function and a procedure is that a function returns a value to the caller. Here is an example that illustrates the syntax for a function and how the code within a function sets the return value for the function (FUNCTION_SIMPLE.VBS).

```
Option Explicit

Dim lngFirst
Dim lngSecond

lngFirst = 10
lngSecond = 20

MsgBox "The sum is: "& AddNumbers(lngFirst, lngSecond)

Function AddNumbers(lngFirstNumber, lngSecondNumber)

    AddNumbers = lngFirstNumber + lngSecondNumber

End Function
```

`AddNumbers` may not be the most useful function in the world, but it serves well to illustrate a couple things:

❑ Notice that this function has two arguments, `lngFirstNumber` and `lngSecondNumber`. The arguments are used inside of the function.

❑ Notice that the way the return value is specified is by referring to the name of the function within the code of the function. That's what is going on in this line.

```
AddNumbers = lngFirstNumber + lngSecondNumber
```

It's as if there is a nondeclared variable inside of the function that has the same exact name as the function itself. To set the return value of the function, you set the value of this invisible variable. You can do this from anywhere inside the function, and you can change the return value of the function repeatedly just as you can with a normal variable. If you set the return value more than once inside the function, the last such line of code to execute before exiting from the function is the one that sets the value.

Let's join together a procedure and a function to demonstrate how functions and procedures are used in a nested fashion (`PROCEDURE_FUNCTION_NESTED.VBS`).

```
Option Explicit

GreetUser

Sub GreetUser
    MsgBox "Hello, "& GetUserName & _
        ". Welcome to our script."
End Sub

Function GetUserName
    GetUserName = InputBox("Please enter your name.")
End Function
```

Notice how the `GreetUser()` procedure calls the `GetUserName()` function. Functions and procedures can work together in this way, which is how programs are built. Break your code up into specific modular building blocks of procedures and functions that do very specific things and then string the building blocks together in a logical manner.

This example brings up a good opportunity to introduce an important principle that's discussed in more detail in the "Design Strategies for Procedures and Functions" section of this chapter. Using the puppetmaster metaphor in the current example, you have designed a puppet (the `GreetUser()` procedure) that uses another puppet (`GetUserName()`) without the puppetmaster (the main script body) needing to be aware of it. This may seem like a good thing, and as far as it goes, it is, but there is a serious flaw in the nested procedure–function design.

The `GreetUser()` procedure has an unnecessary *coupling* to the `GetUserName()` function. What this means is that `GreetUser()` "knows about" and depends on the `GetUserName()` function; it won't work without it. It depends on it because it makes a call to it; `GreetUser()` won't know whom to greet if it does not ask `GetUserName()` for a name.

Some amount of coupling among code modules is necessary and good, but coupling is also something that you want to avoid if you don't need it. The more couplings in your program, the more complex it is. Some complexity is inevitable, but you want to reduce complexity as much as possible. When functions and procedures are coupled together in a haphazard manner, you get what is famously known as "spaghetti code" — that is, code in which it is impossible to trace the logic because the logic twists and turns in a seemingly random pattern.

Here's a different version of the same script that eliminates the unnecessary coupling, and puts some of the control and knowledge back in the hands of the puppetmaster. It may seem that it was a good thing for the `GreetUser` puppet to be smart enough to use the flexible `GetUserName` puppet, but it is better in the long run if `GreetUser` is designed to be self sufficient and not any smarter than it needs to be.

```
Option Explicit

GreetUser GetUserName

Sub GreetUser(strUserName)
    MsgBox "Hello, " & strUserName & _
        ". Welcome to our script."
End Sub

Function GetUserName
    GetUserName = InputBox("Please enter your name.")
End Function
```

The logic of the program is the same, but now you have *decoupled* `GreetUser()` and `GetUserName()`. You do this by restoring the `strUserName` argument to `GreetUser` and instead using the code at the top of the script to put the two functions together without either function "knowing about" the other. Here is the interesting line of code in this script.

```
GreetUser GetUserName
```

The return value from the `GetUserName()` function is fed as the `strUserName` argument of the `GreetUser()` function.

One final note about function syntax: Programmers familiar with other languages may have noticed that there is no way to declare the data type of a function's return value. This makes sense if you remember that VBScript supports only one data type — the `Variant`. Because all variables are `Variants`, there is no need for syntax that specifies the data type of a function.

One way that many VBScript programmers choose to help with code clarity in this regard is to use the same Hungarian type prefixes in front of their function names as they do for their variable names. For example, `GetUserName()` could be renamed `strGetUserName()`. However, if you choose to follow this convention, it is extra important to name your variables and functions so that they are easy to tell apart. Using the verb–noun convention for function names helps, such that it becomes obvious that `strUserName` is a variable and `strGetUserName` is a function.

Calling Procedures and Functions

In the preceding examples of procedures and functions, you may have noticed some differences in the syntax for calling a procedure as opposed to a function. There are indeed differences, and the VBScript compiler is very particular about them.

Legal ways to call a procedure	Illegal ways to call a procedure
`GreetUser "Bill"`	GreetUser("Bill")
`Call GreetUser("Bill")`	Call GreetUser "Bill"

These two legal conventions are functionally equivalent, and whichever you choose is largely a matter of taste. Some people would argue that the second convention (using the `Call` keyword) is clearer while others hate the extra typing. Some people like the second convention because it's more like the old BASIC programming language in which VBScript has its roots. Both conventions are equally common, and Visual Basic and VBScript programmers over time become very accustomed to one or the other. When calling a procedure (as opposed to a function), if you choose not to use the `Call` keyword, then you cannot use parentheses around the argument value you are passing to the procedure. Conversely, if you do want to use the `Call` keyword, then the parentheses are required. That's just the way it is.

You'll notice in this book the first convention is used for the most part, so you can see which way we've chosen. (In fact, if any of the syntax rules in this section seem confusing, just follow the example scripts to see how it's done — or at least how we've chosen to do it.)

The rules for calling functions are a bit different.

Legal ways to call a function	Illegal ways to call a function	Comments
`lngSum = AddNumbers (10, 20)`	`lngSum = AddNumbers 10, 20`	To receive the return value from a function, you must *not* use the `Call` keyword, and you must use parentheses around the argument list. This is illegal without parentheses.
`Call AddNumbers (10, 20)`	`lngSum = Call AddNumbers (10, 20)`	You can use the `Call` keyword if you do not wish to receive the return value of the function, but you must use the parentheses. It's illegal if you use the `Call` keyword when receiving the return value.
`AddNumbers 10, 20`	`AddNumbers (10, 20)`	You can also omit the `Call` keyword and still ignore the return value, but you must omit the parentheses in that case.

This begs the question: Why would you ever want to call a function if you did not want the return value? The code in the preceding two examples might compile, but it looks awfully silly. Generally speaking, functions are functions because they return values and we call functions because we want the values they return.

However, there are cases where it makes sense to ignore the return value and call a function as if it were a procedure. The way you have been using MsgBox() is a good example of this. MsgBox() can be used as either a procedure or a function, depending on why you need it. MsgBox() has dual purpose. It can just display a message for you, which is how you've been using it, or you can use it as a function to find out which button a user clicked on the dialog box. Here is a script that illustrates the two ways of using MsgBox() (MSGBOX_DUAL.VBS).

```
Option Explicit

Dim lngResponse
Dim strUserName

lngResponse = MsgBox("Would you like a greeting?", vbYesNo)

If lngResponse = vbYes Then
    strUserName = GetUserName
    GreetUser strUserName
End If

Sub GreetUser(strUserName)
    MsgBox "Hello, " & strUserName & _
        ". Welcome to our script."
End Sub

Function GetUserName
    GetUserName = InputBox("Please enter your name.")
End Function
```

In this line of code, you use MsgBox() as a function.

```
lngResponse = MsgBox("Would you like a greeting?", vbYesNo)
```

MsgBox() has some optional arguments, one of which is the second argument that allows you to specify if you want the dialog box to offer more buttons than just the OK button. This use of the MsgBox() function produces the dialog box shown in Figure 4-1.

If the user clicks the Yes button, the MsgBox() function returns a certain value (defined as vbYes in this example). If the user clicks Yes, then the familiar GreetUser() procedure is eventually called, in which you can see how you can call MsgBox() as a procedure instead of as a function.

Figure 4-1

Note: `vbYesNo` *and* `vbYes` *from the example are built-in VBScript "named constants," which are like variables with fixed, unchangeable values. (Named constants are covered later in this chapter.)*

Optional Arguments

As you just saw with the `MsgBox()` function in the previous section, procedures and functions can have *optional arguments*. If an argument is optional, then you don't have to pass anything to it. Generally, an optional argument will have a default value if you don't pass anything. Optional arguments always appear at the end of the argument list; mandatory arguments must come first, followed by any optional arguments — but the procedures and functions you write yourself using VBScript cannot have optional arguments. If necessary, you can get around this by defining mandatory arguments and interpreting a certain value (such as `Null`) to indicate that the caller wants that argument to be ignored. This kind of "fake" optional argument can help you sometimes in a bind, but this technique is generally discouraged.

Exiting a Procedure or Function

A procedure or function will exit naturally when the last line of code inside of it is done executing. However, sometimes you want to terminate a procedure sooner than that. In this case, you can use either of the statements `Exit Sub` (for procedures) or `Exit Function` (for functions). The code will stop executing wherever the `Exit` statement appears and the flow of the code will return to the caller.

With the simple functions that have been used as examples, there has not been an obvious place where you would want to use `Exit Sub` or `Exit Function`. Usually these statements are used inside of more complex code in situations where you have reached a logical stopping point or dead end in the logic. That said, many programmers discourage the use of these statements in favor of using a code structure that does not require them. Take this code, for example (`EXIT_SUB.VBS`).

```
Option Explicit

GreetUser InputBox("Please enter your name.")
Sub GreetUser(strUserName)
    If IsNumeric(strUserName) or IsDate(strUserName) Then
        MsgBox "That is not a legal name."
        Exit Sub
```

```
        End If
        MsgBox "Hello, "& strUserName & _
            ". Welcome to our script."
    End Sub
```

Notice the `Exit Sub` in the `GreetUser()` procedure. Some logic has been added that tests to make sure the name is not a number or date, and if it is, it informs the user and uses `Exit Sub` to terminate the procedure. However, many programmers would argue that there is a better way to do this that does not require the use of `Exit Sub`, as in this example (`EXIT_SUB_NOT_NEEDED.VBS`).

```
    Option Explicit

    GreetUser InputBox("Please enter your name.")

    Sub GreetUser(strUserName)
        If IsNumeric(strUserName) or IsDate(strUserName) Then
            MsgBox "That is not a legal name."
        Else
            MsgBox "Hello, "& strUserName & _
                ". Welcome to our script."
        End If
    End Sub
```

Notice that instead of using `Exit Sub` an `Else` clause is used. The principle at work here is to design the procedure to have only one exit point, which is the implicit exit point at the end of the procedure. By definition, a procedure or function with an `Exit` statement has more than one exit point, which some programmers would argue is poor design. The logic behind this principle is that procedures with multiple exit points are more prone to bugs and harder to understand.

Don't worry too much about whether your code conforms to some design ideal — especially in small, simple scripts such as these. The more important consideration is the idea that the use of Exit Sub and Exit Function are directly tied to the logic flow of your script. Because they can be used to interrupt the flow of logic and produce "jumps" in the code, overuse can lead to logic that is hard to follow and prone to bugs. This is why some people caution against their use as a general matter.

Variable Scope, Declaration, and Lifetime

Variable *scope* and *lifetime* are closely related concepts. A variable's scope is a kind of box in which a variable is valid and accessible; outside of the box, the variable is not visible or accessible, and the variable itself cannot see or interact outside of its box. The *scope* of a variable is directly tied to the *lifetime* of that variable. (The concept of variable lifetime is covered in more detail in the next section.)

Understanding Variable Scope

There are three types of variable scope in VBScript:

❑   **Script-level scope:** The variable is available to all of the code in a script file. Variables declared in the "main body" of a script file (like a Windows Script Host `.VBS` file or an Active Server Pages `.ASP` file) automatically have script-level scope.

❏ **Procedure-level scope:** The variable is available only to the procedure or function in which it is declared. Other code outside of the procedure, even if that code resides in the same script file, cannot access a procedure-level variable. Procedure-level scope is also known as "local" scope, and programmers commonly use the term "local variable" to refer to a variable declared at the procedure level.

❏ **Class-level scope:** This is a special construct that contains a logic grouping of properties and methods. In VBScript, classes are defined in a script using the `Class...End Class` block definition statements. A variable that is declared using the `Private` statement in the main body of the class definition has class-level scope. This means that other code in the class can access the variable, but code outside of the class definition, even if that code resides in the same script file, cannot access the variable. Class-level scope is covered in Chapter 8.

There are three statements that you can use to declare variables: `Dim`, `Private`, and `Public`. (The `ReDim` statement that was introduced in the previous chapter also falls into this category of statements, but it is specifically used for the "redimensioning" of already declared array variables.) You use these declaration statements in different situations, depending on the scope of the variable being declared:

❏ `Dim`: Use this statement to declare variables with either script or procedure-level scope. Any variable declared at the script level is automatically available to the entire script file, regardless of whether `Dim`, `Private`, or `Public` is used to declare it. In order to declare a variable inside of a procedure (also known as a *local variable*), you must use `Dim`. Using `Public` and `Private` is not allowed inside of a procedure. If used at the class level, `Dim` has the exact same effect as `Public`.

❏ `Private`: Use the `Private` statement at either the script- or class-level scope, but not inside of procedures or functions. If used at the script level, it has the exact same effect as using `Dim` or `Public`. Any variable declared at the script level is automatically available to the entire script file, regardless of whether `Dim`, `Private`, or `Public` was used to declare it. Although VBScript does not require it, many programmers prefer to use the `Private` statement to declare variables at the script level, and to reserve `Dim` for local variables within procedures and functions. In order to declare a private class-level variable, you must use `Private`. Any variable declared at the class level with either `Dim` or `Public` is automatically available as a public property of the class.

❏ `Public`: You may use the `Public` statement to declare variables with script-level scope, but in effect it is exactly the same as either `Dim` or `Private`. The only place that `Public` is really meaningful is at the class level. A variable declared at the class level with `Public` is made available as a public property of the class. The reason that `Public` is not meaningful at the script level is that, with the exception of "script components" (see Chapter 16), variables are not available outside the script file in which they reside. Therefore, the only place it really makes sense to use `Public` is for creating public properties for a class. However, note that many VBScript programmers discourage the use of `Public` variables in a class and prefer instead to use a combination of a `Private` class-level variable and `Property Let`, `Set`, and `Get` procedures (see Chapter 8).

Many rules were packed in these three points (and again, the examples you'll get to soon will make the rules clearer), so the following guidelines might make it easier to keep track of when to use `Dim`, `Private`, and `Public`.

❑ Use `Dim` either at the procedure level to declare variables that are local to that procedure or at the script level. `Dim` is sort of the all-purpose keyword for declaring variables. In non-class-based scripts and scripts that are not used as Windows Script Components, `Private` and `Public` don't have any effect different than that of `Dim`.

❑ If you want, you can use `Private` at the script level (instead of `Dim`) to declare variables that will be available to the whole script. Use of `Private` becomes more important at the class level to declare variables that are available only within a class.

❑ Use `Public` only to declare public properties for a class, but also consider the option of using a `Private` variable in combination with `Property Let`, `Set`, and `Get` procedures. Even though `Dim` has the same effect as `Public` at the class level, it is more explicit, and therefore preferable, to not use `Dim` at the class level.

Before moving on to the topic of variable lifetime, the discussion turns to a few more tidbits about declarations.

Understanding Variable Declaration

VBScript allows you to put more than one variable declaration on the same line, but from a style standpoint, it is generally preferable to limit variable declarations to one per line, as the example scripts have, but this is not an absolute rule. For example, script programmers who are writing scripts that are downloaded over the Web as part of an HTML file often prefer to put multiple declarations on a single line because it makes the file a little smaller. Sometimes, though, a programmer simply prefers to have more than one variable in a single declaration. This is one of those stylistic things on which programmers simply differ. It's nothing to get worked up about.

Here is an example of a valid multi-variable declaration.

```
Dim strUserName, strPassword, lngAge
```

And here is one using `Private` instead of `Dim`. The rules are the same whether you are using `Dim`, `Private`, or `Public`.

```
Private strUserName, strPassword, lngAge
```

Note, however, that you cannot mix declarations of differing scope on the same line. If you want to declare some `Private` and `Public` variables in a class, for example, you must have two separate lines.

```
Private strUserName, strPassword
Public lngAge, datBirthday, boolLikesPresents
```

Finally, VBScript places a limit on the number of variables you can have within a script or procedure. You cannot have more than 127 procedure-level variables in any given procedure, and you cannot have more than 127 script-level variables in any given script file. This should not cause you any trouble, however. If you are using this many variables in a script or procedure, you might want to rethink your design and break that giant procedure up into multiple procedures. And if you really do have that much data, consider organizing them into classes, each of which can have multiple properties.

Variable Lifetime

Lifetime refers to the span of time that a variable is in memory and available for use while the script is executing. The life of a variable only lasts as long as its scope. A variable with procedure-level scope is only alive as long as that procedure is executing. When the procedure is finished, the memory that was holding that variable is released as if the variable never existed. Similarly, a variable with script-level scope is alive as long as the script is running. And likewise, a variable with class-level scope is alive only while some other code uses an object based on that class.

By limiting a variable's scope, you also limit its lifetime. Here is an important principle to keep in mind: You should limit a variable's lifetime, and therefore its scope, as much as you can. Because a variable takes up memory, and therefore operating system and script engine resources, you should . keep it alive only as long as you need it. By declaring a variable within the procedure in which it will be used, you keep the variable from taking up resources when the procedure in which it resides is not being executed.

Really, though, resource consumption is not the most important reason for limiting variable scope; limiting scope decreases the chance for programming errors and makes code more understandable and maintainable. If you have a script with several procedures and functions, and all of your variables are declared at the script level so that any of those procedures and functions can change the variables, you've created a situation in which any code can change any variable at any time, and this can become very difficult for a programmer to keep up with.

Simply following good principles of modularlaization to code well-designed procedures and functions will take care of scope and lifetime issues naturally — no extra effort required. If your script's logic is broken into smaller chunks (procedures and functions), each chunk becomes a natural scope boundary for its data. Make use of local variables and procedure parameters as much as possible so that each procedure only has visibility to the data that it absolutely needs.

Look at an example that illustrates variable scope and lifetime (SCOPE.VBS):

```
Option Explicit

Private datToday

datToday = Date
MsgBox "Tommorrow's date will be "& AddOneDay(datToday) & "."

Function AddOneDay(datAny)
    Dim datResult
    datResult = DateAdd("d", 1, datAny)
    AddOneDay = datResult
End Function
```

This script contains a function called AddOneDay(). The variable datResult is declared with Dim inside the function and has procedure-level scope, which means that it is not available to any of the code outside of the function. The variable datToday is declared with Private and has script-level scope. The variable datResult is active only while the AddOneDay() function is executing, whereas the datToday variable is active for the entire lifetime of the script.

Design Strategies for Scripts and Procedures

Take another look at the last example (SCOPE.VBS). Note that you could have instead designed this script this way (SCOPE_BAD_DESIGN.VBS).

```
Option Explicit

Private datToday

datToday = Date
AddOneDay
MsgBox "Tommorrow's date will be " & datToday & "."

Sub AddOneDay()
    datToday = DateAdd("d", 1, datToday)
End Sub
```

This code is 100 percent legal and valid, and the ultimate result is the same as the original. Because datToday has script-level scope, it is available to the code inside of AddOneDay() (which you've now changed from a function to a procedure); you simply designed AddOneDay() to change datToday directly. It does work, but this kind of technique creates some problems.

You've lost the reusability of the AddOneDay function. Now AddOneDay() is "tightly coupled" to the script-level variable datToday. If you want to copy AddOneDay() and paste it into another script so you can reuse it, you've made your job a lot more difficult. When AddOneDay() was a stand-alone function with no knowledge of any data or code outside of itself, it was totally portable, generic, and reusable.

Limiting Code that Reads and Changes Variables

The point is not to avoid using script-level variables altogether. And it is not inherently bad to have a procedure refer to a script-level variable. It's all in *how* you go about doing it. The strategy you want to employ is to *limit* the number of places in your script that directly read and change script-level variables. You also want to make it as obvious as possible so that other people reading your code can see how it works.

Recall the puppetmaster and his puppets. If the puppets are meddling with the puppetmaster's script-level data too much, then the puppetmaster will have a harder time keeping tracking of things, making sure that mistakes don't happen.

Take a look at this script (SENTENCE_NO_PROCS.VBS).

```
Option Explicit

Dim strSentence
Dim strVerb
Dim strNoun

'Start the sentence
strSentence = "The "
```

(continued)

```
'Get a noun from the user
strNoun = InputBox("Please enter a noun (person, " & _
    "place, or thing).")

'Add the noun to the sentence
strSentence = strSentence & Trim(strNoun) & " "

'Get a verb from the user
strVerb = InputBox("Please enter a past tense verb.")

'Add the verb to the sentence
strSentence = strSentence & Trim(strVerb)

'Finish the sentence
strSentence = strSentence & "."

'Display the sentence
MsgBox strSentence
```

This essentially useless script goes through a series of steps to build a simple sentence based on input from the user. All of the code is in a single block with no procedures or functions, and the code shares access to script-level variables.

Breaking Code into Procedures and Functions

Here is the same procedure broken into procedures and functions along the lines of our puppetmaster and puppets metaphor (SENTENCE_WITH_PROCS.VBS).

```
Option Explicit

Dim strSentence

strSentence = "The "
strSentence = strSentence & GetNoun & " "
strSentence = strSentence & GetVerb
strSentence = strSentence & GetPeriod
DisplayMessage strSentence

Function GetNoun
    GetNoun = Trim(InputBox("Please enter a noun (person, place, or thing)."))
End Function

Function GetVerb
    GetVerb = Trim(InputBox("Please enter a past tense verb."))
End Function

Function GetPeriod
    GetPeriod = "."
End Function

Sub DisplayMessage(strAny)
    MsgBox strAny
End Sub
```

In this version you have a single script-level variable with a block of code at the top that coordinates the logic leading to the goal of the script: to build a sentence and display it to the user. The code at the top of the script uses a series of functions and one procedure to do the real work. Each function and procedure has a very specific job and makes no use of any script-level data. All of the functions and procedures are "dumb" in that they do not have any "knowledge" of the big picture. This makes them less error prone, easier to understand, and more reusable.

Another benefit is that you do not have to read the whole script to understand what's going on in this script. All you have to do is read these five lines and you have the entire big picture.

```
strSentence = "The "
strSentence = strSentence & GetNoun & " "
strSentence = strSentence & GetVerb
strSentence = strSentence & GetPeriod
DisplayMessage strSentence
```

If, after getting the big picture, you want to dive into the specific details of how a particular step is accomplished, you know exactly where in the script to look. Even though this is a silly example not rooted in the real world, it illustrates the technique of strategically modularizing your scripts.

General Tips for Script Design

Here are some general principles to aid you in your script designs:

❏ Simple script files that perform one specific job with a limited amount of code can be written as a single block of code without any procedures or functions.

❏ As script files become more complex, look for ways to break the logic down into subparts using procedures, functions, and/or classes.

❏ As you break the logic into subparts, keep the coordinating code at the top of the script file.

❏ Design each procedure and function so that it has a very specific job and does only that job. Give the procedure a good descriptive name that indicates what job it does.

❏ Design each procedure and function so that it does not need to have any "knowledge" of the script file's "big picture." In other words, individual procedures and functions should be "dumb," only knowing how to do their specific job.

❏ As much as possible, keep the procedures and functions from reading or writing to script-level variables. When procedures and functions need access to some data that is stored in a script-level variable, include it as an argument rather than accessing the script-level variable directly.

❏ If the value of a script-level variable needs to be changed, use the coordinating code at the top of the script file to make the change.

ByRef and ByVal

There is one concept that was skipped during the introduction to procedure and function arguments: passing arguments *by reference* versus passing arguments *by value*. An argument is defined either by reference or by value depending on how it is declared in the procedure or function definition. A by-reference argument is indicated with the ByRef keyword, whereas a by-value argument can either be indicated with the `ByVal` keyword or by not specifying either `ByRef` or `ByVal` — that is, if you do not specify one or the other explicitly; `ByVal` is the default.

So what does all this mean exactly? You have probably noticed that when a variable is passed to a procedure or function as an argument that the code in the procedure can refer to that argument by name like any other local variable in that procedure. Specifying that an argument is by-value means that the code in the procedure cannot make any permanent changes to the value of the variable.

With by-value, the code in a procedure can change the argument, but the changes are temporary; as soon as the procedure terminates, the changes to that variable/argument are discarded along with all the other local variables the procedure was using. On the other hand, with by-reference, it's more like the caller is sharing a variable with the procedure or function being called; any changes the procedure makes to the by-reference argument are "permanent" in the sense that they are still there when control returns back to the calling code.

Let's look at some examples. Here is a procedure with two arguments, one `ByVal` and one `ByRef` (BYREF_BYVAL.VBS).

```
Option Explicit

Dim lngA
Dim lngB

lngA = 1
lngB = 1

ByRefByValExample lngA, lngB

MsgBox "lngA = " & lngA & vbNewLine & _
    "lngB = " & lngB

Sub ByRefByValExample(ByRef lngFirst, ByVal lngSecond)
    lngFirst = lngFirst + 1
    lngSecond = lngSecond + 1
End Sub
```

Running this code produces the dialog box shown in Figure 4-2.

Figure 4-2

Notice the following about this code:

❑ The `lngA` and `lngB` variables are declared at the script level, outside of the `ByRefByValExample()` procedure and both are initialized to a value of 1.

❑ The `lngFirst` argument is declared as `ByRef` and `lngSecond` as `ByVal`.

❑ Both arguments are incremented by 1 inside of the procedure.

❑ In the dialog box, only `lngA` (which was passed by reference) has a value of 2 after the procedure terminates.

Only `lngA` was changed because only `lngA` was passed by reference. Because `lngB` was passed by value, changes made to it inside of the `ByRefByValExample()` procedure are not reflected in the variable outside of the procedure.

Most of the time (you could even say almost all of the time), you will want to use `ByVal` for your procedure and function arguments. For many of the same reasons discussed in the previous sections about variable scope and lifetime, it is just plain safer and straightforward to use `ByVal`. There is nothing inherently wrong with `ByRef`, and there are sometimes good reasons to use it that are too involved to get into, but stick with `ByVal` until you run into a situation where you feel you need `ByRef`.

For example, here is a script that is using `ByRef` even though it does not have to (BYREF.VBS).

```
Option Explicit

Dim strWord

strWord = "alligator"
AppendSuffix strWord
MsgBox strWord

Sub AppendSuffix(ByRef strAny)
    strAny = strAny & "XXX"
End Sub
```

Here is a better example that eliminates the need for `ByRef` (BYVAL.VBS).

```
Option Explicit

Dim strWord

strWord = "alligator"
strWord = AppendSuffix(strWord)
MsgBox strWord

Function AppendSuffix(ByVal strAny)
    AppendSuffix = strAny & "XXX"
End Function
```

This example changes the procedure to a function such that the `ByRef` keyword is no longer needed. Note also that the `ByVal` keyword in this example is optional; leaving it out has the same effect because `ByVal` is the default.

Literals and Named Constants

This section introduces a concept that has known some controversy among programmers. When is it okay to use literals in your code, and when is it better to use a named constant instead? On one extreme, you have programmers who never use named constants in place of literals (either by choice or because they're not aware of the technique). On the other extreme, you have programmers who never use literals anywhere, but always use named constants instead. In the middle, there is a balance that allows for some use of literals, but leans toward the use of named constants when doing so increases clarity and reduces the likelihood of typing mistakes.

After reading the discussion given in the next section, you should have a good feel for where you stand on the literals and named constants controversy. It's a good idea to understand the benefits of using named constants, and what the risks are in not using them, so that you can decide for yourself when it's a good idea to use them.

What Is a Literal?

A *literal* is any piece of static data that appears in your code that is not stored in a variable or named constant. Literals can be strings of text, numbers, dates, or Boolean values. For example, the word `"Hello"` in the following code is a literal.

```
Dim strMessage

strMessage = "Hello"
MsgBox strMessage
```

The date `08/31/69` in the following code is also a literal.

```
Dim datBirthday

datBirthday = #08/31/69#
MsgBox "My birthday is " & datBirthday & "."
```

The string `"My birthday is "` is also a literal. Literals do not need to be stored in a variable to be considered a literal. And for one more example, the value `True` in the following code is also a literal.

```
Dim boolCanShowMsg

boolCanShowMsg = True
If boolCanShowMsg Then
    MsgBox "Hello there."
End If
```

Many times, literals are just fine in your code, especially for simple scripts without a lot of code or complexity. Programmers use literals all the time. They are not inherently bad. However, there are many instances when the use of a named constant is preferable to using a literal.

What Is a Named Constant?

A *named constant* is similar to a variable, in that it is a name (or a "symbol") for a data storage location in memory. The difference is that a constant, as the name suggests, cannot be changed at runtime. A variable is dynamic. While the code is running, any code within a variable's scope can change the value of it to something else. A named constant, on the other hand, is static. Once defined, it cannot be changed by any code during runtime.

In VBScript, you define a constant in your code using the `Const` statement. Here's an example (NAMED_CONSTANT.VBS).

```
Option Explicit

Const GREETING = "Hello there, "

Dim strUserName strUserName = InputBox("Please enter your name.")
If Trim(strUserName) <> "" Then
  MsgBox GREETING & strUserName & "."
End If
```

If the user types in the name `"William"`, then this code results in the dialog box shown in Figure 4-3.

Figure 4-3

The `Const` statement defines the named constant called GREETING. The name of the constant is in all capital letters because this is the generally accepted convention for named constants. Defining constant names in all capital letters makes them easy to differentiate from variables, which are generally typed in either all lowercase or mixed case. Additionally, because constants are usually written in all capital letters, distinct words within the constant's name are usually separated by the underscore (_) character, as in this example (NAMED_CONSTANT2.VBS).

```
Option Explicit

Const RESPONSE_YES = "YES"
Const RESPONSE_NO = "NO"

Dim strResponse

strResponse = InputBox("Is today a Tuesday? Please answer Yes or No.")
strResponse = UCase(strResponse)
If strResponse = RESPONSE_YES Then
  MsgBox "I love Tuesdays."
ElseIf strResponse = RESPONSE_NO Then
  MsgBox "I will gladly pay you Tuesday for a hamburger today."
Else
  MsgBox "Invalid response."
End If
```

Constants also have scope, just like variables. While you cannot use the Dim statement to declare a constant, you can use Private and Public in front of the Const statement. However, these scope qualifications are optional. A constant declared at the script level automatically has script-level scope (meaning it is available to all procedures, functions, and classes within the script file). A constant declared inside of procedure or function automatically has procedure-level (a.k.a. local) scope (meaning that other code outside of the procedure cannot use the constant).

You can also declare multiple constants on one line, like so:

```
Const RESPONSE_YES = "YES", RESPONSE_NO = "No"
```

Finally, you cannot use variables or functions to set the value of a constant, because that would require the value to be set at runtime. The value of a constant must be defined at design time with a literal value, as in the aforementioned examples. For example, this would not be valid:

```
Dim strMessage
Const SOME_VALUE = strMessage
```

Benefits of Named Constants

The following list examines some of the benefits that named constants offer.

❏ Named constants can decrease bugs. If you are repeating the same literal value many times throughout your code, the probability of misspelling that literal goes up every time you type it. If you type the constant's name in place of the literal throughout your code, you can just as easily misspell that, but the script engine catches this error at runtime (as long as you use Option Explicit), whereas a misspelling of the literal itself might go unnoticed for quite some time.

❏ Named constants can increase clarity. Some of the literals used in the previous examples were mostly clear all by themselves, and adding a constant did not really make their meaning more clear. However, using a literal in your code can often hide meaning when the purpose of the literal is not immediately apparent from reading the code. This is especially true with literals that are numbers. A number by itself does not suggest its purpose for being in the code, and using a constant in its place can make that meaning clear.

❏ If the literal being replaced by the constant is especially long, or otherwise cumbersome to type, using the constant makes it a lot easier to type your code. For example, if you needed to insert a large multi-paragraph legal disclaimer at various points in your scripts, it's a good idea to replace that large block of text with a short named constant that's much easier to type.

Guidelines for Named Constants

This section discusses a couple of guidelines you should follow for named constants.

> **Named Constant Guideline #1: If you are using a literal only once, it's probably okay to use it instead of creating a named constant.**

Named Constant Guideline #1 is especially true when you consider constants used in HTML-embedded script code, which must be downloaded over the Web. If you always used named constants in place of literals in client-side Web scripting, you could easily increase the size of the file that the user has to download to a point that is noticeable. And even in a server-side Web scripting scenario (where the script code is not downloaded to the user's browser), using constants everywhere can slow down the script execution. This is because the script engine has to process all the constants before it can execute the code that uses them.

However, if you are using the same literal over and over throughout the script, then replacing it with a named constant can really increase the readability of the code, and reduce mistakes from misspellings of the literal. A great technique in server-side Web ASP (Active Server Pages) scripting (see Chapter 20) is to put named constants in an "include" file that can be reused in multiple scripts. Named constants are important, but sometimes you have to weigh the tradeoff.

> **Named Constant Guideline #2: If using a named constant in place of a literal will make the meaning of the code more clear, use the named constant.**

Named Constant Guideline #2 is especially true for literals that are numbers and dates.

When you are working with arrays, using named constants in place of the array subscripts is a really good idea (see also the next section of this chapter).

Built-In VBScript Constants

Many VBScript hosts, such as the Windows Script Host and Active Server Pages, support the use of constants that are built into VBScript. These are especially helpful for two reasons: First, it can be hard to remember a lot of the seemingly arbitrary numbers that many of the VBScript functions and procedures use as parameters and return values; and second, using these named constants makes your code a lot easier to read. You saw some examples of built-in named constants related to the VarType() and MsgBox() functions.

Appendix D of this book contains a list of many of the named constants that VBScript provides for you for free. You'll notice that many of these constants are easy to identify by the prefix vb. Also, you'll notice that these constants are usually written in mixed case, rather than all uppercase. By way of example, take a look at some constants you can use in an optional parameter of the MsgBox() function (see Appendix A for details on the MsgBox() function).

Thus far, you have used the first parameter of MsgBox() multiple times throughout the book. This first parameter is the message that you want displayed in the dialog box. The MsgBox() function also takes several optional parameters, the second of which is the "buttons" parameter, which lets you define different buttons and icons to appear on the dialog box. Here's an example.

```
MsgBox "The sky is falling!", 48
```

This code produces the dialog box shown in Figure 4-4.

Figure 4-4

By passing the number 48 to the second argument of MsgBox(), you told the function that you want the exclamation point icon to appear on the dialog box. Instead of using the not-so-clear number 48, you could have used the vbExclamation named constant instead.

```
MsgBox "The sky is falling!", vbExclamation
```

This code results in the exact same dialog box, but it's much clearer from reading the code what you're trying to do. Take a look at Appendix D to get a sense for the other intrinsic VBScript constants. They come in handy once you learn a few of the more common ones, like vbExclamation and vbNewLine.

Summary

In this chapter you dove deeper into some of the details of VBScript variables. VBScript does not force you to declare variables before using them, but it is highly recommended that you include the Option Explicit statement at the top of all of your scripts so that VBScript will force variable declaration. Whether using Option Explicit or not.

VBScript has some rules for how you can name variables, including that variable names must start with a letter and cannot include most special characters.

This chapter also formally introduced procedures and functions, including the syntax for defining them and design principles on how to best make use of them. Once the concept of using procedures and functions to put boundaries around certain blocks of code was introduced, it was explained how those boundaries define variable scope and lifetime.

This chapter discussed the ByRef and ByVal keywords that can be used when declaring arguments for a procedure or function and closed by introducing named constants, which can, and often should, be used in your code in place of literal values.

Control of Flow

The VBScript language provides certain mechanisms to allow you to manipulate the execution of the code in your script. For example, you can use *branching logic* to skip some lines of code. You can also execute some lines of code multiple times through the use of *looping logic*. The common term for the way in which you use these techniques is called *control of flow*.

Branching logic is implemented in VBScript with statements such as `If`, `Else`, and `Select Case`. Loops are defined with the `For`, `Do`, and `While` blocks. The sections in this chapter prepare you with all of the information you need on branching and looping, which are as essential to programming as variables. If you are relatively new to programming, this is an important chapter. Like all of the chapters up to this point, this chapter explains essential programming fundamentals while also teaching you the VBScript-specific techniques and syntax.

If you are an experienced programmer in another language, you might only skim this chapter for some of the VBScript particulars. VBScript's branching and looping capabilities are basically the same as any mature procedural language, and are virtually identical to Visual Basic's. If you are looking only for syntax details, the language reference in Appendix A might be your best source of information.

Branching Constructs

Branching is the process of making a decision in your code and then, based on that decision, executing one block of code, but not others. If you have been reading along since the beginning of the book, you have seen the most common VBScript branching construct, `If...End If`, many times already. This chapter covers `If...End If` in detail along with another branching construct, `Select...End Select`.

`If...End If` and `Select...End Select` are both used to define a code block, which is a section of code that is bounded by beginning and ending statements. In the case of an `If` block, the beginning of it is defined by an `If` statement, and the end is defined by an `End If` statement. `Select...End Select` follows the same pattern. VBScript requires that both the beginning and the ending statements be there as a pair. If you forget to include the ending statement, VBScript produces a syntax error at runtime.

It's a good idea to get in the habit of typing both the beginning and ending statements first, before you type the code that goes between them. This ensures that you won't forget to type the ending statement, especially if the code that goes between the statements is rather involved. This is also especially helpful if you plan to nest multiple code blocks within each other.

The "If" Branch

The `If...End If` construct can be very simple, or it can become fairly complicated. In its simplest form, it requires this syntax.

```
If <expression> Then
    <other code goes here>
End If
```

In place of `<expression>` you can use anything that results in a `True` or `False` answer (also known as a Boolean expression). This can be a mathematical equation.

```
If 2 + 2 = 4 Then
    <other code goes here>
End If
```

Or it can be a function that returns `True` or `False`.

```
If IsNumeric(varAny) Then
    <other code goes here>
End If
```

Or it can use more complicated Boolean logic.

```
If strMagicWord = "Please" And (strName = "Hank" Or strName = "Bill") Then
    <other code goes here>
End If
```

You can also use the `Not` statement to reverse the `True` or `False` result of the expression.

```
If Not IsNumeric(varAny) Then
    <other code goes here>
End If
```

You can add another dimension to the `If` construct by adding an `Else` block. The `Else` block will be executed if the result of the `If` expression is `False`.

```
If IsNumeric(varAny) Then
    <other code goes here>
Else
    <some other code goes here>
End If
```

Many times, however, the decision you are trying to make does not involve a simple either/or evaluation. In that case, you can add as many `ElseIf` blocks as you like.

```
If IsNumeric(varAny) Then
    <other code goes here>
ElseIf IsDate(varAny) Then
    <some other code goes here>
ElseIf IsEmpty(varAny) Then
    <some other code goes here>
Else
    <some other code goes here>
End If
```

If the first expression returns `False`, then the execution moves to the first `ElseIf` evaluation. If that returns `False`, then the execution moves on to the second `ElseIf` evaluation. If that returns `False`, then the execution falls into the code in the `Else` block. The `ElseIf` line must end with the word `Then`, just as the initial `If` line must. The `Else` block is always optional and must come last.

```
If IsNumeric(varAny) Then
    <other code goes here>
ElseIf IsDate(varAny) Then
    <some other code goes here>
ElseIf IsEmpty(varAny) Then
    <some other code goes here>
End If
```

You can also nest `If...End If` blocks within each other.

```
If IsNumeric(varAny) Then
    If varAny > 0 Then
        <code goes here>
    ElseIf varAny < 0 Then
        <code goes here>
    Else
        <code goes here>
    End If
Else
    <some other code goes here>
End If
```

You can nest as deeply as you like, but beware of nesting too deeply, because the logic of the code can become unmanageable and hard to follow. Studies have shown that most humans have a hard time keeping track after nesting gets more than three or four levels deep.

Keep in mind that a `Select...End Select` block (which is introduced in the next section) is often an alternative to an `If...End If` block with a lot of `ElseIf` clauses in the middle. However, the `ElseIf` construct is more flexible, because each different `ElseIf` line can evaluate something totally different, whereas a `Select...End Select` block must consider different possible results to the *same* expression. Because the `If...ElseIf...End If` is more flexible, you can always use it in place of `Select...End Select`. However, the reverse is not true. You can only use `Select...End Select` to evaluate different variations of the *same* expression.

Here is a sequence of `ElseIf` blocks that evaluate totally different expressions.

```
If boolFirst Then
    <other code goes here>
ElseIf boolSecond Then
    <some other code goes here>
ElseIf boolThird Then
    <some other code goes here>
ElseIf lngTest = 1 Then
    <some other code goes here>
ElseIf strName = "Bill" Then
    <some other code goes here>
End If
```

The "Select Case" Branch

As mentioned in the previous section, the `Select...End Select` construct is useful when you are evaluating different possible results to the same expression. `Select...End Select` has the following syntax.

```
Select Case <expression>
    Case <possibility 1>
        <code goes here>
    Case <possibility 2>
        <other code goes here>
    Case <possibility 3>
        <other code goes here>
    Case <possibility n>
        <other code goes here>
    Case Else
        <other code goes here>
End Select
```

Notice that you are evaluating the same expression multiple times, whereas the `If...ElseIf...End If` block allows you to evaluate different expressions. Notice also that after all the tests are made, you can include an optional `Case Else` block that will execute if none of the other possibilities return `True`. Let's look at a more concrete example.

```
Select Case VarType(varAny)
    Case vbString
        <code goes here>
    Case vbLong
        <code goes here>
    Case vbBoolean
        <code goes here>
    Case Else
        <code goes here>
End Select
```

The first line evaluates the expression `VarType(varAny)`; then each subsequent `Case` statement checks for each of many possible results. Finally, if none of the `Case` statements evaluates to `True`, then the `Case Else` block is executed. Note that you can accomplish this same thing with an `If...ElseIf...End If` block.

```
If VarType(varAny) = vbString Then
    <code goes here>
ElseIf VarType(varAny) = vbLong Then
    <code goes here>
ElseIf VarType(varAny) = vbBoolean Then
    <code goes here>
Else
    <code goes here>
End If
```

However, this has the disadvantage that the expression `VarType(varAny)` is executed for *every* `ElseIf` block, whereas with the `Select...End Select`, it is evaluated only once, which is more efficient. Some programmers would also argue that the `Select Case` block is more elegant and readable than a series of `ElseIf` statements.

It is a good idea to always consider including a `Case Else` block in your `Select Case` blocks — even if you cannot conceive of a situation where the `Case Else` would be executed. This is a good idea for two reasons:

❑ If the input data or code for your script changes unexpectedly, and the `Case Else` block does suddenly start executing, your code will catch it — whereas without the `Case Else` block you might never catch it. This is useful when you are expecting a limited set of input values for which you are checking, with the `Case Else` block catching any other input data that does not match the expected set of values.

❑ Including a `Case Else` block can add documentation to the code about why the `Case Else` block is never intended to be executed. It's a common convention to include a `Case Else` block that contains nothing other than a comment stipulating why the programmer expects the `Else` condition to never exist. Here's an example that uses both a comment and an error message.

```
Select Case lngColor
    Case vbRed
        <code goes here>
    Case vbGreen
        <code goes here>
    Case vbBlue
        <code goes here>
    Case Else
        'We never use anything but Red, Green, and Blue
        MsgBox "Illegal color encountered: " & lngColor, _
                vbExclamation
End Select
```

You can also nest `Select...End Select` blocks within one another, and you can nest `If...End If` blocks (or any other kind of code) inside the `Select...End Select` as well.

```
Select Case VarType(varAny)
    Case vbString
        Select Case varAny
            Case "Test1"
                If Trim(strUserName) = "" Then
                    <code goes here>
                Else
                    <code goes here>
                End If
            Case "Test2"
                <code goes here>
            Case "Test3"
                <code goes here>
        End Select
    Case vbLong
        <code goes here>
    Case vbBoolean
        <code goes here>
    Case Else
        <code goes here>
End Select
```

Note that while you only have two levels of nesting here, it looks like four because of the two-level structure of the Select Case *block. Nesting* Select Case *blocks more than a few levels can be particularly damaging to clarity for this reason.*

Loop Constructs

Whereas branching is the process of making a decision on whether to execute one block of code or another, looping is the process of repeating the same block of code over and over.

VBScript provides four looping constructs that you can use in different situations. In the view of most Visual Basic and VBScript programmers, however, one of these loop constructs, the While...Wend loop, has been supplanted by the more intuitive, powerful, and flexible Do...Loop. For this reason, this chapter emphasizes the remaining three loops. However, in the interest of completeness, the syntax for the While...Wend loop is covered at the end of the chapter.

Once you remove While...Wend from consideration (which you're mostly doing for simplicity's sake, not because there is anything wrong with it), each of the remaining three loop constructs is ideal for a different type of loop. Each of the following sections explains the syntax for these loops, as well as when you would use one loop or another.

For...Next

The For...Next loop is ideal for two situations:

❑ When you want to execute a block of code repeatedly a known, finite number of times.

❑ When you want to execute a block of code once for each element in a complex data structure such as an array, file, or database table. (However, the For Each...Next loop is specifically designed for another kind of complex data structure, the collection.)

First take a look at how to use the `For...Next` loop to execute a block of code a known number of times (`FOR_LOOP_SIMPLE.VBS`).

```
Option Explicit

Dim lngIndex

For lngIndex = 1 To 5
    MsgBox "Loop Index: " & lngIndex
Next
```

Running this code produces, in succession, the five dialog boxes shown in Figures 5-1 through 5-5.

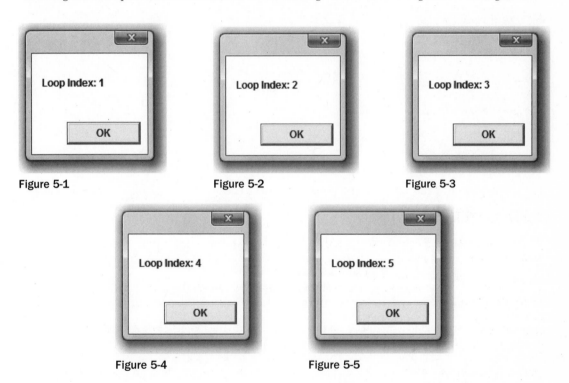

Figure 5-1   Figure 5-2   Figure 5-3

Figure 5-4   Figure 5-5

The first thing to notice is that in order to use the `For...Next` loop, you need a loop variable — also known as a loop index. The variable `lngIndex` serves this purpose. The statement `For lngIndex = 1 To 5` means that this loop will execute five times. As you can see from the dialog boxes that appear, the value of `lngIndex` matches each step in the traversal from the number 1 to the number 5. After looping for the fifth time, the loop stops and the code moves on. Note that you don't need to start at 1 in order to loop five times (`FOR_LOOP_NOT_ONE.VBS`).

```
Option Explicit
Dim lngIndex

For lngIndex = 10 To 14
    MsgBox "Loop Index: " & lngIndex
Next
```

This still loops five times, but instead of starting at 1, it starts at 10. As the loop iterates, lngIndex has a value of 10, then 11, then 12, and so on to 14.

You can also use the Step keyword to skip numbers (FOR_LOOP_STEP.VBS).

```
Option Explicit

Dim lngIndex

For lngIndex = 10 To 18 Step 2
    MsgBox "Loop Index: " & lngIndex
Next
```

Once again, this still loops five times but, because you specified Step 2, it skips every other number. On the first loop, lngIndex has a value of 10, then 12, then 14, and so on to 18. You can use any increment you like with the Step keyword (FOR_LOOP_STEP_100.VBS).

```
Option Explicit

Dim lngIndex

For lngIndex = 100 To 500 Step 100
    MsgBox "Loop Index: " & lngIndex
Next
```

You can also use the Step keyword to cause the loop to go backward (FOR_LOOP_BACKWARDS.VBS).

```
Option Explicit

Dim lngIndex

For lngIndex = 5 To 1 Step -1
    MsgBox "Loop Index: " & lngIndex
Next
```

Because you used a negative number with the Step keyword, the loop goes downward through the numbers. Notice that for this to work, the increment range must specify the larger number first.

You are not limited to using negative numbers with the Step keyword. The loop itself can loop through negative numbers, like this (FOR_LOOP_NEGATIVE.VBS):

```
Option Explicit

Dim lngIndex

For lngIndex = -10 To -1
    MsgBox "Loop Index: " & lngIndex
Next
```

Or like this (FOR_LOOP_NEGATIVE2.VBS):

```
Option Explicit

Dim lngIndex

For lngIndex = -10 To -20 Step -2
    MsgBox "Loop Index: " & lngIndex
Next
```

You can also nest loops inside one another (FOR_LOOP_NESTED.VBS).

```
Option Explicit

Dim lngOuter
Dim lngInner

For lngOuter = 1 to 5
    MsgBox "Outer loop index: " & lngOuter

    For lngInner = 10 to 18 Step 2
        MsgBox "Inner loop index: " & lngInner
    Next
Next
```

So what do you do when you *don't* know exactly how many times you want to loop? This is a common situation. It often comes up when you need to traverse an array (see Chapter 3), a string, or any other kind of structure. Take a look at an example (EXTRACT_FILE_NAME.VBS).

```
Option Explicit

Dim lngIndex
Dim lngStrLen
Dim strFullPath
Dim strFileName

'This code will extract the filename from a path

strFullPath = "C:\Windows\Temp\Test\myfile.txt"
lngStrLen = Len(strFullPath)

For lngIndex = lngStrLen To 1 Step -1
    If Mid(strFullPath, lngIndex, 1) = "\" Then

    strFileName = Right(strFullPath, _
            lngStrLen - lngIndex)
        Exit For
    End If
Next

MsgBox "The filename is: " & strFileName
```

Running this code produces the dialog box shown in Figure 5-6.

The filename is: myfile.txt

OK

Figure 5-6

Some new elements have been added in this example. The Len() function is a built-in VBScript function that returns the number of characters in a string. The Mid() function extracts one or more bytes from the middle of a string. The first parameter is the string to extract from; the second parameter is the character at which to start the extraction; the third parameter is how many characters to extract. The Right() function is similar to Mid(), except that it extracts a certain number of the rightmost characters in a string. Finally, the Exit For statement breaks you out of a loop. This is very handy when you know that you don't need to loop anymore.

Notice how you use the length of the strFullPath variable to drive how many times you need to loop. When you started, you did not know how many times you needed to go around, so you used the length of the structure you needed to traverse (in the case, a string) to tell you how many times to loop. Notice also how you traverse the string backward so that you can search for the last backslash character ("\") in the strFullPath variable. Once you find the backslash, you know where the filename begins. Once you use the Right() function to extract the filename into the strFileName variable, you don't need the loop anymore (you've accomplished your goal), so you use Exit For to break out of the loop. Exit For jumps the execution of the code to the very next line after the Next statement.

It is useful to note that the preceding example does not demonstrate the most efficient way to extract the filename from a path. The example is for demonstrating how to use a For...Next loop to move through a data structure of a size that is unknown at design time. Now take a look at a more efficient way to accomplish the same task, which is instructive in that it is not uncommon that you can discover other ways of accomplishing what only looked possible with a loop. The following code is much faster, especially in the case of a long filename (EXTRACT_FILE_NAME_NO_LOOP.VBS).

```
Option Explicit

Dim strFileName
Dim strFullPath

strFullPath = "C:\MyStuff\Documents\Personal\resume.doc"
strFileName = Right(strFullPath, _Len(strFullPath) - InStrRev(strFullPath,"\"))

MsgBox "The filename is: " & strFileName
```

There is almost always more than one way to solve the same problem. Loops are very handy and an integral part of programming, but they are also expensive from a performance standpoint. The second example is better for two reasons: One, there are less lines of code; and two, because it does not use a loop to repeat the same lines of code over and over, it finds the answer much faster.

For Each...Next

The `For Each...Next` loop is a special kind of loop that is specifically used for traversing collections. A *collection*, as the name suggests, is a collection of data, almost like an array. A collection most often contains objects of the same type (even though collections can be collections of virtually any kind of data). For example, built into the VBScript runtime objects `FileSystemObject` (see Chapter 7) is the `Folder` object, which represents a directory in a file system. The `Folder` object has a `Files` collection, which is exposed as a property. Inside the `Folder.Files` collection are zero or more `File` objects. You can use a `For Each...Next` loop to move through each of the `File` objects in the `Folder.Files` collection.

With the `For Each...Next` loop, you cannot directly control how many times the loop will go around. This is dependent upon how many objects are in the collection you are traversing. However, you can still use the `Exit For` statement to break out of the loop at any time. You can figure out when to use `Exit For` by testing for some condition, or using an extra counter variable to count how many times you've gone through the loop.

The next example uses the `FileSystemObject` and related objects, which are introduced formally in Chapter 7. In this example (`FSO_FIND_FILE.VBS`), you attempt to locate the `AUTOEXEC.BAT` file on your system. (Don't worry, it's safe to try out this code — there is no danger of harming your `AUTOEXEC.BAT` file.)

```vbscript
Option Explicit

Dim objFSO
Dim objRootFolder
Dim objFileLoop
Dim boolFoundIt

Set objFSO = _
    WScript.CreateObject("Scripting.FileSystemObject")
Set objRootFolder = objFSO.GetFolder("C:\")
Set objFSO = Nothing

boolFoundIt = False
For Each objFileLoop In objRootFolder.Files

    If UCase(objFileLoop.Name) = "AUTOEXEC.BAT" Then
        boolFoundIt = True
        Exit For
    End If

Next

Set objFileLoop = Nothing
Set objRootFolder = Nothing

If boolFoundIt Then
    MsgBox "We found your AUTOEXEC.BAT file in "& _
        "the C:\ directory."
Else
    MsgBox "We could not find AUTOEXEC.BAT in " & _
        "the C:\ directory."
End If
```

Don't worry about any syntax that may be unfamiliar to you. Concentrate instead on the syntax of the `For Each...Next` loop block. The `objRootFolder` variable holds a reference to a `Folder` object, which has a `Files` collection. The `Files` collection is a collection of `File` objects. So what VBScript is telling you to do is "take a look at each `File` object in the `Files` collection." Each time the loop goes around, the loop variable, `objFileLoop`, will hold a reference to a different `File` object in the `Files` collection. If the `Files` collection is empty, then the loop will not go around at all. Notice how you use the `Exit For` statement to break out of the loop once you've found the file you're looking for.

The preceding script example is intended to demonstrate the use of the `For Each...Next` loop to traverse a collection of objects. Just as in the previous section, using a loop in this way is not necessarily the best way to see if a file exists. For example, this is much faster and more compact (`FSO_FIND_FILE_NO_LOOP.VBS`):

```
Option Explicit

Dim objFSO

Set objFSO = _WScript.CreateObject("Scripting.FileSystemObject")

If objFSO.FileExists("C:\AUTOEXEC.BAT") Then
    MsgBox "We found your AUTOEXEC.BAT file in the " & _
        "C:\ directory."
Else
    MsgBox "We could not find AUTOEXEC.BAT in " & _
        "the C:\ directory."
End If

Set objFSO = Nothing
```

You might be thinking that we're trying to send the message that you should not use loops, that there is always a better way. This is not the case. Loops are extremely useful and many well-written scripts use them often. Programming is most often about using some kind of data, and often meaningful data is stored in complex structures like arrays and collections. If you need to root around inside that data to do what you need to do, the loop is your friend. However, as mentioned, many times a loop seems like the obvious solution, but there may be a more elegant, less expensive alternate solution.

Before you move on to the `Do` loop, please note that even though the `For Each...Next` loop is most often used to loop through collections, it can also be used to loop through all the elements of an array. No matter how many elements or dimensions the array has, the `For Each...Next` loop touches each and every one of them. Here is an example of using the `For Each...Next` loop to traverse a single dimension array (`FOR_EACH_ARRAY.VBS`).

```
Option Explicit

Dim astrColors(3)
Dim strElement

astrColors(0) = "Red"
astrColors(1) = "Green"
astrColors(2) = "Blue"
astrColors(3) = "Yellow"

For Each strElement In astrColors
    MsgBox strElement
Next
```

Do Loop

The Do loop is the most versatile of all the loop constructs. This is because you can easily make it loop as many times as you like based on any criteria you like.

Executing the Block at Least Once

The power of the Do loop is in the use of the While and Until keywords. You can use While or Until at either the beginning of the loop or the end of the loop to control whether the loop will go around again. Take a look at a simple script that uses a Do loop (DO_WHILE.VBS).

```
Option Explicit

Dim boolLoopAgain
Dim lngLoopCount
Dim strResponse

boolLoopAgain = False
lngLoopCount = 0
Do
    boolLoopAgain = False
    lngLoopCount = lngLoopCount + 1

    strResponse = InputBox("What is the magic word?")
    If UCase(Trim(strResponse)) = "PLEASE" Then
        MsgBox "Correct! Congratulations!"
    Else
        If lngLoopCount < 5 Then
            MsgBox "Sorry, try again."
            boolLoopAgain = True
        Else
            MsgBox "Okay, the word we wanted was 'Please'."
        End If
    End If
Loop While boolLoopAgain
```

Using a Do loop in this way to process user input is a common technique. You need to ask the user something, but he or she might enter illegal data. You need a way to check the input and, if necessary, loop back and ask the user to enter it again.

Notice the following about this code:

❏ The Do statement marks the beginning of the loop block, and the Loop statement defines the end of the block. The While statement, however, places a condition on the Loop statement. The loop only goes around again if the expression following the While statement is True. In this case, the expression is a variable called boolLoopAgain, which has the Boolean subtype, but it could be any expression that evaluates to or returns a True or False response.

❏ You initialize the boolLoopAgain variable to False before the loop starts. This accomplishes two things: It establishes the subtype of the variable as Boolean, and it guarantees that the loop only goes around again if some piece of code inside the loop explicitly sets the variable to True. If the user guesses wrong, then you set boolLoopAgain to True, guaranteeing that the loop goes around at least one more time and so you can ask the user to guess again.

❑   You use a loop counter variable, lngLoopCount, to make sure that the loop does not go around forever and drive the user crazy if he or she can't guess the magic word. Using a loop counter variable is optional, and not part of the Do...Loop syntax, but it's a good idea if there's a chance that the loop might go around indefinitely.

Using this particular loop structure — with the Do statement by itself at the beginning, and the While condition attached to the Loop statement at the end — has an important implication: Because you did not place a condition on the Do statement, the code inside the loop is guaranteed to execute *at least once*. This is what you want in this case, because if you did not execute the code at least one time, the user would never get asked the question "What is the magic word?".

Testing a Precondition

Sometimes, though, you only want the code inside the loop to execute if some precondition is True; if that precondition is False, then you don't want the loop to execute at all. In that case, you can place the While statement at the beginning of the loop. If the Do While condition is False, then the loop does not go around even once.

In the following example, you use the FileSystemObject to open a text file. You access the text file using a TextStream object. When you open a file in the form of a TextStream object, the TextStream object uses a "pointer" to keep track of its place in the file as you move through it. When you first open the file, the pointer is at the beginning of the file. (The pointer is not physically placed in the file — it exists only in memory in the TextStream object.) You can move through the file line by line using the TextStream.ReadLine method.

Each time you call ReadLine, the pointer moves one line down in the file. When the pointer moves past the last line in the file, the TextStream.AtEndOfStream property will have a value of True. That's when you know you're done reading the file. There is a possible problem, though: When you open a text file, you're not sure if it actually contains any data. It might be empty. If it is, then you don't want to call ReadLine, because this will cause an error. However, you'll know that the file is empty if the AtEndOfStream property is True right after opening the file. You can handle this nicely by placing the calls to ReadLine inside of a Do loop.

If you want to try out this code, just create a text file and put the following lines in it (the downloadable code contains a file called TESTFILE.TXT):

```
Line 1
Line 2
Line 3
Line 4
Line 5
```

Save the file to your hard drive in the same location as the following script (DO_WHILE_READ_FILE.VBS). The script assumes that TESTFILE.TXT is in the same directory as the script file. While you're reading this code, don't worry if you're not familiar with the particulars of the FileSystemObject and TextStream objects, which are covered in detail in Chapter 7. Just pay attention to the way you use the While condition in conjunction with the Do statement.

```
Option Explicit

Dim objFSO
Dim objStream
Dim strText

Set objFSO = _
    WScript.CreateObject("Scripting.FileSystemObject")
Set objStream = objFSO.OpenTextFile("testfile.txt")
Set objFSO = Nothing

strText = ""
Do While Not objStream.AtEndOfStream
    strText = strText & objStream.ReadLine & vbNewLine
Loop
Set objStream = Nothing

If strText <> "" Then
    MsgBox strText
Else
    MsgBox "The file is empty."
End If
```

Running this code results in the dialog box shown in Figure 5-7.

Figure 5-7

You can see that by placing the While condition at the *beginning* of the loop, you can decide whether you want the loop to go around even once. If the file is empty, then you don't want to try reading any lines. Because you have no condition on the Loop statement, when the loop reaches the end, the code jumps back up to the Do line. However, if the Do While expression returns False, the loop does not execute again, and the code jumps back down to the line immediately following the Loop line.

The objStream.AtEndOfStream property is True only when the end of the file is reached. As long as you have not reached the end of the file, you want to keep looping. If you start out at the end of the file because the file is empty, you don't want to loop at all.

Going back to the first Do loop example, for the record, note that you *could* have put the While statement with the Do and accomplished the same thing (DO_WHILE2.VBS).

```
Option Explicit

Dim boolLoopAgain
Dim lngLoopCount
Dim strResponse

boolLoopAgain = True
lngLoopCount = 0
Do While boolLoopAgain
    boolLoopAgain = False
    lngLoopCount = lngLoopCount + 1

    strResponse = InputBox("What is the magic word?")
    If UCase(Trim(strResponse)) = "PLEASE" Then
        MsgBox "Correct! Congratulations!"
    Else
        If lngLoopCount < 5 Then
            MsgBox "Sorry, try again."
            boolLoopAgain = True
        Else
            MsgBox "Okay, the word we wanted was 'Please'."
        End If
    End If
Loop
```

Compare the first Do loop example with this one. Both examples accomplish exactly the same thing: The loop executes at least once, and it only loops again if the code inside the loop says that you should. The difference with this second technique is that you started off by initializing boolLoopAgain to True, which guarantees that the loop executes at least once.

Choosing Between Until and While

As you can see, the Do loop is quite versatile, and how you accomplish one thing or another is largely a matter of preference. That said, one could make a pretty good argument that the first version of this code is preferable because the Do statement all by itself makes it obvious that the loop is going to execute at least once, whereas this second example is a little bit tricky.

All else being equal, if there are two ways of coding something, the more explicit method is almost always preferable.

So the first question you need to answer when considering the use of the Do loop is, do I want the code to execute at least once, no matter what? If the answer to this question is yes, then it's best to place your condition at the end of the loop. Otherwise, put the condition at the beginning of the loop.

However, there is a second question: Should you use the While statement for the condition, or its cousin, the Until statement? The answer is also largely a matter of preference. Although the While and Until statements are slightly different, they pretty much do the same thing. The main difference is one of semantics, and people generally fall into the habit of using one or the other, based on which syntax makes the most intuitive sense to them. However, one usually tends to be clearer than another in a given situation.

Here's how Microsoft's VBScript documentation describes the Do loop (we added the **bold** emphasis):

*Repeats a block of statements **while** a condition is True or **until** a condition becomes True.*

As you can see, the distinction between While and Until is rather fuzzy. The easiest way to explain the difference is to modify the previous two examples replacing While with Until. You'll see that the consideration of whether to execute the loop *at least once* remains the same. However, the implementation is slightly different. Here's the first example, modified to use Until instead of While (DO_UNTIL.VBS).

```
Option Explicit

Dim boolLoopAgain
Dim lngLoopCount
Dim strResponse

boolLoopAgain = False
lngLoopCount = 0
Do
    boolLoopAgain = False
    lngLoopCount = lngLoopCount + 1

    strResponse = InputBox("What is the magic word?")
    If UCase(Trim(strResponse)) = "PLEASE" Then
        MsgBox "Correct! Congratulations!"
    Else
        If lngLoopCount < 5 Then
            MsgBox "Sorry, try again."
            boolLoopAgain = True
        Else
            MsgBox "Okay, the word we wanted was 'Please'."
        End If
    End If

Loop Until boolLoopAgain = False
```

It may look like the same code, but the difference is that you must test for a False value in your Until clause, whereas you tested for a True value in your While clause. When you read the line Loop While boolLoopAgain, does it make more sense than Loop Until boolLoopAgain = False? If the While syntax makes more sense to you, maybe you can fix that by changing the name of your variable (DO_UNTIL_BETTER_NAME.VBS).

```
Option Explicit

Dim boolStopLooping
Dim lngLoopCount
Dim strResponse

boolStopLooping = True
lngLoopCount = 0
Do
    boolStopLooping = True
    lngLoopCount = lngLoopCount + 1

    strResponse = InputBox("What is the magic word?")
    If UCase(Trim(strResponse)) = "PLEASE" Then
```

(continued)

```
            MsgBox "Correct! Congratulations!"
        Else
            If lngLoopCount < 5 Then
                MsgBox "Sorry, try again."
                boolStopLooping = False
            Else
                MsgBox "Okay, the word we wanted was 'Please'."
            End If
        End If

    Loop Until boolStopLooping = True
```

Does the Until syntax make a little more sense now? The point is you can use either While or Until to accomplish what you need to — it's just a matter of what makes more sense in a given situation. Look at your file reading example again, this time using Until instead of While (DO_UNTIL_READ_FILE.VBS).

```
Option Explicit

Dim objFSO
Dim objStream
Dim strText

Set objFSO = _WScript.CreateObject("Scripting.FileSystemObject")
Set objStream = objFSO.OpenTextFile("testfile.txt")
Set objFSO = Nothing

strText = ""
Do Until objStream.AtEndOfStream
    strText = strText & objStream.ReadLine & vbNewLine
Loop
Set objStream = Nothing

If strText <> "" Then
    MsgBox strText
Else
    MsgBox "The file is empty."
End If
```

The Until syntax might make this clearer. People sometimes have an easier time thinking in terms of positives, and the syntax Do While Not objStream.AtEndOfStream may be more or less clear to you than Do Until objStream.AtEndOfStream. It's up to you, though. VBScript doesn't care. And if you use good variable names, stick to straightforward logic, and make good use of indenting and white space; your fellow programmers most likely won't care either.

Breaking Out of a Do Loop

Before we move on to While...Wend, we need to mention the Exit Do statement. Like Exit For, you can use Exit Do to break out of a Do loop at any point. You can have as many Exit Do statements inside your loop as you like. Here's an example, yet another variation on your "magic word" example (DO_WHILE3.VBS).

```
Option Explicit

Dim boolLoopAgain
Dim lngLoopCount
Dim strResponse

boolLoopAgain = False
lngLoopCount = 0
Do
    boolLoopAgain = False
    lngLoopCount = lngLoopCount + 1

    strResponse = InputBox("What is the magic word?")
    If UCase(Trim(strResponse)) = "PLEASE" Then
        MsgBox "Correct! Congratulations!"
        Exit Do
    Else
        If lngLoopCount < 5 Then
            MsgBox "Sorry, try again."
            boolLoopAgain = True
        Else
            MsgBox "Okay, the word we wanted was 'Please'."
            Exit Do
        End If
    End If

Loop While boolLoopAgain
```

Instead of setting `boolLoopAgain` to `False`, you just execute an `Exit Do`, which has the same effect in that you won't go around the loop again. When the `Exit Do` statement executes, the code jumps out of the loop, to the line of code immediately following the last line of the loop block (in the example, there is no code after the loop, so the script ends). However, while this example illustrates the proper syntax for `Exit Do`, you did not necessarily make your magic word code any better by using it.

Remember the procedures and functions discussion in Chapter 4? When discussing the `Exit Sub` and `Exit Function` statements, it is stated that you should use them carefully and that there is usually a way to organize your code so that you do not have to use them. The potential problem with using `Exit Sub` and `Exit Function` is that the logic can become hard to follow because of the jumping out of the flow. The same principle applies to `Exit Do`.

If you compare the original magic word code to this new version, in the original you used the `boolLoopAgain` statement in conjunction with `If` conditions to control the loop. The logic flows from top to bottom in a linear fashion. The new code with the `Exit Do` statements has lost that elegance and clarity.

A final note about `Exit Do` (and the other loop `Exit` statements as well): If you are working with nested loops, an `Exit Do` executed in the *inner* loop *does not* break out of the *outer* loop as well — only from the loop in which the `Exit Do` was executed.

While...Wend

As was mentioned at the beginning of the chapter, the `While...Wend` loop is an older loop syntax from early versions of BASIC and Visual Basic. Programmers often prefer the `Do` loop (see previous section) over the `While...Wend` loop, which is not nearly as versatile. This is not to say that it is not perfectly valid to use it, and many programmers use it often. It works fine, it's simple, and Microsoft certainly has not given any indication that they plan to remove support for it. It has simply fallen out of vogue. In the interest of completeness, here's an example of the `While...Wend` syntax (`WHILE_WEND.VBS`).

```
Option Explicit

Dim lngCounter

lngCounter = 0
While lngCounter <= 20
    lngCounter = lngCounter + 1
    '<other code goes here>
Wend
```

Unlike the `Do` loop, you do not have the option of using either `While` or `Until`, nor can you place the condition at the end of the loop. The condition for whether to loop again can only be placed at the beginning of the loop, as you see here. Finally, a significant limitation of the `While...Wend` loop is that there is no equivalent to `Exit For` or `Exit Do`, meaning you cannot forcibly break out of the loop.

Summary

This chapter covered the topic of *control of flow*, which involves branching and looping. *Branching* is the technique of checking conditions, making a decision, and executing (or not executing) a block of code based on that decision. Following are the branching constructs in VBScript:

```
If ...ElseIf ...Else ...End If

Select Case ...End Select
```

Looping is the technique of repeating the same block of code over again. The looping constructs in VBScript are as follows:

```
For ...Next
For Each ...Next
Do ...Loop While
Do While ...Loop
Do ...Loop Until
Do Until ...Loop
While ...Wend
```

6

Error Handling
and Debugging

No explanation or tutorial of a programming language is complete without thorough coverage of *error handling* (also known as *exception handling*). It is of course important to learn the syntax of a language and to use correct logic in your programs. What truly gives a program or script professional polish — what separates throwaway from production quality — is error handling.

Writing a computer program, even a simple one, is a delicate matter. You have to get the syntax exactly right. You have to place the quote marks and the parentheses just so. You have to name the files in a particular way. You have to follow a certain kind of logic.

What's more, your program does not exist in a vacuum. A VBScript program can interact directly or indirectly with the scripting host, the operating system, the user, the network, and the Internet. A script is beset by the possibility of full disks, invalid user entries, scrambled file formats, and the electricity suddenly dropping out. Things can, and will, go wrong.

Error handling is the programmer's main line of defense against this inherent unpredictability. The term error handling refers not only to how a program responds when an error occurs, but also to how it prevents errors from happening in the first place.

The topic of *debugging* goes hand in hand with that of error handling. Debugging, as the name suggests, is the process of detecting, locating, and removing bugs from a program. The *removing* part of that process is most often the easiest part. The real art of debugging is in the use of tools and techniques for finding a bug in the first place. Basic proficiency with debugging brings with it a reduction in frustration and an increase in productivity. If you are charging your clients by the hour, or if you are working in a high-pressure situation, the ability to track down a bug quickly is of key importance.

This chapter delves into the closely related subjects of error handling and debugging. If you are a new programmer, this chapter explains not only the VBScript mechanics of error handling and debugging, but also the universal principles and techniques at work. If you are an experienced programmer in other programming languages, this chapter is still worth your while; error handling and debugging in VBScript are quite unique and likely different from your experience with other languages. In fact, it's fair to characterize error handling as VBScript's primary area of weakness.

Note that error handling associated with the Script Control (Chapter 21) is slightly different than with other VBScript hosts; in the Script Control you can also allow the host application to handle runtime errors. For more specific information, see Chapter 21.

Types of Errors

Three types of errors can burrow their way into your lovingly crafted VBScript code. *Syntax errors* halt the execution of the script. *Runtime errors* invoke an error handler, giving you the opportunity to do something about the error — or at least display it attractively. *Logic errors* generally cause strange and unexpected things to happen while the program is running, from contaminating data, confusing users, causing other logic and runtime errors to occur, or obscuring the real source of a problem.

Syntax Errors

VBScript, like all other programming languages, follows set rules for the construction of statements. Before the script runs, the script engine parses all of the code, converting it into tokens. When an unrecognizable structure or an expression is encountered (for example, if you mistype a keyword or forget to close a loop), a syntax error (also known as a *compilation error*) is generated. Luckily, you can usually catch syntax errors during the development phase, with minimal testing of the code.

Here is an example script that, when run under the Windows Script Host, produces the syntax error displayed in Figure 6-1.

Figure 6-1

```
Option Explicit

Dim x
If x > 0
    MsgBox "That number is high enough."
End If
```

Most of the time, the information in the error display makes it obvious where the problem is — in this case, a missing Then keyword on line 4. How the syntax error displays depends on which host the script is run under. For example, scripts running under the Windows Script Host display by default in a message box.

Syntax errors (and runtime errors) are easier to spot than logic errors (which you'll look at shortly) because they always result in an error message; in fact, in most cases the display of a syntax error message is out of your control. That's good news, because as you see in Figure 6-1, the error message pretty much points you to exactly what's wrong and where. With a basic understanding of VBScript, syntax errors are not a major concern.

Syntax errors tend to pop up in several circumstances:

❑   When something is missing from the code — parentheses, keywords (especially those that define blocks), parameters — or when some element of this code is simply out of place

❑   When a keyword, statement, or procedure call is misspelled or used incorrectly

❑   When you try to use a Visual Basic or VBA keyword or function that is not implemented by VBScript

❑   When you use keywords that are not supported by a particular version of the script engine. (In theory, certain keywords may be phased out, and others added, but in the history of this book we're not aware of any changes of this nature; VBScript has been very consistent with regard to backward compatibility.)

As you may expect, dynamic code executed using the `Eval`, `Execute`, and `ExecuteGlobal` functions is not parsed at the same time as normal script code. Dynamic code is not parsed until the call to one of these functions, and so syntax errors in dynamic code are not reported until that time. Special attention must be paid when generating dynamic code. Ideally, you would be able to test all of your dynamically generated code before releasing to users, but because dynamic code often includes input from outside sources, it is not always possible to anticipate syntax errors.

Appendix E shows all 49 of VBScript's syntax errors and their codes. All of these errors, with the exception of the first two — Out of Memory *and* Syntax Error *— are relatively easy to diagnose and correct (though sometimes diagnosis can be tricky when you have a lot of nested elements or hard to follow code).*

Runtime Errors

The second, and most common type of error is the runtime error, which occurs when a command attempts to perform an action that is invalid. A runtime error is different from a syntax error in that the offending code looks syntactically fine to the script engine, but has some kind of problem when it is executed. That is, the error does not offend the VBScript runtime engine during compilation; rather, the runtime engine has a problem with the execution of the code.

Runtime errors can be divided into three categories:

❑   Native VBScript runtime errors

❑   Non-VBScript runtime errors

❑   Variable declaration runtime errors related to the Option Explicit directive

In all three cases, the result is the same: An error occurs while the script is running. What differentiates the three types is what causes an error — and how you can prevent them.

Native VBScript Runtime Errors

For example, a runtime error occurs if you try to divide by zero (ERR_DIVIDE_BY_ZERO.VBS).

```
Option Explicit

Dim x
x = 200/0
MsgBox "The answer is: " & x
```

This code, run under the Windows Script Host, produces the error displayed in Figure 6-2.

Figure 6-2

Figure 6-3 shows the same error from the same script, but this time the script was launched from the command line (see Chapter 15, "The Windows Script Host").

```
G:\Windows\system32\cmd.exe

Microsoft Windows [Version 6.0.5384]
(C) Copyright 1985-2005 Microsoft Corp.

G:\Users\dread>c:

C:\>cd\script

C:\script>cscript test.vbs
Microsoft (R) Windows Script Host Version 5.6
Copyright (C) Microsoft Corporation 1996-2001. All rights reserved.

C:\script\test.vbs(4, 1) Microsoft VBScript runtime error: Division by zero

C:\script>_
```

Figure 6-3

As with the syntax error, the default error display of this runtime error gives fairly specific information about what went wrong. What distinguishes this example from a syntax error is that there is nothing wrong with the syntax of this code. Instead, the code is trying to do something that computers don't like: dividing by zero.

Another common example of a runtime error is passing the Null value to a function that does not like nulls, as in this example.

```
Option Explicit

Dim x
x = Null
MsgBox x
```

This code produces an Invalid use of Null runtime error on line 4. The MsgBox() function does not accept Null as a valid input value. Null values often cause problems when passed to built-in VBScript functions; so when your script takes in data from user input, a file, or a database, you have the opportunity to test for (or eliminate the possibility of) a Null value before it causes a problem.

One common technique is to take advantage of VBScript's implicit type coercion (see Chapter 3) to get rid of the Null.

```
Option Explicit

Dim x
x = GetValueFromDatabase()
MsgBox "" & x
```

GetValueFromDatabase() is a fictional function that, because databases have an explicit mechanism for storing Null values, might return a *Null*. This code accounts for this fact by appending an empty string (" ") to the value of *x*. When VBScript executes this code, the concatenation of the empty string causes the *Null* subtype of *x* to convert to the *String* subtype. You can use this trick with any potentially Null or numeric value to turn it into a String. A little defensive programming can prevent many runtime errors from ever occurring.

The tricky thing with runtime errors is that it takes some time for a programmer in any language or platform to learn the particular things that can cause runtime errors. Unfortunately, it would take an entire book, at least the size of this one, to cover all of the possible scenarios for runtime errors, especially when you consider all of the hosts under which VBScript can be run and all of the commercial and custom components that VBScript can use. A little knowledge and experience, though, goes a long way.

Here are three tips to help you with runtime errors:

❑ The first time you use a function, read the documentation for that function to look for possible traps that can lead to runtime errors, and then code defensively to prevent those errors.

❑ Test as much as you can. One thing that's nice about script code is that it's easy to copy-and-paste sections of it to try out. Try keeping a file called test.vbs open in your text editor. Any time you want to try something out, paste it in there, run the script, and see what happens. For example, you can find out what would happen if you pass a Null to a certain function.

❑ If you are plagued by a runtime error for which you don't have an explanation, search online knowledge bases and discussion forums; chances are someone has already encountered that error and can tell you what's causing it. If the error message is long, use some significant and unique fragment of the error message to search on; try putting the text in quotes to tell the search engine to match on the whole phrase, and be careful not to embed any text in your search phrase that is unique to your situation or environment.

Non-VBScript Runtime Errors

The two examples of runtime errors you've seen so far — a divide by zero error and a `Null` value passed to the `MsgBox()` function — are produced by the VBScript runtime engine (which you can tell by the `Source` value of `"Microsoft VBScript runtime error"` in Figure 6-2). However, not all runtime errors come from VBScript itself. In fact, depending on the complexity of the project, it is safe to say that most errors you encounter as a VBScript programmer are not produced by the VBScript engine. Instead, these errors often come from other sources — namely, scripting hosts such as Internet Information Service (IIS) and external components such as Microsoft's ActiveX Data Objects (ADO). Runtime errors can even be raised by other VBScript scripts because any script can use the `Err.Raise()` method to generate runtime errors. (`Err.Raise()` is covered later in this chapter.)

The method of dealing with nonnative VBScript runtime errors is the same as for native ones. Ideally, the error message gives you enough information to make the cause of the error obvious. For example, Microsoft's ADO data access component (see Appendix J) has a runtime error with the description `"The specified table does not exist"`. The cause of this error is pretty clear from the description; evidently, the offending code referred to a database table that does not exist, which is perhaps the result of a misspelling in the code.

However, ADO also has several other runtime errors with descriptions such as `"Unspecified error"`, `"Operation aborted"`, and even the super helpful `"Errors occurred"`. What are you supposed to do when faced with such ambiguous information? Unfortunately, the only way to work past these errors is through a combination of detective work, testing, and trial and error. When a runtime error message does not offer useful hints as to what's going on, your best bet is to turn to online knowledge bases such as the one at microsoft.com and online discussion forums such as those offered at `p2p.wrox.com`.

Start by searching these resources for information about the error. If you can't find instances of people having encountered and fixed the error before, then post a description of your problem so that other developers can offer help. When you post, be sure to include code samples and as much information as possible about the context of what you are trying to do. The annoyance of runtime errors is an unfortunate downside of being a programmer, but not an insurmountable one, especially with the help of your fellow developers around the world.

Errors Related to Option Explicit

As discussed in Chapter 4, the use of the `Option Explicit` statement is critical to your success as a VBScript programmer. It is your best defense against strange, difficult to detect errors that can result from misspellings of variable names and mistakes related to a variable's scope. When you use `Option Explicit`, if your code refers to a variable that has not been declared (or that has not been declared with the correct scope) then VBScript will produce an error, thereby allowing you to fix a problem that otherwise may not have been detected at all.

However, the error you receive in these situations will be a runtime error — not a syntax error as you might expect from an error related to variable declaration. VBScript will report only the `"Variable is` undefined" runtime error when the offending code is executed, not when the code is compiled. This means that, even if you use Option Explicit (which is highly recommended), you need to test your code fully before putting it into production.

Take a look at a quick example to illustrate why. The following Windows Script Host code (OPT_EXPL_ERROR.VBS), which uses the Option Explicit statement, has a missing variable declaration for the lngDay variable in the SpecialNovemberProcessing() procedure:

```
Option Explicit

Dim datToday
Dim lngMonth

datToday = Date()
lngMonth = DatePart("m", datToday)
If lngMonth = 11 Then
    SpecialNovemberProcessing(datToday)
End If

Private Sub SpecialNovemberProcessing(datAny)
    lngDay = DatePart("d", datAny)
    MsgBox "Today is day " & lngDay & " of November."
End Sub
```

As you can see from the code, the SpecialNovemberProcessing() procedure is only called when the month of the current system date is November. If you run this code when your system date is anything other than November, VBScript does not detect the variable declaration problem with lngDay in SpecialNovemberProcessing(). If you wrote this code and tested it with a non-November month, then SpecialNovemberProcessing() would never be called. However, after you have released the code to production and November finally rolls around, this code will produce a "Variable is undefined" runtime error, and you will have an embarrassing production error on your hands. If you are reading these words in a month that is not November, and you want to see this behavior in action, first run this script and you'll see that no error is produced. Then, change the 11 in this line to match whatever month your system clock says it is.

```
If lngMonth = 11 Then
```

Run the script after making the change, and you'll see that VBScript generates a "Variable is undefined" runtime error.

The way to prevent this from happening is to fully test your code to make sure that all paths of execution are exercised. Check your code for procedures and functions that are called only under certain conditions, and then force those conditions to exist so that you can make sure all of your code executes properly.

Logic Errors

You can think of a logic error as a kind of *hidden* error. Logic errors, in general, do not produce any kind of error message. Instead, a logic error produces what programmers often call, with some sarcasm, "undesirable results." For example, if you write a sales tax calculation script for processing orders on your ASP-based web site, and that script incorrectly calculates the tax amount, that's a logic error — otherwise known as a bug. No error message is produced, but the program is wrong all the same. One could definitely make an argument that logic errors are the worst kind of error because they can go undetected for a long time, and, as in the example of miscalculated sales tax, can even cause serious legal and financial problems.

The computer generally cannot detect a logic error for you. Only careful examination, testing, and validation of a program can detect logic errors. The best way to deal with logic errors is to avoid them in the first place. The oldest and most common method for logic error prevention is requirements and design specifications, which are detailed descriptions (in the form of words and/or diagrams) of how a program needs to work. A requirements specification stays as close to normal human vocabulary as possible, without describing actual technical details, so that nontechnical subject matter experts can verify the requirements. A design specification is generally produced after the requirements specification and describes the details of the technical implementation that "solves" the requirements. Specifications need not be formal to be effective; often a design sketch and punch list on a whiteboard will do the trick.

By producing specifications, you can avoid many logic errors by ensuring that you fully understand the problem and the proposed solution *before* you start writing code. However, even with perfect specifications, logic errors can still creep into your code. You might accidentally use a "plus" operator instead of "minus," or a "greater than" operator instead of "less than." You might just plain forget to implement the special sales tax processing rules for a particular locale, even if those rules are clearly spelled out in the specifications. We're all human. Logic errors can also result from improper use of the programming language. For example, a VBScript programmer who does not understand the subtleties of the *Variant* subtypes and implicit type coercion described in Chapter 3 could introduce logic errors into a script and not even understand why.

Because some amount of logic errors are inevitable in all but the most trivial programs, thorough testing of program code is essential. The programmer has the first responsibility to perform some basic testing of his or her code, and ideally the programmer will have professional testers who can follow up with more methodical and thorough testing. Ideally, such testing is based on the requirements and design specifications of the code.

In addition to upfront specifications and after-the-fact testing, another preventative measure against logic errors is what is known as defensive programming. Defensive programming involves checking assumptions about the expected program flow and either (a) generating runtime errors when those checks fail, or (b) including extra code that fixes the problem. For example, if you are writing a function that takes a numeric argument, and your logic requires that the argument must be greater than zero, include a double-check at the top of the function that ensures that the argument is greater than zero. If the check fails, you can choose to generate a custom runtime error or, depending on the situation, do something to fix the offending numeric argument. (Custom runtime errors are discussed later in this chapter.)

The greater the complexity, the more likely that logic errors will be introduced. If you are working on a particularly complex problem, break the problem down into manageable chunks, in the form of procedures, functions, classes, and so on, as discussed in Chapter 4. When the solution to a problem is decomposed into smaller modules, it becomes easier to hold in your head all at once while simultaneously allowing you to focus your attention on one small aspect of the problem at a time.

Error Visibility and Context

A key aspect of understanding and managing runtime errors is knowledge of where your code is running and what happens when an error occurs. The following sections briefly describe some of the more typical situations. Later in the chapter you're introduced to error trapping techniques, which you can use to catch errors when they occur and control what happens after that point.

Windows Script Host Errors

Throughout the book so far, the example scripts you've been using are intended for running under the Windows Script Host (WSH), which is built into Windows. As you can see in Figures 6-1, 6-2, and 6-3, WSH has an automatic error display mechanism. For an *interactive* script where the person running it is sitting in front of the computer launching the script, this default error display may be sufficient. If an error occurs, WSH displays it in a dialog box (or as plain text on the command line, depending on how the script was launched), and the human operator can decide what to do at that point.

However, often a WSH script runs automatically, perhaps on a schedule, with no human operator sitting in front of the computer. In this case, you can control to some degree what happens when an error occurs instead of using WSH's default error display mechanism. The section "Handling Errors" later in this chapter discusses various techniques.

Server-Side ASP Errors

A server-side ASP error can occur when IIS is processing ASP code. ASP code runs on the server to produce web pages and other Web-friendly files that are pushed out to the browser. Even though the code is executed on the server, paradoxically the default mechanism of displaying an error is inside the web browser — that is, the web server pushes the error out to the browser unless told to do otherwise. If you think about it, this makes sense. Without the browser, IIS is invisible. Its whole purpose is to push content to the browser. There is no terminal in which to display an error on the server, and even if there were, most of the time no one is sitting there watching the server.

However, IIS does not leave you powerless when it comes to error display. The section later in this chapter called "Presenting and Logging Errors" describes a technique you can use to display how and whether detailed error information is displayed in the browser when a server-side error occurs. However, please also see the section in this chapter called "Server-Side ASP Errors" for additional information about customizing classic ASP runtime errors for Internet Information Services version 7.0 running under Windows Vista.

Client-Side VBScript Errors in Internet Explorer

Because client-side VBScript code runs inside of the Internet Explorer browser, naturally you would expect errors to display in the browser. That is the case, but your users will very likely have their browsers set up so that they never see a client-side VBScript (or JavaScript or JScript for that matter) error when it occurs. Figure 6-4 shows the Advanced tab on the Internet Options dialog box for Internet Explorer 7, with the *"Display a notification about every script error"* option highlighted.

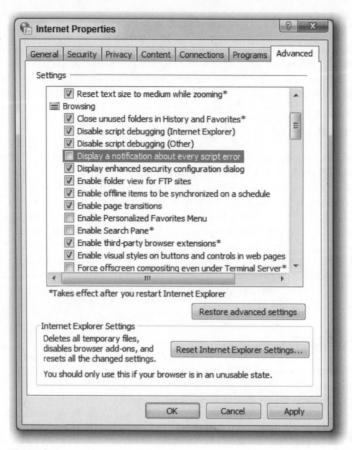

Figure 6-4

As you can see, users may or may not have error display turned on in the browser. It's safe to assume that your users do not have this option turned on because having it turned on becomes annoying after awhile. If an error message popped up in your browser every time you browsed to a web page with a client-side script error, clicking the OK button all the time would drive you crazy. When error display is turned off, a small yellow triangle with an exclamation point (!) appears in the status bar at the bottom of the browser window. This is the user's only indication that an error has occurred, and the actual error message only comes up if the user happens to notice the yellow icon and clicks it.

However, it is important to consider the likely possibility that users of your web page will not *care* what the error is. There is nothing that they can do about it anyway. All they know is that the page is not working. This situation underlines the importance of thoroughly testing all of your browser-based VBScript code.

Handling Errors

What exactly does *error handling* mean? In the purest definition, it means taking an active, rather than passive, approach when responding to errors, including having extra code built into your script to deal with errors in case they occur. This can take the form of a *global* error handling scheme that does something such as:

❑ Display the error to a user

❑ Log the error to a file, database, or the Windows Event Log

❑ Email the error to a system administrator

❑ Page the system administrator

❑ Some combination of all of the these

In addition to a *global* error handling scheme, such as a custom 500.100 error page in an ASP web site, you can trap for specific errors at specific points. For example, trying to connect to a database is a common point where errors occur. The password a user enters might be wrong, or the database might have reached the maximum allowable connections, or the network might be down. Knowing that connecting to a database is error prone, the experienced VBScript programmer can put a specific error trap in his or her code in the place where the code attempts a database connection.

The remainder of this section introduces the elements necessary for handling errors in your VBScript programs.

Using the Err Object

The Err object is what is described in Microsoft's VBScript documentation as an "intrinsic object with global scope," which means that it is always available to any VBScript code. You don't need to declare a variable to hold an Err object, nor is there a need to instantiate it using CreateObject() or New. There is exactly one Err object in memory at all times while a VBScript program is running.

The Err object contains information about the last error that occurred. If no error has occurred, the Err object is still available, but it doesn't contain any error information. Error information is stored in the properties of the Err object; some of which are given in following table.

The properties and methods of the Err object are described in more detail in Appendix E.

Description	Holds a Textual Description of the Last Error that Occurred
Number	Holds the number of the last error that occurred.
Source	Holds a textual description of the source of the last error that occurred; usually this is the name of the component from where the error originated.
HelpFile	If the source of the error has an associated Windows help file, holds the pathname of the help file.
HelpContext	If the source of the error has an associated Windows help file, holds a unique identifier.

The Err object also has two methods. The first is the Clear() method, which erases all of the properties of the Err object so that the information about the last error is thrown away. The second is the Raise() method, which you can use in your VBScript code to generate custom runtime errors. The next section about the On Error statements goes into more detail on how you can use the Err object and its properties and methods to handle errors in your VBScript programs. In addition, the section later in this chapter called "Generating Custom Errors" explains the use of the Err.Raise() method.

Using the On Error Statements

Unfortunately, VBScript does not have the robust, structured error handling mechanism offered by other programming languages such as Visual Basic, C++, Java, and the .NET languages. This is one of VBScript's most glaring shortcomings, and unfortunately Microsoft has not made any improvements in this area over the years, even though it continues to feature VBScript as *the* scripting language of Windows. It is not a stretch to characterize VBScript's error handling mechanism as awkward and limiting. In fact, if you don't understand how it works and use it properly, it can cause you to not even be aware that dozens of errors might be occurring in your code. That's why this chapter is so important.

By default, a VBScript program does not have any error handling at all (which, to be fair, is also the default state of many other languages — that is, by default, if your code does nothing to "handle" an error, the host, runtime, or operating system will handle it). All of the example scripts in the book so far are in this default state. As described at the beginning of this chapter, if an error occurs, whatever error display mechanism the script host uses takes over and, in most cases, simply displays the error information to the user.

Understanding VBScript Error Control

A useful way to think about the explicit VBScript error control that you can wield in your code is this:

Imagine there is a switch that controls the error control setting for the entire script; this switch only has two positions. The default position of the switch is On. When the switch is On, any error that occurs is immediately reported. When the switch is Off, any error that occurs is essentially ignored (that is, unless you specifically check to see if an error occurred). This WSH script (ERR_DIVIDE_BY_ZERO.VBS) from the beginning of the chapter that causes a divide by zero error is using the default On position.

```
Option Explicit

Dim x
x = 200/0
MsgBox "The answer is: " & x
```

When the script engine tries to execute line 4, it hits the divide by zero error and immediately displays the error, as shown in Figures 6-2 and 6-3.

If you want to flip the error control switch to the Off position, you can add the On Error Resume Next statement to the top of the script, like so (ERR_DBZ_RESUME_NEXT.VBS):

```
Option Explicit

On Error Resume Next
Dim x
x = 200/0
MsgBox "The answer is: " & x
```

If you run this code, instead of displaying the divide by zero error, VBScript ignores that error and continues executing the next line. The message box pops up, but because the value of x is never initialized, the value shown after "The answer is: " is blank. The divide by zero error still occurs, but with the switch in the Off position; VBScript doesn't tell you about it.

You can perhaps imagine how flipping the global error control switch to the Off position with On Error Resume Next could get you into trouble. What if the x = 200/0 line was part of a much larger algorithm calculating the price of an expensive product sold by your company? If you had used On Error Resume Next in this manner to suppress error, then you might never find the error and the price of the product could be way off.

Flipping the Error Handling Switch

We are not trying to say that On Error Resume Next is inherently bad. Rather, because On Error Resume Next globally suppresses errors for your *entire* script — including all procedures, functions, classes, and (with ASP) include files — it is very dangerous and must be used carefully. We can propose with confidence the following two rules:

❑   Unless you have a very good reason, never suppress all errors by simply placing the On Error Resume Next statement at the top of your script.

❑   If, in the body of your script, you use the On Error Resume Next statement to temporarily disable error reporting, make sure you use a corresponding On Error GoTo 0 statement to enable it again. In other words, if you flip the switch to Off, be sure to flip it back to On again as soon as it makes sense.

What is On Error GoTo 0, which is mentioned in that second rule? Just as On Error Resume Next flips the error reporting to the switch to the Off position, On Error GoTo 0 turns it back to On. The second rule states explicitly what is implicit in the first rule: In general, don't use On Error Resume Next by itself, without a subsequent On Error GoTo 0 statement to flip the switch back to On.

Used together with the Err object (introduced in the previous section), you can use the two On Error statements to add specific error traps to your code. The following script (ERR_TRAP.VBS) demonstrates an error trap using On Error Resume Next and On Error GoTo 0 together. (The example also demonstrates the Err.Raise() method, which is discussed in detail in the "Generating Custom Errors" section later in this chapter.) The script also contains an incomplete procedure called DisplayError(), which will be populated with real code in the next section.

```
Option Explicit
Dim x

On Error Resume Next
x = GetValueFromDatabase()
If Err.Number = 0 Then
    MsgBox "The value of x is: " & x
Else
    DisplayError
End If
On Error GoTo 0

Private Function GetValueFromDatabase()

    'Deliberately create an error for
    'demonstration purposes.
    Err.Raise vbObjectError + 1000, _
        "GetValueFromDatabase()", _
        "A database error occurred."

End Function

Private Sub DisplayError()
    'Stub procedure. We will fill this in
    'with a proper error display.
    MsgBox "An error occurred."
End Sub
```

The part of this code that you want to focus on is the block that begins with the On Error Resume Next statement and ends with the On Error GoTo 0 statement. By surrounding this block of code with these two statements, the programmer who wrote this code is saying "There is a good chance an error might occur right here, so I'm going to set a trap for it."

The line of code that the programmer is worried about is this one.

```
x = GetValueFromDatabase()
```

This fake GetValueFromDatabase() function was created to illustrate the point that database-related calls are often prone to errors. When databases are involved, there are just a lot of things that could go wrong, more so than in most other situations. The same could be said of interactions with the Windows file system, the Internet, email, networks, or other external components or services that are out of your control. Over time, programmers develop a sixth sense about hot spots for potential errors.

In this case, the programmer was correct: If you run the full downloaded script, you will see that the fake GetValueFromDatabase() function does raise an error. Whenever an error occurs, the Err object's properties are populated with information about the error. Generally, you can count on the fact that if an error occurs, the Err.Number property will be some number greater than or less than zero. So the line immediately after the call to GetValueFromDatabase() checks the Err.Number property.

If the error number is 0, then the code assumes that no error occurred and proceeds with its normal path of execution — in this case, displaying the value of the variable x. If an error does occur, as indicated by the non-zero value in the Err.Number property, the script attempts to gracefully display the error before continuing. (You'll put some meaningful code in this `DisplayError()` procedure in the next section, "Presenting and Logging Errors.")

Setting Traps for Errors

What your script does after an error occurs really depends on the situation. You may want to log the error to a file or hide the error from the user. You may want to retry the operation a few times before giving up. You may want to send an email to the system administrator. You may want to continue execution of the script after the error or stop the script. The choice is up to you.

The key point here is this: If the programmer had not set a trap for this error and taken the action he or she chose (in this case, displaying the error), he or she would not have had any control over the situation. The VBScript host would have followed its default error handling path, as illustrated with the script errors at the beginning of this chapter. Anticipate the "hot spots" for likely errors, set traps to catch possible errors, and control the outcome based on the needs of your script's requirements.

Here are the steps for setting an error trap.

1. Use the `On Error Resume Next` statement on the line immediately before the line you suspect might raise an error. (This assumes that you have been careful not to use `On Error Resume Next` to turn off error handling for the whole script.)

2. On the line immediately after the suspect line, check the value of `Err.Number`. If it is zero, you can safely assume that no error has occurred and proceed as normal. If the value is anything other than zero, an error has occurred and you have to "handle" the error somehow (see next section). There are many choices for what to do, including displaying the error information to the user, logging it, emailing it, using a `Do` loop with a retry counter variable to try again a few times, or hide the error completely by ignoring it.

3. After you have handled the error, or determined that there was no error, it is very important to use the `On Error GoTo 0` statement to put VBScript back into its default mode of handling errors for you. If you do not follow the `On Error Resume Next` statement with a corresponding `On Error GoTo 0` statement, then you will, without realizing it, suppress possible errors later in your script, which can lead to difficult-to-find bugs.

It is unfortunate that VBScript's error handling is designed so that the programmer is forced to watch out for error *hot spots* and set very specific traps to catch the errors so that they can be handled elegantly — rather than having VBScript or its host take over and stop your script dead in its tracks. The more flexible error handling schemes of other programming languages have ways of setting *generic traps* for errors so that you are always in control. For example, this is a generic trap in the Visual Basic.NET language:

```
Try
    DoTheFirstThing()
    DoTheSecondThing()
    DoTheThirdThing()
Catch ex As Exception
    MessageBox.Show("An error occurred: " & ex.ToString()
End Try
```

VBScript does not have any generic error trapping mechanism such as this. (However, the custom `500.100` ASP error page in IIS, introduced later in this chapter, is a generic error handling mechanism for an entire web application; other VBScript hosts might offer other kinds of mechanisms for handling errors.)

You may have already seen the big problem here: If VBScript does not give you a way of generically trapping errors, are you supposed to put specific error traps after every single line of code you write? Obviously, doing this for *every* line of code is not practical, but unfortunately you *do* have to use these error traps in places where errors are likely. You just have to trust that, given proper use of VBScript, your calls to generic functions such as `MsgBox()` and `InStr()` are not going to raise errors, but when you're dealing with those hot spots mentioned earlier, error traps are a good idea for production code. It's not quite as bad as it sounds. Within any given script, you have some hot spots, but hopefully not so many that you go crazy writing traps.

Here is an illustration of a section of script code with several possible hot spots in a row.

```
On Error Resume Next

DoTheFirstThing
If Err.Number <> 0 Then
    MsgBox "An error occurred: " & Err.Number & " - " & Err.Description & _
        " - " & Err.Source
    On Error GoTo 0
    WScript.Quit
End If

DoTheSecondThing
If Err.Number <> 0 Then
    MsgBox "An error occurred: " & Err.Number & " - " & Err.Description & _
        " - " & Err.Source
    On Error GoTo 0
    WScript.Quit
End If

DoTheThirdThing
If Err.Number <> 0 Then
    MsgBox "An error occurred: " & Err.Number & " - " & Err.Description & _
        " - " & Err.Source
    On Error GoTo 0
    WScript.Quit
End If

On Error GoTo 0
```

What you have here is a script with multiple hot spots, and therefore multiple traps. Notice how each trap includes a call to the Windows Script Host `WScript.Quit` command, which prevents the script from executing any further; the idea is that if something unexpected has happened, you don't want any of the code below to try to execute — all bets are off, as the saying goes.

Depending on the situation, this script could be improved further by replacing `WScript.Quit` with a call to another procedure in the script called `DoCleanup`, in which you might make sure the open files are closed, database connections are released, errors are logged, data is saved, email notifications are sent, and so on. Then you can call `WScript.Quit` at the end of `DoCleanup`. This is a way to achieve some semblance of a centralized error handling facility, and it also addresses the topic of *cleaning up*, which is important in some scripts, especially those that utilize external resources such as a file system, operating system, or database.

The previous code demonstrates good usage of traps, but does have one longer-term weakness: If someone comes along and changes this code, perhaps inserting some new code before the call to

`DoTheSecondThing()`, without reading the whole thing carefully, that programmer might not realize that he or she is adding code in an error where the error handling switch is "off." Some might call the following improved version overkill, but it's the safest technique because each hot spot is a self-contained trap that can be copied, pasted, moved around, and so on:

```
On Error Resume Next
DoTheFirstThing
If Err.Number <> 0 Then
    MsgBox "An error occurred: " & Err.Number & " - " & Err.Description & _
        " - " & Err.Source
    On Error GoTo 0
    WScript.Quit
End If
On Error GoTo 0

On Error Resume Next
DoTheSecondThing
If Err.Number <> 0 Then
    MsgBox "An error occurred: " & Err.Number & " - " & Err.Description & _
        " - " & Err.Source
    On Error GoTo 0
    WScript.Quit
End If
On Error GoTo 0

On Error Resume Next
DoTheThirdThing
If Err.Number <> 0 Then
    MsgBox "An error occurred: " & Err.Number & " - " & Err.Description & _
        " - " & Err.Source
    On Error GoTo 0
    WScript.Quit
End If
On Error GoTo 0
```

Some readers may already have observed the opportunity to move the error handling logic down into each of the "DoThe" procedures, thereby simplifying the main logic flow of the script:

```
DoTheFirstThing
DoTheSecondThing
DoTheThirdThing
```

However, many people would consider it poor form to trap and display errors in a generic manner in a subprocedure. The design principle at work in that point of view is that the subprocedures should remain ignorant about the handling of the errors, which should be left up to the main flow of the script (recall the puppetmaster-and-puppets metaphor from Chapter 4). The most important thing is to choose a sound error handling technique that works for you, apply it consistently, and do what you can to make it easy for the next programmer to come along to figure out what's going on in your code.

Presenting and Logging Errors

As discussed in the previous section, when you have *trapped* an error, you have to do something with it. This *doing something* is usually referred to as *handling* the error, which means you are going to respond to the error in some specific way other than letting the VBScript host handle the error on your behalf.

The most common error handling technique is to display the error to your users. As demonstrated at the beginning of this chapter, if you do not use the On Error Resume Next statement, VBScript's default error handling (depending on the host) is generally to display the error to the user somehow. So if VBScript will display the error for you, why add your own error handling and display code? There are two good reasons: control and cosmetics.

❏ **Control:** If you do not use the error trapping technique described in the previous section, then you are giving all error handling control to the VBScript host. Yes, the host displays the error for you, but it also stops your script at the exact point the error occurred. If you had a file open, you won't get a chance to close it. If you're in the middle of a database update, your connection to the database, along with your data, is thrown away. If you're in the middle of collecting a large amount of information from the user, all of that work on the user's part is lost. Allowing the VBScript host to handle all errors for you is often not the best technique.

❏ **Cosmetics:** This has to do with how the error displays. The error display in, for example, the WSH, is not the most friendly in the world. Your users might miss the important information buried in the daunting error display dialog box. By writing your own procedure to display errors in your WSH scripts, you can present a more professional face to your users. Try adding some code to the DisplayError procedure you saw in one of the example scripts (ERR_TRAP.VBS) from the previous section.

```
Private Sub DisplayError(lngNumber, strSource, strDescription)
    MsgBox "An error occurred. Please write down " & _
        "the error information displayed below " & _
        "and contact your system administrator: " & _
        vbNewLine & vbNewLine & _
        "Error Description: " & strDescription & vbNewLine & _
        "Error Number: " & lngNumber & vbNewLine & _
        "Error Source: " & strSource, _
        vbExclamation
End Sub
```

This looks like a lot of code, but really you're just stringing together a nice, friendly message with line breaks and white space, as shown in Figure 6-5. Other than the improved appearance, you're basically displaying the same information that VBScript would have by default.

Figure 6-5

Beyond displaying the error, you have other options as well. In fact, if your script runs unattended, you might not want to display the error at all because you have no one sitting there to click the OK button. One of the most popular techniques is to log the error to a file, a database, or the Windows Event Log. You can also email the error to a system administrator, or even page the system administrator on his or her beeper. You could get really fancy and send a message to a web site that reboots the server in your back office. How elaborate you get, and what ways you choose to respond, is really dependent upon the situation — in particular, how important the script is and what bad things might happen if an error occurs without anyone noticing.

Unfortunately, there's not enough space in this chapter to demonstrate all of the possible techniques for logging, emailing, and so on, but none of these ideas are beyond the capabilities of VBScript and the companion components described in this book and elsewhere. You can use the `FileSystemObject` library (see Chapter 7) to open an error log file and append to the end of it. You can use Microsoft Outlook and Exchange to send an email or beeper message. You can use IIS to redirect to another web page.

It should also be noted that sometimes doing nothing is appropriate when you have trapped an error — that is, you may decide to in effect suppress the error and keep going, as in the following example:

```
On Error Resume Next
'Call a procedure whose errors we do not care about
DoSomething
On Error GoTo 0
'...script code continues...
```

Sometimes you want to trap and/or suppress certain errors while allowing other errors to be handled more generally:

```
On Error Resume Next
DeleteFile("somefile.txt")
If Err.Number > 0 Then
    If InStr(Err.Description, "file does not exist") > 0 Then
        'Ignore error
    Else
        DisplayError
    End If
End If
On Error GoTo 0

'...script code continues...
```

The key thing to keep in mind is to retain control of your application, its behavior, and its appearance by taking a proactive stance about what you want to do when errors occur.

Displaying Server-Side ASP Errors

One common VBScript-related error handling situation bears special mention: the display of server-side ASP errors using IIS. In versions of Internet Information Services prior to 7.0 released with Microsoft

Windows Vista (somewhere along the way, Microsoft changed the name from Internet Information Server to Internet Information *Services*), IIS will by default push ASP syntax and runtime errors out to the browser using a built-in template HTML page. Figure 6-6 shows a divide by zero runtime error for an ASP page viewed under Windows XP from an older version of IIS.

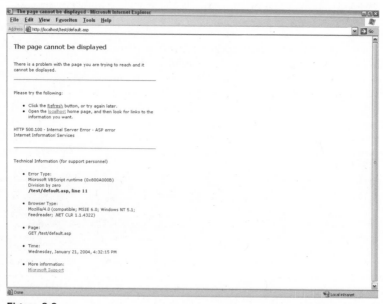

Figure 6-6

As you can see, the normal error information displays as you would expect (although it's kind of buried in the fine print of the page): the error number, description, source, and so on. In addition, the display includes information about the page that caused the error and about the requesting browser. It's nice that IIS has this built-in error display feature, but this default page is not the most attractive in the world, and almost certainly does not fit in with the look and feel of the rest of your web site.

It appears that Microsoft has reconsidered the default error display shown in Figure 6-6 to be a security vulnerability because it reveals information that could be useful to hackers. In newer versions, IIS reveals much less information to the client browser. The default message is simple, vague, and transmitted in plain text: "An error occurred on the server when processing the URL. Please contact the system administrator." You can see this message if you browse to a classic ASP page with a runtime error using a non-Microsoft browser, or with Microsoft's Internet Explorer browser with "friendly error messages" turned off. If the IE "Show friendly HTTP error messages" is turned on (which it is by default), then the error display is more attractive, but equally vague — though, as shown in Figure 6-7, you do get to see the 500 error code.

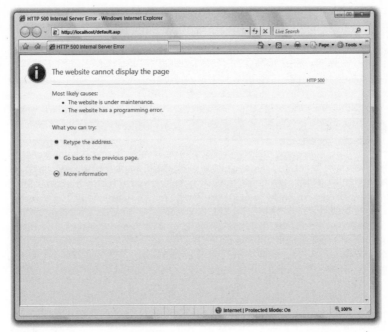

Figure 6-7

A Note about ASP and ASP.NET

VBScript is the default, and most popular, language of what many people today refer to as *classic ASP*, which distinguishes it from ASP.NET, which is Microsoft's next generation implementation of the Active Server Pages concept. In ASP.NET, VBScript is no longer used as the default language (most people use VB.NET or C#), though the ASP.NET runtime engine and Microsoft's newest versions of Internet Information Services are backward compatible with classic ASP web sites written in VBScript. We keep the *VBScript Programmer's Reference* up to date to support the programmers with this information because of the thousands (probably millions) of lines of ASP code still in use around the world.

Previous editions of *VBScript Programmer's Reference* have included information about creating your own custom page for trapping, handling, and displaying ASP runtime errors. Unfortunately, for IIS 7 running under Windows Vista, we have had no success installing a custom 500.100 page, or even affecting in any way the handling of 500.100 runtime errors in classic ASP pages. It appears that Microsoft has locked this down so tight that even the administration interface that is intended to allow you to configure the handling of runtime errors does not have any effect. This may turn out to be a bug, or we may find out later that there is a switch hidden somewhere to allow it to work.

(continued)

A Note about ASP and ASP.NET *(continued)*

We are still including this information in the book because it is an important topic and still relevant to pre-version-7 releases of IIS that are still in wide use. In addition, if and when this issue is resolved for IIS 7 under Windows Vista (or perhaps under the forthcoming Windows Server code named "Longhorn"), the procedure for configuring custom handling of classic ASP 500.100 errors will likely be very similar to what we describe in this chapter.

You do not, however, have to accept the default 500.100 error display page; you can make your own. For each web site hosted by your IIS server, you can set up custom error handler pages for each type of error that can occur. As you can see in Figure 6-6, the error type for a server-side ASP code error is HTTP 500.100 - Internal Server Error - ASP error. (Figure 6-7 shows how IIS 7 running under Windows Vista suppresses this detailed error code information.) The 500.100 error page displays ASP and VBScript runtime errors, as well as errors raised by other code called by your ASP code. If you want to provide an error display page of your own, you can replace the default error page in IIS for 500.100 ASP errors (and many other kinds of errors as well, though errors other than 500.100 are not in the scope of this discussion).

Figure 6-8 shows the web site properties screen for the IIS default web site. Each web site configured in IIS has its own unique properties, so you can set up different custom error display pages for each of your web sites. For the web site properties in Figure 6-8, the default 500.100 error page is configured. By clicking the Edit Properties button, you can point to a different error display file. (See Chapter 20 or the IIS documentation for more information about configuring your web site.)

Figure 6-8

Before you can replace the default 500.100 page, however, you must create a new custom page of your own with which to replace it. If you have at least a basic grasp of basic ASP concepts (see Chapter 20), then you can a copy the default 500-100.asp web page, the location of which is highlighted in Figure 6-8, and customize it, or simply use it as a guide for working the desired logic into your site's ASP template.

The key in a 500.100 page is to use the Server.GetLastError() method to get a reference to an ASPError object, which is very similar to the native VBScript Err object. The ASPError object has properties like Number, Description, and Source, just like the Err object. In addition, the ASPError object has properties called ASPCode and ASPDescription that return more detailed information if the error was an ASP-specific error raised by IIS. There are even File, Line, and Column properties to provide information on exactly where the error occurred. The following code snippet illustrates how to get a reference to an ASPError object.

```
<%
Option Explicit

Dim objASPError

Set objASPError = Server.GetLastError
%>
```

It's a safe assumption (though not a guarantee) that Server.GetLastError will return a fully populated ASPError object — otherwise the 500.100 page would not have been called. Now that you have a reference to an ASPError object, you can embed code such as the following within the HTML of your new custom error page to display the various properties of the ASPError object.

```
Response.Write "Number: " & _
    Server.HTMLEncode(objASPError.Number) & "<br>"
Response.Write "Description: " & _
    Server.HTMLEncode(objASPError.Description) & "<br>"
Response.Write "Source: " & _
    Server.HTMLEncode(objASPError.Source) & "<br>"
```

You can also embed the calls to the ASPError properties between <%...%> tokens, if that is your preferred style.

This is a very simple example and, as you will see, if you read the default 500-100.asp file, you can get quite elaborate with the design. A custom error page is a great way to centralize your error handling code. Keep in mind that because this is *your* ASP error display page on *your* web site, you can use the error information in the ASPError object any way you like. You could provide an input field and a button to allow the user to type in comments and email them and the error information to you. You might even decide to hide the ugly details of the error from your users, replacing it with a simple "Sorry, the web site had a problem" message, and logging the error in the background. You can also include code for handling specific errors, taking different actions depending on the error number. As in any error handling situation, it's all up to you.

If your web site already has an established look and feel, it's a good idea to design your error page to match the rest of your web site. This reduces the surprise of your users if ASP errors do occur on your web site because the error display won't make them feel like they've been suddenly kicked out of your web site.

Generating Custom Errors

So far, this chapter has discussed how, when, and why to *react* to errors. However, VBScript also provides the ability to create errors yourself, which, believe it or not, is sometimes the best thing to do — after all, errors are a way of communicating that something has gone wrong, and there's no reason your scripts can't be smart enough to detect that something has gone wrong. Any VBScript code you write can at any time stop execution and generate an error. The key to this ability is the `Raise` method of the *Err* object introduced earlier in this chapter.

Using Err.Raise

Recall from earlier that the `Err` object is always available and is of global scope. That means you can refer to it any time you want without having to declare a variable for it. The following code demonstrates a call to `Err.Raise()`:

```
Err.Raise vbObjectError + 10000, _
    "MyScript.MyFunction", _
    "The Age argument of MyFunction may not be greater than 150."
```

In this code example you use the first three arguments of the `Err.Raise()` method.

❏ The first argument is the error number. You are free to use any error number between 0 and 65535, but using zero is not recommended because, as illustrated earlier in this chapter, many programmers consider 0 as the absence of an error. In addition, Microsoft strongly recommends that you add the value of the `vbObjectError` constant to your error number. The detailed explanation of why this is necessary is out of the scope of this book, but to summarize, adding `vbObjectError` to your error number makes sure your error number does not clash with "official" Microsoft Windows error numbers.

❏ The second argument is the error source. This is an optional parameter that many people omit or leave blank, but if you are raising an error from a specific script, page, and/or function, including some kind of description of where the error originated is a good idea. A programmer who receives your error (maybe even yourself) will thank you someday for filling in the `Source` argument.

❏ The third argument is the error description. It's a good idea to be as specific as possible in your description. Include any additional information you can think of that would be helpful to someone trying to diagnose and eradicate the cause of your error. Remember those useless ADO error descriptions mentioned earlier in the chapter? Don't stick yourself or your fellow programmers with useless messages like `"Errors occurred or Undefined error"`.

The `Err.Raise()` method accepts two additional arguments that are seldom used in a VBScript context: `helpfile` and `helpcontext`. If your VBScript project does have a companion Windows help file, by all means include the path to it in the `helpfile` argument. And if your help file has a specific section that explains the cause and solution for your custom error, then providing the "context id" for that section is a great idea, too.

When Not to Use Err.Raise

Now that you know *how* to generate a custom error, the obvious follow-up questions are *why* and *when* to raise a custom error.

First, though, let's talk about when it's *not* a good idea to raise custom errors. Errors are generally created for the benefit of other programmers. When something goes wrong (like a lost database connection), or when a program tries to do something illegal (like dividing by zero), an error is the most common way to inform a program or programmer of that fact. While your users generally will not appreciate seeing errors, in the big picture it is generally better that they know that something is wrong, even if they don't understand it or know how to fix it.

Ideally, the only time a user should see an error is when something unexpected occurred either in your script or in something outside of your script, like a component or Windows itself. Furthermore, you want errors to make it only as far as the user's eyes when you did not have a specific way of dealing with the error. (For example, if your script received an error indicating a lost database connection, you can try to reconnect to the database rather than stopping your script and displaying the error to the user.)

It is useful to distinguish between an error and a *problem message*. Certainly, there are times that you must communicate bad news to your user, or ask your user to fix some problem. You see this all the time on web pages with forms. If you forget to fill in a certain field, the web page tells you about it so that you can fix the problem. This kind of problem message is different from an error.

Remember the script at the beginning of this chapter that caused a divide by zero error? What if you had a script asking the user to enter a number, which your script will divide into 100, like so:

```
Option Explicit

Dim x, y

x = InputBox("Please enter a number to divide into 100.")
y = 100 / x
MsgBox "100 divided by " & x & " is " & y & "."
```

What if the user enters 0? With this code as is, run under the WSH, the user will see an unfriendly divide by zero error, as seen in Figure 6-2.

Suppose, instead, you tested the value that the user typed in before attempting the division, as in this script (PROBLEM_MESSAGE.VBS).

```
Option Explicit

Dim x, y

x = InputBox("Please enter a number to divide into 100.")
If x <> 0 Then
    y = 100 / x
    MsgBox "100 divided by " & x & " is " & y & "."
Else
    MsgBox "Please enter a number other than zero."
End If
```

This time, the user sees a nice, friendly *problem message* instead of an ugly, scary error. Users would always prefer to see a cordial message that informs them of what they can do to fix a problem rather than an error that leaves them feeling stupid and helpless.

The point of all this is to say that it is not a good idea to abuse `Err.Raise()` by using it to inform your users of when they have done something wrong. Instead, as described in the next section, use `Err.Raise()` to catch programming problems or to report problems in the environment. The following script (ERR_MSG_UGLY.VBS) illustrates how not to use `Err.Raise`. The error description is sarcastic, but it reflects how your users will feel if you use `Err.Raise()` in this way.

```
Option Explicit

Dim x, y

x = InputBox("Please enter a number to divide into 100.")
If x <> 0 Then
    y = 100 / x
    MsgBox "100 divided by " & x & " is " & y & "."
Else
    Err.Raise vbObjectError + 15000, _
        "ERR_MSG_UGLY.VBS", _
        "Hey, stupid, you can't enter a zero! It will " & _
        "cause a divide by zero error!"
End If
```

When to Generate Custom Errors

Now that you know *how* to generate custom errors — and when *not* to — the question that is left is when you *should* generate a custom error. The answer has to do with the assumptions that your script makes. Whenever you write computer programs, you're forced to operate on a set of assumptions. Different types of programs running in different types of environments have different sets of assumptions, but assumptions are always there.

Certain assumptions are foundational: You assume a certain operating system and computer configuration; you assume the ability to open files for reading and writing; you assume a certain database configuration; you assume that the `Customer` table is structured in a certain way; you assume that the web server works in a certain way.

Other assumptions are more specific, and often take the form of rules. For example, imagine that there is a rule baked into the design of your retail order management system that the `CustomerID` primary key in the `Customer` table is never less than or equal to zero and that the number matches an actual record in the `Customer` table. So your `LoadCustomer()` function, which takes a `CustomerID` argument to load a particular customer from the database, operates on an assumption that this rule is being followed. However, if there is any chance that the `CustomerID` passed to the `LoadCustomer()` function might violate this rule, it's a good idea for the programmer of the `LoadCustomer()` function to test the value of `CustomerID` to see if it is operating according to the rule:

```
Private Function LoadCustomer(CustomerID)
    If CustomerID <= 0 Then
        Err.Raise vbObjectError + 12000, _
            "LoadCustomer", _
            "The CustomerID argument must be greater than 0."
```

```
    End If

    '...code continues...
End Function
```

A rule was broken; an assumption failed. Generate an error. That is the most basic answer to the questions of *when* and *why* to generate custom errors.

Before you look at a specific example, reconsider the previous section, which explained that it is *not* a good idea to use custom errors as a way to tell your users about things they have done wrong. Instead, use more friendly and helpful *problem messages*, which are not the same as *errors* per se. The distinction between this advice from the previous section about when *not* to use errors to report a problem and the advice in this section about when you *do* want to use errors to report a problem is one of *audience*.

Take another look at the same ERR_MSG_UGLY.VBS script you saw earlier:

```
Option Explicit

Dim x, y

x = InputBox("Please enter a number to divide into 100.")
If x <> 0 Then
    y = 100 / x
    MsgBox "100 divided by " & x & " is " & y & "."
Else
    Err.Raise vbObjectError + 15000, _
        "ERR_MSG_UGLY.VBS", _
        "Hey, stupid, you can't enter a zero! It will " & _
        "cause a divide by zero error!"
End If
```

Besides the obviously rude wording of the error message (which of course demonstrates the true effect of unhandled errors on users) the real reason this technique is undesirable is that the audience of the error in this script is the user. Ideally, you don't want to use errors to communicate with your users. If you must report bad news to the user or tell him or her that he or she did something against the assumptions/rules of your script, you want to do this in a more friendly and helpful manner. The reason the *audience* of this script is the user is that the Err.Raise() method is being used in code that is directly interacting with a user — as opposed to lower-level code, in a subprocedure or class method.

However, when the audience of a block of code is other code (or to put it another way, the programmer himself or herself), then an error is appropriate — because you can assume that the programmer is equipped to do something about an error. Take a look at this reworking of the script (ERR_MSG_NICE.VBS).

```
Option Explicit

Dim x, y

x = InputBox("Please enter a number to divide into 100.")
On Error Resume Next
y = DivideNumbers(100, x)
If Err.Number = (vbObjectError + 15000) Then
    On Error GoTo 0
```

(continued)

```
        MsgBox "Please enter a number other than zero."
    Else
        On Error GoTo 0
        MsgBox "100 divided by " & x & " is " & y & "."
    End If

Private Function DivideNumbers(dblNumber, dblDivideBy)

    If dblDivideBy = 0 Then
        Err.Raise vbObjectError + 15000, _
            "ERR_MSG_NICE.DivideNumbers()", _
            "Division by zero not allowed. "
    Else
        DivideNumbers = dblNumber / dblDivideBy
    End If

End Function
```

This example is a little contrived, because the script could have just checked to see if the value entered by the user was zero before calling the DivideNumbers() function. However, the division code was moved into a function called DivideNumbers() so that you could demonstrate how the audience for a custom error is other code, not users. In terms of audience, the main part of the script (outside the DivideNumbers() function) is directly interacting with the user. The DivideNumbers() function, on the other hand, is lower down in the script, interacting only with other code in the main part of the script that called it. Because the audience of the lower-level DivideNumbers() function is other code, if something goes wrong, the best way for DivideNumbers() to tell the other code about it is with a runtime error.

However, the main code that is interacting with the user anticipates that this error could come back from the DivideNumbers() function and has a trap to catch it if it does. The whole purpose of the error trap is to turn the unfriendly runtime error into a friendly problem message for the user. The outer edge code and the lower-level code are communicating the same problem in two different ways based on the audience.

The other thing to take notice of with the DivideNumbers() function is that it is proactively verifying assumptions. This is what programmers call defensive programming, which involves anticipating problems and failed assumptions as early as possible. It is as if the programmer of DivideNumbers() said to himself or herself, "The primary purpose of this function is to divide two numbers. The division operation has an assumption/rule that division by zero is not allowed. Therefore, I am going to test this assumption, and if the test fails, I will raise an error." Though contrived, this demonstrates one of the primary situations in which it is good to generate custom errors from your code.

Before moving on, consider another situation in which generating a runtime error would be appropriate. In the previous example, the DivideNumbers() function is doing a before-the-fact verification of an assumption: Before you try to do the division, make sure that's not going to be an illegal operation. In other situations you must instead report failed assumptions after the fact. Consider a function called GetCustomerName(), which takes a CustomerID argument and returns a customer's name as a String. The function uses the CustomerID value to query the Customer table in a database. If the customer record is found based on the CustomerID argument, the function returns the customer's name from the database record. What if, however, no Customer record was found with that CustomerID?

One way to handle this is for `GetCustomerName()` to use `Err.Raise()` to generate a custom `"No Customer record with specified CustomerID"` runtime error. Then the code that calls `GetCustomerName()` can respond to this error in whatever way is appropriate given the situation. You can generate other examples along these same lines. For example, if a procedure called `OpenFile()` can't find the requested file, it might generate a `"File Not Found"` error. Or if a procedure called `WriteFile()` is denied access to the specified file based on security settings in the file system, it might generate a `"Permission denied"` error.

At this point, you've discovered how to generate custom errors using `Err.Raise()`, when and why to generate them, and when not to. Other than the syntax rules for the `Err.Raise()` method, none of the restrictions or suggestions offered are built into VBScript itself. Instead, the chapter has concentrated on sound error handling principles and techniques followed by programmers in many different languages. Learning and understanding these principles and techniques is an essential part of writing programs with a professional polish.

Debugging

The term *debugging* refers to the activity of a programmer trying to figure out the cause of a problem (or "bug") in his or her program, and then taking steps to eliminate the problem. There are two steps to this process: identifying the problem and fixing the problem. Although the formal sense of the term debugging refers to both steps (finding followed by fixing), the discussion in this section focuses on the finding step, which involves a certain amount of detective work and puzzle solving.

What Is a Debugger?

A *debugger* is a tool to help programmers gain visibility into the running of a program and follow the logic of the code as it is executed line by line at runtime. This can aid not only in finding bugs, but also in simply understanding a program, especially if the logic twists and turns in ways that are difficult to comprehend by simply reading the code. If you can follow along with the code as it runs, you can more easily see how it works — where it branches, where it loops, where it skips over a section of the code, where the value of a variable changes or fails to change.

A debugger sits in between the compiler and/or runtime engine and the actual running program. Without a debugger, your only visibility into what's going on in your code is the output it generates. A debugger gives you a window into what's actually going on in the background as the code is run line by line.

Most programming languages offer some kind of debugger, and VBScript is no different. A debugging tool gives you various capabilities to help in watching and interacting with your code as it executes. The following bullet points describe features typically offered by a debugging tool. The intention in providing this information is to give you an idea of what a debugger is, in case you've never used one before. In the sections that follow, we discuss various aspects of debugging and debuggers that are specific to VBScript, including a full reference for the Microsoft Script Debugger tool at the end of the chapter.

- ❏ **A way to specify a certain line of code on which to pause program execution.** The line of code you specify is called a *breakpoint*. For example, if the problem you are having is deep down in the code in your `CalculatePrice()` function, you mark a certain line in the `CalculatePrice()` function as a breakpoint. The program runs up until the breakpoint is reached, at which point it pauses execution, showing you the breakpoint line.

❏ **A way to step through your code one line at a time.** Once the debugger pauses the program at a certain line because of a watch or breakpoint, the debugger allows you to slowly and deliberately execute the code one line at a time so you can follow along with the logic of the program as it executes. Debuggers usually have three "step" options: *Step Into*, *Step Over*, and *Step Out*. Which one you use depends on what you want to do — or more specifically, exactly which code you want to see.

❏ **Step Into** brings the debugger into a procedure or function, if one is being called and if the code for it is in the scope of the debugger; in other words, you can't Step Into the VBScript MsgBox() function, because the VBScript runtime does not make that code available to the debugger. This is useful when you suspect the procedure being called might have a problem.

❏ **Step Over** does the opposite: If the line you are on calls a procedure or function, the debugger executes it without stepping into it. This is useful when you are confident that the procedure being called is not part of the problem you're debugging.

❏ **Step Out** finishes the execution of a lower-level procedure or function and then pauses again at the next line of code after the call to that procedure or function. This is useful if you've stepped into a procedure, and then decided that you don't need to step through the rest of it.

Remember that the code always executes whether the debugger is showing it to you or not. If you Step Over or Step Out, the code you "skip" in the debugger still executes.

❏ **A way to view the value of all variables active at any given point in the code.** While code execution pauses, the debugger generally has some way to view all active variables at that point in the code and to determine their values. A good debugger even allows you to change the value of a variable so that you can experiment and observe the effects as you step through the code.

❏ **A way to view the "call stack."** The *call stack* is the nested sequence of function and procedure calls that lead to a certain point in the code. For example, if the debugger pauses because of a breakpoint in the CalculatePrice() function, the debugger's call stack window shows you that the Main() procedure called the LoadOrder() procedure, which called the CalculateOrder() procedure, which called the CalculateLineItem() procedure, which called the CalculatePrice() function in which the debugger is paused. The call stack tells you how you got to where you are:

```
Main
     LoadOrder
          CalculateOrder
               CalculateLineItem
                    CalculatePrice
```

Please note that the Microsoft Script Debugger does not have two options that developers are accustomed to having in a debugger:

—It does not have a Locals Window, which is a graphical display of all active variables active at a breakpoint. (You can, however, use the Command Window in the Script Debugger to query the value of any in-scope variables.)

—It does not have Watch functionality, which is a way to set up a dynamic breakpoint based on a change in the value of a certain variable or variables.

Please see the section "Using the Microsoft Script Debugger" at the end of this chapter for a full reference of the features of the Microsoft Script Debugger.

VBScript Debugging Scenarios

The following sections explore the details of debugging your VBScript code under the following scenarios:

❑   Scripts hosted by the Windows Script Host (WSH)

❑   Client-side Web scripts running in Internet Explorer (IE)

❑   Server-side Active Server Pages (ASP) Web scripts running under Internet Information Services (IIS)

❑   When a debugger is not available or convenient

Microsoft offers a freely downloadable product called the Microsoft Script Debugger. This debugger is integrated with the three major VBScript hosts covered in this book: Windows Script Host, Internet Explorer, and Internet Information Services/ASP.

After you learn how to use the Script Debugger in the WSH, IE, and ASP scenarios, in the section called "Debugging without a Debugger," you examine some ways that you can accomplish debugging tasks when the Script Debugger is not available or not convenient.

> A note on debugging classic ASP using Microsoft's latest .NET-oriented versions of Visual Studio: Unfortunately, it does not appear that you can load classic ASP pages into the Visual Studio debugger. Long story short, the limitation centers on the way different types of "resources" are handled in the IIS architecture — IIS sees ASP and ASP.NET pages as distinct kinds of resources, so IIS never gives the ASP.NET runtime engine a chance to even know that a classic ASP page is executing, even if that ASP page is in the same web site as the ASP.NET application. The same limitation is to blame for classic ASP and ASP.NET web sites not seeing each other's session state on the server.

Debugging WSH Scripts with the Microsoft Script Debugger

This section introduces the basics of activating the Microsoft Script Debugger for scripts running under the WSH. It covers how to *activate* the debugger when running a WSH script. Because the usage of the Script Debugger, once activated, is basically the same no matter which host you're running under, usage details are covered separately in a later section called "Using the Microsoft Script Debugger." This section also assumes that you have read the earlier section "What Is a Debugger?" which explains the basic terms and concepts of a debugging tool.

Downloading and Enabling the Debugger

If you have not done so yet, you can download the Script Debugger for free from `msdn.microsoft .com/scripting` (be sure to get the version that matches your version of Windows). Even though the installation program does not require it, it's a good idea to reboot your machine after installing the Script Debugger.

Unlike IE and ASP/IIS scripts (see next two sections), enabling the debugger is not a configuration option. The WSH is automatically aware of the debugger. However, the WSH `wscript.exe` and `cscript.exe` programs require special command-line switches to enable the debugger when running a script. (See Chapter 15 for more details on `wscript.exe` and `cscript.exe`.)

Running the Debugger

Normally, for non-command-line scripts, if you want to run a WSH script you would probably just double-click the `.vbs` file in Windows Explorer. However, if you want to debug a non-command-line WSH script, you have to launch the script using `wscript.exe` directly. The most straightforward way to do this is with the `Run` option on the Windows `Start` menu. If you work with command-line scripts, you are already accustomed to launching your scripts with `cscript.exe`. In that case, all that's required to enable the debugger is to add an additional switch to your normal `cscript.exe` command lines.

Both `wscript.exe` and `cscript.exe` accept two debugging related switches. The behavior is the same for both `wscript.exe` and `cscript.exe`. The `//x` switch launches the script in the debugger, making an automatic breakpoint on the first line of the script. The `//d` switch launches the script as normal, but in a "debug aware" mode, meaning that the debugger is only activated if one of two things happens: if an unhandled error occurs or if the `Stop` statement is encountered.

> There is one quirk with the WSH and the Script Debugger: For debugging to work, you must already have the Script Debugger running when you launch the script. You must start the Script Debugger manually. The executable file for the latest version of the Script Debugger that runs under Windows 2000 and Windows XP is `msscrdbg.exe`. The default installation location is `C:\Program Files\ Microsoft Script Debugger`, but may be installed in a different folder on your computer.

Switch Examples

Take a look at a few switch examples. Although these examples use `wscript.exe`, the information applies equally to `cscript.exe`. Once you've located `msscrdbg.exe`, double-click it to launch the debugger. You may want to create a shortcut for it to make it easier to launch in the future. The examples in this section assume that you already have the debugger running.

The first example illustrates how to launch a script in the debugger with a script that does not have any preset breakpoints or runtime errors:

1. The downloadable code for this chapter includes a script called `WSH_DEBUG_X.VBS`. Place this file in a folder on your hard drive and use the Start ➪ Run menu option with this command.

```
wscript //x c:\scripts\WSH_DEBUG_X.VBS
```

2. Change the path for the script to match where you've placed it on your hard drive.

3. Run the command. When you do so, you should see a window such as the one shown in Figure 6-9.

Microsoft Script Debugger - [Read only: WSH_DEBUG_X.VBS [break]]

File   Edit   View   Debug   Window   Help

File | Edit | Debug

```
Option Explicit

Dim x, y, z

x = 5
y = 100
z = y / x
MsgBox y & " divided by " & x & " equals " & z & "."
```

Ready   Ln 5

Figure 6-9

This is the Microsoft Script Debugger in an active debugging session, stopped at a breakpoint. The //x command line switch tells WSH to run the script in the debugger with a breakpoint on the very first line. When you use the //x switch, you are in essence saying that you want to debug your whole script from the very beginning. With //x, it is not necessary to manually specify any breakpoints (for example, you don't need to use the Stop statement — see the section "Activating the Debugger with the Stop Statement" later in this chapter).

The section "Using the Microsoft Script Debugger" describes all the debugging options you have at this point, so feel free to skip ahead to that section or just play around with some of the options on the Debug *menu or toolbar. When you are done, you can click the* Run *or* Stop Debugging *menu or toolbar option before moving on to the next example.*

If you can imagine this script as much larger, you can also imagine that you might not want to use the //x switch to debug the script starting right at the top. Instead, you might only want the debugger to come up if: (a) An error occurs, or (b) WSH reaches a manual breakpoint that you have inserted into the code. Otherwise, you might be forced to step through dozens of lines of code before reaching the point in your script that you really want to debug. The //d switch, instead of the //x switch is what you need.

Let's look at situation (a) first. The script WSH_DEBUG_ERR.VBS contains a divide by zero error. Run a command such as the one in the following example from the Start ⇨ Run menu (notice that you're using the //d switch now instead of the //x switch).

```
wscript //d c:\scripts\WSH_DEBUG_ERR.VBS
```

As you can see in Figure 6-10, this time the debugger stops on the line with the divide by zero error. This gives you the opportunity to use the debugger to observe what happened to cause the error and experiment with ways to fix it. Because you used the //d switch, if this script had not contained any errors, you would have never seen the debugger at all. The //d switch says to WSH, "Only bring up the debugger if I need it," whereas the //x switch says, "Bring up the debugger no matter what, and break on the first line."

Figure 6-10

You can also use the //d switch when you want the debugger to come up on a preset breakpoint. For this purpose, VBScript offers the Stop statement, which is a command to tell the host to activate the debugger, pausing execution on the line with the Stop statement. If no debugger is available, the VBScript runtime ignores the Stop statement. For example, if you run a WSH script that contains a Stop statement *without* using the //d switch, WSH ignores the Stop statement and does not bring up the debugger.

Setting a manual breakpoint with the Stop statement is useful when you want a script to run up to a certain point where you want to pause execution. If you are debugging a fairly large script, this ability is a huge timesaver, especially if the point from which you want to debug is deep down in the script. The file WSH_DEBUG_STOP.VBS contains a Stop statement. If you run it with this command line, you see that the debugger comes up with a breakpoint on exactly the line with the Stop statement.

```
wscript //d c:\scripts\WSH_DEBUG_STOP.VBS
```

You've now seen how you can control the activation of a debugging session for WSH scripts in the Script Debugger. The following two sections explain the same concepts for Internet Explorer web page scripts and server-side ASP web pages.

If you want to get into the details of how the Script Debugger works once you have started a debugging session, you can skip ahead to the section called "Using the Microsoft Script Debugger."

Debugging Client-Side Web Scripts with the Microsoft Script Debugger

This section introduces the basics of activating the Microsoft Script Debugger for client-side Web scripts running in IE. It only explains how to *activate* the debugger for a script embedded in a web page opened in IE.

Because the usage of the Script Debugger, once activated, is basically the same no matter which host you're running under, usage details are covered separately in a later section called "Using the Microsoft Script Debugger." The current section also assumes that you have read the previous section "What Is a Debugger?" which explains the basic terms and concepts of a debugging tool.

If you have not done so yet, you can download the Script Debugger for free from `msdn.microsoft` `.com/scripting` (be sure to get the version that matches your version of Windows).

Enabling the Script Debugger

Once you've downloaded and installed the Script Debugger, the first thing you do to debug VBScript in a client-side web page is enable the debugging option in Internet Explorer (which, as far as we know is the only browser that supports VBScript; many Windows-based organizations choose to develop applications that are dedicated to IE as a client). Figure 6-11 shows the Advanced tab of the Internet Options dialog box for IE7. Notice that the option Disable script debugging has been unchecked. This enables the debugger. The next question is how to get it to come up so that you can do some debugging.

Figure 6-11

Activating the Debugger with an Error

Once you install and enable the Script Debugger, any time an error occurs in any of the VBScript code embedded in a page, you have an opportunity to activate the debugger. Take a look at this HTML page, which contains a script with a divide by zero error (IE_DEBUG_ERR.HTML).

```
<!DOCTYPE HTML PUBLIC "-//W3C//DTD HTML 4.0 Transitional//EN">
<html>
    <head>
        <meta http-equiv="Content-Type" content="text/html;
         charset=UTF-8" />
        <title>VBScript Programmer's Reference - IE Debugger
            Example</title>
        <script type="text/vbscript" language="VBScript">
            Sub cmdTest_OnClick
                Dim x, y, z
                x = 0
                y = 100
                z = y / x
                txtResult.Value = z
            End Sub
        </script>
    <head>
    <body>
    <h2>IE Script Debugger Example: Activate Debugger with
        Error<br></h2>
    This button will call a script that contains a coding error.<br>
    If the IE "Disable script debugging" option is turned off, the
    debugger will be active on the line of code with the error.
    </h2>
    <input type="button" name="cmdTest" value="Run Test"><br><br>
    <b>Test Result:</b> <input type="text" name="txtResult"
        id="txtResult">
    </body>
</html>
```

Notice that the button called cmdTest, which activates the script called cmdTest_OnClick. cmdTest_OnClick, contains a divide by zero error. (If you are not familiar with the basics of embedding VBScript in an HTML page, please see Chapter 10.) This code produces the web page shown in Figure 6-12.

If you click the Run Test button, you see a dialog box such as the one shown in Figure 6-13.

If you click the Yes button, you see a window similar to the one shown in Figure 6-14.

As you can see in Figure 6-14, the line with the error is highlighted, with an arrow off to the left pointing to the same line. These indicators mean that the code has paused execution at this point. You now have an active debugging session for this web page. The section "Using the Microsoft Script Debugger" describes all the debugging options you have at this point, so feel free to skip ahead to that section or just play around with some of the options on the Debug menu or toolbar. When you are done, you can click the Run or Stop Debugging menu or toolbar option before moving on to the next example.

Figure 6-12

Figure 6-13

Activating the Debugger with the Stop Statement

You can also force the activation of the Script Debugger in an Internet Explorer session using the Stop statement. Stop is a special VBScript keyword that applies only when script debugging is enabled in the current host (in this case, IE). If no debugger is active, the VBScript runtime engine ignores the Stop statement. (However, particularly for client-side scripts, you don't want to leave any stray Stop statements in your code because your end users might end up looking at a debugger and wondering what the heck is going on.)

Figure 6-14

The following code snippet is from another version of the same page from the previous section, this time with the divide by zero error removed and the `Stop` statement inserted into the code (`IE_DEBUG_STOP.HTML`).

```
<script type="text/vbscript" language="VBScript">
    Sub cmdTest_OnClick
        Dim x, y, z
        Stop
        x = 5
        y = 100
        z = y / x
        txtResult.Value = z
    End Sub
</script>
```

If you click the Run Test button on this page, the Script Debugger comes up automatically, with execution paused on the line with the `Stop` statement. The `Stop` statement is useful when you're editing your script and know in advance that you want to set a breakpoint at a certain point in the script. The next section explains how to set a breakpoint once the page is already open in IE.

Activating the Debugger with a Manual Breakpoint

If you already have a web page with a script open in IE, you can use the View ➪ Script Debugger ➪ Open menu in IE to open the debugger before the script starts executing. However, this technique works only if you are debugging a script that is executed *on demand* — for example, with the click of a button on the page. If the script is one that runs automatically when the page is loaded, you must use the `Stop` statement to set a breakpoint.

The page IE_DEBUG_MANUAL.HTML (which, like all examples in this book, is downloadable from wrox.com) is just like the page examples used in the previous example, except that it does not contain a Stop statement or divide by zero error. If you open this page in IE, you can use the View ⇨ Script Debugger ⇨ Open menu to open the debugger. The debugger window opens, displaying the page with your cmdTest_OnClick procedure.

At this point, you can use the Toggle Breakpoint menu or toolbar option to set a breakpoint on any line in the script you want. Then return to the browser and click the Run Test button. The Script Debugger window comes back and pauses on the line where you set your breakpoint.

Debugging ASP with the Microsoft Script Debugger

This section introduces the basics of activating the Microsoft Script Debugger for server-side ASP pages running in IIS. It only explains how to *activate* the debugger for ASP pages.

Because the usage of the Script Debugger, once activated, is basically the same no matter which host you're running under, usage details are covered separately in a later section called "Using the Microsoft Script Debugger." This section also assumes that you've read the earlier section "What Is a Debugger?" which explains the basic terms and concepts of a debugging tool. This section also assumes that you are familiar with the basics of administering IIS.

If you have not done so yet, you can download the Script Debugger for free from msdn.microsoft.com/scripting (be sure to get the version that matches your version of Windows).

What about the Visual Interdev Debugger?

Visual Interdev, an ASP development tool that at one time, in pre-.NET days, shipped with Microsoft Visual Studio, also includes a debugger that ASP programmers can use to debug ASP web sites. Programmers who have Visual Interdev available may choose to use that debugger instead of the free Script Debugger. The Visual Interdev debugger does offer some functionality that the Script Debugger does not offer, namely the Locals window, Watches, and "Advanced Breakpoints." Launching the debugger in Interdev is a little different than what this section describes (please consult the Visual Interdev documentation), but once the debugger is activated, the general capabilities and techniques described in this section and the "Using the Microsoft Script Debugger" section (given later) apply equally well to Visual Interdev and the Script Debugger.

Enabling ASP Debugging

For your IIS-hosted web site to allow you to debug ASP pages, you must explicitly enable this capability. You do this using the IIS administration tool (for IIS versions 5.x and 6.0 — see note below about IIS 7 and Windows Vista), which on the latest versions of Windows is available through the "Administrative Tools" Control Panel applet. To enable this feature, do the following:

1. Right-click the web site you want to debug and choose the Properties menu option.
2. Go to the Home Directory tab.

3. Click the `Configuration` button in the lower right corner of the Home Directory tab. This brings up the Application Configuration dialog box.

4. On the Application Configuration dialog box, click the Debugging tab.

5. On the Debugging tab, make sure the `Enable ASP server-side script debugging` option is selected. (You can ignore the `Enable ASP client-side script debugging` option; it does nothing.)

After enabling this option (if it was not already enabled), it's a good idea to reboot your machine before trying to use the Script Debugger with ASP. Under ideal circumstances, these steps described are all that is required to enable ASP debugging. However, see the note nearby about ASP debugging with IIS 7 under Windows Vista.

> **Unfortunately, in preparation for the third edition of this book, the authors were never able to get ASP server-side script debugging to work under IIS 7 running Windows Vista. The experience was similar to the one documented earlier in this chapter regarding custom `500.100` pages under IIS 7: The configurations options are there, and you can change them, but they seem to have no effect. Possibly, after this book goes to press, a solution will emerge for this issue, but the authors were not able to uncover one.**

If you are having trouble, the Microsoft "Knowledge Base" (`support.microsoft.com`) does have some articles that may help you. Using the Knowledge Base Search function, search for article IDs 252895, 192011, 244272, 284973, and 312880. If you are still experiencing trouble, try the discussion groups at `p2p.wrox.com` or `www.microsoft.com/communities/newsgroups/en-us/`.

Be sure to turn off the `Enable ASP server-side script debugging` option for your web site before you release the web site to users. You do not want the debugger to launch when actual users are browsing your web site. In fact, it's a good idea to perform ASP debugging only on your development machine and never on the actual server hosting your production web site.

Activating the Debugger

Just as with WSH and IE script debugging, the Script Debugger with ASP pages is activated under two circumstances:

❑ When an unhandled runtime error occurs

❑ When IIS encounters a `Stop` statement in a page's VBScript code

The previous two sections of this chapter on WSH and IE debugging demonstrate how the debugger activates when it encounters a runtime error, such as a divide by zero error. This works exactly the same with ASP debugging. If you enable ASP debugging for your site's ASP code and IIS encounters a line of code that causes an unhandled runtime error, then the debugger comes up with a breakpoint on that line. If you want to see this work, modify the `asp_debug_stop.asp` page (described later) by commenting out the `Stop` statement and changing the value of x to 0. This triggers a divide by zero error.

The downloadable code for this chapter includes a file called `asp_debug_stop.asp` that demonstrates how to activate the Script Debugger with ASP using the `Stop` statement. To try out this example, you need to install the `asp_debug_stop.asp` file in IIS. Make sure that you install it on a machine that, as described in the previous section has:

❑ IIS installed

❑ The Script Debugger installed

❑ At least one running web site (the "Default Web Site" will do) with server-side ASP debugging enabled.

This is what the top of `asp_debug_stop.asp` looks like, before the `<HTML>` tag.

```
<%@ Language=VBScript %>
<% Option Explicit %>
<%
Dim strResult

Call Main()

Sub Main
    Dim x, y, z

    Stop
    x = 5
    y = 100
    z = y / x
    strResult = z
End Sub
%>
```

Notice the `Stop` statement inside the `Main()` procedure. As with any other script, this causes the debugger to pause at this point in the code.

Once you have `asp_debug_stop.asp` installed under a running web site on your machine, use IE to browse to that page using `http://localhost/` as the beginning of the URL. As soon as you do, the Script Debugger should come up, paused on the line with the `Stop` statement. This means that you are now in an active debugging section, with the functionality described in the next section, "Using the Microsoft Script Debugger," available to you.

If, for some reason, the debugger does not come up, but the page *does* successfully come up in the browser, please see the previous section, "Enabling ASP Debugging," for configuration and trouble-shooting tips.

Debugging without a Debugger

When you are without the benefits of a debugger, some basic techniques can assist with debugging, whether you want to find a problem or just understand how a program works. Not all techniques, however, are available or useful in all hosts. As this section discusses techniques, it identifies which ones are available in the three most common VBScript hosts: WSH, IIS with ASP, and IE.

Some of these techniques are useful when a debugger is available and you do not necessarily need to wait to implement them until you have a debugging problem. Once you determine which of these techniques is useful to you, you can build them into your application from the beginning.

Using a Global Debug Flag

This is a technique available in any host, though the implementation differs depending on the host. The global debug flag allows you to run your script in two different modes:

❑ **Debug mode:** The script may output various messages about what is going on in the program (see "Outputting Debug Messages"). This mode is only for the benefit of the programmer or tester, not for end users.

❑ **Production mode:** Output messages are suppressed.

A global debug flag is simply a `Boolean` variable that has global scope in your script. For example, you might call this variable `gblnDebug`. Many people prefer to implement a debug flag as a named constant, in which case you might instead call it `DEBUG_MODE`. (The named constant convention is used because it is more reliable in that its value cannot be changed while the script is running.) In some hosts, such as IIS with ASP, you don't use a variable at all, but rather a custom property of the `Application` object.

Once you define a global debug flag anywhere in your script, you can insert code that executes only when the flag is equal to `True`. It's important to have only one place in your script that sets the value of the flag so that it is consistently either `"On"` or `"Off"` throughout the script (`True` means `"On"` and `False` means `"Off"`). The code to implement the other techniques discussed later, such as outputting debug messages, goes inside of an `If...End If` block that checks the value of the global debug flag.

Here is a simple example of a debug flag implemented in a WSH script (`WSH_NODEBUG_FLAG.VBS`).

```
Option Explicit

Private Const DEBUG_MODE = True

If DEBUG_MODE Then
    MsgBox "Script starting."
End If


MsgBox "Non-debug script code executing here."

If DEBUG_MODE Then
    MsgBox "Script ending."
End If
```

Here you have a named constant called `DEBUG_MODE` that, because it is declared at the top of the script, has global scope. Then, you have two debug messages at the beginning of the script and the end of the script. (See the next section for more information about debug messages.) These messages are only displayed when `DEBUG_MODE` is `True`. The programmer can then change the value of the `DEBUG_MODE` constant to `True` or `False`, depending on whether he or she wants to see the debug messages or not. Of course, you have to be careful that you set the flag to `False` before releasing a script to production.

Implementing a debug flag in with ASP or IE is a little trickier. With ASP, the most common technique is to use the `Application_OnStart` procedure in the `global.asa` file to add a custom property to the `Application` object's `Contents` collection. (See Chapter 20 for more information on these ASP concepts.) Then, anywhere in your ASP application, you can check the value of the debug flag on the `Application` object. Here is an example of what the code looks like in `global.asa` to create and set the debug flag.

```
Sub Application_OnStart
    Application("DEBUG_MODE") = True
End Sub
```

Because the `Contents` collection is the default property of the `Application` object, it is conventional to not refer to it directly. Instead, as you see here, just follow the `Application` with parentheses. The `Contents` collection automatically adds a property called `"DEBUG_MODE"` with the specified value (in this case `True`). Again, just as with the WSH example, the programmer changes the value of the flag to switch back and forth between debug mode and production mode. Finally, because the `Application_OnStart` procedure executes only when the web site stops and restarts, many programmers also create a special-purpose ASP page to change the value of the flag while the application is running.

Using a debug flag in IE is tricky because your scripts are running in the browser on a client machine. How you implement a debug flag for visibility in IE depends on how you are producing your web pages. If your pages are static or generated by some kind of publishing tool, you need to declare a variable in each page or template, and then change the value through the search-and-replace function in your code editor, or whatever makes sense given your toolset.

If your pages are dynamically generated through ASP, then it's a little easier. Make sure that each HTML page you produce includes a declaration for the debug flag variable with page-level scope. This ensures, for example, that all of the scripts on your page can read the variable to include debug messages in the page output. One way to accomplish this is to put the variable declaration and value setting in an include file that all your ASP pages use. To make maintenance of the flag as easy as possible, tie the setting of its value to a `"DEBUG_MODE"` flag on the `Application` object, as described earlier.

Outputting Debug Messages

What a debugging tool offers is visible program information, such as variable values, when variable values change and what the path(s) of execution is through the code. Because you do not have that visibility when a debugger is not available to you, you need to gain some visibility, the best way being through *debug messages*.

You use debug messages for any number of purposes, depending on what information you need:

❑ You can output debug messages in the form of log entries, which provide a view into the sequence of events in your script. A debug message log entry might report significant program events such as the beginning and ending of a script, an entry into a certain function, a connection to a database, the opening of a file, steps in a larger process, or the changing of certain variables. It can be simple or elaborate, depending on your needs.

❑ You can track changes to important variables. If you suspect that a certain variable is, because of a logic error in your code, changing to the wrong value at the wrong time, you can output a message each time the value changes. This can substitute for the "watch" feature of a debugger.

❑ Debug messages are also useful for displaying the total state of your program. For example, in an ASP program you can output all the values stored on the `Request`, `Response`, `Session`, and/or `Application` objects at the bottom of each page (see later). Or, if you are using an array or `Dictionary` to store a series of values, you can output all of the values in a debug message.

Debug messages can take different forms. Like debug flags, the implementation depends on the host:

❑ The simplest way to output a debug message is with the `MsgBox()` function, which displays a dialog box and pauses the execution of the code until the `OK` button is clicked. However, the `MsgBox()` function is really useful only for scripts running in WSH or IE.

❑ For WSH scripts, it's actually preferable to use the `Echo` method of the `WScript` object (see Chapter 15 for detailed information on the intrinsic WSH objects) instead of `MsgBox()`. The advantage of this is that you can choose to run the script either with `wscript.exe`, in which case the `Echo` method displays the message with a dialog box, or with `cscript.exe`, in which case the message outputs to the console window (see Chapter 15). If you use `Echo` a lot in your script, running it under `cscript` keeps you from having to click the `OK` button over and over.

This code fragment shows a debug message implemented with the `Echo` method.

```
If DEBUG_MODE Then
    WScript.Echo "Current order status: " & gstrOrderStatus
End If
```

❑ Yet another way to output debug messages in WSH is to use the `StdOut` property of the `WScript` object, which is implemented as a `TextStream` object (see Chapter 7). However, you can use only `StdOut` with WSH scripts that are exclusively run in the console window with `cscript.exe`. Using `StdOut` under `wscript.exe` will cause an error. Here is a code fragment that uses `StdOut` for debug messages.

```
Dim objStdOut

If DEBUG_MODE Then
    objStdOut = WScript.StdOut
End If
...

If DEBUG_MODE Then
    objStdOut.WriteLine "Current order status: " & _
        gstrOrderStatus
End If
```

❑ In WSH scripts you can also use the `LogEvent()` method of the `WshShell` object to add events to the Windows Event Log. `LogEvent()` can be used under `wscript.exe` or `cscript.exe`.

❑ Because ASP scripts run on the server, `MsgBox()` is not a good way to implement debug messages when IIS is the host. In addition, the WSH `WScript` and `WshShell` objects are not available in ASP. Instead, with ASP the best thing to do is either include debug messages in the body of the HTML page or log them to a file, database, or the Windows Event Log.

One powerful technique is to create an include file for use in all of your ASP pages that contain a standard section of debug info at the bottom of every generated HTML page. When the web site is running in debug mode, the HTML will include the debug section. When in production mode, the debug section is omitted so that your users never see it.

This debug info section could be as simple or as fancy as you require. Most commonly, programmers will at least include information such as the names and values of all of the properties in the `Contents` collections of the `Session` and `Application` objects and the values stored in the `Form`, `Cookies`, `QueryString`, and `ServerVariables` properties of the `Request` object (see Chapter 20). If you have any other variables that store particularly important information, then you can include the values of these variables as well.

Homemade Assertions

VBScript unfortunately does not support a feature called *assertions*, which is included in many other languages such as Visual Basic and VB.NET. An assertion is a test of an assumption in the form of a `True/False` expression. For example, if in the middle of a complex algorithm you want to make sure that a certain variable is equal to a certain value at a certain point, to verify that the algorithm works properly, you can add an assertion that tests the value of the variable. The assertion expression is evaluated only when the program is running in debug mode. In a language with a debugger and full support for assertions, the failure of the assertion would trigger a breakpoint pause in the debugger.

Although VBScript does not natively support assertions, you can still "roll your own." The following code fragment illustrates an assertion in a WSH script.

```
If DEBUG_MODE Then
    If gstrOrderStatus <> "PENDING" Then
        WScript.Echo "***INVALID ORDER STATUS AT THIS POINT***"
    End If
End If
```

Inserting Temporary Test Code

You can also include *test code* that you want to execute only while in debug mode. This is especially useful when you are trying to track down a stubborn logic bug in your code. A good debugger allows you to pause the code at a certain point and execute test code that is not normally part of the program. Once again, if you do not have a debugger, you can use a debug flag to execute only test code while running in debug mode.

```
If DEBUG_MODE Then
    'Test code to illegally change order status to verify status tracking logic.
    'A status of NEW would not normally be allowed at this point.
    gstrOrderStatus = "NEW"
End If
```

You might also want to mark these blocks of test code with a unique value in a comment so that you can use your editor's Search function to find and eliminate them later.

Using the Microsoft Script Debugger

The three previous sections describe how to activate the Script Debugger into a debugging session under the WSH, IE, and IIS. Once you have activated the debugger, the activities you can perform are pretty much the same regardless of which host you are running under. The following sections describe the basics of the Script Debugger functionality, including why and when a particular function is useful.

The examples in the following sections are based on a WSH script debugging session with the file `WSH_DEBUG_EXAMPLE.VBS`, which is part of the downloadable code for this chapter. Where necessary, this section points out relevant differences in debugging activities under IE and/or IIS.

If you want to follow along with the examples, start a debugging session using the `//x` command-line switch with `wscript.exe`, as described earlier in the chapter. (If you want, you can also run it under `cscript.exe`; the behavior of the debugger is the same in either case.) Running the script with the `//x` switch activates the debugger, paused at the very first line of code, as shown in Figure 6-15. As mentioned before, when debugging a WSH script, you must have the Script Debugger already running when you launch the script.

Figure 6-15

Also, for your reference, here is the code for `WSH_DEBUG_EXAMPLE.VBS`.

```
Option Explicit

Const FILE_NAME = "WSH_DEBUG_TEST_FILE.TXT"
Const COPY_SUFFIX = "_COPY"
Const OVERWRITE_FILE = True

'***** Main Code

Dim objFSO
Dim strExtension
Dim blnFileExists
Dim strNewFileName
Dim strScriptPath

Set objFSO = CreateObject("Scripting.FileSystemObject")
strScriptPath = GetScriptPath()
blnFileExists = VerifyFile(strScriptPath, FILE_NAME)
```

```
If blnFileExists Then
    strExtension = GetExtension(FILE_NAME)
    strNewFileName = MakeNewFileName(FILE_NAME, _
        strExtension, COPY_SUFFIX)
    CopyFile strScriptPath & FILE_NAME, _
        strScriptPath & strNewFileName, _
        OVERWRITE_FILE
Else
    On Error GoTo 0
    Err.Raise vbObjectError + 10000, _
        "WSH_DEBUG_EXAMPLE.VBS", _
        "Expected file " & FILE_NAME & " not found."
End If

'***** Supporting procedures and functions

Private Sub CopyFile(strFileName, strNewFileName, blnOverwrite)
    objFSO.CopyFile strFileName, strNewFileName, blnOverwrite
End Sub

Private Function GetExtension(strFileName)
    GetExtension = objFSO.GetExtensionName(strFileName)
End Function

Private Function GetScriptPath
    Dim strPath

    strPath = objFSO.GetAbsolutePathName(WScript.ScriptFullName)
    strPath = Left(strPath, _
        Len(strPath) - Len(objFSO.GetFileName(strPath)))
    GetScriptPath = strPath
End Function

Private Function VerifyFile(strPath, strFileName)
    VerifyFile = objFSO.FileExists(strPath & strFileName)
End Function

Private Function MakeNewFileName(strFileName, strExtension, strSuffix)
    MakeNewFileName = Left(strFileName, Len(strFileName) _
        - (1 + Len(strExtension))) & strSuffix & _
        "." & strExtension
End Function
```

The code is a bit more complex than it needs to be, but that is deliberate in order to create interesting debugging opportunities for the examples given later.

Setting Breakpoints

WSH_DEBUG_EXAMPLE.VBS does not contain any manual breakpoints using the Stop statement. However, because you launched the script using the //x switch, the debugger has set an automatic breakpoint on the first line of the script. You can easily identify the breakpoint because it is highlighted in yellow and has a yellow arrow next to it in the left column of the debugger window.

Now that you're in a debugging session, you can set more breakpoints in the script for this session. You do this using your mouse or your keyboard arrow keys, placing the cursor on some other line below the current line. For example, place it on this line.

```
If blnFileExists Then
```

Once the cursor is on the line of your choosing, click the Toggle Breakpoint option on the Debug menu or toolbar. Your line should now be highlighted in red with a red circle in the column to the left. The purpose of a breakpoint is to tell the debugger to pause execution on the specified line. This implies that the debugger is running through the code, which is different than your stepping through the code one line at a time (discussed next). If you are stepping through the code, breakpoints don't really do anything for you because you are by definition stopping on each line of code.

Therefore, to see your new breakpoint in action, click the Run option on the Debug menu or toolbar. Clicking the Run option is, in effect, telling the debugger to run through the code, only stopping if the debugger encounters one of three things:

❑   A breakpoint like the one you just defined

❑   An unhanded error

❑   The end of the script (in which case the debugging session ends)

After you click the Run option, code execution should pause on the breakpoint you defined. The only reason the breakpoint would not work is if you chose a line that is inside of a conditional If...Then or Select Case block that does not get executed.

Breakpoints are useful when you want to skip down to examine a deeper part of the script. You can step one line at a time down to the line you want to examine, but that can become very tedious in any script that is more than a few lines, especially if you're debugging it more than once. So the recommended technique is this: Get in the habit of starting the debugger with the //x switch, which gives you the opportunity to decide what to do once you're in the debugger. You can decide to step line by line, scroll down to find a place for a manual breakpoint, or click Run to skip ahead to a breakpoint or error that you already know is there.

Stepping Through Code

You should understand that the yellow-highlighted line of code with the yellow arrow (see Figure 6-15) has not executed yet; the debugger paused on a line of code before executing it. Once the debugger is paused on a certain line of code, you can *step through* the code. *Stepping* means executing each line of code one at a time; generally the user clicks or presses a key to advance each line. If you click one of the debugger's step options, the highlighted line of code executes and the highlight moves down to the next line.

The Script Debugger provides three different kinds of stepping.

❑   **Step Into** means that you want to execute the currently highlighted line of code. The *into* part of Step Into means that if that line of code calls a procedure or function within the scope of the debugger, the debugger *steps into* that function, pausing on the first line of code inside of that procedure or function. (This is in contrast to *Step Over*, described next.) Notice the definition doesn't say that the debugger steps into *every* procedure or function — only those that are *in the scope of the debugger*, which means that the code for the function must be available to the debugger for the debugger to step into it. In general, this means that the procedure or function must be within the same script you are debugging (or, in the case of ASP, in an include file).

To try out a Step Into example, start a debug session with the WSH_DEBUG_EXAMPLE.VBS script and use the //x option. When the script comes up in the debugger, set a breakpoint on this line of code and click the Run option.

```
blnFileExists = VerifyFile(FILE_NAME)
```

The debugger pauses on this line because you set a breakpoint on it. If you now click the Step Into option on the Debug menu or toolbar, the debugger pauses execution on the first line within the VerifyFile() function.

❑ **Step Over** means that you want to execute the currently highlighted line of code *without* stepping into any procedures or functions called by that line. For example, if the highlighted line calls a function that you are already familiar and comfortable with, then stepping into that function is a waste of your time. In this situation, you use the Step Over option instead of Step Into.

Going back to the previous example, if you had clicked the Step Over option instead of Step Into, the debugger would go to the next line after the highlighted line without pausing on any of the lines in the VerifyFile() function. Keep in mind that the VerifyFile() function still executes; the difference is that the debugger does not bring you into VerifyFile().

❑ **Step Out** means that you want the debugger to execute the rest of the current procedure or function without going through it line by line. The debugger then pauses on the next line after the line that called the procedure or function you are stepping out of. In the previous example, if you used Step Into to go into the VerifyFile() function, you could use Step Out to complete the execution of the VerifyFile() function, and then pause again at the line after the VerifyFile() call, which is this line.

```
If blnFileExists Then
```

The Step Out option is particularly useful when you accidentally click Step Into instead of Step Over. A quick click of Step Out gets you back to where you were as if you had used Step Over instead of Step Into.

Keep in mind that even when using Step Over, if the procedure or function you are stepping over has an unhandled error inside of it, the debugger pauses on the line of code that is about to cause the error. The debugger always stops for unhandled errors.

Using the Command Window

The *Command Window* is one of the most powerful features of the Script Debugger (in other Microsoft debuggers, this is also known as the Immediate Window). While the debugger pauses on a line of code, you can use the Command Window to view the value of in-scope variables, change the value of those variables, and execute actual VBScript code while the main script is paused. To enable the Command Window, choose the Command Window option on the View menu. Some examples follow.

If you followed along with the previous example and want to follow along with the next example, restart WSH_DEBUG_EXAMPLE.VBS *with a fresh debugging session using the* //x *option.*

Set a breakpoint on this line in the script and click the Run option.

```
If blnFileExists Then
```

This line of code, where you've paused execution with your breakpoint, comes after the following line:

```
blnFileExists = VerifyFile(strScriptPath, FILE_NAME)
```

This means that at the point you've paused, the value of blnFileExists is already set by the VerifyFile() function. Presuming that everything is set up correctly and WSH_DEBUG_TEST_FILE.TXT is in the same directory as your script, blnFileExists should have a value of True. While the debugger is paused, you can prove this using the Command Window. The Command Window supports a special function using the question mark character (?) that displays the value of any in-scope variable. If you type ? blnFileExists into the Command Window and press the Enter key, the Command Window displays the value of True, as shown in Figure 6-16.

Figure 6-16

Using the ? operator is one of the most typical things you will do in the Command Window. Together with breakpoints, this is a powerful capability that allows you to see the overall state of your entire script at any point you want. But viewing the value of a variable is not the only thing you can do in the Command Window.

Suppose you want to test to make sure that the Err.Raise() call in the Else block is working as you expect. Making sure that you exercise all of the logic pathways through your code is an important part of testing your scripts before releasing them. Under normal circumstances, the Else block is not tested unless you renamed or remove WSH_DEBUG_TEST_FILE.TXT. However, using the Command Window, you can change the value of blnFileExists to False just to make sure the Else block is executed at least once. To do this, type blnFileExists = False into the Command Window, just as if you were typing a normal line of VBScript code, and press the Enter key. This operation is shown in Figure 6-17.

Now, you've changed the value of blnFileExists right in the middle of our debugging session. If you click the Run option, the debugger breaks on the Err.Raise() call (because this amounts to an unhandled runtime error). At this point you can use the Command Window to examine the value of the Err object to see what error is occurring, as shown in Figure 6-18.

This should give you an idea of the power of the Command Window. In addition to doing simple things such as changing the value of variables, you can call methods on in-scope objects in your script, and call other procedures and functions within the script. You can even write and execute a mini-script right in the Command Window, as shown in Figure 6-19.

Figure 6-17

Figure 6-18

Figure 6-19

Keep in mind that you can also use the Command Window to access the *intrinsic objects* available in the VBScript host. The `Err` object is an example of an intrinsic object that is available in all hosts, but each host has a unique set of intrinsic objects that are available only in that host. For example, WSH has the `WScript` object. ASP has the `Request` and `Response` objects. You can access these objects, like any other object in scope while the debugger is paused, through the Command Window.

Viewing the Call Stack

A *call stack* is a hierarchical list of the chain of execution in a program. As one function calls another function that calls another function, VBScript keeps track of this calling order so that as each function completes, VBScript can go backward *up the stack*. Sometimes when you are paused inside of a procedure or function you might not be exactly sure how the path of execution got to that point. This is where the Call Stack window in the Script Debugger can help. Take a look at an example.

If you followed along with the previous example and wish to follow along with the next example, restart `WSH_DEBUG_EXAMPLE.VBS` *with a fresh debugging session using the* `//x` *option.*

1. Set a breakpoint on this line of code inside of the `GetScriptPath()` function.

```
strPath = objFSO.GetAbsolutePathName(WScript.ScriptFullName)
```

2. Click the Run option, and the debugger pauses on this line of code.

3. Click the Call Stack option on the View menu. The Call Stack window appears and should look something like Figure 6-20.

Figure 6-20

The call stack reads from the bottom up. (That's why they call it a stack, like a stack of plates or books — first thing in goes on the bottom, last thing in goes on top.) In Figure 6-20, `"VBScript global code"` means that the path of execution started in the *root* of the script, outside of any named procedure or function. Above that, the line with `GetScriptPath` tells you that right now you're in the `GetScriptPath()` function. This simple example does not look like much, but when you have a complex script with many levels of procedures and functions calling each other, the Call Stack window is very helpful for getting your bearings.

Summary

This chapter covered a lot of ground. In the first half of the chapter, you discovered:

❑   Why it is important to care about errors, error handling, and debugging.

❑   The different types of errors a script can encounter: syntax errors, runtime errors, and logic errors.

❑   The three primary VBScript hosts (WSH, IE, and IIS) and how errors and error handling are different between them.

❑   The concept of error handling, which means taking a proactive stance as a programmer to ensure that you are testing risky assumptions and that your script can at least fail gracefully if things go horribly wrong.

❑   The concept of generating custom errors. Strategies for when and how to use `Err.Raise()` were also introduced.

The second half of the chapter moved away from errors and error handling into debugging. Debugging is the process of figuring out the cause of a problem or error in a script, and then taking steps to fix it. One of the most important tools in debugging is a debugger. A debugger is a tool that allows you to interactively execute a program line by line, and lets you see the values of variables and even change them. You discovered:

❑   General debugging terms such as breakpoints, stepping through code, and call stacks.

❑   The various debugging techniques that do not involve a debugging tool.

❑   The freely downloadable Microsoft Script Debugger that you can use with the three major VBScript hosts (WSH, IE, and IIS).

❑   The features that the Script Debugger offers that can help you find problems in a script or just understand the code better. These features are the same no matter which host you are using.

Bugs, errors, exceptions, and failed assumptions are inevitable. If you want your programs to have a professional polish, and if you want to make the process of finding and eliminating the inevitable problems to be as short and painless as possible, this is an important chapter to read. A thorough understanding of errors, error handling, and debugging is the mark of a professional programmer.

7

The Scripting
Runtime Objects

This chapter introduces some powerful objects that are available for use in your VBScript code. You can think of these as utility objects, because they are designed to be reusable in a variety of situations. This chapter also introduces the `Dictionary` object, which is a useful and more versatile replacement for arrays, as well as the family of objects in the `FileSystemObject` hierarchy. The objects in the `FileSystemObject` family offer pretty much everything you need for interacting with the Windows file system.

This chapter starts off with a brief overview of the basic syntax, rules, and recommendations for using objects in VBScript. For those who have been working through the previous chapters on VBScript fundamentals, the first sections of this chapter continue along that course. The rest of the chapter introduces some powerful objects you will find useful in many of your scripts. If you are already familiar with the basics of using objects in VBScript, and if you are looking primarily for how-to information on the runtime objects, you may want to skip ahead to those sections of the chapter.

What Are Runtime Objects?

These objects are described as *runtime objects* because they exist in a separate component, apart from the core VBScript interpreter. They are not an official part of the VBScript language. (In fact, because they are in a separate component — commonly referred to as the "scripting runtime" — they can also be invoked from Visual Basic or any other COM-enabled language.) These runtime objects are automatically available to you pretty much anywhere you would use VBScript, be it in Office, Active Server Pages, or the Windows Script Host. So while it's interesting to know that these runtime objects are not officially part of VBScript, it is not essential knowledge. However, the distinction is helpful given that the official Microsoft scripting documentation has the runtime objects information in a separate section labeled "Script Runtime."

Please note that there are a few other objects that are similar to the runtime objects that this chapter won't be discussing: the built-in VBScript objects. These are referred to as built-in because, unlike the runtime objects, they are an inherent part of VBScript (they are also sometimes called intrinsic objects). However, these objects are covered in detail elsewhere in the book. For information on the built-in Debug *and* Err *objects, please refer to Chapter 6. For information on the built-in* RegExp *object and its cousin the* Match *object, please refer to Chapter 9, which covers regular expressions in detail.*

Object Basics

The next few sections cover some basic concepts for using objects in your VBScript programs. This information will equip you to make use of the scripting runtime objects, but it also pertains equally to objects from other components and hosts.

Creating Objects

Throughout the example scripts in this chapter, you'll use the scripting runtime objects to accomplish various tasks. This section quickly goes over the syntax for creating (also known as *instantiating*) objects. Objects are a bit different than other data types because you must create them explicitly. With a normal numeric variable, for example, you just use the equals (=) operator to put a number into it. With objects, however, you must first use a separate command to create the object, after which you can use the object in your code.

When an object is instantiated, a copy of that type of object is created in memory, with a "pointer" (also known as a *reference*) to the object stored in the variable you have declared for it. You must declare a variable in order to instantiate and store a reference to an object. You use the Set command in conjunction with the CreateObject() function to instantiate an object and store a reference in a declared VBScript variable. Here is an example (CREATE_OBJECT.VBS).

```
Option Explicit

Dim objDict

Set objDict = CreateObject("Scripting.Dictionary")

MsgBox "The Dictionary object holds this many items: " & _
    objDict.Count
```

This code declares a variable to hold the object (objDict), and then uses the Set command and the CreateObject() function to instantiate the object initializing the value of an object variable. This is the only use for the Set command. The call to MsgBox() then displays the value of the object's Count property.

The Set command tells VBScript that you intend to use the objDict variable to store an object reference, but the CreateObject() function actually does the real work of creating the object. Whenever you use CreateObject(), you must pass into it the identifier of the object you want to instantiate (it is often referred to as the *prog id* of the object), in this case "Scripting.Dictionary". Scripting is the name of the library in which the object's class definition is stored (in this case the scripting runtime library), and Dictionary is the formal name of the class. Whenever you want to instantiate an object of a particular type, you just have to know the library and class name of the object (which together comprise the prog id) so that you can pass it to `CreateObject()`. The documentation for any object you want to use should tell you this information.

Not all objects can be instantiated directly in this way. Many libraries, including the scripting runtime, have certain objects that can only be created directly by another object in the library. With these types of objects, you cannot use the `CreateObject()` function to instantiate them. Instead, one of the other objects in the library must create them for you. That is, you can use the objects, but you have to go through an intermediary in order to create them. The `FileSystemObject` is such an intermediary; you'll get into `FileSystemObject` in detail later in this chapter, but for a moment let's jump ahead to give an example of an object type that cannot be directly instantiated: the scripting runtime's `Folder` object. Only the `CreateFolder()` or `GetFolder()` methods of the `FileSystemObject` can create a `Folder` object for you. The following code illustrates how this works using the `GetFolder()` method (`NOT_DIRECTLY_CREATABLE.VBS`).

```
Option Explicit

Dim objFSO
Dim objFolder

Set objFSO = CreateObject("Scripting.FileSystemObject")
Set objFolder = objFSO.GetFolder("C:\")

If objFolder.IsRootFolder Then
    MsgBox "We have opened the root folder."
End If
```

Note that Windows security settings and the permissions assigned to your Windows user account may produce a runtime error trying to open a reference to the root of the C: drive.

Properties and Methods

Objects have two different elements that you can access with your code: properties and methods. A *property* is a special kind of public variable that is attached to an object; it is a placeholder for a value associated with that object. A property may hold any type of data, from strings to numbers to dates. A property may also hold a reference to another object. Some properties are read-only, while others can be set with your code. To find out which ones are read-only and which ones can be changed, you need to familiarize yourself with the object through its documentation.

You saw two examples of properties in the previous section: the `Dictionary` *object's* `Count` *property and the* `Folder` *object's* `IsRootFolder` *property. You'll see more later in this chapter.*

A *method* is simply a procedure or function that is attached to an object. You can call methods just as you would any other procedure or function (see Chapter 4). You saw one example of a method in the last code example from the previous section: the `FileSystemObject`'s `GetFolder()` method, which is a function that returns a `Folder` object.

Just as in the previous examples, when calling a property or method of an object you must use the name of the variable that holds the object, followed by a period, and then by the name of the property or method.

The "With" Keyword

The With keyword is a handy shortcut that can save you some typing. When you are referring to the same object more than once in a block of code, you can surround the block of code with the With...End With construct. Here is an example (WITH_BLOCK.VBS).

```
Option Explicit

Dim objFSO
Dim objFolder
Set objFSO = CreateObject("Scripting.FileSystemObject")
Set objFolder = objFSO.GetFolder("C:\Program Files")

With objFolder
    MsgBox "Here are some properties from the " & _
        "Folder object:" & _
        vbNewLine & vbNewLine & _
        "Path: " & .Path & vbNewLine & _
        "DateCreated: " & .DateCreated & vbNewLine & _
        "DateLastAccessed: " & .DateLastAccessed & _
        vbNewLine & _
        "DateLastModified: " & .DateLastModified
End With
```

Notice how you surround the last block of code with With and End With. In the With statement, you refer to the objFolder object variable, which means that within that block of code you can refer to the Path, DateCreated, DateLastAccessed, and DateLastModified properties without having to refer to the objFolder variable by name each time. The With statement is a convenience that can save you some typing and make your code look a bit cleaner. Using this construct, though, is totally optional.

Objects Can Have Multiple References

Behind the scenes, an object variable does not really contain the copy of the object. The object itself is held elsewhere in the computer's memory, and the variable only holds a reference to the object, not the object itself. The object is stored in a part of memory that the VBScript runtime engine manages. The reason this technical distinction is important is that you need to be aware of when you are dealing with two different objects versus when you are dealing with two references to the same object. Take a look at this example (REF_TWO_OBJECTS.VBS).

```
Option Explicit

Dim objDict1
Dim objDict2

Set objDict1 = CreateObject("Scripting.Dictionary")
Set objDict2 = CreateObject("Scripting.Dictionary")

objDict1.Add "Hello", "Hello"

MsgBox "The first Dictionary object holds this many " & _
    "items: " & objDict1.Count & vbNewLine & _
    "The second Dictionary object holds this many " & _
    "items: " & objDict2.Count
```

This code produces the dialog box shown in Figure 7-1.

Figure 7-1

You have two variables, objDict1 and objDict2, and you use Set and CreateObject() to instantiate two separate Dictionary objects. Then you use the Dictionary object's Add() method to add a string to objDict1 (you'll get to the details of the Dictionary object later in this chapter). Notice, however, that you did not add any items to objDict2. This is reflected in the dialog box, where you see that objDict1 has a Count of 1 whereas objDict2 has a Count of 0, because you did not add anything to objDict2. Now, take a look at this code (REF_ONE_OBJECT.VBS).

```
Option Explicit

Dim objDict1
Dim objDict2

Set objDict1 = CreateObject("Scripting.Dictionary")
Set objDict2 = objDict1
objDict1.Add "Hello", "Hello"

MsgBox "The first Dictionary object holds this many " & _
    "items: " & objDict1.Count & vbNewLine & _
    "The second Dictionary object holds this many " & _
    "items: " & objDict2.Count
```

This code produces the dialog box shown in Figure 7-2.

Figure 7-2

Notice that you only use `CreateObject()` one time, with `objDict1`. The next line is the key line of code in this example.

```
Set objDict2 = objDict1
```

This line sets `objDict2` equal to `objDict1`, which means that two variables are holding references to *the same object*. That is why the `Count` properties of both `objDict1` and `objDict2` have a value of 1, even though you only call the `Add()` method on `objDict1`. Because both variables hold references to the same object, it does not matter which variable you use to make a change to that object — both variables reflect the change.

Object Lifetime and Destroying Objects

When it comes to the issue of variable *lifetime* (see Chapter 4), object variables are a little different than other kinds of variables. The key to understanding this difference lies in the two facts introduced in the previous section of this chapter: First, an object variable only holds a reference to the object, not the object itself; and second, multiple variables can each hold a reference to the same object.

An object stays active in memory as long as one or more variables hold a reference to it. As soon as the *reference count* goes down to zero, the object destroys itself automatically. An object can lose its reference to an object in one of two ways:

❑ If a variable goes out of *scope* (see Chapter 4).

❑ If a line of code explicitly "empties out" the object variable by setting it to the special value of `Nothing`. Take a look at an example (`REF_NOTHING.VBS`).

```
Option Explicit

Dim objDict1
Dim objDict2

Set objDict1 = CreateObject("Scripting.Dictionary")
'The object now exists and has a reference count of 1
Set objDict2 = objDict1
'The object now has a reference count of 2

objDict1.Add "Hello", "Hello"

MsgBox "The first Dictionary object holds this many " & _
    " items: " & objDict1.Count & vbNewLine & _
    "The second Dictionary object holds this many " & _
    "items: " & objDict2.Count

Set objDict1 = Nothing
'The object still exists because objDict2 still
'holds a reference
Set objDict2 = Nothing
'The object's reference count has now gone down to 0,
'so it has been destroyed.
```

As you read this code, follow along with the comments to see the reference count and lifetime of the object. Notice how you use this syntax to eliminate a variable's reference to the object.

```
Set objDict1 = Nothing
```

Nothing is a special value, which you can only use with object variables. By setting an object variable to Nothing, you are basically saying "I don't need this object reference anymore." It is important to note that the two lines of code you added to this script setting the two variables to Nothing are, in this specific example, unnecessary. This is because, as previously mentioned, an object is destroyed automatically when the reference variables naturally go out of scope. objDict1 and objDict2 go out of scope when the script ends, so in this short script the Nothing lines are not necessary.

However, it is important to use Nothing in longer scripts. The principle to keep in mind is that you do not want to have objects in memory any longer than you need them. Objects take up a relatively large amount of resources, so you want to instantiate them right before you need them and destroy them as soon as you don't need them anymore. This example script from Chapter 5 illustrates this principle (FSO_FIND_FILE.VBS from Chapter 5).

```
Option Explicit

Dim objFSO
Dim objRootFolder
Dim objFileLoop
Dim boolFoundIt

Set objFSO = _
    WScript.CreateObject("Scripting.FileSystemObject")
Set objRootFolder = objFSO.GetFolder("C:\")
Set objFSO = Nothing

boolFoundIt = False
For Each objFileLoop In objRootFolder.Files
    If UCase(objFileLoop.Name) = "AUTOEXEC.BAT" Then
        boolFoundIt = True
        Exit For
    End If
Next
Set objFileLoop = Nothing
Set objRootFolder = Nothing

If boolFoundIt Then
    MsgBox "We found your AUTOEXEC.BAT file in " & _
        "the C:\ directory."
Else
    MsgBox "We could not find AUTOEXEC.BAT in " & _
        "the C:\ directory."
End If
```

Note that Windows security settings and the permissions assigned to your Windows user account may produce a runtime error trying to open a reference to the root of the C: drive.

Take a look at this line in relation to the rest of the script.

```
Set objFSO = Nothing
```

189

The reason for this line is that at that point you don't need `objFSO` anymore. The only reason you need it is to call the `GetFolder()` method to get a `Folder` object. Once you have the `Folder` object, `objFSO` is of no more use to you, so you follow the principle of limiting object lifetime as much as possible to `objFSO` to `Nothing`.

> *For more information on the* `Nothing` *keyword, the* `Is Nothing` *statement, and the* `IsObject()` *function, please see Chapter 3.*

The Dictionary Object

Chapter 3 introduced the *array*, which is a unique data type that allows you to store multiple separate values in a single variable. The `Dictionary` object offers similar functionality, but in a different way. You may remember the phone list example from Chapter 3. The phone list was a simple two-dimensional array of names and phone numbers, as shown in the following table. The left column and top row show the subscripts of the array.

	0	1	2
0	Williams	Tony	404-555-6328
1	Carter	Ron	305-555-2514
2	Davis	Miles	212-555-5314
3	Hancock	Herbie	616-555-6943
4	Shorter	Wayne	853-555-0060

One problem with this data structure is that there is not an easy way to search the array — for example, a search for a certain name by phone number or a certain phone number by name. One way is to loop through the whole array and check the appropriate "columns" to see if you've found the "row" you want. There are also other, more advanced, ways to search this array, but they have to be programmed manually.

The `Dictionary` object solves this problem by providing an *associative array*, which means that each item (or "row," if it helps you to think about it that way) in the array has a unique *key* associated with it. So instead of having to search for an item in the dictionary, you can simply ask for it using the key. A `Dictionary` object can hold any type of data, from simple data types such as strings and dates to complex data types such as arrays and objects.

> *This section covers the basics of the* `Dictionary` *object, including an overview and examples. For a complete reference of the* `Dictionary` *object's properties and methods, please consult Appendix F.*

Overview

Let's use the phone list example to show how things can be done differently using a `Dictionary` object instead of an array. In this example, you get a little fancy and store arrays of phone list entries in a dictionary, and for each entry, you use the phone number as the key. This allows you to keep the list information structured (separated into last name, first name, and phone number) while also giving you the ability to find a row quickly using the phone number as the key.

In Chapter 8, which has a discussion on creating your own VBScript classes, you extend the phone list yet again by using a custom PhoneEntry *class for each entry instead of the array.*

This code populates the dictionary with your phone list (DICT_FILL_LIST.VBS).

```
Option Explicit

Const LAST = 0
Const FIRST = 1
Const PHONE = 2

Dim dicPhoneList

Set dicPhoneList = CreateObject("Scripting.Dictionary")
FillPhoneList
Sub FillPhoneList

    Dim strItemAdd(2,0)
    Dim strKey

    'Populate the list, using phone number as the key.
    'Add values to temp array, then add temp
    'array to dictionary.
    strItemAdd(LAST, 0) = "Williams"
    strItemAdd(FIRST, 0) = "Tony"
    strItemAdd(PHONE, 0) = "404-555-6328"
    strKey = strItemAdd(PHONE, 0)
    dicPhoneList.Add strKey, strItemAdd

    strItemAdd(LAST, 0) = "Carter"
    strItemAdd(FIRST, 0) = "Ron"
    strItemAdd(PHONE, 0) = "305-555-2514"
    strKey = strItemAdd(PHONE, 0)
    dicPhoneList.Add strKey, strItemAdd

    strItemAdd(LAST, 0) = "Davis"
    strItemAdd(FIRST, 0) = "Miles"
    strItemAdd(PHONE, 0) = "212-555-5314"
    strKey = strItemAdd(PHONE, 0)
    dicPhoneList.Add strKey, strItemAdd

    strItemAdd(LAST, 0) = "Hancock"
    strItemAdd(FIRST, 0) = "Herbie"
    strItemAdd(PHONE, 0) = "616-555-6943"
    strKey = strItemAdd(PHONE, 0)
    dicPhoneList.Add strKey, strItemAdd

    strItemAdd(LAST, 0) = "Shorter"
    strItemAdd(FIRST, 0) = "Wayne"
    strItemAdd(PHONE, 0) = "853-555-0060"
    strKey = strItemAdd(PHONE, 0)
    dicPhoneList.Add strKey, strItemAdd

End Sub
```

First, you declare some named constants to make the array subscripts more clear. Then you declare a script-level variable called dicPhoneList for the Dictionary, which you instantiate using the CreateObject() function. Then you call the FillPhoneList() procedure, which populates the script-level Dictionary. For each list entry, FillPhoneList() builds a simple array, which you declared as a local variable, sets the key using the phone number, and stores the entry in the Dictionary.

Notice that the Add() method takes two arguments. The first is the key for the item you want to add and the second is the item value itself, in this case an array that holds one phone list entry, including last name, first name, and phone number.

Now, extend this script to do something useful with the Dictionary object (DICT_RETRIEVE_LIST.VBS).

```
Option Explicit

Const LAST = 0
Const FIRST = 1
Const PHONE = 2

Dim dicPhoneList

Set dicPhoneList = CreateObject("Scripting.Dictionary")
FillPhoneList
SearchPhoneList

Sub FillPhoneList

    Dim strItemAdd(2,0)
    Dim strKey

    'Populate the list, using phone number as the key.
    'Add values to temp array, then add temp
    'array to dictionary.

    strItemAdd(LAST, 0) = "Williams"
    strItemAdd(FIRST, 0) = "Tony"
    strItemAdd(PHONE, 0) = "404-985-6328"
    strKey = strItemAdd(PHONE, 0)
    dicPhoneList.Add strKey, strItemAdd

    strItemAdd(LAST, 0) = "Carter"
    strItemAdd(FIRST, 0) = "Ron"
    strItemAdd(PHONE, 0) = "305-781-2514"
    strKey = strItemAdd(PHONE, 0)
    dicPhoneList.Add strKey, strItemAdd

    strItemAdd(LAST, 0) = "Davis"
    strItemAdd(FIRST, 0) = "Miles"
    strItemAdd(PHONE, 0) = "212-555-5314"
    strKey = strItemAdd(PHONE, 0)
    dicPhoneList.Add strKey, strItemAdd

    strItemAdd(LAST, 0) = "Hancock"
    strItemAdd(FIRST, 0) = "Herbie"
    strItemAdd(PHONE, 0) = "616-555-6943"
```

```
        strKey = strItemAdd(PHONE, 0)
        dicPhoneList.Add strKey, strItemAdd

        strItemAdd(LAST, 0) = "Shorter"
        strItemAdd(FIRST, 0) = "Wayne"
        strItemAdd(PHONE, 0) = "853-555-0060"
        strKey = strItemAdd(PHONE, 0)
        dicPhoneList.Add strKey, strItemAdd

End Sub

Sub SearchPhoneList

Dim strPhone
    Dim strItemRead

    strPhone = InputBox("Please enter a phone number " & _
        "(XXX-XXX-XXXX) with which to search the list.")

    If dicPhoneList.Exists(strPhone) Then
        strItemRead = dicPhoneList.Item(strPhone)
        MsgBox "We found that entry:" & vbNewLine & _
            vbNewLine & _
            "Last: " & strItemRead(LAST,0) & vbNewLine & _
            "First: "& strItemRead(FIRST,0) & vbNewLine & _
            "Phone: " & strItemRead(PHONE,0)
    Else
        MsgBox "That number was not found in the " & _
                "phone list."
    End If

End Sub
```

A new procedure has been added, called SearchPhoneList(), which asks the user for a phone number in the proper format, and checks the dictionary to see if there is an entry for that number. If there is, the code displays the entry in a dialog box. You use the Exists() method to check if the number was used as a key value in the dictionary. Exists() returns a Boolean True if the key has a match in the dictionary, False if not. If Exists() returns True, then the code can use the Item property with confidence to retrieve the phone list entry.

Notice that when you retrieve the array from the dictionary, you put it into a variable (strItemRead) *before* you start using the array subscripts to get the values from inside the array. This is an optional technique, but one that makes your code a little easier to read. It's optional because VBScript can figure out for you that there is an array stored in the dictionary item without you having to feed the array into the strItemRead "holding variable" first. The following alternative syntax achieves the exact same result without the extra variable:

```
If dicPhoneList.Exists(strPhone) Then
    With dicPhoneList
        MsgBox "We found that entry:" & vbNewLine & _
            vbNewLine & _
            "Last: " & .Item(strPhone)(LAST,0) & _
```

(continued)

```
                    vbNewLine & _
                    "First: " & .Item(strPhone)(FIRST,0) & _
                    vbNewLine & _
                    "Phone: " & .Item(strPhone)(PHONE,0)

        End With
    Else
        MsgBox "That number was not found in the " & _
            "phone list."
    End If
```

This is the key syntax in this example (notice that the code at this point is inside of a `With` block).

```
.Item(strPhone)(LAST,0)
```

Because you know in advance that there is an array stored in the dictionary, you can just follow the call to the `Item` property with the array subscripts you want. VBScript does the work behind the scenes. The "holding variable" is optional. Different programmers will prefer one convention over the other, and you can choose whichever you prefer.

Three Different Ways to Add

Let's look at some additional syntactic variations that are possible with the `Dictionary` object. All of the following are valid ways to add a new item to a dictionary.

```
dicAnimals.Add "12345", "Cat"

dicAnimals.Item("45678") = "Dog"

dicAnimals("98765") = "Goldfish"
```

The first line is the syntax that's been demonstrated already, using the `Add()` method. This is the most explicit syntax, but somehow not as much fun as the methods used in the second or third lines, which both take advantage of two particular behaviors of the `Dictionary` object: one, because `Item` is a property (as opposed to a method), you can bypass the `Add()` method and just set the `Item` property directly using the equals operator (=); and the other, if you pass a key value to the `Item` property that is *not* found in the `Dictionary`, the `Dictionary` object adds that key to the list behind the scenes.

Behavior number two makes possible the syntax in those second and third lines. However, this trick is a double-edged sword. This same behavior also holds true when you are simply *reading* from the `Item` property. If you use a line such as the following to retrieve a value from a dictionary, and the key you pass in does not exist in the dictionary already, then you just added an empty item to the dictionary even though you probably did not intend to.

```
strAnimalName = dicAnimals.Item("72645")
```

That is why it is important to use the `Exists()` method first to ensure that the key you are about to use is really in the dictionary.

```
If dicAnimals.Exists("72645") Then
    strAnimalName = dicAnimals.Item("72645")
End If
```

One could certainly argue in favor of the idea that this is a poor design choice, but that's the way it works.

Finally, going back to that third syntax of adding to a dictionary:

```
dicAnimals("98765") = "Goldfish"
```

What this syntax is taking advantage of is the fact that the Item property is the *default property* of the Dictionary object. When a property is an object's default property, referring to it by name is optional. The second syntax refers to it by name, and the third takes the shortcut. All three of these syntactical conventions are valid and acceptable.

The CompareMode Property

The CompareMode property controls which "mode" the dictionary's Item property uses when comparing key values for equality. The options are "Text" (1; vbTextCompare; the default), "Binary" (0; vbBinaryCompare), and "Database" (2; vbDatabaseCompare).

The main thing you have to think about when it comes to the CompareMode property is whether or not you want your key comparisons in the Item method to be case-sensitive. If case-*in*sensitive is fine, then you can accept the default value of vbTextCompare (1). If, on the other hand, you want comparisons to be case-sensitive, change this property to vbBinaryCompare (0). Take a look at the following code:

```
dicAnimals.Add "abc", "Cat"
dicAnimals.Add "def", "Dog"
dicAnimals.Add "ABC", "Goldfish"
```

If you use vbTextCompare, then the third line of this code will produce an error stating that you are trying to add a duplicate key to the dictionary. This will occur because with vbTextCompare, "abc" and "ABC" are seen as equivalent. If, however, you use vbBinaryCompare, then the third line will *not* produce an error because "abc" and "ABC" are seen as distinct values.

The Item Property

You've seen the Item property in action in several of the earlier examples. Item is the gateway to the data storage inside the Dictionary object. To read from the Item property, you can access it directly with a particular key, or you can *enumerate* the Items collection with a For Each loop to access each dictionary item in order. Item can be used in three ways:

❑   To add a new item to the dictionary; if key value is not already in the dictionary, it is added automatically

❑   To update the value of an item already in the dictionary

❑   To read or retrieve the value of an item already in the dictionary

Whenever accessing the Item property directly (as opposed to indirectly through enumeration with a For Each loop), you must pass the Key argument, which can be any unique string or integer. The key value determines from which item in the dictionary it writes or reads.

The following is an example syntax for the `Item` property:

```
'Add an item to the dictionary
dicAnimals.Item("1234") = "Cat"

'Update an item already in the dictionary
dicAnimals.Item("1234") = "Feline"

'Read an item from the dictionary
strAnimalName = dicAnimals.Item("1234")
```

`Item` is the default property, which means that referring to it by name is optional.

The Exists Method

You can use the `Exists()` method to check if a key is already in the dictionary. If you are not positive that the key is in the dictionary, it is important to use the `Exists()` method before reading from the `Item` property. This is because the `Item` property adds the key if there is not a match. It is also wise to check the `Exists()` method before calling the `Remove()` method, because `Remove()` raises an error if the key does not exist in the dictionary.

In this example given previously in this chapter, you check `Exists()` before accessing `Item`.

```
If dicAnimals.Exists("72645") Then
    strAnimalName = dicAnimals.Item("72645")
End If
```

If you are developing or supporting a classic ASP web site, consider investigating Microsoft's obscure, but useful, `LookupTable` object. It is an alternative to the `Dictionary` object that offers similar functionality, with the added advantage of being "free threaded," which means that it can be safely attached to the ASP `Application` or `Session` variables; in fact, programmers at Microsoft created the `LookupTable` expressly for that purpose.

The FileSystemObject Library

The remainder of this chapter is dedicated to the `FileSystemObject` (FSO) library. This chapter does not contain a complete and detailed reference for all of the FSO objects, properties, and methods. Appendix F does, however, contain a complete reference. If you need quick lookup for a particular property or method, Appendix F is the place. As for the current chapter, the following sections start with an overview of the FSO library, after which they demonstrate, including example code, some common tasks such as opening and reading a text file; writing to a text file; and creating and copying files and folders.

Why FileSystemObject?

Quite often scripts need the ability to create a file, read a file, find a file or folder, check for the existence of a certain drive, and so on. For security reasons, none of this functionality is built into the core VBScript language. However, all of this functionality and more are available from the scripting runtime's `FileSystemObject` library. The `FileSystemObject` is a kind of "master object" that serves as the access point for a family of objects. All of the objects in the FileSystemObject hierarchy work together to provide functionality for accessing and manipulating the Windows file system.

The FileSystemObject (FSO) is intended for use with the Windows Script Host, Active Server Pages, and other "safe" hosts. By default, access to the FileSystemObject is blocked from scripts running inside of the Internet Explorer browser. These security settings can be changed to allow browser scripts to use the FileSystemObject, but it is not recommended that you do so. It is also not recommended that you ask your users to do so.

The FSO object model consists of the objects and collections shown in the following table.

Object or Collection	Description
FileSystemObject	This is the main, or "root," object. To use any of the FSO objects, you must first create a FileSystemObject, at which point you can use its properties and methods to perform various functions and access the other objects. Example properties and methods: CopyFile, CreateFolder, FileExists, Drives.
Drive	A Drive object represents a logical or physical drive mapped on the host computer. The drive can be a hard disk, CD-ROM drive, or even a RAM drive. Example properties and methods: DriveLetter, AvailableSpace, RootFolder.
Drives	A Drives Collection is a child of FileSystemObject and holds zero or more Drives objects. The only way to obtain a reference to a valid Drives object is through the FileSystemObject .Drives property. All drives are included, regardless of type. Removable-media drives do not need to have media inserted to appear. Drives has two properties: Count and Item.
File	A File object represents a file that exists in a folder on a drive. There are two ways to obtain a File object: One is from the FileSystemObject.GetFile() method and the other is from the Folder.Files collection. The File object is easily confused with the TextStream object, which represents a stream of text going into or coming out of a file, but not the file itself. Example properties and methods: DateCreated, ParentFolder, Copy, Delete.
Files	The Files collection is a child of the Folder object. The only way to obtain a valid Files object is through the Folder.Files property. This collection has only two properties: Count and Item.
Folder	A Folder represents a folder on a drive. You can obtain a reference to a Folder object through the Drive.RootFolder and the CreateFolder(), GetFolder(), and GetSpecialFolder() methods of FileSystemObject. Example properties and methods: IsRootFolder, ParentFolder, Drive, Files, SubFolders.

(continued)

Object or Collection	Description
Folders	The Folders collection stores a list of Folders objects. You can obtain a Folders object only through the Folder.SubFolders property. This collection has only two properties and one method: Count, Item, and Add. The Add() method allows you to add a new subfolder (as a Folder object) to the collection.
TextStream	A TextStream object represents a series of text, either being read from a file, written to a file, or going to or coming from the Windows "standard I/O." You can obtain a TextStream object via the File.OpenAsTextStream() and Folder.CreateTextFile() methods, as well as the CreateTextFile(), OpenTextFile(), and GetStandardStream() methods of FileSystemObject. Internally, a TextStream object has a line pointer and a character pointer. When reading or writing a file as a TextStream, you move through the file from top to bottom *only once*, character-by-character and/or line-by-line. Example properties and methods: Read, Write, ReadLine, WriteLine, AtEndOfLine.

Using Collections

The FileSystemObject hierarchy contains a few Collection type objects — a subject not yet discussed. What is a Collection? A Collection is a special type of object much like the Dictionary object, in that it stores a key-indexed group of data. VBScript does not natively support generic Collection objects, but many COM-based libraries, such as the scripting runtime discussed in this chapter, will use Collection objects. In other words, VBScript does not let you create your own Collection objects, but it supports the use of Collection objects defined in other COM libraries.

There is no real mystery to a Collection if you already understand the Dictionary. Like Dictionary, Collection has Count and Item properties, and you can enumerate the Item property using a For Each loop. However, Collection does not have some of the niceties of the Dictionary such as the Exists() and RemoveAll() methods. You'll see examples of the syntax throughout the remainder of this chapter as we discuss FSO collections such as Drives, Folders, and Files.

Understanding FileSystemObject

The FSO objects are a little strange to some programmers at first because the root object, FileSystemObject, is the access point for everything else. Before you can do anything with drives or folders or files, you must first create a FileSystemObject. Either directly or indirectly, for everything you want, you have to start by going through FileSystemObject. Take a look at the properties, and especially, methods of FileSystemObject and you will see all of the tasks it can perform and data it can provide.

The most important thing to keep in mind is that if you want access to any object other than FileSystemObject itself, then you have to get that object directly or indirectly through one or more of the properties and methods of FileSystemObject. Sometimes you have to "drill down" through the levels of objects to get what you want, and at other times, FileSystemObject will have a method that does exactly what you need.

The next two examples accomplish the same task. The goal is to locate the AUTOEXEC.BAT file and display the date and time it was last changed. This first example uses an indirect, drill-down methodology (GET_AUTOEXEC_1.VBS).

```
Option Explicit

Dim objFSO
Dim objCDrive
Dim objRootFolder
Dim objFileLoop
Dim objAutoExecFile
Set objFSO = CreateObject("Scripting.FileSystemObject")
Set objCDrive = objFSO.GetDrive("C")
Set objRootFolder = objCDrive.RootFolder

For Each objFileLoop in objRootFolder.Files
    If UCase(objFileLoop.Name) = "AUTOEXEC.BAT" Then
        Set objAutoExecFile = objFileLoop
        Exit For
    End If
Next

If IsObject(objAutoExecFile) Then
    MsgBox "The autoexec.bat was last changed on: "& _
        objAutoExecFile.DateLastModified
Else
    MsgBox "Could not find autoexec.bat."
End If
```

This code starts at the top of the hierarchy, drills into the drive level, the folder level, and then the file level — a lot of trouble to find one file, especially when you know right where the file should be. But there is a much simpler way to solve the same problem, one that takes advantage of the direct method provided by FileSystemObject (GET_AUTOEXEC_2.VBS).

```
Option Explicit

Dim objFSO
Dim objAutoExecFile

Set objFSO = CreateObject("Scripting.FileSystemObject")
Set objAutoExecFile = objFSO.GetFile("C:\autoexec.bat")

MsgBox "The autoexec.bat was last changed on: "& _
    objAutoExecFile.DateLastModified
```

If you find yourself going to a lot of trouble to accomplish a task, take a step back, look through the various FSO objects, properties, and methods and you might find a more direct way.

Creating a Folder

There are two different ways to create a folder. Which one you choose depends on what you are doing otherwise in your script. If you are already working with a `Folder` object that represents the folder in which you want to create the new folder, you can use the `Folder.SubFolders.Add()` method, like so (FSO_CREATE_FOLDER.VBS):

```
Option Explicit

Dim FSO
Dim objFolder

Set FSO = CreateObject("Scripting.FileSystemObject")
Set objFolder = FSO.GetFolder("C:\")
If Not FSO.FolderExists("C:\TestVBScriptFolder") Then
    objFolder.SubFolders.Add "TestVBScriptFolder"
    MsgBox "The C:\TestVBScriptFolder folder was " & _
        "created successfully."

End If
```

If you run this script on your computer, you can run the FSO_CLEANUP.VBS *script to remove the folder that was created.*

The preceding example, as mentioned, is the most practical if you already have a `Folder` object that you are working with. However, there is a quicker way to create a new folder if you don't otherwise have any need for a `Folder` object. The following code simply uses the `FileSystemObject.CreateFolder()` method (FSO_CREATE_FOLDER_QUICK.VBS):

```
Option Explicit

Dim FSO

Set FSO = CreateObject("Scripting.FileSystemObject")

FSO.CreateFolder("C:\TestVBScriptFolder")

MsgBox "The C:\TestVBScriptFolder folder was " & _
    "created successfully."
```

Note: If you run this script on your computer, you can run the FSO_CLEANUP.VBS *script to remove the folder that was created.*

This script accomplishes the same thing but without using the `Folder` object. As mentioned previously, with FSO, you can often perform the same task using one of `FileSystemObject`'s methods or one of the other FSO objects.

Copying a File

Copying a file is pretty simple. The `FileSystemObject` object has a method called `CopyFile()` exactly for this purpose. The following script copies a file that is assumed to exist in the same directory as the script file (`FSO_COPY_FILE.VBS`). If you downloaded all of the code for this chapter in the same directory, the file you are copying should be there.

```
Option Explicit

Dim FSO

Set FSO = CreateObject("Scripting.FileSystemObject")

If FSO.FileExists("TEST_INPUT_FILE.TXT") Then
    FSO.CopyFile "TEST_INPUT_FILE.TXT", _
        "TEST_INPUT_FILE_COPY.TXT", True
End If
```

If you run this script on your computer, you can run the `FSO_CLEANUP.VBS` *script to remove the file that was created.*

Notice that you check `FileExists()` first because if the file you are copying does not exist, then `CopyFile()` raises an error. Also notice that you have passed `True` for the `overwrite` argument, which means that you want to overwrite the file if it already exists. If you did not want to overwrite it, you would want to use `FileExists()` to check first.

The previous example assumes that the source and destination are both in the same directory as the script. You can also use full pathnames for both the file being copied and the target file.

```
FSO.CopyFile "\\ A_Network_Folder\Customers.xls", _
    "C:\MyFolder\Spreadsheets\Customers.xls", True
```

You can also omit the filename from the target path if you want to use the same filename. In fact, omitting the filename is a requirement if you use wildcard characters in the source path:

```
FSO.CopyFile "\\A_Network_Folder\*.xls", _
    "C:\MyFolder\Spreadsheets\", True
```

Notice the trailing backslash (\) that you have on the target path. This is critical because it signals the `CopyFile()` method that `Spreadsheets` is a folder. Without the trailing backslash, `CopyFile()` assumes that `Spreadsheets` is a file you want it to create. Note also that wildcard characters are not allowed for the target path.

After you have copied a file, you can access it using either the `FileSystemObject.GetFile()` method (which returns a `File` object) or find the file in the `Folder.Files` collection. Or, if the file you've copied is a text file and you need to read from or write to the file, you can open it as a `TextStream` (see the "Reading a Text File" and "Writing to a Text File" sections later in this chapter).

Copying a Folder

Copying a folder is much like copying a file, but it's a bit more complex because a folder can contain multiple items, including subfolders and files. Also, you might want to copy more than one folder, in which case you may be able to use wildcard characters to identify the folders you want to copy. Here is a simple example:

```
Option Explicit

Dim FSO

Set FSO = CreateObject("Scripting.FileSystemObject")

If FSO.FolderExists("C:\TestVBScriptFolder") Then
    FSO.CopyFolder "C:\TestVBScriptFolder", _
        "C:\Program Files\", True
End If
```

If you run this script on your computer, you can run the FSO_CLEANUP.VBS *script to remove the folder that was created.*

Because you did not include any wildcard characters in the source path, the CopyFolder() method assumes that TestVBScriptFolder is the one you want to copy, and it looks for a folder with exactly that name. If, however, you had wanted to copy any folders in the C:\ folder that start with the string TestVBScript, you could use wildcard characters.

```
FSO.CopyFolder "C:\TestVBScript*", _"C:\Program Files\", True
```

However, it is important to understand that the wildcard characters used with the CopyFolder() method are *only* used to match folders — not files. If you want to copy some files and not others, then you must use the CopyFile() method (see previous section).

You also have to be careful when copying folders with multiple files and subfolders into an existing hierarchy of identical folders and files. If any of those folders and files have the read-only attribute turned on, then the CopyFolder() method will raise an error, even if you pass True for the overwrite argument. If you suspect that some target folders or files might have the read-only attribute turned on, you can use the Folder.Attributes and/or File.Attributes property to check first (see Appendix F).

Reading a Text File

It is often necessary to open a text file and either retrieve a specific piece of data from it, or simply feed the entire file contents into another data structure. This section looks at examples for both of these situations. Both of the scripts in this section assume that a file called TEST_INPUT_FILE.TXT exists in the same directory as the scripts. If you downloaded all of the code for this chapter, you should have everything you need.

You can see the contents of TEST_INPUT_FILE.TXT as follows. Each field is separated by a tab character. Each line ends with a standard Windows end-of-line character-pair.

```
OrderID=456    CustID=123    ItemID=765
OrderID=345    CustID=987    ItemID=149
OrderID=207    CustID=923    ItemID=592
```

The first example opens this file and looks for a specific piece of data (FSO_READ_FILE_SEEK.VBS). Much of the code here has to do with parsing the data in the file, so if you want to focus on how you actually open and read the file, follow the objStream variable, which holds a TextStream object. The interesting part of this code is in the GetCustIDForOrder() function, which opens a text file, searches for some particular data, and returns it.

```
Option Explicit

Const ORDER_ID_TO_FIND = "345"
Dim strCustID

strCustID = ""
strCustID = GetCustIDForOrder(ORDER_ID_TO_FIND)
If strCustID <> "" Then
    MsgBox "The CustomerID for Order "& _
        ORDER_ID_TO_FIND & " is: " & strCustID
Else
    MsgBox "We could not find OrderID "& _
        ORDER_ID_TO_FIND & "."
End If

Function GetCustIDForOrder(strOrderIDSeek)

    Const TristateFalse = 0
    Const ForReading = 1
    Const ORDER_FIELD = "OrderID="
    Const CUST_FIELD = "CustID="
    Const FILE_NAME = "TEST_INPUT_FILE.TXT"

    Dim FSO
    Dim objStream
    Dim strLine
    Dim lngFirstTab
    Dim lngSecondTab
    Dim strOrderID
    Dim strCustID

    strCustID = ""

    Set FSO = CreateObject("Scripting.FileSystemObject")

    If FSO.FileExists(FILE_NAME) Then
        Set objStream = FSO.OpenTextFile(FILE_NAME, _
            ForReading, False, TristateFalse)
    Else
        MsgBox "Could not find " & FILE_NAME & "."
        GetCustIDForOrder = ""
        Exit Function
    End If

    Do While Not objStream.AtEndOfStream
        strLine = objStream.ReadLine
        lngFirstTab = InStr(Len(ORDER_FIELD), strLine, _
            vbTab, vbBinaryCompare)
        strOrderID = Mid(strLine, Len(ORDER_FIELD) + 1, _
            lngFirstTab - Len(ORDER_FIELD) - 1)
        If strOrderID = strOrderIDSeek Then
```

(continued)

```
                lngSecondTab = InStr(lngFirstTab + 1, strLine, _
                    vbTab, vbBinaryCompare)
                strCustID = Mid(strLine, lngFirstTab + _
                    Len(CUST_FIELD) + 1, _
                    lngSecondTab - (lngFirstTab + _
                    Len(CUST_FIELD)))
            Exit Do
        End If
    Loop
objStream.Close
    GetCustIDForOrder = strCustID

End Function
```

After using `FileExists()` to ensure that your input file is where you expect it to be, you use this line to open the file as a `TextStream` object:

```
Set objStream = FSO.OpenTextFile("TEST_INPUT_FILE.TXT", _
    ForReading, False, TristateFalse)
```

You tell the `OpenTextFile()` method which file you want to open, that you want to open it for reading (as opposed to writing), that you don't want to create it if it does not exist, and that you want to open it in ASCII mode. (Please see Appendix F for a detailed explanation of these arguments.) After this point, you have an open `TextStream` object in your `objStream` variable. The line pointer and the character position pointer are both at the beginning of the file. When processing a file, you have three options:

❑   Use the `ReadAll()` method to feed the entire file into a string variable, after which you can parse the variable using a variety of methods.

❑   Use a loop and the `Read()` method to move through the file, one character at a time.

❑   Use a loop and the `ReadLine()` method to move through the file one line at a time, parsing each line as necessary.

Which method you choose depends on what is in the file, how it is structured (if it is structured), and what you need to do with the data. The example file is structured as a series of fields that repeat on a line-by-line basis. So this example opted to use the `ReadLine()` method:

```
Do While Not objStream.AtEndOfStream
    strLine = objStream.ReadLine
    ...<<code ommitted>>...
Loop
objStream.Close
```

By setting up the `Do` loop this way, you ensure two things: one, that you start the loop only if the opened file is not totally empty; and the other, that looping stops once the last line of the file has been read. The other thing that makes this work is that when the `ReadLine` method is called, the line pointer in `objStream` automatically moves ahead by one. A `TextStream` object always moves the pointers ahead automatically as you read the file. Finally, notice that you call the `Close()` method on the `TextStream` object as soon as you're done with it; it's a good idea to call the `Close()` method for any file you open.

We'll only comment briefly on these lines, which we omitted from the previous code snippet of the `ReadLine` loop.

```
    lngFirstTab = InStr(Len(ORDER_FIELD), strLine, _
        vbTab, vbBinaryCompare)
    strOrderID = Mid(strLine, Len(ORDER_FIELD) + 1, _
        lngFirstTab - Len(ORDER_FIELD) - 1)
    If strOrderID = strOrderIDSeek Then
        lngSecondTab = InStr(lngFirstTab + 1, strLine, _
            vbTab, vbBinaryCompare)
        strCustID = Mid(strLine, lngFirstTab + _
            Len(CUST_FIELD) + 1, _
            lngSecondTab - (lngFirstTab + _
            Len(CUST_FIELD)))
        Exit Do
    End If
End If
```

What's happening here is that you're using the `InStr()`, `Mid()`, and `Len()` functions to parse the contents of each line, looking for specific known field markers. Other similar functions such as `Left()` and `Right()` are useful also, depending on the situation. You can learn about the details of how these functions work in Appendix A.

The particular techniques employed in this code depend on the fact that you know how the file should be structured. You know the field names and the fact that the field delimiter is the tab character. For a production-quality script, you would also want to include some defensive code to ensure graceful handling of files that are not formatted as expected.

Writing to a Text File

Creating a new text file is about as straightforward as reading from one. The steps are simple: Open a new text file in a specified location, write data to it, and close the file. All of this is done through the `TextStream` object. This simply demonstrates the three steps (`FSO_CREATE_FILE.VBS`):

```
Option Explicit

Dim FSO
Dim objStream

Const TristateFalse = 0
Const FILE_NAME = "CREATE_FILE_TEST.TXT"

Set FSO = CreateObject("Scripting.FileSystemObject")

Set objStream = FSO.CreateTextFile(FILE_NAME, _
    True, TristateFalse)

With objStream
    .WriteLine "Test Line 1"
    .WriteLine "Test Line 2"
    .WriteLine "Test Line 3"
    .Close
End With

MsgBox "Successfully created " & FILE_NAME & "."
```

If you run this script on your computer, you can run the FSO_CLEANUP.VBS *script to remove the file that was created.*

Because in this case you're creating a new, blank text file, you use the FileSystemObject .CreateTextFile() method. You pass True for the overwrite argument so that if a file of the same name is already there, it's replaced by the new file. Then you use the TextStream.WriteLine() method to add one line at a time to the file. You could have also used the Write() method to add the data all at once or a little bit at a time (adding multiple lines at once if you'd liked). The WriteBlankLines() method is also available. Finally, you use the Close() method to close the file.

Sometimes you need to write to a file that already exists rather than create a new one. Unfortunately, the TextStream object, as is, only supports two ways to write to an existing file: one, appending data to the end of an existing text file, and the other, starting at the beginning of an existing file, which throws out all existing data in the file. The following example demonstrates how to append to an existing file. As for the ability to start writing at the beginning (which unfortunately means you also have to throw out all existing data in the file), this is of course not that useful; you might as well just use CreateTextFile() to open a new blank file.

So let's take a look at an example of appending to an existing file (FSO_APPEND_FILE.VBS). This script assumes that you have run FSO_CREATE_FILE.VBS first.

```
Option Explicit

Dim FSO
Dim objStream

Const ForAppending = 8
Const TristateFalse = 0
Const FILE_NAME = "CREATE_FILE_TEST.TXT"

Set FSO = CreateObject("Scripting.FileSystemObject")

If Not FSO.FileExists(FILE_NAME) Then
    MsgBox "Could not find " & FILE_NAME & ". "& _
        "Please run FSO_CREATE_FILE.VBS first."
Else
    Set objStream = FSO.OpenTextFile(FILE_NAME, _
        ForAppending, False, TristateFalse)

    With objStream
        .WriteLine "Appended Line 1"
        .WriteLine "Appended Line 2"
        .WriteLine "Appended Line 3"
        .Close
    End With

    MsgBox "Successfully appended to " & FILE_NAME & "."
End If
```

This code is very similar to the code for creating a new text file. Instead of using CreateTextFile(), you use OpenTextFile(), passing it the ForAppending value for the iomode argument (see Appendix F). Then you use the WriteLine() and Close() methods just as before. Adding new data to the file is basically the same as for creating a new file, except that you are instead adding to the end of an existing file. In some cases, you might prefer to get all of the new data into a single string variable and passing to the `Write()` *method.*

There are two common writing-related tasks that the `TextStream` object *does not* support: inserting data at the beginning of an existing file, and adding data somewhere in the middle of an existing file. To accomplish these, you have to write some code of your own to open the file for reading, get the contents into one or more variables, close the file, add or remove whatever data you need, and then write it all back as a new file.

Summary

This chapter started with an overview of the basic syntax and techniques for using objects in VBScript. This overview included an explanation of the `CreateObject()` function, object lifetime reference counts, and object destruction.

This chapter also introduced the scripting runtime objects, which is a set of objects that exist in a separate library apart from core VBScript, but which are available almost anywhere VBScript can be hosted. The scripting runtime is divided into the `Dictionary` object and the `FileSystemObject`, which acts as the gateway to a family of related objects. The focus in this chapter was to explain why these objects are useful, how they are designed, and how to perform common tasks. For a complete reference of the scripting runtime objects, please consult Appendix F.

The `Dictionary` object provides an associated array, allowing you to store a series of data of any type: strings, numbers, arrays, objects, and so on. Each item added to a `Dictionary` object must be given a key value, which must be unique within the dictionary. The key can then be used to retrieve the item from the dictionary later.

The `FileSystemObject` library offers a variety of objects that allow you to interact with the Windows file system. Features include: creating and editing text files; creating folders; copying, moving, and deleting files and folders; "drilling down" into the hierarchy of drives, folders, subfolders, and files; reading file attributes; and more.

Classes in VBScript (Writing Your Own COM Objects)

Even though the feature has existed for some time, most people don't know that you can define classes in VBScript. This gives VBScript programmers a powerful tool, especially in more extensive script-based projects. Granted, classes defined in VBScript do not have the more properly object-oriented capability of Java, C++, VB.NET, or even Visual Basic 6, but they do let the VBScript programmer take advantage of a few of the object oriented benefits available when programming in those other languages.

If you've skipped previous chapters and are not familiar with how to use COM objects from VBScript, then you might benefit from reading the first sections of Chapter 7 before tackling this chapter. This chapter assumes that you are familiar with the basics of instantiating objects and calling their properties and methods.

Objects, Classes, and Components

Before you get too far into how to write your own classes in VBScript, and where you can make use of them, this section covers some terminology. Few technical terms in recent years have been misused, obscured, morphed, and confused more than *class*, *object*, and *component*. Often the terms are used interchangeably, even though they do have distinct meanings. This lack of clarity drives object-oriented purists crazy, but it also makes these waters difficult for beginners to navigate. Let's clear the fog a little bit.

In the strict sense, an *object* is an in-memory representation of a complex data and programming structure that can exist only while a program is running. A good analogy is an array, which is also a complex data structure that exists only at runtime. When in a programming context you refer to an array, it is clear to most people that you mean the in-memory data structure. Unfortunately, when programmers use the word object, it is not always clear that they are using the strict definition of the term, referring to a construct in memory at runtime.

An object is different from an array in several ways, the most important being that unlike an array an object does more than just store complex data (in the form of *properties*); objects also have "behavior" — that is, "things it knows how do when asked" — which are exposed as *methods*. Properties can store any kind of data, and methods can be either procedures or functions. The idea of bringing the data and the behavior together in an object is that you can design your program so that the data that needs to be manipulated and the code that manipulates it are close to each other.

A *class* is a template for an object. Whereas an object exists only in memory at runtime, a class is a programming construct that you can only work on directly at design time. A class is the code, and an object is the use of that code while a program is running. If you want to use an object at runtime, you have to first define a class at design time. Objects are created at runtime based on templates that classes provide. (These are all different ways of saying the same thing.) For example, you could write a class called `Customer`. Once the class definition is saved, you could then use other code to create a thousand `Customer` objects in memory. This concept is illustrated in Figure 8-1.

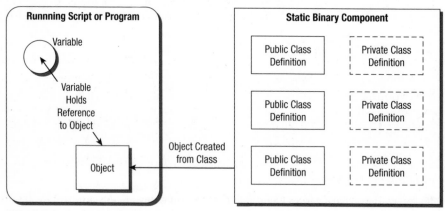

Figure 8-1

Many people, however, use the terms *class* and *object* interchangeably, like so: "I coded the Customer object, and then created a thousand Customer objects and sorted them by total sales." As mentioned, this can create some confusion for beginners, but over time you can learn to use the context to figure out what is meant.

A *component* is nothing more than a packaging mechanism, a way of compiling one or more related classes into a binary file that can be distributed to one or more computers. You can see that the classes used to create the object in Figure 8-1 are stored inside of a component. In the Windows operating system, a component usually takes the form of a `.DLL` or `.OCX` file. The scripting runtime library introduced in Chapter 7 is a perfect example of a component. When a programmer writes some classes that are related to each other in some way, and he or she wants people to use those classes to create objects at runtime, she would probably package and distribute the classes as a component. A single program or script might make use of dozens of different classes from different components.

Components are not the only way to make use of classes, however. Figure 8-1 shows only one possible scenario (albeit a very common one). In a Visual Basic application, for example, you can write classes that are compiled within the application itself, and are never exposed to the outside world. The classes exist only inside that application, and the sole purpose is to serve the needs of that application. In that case, you would tend not to consider those classes to be part of the component, because they are not exposed publicly.

People are finding that it is often much more productive and forward thinking to package their classes into a component that can exist outside of the application. The thinking is that you might find a use for one or more of those classes later, and having them in a more portable component makes them much easier to reuse. In VBScript, you can use both techniques: You can create classes within a script that only that script can use (which is covered in this chapter), or you can package your classes as a Windows Script Component (see Chapter 16).

The Class Statement

The key to creating VBScript classes is the `Class` statement. Similar to the way the `Function...End Function` or `Sub...End Sub` statement pairs block off the boundaries of a procedure, the `Class` and `End Class` statements block off the boundaries of a class. You can use multiple blocks of `Class...End Class` blocks in a single script file to define multiple classes (however, classes cannot be nested in VBScript).

If you are coming to VBScript from another language, you are probably accustomed to defining classes in their own separate files. However, this is not the case with VBScript classes. In general, you must define a VBScript class in the same script file as the script code that creates an instance of it.

This may seem like a pretty big limitation — because part of the purpose of creating a class is easy code portability and centralized reuse — but there are two other options.

- ❏ You can package one or more VBScript classes in a Windows Script Component, discussed in detail in Chapter 16.

- ❏ You can use the Active Server Pages (ASP) # `INCLUDE` directive to store a class definition in one file and include it in multiple ASP pages. VBScript classes in your ASP scripts are discussed in Chapter 20.

In this chapter, however, we're limiting the discussion of classes to those defined within the same script file as the code that makes use of the class.

Other than this same-script-file difference, Visual Basic programmers will not have any trouble adjusting to VBScript classes. Except for the differences between the Visual Basic and VBScript languages, the structure and techniques for VBScript classes are pretty much the same as for Visual Basic. Here is the fundamental syntax for the `Class` statement.

```
Class MyClass

    <rest of the class code will go here>

End Class
```

You would, of course, replace `MyClass` with the name of the class you are defining. This class name must be unique within the script file, as well as within any classes that are brought into the same scope through "include directives." The class name must also not be the same as any of the VBScript reserved words (such as `Function` or `While`).

Defining Properties

When a script creates an object based on a class, properties are the mechanisms through which data is stored and accessed. Through properties, data can be either stored in the object or retrieved from the object.

Private Property Variables

The best way to store the value of a property is in a private property variable. This is a variable that is defined at the class level (at the beginning of the class). This variable is private (that is, it is not directly accessible to code outside of the class) and holds the actual value of the property. Code that is using a class will use `Property Let`, `Set`, and `Get` procedures to interact with the property, but these procedures are merely gatekeepers for the private property variable.

You define a private property variable like so:

```
Class Customer

    Private mstrName

    <rest of the class code will go here>

End Class
```

For the variable to have private, class-level scope, you must declare it with the `Private` statement. The *m* prefix is the *Hungarian* notation to indicate that the scope of the variable is *module level*, which is another way of saying *class level*. Some texts will advocate the use of the *c* prefix (as in `cstrName`) to indicate *class*-level scope. However, we do not recommend this approach as it is easily confused with the prefix that Visual Basic programmers often use for the `Currency` data type.

For more on Hungarian notation, see Chapter 3.

Property Let

A `Property Let` procedure is a special kind of procedure that allows code outside of a class to place a value in a private property variable. A `Property Let` procedure is similar to a VBScript `Sub` procedure in that it does not return a value. Here is the syntax.

```
Class Customer

    Private mstrName

    Public Property Let CustomerName(strName)
        mstrName = strName
    End Property

End Class
```

Notice that instead of using the Sub or Function statements to define the procedure, Property Let is used. A Property Let procedure must accept at least one argument. Omitting this argument defeats the whole purpose of the Property Let procedure, which is to allow outside code to store a value in the private property variable. Notice how the code inside the property procedure saves that strName value passed into the procedure in the private property variable mstrName. You are not required to have any code at all inside the procedure, but not storing the value passed into the procedure in some sort of class-level variable or object would tend to, once again, defeat the whole purpose of the Property Let procedure.

Conversely, you can have as much additional code in the procedure as you like. In some cases, you might want to do some sort of validation before actually assigning the passed-in value in the private property variable. For example, if the length of the customer name value was not allowed to exceed 50 characters, you could verify that the strName argument value does not exceed 50 characters, and, if it did, use the Err.Raise() method (see Chapter 6) to inform the calling code of this violation.

Finally, a property procedure must end with the End Property statement (just as a Function procedure ends with End Function, and a Sub procedure ends with End Sub). If you wanted to break out of a property procedure, you would use the Exit Property statement (just as you would use Exit Function to break out of a Function, and Exit Sub to break out of a Sub).

Property Get

A Property Get procedure is the inverse of a Property Let procedure. While a Property Let procedure allows code outside of your class to write a value to a private property variable, a Property Get procedure allows code outside of your class to read the value of a private property variable. A Property Get procedure is similar to a VBScript Function procedure in that it returns a value. Here is the syntax.

```
Class Customer

    Private mstrName

    Public Property Let CustomerName(strName)
        mstrName = strName
    End Property

    Public Property Get CustomerName()
        CustomerName = mstrName
    End Property

End Class
```

Like a VBScript Function procedure, a Property Get procedure returns a value to the calling code. This value is typically the value of a private property variable. Notice how the name of the Property Get procedure is the same as the corresponding Property Let procedure. The Property Let procedure stores a value in the private property variable, and the Property Get procedure reads it back out.

The Property Get procedure does not accept any arguments. VBScript allows you to add an argument, but if you are tempted to do this, then you must also add an additional argument to the property's corresponding Property Let or Property Set procedure (if there is one). This is because a Property Let/Set procedure must always have *exactly one more* argument than its corresponding Property Get procedure.

Adding an extra argument to a `Property Let/Set` procedure is extremely awkward, and asking the code that uses your class to accommodate more than one argument in a `Property Let` procedure is very bad form. If you feel you have a need for a `Property Get` procedure to accept an argument, you are much better off adding an extra property to fulfill whatever need the `Property Get` argument would have fulfilled.

If your `Property Get` procedure returns a reference to an object variable, then you may want to use the `Set` statement to return the value. For example:

```
Class FileHelper

    'Private FileSystemObject object
    Private mobjFSO

    Public Property Get FSO()
        Set FSO = mobjFSO
    End Property

End Class
```

However, because all VBScript variables are `Variant` variables, the `Set` syntax is not strictly required. This syntax would work just as well.

```
Class FileHelper

    'Private FileSystemObject object
    Private mobjFSO

    Public Property Get FSO()
        FSO = mobjFSO
    End Property

End Class
```

It's a good idea to use the `Set` syntax, though, because it makes it clearer that the corresponding `Property Get` procedure is returning a reference to an object variable.

Property Set

A `Property Set` procedure is very similar to a `Property Let` procedure, but the `Property Set` procedure is exclusively for object-based properties. When the property needs to store an object (as opposed to a variable with a numeric, `Date`, `Boolean`, or `String` subtype), you can provide a `Property Set` procedure instead of a `Property Let` procedure. Here is the syntax for a `Property Set` procedure.

```
Class FileHelper

    'Private FileSystemObject object
    Private mobjFSO

    Public Property Set FSO(objFSO)
        Set mobjFSO = objFSO
    End Property

End Class
```

Functionally, `Property Let` and `Property Set` procedures do the same thing. However, the `Property Set` procedure has two differences:

- It makes it clearer that the property is an object-based property (any technique that makes the intent of the code more explicit is preferable over any other equally correct technique).

- Code outside of your class must use the `Set Object.Property = Object` syntax in order to write to the property (also a good thing, because this is the typical way of doing things).

For example, here is what code that uses an object based on the preceding class might look like.

```
Dim objFileHelper
Dim objFSO

Set objFSO = _WScript.CreateObject("Scripting.FileSystemObject")
Set objFileHelper = New FileHelper
Set objFileHelper.FSO = objFSO
```

Notice that when the last line writes to the `FSO` property, it uses the `Set` statement. This is required because the `FileHelper` class used a `Property Set` procedure for the `FSO` property. Without the `Set` statement at the beginning of the last line, VBScript would produce an error. When a property on a class is object based, it is typical to use a `Property Set` procedure. Most programmers using your class will expect this.

That said, because all VBScript variables are `Variant` variables, it is perfectly legal to use a `Property Let` procedure instead. However, if you provide a `Property Let` procedure *instead* of a `Property Set` procedure, code that uses your class *cannot* use the `Set` statement to write to the property (VBScript will produce an error if they do), and this causes a trip-up for programmers who are accustomed to using the `Set` syntax. To be very thorough, and cover both bases, you can provide both a `Property Let` and a `Property Set` for the same property, like so:

```
Class FileHelper

    'Private FileSystemObject object
    Private mobjFSO

    Public Property Set FSO(objFSO)
        Set mobjFSO = objFSO
    End Property

    Public Property Let FSO(objFSO)
        Set mobjFSO = objFSO
    End Property

End Class
```

The `Set` syntax inside of the `Property Set` and `Let` is optional. Because you write directly to the `Variant` private property variable, you can use either. This example is the functional equivalent of the previous example.

```
Class FileHelper

    'Private FileSystemObject object
    Private mobjFSO

    Public Property Set FSO(objFSO)
        mobjFSO = objFSO
    End Property

    Public Property Let FSO(objFSO)
        mobjFSO = objFSO
    End Property

End Class
```

Making a Property Read-Only

You can make a property on a class read-only in one of two ways:

❑   By providing only a `Property Get` procedure for the property

❑   By declaring the `Property Get` procedure as `Public` and the `Property Let` procedure as `Private`

Here is the first technique.

```
Class Customer

    Private mstrName

    Public Property Get CustomerName()
        CustomerName = mstrName
    End Property

End Class
```

Notice the absence of a `Property Let` procedure. Because you have not provided a `Property Let` procedure, code outside of the class cannot write to the `CustomerName` property.

Here is the second technique.

```
Class Customer

    Private mstrName

    Private Property Let CustomerName(strName)
        mstrName = strName
    End Property

    Public Property Get CustomerName()
        CustomerName = mstrName
    End Property

End Class
```

The `Property Get` procedure is declared with the `Public` statement, and the `Property Let` procedure is declared with the `Private` statement. By declaring the `Property Let` as `Private`, you have effectively hidden it from code outside of the class. Code inside of the class can still write to the property through the `Property Let` procedure, but in this simple example, it is of limited usefulness because code inside of the class can write directly to the private property variable, so there is little need for the private `Property Let` procedure.

The exception to this is when you have code inside of the `Property Let` procedure that is performing validations and/or transformations on the value being placed in the property. If this is the case, then there might be a benefit in code inside the class using the private `Property Let` procedure rather than writing directly to the private property variable.

The first method (providing only a `Property Get`) is the more typical method of creating a read-only property.

Making a Property Write-Only

The two techniques for making a property write-only are the exact reverse of the two techniques for making a property read-only (see previous section):

❑   You can omit the `Property Get` procedure and provide only a `Property Let` procedure.

❑   You can declare the `Property Let` procedure with the `Public` statement, and declare the `Property Get` with the `Private` statement.

Public Properties without Property Procedures

You can provide properties for your class without using `Property Let`, `Set`, and `Get` procedures. This is accomplished through the use of public class-level variables. For example, this code

```
Class Customer

    Private mstrName

    Public Property Let CustomerName(strName)
        mstrName = strName
    End Property

    Public Property Get CustomerName()
        CustomerName = mstrName
    End Property

End Class
```

is the functional equivalent of this:

```
Class Customer

    Public Name

End Class
```

The second option looks a lot more attractive. It has a lot less code and from a functionality and syntax standpoint, it is perfectly legal. However, many VBScript programmers strongly prefer using private property variables in combination with `Property Let`, `Set`, and `Get` procedures, as discussed in the previous sections.

Other programmers prefer to use public class-level variables instead of `Property Let`, `Set`, and `Get` procedures. The main advantage of using public class-level variables to create class properties is that this method takes a lot less code. However, not using `Property Let`, `Set`, and `Get` procedures also has some serious disadvantages that you should consider.

Unless you want the code that uses your class to use awkward syntax such as `objCustomer.mstrName = "ACME Inc."`, you cannot use Hungarian scope or subtype prefixes on your class-level variables. If you agree with the theory that Hungarian prefixes add value to your code, this tends to make the code less readable and understandable.

❑   You cannot use the techniques described in previous sections of this chapter for making properties read-only or write-only.

❑   Code outside of your class can write to any property at any time. If you have certain circumstances where it is valid to write to a certain property, and others where it's invalid to write to a certain property, the only way you can enforce this is through `Property Let` procedures that have code in them to check for these valid and invalid circumstances. You never know when code outside the class might be changing the values of properties.

❑   Without `Property Let` procedures, you cannot write code to validate or transform the value being written to a property.

❑   Without `Property Get` procedures, you cannot write code to validate or transform the value being read from a property.

That said, if you can live with these disadvantages, you certainly can declare your properties as public class-level variables and change them to use `Property Let`, `Set`, and `Get` procedures later if the need arises. However, one could make an argument that it's better to do it the "right" way from the start. This is one of those issues where good programmers will simply have a difference of opinion, but you'll find more programmers who prefer `Property Let`, `Set`, and `Get` procedures over public class-level variables.

Often, however, you are creating a simple class for use within a single script. In such situations, it may be more acceptable to take some shortcuts so that the code is simpler and easier to write. In these cases, you may decide to forgo `Property Let`, `Set`, and `Get` procedures and just use public variables.

Defining Methods

A *method* is a different name for functions and procedures, which has been discussed throughout this book. When a function or procedure is part of a class, you call it a method instead. If you know how to write `Function` and `Sub` procedures (see Chapter 4), then you know how to write methods for a class. There is no special syntax for methods, as there is for properties. Your primary consideration is whether to declare a `Function` or `Sub` in a class as `Public` or `Private`.

Simply put, a class method that is declared with the `Public` statement will be available to code outside or inside the class, and a method that is declared with the `Private` statement will be available only to code inside the class.

The example script `SHOW_GREETING.VBS` contains a class called `Greeting`, which can be used to greet the user with different types of messages. The class uses both public and private methods. As you can see in the code for the `Greeting` class, methods defined in a class use the same syntax as any other VBScript procedure or function. The only new consideration with class methods is whether to make them public or private.

```
Class Greeting

    Private mstrName

    Public Property Let Name(strName)
        mstrName = strName
    End Property

    Public Sub ShowGreeting(strType)
        MsgBox MakeGreeting(strType) & mstrName & "."
    End Sub

    Private Function MakeGreeting(strType)
        Select Case strType
            Case "Formal"
                MakeGreeting = "Greetings, "
            Case "Informal"
                MakeGreeting = "Hello there, "
            Case "Casual"
                MakeGreeting = "Hey, "
        End Select
    End Function

End Class
```

Code that is outside of this class can call the `ShowGreeting()` method, which is public, but cannot call the `MakeGreeting()` method, which is private and for internal use only. The code at the top of the `SHOW_GREETING.VBS` example script makes use of the class.

```
Dim objGreet
Set objGreet = New Greeting

With objGreet
    .Name = "Dan"
    .ShowGreeting "Informal"
    .ShowGreeting "Formal"
    .ShowGreeting "Casual"
End With
Set objGreet = Nothing
```

Running this script results in the dialog boxes shown in Figures 8-2 through 8-4.

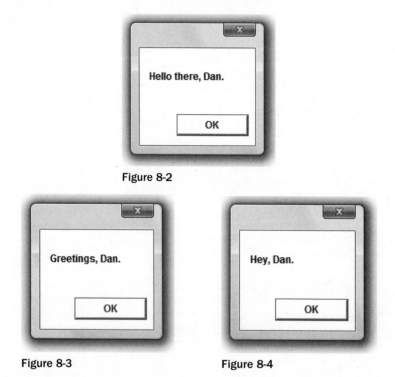

Figure 8-2

Figure 8-3   Figure 8-4

> *Note to Visual Basic programmers: VBScript does not support the* `Friend` *keyword for defining properties and methods.*

Class Events

An *event* is a special kind of method that is called automatically. In any given context, the classes with which you are working may support one or more events. When an event is supported in a given context, you can choose to write an *event handler*, which is a special kind of method that will be called whenever the event "fires." For example, in a web browser, when the user clicks a button, VBScript code in the page can respond to the `OnClick` event of that button.

Any VBScript class that you write automatically supports two events: `Class_Initialize` and `Class_Terminate`. Providing event handler methods in your class is optional. If you include event handler methods in your class, then they are called automatically; if you don't, nothing happens when these events fire — which is not a problem at all if you have no good reason to provide handler methods.

The Class_Initialize Event

The `Class_Initialize` event "fires" in your class when some code instantiates an object that is based on your class. It always fires when an object based on your class is instantiated, but whether your class contains any code to respond to it is up to you. If you do not want to respond to this event, you can simply choose to omit the event handler for the event. Here is an example class that contains a `Class_Initialize` event handler.

```
Class FileHelper

    'Private FileSystemObject object
    Private mobjFSO

    Private Sub Class_Initialize
        Set mobjFSO = _
            WScript.CreateObject("Scripting.FileSystemObject")
    End Sub

    '<<rest of the class goes here>>

End Class
```

As in this example, initializing class-level variables is a fairly typical use for a `Class_Initialize` handler. If you have a variable that you want to make sure has a certain value when your class first starts, you can set its initial value in the `Class_Initialize` event handler. You might also use the `Class_Initialize` event to do other preliminary things, such as opening a database connection, or opening a file.

The syntax for blocking off the beginning and ending of the `Class_Initialize` event handler must be exactly as you see it in this example. Your code can do just about whatever you please inside the event handler, but you do not have the flexibility of giving the procedure a different name. The first line of the handler must be `Private Sub Class_Initialize`, and the last line must be `End Sub`. Really, the event handler is a normal VBScript subprocedure, but with a special name.

> *Technically, you can also declare the event handler with the* `Public` *statement (as opposed to* `Private`*), but event handlers are generally private. If you make it public, code outside of the class can call it like any other method any time it liked, which is not generally desirable.*

There can only be exactly one `Class_Initialize` event handler in a given class. You can omit it if you don't need it, but you can't have more than one.

The Class_Terminate Event

The `Class_Terminate` event is the inverse of the `Class_Initialize` event (see previous section). Whereas the `Class_Initialize` event fires whenever an object based on your class is instantiated, the `Class_Terminate` event fires whenever an object based on your class is destroyed. An object can be destroyed in either of two ways:

- ❑ When some code explicitly assigns the special value `Nothing` to the last object variable with a reference to the object

- ❑ When the last object variable with a reference to the object goes out of scope

When either of these things occurs, the `Class_Terminate` event fires immediately before the object is actually destroyed. (For more information about object lifetime and references, please see Chapter 7.)

Here is the example `FileHelper` class that you saw in the previous section, this time with a `Class_Terminate` event handler added.

```
Class FileHelper

    'Private FileSystemObject object
    Private mobjFSO

    Private Sub Class_Initialize
        Set mobjFSO = _
        WScript.CreateObject("Scripting.FileSystemObject")
    End Sub

    Private Sub Class_Terminate
        Set mobjFSO = Nothing
    End Sub

    '<rest of the class goes here>

End Class
```

In this example, you use the Class_Terminate event handler to destroy the object that you instantiated in the Class_Initialize event. This is not strictly necessary, because when the FileHelper object is destroyed, the private mobjFSO variable goes out of scope and the script engine destroys it for us. However, some programmers prefer to explicitly destroy all objects that they instantiate, and this is useful for an example.

You might also use the Class_Terminate event to close a database connection, close a file, or save some information in the class to a database or file. The same syntactical restrictions that apply to Class_Initialize event handlers apply to Class_Terminate event handlers.

Class-Level Constants

For reasons that are unclear, VBScript does not support named constants declared at the class level. That is, you cannot use the Const statement within a class so that the constant variable is available throughout the class, or from outside the class. For example, this code produces a compile error.

```
Option Explicit

Dim objTest

Set objTest = new ConstTest
objTest.SayHello
Set objTest = Nothing

Class ConstTest

    Private Const TEST_CONST = "Hello there."

    Public Sub SayHello
        MsgBox TEST_CONST
    End Sub

End Class
```

The compile error occurs on this line.

```
Private Const TEST_CONST = "Hello there."
```

The reason is that this statement is scoped at the class level, which means that it is declared within the class, but not within any of the properties or methods of the class. (The Const statement is legal within a property or method, but it will of course have only local scope within that property or method.) There is a workaround, however, as shown in this example.

```
Option Explicit

Dim objTest

set objTest = new ConstTest
objTest.SayHello

Class ConstTest

    Private TEST_CONST

    Private Sub Class_Initialize
        TEST_CONST = "Hello there."
    End Sub

    Public Sub SayHello
        MsgBox TEST_CONST
    End Sub

End Class
```

This workaround creates a pseudo-constant. Instead of declaring TEST_CONST with the Const statement, you declare it as a normal, private class-level variable (you could have made it public as well). Then in the Class_Initialize event handler, you give the TEST_CONST variable the "constant" value that you want. There is a small danger in this, however, because code inside your class can still change the value of the TEST_CONST variable. However, using the all-caps naming convention might help prevent this from happening (most programmers are accustomed to equating all-caps with a named constant). You'll just have to make sure the code inside the class behaves itself.

Please note that in earlier versions of VBScript, class-level constants were also not supported. However, strangely, they would not cause a compile error; their values would simply be ignored. If you are using a version of VBScript that does not produce the compile error, you essentially still have the same problem, and the same workaround will do the trick.

Building and Using a Sample VBScript Class

Chapter 3 showed how to use an array to store a list of names and phone numbers. Later, Chapter 7 showed how to store a phone list in a series of one-element arrays in the scripting runtime's Dictionary object. Now, for the remainder of this chapter, you will further adapt the phone list example to use

VBScript classes. In much the same way as the example code from Chapter 7, the code you develop now will accomplish the following:

❏ Provide a data structure to store a phone list entry.

❏ Provide a data structure to store a list of phone list entries.

❏ Provide a way to locate and display a phone list entry.

The example script you will develop has the following elements:

❏ A ListEntry class to store a single phone list entry. This class also knows how to display its own data.

❏ A PhoneList class that uses an internal Dictionary object to store a series of ListEntry objects. This class, which uses the phone number value as the key for the dictionary, also supports the retrieval and the display of an individual entry.

❏ Support for non-class-based code that uses the two aforementioned classes to populate a phone list and asks the user for a phone number to locate and display.

You might remember from the Chapter 7 example that all of this same functionality was provided, but it was all done without classes. With that in mind, the purpose of this chapter's evolution of the Chapter 7 code is to illustrate how classes are used to create more readable, generic, and reusable code that is more tolerant to future changes. You can read, execute, and experiment with this script in the PHONE_LIST_CLASS.VBS file, which, along with all of the rest of the code for this book, can be downloaded from the wrox.com web site.

First, take a look at the ListEntry class.

```
Class ListEntry

    Private mstrLast
    Private mstrFirst
    Private mstrPhone
    Public Property Let LastName(strLastName)
        If IsNumeric(strLastName) or _
            IsDate(strLastName) Then
            Err.Raise 32003, "ListEntry", _
                "The LastName property may not " & _
                "be a number or date."
        End If

        mstrLast = strLastName
    End Property
    Public Property Get LastName
        LastName = mstrLast
    End Property

    Public Property Let FirstName(strFirstName)
        If IsNumeric(strFirstName) or _
            IsDate(strFirstName) Then
            Err.Raise 32004, "ListEntry", _
                "The FirstName property may not " & _
```

```
                    "be a number or date."
        End If

        mstrFirst = strFirstName
    End Property
    Public Property Get FirstName
        FirstName = mstrFirst
    End Property

    Public Property Let PhoneNumber(strPhoneNumber)
        mstrPhone = strPhoneNumber
    End Property
    Public Property Get PhoneNumber
        PhoneNumber = mstrPhone
    End Property

    Public Sub DisplayEntry
        MsgBox "Phone list entry:" & vbNewLine & _
            vbNewLine & _
            "Last: " & mstrLast & vbNewLine & _
            "First: " & mstrFirst & vbNewLine & _
            "Phone: " & mstrPhone

    End Sub

End Class
```

This class has three properties: LastName, FirstName, and PhoneNumber. Each property is implemented using a private property variable, along with Property Let and Get procedures. Because the class has both Let and Get procedures for each property, the properties are both readable and writeable. Notice also that in the Property Let procedures for LastName and FirstName, you are checking to make sure that outside code does not store any numeric or date values in the properties. If an illegal value is passed in, the code raises an error (see Chapter 6).

Checking for numbers and dates is a somewhat arbitrary choice of something to validate; the primary purpose in this example is to illustrate how important it is to use your Property Let procedures to ensure that programmers do not store any data in a property that does not belong. This technique is especially important given VBScript's lack of data type enforcement; because all variables have the Variant data type, any variable can hold any value.

Please note that you could have chosen many other types of validation. You could have checked for data length (minimum or maximum), special characters that might be illegal, proper formatting, and so on. For example, you could have also added a check to the PhoneNumber Property Let that verifies the format xxx-xxx-xxxx. Or you could have added a "transformation" that converts the phone number into that format if it already wasn't. What kinds of validations and transformations you choose depends on the situation. The point is to test the assumptions inherent in the rest of your code to avoid bugs and errors.

The ListEntry class has one method: DisplayEntry, which uses the MsgBox() function to display the properties of a list entry. The example chose to put this code in the ListEntry class because of the general principle that a class should provide functionality that it is "natural" for that class to know how to do. The ListEntry class "knows" the last name, first name, and phone number. Therefore, to keep the code that manipulates data as close as possible to where the data is stored, you put the `DisplayEntry()` method on the `ListEntry` class.

In object-oriented parlance, this is called *separation of concerns* or *responsibility-based design*. Each class has a set of *things* it needs to *know* and to *know how to do*. You want to design your classes so that the separations between them are logical and not anymore intertwined than necessary. The less one class *knows* about other classes, the better.

However, sometimes you have functionality that you expressly *do not* want a class to know how to do. The idea is to keep your classes as generic as possible, so that you can use them in multiple ways in multiple contexts. You'll see examples of this as you continue to build your code.

Moving on, this is the second class, `PhoneList`:

```
Class PhoneList

    Private objDict

    Private Sub Class_Initialize
        Set objDict = CreateObject("Scripting.Dictionary")
    End Sub
    Private Sub Class_Terminate
        Set objDict = Nothing
    End Sub


    Public Property Get ListCount
        ListCount = objDict.Count
    End Property

    Public Function EntryExists(strPhoneNumber)
        EntryExists = _
            objDict.Exists(strPhoneNumber)
    End Function

    Public Sub AddEntry(objListEntry)
        If TypeName(objListEntry) <> "ListEntry" Then
            Err.Raise 32000, "PhoneList", _
                "Only ListEntry objects can be stored " & _
                "in a PhoneList class."
        End If
        'We use the PhoneNumber property as the key.
        If Trim("" & objListEntry.PhoneNumber) = "" Then
            Err.Raise 32001, "PhoneList", _
                "A ListEntry object must have a " & _
                "phone number to be added to the " & _
                "phone list."
        End If
        objDict.Add objListEntry.PhoneNumber, objListEntry
    End Sub

    Public Sub DisplayEntry(strPhoneNumber)
        Dim objEntry

        If objDict.Exists(strPhoneNumber) Then
```

```
                    Set objEntry = objDict(strPhoneNumber)
                    objEntry.DisplayEntry
             Else
                    Err.Raise 32002, "PhoneList", _
                          "The phone number'" & strPhoneNumber & _
                          "' is not in the list."
             End If
      End Sub

 End Class
```

The first thing to notice about this class is that internally it uses a private `Dictionary` object to store the phone list. This is a powerful technique for two reasons:

❑   It illustrates how your classes can *borrow* the functionality of other classes.

❑   The fact that you don't expose the internal `Dictionary` object to any code outside of the `PhoneList` class means that scripts that use the `PhoneList` class do not need to have any knowledge of how the `PhoneList` class stores the data.

If you want to change the `Dictionary` to some other data storage method (such as an array, hash table, text file, and so on), you could do so without breaking any other code that uses the `PhoneList` class. Next, as illustrated earlier in this chapter, notice you're using the `Class_Initialize` and `Class_Terminate` events to control the lifetime of the internal `Dictionary` object (objDict). This allows the rest of the class to assume that there is always a `Dictionary` object to use.

Next, you have a `Property Get` procedure called `ListCount` and a method called `EntryExists`. The `ListCount` property is a "wrapper" for the `objDict.Count` property, and likewise `ExtryExists` is a wrapper for the `objDict.Exists` method. You could have chosen to expose other `Dictionary` properties and methods as well. However, be careful about this because you don't want to lose your future flexibility to change out the `Dictionary` object with another data storage structure.

For example, you could make things really easy and just expose `objDict` as a property and let outside code use it directly as a dictionary. However, if you did that, outside code would become too "tightly coupled" to the internals of your class — meaning that outside code would have too much "knowledge" about how your class works internally. As much as possible, you want the `PhoneList` class to be a "black box"; you can use the functionality of a black box, you can know what goes in and what comes out, but you can't see what's inside the box that makes it all work.

Next you have the `AddEntry()` method. This method really does only one thing: It calls the dictionary's `Add()` method, using the phone number of the list entry as the key for the dictionary.

```
objDict.Add objListEntry.PhoneNumber, objListEntry
```

Notice that you store the `ListEntry` object itself in the dictionary, just as in Chapter 7 you stored a phone list entry array in the dictionary.

However, this is the last line of the method. All of the code that comes before it is validation code. The idea here is that you want to test and document the assumptions that the method makes. This method has two important implicit assumptions:

❑   That only `ListEntry` objects are stored in the `PhoneList` class

❑   That the `PhoneNumber` property is used as the key

To test these assumptions:

❑   Use the `TypeName` function to check that the outside code is passing a `ListEntry` object, and not some other kind of data. This is necessary because, given VBScript's lack of data type enforcement, you need to do your own validation.

❑   Check that the `ListEntry` object has a non-blank value in the `PhoneNumber` property. This way, you can make sure that you have something that can be used as a key.

There are other assumptions that you could have tested as well, but these are the two that are most likely to produce strange bugs or error messages that make it difficult for programmers using your classes to figure out what they are doing wrong. These clear error messages document for all concerned what the important assumptions are.

Finally, `PhoneList` has a method called `DisplayEntry`. Now wait a minute — didn't you also have a `DisplayEntry` method on the `ListEntry` class? Why two methods that apparently do the same thing?

It all comes down to design options. There is not necessarily a "correct" way to design these classes. The `DisplayEntry` method of the `PhoneList` class "delegates" the responsibility of displaying of an entry to the `ListEntry.DisplayEntry()` method, as you can see in these lines.

```
If objDict.Exists(strPhoneNumber) Then
    Set objEntry = objDict(strPhoneNumber)
    objEntry.DisplayEntry
```

So even though you have two methods, there is not really any duplication because the code that does the actual displaying only exists in the `ListEntry` class. The implicit design decision you made was to specialize the `PhoneList` class with methods (such as `DisplayEntry()`) that allow programmers to do specific things with phone list entries (such as displaying them), as opposed to going with a more generic approach that just exposes the list of entries, allowing the outside code to do the work embodied in the preceding three lines of code — that is, finding the correct entry and telling it to display itself. Both designs are valid, and nothing in the chosen design prevents you from extending these classes in any number of ways in the future.

Now that you have the two classes, you can look at some code that makes use of these classes (again, all of this code can be found in `PHONE_LIST_CLASS.VBS`).

```
Option Explicit

Dim objList

FillPhoneList
On Error Resume Next
objList.DisplayEntry(GetNumberFromUser)

If Err.Number <> 0 Then
    If Err.Number = vbObjectError + 32002 Then
        MsgBox "That phone number is not in the list.", _
            vbInformation
    Else
        DisplayError Err.Number, Err.Source, _
            Err.Description
    End If
End If

Public Sub FillPhoneList
    Dim objNewEntry

    Set objList = New PhoneList

    Set objNewEntry = New ListEntry
    With objNewEntry
        .LastName = "Williams"
        .FirstName = "Tony"
        .PhoneNumber = "404-555-6328"
    End With
    objList.AddEntry objNewEntry
    Set objNewEntry = Nothing

    Set objNewEntry = New ListEntry
    With objNewEntry
        .LastName = "Carter"
        .FirstName = "Ron"
        .PhoneNumber = "305-555-2514"
    End With
    objList.AddEntry objNewEntry
    Set objNewEntry = Nothing

    Set objNewEntry = New ListEntry
    With objNewEntry
        .LastName = "Davis"
        .FirstName = "Miles"
        .PhoneNumber = "212-555-5314"
    End With
    objList.AddEntry objNewEntry
    Set objNewEntry = Nothing

    Set objNewEntry = New ListEntry
    With objNewEntry
        .LastName = "Hancock"
        .FirstName = "Herbie"
```

(continued)

```
                    .PhoneNumber = "616-555-6943"
        End With
        objList.AddEntry objNewEntry
        Set objNewEntry = Nothing

        Set objNewEntry = New ListEntry
        With objNewEntry
            .LastName = "Shorter
            .FirstName = "Wayne"
            .PhoneNumber = "853-555-0060"
        End With
        objList.AddEntry objNewEntry
        Set objNewEntry = Nothing

    End Sub

    Public Function GetNumberFromUser
        GetNumberFromUser = InputBox("Please enter " & _
            "a phone number (XXX-XXX-XXXX) with " & _
            "which to search the list.")
    End Function
```

Running this code and entering the phone number 404-555-6328 results in the dialog box shown in Figure 8-5.

Figure 8-5

Running the code again and entering an invalid phone number results in the dialog box shown in Figure 8-6.

Figure 8-6

The most important point to take away from this elaborate example can be found in these two simple lines of code (without the error handling related code).

```
FillPhoneList
objList.DisplayEntry(GetNumberFromUser)
```

These two lines represent the total logic of the script: Create a phone list, fill it up, ask the user for a phone number to search for, and display the entry. This is the beauty of breaking the code up into separate classes and procedures. If you make your classes and procedures as generic as possible, then the code that actually strings them together to do something useful is relatively simple and easy to understand and change — not to mention easy to reuse in many ways.

The `FillPhoneList()` procedure creates a `PhoneList` object (`objList`) and fills it up with entries. Imagine the phone list entries coming from a database table, a file, or from user entry. `FillPhoneList()` uses a "temporary object variable" called `objNewEntry`. For each entry in the list, it instantiates `objNewEntry`, fills it with data, then passes it to the `objList.AddEntry()` method.

Notice that you use the `New` keyword in `FillPhoneList` to instantiate objects from your custom VBScript classes.

```
Set objList = New PhoneList
```

and

```
Set objNewEntry = New ListEntry
```

What happened to the `CreateObject()` function? `CreateObject()` is only for use in instantiating non-native VBScript objects (such as `Dictionary` and `FileSystemObject`), whereas you must use `New` to instantiate a custom VBScript class that exists in the same script file. The reasons behind this are complex, so keep this simple rule in mind: If you are instantiating an object based on a custom VBScript class, use `New`; otherwise, use `CreateObject`.

The `GetNumberFromUser()` function is very simple. It uses the `InputBox()` function to prompt the user for a phone number and returns whatever the user entered. The code at the top of the script then passes this value to `objDict.DisplayEntry()`. If the entry exists, the `ListEntry` object displays itself. If not, `objDict.DisplayEntry()` returns an error.

You can use the `PhoneList` and `ListEntry` classes in many ways for any number of purposes. As new needs arise, you can extend the classes without breaking any code that is already using them. Any future programmers who come to the script will have a very easy time understanding what the script is doing. After all, it's all in these two lines of code.

```
FillPhoneList
objList.DisplayEntry(GetNumberFromUser)
```

If a programmer wants to further understand the low-level details of how the script works, he or she can choose to read the rest of the code, digging into the procedures and the classes. But in many cases, that is unnecessary, unless the programmer needs to fix a bug or add some functionality. If all a programmer wants to know is *What does this script do?* the answer is right there in those two simple lines.

Summary

This chapter explained how to develop classes in native VBScript. This is a powerful ability that allows you to create scripts that are object oriented in nature, which, when properly designed, can give you greater understandability, maintainability, flexibility, and reuse. A VBScript class is defined using the `Class...End Class` block construct. In general, classes must be defined within the same script file as the code that will make use of them. (For an alternative technique, please see Chapter 16 for information on Windows Script Components.)

Classes can have properties and methods. Properties are defined using either public variables or special procedure constructs called `Property Let`, `Get`, and `Set` procedures. Using private property variables and different combinations of `Let`, `Get`, and `Set` procedures, you can control whether properties are read-only, write-only, or both. Methods are defined like normal procedures and functions, and can be either public or private.

The final section of this chapter gave a detailed class-based example, including explanations of the design and programming techniques. The example is an extension of the phone list examples used in Chapters 3 and 7.

Regular Expressions

Version 5 and later of VBScript fully support regular expressions. Before that, this was one feature that was sorely lacking within VBScript, and one that made it inferior to other scripting languages, including JavaScript. This chapter begins with a brief introduction to regular expressions before taking a look at what regular expressions have to offer the programmer. It then looks at how to make use of regular expressions in VBScript code.

Introduction to Regular Expressions

Regular expressions provide powerful facilities for character pattern-matching and replacing. Before the addition of regular expressions to the VBScript engine, performing a search-and-replace task throughout a string required a fair amount of code, comprising mainly of loops, `InStr`, and `Mid` functions. Now it is possible to do all this with one line of code using a regular expression.

If you've programmed in the past using another language (C#, C++, Perl, awk, or JavaScript — even Microsoft's own JScript had support for regular expressions before VBScript did), regular expressions won't be new to you. However, one thing that experienced programmers need to know in order to leverage regular expressions in VBScript is that VBScript does not provide support for regular expression constants (like `/a pattern/`). Instead, VBScript uses text strings assigned to the `Pattern` property of a `RegExp` object. In many ways this is superior to the traditional method because there is no new syntax to learn. But if you are used to regular expressions from other languages, especially client-side JavaScript, this is something you may not expect.

> *Now, many Windows-based text editors have followed in the footsteps of the Unix text editor vi and support regular expression searches. These include UltraEdit-32 (www.ultraedit.com) and SlickEdit (www.slickedit.com).*

Regular Expressions in Action

The quickest and easiest way to become familiar with regular expressions is to look at a few examples. Here is probably one of the simplest examples of a regular expression in action involving find-and-replace.

```
Dim re, s
Set re = New RegExp
re.Pattern = "France"
s = "The rain in France falls mainly on the plains."
MsgBox re.Replace(s, "Spain")
```

Nothing spectacular — but it is a powerful foundation to build up from. Here's how the code works.

1. Create a new regular expression object.

```
Set re = New RegExp
```

2. Set the key property on that object. This is the pattern that you want to match.

```
re.Pattern = "France"
```

3. The following line is the string you will be searching:

```
s = "The rain in France falls mainly on the plains."
```

This line is the powerhouse of the script in that it does the real work. It asks the regular expression object to find the first occurrence of `"France"` (the pattern) within the string held in variable s and to replace it with `"Spain"`.

4. Once you've done that, you use a message box to show off your great find-and-replace skills.

```
MsgBox re.Replace(s, "Spain")
```

5. When the script is run, the final output should be as shown in Figure 9-1.

Figure 9-1

Now, it's all well and good hard-coding the string and searching criteria straight from the start, but you can add more flexibility by making the script accept the string and the find-and-replace criteria from an input.

```
Dim re, s, sc
Set re = New RegExp
s = InputBox("Type a string for the code to search")
re.Pattern = InputBox("Type in a pattern to find")
sc = InputBox("Type in a string to replace the pattern")
MsgBox re.Replace(s, sc)
```

This is pretty much the exact same code as before, but with one key difference. Instead of having everything hard-coded into the script, you introduce flexibility by using three input boxes in the code.

```
s = InputBox("Type a string for the code to search")
re.Pattern = InputBox("Type in a pattern to find")
sc = InputBox("Type in a string to replace the pattern")
```

The final change to the code is in the final line enabling the `Replace` method to make use of the `sc` variable.

```
MsgBox re.Replace(s, sc)
```

This lets you manually enter the string you want to be searched, as shown in Figure 9-2.

Figure 9-2

Then you can enter the pattern you want to find (see Figure 9-3).

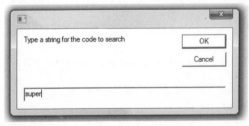

Figure 9-3

Finally, enter a string to replace the pattern (see Figure 9-4).

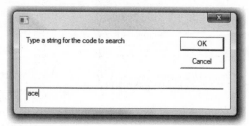

Figure 9-4

This lets you try out something that you might already be thinking; what happens if you try to find and replace a pattern that doesn't exist in the string? In fact, nothing happens, as shown here.

1. Type in the string as shown in Figure 9-5.

Figure 9-5

2. Enter a search for a pattern that doesn't exist (something that doesn't appear in the string). In Figure 9-6, the string "JScript" was used.

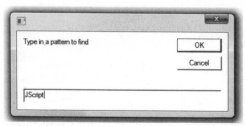

Figure 9-6

3. In the next prompt, enter a string to replace the nonexistent pattern. Because no replacement is carried out, it can be anything. In Figure 9-7, the string "JavaScript" was used. Notice what happens. Nothing. As you can see in Figure 9-8, the initial string is unchanged.

Figure 9-7

Figure 9-8

Building on Simplicity

Obviously the examples that you've seen so far are quite simple ones, and to be honest, you could probably do everything done here just as easily using VBScript's string manipulation functions. But what if you wanted to replace all occurrences of a string? Or what if you wanted to replace all occurrences of a string but only when they appear at the end of a word? You need to make some tweaks to the code. Take a look at the following code:

```
Dim re, s
Set re = New RegExp
re.Pattern = "\bin"
re.Global = True
s = "The rain in Spain falls mainly on the plains."
MsgBox re.Replace(s, "in the country of")
```

This version has two key differences:

❑   It uses a special sequence (\b) to match a word boundary (you can see all the special sequences available in the section "Regular Expression Characters" later in this chapter). This is demonstrated in Figure 9-9.

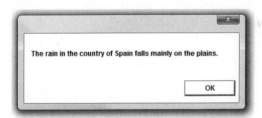

Figure 9-9

Suppose you left the \b out, like this:

```
Dim re, s
Set re = New RegExp
```

```
re.Pattern = "in"
```

```
re.Global = True
s = "The rain in Spain falls mainly on the plains."
MsgBox re.Replace(s, "in the country of")
```

Without this, the "in" part of the words "rain", "Spain", "mainly", and "plains" are changed to "in the country of" also. This would give, as you can see in Figure 9-10, some very funny, but undesirable, results.

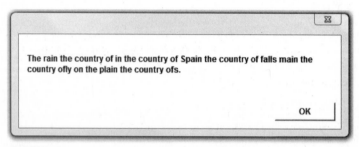

The rain the country of in the country of Spain the country of falls main the country ofly on the plain the country ofs.

OK

Figure 9-10

❑   By setting the Global property, you ensure that you match all the occurrences of "in" that you want.

```
Dim re, s
Set re = New RegExp
re.Pattern = "in"
```

```
re.Global = True
```

```
s = "The rain in Spain falls mainly on the plains."
MsgBox re.Replace(s, "in the country of")
```

Regular expressions provide a very powerful language for expressing complicated patterns like these, so let's get on with learning about the objects that allow you to use them within VBScript.

The RegExp Object

The RegExp object is the object that provides simple regular expression support in VBScript. All the properties and methods relating to regular expressions in VBScript are related to this object.

```
Dim re
```

```
Set re = New RegExp
```

This object has three properties and three methods, as shown in the following table.

Properties	`Global` property
	`IgnoreCase` property
	`Pattern` property
Methods	`Execute` method
	`Replace` method
	`Test` method

The following sections go into these properties and methods in greater detail. In addition, you learn about regular expression characters, which you can use in your patterns.

Global Property

The `Global` property is responsible for setting or returning a Boolean value that indicates whether or not a pattern is to match all occurrences in an entire search string or just the first occurrence.

Code	`object.Global [= value ]`
Object	Always a `RegExp` object.
Value	There are two possible values: `True` and `False`.
	If the value of the `Global` property is `True`, then the search applies to the entire string; if it is `False`, then it does not. Default is `False` — not `True` as documented in some Microsoft sources.

The following example uses the `Global` property to ensure that all occurrences of `"in"` were changed.

```
Dim re, s
Set re = New RegExp
re.Pattern = "\bin"

re.Global = True

s = "The rain in Spain falls mainly on the plains."
MsgBox re.Replace(s, "in the country of")
```

IgnoreCase Property

The `IgnoreCase` property sets or returns a Boolean value that indicates whether or not the pattern search is case-sensitive.

Code	`object.IgnoreCase [= value ]`
Object	Always a `RegExp` object.
Value	There are two possible values: `True` and `False`.
	If the value of the `IgnoreCase` property is `False`, then the search is case-sensitive; if it is `True`, then it is not. Default is `False` — not `True` as documented in some Microsoft sources.

Continuing with the example, look at the `Global` property earlier; if the string you want to match has "In" capitalized, you must tell VBScript to ignore the case when it does the matching.

```
Dim re, s
Set re = New RegExp
re.Pattern = "\bin"
re.Global = True
re.IgnoreCase = True
s = "The rain In Spain falls mainly on the plains."
MsgBox re.Replace(s, "in the country of")
```

Pattern Property

The `Pattern` property sets or returns the regular expression pattern being searched.

Code	`object.Pattern [= "searchstring"]`
Object	Always a `RegExp` object.
`searchstring`	Regular string expression being searched for. May include any of the regular expression characters — optional.

All the preceding examples used `Pattern`.

```
Dim re, s
Set re = New RegExp
re.Pattern = "\bin"
re.Global = True
s = "The rain in Spain falls mainly on the plains."
MsgBox re.Replace(s, "in the country of")
```

Regular Expression Characters

The real power of regular expressions comes not from using strings as patterns, but from using special characters in the pattern. What follows is a table that shows the characters that you can use along with a description of what each of the characters does in code.

Capitalized special characters do the opposite of their lowercase counterparts.

Character	Description
\	Marks the next character as either a special character or a literal.
^	Matches the beginning of input.
$	Matches the end of input.
*	Matches the preceding character zero or more times.
+	Matches the preceding character one or more times.

Character	Description
?	Matches the preceding character zero or one time.
.	Matches any single character except a newline character.
(pattern)	Matches *pattern* and remembers the match. The matched substring can be retrieved from the resulting Matches collection, using Item [0]...[n]. To match the parentheses characters themselves, precede with slash — use "\("or"\)".
(?:pattern)	Matches *pattern* but does not capture the match, that is, it is a noncapturing match that is not stored for possible later use. This is useful for combining parts of a pattern with the "or" character (│). For example, "anomal(?:y│ies)" is a more economical expression than "anomaly│anomalies".
(?=pattern)	Positive lookahead matches the search string at any point where a string-matching *pattern* begins. This is a noncapturing match, that is, the match is not captured for possible later use. For example, "Windows (?=95│98│NT│2000│XP│Vista)" matches "Windows" in "Windows Vista" but not "Windows" in "Windows 3.1".
(?!pattern)	Negative lookahead matches the search string at any point where a string not matching *pattern* begins. This is a noncapturing match, that is, the match is not captured for possible later use. For example, "Windows (?!95│98│NT│2000│XP│Vista)" matches "Windows" in "Windows 3.1" but does not match "Windows" in "Windows Vista".
x│y	Matches either x or y.
{n}	Matches exactly n times (n must always be a nonnegative integer).
{n,}	Matches at least n times (n must always be a nonnegative integer — note the terminating comma).
{n,m}	Matches at least n and at most m times (m and n must always be nonnegative integers).
[xyz]	Matches any one of the enclosed characters (xyz represents a character set).
[^xyz]	Matches any character not enclosed (^xyz represents a negative character set).
[a-z]	Matches any character in the specified range (a-z represents a range of characters).
[m-z]	Matches any character not in the specified range (^m-z represents a negative range of characters).
\b	Matches a word boundary, that is, the position between a word and a space.
\B	Matches a nonword boundary.
\d	Matches a digit character. Equivalent to [0-9].
\D	Matches a nondigit character. Equivalent to [^0-9].

(continued)

Character	Description
\f	Matches a form-feed character.
\n	Matches a new-line character.
\r	Matches a carriage return character.
\s	Matches any white space including space, tab, form-feed, and so on. Equivalent to "[\f \n \r \t \v]".
\S	Matches any nonwhite space character. Equivalent to [^\f \n \r \t \v]".
\t	Matches a tab character.
\v	Matches a vertical tab character.
\w	Matches any word character including underscore. Equivalent to "[A-Za-z0-9_]".
\W	Matches any nonword character. Equivalent to "[^A-Za-z0-9_]".
\.	Matches .
|	Matches	
\{	Matches {
\}	Matches }
\\	Matches \
\[	Matches [
\]	Matches]
\(	Matches (
\)	Matches)
$ num	Matches num, where num is a positive integer. A reference back to remembered matches.
\n	Matches n, where n is an octal escape value. Octal escape values must be 1, 2, or 3 digits long.
\uxxxx	Matches the ASCII character expressed by the UNICODE xxxx.
\xn	Matches n, where n is a hexadecimal escape value. Hexadecimal escape values must be exactly two digits long.

Many of these codes are self-explanatory, but some examples would probably help with others.

Matching a Whole Class of Characters

You've already seen a simple pattern:

```
re.Pattern = "in"
```

Often it's useful to match any one of a whole class of characters. You do this by enclosing the characters that you want to match in square brackets. For example, the following example replaces any single digit with a more generic term.

```
Dim re, s
Set re = New RegExp
re.Pattern = "[23456789]"
s = "Spain received 3 millimeters of rain last week."
MsgBox re.Replace(s, "many")
```

The output from this code is shown in Figure 9-11.

Spain received many millimeters of rain last week.

OK

Figure 9-11

In this case, the number "3" is replaced with the text "many". As you might expect, you can shorten this class by using a range. This pattern does the same as the preceding one but saves some typing.

```
Dim re, s
Set re = New RegExp
re.Pattern = "[2-9]"
s = "Spain received 3 millimeters of rain last week."
MsgBox re.Replace(s, "many")
```

Replacing Digits and Everything but Digits

Replacing digits is a common task. In fact, the pattern [0-9] (covering all the digits) is used so often that there is a shortcut for it: \d is equivalent to [0-9].

```
Dim re, s
Set re = New RegExp
re.Pattern = "\d"
s = "a b c d e f 1 g 2 h ... 10 z"
MsgBox re.Replace(s, "a number")
```

The string with the replaced characters is shown in Figure 9-12.

Figure 9-12

But what if you wanted to match everything except a digit? Then you can use negation, which is indicated by a circumflex (^) used within the class square brackets.

Using ^ outside the square brackets has a totally different meaning and is discussed after the next example.

Thus, to match any character other than a digit you can use any of the following patterns:

```
re.Pattern = "[^,0-9]" 'the hard way
re.Pattern = "[^\d]" 'a little shorter
re.Pattern = "[\D]" 'another of those special characters
```

The last option here uses another of the dozen or so special characters. In most cases these characters just save you some extra typing (or act as a good memory shorthand) but a few, such as matching tabs and other nonprintable characters, can be very useful.

Anchoring and Shorting a Pattern

There are three special characters that anchor a pattern. They don't match any characters themselves but force another pattern to appear at the beginning of the input (^used outside of [ ]), the end of the input ($), or at a word boundary (you've already seen \b).

Another way by which you can shorten your patterns is using repeat counts. The basic idea is to place the repeat after the character or class. For example, the following pattern, as shown in Figure 9-13, matches both digits and replaces them.

```
Dim re, s
Set re = New RegExp
re.Pattern = "\d{3}"
s = "Spain received 100 millimeters of rain in the last 2 weeks."
MsgBox re.Replace(s, "a whopping number of")
```

Figure 9-13

Without the use of the pattern repeat count in the code, Figure 9-14 shows that the output would leave the "00" in the final string.

Figure 9-14

```
Dim re, s
Set re = New RegExp
re.Pattern = "\d"

s = "Spain received 100 millimeters of rain in the last 2 weeks."
MsgBox re.Replace(s, "a whopping number of")
```

Note also that you can't just set re.Global = True because you'd end up with four instances of the phrase "a whopping number of" in the result. The result is shown in Figure 9-15.

Figure 9-15

```
Dim re, s
Set re = New RegExp
```

```
re.Global = True
re.Pattern = "\d"
```

```
s = "Spain received 100 millimeters of rain in the last 2 weeks."
MsgBox re.Replace(s, "a whopping number of")
```

Specifying a Minimum Number or Range of Matches

As the previous table shows, you can also specify a minimum number of matches {min} or a range {min, max,}. Again, a few repeat patterns are used so often that they have special short cuts.

```
re.Pattern = "\d+" 'one or more digits, \d{1, }
re.Pattern = "\d*" 'zero or more digits, \d{0, }

re.Pattern = "\d?" 'optional: zero or one, \d{0,1}
```

```
Dim re, s
Set re = New RegExp
re.Global = True
```

```
re.Pattern = "\d+"
```

```
s = "Spain received 100 millimeters of rain in the last 2 weeks."
MsgBox re.Replace(s, "a number")
```

The output of the last code is shown in Figure 9-16. Notice how the string "100" is replaced with text.

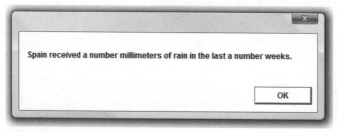

Figure 9-16

```
Dim re, s
Set re = New RegExp
re.Global = True
```

```
re.Pattern = "\d*"
s = "Spain received 100 millimeters of rain in the last 2 weeks."
MsgBox re.Replace(s, "a number")
```

The output of the preceding code is shown in Figure 9-17. Here the string "a number" is inserted between each character except for numbers that have been replaced with the string.

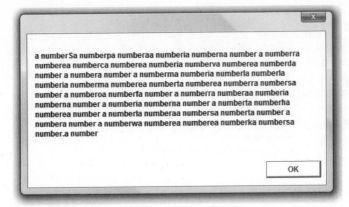

Figure 9-17

```
Dim re, s
Set re = New RegExp
re.Global = True

re.Pattern = "\d?"

s = "Spain received 100 millimeters of rain in the last 2 weeks."
MsgBox re.Replace(s, "a number")
```

The output of the preceding code is shown in Figure 9-18. Here again the string "a number" is inserted between each character except for numbers that have been replaced with the string.

Figure 9-18

Remembered Matches

The last special characters to discuss are remembered matches. These are useful when you want to use some or all of the text that matched your pattern as part of the replacement text — see the `Replace` method for an example of using remembered matches.

To illustrate this, and bring all this discussion of special characters together, let's do something more useful. You want to search an arbitrary text string and locate any URLs within it. To keep this example simple and reasonable in size, you'll only be searching for the `"http:"` protocols, but you'll be handling some of the vulgarities of DNS or domain names, including an unlimited number of domain layers. Don't worry if you "don't speak DNS"; what you know from typing URLs into your browser will suffice.

The code uses yet another of the `RegExp` object's methods that you'll see in more detail in the next section. For now, you need only know that `Execute` simply performs the pattern match and returns each match via a collection. Here's the code.

```
Dim re, s
Set re = New RegExp
re.Global = True
re.Pattern = "http://(\w+[\w-]*\w+\.)*\w+"
s = "http://www.kingsley-hughes.com is a valid web address. And so is "
s = s & vbCrLf & "http://www.wrox.com. And "
s = s & vbCrLf & "http://www.pc.ibm.com - even with 4 levels."
Set colMatches = re.Execute(s)
For Each match In colMatches
    MsgBox "Found valid URL: " & match.Value
Next
```

As you'd expect, the real work is done in the line that sets the actual pattern. It looks a bit daunting at first, but it's actually quite easy to follow. Let's break it down.

1. The pattern begins with the fixed string `http://`. You then use parentheses to group the real workhorse of this pattern. The following highlighted pattern will match one level of a DNS, including a trailing dot:

    `re.Pattern = "http://(`**`\w[\w-]*\w`**`\.)*\w+"`

    This pattern begins with one of the special characters you looked at earlier, `\w`, which is used to match `[a-zA-Z0-9]`, or in English, all the alphanumeric characters.

2. Use the class brackets to match either an alphanumeric character or a dash. This is because DNS can include dashes. Why didn't you use the same pattern before? Simple — because a valid DNS cannot begin or end with a dash. You allow zero or more characters from this expanded class by using the * repeat count.

    `re.Pattern = "http://(\w`**`[\w-]*`**`\w.` `.*\w+"`

3. You again strictly want an alphanumeric character so your domain name doesn't end in a dash. The last pattern in the parentheses matches the dots (.) used to separate DNS levels.

You can't use the dot alone because that is a special character that normally matches any single character except a new line. Thus, you "escape" this character, by preceding it with a slash \.

4. After wrapping all that in parentheses, just to keep your grouping straight, you again use the * repeat count. So the following highlighted pattern will match any valid domain name followed by a dot. To put it another way, it will match one level of a fully qualified DNS.

```
re.Pattern = "http://(\w[\w-]*\w\.)*\w+"
```

5. You end the pattern by requiring one or more alphanumeric characters for the top-level domain name (for example, the com, org, edu, and so on).

```
re.Pattern = "http://(\w[\w-]*\w\.)*\w+"
```

Execute Method

This method is used to execute a regular expression search against a specified string and returns a Matches collection. This is the trigger in the code to run the pattern matching on the string.

Code	object.Execute(*string*)
Object	Always a RegExp object.
String	The text string that is searched for — required.

The actual pattern for the regular expression search is set using the Pattern property of the RegExp object.

```
Dim re, s
Set re = New RegExp
re.Global = True
re.Pattern = "http://(\w+[\w-]*\w+\.)*\w+"
s = "http://www.kingsley-hughes.com is a valid web address. And so is "
s = s & vbCrLf & "http://www.wrox.com. And " s = s & vbCrLf &
"http://www.pc.ibm.com - even with 4 levels."

Set colMatches = re.Execute(s)

For Each match In colMatches
    MsgBox "Found valid URL: " & match.Value
Next
```

Note the difference with other languages that support regular expressions that treat the results of Execute as a Boolean to determine whether or not the pattern was found. As a result of this difference, you'll quite often see examples that have been converted from another language that simply don't work in VBScript!

Some of Microsoft's own documentation has been known to contain such errors, most of which have hopefully been corrected by now.

Remember the result of `Execute` is always a collection, possibly even an empty collection. You can use a test like `if re.Execute(s).count = 0`, or better yet use the `Test` method, which is designed for this purpose.

Replace Method

This method is used to replace text found in a regular expression search.

Code	`object.Replace(string1, string2)`
Object	Always a `RegExp` object.
`string1`	This is the text string in which the text replacement is to occur — required.
`string2`	This is the replacement text string — required.

The `Replace` method returns a copy of `string1` with the text of `RegExp.Pattern` replaced with `string2`. If no match is found in the string, a copy of `string1` is returned unchanged.

```
Dim re, s
Set re = New RegExp
re.Pattern = "http://(\w+[\w-]*\w+\.)*\w+"
s = "http://www.kingsley-hughes.com is a valid web address. And so is "
s = s & vbCrLf & "http://www.wrox.com. And "
s = s & vbCrLf & "http://www.pc.ibm.com - even with 4 levels."

MsgBox re.Replace(s, "** TOP SECRET! **")
```

The output of the preceding code is shown in Figure 9-19.

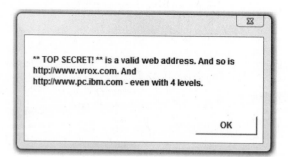

Figure 9-19

The `Replace` method can also replace subexpressions in the pattern. To accomplish this, you use the special characters `$1`, `$2`, and so on, in the replace text. These "parameters" refer to remembered matches.

Backreferencing

A remembered match is simply part of a pattern. This is known as *backreferencing*. You designate which parts you want to store into a temporary buffer by enclosing them in parentheses. Each captured submatch is stored in the order in which it is encountered (from left to right in a regular expressions pattern). The buffer numbers where the submatches are stored begins at 1 and continues up to a maximum of 99 subexpressions. They are then referred to sequentially as $1, $2, and so on.

You can override the saving of that part of the regular expression using the noncapturing metacharacters "?:", "?=", or "?!".

In the following example, the first five words (consisting of one or more nonwhite space characters) are remembered, and then only four of them are displayed in the replacement text:

```
Dim re, s
Set re = New RegExp
re.Pattern = "(\S+)\s+(\S+)\s+(\S+)\s+(\S+)\s+(\S+)"
s = "VBScript is not very cool."
MsgBox re.Replace(s, "$1 $2 $4 $5")
```

The output of the preceding code is shown in Figure 9-20.

VBScript is very cool.

OK

Figure 9-20

Notice how in the preceding code you've added a (\S+)\s+ pair for each word in the string. This is to give the code greater control over how the string is handled. With this, you prevent the tail of the string from being added to the end of the string displayed. Take great care when using backreferencing to make sure that the outputs you get are what you expect them to be to!

Test Method

The `Test` method executes a regular expression search against a specified string and returns a Boolean value that indicates whether or not a pattern match was found.

Code	`object.Test(string)`
Object	Always the name of the RegExp object.
String	The text string upon which the regular expression is executed — required.

The Test method returns True if a pattern match is found and False if no match is found. This is the preferred way to determine if a string contains a pattern. Note you often must make patterns case insensitive, as in the following example:

```
Dim re, s
Set re = New RegExp
re.IgnoreCase = True
re.Pattern = "http://(\w+[\w-]*\w+\.)*\w+"
s = "Some long string with http://www.wrox.com buried in it."
If re.Test(s) Then
    MsgBox "Found a URL."
Else
    MsgBox "No URL found."
End If
```

The output of the preceding code is shown in Figure 9-21.

Figure 9-21

The Matches Collection

The Matches collection contains regular expression Match objects.

The only way to create this collection is by using the Execute method of the RegExp object. It is important to remember that the Matches collection property is read-only, as are the individual Match objects.

For more on RegExp *objects, see the section "The RegExp Object."*

When a regular expression is executed, zero or more Match objects result. Each Match object provides access to three things:

❑   The string found by the regular expression

❑   The length of the string

❑   An index to where the match was found

Remember to set the Global property to True or your Matches collection can never contain more than one member. This is an easy way to create a very simple but hard to trace bug!

```
Dim re, objMatch, colMatches, sMsg
Set re = New RegExp
re.Global = True re.Pattern = "http://(\w+[\w-]*\w+\.)*\w+" s =
"http://www.kingsley-hughes.com is a valid web address. And so is "
s = s & vbCrLf & "http://www.wrox.com. As is "
s = s & vbCrLf & "http://www.wiley.com."
```

```
Set colMatches = re.Execute(s)
sMsg = ""
For Each objMatch in colMatches
    sMsg = sMsg & "Match of " & objMatch.Value
    sMsg = sMsg & ", found at position " & objMatch.FirstIndex & " of
the string."
    sMsg = sMsg & "The length matched is "
    sMsg = sMsg & objMatch.Length & "." & vbCrLf
Next
MsgBox sMsg
```

Matches Properties

Matches is a simple collection and supports just two properties:

1. Count returns the number of items in the collection.

```
Dim re, objMatch, colMatches, sMsg
Set re = New RegExp
re.Global = True re.Pattern = "http://(\w+[\w-]*\w+\.)*\w+"
s = "http://www.kingsley-hughes.com is a valid web address. And so is "
s = s & vbCrLf {\&} "http://www.wrox.com. As is "
s = s & vbCrLf & "http://www.wiley.com."
Set colMatches = re.Execute(s)
```

```
MsgBox colMatches.count
```

The output of the preceding code is shown in Figure 9-22.

Figure 9-22

2. `Item` returns an item based on the specified key.

```
Dim re, objMatch, colMatches, sMsg
Set re = New RegExp
re.Global = True re
re Pattern = "http://(\w+[\w-]*\w+\.)*\w+"
s = "http://www.kingsley-hughes.com is a valid web address. And so is "
s = s & vbCrLf & "http://www.wrox.com. As is " s = s & vbCrLf _
& "http://www.wiley.com."
Set colMatches = re.Execute(s)
```

```
MsgBox colMatches.item(0)
MsgBox colMatches.item(1)
MsgBox colMatches.item(2)
```

The Match Object

`Match` objects are the members in a `Matches` collection. The only way to create a `Match` object is by using the `Execute` method of the `RegExp` object. When a regular expression is executed, zero or more `Match` objects can result. Each `Match` object provides the following:

❑ Access to the string found by the regular expression

❑ The length of the string found

❑ An index to where in the string the match was found

The `Match` object has three properties, all of which are read-only: `FirstIndex`, `Length`, and `Value`. These properties are detailed next.

FirstIndex Property

The `FirstIndex` property returns the position in a search string where a match occurs.

Code	`object.FirstIndex.`
Object	Always a `Match` object.

The `FirstIndex` property uses a zero-based offset from the beginning of the search string. To put it in plain English, the first character in the string is identified as character zero (0).

```
Dim re, objMatch, colMatches, sMsg
Set re = New RegExp
re.Global = True
re.Pattern = "http://(\w+[\w-]*\w+\.)*\w+" s = "http://www.kingsley-hughes.com _
is a valid web address. And so is"
s = s & vbCrLf & "http://www.wrox.com. As is " s = s & vbCrLf _
& "http://www.wiley.com."
Set colMatches = re.Execute(s)
sMsg = ""
```

```
For Each objMatch in colMatches
    sMsg = sMsg & "Match of " & objMatch.Value
    sMsg = sMsg & ", found at position " & objMatch.FirstIndex & " of the string. "
    sMsg = sMsg & "The length matched is "
    sMsg = sMsg & objMatch.Length & "." & vbCrLf
Next
MsgBox sMsg
```

Length Property

The `Length` property returns the length of a match found in a search string.

Code	`object.Length.`
Object	Always a `Match` object.

Here is an example of the Length property in action.

```
Dim re, objMatch, colMatches, sMsg
Set re = New RegExp
re.Global = True re.Pattern = "http://(\w+[\w-]*\w+\.)*\w+"
s = "http://www.kingsley-hughes.com is a valid web address. And so is "
s = s & vbCrLf & "http://www.wrox.com. As is "
s = s & vbCrLf & "http://www.wiley.com."
Set colMatches = re.Execute(s)
sMsg = ""
For Each objMatch in colMatches
    sMsg = sMsg & "Match of " & objMatch.Value
    sMsg = sMsg & ", found at position " & objMatch.FirstIndex & "
of the string. "
    sMsg = sMsg & "The length matched is "
    sMsg = sMsg & objMatch.Length & "." & vbCrLf
Next
MsgBox sMsg
```

Value Property

The `Value` property returns the value or text of a match found in a search string.

Code	`object.Value.`
Object	Always a `Match` object.

Here is an example of the Value property in action.

```
Dim re, objMatch, colMatches, sMsg
Set re = New RegExp
re.Global = True re.Pattern = "http://(\w+[\w-]*\w+\.)*\w+"
s = "http://www.kingsley-hughes.com is a valid web address. And so is "
s = s & vbCrLf & "http://www.wrox.com. As is "
s = s & vbCrLf & "http://www.wiley.com."
Set colMatches = re.Execute(s) sMsg = ""
For Each objMatch in colMatches

    sMsg = sMsg & "Match of " & objMatch.Value

    sMsg = sMsg & ", found at position " & objMatch.FirstIndex & "
of the string. "
    sMsg = sMsg & "The length matched is "
    sMsg = sMsg & objMatch.Length & "." & vbCrLf
Next
MsgBox sMsg
```

A Few Examples

You've covered a lot of theory in the past few pages but, although theory is great, you might like to see regular expressions in action. The remaining part of this chapter gives a few examples of how you can make use of regular expressions to solve real-life problems.

Validating Phone Number Input

Validating inputs prevents a user from entering bogus or dubious information. One piece of information that many developers need to make sure of is a telephone number entered correctly. While you cannot write a script to actually check if a number is a valid phone number, you can use script and regular expressions to enforce a format on the input, which helps to eliminate false entry.

Here is a simple code sample for validating that a standard U.S. phone number entered conforms to the format (XXX) XXX-XXXX.

```
Dim re, s, objMatch, colMatches
Set re = New RegExp
re.Pattern = "\([0-9]{3}\)[0-9]{3}-[0-9]{4}"
re.Global = True
re.IgnoreCase = True
s = InputBox("Enter your phone number in the following Format (XXX) XXX-XXXX:")
If re.Test(s) Then
    MsgBox "Thank you!"
Else
    MsgBox "Sorry but that number is not in a valid format."
End If
```

The code is simple, but again it is the pattern that does all the hard work. Depending on the input, you can get one of two possible output messages, shown in Figures 9-23 and 9-24.

Figure 9-23

Figure 9-24

If you want to make this script applicable in countries with other formats, you must do a little work on it, but customizing it isn't difficult.

Breaking Down URIs

Here is an example that can be used to break down a Universal Resource Indicator (URI) into its component parts. Take the following URI:

```
www.wrox.com:80/misc-pages/support.shtml
```

You can write a script that will break it down into the protocol (ftp, http, and so on), the domain address, and the page/path. To do this, use the following pattern:

```
"(\w+):\ / \ /([^ / :]+)(:\d*)?( [^ # ]*)"
```

The following code carries out the task:

```
Dim re, s Set
re = New RegExp
re.Pattern = "(\w+):\ / \ /( [^ /:]+)(:\d*)?( [^ # ]*)"
re.Global = True
re.IgnoreCase = True
s = "http://www.wrox.com:80/misc-pages/support.shtml"
MsgBox re.Replace(s, "$1")
MsgBox re.Replace(s, "$2")
MsgBox re.Replace(s, "$3")
MsgBox re.Replace(s, "$4")
```

Testing for HTML Elements

Testing for HTML elements is easy; all you need is the right pattern. Here is one that works for elements with both an opening and closing tag.

```
"<(.*)>.*<\/\1>"
```

How you script this depends on what you want to do. Here is a simple script just for demonstration purposes. You could refine this code to look for specific elements or carry out basic error checking.

```
Dim re, s
Set re = New RegExp
re.IgnoreCase = True
re.Pattern = "<(.*)>.*<\ / \1>"
s = "<p>This is a paragraph</p>"
If re.Test(s) Then
    MsgBox "HTML element found."
Else
    MsgBox "No HTML element found."
End If
```

Matching White Space

Sometimes it can be really handy to match white space, that is, lines that are either completely empty, or that only contain white space (spaces and tab characters). Here is the pattern you would need for that.

```
"^[ \t]*$"
```

That breaks down to the following:

```
^ —Matches the start of the line.
[\t]*—Match zero or more space or tab (\t) characters.
$ —Match the end of the line.
```

```
Dim re, s, colMatches, objMatch, sMsg
Set re = New RegExp
re.Global = True re.Pattern = "^[ \t]*$"
s = " "
Set colMatches = re.Execute(s)
sMsg = ""
For Each objMatch in colMatches
    sMsg = sMsg & "Blank line found at position " & _
objMatch.FirstIndex & " of the string."Next
MsgBox sMsg
```

Matching HTML Comment Tags

When you get to the section on Windows Script Host in a later chapter (Chapter 15), you learn how to use VBScript and Widows Script Host to work with the file system. Once you can do this, reading and modifying files becomes within your reach. One good application of regular expressions might be to look for comment tags within an HTML file. You could then choose to remove these before making the files available on the Web.

Here is a script that can detect HTML comment tags.

```
Dim re, s
Set re = New RegExp
re.Global = True
re.Pattern = "^.*<!--.*-->.*$"
s = " <title>A Title</title> <!-- a title tag -->"
If re.Test(s) Then
    MsgBox "HTML comment tags found."
Else
    MsgBox "No HTML comment tags found."
End If
```

With a simple modification to the pattern and the use of `Replace` method, you can get the script to remove the comment tag altogether.

```
Dim re, s
Set re = New RegExp
re.Global = True

re.Pattern = "(^.*)(<!--.*-->)(.*$)"

s = " <title>A Title</title> <!-- a title tag -->"
If re.Test(s) Then
    MsgBox "HTML comment tags found."
Else
    MsgBox "No HTML comment tags found."
End If

MsgBox re.Replace(s, "$1" & "$3")
```

Summary

This chapter covered, in depth, regular expressions and how they fit into the world of VBScript. It showed you how to use regular expressions to carry out effective, flexible pattern matching within text strings. It also showed examples of what can be done by effectively integrating regular expressions with script together with examples of customizable find and replace within text strings as well as input validations.

Learning to use regular expressions can seem a bit daunting, and even those comfortable with programming sometimes find regular expressions forbidding and choose instead less flexible solutions. However, the power and flexibility that regular expressions give to the programmer are immense and your efforts will be quickly rewarded!

10

Client-Side Web Scripting

In this chapter, you take VBScript straight to your web site visitor's browser. You take a look at how VBScript and Internet Explorer can be combined on the client side to create interesting and exciting HTML pages for your visitors.

Going straight for the client side is the easiest, low-tech, no-special-server needed way to get VBScript-enabled pages to the visitor. You can do it using any server, with no Active Server Pages (ASP) needed.

In this chapter you learn what you need to deliver VBScript-enabled content straight to the browser, as well as find out how it works and what you can do with it. You start by exploring the tools you'll need to write client-side VBScript.

Tools of the Trade

Creating HTML web pages requires nothing more than a text editor to type in your HTML code and a web browser to view it. To check that visitors to your web site see things the way you intend, you need to use the same browser or browsers as they are using. This is easy when you are dealing with Firefox or Opera because you can have many different versions installed on one system. Internet Explorer (IE) is a different case. Because it couples so tightly with the operating system, you can only have one version of Internet Explorer per machine.

A Little History Lesson

IE5 did have a compatibility mode that allowed you to launch IE5 acting as IE4. To use IE5's IE4 compatibility mode you did need to have IE4 installed on the machine prior to installing IE5, and you had to choose the IE4 compatibility mode option during the IE5 setup. For more details, see Microsoft Knowledge Base article 197311. Note that IE6 and IE7 have no such feature.

The same version of a browser may support different features or behave differently depending on the operating system. For example, IE4 on the Mac does not support ActiveX. Never assume that because something works on one browser or platform then it will work on them all.

It is quite possible to create all your pages using Windows Notepad. Many web developers do, and this has the advantage of being free (with Windows) and simple to use. However, creating a whole web site (especially if it is a large one) using just Notepad is needlessly complicated, when there are plenty of tools available specifically for web page creation. Most seasoned web designers have some kind of HTML editor that they use and probably swear by. If you're planning to do a lot of VBScripting and haven't decided on a tool to use, there are a few features that you might like to look out for. Features such as:

- ❑ **Syntax highlighting:** This makes the VBScript code much easier to read by color-coding-specific language keywords.

- ❑ **Automatic code completion:** This gives a list of available properties and methods associated with an HTML tag or an ActiveX control.

- ❑ **In-built support for event scripting:** This lists the events available for a particular tag or ActiveX control and even writes the code framework to handle the event.

Be careful of *WYSIWYG* HTML editors. Many WYSIWYG web page design applications also have a tendency to rearrange your carefully crafted HTML tags and code. Because of this, many developers start off by building the skeleton of the web site using a WYSIWYG page design tool and then switch back to Notepad or another simpler text-based editor to hand-code the scripts.

The Evolution of Scripting

Client-side scripting gives the web developer two separate abilities:

- ❑ The ability to manipulate elements within an HTML page
- ❑ The ability to interact with the user

It also provides the "glue" with which to bind and work with ActiveX components embedded in the page.

Client-side scripting, in the form of *JavaScript* 1.0, first emerged with the release of Netscape Navigator 2. Although very primitive and restrictive in comparison to the scripting capabilities of a modern Internet browser, it did mean that an HTML page was no longer just a static page consisting of information designed to be passively viewed by the end user, but that they were now active and able to act more like a conventional application.

Prior to Dynamic HTML (DHTML), the most important use of scripting was for the purposes of form validation. Forms have been supported since the very first browsers, back in the days when just being able to combine text and images on the same web page was considered the pinnacle of excitement.

However, forms have always presented problems. The problem that most web developers wish they could do something about was that there was no way to check whether the information the user had entered into a form field was actually valid — until after they had submitted it to the server. On receiving the submit form, the developer could easily check the validity of the data with a server-side component (usually a CGI program). However, it was always thought that it would be much more user-friendly and efficient to catch as many form errors as possible before getting to this stage. It would be much better if the user could be notified of any mistakes before the information was submitted to the server. Client-side scripting gives us the power to do precisely that.

Scripting in the earlier browsers also enabled a few simple special effects. The most popular amongst these were scrolling text in the status bar and image rollovers. However, once a page was loaded it was still essentially static. Some primitive responses to user interaction of the page were indeed possible, but nothing that could genuinely be called "dynamic" was possible. Any elements that were on the page were there to stay and could not be changed. Adding new elements to an existing page was also impossible.

As you will see in Chapter 14, all this changed with DHTML, particularly that supported by Microsoft's Internet Explorer 4, 5, 6, and 7. Including script into your page simply involves using the <script> tag. In theory there is no restriction concerning where you can place a script in an HTML page but normally you will place most of your scripts inside the <head> tag of an HTML page.

As a very simple example, the following script shows a message box when the page is loaded:

```
<html>
<head>
<title>A sample page</title>
<script language="VBScript">
    MsgBox "Hello World"
</script>

</head>

<body>
<h1>A page containing VBScript</h1>
</body>

</html>
```

Note that you use the `language` attribute to tell the browser to interpret the script as VBScript. JavaScript is the default language of Internet Explorer.

Notice something important about this script — it's not connected to any event in the browser and as such fires as soon as the browser reaches it when parsing the page.

Different Scripting Languages

The browser wars between Microsoft and Mozilla (and Netscape) have left us with a (sometimes confusing) array of scripting languages and standards.

The following table details which language is supported by a particular instance of Internet Explorer.

Browser Version	Microsoft
2	None
3	JScript 1, VBScript 1
4	JScript 3, VBScript 3
5	JScript 5, VBScript 5
6	JScript 5, VBScript 5
7	JScript 5, VBScript 5

This table relates to Windows platforms only. Internet Explorer for the Macintosh does not support VBScript.

Your choice of scripting language is ultimately limited by which browsers your pages must be compatible with. Although it is possible to include different client-side scripting languages in a page, it can quickly become confusing.

Things are a lot better nowadays than they once were, with Internet Explorer currently commanding an enormous lead over the other browsers in terms of browser numbers in use. However, even with one browser having massive dominance over the others, it's still hard for developers to shed their browser burdens and develop for one browser alone. However, greater problems loom on the horizon for web developers as a greater number of browsers (such as Opera and Mozilla) enter the market along with more diverse platforms (especially Linux-based platforms). On the plus side, with Netscape now pretty much out of the picture and Microsoft, Mozilla, and Opera paying more attention to standards, things are easier for developers.

There is one group of developers that have it easier than others when it comes to deciding what standards to support — the intranet developer. The intranet developer is in the enviable position of being able to know pretty well what browser and scripting language others are using and can develop pages and scripts that are perfectly suited to the target browser that is used. This makes the intranet developer's job a lot easier than that of an Internet developer.

JavaScript, JScript, and ECMAScript

JavaScript was first developed by Netscape and was introduced to the development community in Netscape Navigator 2. Although named JavaScript, it in fact has no connection with the development of the Java language, although its syntax can resemble that of Java. The original name for JavaScript was *LiveScript* but this was quickly changed to make it sound cooler and because developers wanted to reinforce the link that JavaScript could be used to control Java applets in a web page. This did nothing to discourage the link between Java and JavaScript and it persists to this day.

Because Netscape owned the name JavaScript, when Microsoft released its version of JavaScript with IE3 it had to be called something else. Microsoft chose JScript. JScript 1 had a remarkably similar set of features to that of Netscape's JavaScript 1.0. With their next release, Microsoft jumped a version to JScript 3, which again is very similar to (although not totally compatible with) JavaScript 1.2. In keeping with the skipping of version numbers, IE5 saw the release of JScript 5, which incorporates some of the features of JavaScript 1.3. Netscape released JavaScript 1.3 and 1.4 with Netscape Communicator 4 and then skipped a browser version altogether and went straight to Netscape 6 and JavaScript 1.5.

All the subtle (and sometimes not so subtle) differences between Netscape's and Microsoft's versions of JavaScript produced no end of headaches for developers who weren't really interested in marketing hype and one-upmanship. They just wanted to get the job done and utilize the power the languages offered, while remaining as browser neutral as they were able. There's nothing more frustrating than spending time developing and designing an all-singing, all-dancing web page, only to find that it needs to be significantly tweaked and rewritten to run on browser X, version Y, and platform Z.

To aid the developer, steps have been made toward compatibility between the various dialects of JavaScript, in the form of ECMAScript. The European Computer Manufacturers Association (ECMA) in December of 1999 released a standard for JavaScript ECMA-262, and hence ECMAScript. Microsoft's JScript 5 and Netscape's JavaScript 1.5 (along with the script engine supplied with the Opera browser) is fully compatible with ECMA-262. (The Opera script engine goes further and even adds support for a number of nonstandardized JavaScript/JScript objects.)

We're now at a position where Internet Explorer, Firefox, and Opera all fully support JavaScript, but VBScript is still only supported by Internet Explorer.

VBScript

Given that you already have a fully featured scripting language in the form of JavaScript (in all of its forms and incarnations), why use VBScript?

Well, first, if you're a Visual Basic or VBA (Visual Basic for Applications, the version of Visual Basic supported with many Microsoft products, such as Microsoft Office) developer, then you'll feel right at home with VBScript, which is a subset of VBA. With such similarity (and this book!), you'll quickly be ready to create sophisticated Web applications. JavaScript's syntax is arguably less intuitive and more obtuse than that of VBScript, and tends to be less forgiving of simple "mistakes" such as case sensitivity.

In terms of what VBScript and JavaScript can actually do, there is little to choose between the two. Almost everything that can be achieved in one language can be achieved in the other; however, sometimes clever and intuitive workarounds are necessary. Although not compliant with the ECMA standard at all (because it's a different language), Microsoft has made clear their intention that VBScript will continue to match JavaScript in terms of functionality.

There are important differences between VBScript and VBA. VBScript is an untyped language, which means that all variables are variants and don't have an explicit type (such as integer or string).

In fact, they do have subtypes that you can (and often need to) use. Conversion functions such as CLng, CStr, *and* CInt *make explicit the subtype you're dealing with.*

If you are used to using VBA, one difference that you will certainly find when moving to VBScript is that error handling is a lot less powerful.

Responding to Browser Events

Most of the client-side scripting you'll do involves handling events raised by objects in the page. It could be the onLoad event of the page itself, onSubmit event of a form, the onClick event of an image, or an event raised by an ActiveX control that you have embedded in your page. The reference section of the book includes a listing of objects and the events they support.

Adding an Event Handler

The easiest way to add an event handler in Internet Explorer is to define a Sub or Function to handle it inside a `<script>` block. The name for the Sub or Function must be of the form elementName_eventname. Also note in the following example the use of the VBScript Me object, which references the object (for example, an HTML tag or ActiveX control) that caused the event to fire.

```
<html>
<head>
<title>A sample page</title>
<script language="VBScript">
    Sub cmdFireEvent_onclick
        MsgBox Me.Name & " made me pop this message up!"
    End Sub
</script>

</head>

<body>
<input type="button" name="cmdFireEvent" value="Trigger">
</body>

</html>
```

Clicking the button generates the message box displayed in Figure 10-1.

Figure 10-1

An alternative way of doing the same thing is to use the for and event properties of the `<script>` tag. All the code inside the `<script>` tags executes when the event fires.

```
<html>
<head>
<title>A sample page</title>
<script for="cmdFireEvent" event="onclick"
language="VBScript">
MsgBox Me.Name & " made me pop this message up!"
</script>

</head>
```

```
<body>
<input type="button" name="cmdFireEvent" value="Trigger">
</body>

</html>
```

Different code, but as Figure 10-2 shows, the result is the same.

Figure 10-2

Adding an Event Handler That Passes Parameters

If you want to pass parameters to your event handling subroutine, then you must define a Sub or Function and call that in your element's onEvent embedded inside the tag. You must not name your subroutine elementName_EventName or the browser will get confused with the first way you saw in the example that defines the event in the last section.

Because you're calling a separate subroutine (and not directly defining an event handler), the Me object if used inside the subroutine won't point to the element that caused the event to fire. It will, however, behave "correctly" in the procedure that calls the function; so from here you can pass Me to the Sub as one of its parameters.

```
<html>
<head>
<title>A sample page</title>
```

```
<script language="VBScript">
Sub DoSomething(theElement,theNumber)
MsgBox theElement.Name & " made me fire"
MsgBox "Today's number is the number " & theNumber
End Sub
</script>
```

```
</head>

<body>
```

```
<input type="button" name="cmdFireEvent" Value="Trigger" onClick="DoSomething
Me,99">
```

```
</body>

</html>
```

Here, the subroutine is called DoSomething, and it's called from the onclick event of the input button with two parameters. Me works fine in the event handler, but note that if you were to try to refer directly to Me in the DoSomething procedure, it would have no meaning because the DoSomething procedure is a stand-alone Sub.

Figures 10-3 and 10-4 show the message boxes generated by this code.

Figure 10-3

Figure 10-4

Cancelling Events

Some events, such as those associated with link tags and forms, can be cancelled. If, for example, the user has entered an invalid value in a form, then you don't want the form to submit because you know that it will fail to process at the server side if it contains bogus information. Instead, you want to stop the event in its tracks and notify the user.

To do this, you normally need to return a value of False to cancel the action. As only functions (not subroutines) can have return values, you need to define your event handler code as a function.

```
<html>
<head>
<title>A sample page containing a form</title>

<script language="VBScript">

Function form1_onsubmit()
' Has the user entered something?

If form1.txtNumber.value = "" Then
MsgBox "You must enter a value!"
form1_onsubmit = false
' Is it a valid number?

ElseIf Not IsNumeric(form1.txtNumber.value) Then
MsgBox "You must enter a number!"
form1_onsubmit = false
' Is the value in the correct range?

ElseIf form1.txtNumber.value > 10 Or _
form1.txtNumber.value < 1 Then
MsgBox "Invalid number!"
form1_onsubmit = false

Else
'Form submit can continue
MsgBox "Valid Number. Thank you!"
End If
End Function
</script>

</head>

<body>

<form action="" method="POST" id="form1" name="form1">
Enter a number from 1 to 10
<input type="text" id="txtNumber" name="txtNumber">
<br>
<input type="submit" value="Submit" id="submit1" name="submit1">
</form>

</body>

</html>
```

Depending on the input, the script generates the appropriate message. The user can enter nothing, a number outside of the appropriate range, or a number in the right range and the appropriate message is displayed accordingly. These are shown in Figures 10-5, 10-6, and 10-7 respectively.

The Order of Things

With most events in a script it's quite obvious when they will fire. You click a button, and the onclick event fires. However, there are some events that don't fire as a direct response to user interaction. The window_onload event is a good example of this. Any script in your page outside of a subprocedure or

Figure 10-5

Figure 10-6

function will fire as the page is parsed by the browser. But which comes first, the `window_onload` or the parsed code? Also if you have a frameset and frames, what will be the order of the `window_onloads` fire?

To illustrate, look at a simple example. You'll need to create three HTML pages: a page containing the frameset tags and a page for each of the frames.

Figure 10-7

First you have the frameset page, which you'll call `EventOrder.htm`.

```
<html>
<head>
<title>A sample page containing script</title>
<script language="VBScript">
Dim sEventTracker
Dim iEventOrder
iEventOrder = 0

window.Parent.iEventOrder = window.Parent.iEventOrder + 1
window.Parent.sEventTracker = window.Parent.sEventTracker _
  & window.Parent.iEventOrder _
  & " Frameset - First code in Page" & Chr(13) & Chr(10)
Sub window_onload
iEventOrder = iEventOrder + 1
  sEventTracker = sEventTracker & iEventOrder _
    & " Frameset window_onload" & Chr(13) & Chr(10)
End Sub
</script>

</head>

<frameset rows="50%,*">
    <frame src="top.htm" id="fraTop" name="fraTop">
    <frame src="bottom.htm" id="fraBottom" name="fraBottom">
        <noframes>
            <body>
            <p>This page uses frames, but your browser doesn't
                support them.</p>
            </body>
        </noframes>
</frameset>

</html>
```

Next you create the top frame page. Save this page as top.htm.

```html
<html>
<head>
<title>A sample page containing script</title>
<script language="VBScript">
window.Parent.iEventOrder = window.Parent.iEventOrder + 1
window.Parent.sEventTracker = window.Parent.sEventTracker _
   & window.Parent.iEventOrder _
   & " Top frame - First code in Page" & Chr(13) & Chr(10)

Sub cmdCheckForm_onclick
    window.Parent.iEventOrder = window.Parent.iEventOrder + 1
    window.Parent.sEventTracker = window.Parent.sEventTracker _
    & window.Parent.iEventOrder _
    & " Top frame - cmdCheckForm_onclick" & Chr(13) & Chr(10)
    form1.txtEvents.Value = window.Parent.sEventTracker
End Sub

Sub window_onload
    window.Parent.iEventOrder = window.Parent.iEventOrder + 1
    window.Parent.sEventTracker = window.Parent.sEventTracker _
    & window.Parent.iEventOrder _
    & " Top frame - window_onload" & Chr(13) & Chr(10)
End Sub
</script>

</head>

<body>
<form action="some_form_handler.asp" method="post" id="form1" name="form1">
<textarea cols="60" name="txtEvents" rows="10"></textarea>
<input type="button" value="List Events" name="cmdCheckForm">
</form>

<script language="VBScript">
window.Parent.iEventOrder = window.Parent.iEventOrder + 1
window.Parent.sEventTracker = window.Parent.sEventTracker _
   & window.Parent.iEventOrder _
   & " Top frame - Second code in Page" & Chr(13) & Chr(10)
</script>
</body>

<html>
```

Finally, create the page for the bottom frame. Save this as bottom.htm.

```html
<html>
<head>
<title>A sample page containing script</title>
<script language="VBScript">
window.Parent.iEventOrder = window.Parent.iEventOrder + 1
window.Parent.sEventTracker = window.Parent.sEventTracker _
   & window.Parent.iEventOrder _
   & " bottom frame - First code in Page" & Chr(13) & Chr(10)
```

```
Sub window_onload
  window.Parent.iEventOrder = window.Parent.iEventOrder + 1
  window.parent.sEventTracker = window.Parent.sEventTracker _
    & window.Parent.iEventOrder _
    & " bottom frame - window_onload" & Chr(13) & Chr(10)
End Sub
</script>

</head>

<body>
</body>
</html>
```

If you load the page containing the frameset, then click the list events button, the text area fills with details of the `window_onload` events and embedded scripts, listed in the order they fired. This is shown in Figure 10-8.

Figure 10-8

It's perhaps worth noting that the differences between browsers include not just the events each HTML tag has but also the order in which they fire. For example, if you run this code in IE3 you'll find the order in which events fire is different from that of IE5 and IE6. Although the events you've used in the examples are the same for IE4, IE5, IE6, and IE7 you will find other differences between them.

Form Validation

On the web, the most common way to obtain information from a user is an HTML form populated with a variety of form elements (in case you're wondering, email is another option). When you use script, the HTML form can be manipulated and examined using its form object. An HTML page can have one or more forms that you can reference either by name or using the document object's forms array. In most cases it's easier just to refer to a form by name.

To insert an HTML form into a page, the `<form>` *tag is used along with the corresponding* `</form>` *close tag.*

The most important properties of the `<form>` tag are `Action` and `Method`. The `Action` property is the URL where the form will post to, for example an ASP page or a CGI script.

The `Method` property can be either `post` or `get`, and determines how the form's data is transmitted to the server when the form is submitted. If the `Method` property is set to `get`, then the data in the form's elements will be appended to the URL that was specified in the `Action` property. A form `Method` of `post` sends the form's data as a data stream to the server along with the `http` header.

Normally it is the form `post` method that is used most often. HTML 4.0 standard even deprecated the `get` method, although this doesn't stop it from being used. The reason for this is because `get` places a character limit on how much data can be sent and is actually visible in the URL for your users to see, something which you may not want.

Having defined the form tags, you can then populate the form with the HTML controls (commonly referred to as *elements*) available. The most common controls are:

❑   Input boxes

❑   Radio buttons

❑   Select controls

The next thing you need to worry about is how to make sure what the user submits is valid data.

Validating Numerical Input Box Values

The most common criteria for validation of an input box that's being used for the entry of numerical data are:

❑   That the field has been completed

❑   That it contains a numeric value

❑   That the numeric value is within an acceptable range

❑   That it is an integer

You saw a simple example of this earlier on when you looked at cancelling events. The following example describes another approach. If the value entered by the user into `form1`'s element `text1` is an integer between `1` and `10`, then a message box tells you that it's valid. At this point (in real life at least, but not as far as the example is concerned) you would actually submit the form rather than inform the user using a message box the way that's done here. The line `"form1.submit"` (which is currently commented out) in the following code will do this, although to use the code as supplied here, you need to create the page `some_form_handler.asp` for yourself or provide an alternative way to process the form.

If the user has entered invalid data, then the `ValidInteger` function returns a message describing the problem.

```
<html>
<head>
<title>A sample page containing script</title>
<script language="VBScript">
Function ValidInteger(sNumber, iMin, iMax)
    Dim iNumber
    ' Is it a number?

    If IsNumeric(sNumber) Then

        ' Is it an integer?
        If InStr(sNumber,".") = 0 Then

            ' Is it in the correct range?
            If CLng(sNumber) >= iMin And CLng(sNumber) <= iMax Then
            ValidInteger = ""
            Else
            ValidInteger = "You must enter an integer between " _
            & iMin & " and " & iMax
End If

    Else
        ValidInteger = "You must enter a whole number"
    End If

    Else
        ValidInteger = "You must enter a number"
    End If End Function

Sub cmdCheckForm_onclick
    Dim sValidity
    sValidity = ValidInteger(form1.text1.value,1,10)
    If sValidity = "" Then
        MsgBox "Valid"
        'form1.submit
    Else
        MsgBox sValidity
    End If

End Sub
</script>

</head>

<body>
<form action="some_form_handler.asp" method="post" id="form1" name="form1">
    <input id="text1" name="text1">
    <input type="button" value="Button" id="cmdCheckForm" name="cmdCheckForm">
</form>
</body>

</html>
```

The outputs generated by the script contained in this form are again reliant upon the input that the user gives it via the input box. Again, this example isn't very sophisticated but does serve as a starting point for more complex and relevant form validation scripts.

Validating Radio Buttons

The only check for validity you can make with a radio button group is that one element has been selected by the user. You can define one of the elements to be checked by default, simply by putting checked inside one of the radio buttons' tags.

In case you are not familiar with HTML, to define a group of radio buttons you simply create a number of radio buttons and give them the same name.

Some things are too important to be left to defaults, though. Take the example of a radio group for selecting a credit card type. By not using a default, you know that the user has made a positive choice in setting his or her credit card type. Otherwise there is a danger that they could have missed the question, and you would end up with invalid information.

```
<html>
<head>
<title>A sample page containing script</title>
<script language="VBScript">
Function RadioGroupValid(radGroup)
    Dim iElement
    RadioGroupValid = False
    ' Loop through the radio buttons in the group
    For iElement = 0 To radGroup.Length - 1
        ' If one is checked then we have validity
        If radGroup(iElement).Checked = True _
            Then RadioGroupValid = True
    Next
End Function

Sub cmdCheckForm_onclick
    Dim sValidity
    If RadioGroupValid(form1.radCreditCard) Then
        MsgBox "You made a selection. Thank you!"
        'form1.submit
    Else
        MsgBox "You forgot to make a selection. Try again."
    End If
End Sub
</script>

</head>

<body>
<form action="some_form_handler.asp" method="post" id="form1" name="form1">
  Visa
  <input type="radio" id="radCreditCard" name="radCreditCard" value="Visa">
  <br>
  Master Card
  <input type="radio" id="radCreditCard" name="radCreditCard" value="MasterCard">
  <br>
  American Express
  <input type="radio" id="radCreditCard" name="radCreditCard" value="AmericanExpress">
  <br>
```

```
    Other
    <input type="radio" id="radCreditCard" name="radCreditCard" value="Other">
    <br>
    <input type="button" value="Test" id="cmdCheckForm" name="cmdCheckForm">
</form>
</body>

</html>
```

The code in the page loops through each of the radio buttons in the group and checks to see if one is selected. You can also determine how many elements there are in a group using the length property.

When the form is actually posted, the value sent will only be the value of the selected radio button. So if radio button 3 is selected, then radio1=AmericanExpress will be submitted to the server and nothing else.

Validating Select Controls and Dates

An HTML select element can be used in the same way as a Visual Basic combo box or a list box, depending on its size property. If the size property is set to 1, then it acts just like a drop-down combo box, but if its size is set to more than 1, then it becomes a list box.

One common use of the select element is to allow the user to enter a date. It has enormous advantages over using a text box for dates, the main one being its clarity and ease of use for the user. Take the difference between American and British date formatting. Each country has a different format and this has enormous scope for causing problems (in Britain 11/07/2007 is interpreted as the 11th day of July 2007; in America this is November 7th of 2007). Using select controls, you can unambiguously pass the date that you mean without trusting the user to get it the right way around.

In the following example, you validate the date defined by the user selecting from certain boxes. You need to ensure that they don't select an invalid date, such as the 31st of April or the 29th of February in a non–leap year.

```
<html>
<head>
<title>A sample page containing script</title>
<script language="VBScript">
Function CheckDate(sDay, sMonth, sYear)
    On Error Resume Next
    Dim Date1
    ' If invalid date an error will be raised
    Date1 = CDate(sDay & "/" & sMonth & "/" & sYear)
    ' If error number not 0 then invalid date
    If Err.number <> 0 Then
        Err.Clear
        ' Calc days in month by going to next month then
        ' subtract 1 day
        Date1 = DateAdd("m",1,sMonth & "/" & sYear)
        Date1 = DateAdd("d",-1,Date1)
        CheckDate = "There are only " & Day(Date1) _
        & " days in " & sMonth
    Else
        CheckDate = ""
    End If
```

(continued)

277

```
End Function

Sub cmdCheckForm_onclick
    sDateValidityMessage = CheckDate(form1.cboDay.Value, _
        form1.cboMonth.Value, form1.cboYear.Value)
    If sDateValidityMessage <> "" Then
        MsgBox sDateValidityMessage
    Else
MsgBox "That date is valid"
        'form1.submit
    End If
End Sub
</script>

</head>

<body>
<form action="some_form_handler.asp" method="post" id="form1" name="form1">
<select id="cboDay" name="cboDay" size="1">
<option value="1">1
<option value="2">2
<option value="3">3
<option value="4">4
<option value="5">5
<option value="6">6
<option value="7">7
<option value="8">8
<option value="9">9
<option value="10">10
<option value="11">11
<option value="12">12
<option value="13">13
<option value="14">14
<option value="15">15
<option value="16">16
<option value="17">17
<option value="18">18
<option value="19">19
<option value="20">20
<option value="21">21
<option value="22">22
<option value="23">23
<option value="24">24
<option value="25">25
<option value="26">26
<option value="27">27
<option value="28">28
<option value="29">29
<option value="30">30
<option value="31">31
</select>

<select id="cboMonth" name="cboMonth" size=1>
<option value="Jan">Jan
<option value="Feb">Feb
<option value="Mar">Mar
```

```
<option value="Apr">Apr
<option value="May">May
<option value="Jun">Jun
<option value="Jul">Jul
<option value="Aug">Aug
<option value="Sep">Sep
<option value="Oct">Oct
<option value="Nov">Nov
<option value="Dec">Dec
</select>
<select id="cboYear" name="cboYear" size=1>
<option value="2003">2003
<option value="2004">2004
<option value="2005">2005
<option value="2006">2006
<option value="2007">2007
<option value="2008">2008
</select>
<br>
<input type="button" value="Test" id="cmdCheckForm" name="cmdCheckForm">
</form>
</body>
</html>
```

Figure 10-9 shows the result on choosing a valid date, while Figure 10-10 shows the response to selecting an invalid date.

Figure 10-9

Figure 10-10

The Document Object Model in Action

VBScript cannot exist within a vacuum. It is a tool with which you leverage and manipulate the environment of its current context or host, whether that be Windows Script Host and the Windows system, Active Server Pages and Internet Information Server, or a web page and the browser. But what are you actually manipulating? The answer is the Document Object Model.

The *Document Object Model (DOM)* is an all-encompassing term for the programmatic interface to the hierarchy of objects available within a browser and the web page it displays. It maps out each object's associated properties, methods, and events. Objects include the browser itself, a frame's window, the document or web page within that frame and the HTML, XHTML, and XML tags within the page, as well as any plug-ins or embedded ActiveX controls. The DOM also includes a number of collections of objects, such as the forms collection you've already seen in use.

Every browser version has its own DOM, and they vary considerably between Microsoft's Internet Explorer and Netscape's Navigator. There is also considerable variation between different versions of the same browser.

In an effort to bring about a common standard for the DOM, the *World Wide Web Consortium (W3C)* (the body that deals with Web standards) has released a number of standards for defining the DOM.

❏   The W3C's DOM (Level 0) approximated to the level supported by version 3 browsers.

❏   Level 1 DOM specifications, released in October 1998, struck a balance between IE4's DOM and that of Netscape 4's, though IE4's was much closer to the specification. The changes from the Level 0 DOM to Level 1, particularly those supported by IE4, were quite dramatic. The Level 1 specification makes every element within a page a programmable object and exposes its attributes as properties. Microsoft's DOM in IE4 went even further, allowing pages to be updated even after they have been loaded. This puts the "Dynamic" in Dynamic HTML. Prior to this (with the exception of images), once the page was loaded into a browser no further changes were possible.

❑   Level 2 was completed in November 2000. It extended on Level 1 with support for XML 1.0 with namespaces, adding support for Cascading Style Sheets (CSS), events such as user-interface events and tree manipulation events, and enhancing tree manipulation methods (tree ranges and traversal mechanisms). The DOM Level 2 HTML became a W3C recommendation in January 2003.

❑   The new DOM Level 3 supported by IE5 and IE6 is a significantly evolutionary move on from that supported by IE4. Under IE4 almost all tags were programmable, while under IE5 and IE6 all of the tags are individually programmable. Also, new methods introduced in IE5's DOM make dynamically manipulating the page easier in later versions of Internet Explorer than it was under IE4.

DOM Level 3 is currently recommended. Level 3 extends Level 2 by finishing support for XML 1.0 with namespaces, aligning the DOM Core with the XML Infoset, adding support for XML Base, and extending the user-interface events (keyboard). Level 3 also adds support for validation and the ability to load and save a document, explores further mixed markup vocabularies and their implications on the DOM API ("Embedded DOM"), and supports XPath.

You can find the latest information on DOM specification developments on the W3C's web site at `http://www.w3.org/DOM/`.

DOM specifications are all well and good, but as programmers it's the practical implementation you're interested in. Before leaving this chapter it's worth taking a look at the DOM as implemented by IE6.

The Window Object

Right at the top of the HTML, DOM hierarchy is the window object. If your page has no frames, then there is just one window object. If the page contains frames, then each frame has its own window object.

Each window object within a frameset has a parent window object, which is the window object of the page defining the frames. You can access any of the other window objects from script inside a page by using the window object's parent property. After you have a reference to the parent window object you can use that to access not only the window object's properties and methods, but also those of any HTML tags inside that window. You can also use it to access any global VBScript variables or functions.

Take a look at a simple frameset example. You will create three pages:

❑   The first defines a frameset.

❑   The second is the left window's page.

❑   The third is the right window's page.

The first page is called `TopFrame.htm`.

```
<html>
<head>
<title>A sample page containing script</title>
<script language="VBScript">
Dim sName
sName = "Top Frame"

Sub SayWhoIsThis()
    MsgBox "This is the top frame's subprocedure " _
    & "window.SayWhoIsThis"
End Sub
</script>

</head>

<frameset cols="50%,*">
  <frame src="LFrame.htm" name="LFrame">
  <frame src="RFrame.htm" name="RFrame">
</frameset>

</html>
```

The second page is called `LFrame.htm`.

```
<html>
<head>
<script language="VBSCRIPT">
Dim sName
sName = "Left Frame"

Sub SayWhoIsThis()
    MsgBox "This is LFrame's subroutine window.SayWhoIsThis"
End Sub
</script>
<title>Left Frame</title>
</head>
 <body>
<H1>Left Frame</H1>
</body>
</html>
```

The third page is called `RFrame.htm`.

```
<html>
<head>
<script language="VBSCRIPT">
Dim sName
sName = "Right Frame"

Sub SayWhoIsThis()
    MsgBox "This is RFrame's subroutine window.SayWhoIsThis"
End Sub
```

```
Sub button1_onclick
    MsgBox "window.sName = " & window.sName
    window.SayWhoIsThis
End Sub

Sub button2_onclick
    MsgBox "window.Parent.sName = " & window.parent.sName
    window.Parent.SayWhoIsThis
End Sub

Sub button3_onclick
    MsgBox "window.parent.LFrame.sName = " & window.Parent.LFrame.sName
    window.Parent.LFrame.SayWhoIsThis
End Sub

Sub button4_onclick
    MsgBox "window.Parent.LFrame.sName = " & window.Parent.frames(0).sName
  window.Parent.frames(0).SayWhoIsThis
End Sub
</script>
<title>Right Frame</title>
</head>

<body>
<h1>Right Frame</h1>
<input type="button" value="window" name="button1">
<input type="button" value="window.Parent" name="button2">
<input type="button" value="window.Parent.LFrame" name="button3">
<input type="button" value="window.Parent.frames(0)" name="button4">
</body>
</html>
```

If you load `TopFrame.htm` into your browser, you can try out the buttons in the right frame. These demonstrate accessing script in the window object of the right frame, its parent's window, and the left frame.

❑   In the first button's `onclick`, you are accessing the window of the current frame, so you normally don't need to explicitly say it is the window object you are referring to because this is implied. In other words, `sName` is the same as `window.sName`. Bear in mind that you will need to explicitly state some contexts if it's the window object you are referring to.

❑   When the second button is clicked, the top frame page (that is, the right window's parent object) is referenced. This is very handy for defining global variables and functions when you have a multiframe page.

❑   For the third button you access the `sName` and `SayWhoIsThis` function contained in the left frame. When the button is clicked, you do this by referencing the frame called `LFrame` contained by the right window's parent window object. As you can see, navigating the DOM can get a little complex at times and vigilance and care is needed to prevent mistakes.

❑   The fourth button does exactly the same as the third but in a different way to demonstrate another of the DOM's important features: collections.

Collections

The `window` object not only has properties, methods, and events, but like many other objects in the DOM it also has collections. You know from the earlier example that a `window` object can have many child `window` objects, but where are these contained? The answer is in the frames collection. The frames collection is a zero-based array containing references to the frames defined by that window. So in `button4`'s code, you see that the left frame is `window.parent.frames(0)`, which is exactly the same as `window.Parent.LFrame`.

Progressing along the DOM down the hierarchy, you come to the `document` object. Each `window` object contains a `document` object. This can be referenced using the `window` object's `document` property. The `document` object acts as a container for all the `document` objects, such as HTML tags and ActiveX controls, inside your page. Just like the window object, the `document` object has a large number of collections associated with it.

Time to look at an example. Here you create a simple page consisting of a paragraph and a table. Using script, you access collections and properties in the DOM by using the `document.all` collection to set references to various document objects in the page. An alternative is to give all the tags names instead, but you'll find this isn't always possible. There will be times when you won't know the name of a tag and need to access it using collections such as the `all` collection.

```
<html>
<head>
<title>A sample page containing script</title>
<script language="VBScript">
Sub button1_onclick
   Dim theWindow
   Dim theDocument
   Dim thePara
   Dim theTable
   Dim theRow
   Dim theCell

   Set theWindow = window

   Set theDocument = theWindow.document
   MsgBox theDocument.title

   Set thePara = theDocument.all(5)
   MsgBox thepara.innerText

   Set theTable = theDocument.all(6)
   MsgBox theTable.tagName

   Set theRow = theTable.rows(1)
   MsgBox theRow.name

   Set theCell = theRow.all(1)
   MsgBox theCell.innertext
End Sub
</script>
```

```
    </head>

<body>
    <p>A boring paragraph</p>
    <table border="1" "name"="table1">
      <tr>
         <td>Cell 1</td>
         <td>Cell 2</td>
      </tr>
      <tr name="second_row_in_table1">
         <td>Cell 3</td>
         <td>Cell 4</td>
      </tr>
    </table>
<input type="button" value="document.all" name="button1">
</body>

</html>
```

For this code, note the following:

❑ First, you dimension some variables, which you'll set to reference document objects. You're probably thinking that you could reference the objects directly, but creating variables instead will make your code easier to read if you are accessing the property numerous times. Creating the reference to the window and document object is unnecessary for this example, but you've done it to emphasize what it is you're referencing in the DOM.

❑ You set the variable theWindow to reference the window object for your page. Then you use object's document property to set a reference to the document for that page and to display the page's title.

❑ You set the variable thePara to reference the paragraph contained in the document object. Why document.all(5) and not document.all(0)? Well, the all collection of an object references all objects contained by that object. The document includes the HTML tag, head tags, the script tags, the body tags, and so on. The collection starts at zero and as the paragraph is the sixth tag in the page it is document.all(5).

❑ You then use the message box to show the innerText property of the paragraph object.

❑ Next, you set theTable to reference the table in the page. It's the next tag after the paragraph, so it corresponds to document.all(6). You show a message box with the table's tagName property. The tagName is simply the tag definition, so for <table> it's TABLE, for a <p> it's P, and so on. See Figure 10-11 to see an example of the output.

❑ Next, you set theRow to reference the second row in the table. You do this using the rows collection of the table object.

❑ Finally, you obtain a reference to the second cell in the row by using the all collection of the row object. You might have used the cells collection, but this example demonstrates that it's not just documents that have the all collection. In fact, all objects have it if they contain other objects.

Figure 10-11

Hopefully, the examples in this section demonstrated how to access objects in the DOM, and also show that the DOM is a hierarchical collection of objects, with each object in the hierarchy being both an object inside another object and also a container for other objects.

Summary

In this chapter, you took a brief look at what client-side scripting can be put to work on. You saw how to connect events raised by HTML objects to VBScript code. You also saw the relationship between VBScript and JavaScript. In reality neither language is better than the other; it's really determined by what browsers your pages must support and what your previous programming background consists of. VBScript makes an excellent choice for Visual Basic and Microsoft Office VBA programmers who are writing for Internet Explorer.

Validating client-side forms using VBScript was also demonstrated with a variety of common controls and types of data. Finally, you took a tour of the Document Object Model and the various standards associated with it, including those laid out by the W3C and implemented by Microsoft.

The next chapter shows many exciting techniques that use the latest technologies available with IE6 and IE7.

Windows Sidebars
and Gadgets

Windows Vista brings with it a range of new features for both users and developers. One new feature is the Windows Sidebar (see Figure 11-1). Windows Sidebar is the application that allows users to run gadgets on the Windows desktop or docked together as part of the Sidebar window. It also allows users to manage gadgets in the Gadget Gallery.

Figure 11-1

Gadgets might seem complicated at first but they're not (well, they can be but that depends on what you want the gadget to do). Gadgets are created using two things that VBScript developers know well: HTML and script. Gadgets have access to information about their own state and settings as well as about Windows (see Figure 11-2). This means that a gadget can interact with files and folders on the host system. Gadgets can also display settings dialog boxes and store user-specific settings using the `System.Gadget` object.

Figure 11-2

Gadget Basics

All gadgets available for the Sidebar are files that are present on the local computer. If users want more gadgets, they have to be downloaded from the web, email, or by allowing applications to install them. Gadgets are packaged in a `.gadget` file (later you'll discover that this is a renamed `.zip` file), and users install the gadget by double-clicking the file (see Figure 11-3). The installation process informs the user of the risks associated with downloading gadgets (see Figure 11-4), and then extracts all of the files required by the gadget into the appropriate folder for use by the Sidebar.

Figure 11-3   Figure 11-4

Users can run multiple instances of a single gadget simultaneously (see Figure 11-5). A good example of this is the clock gadget; if users want to know the time in multiple time zones, they can run multiple instances of the clock gadget and set each clock to a specific time zone (see Figure 11-6).

Figure 11-5   **Figure 11-6**

Users can interact with gadgets by clicking buttons, images, or text on the gadget (see Figure 11-7), or by dragging and dropping the gadget onto the screen (see Figure 11-8). These user-initiated events are handled in the gadget script.

Figure 11-7   Figure 11-8

Gadget Files

A gadget must contain the following files:

- ❑ **HTML file:** This defines the structure and script for the gadget.
- ❑ **Manifest:** This is an XML file that specifies the core HTML file and defines the gadget's properties, such as name, icon, and description. This file must be called gadget.xml.

Optionally, gadgets may also contain the following files:

- ❑ A settings HTML file
- ❑ Script files
- ❑ Images
- ❑ Style sheets
- ❑ An icon

The two main files needed to create a gadget are the HTML file and the manifest, and we will ignore the other files in this chapter for clarity as they are only required for more advanced gadgets.

The Manifest File

Once you've learned VBScript and you have a clear purpose for what you want your gadget to do, creating a gadget isn't all that difficult. One of the parts that people find the hardest is to create the XML manifest file. This file is a settings and configuration file for your gadget (a bit like .INI files, if you remember these).

Being an XML file, the manifest is a plain text file that can be created using nothing more sophisticated than Windows Notepad. Following is a basic XML manifest file that you can use for your gadgets.

```xml
<?xml version="1.0" encoding="utf-8" ?>

<gadget>
        <name>Gadget Name</name>
        <author>Gadget Author</author>
        <copyright>&#169; 2007</copyright>
        <description>Gadget description</description>
        <icons>
                <icon>icon.png</icon>
        </icons>
        <version value="1.0.0.0" MinPlatformVersion="0.1"></version>
        <sidebar>
                <type>html</type>
                <permissions>full</permissions>
                <code>test.htm</code>
                <website>www.example.com</website>
        </sidebar>
</gadget>
```

The manifest file must be saved with the name `gadget.xml`. No other name will work.

The tags you will need to edit are shown in the following table.

Tag	Description
`<author>`	Gadget author
`<code>`	The name of the HTML file containing the gadget code
`<copyright>`	Copyright information
`<description>`	Brief description of the gadget
`<icon>`	An icon for the gadget (if you don't specify one, a default icon will be used)
`<name>`	Name of the gadget
`<website>`	Web site associated with the gadget

If you take a look at the Gadget Picker in Windows Vista, you will see how the information from many of these tags is used on-screen (see Figure 11-9).

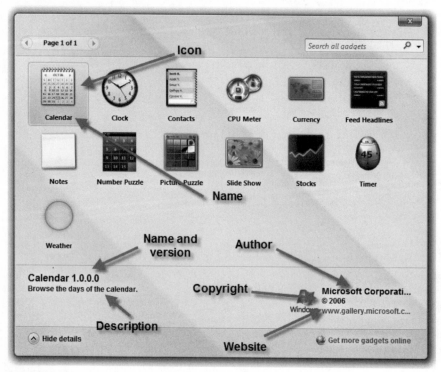

Figure 11-9

Icons

Just a few quick words about creating icons for gadgets:

❑ These icons are regular image files and not Windows icons.

❑ .GIF, .JPG, or .PNG formats can be used (best to use .PNG because this allows for transparency).

❑ The best size for icons is 64 × 64 pixels. Images of another size will be resized down to this.

Building a Gadget

As already mentioned, gadgets are created using HTML files. This means that you are free to use text, images, CSS (Cascading Style Sheets), script (JavaScript, Jscript, and VBScript) and pretty much anything else that you can stuff into an HTML document. With this in mind let's now look at a very simple Sidebar gadget.

```
<html>
<head>
    <title>The "Hello, World!" Gadget</title>
    <style>
        body
        {
            margin: 0;
            width: 145px;
            height: 65px;
        }
        #g1
        {
            width: 145px;
            top: 24px;
            text-align: center;
            font-family: Tahoma;
            font-size: 10pt;
            position: absolute;
        }
    </style>
</head>
<body>
    <span id="g1">
        Hello, World!  Cool, eh?
    <span>
</body>
</html>
```

You'll agree that this is a pretty straightforward web page. Nothing spectacular there at all, and it doesn't even contain any script! So, how do you use this gadget? First, you'll see the manual way.

1.   Make sure that the Windows Sidebar is open. If it isn't, click Start ⇨ All Programs ⇨ Accessories ⇨ Windows Sidebar.

2.   Navigate to your gadgets folder, which is at `%userprofile%\AppData\Local\Microsoft\ Windows Sidebar\Gadgets` (see Figure 11-10).

Some gadgets are stored in the Program Files folder, but gadgets for a specific user are stored in specific user profile folders.

3.   Create a folder here for your gadget. The example uses `test.gadget`. Note that it must contain the `.gadget` extension (see Figure 11-11).

4.   Copy the preceding code into a Notepad file (see Figure 11-12) and save this into the folder you just created. Call this file `test.htm` (see Figure 11-13).

Figure 11-10

Figure 11-11

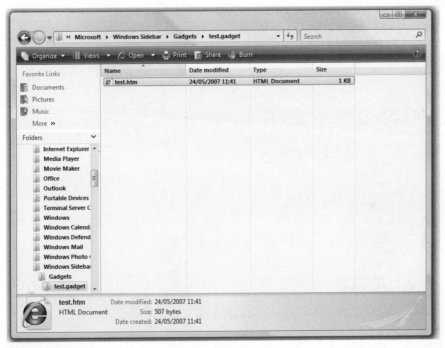

Notepad window showing:

```html
<html>
<head>
    <title>The "Hello, World!"
Gadget</title>
    <style>
        body
        {
            margin: 0;
            width: 145px;
            height: 65px;
        }
        #g1
        {
            width: 145px;
            top: 24px;
            text-align: center;
            font-family: Tahoma;
            font-size: 10pt;
            position: absolute;
        }
    </style>
```

Figure 11-12

Figure 11-13

5. Now it's time to create a manifest file. Here's the one this example is using:

```xml
<?xml version="1.0" encoding="utf-8" ?>

<gadget>
    <name>The "Hello, World!" Gadget</name>
    <author>Gadget Author</author>
    <copyright>&#169; 2007</copyright>
    <description>Gadget description</description>
    <version value="1.0.0.0" MinPlatformVersion="0.1"></version>
    <sidebar>
        <type>html</type>
        <permissions>full</permissions>
        <code>test.htm</code>
        <website>www.example.com</website>
    </sidebar>
</gadget>
```

6. Save the manifest into the folder, remembering to call it `gadget.xml` (see Figure 11-14).

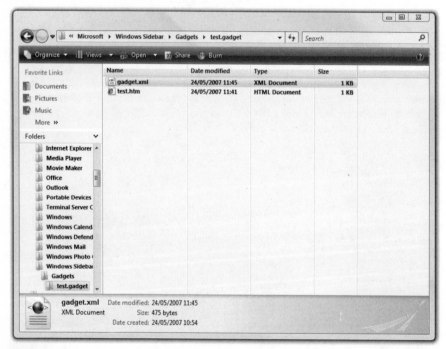

Figure 11-14

You're now ready to load the gadget. These steps are simple but we'll take you through the process nonetheless.

1. Click the + symbol on the Sidebar (see Figure 11-15).

Figure 11-15

2.   Select the Hello, World! gadget from the Gadget Picker (see Figure 11-16). And here it is installed (see Figure 11-17). Doesn't look like much yet.

Some people have difficulty getting the gadget to appear in the Gadget Gallery. A reboot might help. If it doesn't, refer to the section later in this chapter that deals with packaging the gadget for alternative methods to get the gadget to appear in the gallery.

Figure 11-16

Figure 11-17

The gadget is far from perfect, so let's make some alterations. First off, notice how the gadget is wider than the default width of the sidebar (you can see this clearly in Figure 11-18).

Figure 11-18

Not good. Let's drop the width down to 130 pixels.

```html
<html>
<head>
    <title>The "Hello, World!" Gadget</title>
    <style>
        body
        {
            margin: 0;
            width: 130px;
            height: 65px;
        }
        #g1
        {
            width: 130px;
            top: 24px;
            text-align: center;
            font-family: Tahoma;
            font-size: 10pt;
            position: absolute;
        }
    </style>
</head>
<body>
    <span id="g1">
        Hello, World!  Cool, eh?
    <span>
</body>
</html>
```

As you can see from Figure 11-19, this now looks much better.

To refresh a gadget, remove it from the sidebar and then add it again.

Figure 11-19

Now that you have a gadget that fits comfortably into the sidebar, you can experiment with it a little. Just to prove that you can put VBScript into a gadget as simply as you can add it to a web page, here's an example that you should be familiar with:

```html
<html>
<head>
    <title>The "Hello, World!" Gadget</title>
    <style>
        body
        {
            margin: 0;
            width: 130px;
            height: 65px;
        }
        #g1
        {
            width: 130px;
            top: 24px;
            text-align: center;
            font-family: Tahoma;
            font-size: 10pt;
            position: absolute;
        }
    </style>
    <script language="vbscript">
        Sub sub1()
            MsgBox "Hello, World!"
        End Sub
    </script>
</head>
<body>
    <span id="g1">
        <input type="button" value="OK!" onClick="sub1()">
    <span>
</body>
</html>
```

Figure 11-20 shows the result of these changes.

Figure 11-20

What do you think happens when you click the button? Figure 11-21 has the answer!

Figure 11-21

OK, time to write a gadget that does something a little more impressive than bring up a dialog box. Here's the code:

```html
<html>
<head>
    <title>Free space on C Drive</title>
    <style>
        body
        {
            margin: 0;
            width: 130px;
            height: 65px;
        }
        #g1
        {
            width: 130px;
            top: 24px;
            text-align: center;
            font-family: Tahoma;
            font-size: 10pt;
            position: absolute;
        }
    </style>
```

(continued)

```
<script language="vbscript">
Sub Window_OnLoad()
    sub1()
End Sub

Sub sub1()
    strComputer = "."
    Set objWMIService = GetObject("winmgmts:" _
& "{impersonationLevel=impersonate}!\\" & strComputer & "\root\cimv2")
    Set cDisk = objWMIService.ExecQuery _
("Select * from Win32_LogicalDisk Where DeviceID = 'C:'")
        For Each objDisk in cDisk
            g1.InnerHTML = objDisk.FreeSpace
        Next
End Sub
</script>
</head>
<body>
    <span id="g1"><span>
</body>
</html>
```

Here's the portion of the script that pulls figures out to free space on the disk:

```
Sub sub1()
    strComputer = "."
    Set objWMIService = GetObject("winmgmts:" _
& "{impersonationLevel=impersonate}!\\" & strComputer & "\root\cimv2")
    Set cDisk = objWMIService.ExecQuery _
("Select * from Win32_LogicalDisk Where DeviceID = 'C:'")
        For Each objDisk in cDisk

            g1.InnerHTML = objDisk.FreeSpace

        Next
End Sub
```

The problem is, as you can see from Figure 11-22, the figure displayed in megabytes isn't all that handy.

215700MB

Figure 11-22

With a quick modification, the output is shown in megabytes:

```
<script language="vbscript">
Sub Window_OnLoad()
    sub1()
End Sub

    Sub sub1()
        strComputer = "."
        Set objWMIService = GetObject("winmgmts:" _
    & "{impersonationLevel=impersonate}!\\" & strComputer & "\root\cimv2")
        Set cDisk = objWMIService.ExecQuery _
    ("Select * from Win32_LogicalDisk Where DeviceID = 'C:'")
            For Each objDisk in cDisk
                g1.InnerHTML = int(objDisk.FreeSpace / 1048576) & " MB"
            Next
    End Sub
</script>
```

The new output is shown in Figure 11-23.

215700 MB

Figure 11-23

If you want to pull out the percentage of free space left on the drive (which, let's face it, is more useful than just a number) you'll need to tweak the code a little more:

```
<script language="vbscript">
Sub Window_OnLoad()
    sub1()
End Sub

    Sub sub1()
        strComputer = "."
        Set objWMIService = GetObject("winmgmts:" _
    & "{impersonationLevel=impersonate}!\\" & strComputer & "\root\cimv2")
        Set cDisk = objWMIService.ExecQuery _
    ("Select * from Win32_LogicalDisk Where DeviceID = 'C:'")
            For Each objDisk in cDisk
                cDiskFreeSpace = objDisk.FreeSpace
                cDiskTotalSpace = objDisk.Size
                pctCFree = cDiskFreeSpace / cDiskTotalSpace
                g1.InnerHTML = FormatPercent(pctCFree)
            Next
    End Sub
</script>
```

Check out the output in Figure 11-24. Pretty cool, eh?

Figure 11-24

Finally, let's give the code a little tweak so it pulls out the free space of all drives installed on the system and not just the C drive.

```
<html>
<head>
    <title>Free space on C Drive</title>
    <style>
        body
        {
            margin: 0;
            width: 130px;
            height: 75px;
        }
        #g1
        {
            width: 130px;
            top: 15px;
            text-align: center;
            font-family: Tahoma;
            font-size: 10pt;
            position: absolute;
        }
    </style>
    <script language="vbscript">
    Sub Window_OnLoad()
        sub1()
    End Sub
        Sub sub1()
            strComputer = "."
            Set objWMIService = GetObject("winmgmts:" _
        & "{impersonationLevel=impersonate}!\\" & strComputer & "\root\cimv2")
            Set hDisks = objWMIService.ExecQuery _
        ("Select * from Win32_LogicalDisk Where DriveType = 3")
        g1.InnerHTML = ""
                For Each objDisk in hDisks
                    diskFreeSpace = objDisk.FreeSpace
                    diskTotalSpace = objDisk.Size
```

```
                    pctFree = diskFreeSpace / diskTotalSpace
                    g1.InnerHTML = g1.InnerHTML + objDisk.Name + " " _
                + FormatPercent(pctFree) + "<br />"
                Next
        End Sub
    </script>
</head>
<body>
    <span id="g1"><span>
</body>
</html>
```

Figure 11-25 shows this updated code in action.

C: 90.11%
D: 91.27%
E: 99.96%

Figure 11-25

Auto-Refresh a Gadget

One more thing. Currently, the script runs once when the gadget is loaded. This is fine for some scripts but for a script that looks at something that is constantly changing such as free space on a drive, you'd want it to run on a regular basis so that the data is refreshed. Not a problem. All you need to do is add a timer script that refreshes the gadget at regular intervals, say every minute (60,000 milliseconds):

```
<script language="vbscript">
Sub Window_OnLoad()
    sub1()
    timer1 = window.SetInterval("sub1", 60000)

End Sub

Sub sub1()
    strComputer = "."
    Set objWMIService = GetObject("winmgmts:" _
& "{impersonationLevel=impersonate}!\\" & strComputer & "\root\cimv2")
    Set hDisks = objWMIService.ExecQuery _
("Select * from Win32_LogicalDisk Where DriveType = 3")
g1.InnerHTML = ""
        For Each objDisk in hDisks
            diskFreeSpace = objDisk.FreeSpace
            diskTotalSpace = objDisk.Size
            pctFree = diskFreeSpace / diskTotalSpace
            g1.InnerHTML = g1.InnerHTML + objDisk.Name + " " _
        + FormatPercent(pctFree) + "<br />"
        Next
    End Sub
</script>
```

This new line of code uses the SetInterval method to create a timer. This timer causes the gadget to call the sub1 subroutine every 60 seconds (60,000 milliseconds). This, in turn, refreshes the data displayed in the gadget window. Simple!

Here, for completeness, is the final code for this gadget:

```
<html>
<head>
    <title>Free space on C Drive</title>
    <style>
        body
        {
            margin: 0;
            width: 130px;
            height: 75px;
        }
        #g1
        {
            width: 130px;
            top: 15px;
            text-align: center;
            font-family: Tahoma;
            font-size: 10pt;
            position: absolute;
        }
    </style>
    <script language="vbscript">
    Sub Window_OnLoad()
        sub1()
        timer1 = window.SetInterval("sub1", 60000)
    End Sub
        Sub sub1()
            strComputer = "."
            Set objWMIService = GetObject("winmgmts:" _
    & "{impersonationLevel=impersonate}!\\" & strComputer & "\root\cimv2")
            Set hDisks = objWMIService.ExecQuery _
    ("Select * from Win32_LogicalDisk Where DriveType = 3")
        g1.InnerHTML = ""
                For Each objDisk in hDisks
                    diskFreeSpace = objDisk.FreeSpace
                    diskTotalSpace = objDisk.Size
                    pctFree = diskFreeSpace / diskTotalSpace
                    g1.InnerHTML = g1.InnerHTML + objDisk.Name + " " _
                    + FormatPercent(pctFree) + "<br />"
                Next
            End Sub
    </script>
</head>
<body>
    <span id="g1"><span>
</body>
</html>
```

Your gadget is functional. Now that you know how to build this gadget, you can use your skills with CSS and images to tweak it so that it looks more appealing than it currently does. However, these are purely cosmetic elements. You have a working gadget!

Packaging the Gadget

You have your gadget all programmed and tested. How do you package it so that users can download and install it? Well, obviously the method we outlined earlier (messing about in the gadgets folder) isn't going to be popular with people so you need a better way. Microsoft has given you a better way, and it's pretty simple. In fact, there are two ways that you can package a gadget:

❑   Zip up all your gadget files into a ZIP file and change the extension from `.zip` to `.gadget`.

❑   Alternatively, if you don't want to mess about with ZIP archives you can instead use CAB files, again remembering to change `.cab` to `.gadget`. The advantage of using CAB files is that they can be digitally signed for security.

That's it!

Summary

In this chapter you read about two new features of the Windows Vista operating system — the Windows Sidebar and Gadgets. You started by examining the Windows Sidebar and gadgets before moving on to look at the basics of creating a gadget. With the basics in place, you then moved on to actually creating a gadget and the associated manifest file and saw how the changes that you made to the code affected the gadget itself. With a few code tweaks, you turned an example gadget into a useful gadget. Finally, you looked at how to package the gadget so that others can download and install it.

Task Scheduler Scripting

The Windows Task Scheduler allows the user or administrator to schedule a program to be run at a particular time or in response to a specific event. Task Scheduler can also be controlled via script. Windows Vista and Windows Server 2008 ship with the new redesigned Task Scheduler 2.0 and in this chapter you'll see the changes made to Task Scheduler and how to make use of it. Here are some of the new features and capabilities:

❑ Sends automatic email notifications when there are problems with the local or remote system

❑ Launches new diagnostic programs when a problem with Task Scheduler or a scheduled task is detected

❑ Can execute tasks when the PC is unattended

❑ Offers the ability to run tasks in a particular sequence

❑ Carries out actions based on an event logged in the system event log

❑ Configures systems to automatically respond to system problems

❑ Runs tasks in response to system changes of multiple triggers

❑ Configures a system to wake up from standby or hibernation so that routine tasks can be carried out

Task Scheduler 2.0 also includes new tools and features, such as:

❑ Triggers and actions

❑ Credential management

❑ Improved user interface

❑ MMC snap-in

❑ Task settings

❑ Improved scripting support

❑ Task Scheduler XML schema

Working with Task Scheduler

Before you go on to look at the new Task Scheduler scripting objects and some scripting examples, first take a look at how to interact with Task Scheduler from within Windows.

Using the MMC Snap-in

The Task Scheduler user interface and the `Schtasks.exe` command-line tool have both been completely redesigned to leverage the Microsoft Management Console (MMC). The Scheduled Task wizard that was present in previous versions of Windows is now replaced under Windows Vista and Windows Server 2008 with a new MMC-compatible Task Scheduler application that can be run either as a stand-alone application or as an MMC snap-in (see Figure 12-1).

Figure 12-1

You can start the Task Scheduler MMC snap-in in stand-alone mode from the command line or by using the Windows interface.

To start the Task Scheduler from the command line:

1. Click Start ➪ All Programs ➪ Accessories ➪ Command Prompt.

2. At the command prompt, type **Taskschd**.

To run the Task Scheduler from the Windows interface:

1. Click Start ⇨ Control Panel.

2. Click System and Maintenance.

3. Click Administrative Tools.

4. Double-click Task Scheduler to display the Task Scheduler 2.0 interface.

Defining and Creating Tasks in Task Scheduler

In Task Scheduler you can define tasks by selecting specific menus and creating basic tasks with the help of easy-to-use wizards. In this wizard, you define the triggers and actions surrounding your task:

❑   A *trigger* is a set of criteria that, when met, executes a task. Task Scheduler 2.0 incorporates new time and event triggers that allow you to start a single task using multiple triggers. Another powerful new feature of Task Scheduler 2.0 is the ability to trigger a task that is based on an event logged in the event log. This allows you to send an email notification or launch a program automatically when an event occurs (or you can do both). Task Scheduler also logs a task's history in the event log, and the log can be looked at to discover the status of a task. Triggers include:

>   ❑   Time triggers that start tasks at specified times. You can start the task just once, at a specific time, or multiple times based on a specific schedule. The schedule can be configured for daily, weekly, or monthly reoccurrence of the task.

>   ❑   Event triggers that start a task in response to events that occur.

❑   An *action* is the job carried out by the task. Each task can specify one or more actions to complete. If you specify more than one action, they will be run sequentially. The new, improved Task Scheduler 2.0 supports a maximum of 32 actions. You can also use a single task to initiate multiple actions. To do this, you can either set up multiple actions that are run sequentially as part of a single task, or you can create a sequence of tasks with events triggered by the previous task, which launch the next task.

Task Scheduler uses the settings you specify to run the task with respect to conditions that are external to the task itself. These are called task settings and they determine how a task is run, stopped, or deleted. Here are some examples of how task settings can be used:

❑   Retry a task if it fails.

❑   Schedule actions to take if a task fails to run.

❑   Specify when a task must time out (this prevents tasks from running for too long).

❑   Specify the number of times to retry a failed task.

❑   Force a task to stop if it does not end when requested.

❑   Ensure that a task runs when the machine is powered on, if the machine is powered off when a task is scheduled.

❑   Run a task as soon as possible after a scheduled start is missed.

To define your new task settings, follow these steps:

1. From the Action menu, you can select one of the following menus:

   ❏ Connect to Another Computer

   ❏ Create Basic Task

   ❏ Create Task

   ❏ Import Task

   ❏ Display All Running Tasks

2. Select Create Basic Tasks. This fires up the Basic Task Wizard.

3. Click Triggers and select one of the following as shown in Figure 12-2:

   ❏ Daily

   ❏ Weekly

   ❏ Monthly

   ❏ One time

   ❏ When the computer starts

   ❏ When I log on

   ❏ When a specific event is logged

Figure 12-2

4. Specify actions to carry out as shown in Figure 12-3:

    ❑ Start a program (which can be a program or a script)

    ❑ Send an email

    ❑ Display a message

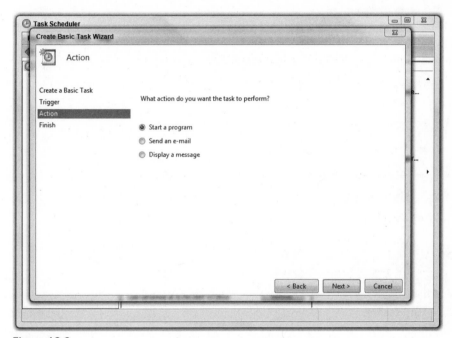

Figure 12-3

The final screen of the Basic Task Wizard is shown in Figure 12-4.

5. Click Finish.

While Task Scheduler 1.0 only supported about 1,000 registered tasks, Task Scheduler 2.0 can handle an unlimited number of registered tasks.

Figure 12-4

Task Scheduler XML Schema

The Task Scheduler schema defines XML-formatted documents that can be used to register tasks with the Task Scheduler service. Developers create their own XML, validate it against this schema, and can use this to register tasks.

This method can be used to import tasks already registered with the Schtasks.exe command-line tool, or to register tasks through other installed programs.

Task Scheduler 2.0 Scripting Objects

The following Task Scheduler scripting objects are available to programmers through both Visual Basic and VBScript.

Action

This scripting object provides common properties that are inherited by all action objects. An action object is created by the ActionCollection.Create method.

Methods

The Action object does not define any methods.

Properties

The `Action` object has the following properties.

Properties	Description
Id	Gets or sets the identifier of the action.
Type	Gets the type of the action.

ActionCollection

This scripting object contains the actions performed by the task.

Methods

The `ActionCollection` has the following methods.

Method	Description
Create	Creates and adds a new action to the collection.
Clear	Clears all the actions from the collection.
Remove	Removes a specified action from the collection.

Properties

The `ActionCollection` object has the following properties.

Properties	Description
Context	Gets or sets the identifier of the principal for the task.
Count	Gets the number of actions in the collection.
Item	Gets a specified action from the collection.
XmlText	Gets or sets an XML-formatted version of the collection.

BootTrigger

This scripting object represents a trigger that starts a task when the system is booted.

Methods

The `BootTrigger` does not define any methods.

Properties

The `BootTrigger` object has the following properties.

Properties	Description
Delay	Gets or sets a value that indicates the amount of time between when the system is booted and when the task is started.
Enabled	Inherited from the `Trigger` object. Gets or sets a Boolean value that indicates whether the trigger is enabled.
EndBoundary	Inherited from the `Trigger` object. Gets or sets the date and time when the trigger is deactivated. The trigger cannot start the task after it is deactivated.
ExecutionTimeLimit	Inherited from the `Trigger` object. Gets or sets the maximum amount of time that the task launched by the trigger is allowed to run.
Id	Inherited from the `Trigger` object. Gets or sets the identifier for the trigger.
Repetition	Inherited from the `Trigger` object. Gets or sets how often the task is run and how long the repetition pattern is repeated after the task is started.
StartBoundary	Inherited from the `Trigger` object. Gets or sets the date and time when the trigger is activated.
Type	Inherited from the `Trigger` object. Gets the type of the trigger.

ComHandlerAction

This scripting object represents an action that fires a handler.

Methods

The `ComHandlerAction` does not define any methods.

Properties

The `ComHandlerAction` object has the following properties.

Properties	Description
ClassId	Gets or sets the identifier of the handler class.
Data	Gets or sets additional data that is associated with the handler.
Id	Inherited from the Action object. Gets or sets the identifier of the action.
Type	Inherited from the Action object. Gets the type of the action.

DailyTrigger

This scripting object represents a trigger that starts a task based on a daily schedule.

Methods

The DailyTrigger does not define any methods.

Properties

The DailyTrigger object has the following properties.

Properties	Description
DaysInterval	Gets or sets the interval between the days in the schedule.
Enabled	Inherited from the Trigger object. Gets or sets a Boolean value that indicates whether the trigger is enabled.
EndBoundary	Inherited from the Trigger object. Gets or sets the date and time when the trigger is deactivated. The trigger cannot start the task after it is deactivated.
ExecutionTimeLimit	Inherited from the Trigger object. Gets or sets the maximum amount of time that the task launched by the trigger is allowed to run.
Id	Inherited from the Trigger object. Gets or sets the identifier for the trigger.
RandomDelay	Gets or sets a delay time that is randomly added to the start time of the trigger.
Repetition	Inherited from the Trigger object. Gets or sets how often the task is run and how long the repetition pattern is repeated after the task is started.
StartBoundary	Inherited from the Trigger object. Gets or sets the date and time when the trigger is activated.
Type	Inherited from the Trigger object. Gets the type of the trigger.

EmailAction

This scripting object represents an action that sends an email.

Methods

The EmailAction does not define any methods.

Properties

The EmailAction object has the following properties.

Properties	Description
Attachments	Gets or sets an array of attachments that is sent with the email.
Bcc	Gets or sets the email address or addresses that you want to Bcc.
Body	Gets or sets the body of the email that contains the email message.
Cc	Gets or sets the email address or addresses that you want to Cc.
From	Gets or sets the email address that you want to send from.
HeaderFields	Gets or sets the header information in the email that you want to send.
Id	Inherited from the Action object. Gets or sets the identifier of the action.
ReplyTo	Gets or sets the email address that you want to reply to.
Server	Gets or sets the name of the server that you use to send email from.
Subject	Gets or sets the subject of the email.
To	Gets or sets the email address or addresses that you want to send to.
Type	Inherited from Action object. Gets the type of the action.

EventTrigger

This scripting object represents a trigger that starts a task when a system event occurs.

Methods

The EventTrigger does not define any methods.

Properties

The EventTrigger object has the following properties.

Properties	Description
Delay	Gets or sets a value that indicates the amount of time between when the system is booted and when the task is started.
Enabled	Inherited from the `Trigger` object. Gets or sets a Boolean value that indicates whether the trigger is enabled.
EndBoundary	Inherited from the `Trigger` object. Gets or sets the date and time when the trigger is deactivated. The trigger cannot start the task after it is deactivated.
ExecutionTimeLimit	Inherited from the `Trigger` object. Gets or sets the maximum amount of time that the task launched by the trigger is allowed to run.
Id	Inherited from the `Trigger` object. Gets or sets the identifier for the trigger.
Repetition	Inherited from the `Trigger` object. Gets or sets how often the task is run and how long the repetition pattern is repeated after the task is started.
StartBoundary	Inherited from the `Trigger` object. Gets or sets the date and time when the trigger is activated.
Subscription	Gets or sets the XPath query string that identifies the event that fires the trigger.
Type	Inherited from the `Trigger` object. Gets the type of the trigger.
ValueQueries	Gets or sets a collection of named XPath queries.

ExecAction

This scripting object represents an action that executes a command-line operation.

Methods

The ExecAction does not define any methods.

Properties

The ExecAction object has the following properties.

Properties	Description
Arguments	Gets or sets the arguments associated with the command-line operation.
Id	Inherited from the Action object, this gets or sets the identifier of the action.
Path	Gets or sets the path to an executable file.
Type	Inherited from the Action object, this gets the type of the action.
WorkingDirectory	Gets or sets the directory that contains either the executable file or the files that are used by the executable file.

IdleSettings

This scripting object specifies how the Task Scheduler performs tasks when the computer is in an idle condition.

Methods

The IdleSettings does not define any methods.

Properties

The IdleSettings object has the following properties.

Properties	Description
IdleDuration	Gets or sets a value that indicates the amount of time that the computer must be in an idle state before the task is run.
RestartOnIdle	Gets or sets a Boolean value that indicates whether the task is restarted when the computer moves into an idle condition more than once.
StopOnIdleEnd	Gets or sets a Boolean value that indicates that the Task Scheduler will terminate the task if the idle state ends before the task is completed.
WaitTimeout	Gets or sets a value that indicates the amount of time that the Task Scheduler will wait for an idle condition to occur.

IdleTrigger

This scripting object represents a trigger that starts a task when an idle condition occurs.

Methods

The IdleTrigger does not define any methods.

Properties

The `IdleTrigger` object has the following properties.

Properties	Description
Enabled	Inherited from the `Trigger` object. Gets or sets a Boolean value that indicates whether the trigger is enabled.
EndBoundary	Inherited from the `Trigger` object. Gets or sets the date and time when the trigger is deactivated. The trigger cannot start the task after it is deactivated.
ExecutionTimeLimit	Inherited from the `Trigger` object. Gets or sets the maximum amount of time that the task launched by the trigger is allowed to run.
Id	Inherited from the `Trigger` object. Gets or sets the identifier for the trigger.
Repetition	Inherited from the `Trigger` object. Gets or sets how often the task is run and how long the repetition pattern is repeated after the task is started.
StartBoundary	Inherited from the `Trigger` object. Gets or sets the date and time when the trigger is activated.
Type	Inherited from the `Trigger` object. Gets the type of the trigger.

LogonTrigger

This scripting object represents a trigger that starts a task when a user logs on.

Methods

The `LogonTrigger` does not define any methods.

Properties

The `LogonTrigger` object has the following properties.

Properties	Description
Delay	Gets or sets a value that indicates the amount of time between when the system is booted and when the task is started.
Enabled	Inherited from the `Trigger` object. Gets or sets a Boolean value that indicates whether the trigger is enabled.
EndBoundary	Inherited from the `Trigger` object. Gets or sets the date and time when the trigger is deactivated. The trigger cannot start the task after it is deactivated.
ExecutionTimeLimit	Inherited from the `Trigger` object. Gets or sets the maximum amount of time that the task launched by the trigger is allowed to run.
Id	Inherited from the `Trigger` object. Gets or sets the identifier for the trigger.
Repetition	Inherited from the `Trigger` object. Gets or sets how often the task is run and how long the repetition pattern is repeated after the task is started.
StartBoundary	Inherited from the `Trigger` object. Gets or sets the date and time when the trigger is activated.
Type	Inherited from the `Trigger` object. Gets the type of the trigger.

MonthlyDOWTrigger

This scripting object represents a trigger that starts a task on a monthly day-of-week schedule.

Methods

The MonthlyDOWTrigger does not define any methods.

Properties

The MonthlyDOWTrigger object has the following properties.

Properties	Description
DaysOfWeek	Gets or sets the days of the week during which the task runs.
Enabled	Inherited from the Trigger object. Gets or sets a Boolean value that indicates whether the trigger is enabled.
EndBoundary	Inherited from the Trigger object. Gets or sets the date and time when the trigger is deactivated. The trigger cannot start the task after it is deactivated.
ExecutionTimeLimit	Inherited from the Trigger object. Gets or sets the maximum amount of time that the task launched by the trigger is allowed to run.
Id	Inherited from the Trigger object. Gets or sets the identifier for the trigger.
MonthsOfYear	Gets or sets the months of the year during which the task runs.
RandomDelay	Gets or sets a delay time that is randomly added to the start time of the trigger.
Repetition	Inherited from the Trigger object. Gets or sets how often the task is run and how long the repetition pattern is repeated after the task is started.
RunOnLastWeekOfMonth	Gets or sets a Boolean value that indicates that the task runs on the last week of the month.
StartBoundary	Inherited from the Trigger object. Gets or sets the date and time when the trigger is activated.
Type	Inherited from the Trigger object. Gets the type of the trigger.
WeeksOfMonth	Gets or sets the weeks of the month during which the task runs.

MonthlyTrigger

This scripting object represents a trigger that starts a task based on a monthly schedule.

Methods

The MonthlyTrigger does not define any methods.

Properties

The MonthlyTrigger object has the following properties.

Properties	Description
DaysOfMonth	Gets or sets the days of the month during which the task runs.
Enabled	Inherited from the Trigger object. Gets or sets a Boolean value that indicates whether the trigger is enabled.
EndBoundary	Inherited from the Trigger object. Gets or sets the date and time when the trigger is deactivated. The trigger cannot start the task after it is deactivated.
ExecutionTimeLimit	Inherited from the Trigger object. Gets or sets the maximum amount of time that the task launched by the trigger is allowed to run.
Id	Inherited from the Trigger object. Gets or sets the identifier for the trigger.
MonthsOfYear	Gets or sets the months of the year during which the task runs.
RandomDelay	Gets or sets a delay time that is randomly added to the start time of the trigger.
Repetition	Inherited from the Trigger object. Gets or sets how often the task is run and how long the repetition pattern is repeated after the task is started.
RunOnLastDayOfMonth	Gets or sets a Boolean value that indicates that the task runs on the last day of the month.
StartBoundary	Inherited from the Trigger object. Gets or sets the date and time when the trigger is activated.
Type	Inherited from the Trigger object. Gets the type of the trigger.

NetworkSettings

This scripting object provides the settings that the Task Scheduler service uses to obtain a network profile.

Methods

The NetworkSettings object does not define any methods.

Properties

The NetworkSettings object has the following properties.

Properties	Description
Id	Gets or sets a GUID value that identifies a network profile.
Name	Gets or sets the name of a network profile. The name is used for display purposes.

Principal

This scripting object provides the security credentials for a principal.

Methods

The `Principal` object does not define any methods.

Properties

The `Principal` object has the following properties.

Properties	Description
DisplayName	Gets or sets the name of the principal that is displayed in the Task Scheduler user interface (UI).
GroupId	Gets or sets the identifier of the user group that is required to run the tasks that are associated with the principal.
Id	Gets or sets the identifier of the principal.
LogonType	Gets or sets the security logon method that is required to run the tasks that are associated with the principal.
RunLevel	Gets or sets the identifier that is used to specify the privilege level that is required to run the tasks that are associated with the principal.
UserId	Gets or sets the user identifier that is required to run the tasks that are associated with the principal.
Type	Gets the type of the action.

RegisteredTask

This scripting object provides the methods that are used to run the task immediately, get any running instances of the task, get or set the credentials that are used to register the task, and the properties that describe the task.

Methods

The `RegisteredTask` has the following methods.

Method	Description
GetInstances	Returns all instances of the registered task that are currently running.
GetSecurityDescriptor	Gets the security descriptor that is used as credentials for the registered task.
GetRunTimes	Gets the times that the registered task is scheduled to run during a specified time.
SetSecurityDescriptor	Sets the security descriptor that is used as credentials for the registered task.
RunEx	Runs the registered task immediately using specified flags and a session identifier.
Stop	Stops the registered task immediately.
Run	Runs the registered task immediately.

Properties

The `RegisteredTask` object has the following properties.

Properties	Description
Definition	Gets the definition of the task.
Enabled	Gets or sets a Boolean value that indicates if the registered task is enabled.
LastRunTime	Gets the time the registered task was last run.
LastTaskResult	Gets the results that were returned the last time the registered task was run.
Name	Gets the name of the registered task.
NextRunTime	Gets the time when the registered task is next scheduled to run.
NumberOfMissedRuns	Gets the number of times the registered task has missed a scheduled run.
Path	Gets the path to where the registered task is stored.
State	Gets the operational state of the registered task.
Xml	Gets the XML-formatted registration information for the registered task.

RegisteredTaskCollection

This scripting object contains all the tasks that are registered.

Methods

The `RegisteredTaskCollection` object does not define any methods.

Properties

The `RegisteredTaskCollection` object has the following properties.

Properties	Description
Count	Gets the number of registered tasks in the collection.
Item	Gets the specified registered task from the collection.

RegistrationInfo

This scripting object provides the administrative information that can be used to describe the task.

Methods

The `RegistrationInfo` object does not define any methods.

Properties

The `RegistrationInfo` object has the following properties.

Properties	Description
Author	Gets or sets the author of the task.
Date	Gets or sets the date and time when the task is registered.
Description	Gets or sets the description of the task.
Documentation	Gets or sets any additional documentation for the task.
SecurityDescriptor	Gets or sets the security descriptor of the task.
Source	Gets or sets where the task originated.
URI	Gets or sets the URI of the task.
Version	Gets or sets the version number of the task.
XmlText	Gets or sets an XML-formatted version of the registration information for the task.

RegistrationTrigger

This scripting object represents a trigger that starts a task when the task is registered or updated.

Methods

The `RegistrationTrigger` does not define any methods.

Properties

The `RegistrationTrigger` object has the following properties.

Properties	Description
Delay	Gets or sets a value that indicates the amount of time between when the system is booted and when the task is started.
Enabled	Inherited from the `Trigger` object. Gets or sets a Boolean value that indicates whether the trigger is enabled.
EndBoundary	Inherited from the `Trigger` object. Gets or sets the date and time when the trigger is deactivated. The trigger cannot start the task after it is deactivated.
ExecutionTimeLimit	Inherited from the `Trigger` object. Gets or sets the maximum amount of time that the task launched by the trigger is allowed to run.
Id	Inherited from the `Trigger` object. Gets or sets the identifier for the trigger.
Repetition	Inherited from the `Trigger` object. Gets or sets how often the task is run and how long the repetition pattern is repeated after the task is started.
StartBoundary	Inherited from the `Trigger` object. Gets or sets the date and time when the trigger is activated.
Type	Inherited from the `Trigger` object. Gets the type of the trigger.

RepetitionPattern

This scripting object defines how often the task is run and how long the repetition pattern is repeated after the task is started.

Methods

The `RepetitionPattern` object does not define any methods.

Properties

The `RepetitionPattern` object has the following properties.

Properties	Description
Duration	Gets or sets how long the pattern is repeated.
Interval	Gets or sets the amount of time between each restart of the task.
StopAtDurationEnd	Gets or sets a Boolean value that indicates if a running instance of the task is stopped at the end of the repetition pattern duration.

RunningTask

This scripting object provides the methods to get information from and control a running task.

Methods

The RunningTask has the following methods.

Method	Description
Refresh	Refreshes all of the local instance variables of the task.
Stop	Stops this instance of the task.

Properties

The RunningTask object has the following properties.

Properties	Description
CurrentAction	Gets the name of the current action that the running task is performing.
EnginePID	Gets the process ID for the engine (process) that is running the task.
InstanceGUID	Gets the GUID for this instance of the task.
Name	Gets the name of the task.
Path	Gets the path to where the registered task is stored.
State	Gets the state of the running task.

RunningTaskCollection

This scripting object provides a collection that is used to control running tasks.

Methods

The RunningTaskCollection object does not define any methods.

Properties

The `RunningTaskCollection` object has the following properties.

Properties	Description
Count	Gets the number of running tasks in the collection.
Item	Gets the specified running task from the collection.

SessionStateChangeTrigger

This scripting object triggers tasks for console connect or disconnect, remote connect or disconnect, or workstation lock or unlock notifications.

Methods

The `SessionStateChangeTrigger` does not define any methods.

Properties

The `SessionStateChangeTrigger` object has the following properties.

Properties	Description
Delay	Gets or sets a value that indicates the amount of time between when the system is booted and when the task is started.
Enabled	Inherited from the `Trigger` object. Gets or sets a Boolean value that indicates whether the trigger is enabled.
EndBoundary	Inherited from the `Trigger` object. Gets or sets the date and time when the trigger is deactivated. The trigger cannot start the task after it is deactivated.
ExecutionTimeLimit	Inherited from the `Trigger` object. Gets or sets the maximum amount of time that the task launched by the trigger is allowed to run.
Id	Inherited from the `Trigger` object. Gets or sets the identifier for the trigger.
Repetition	Inherited from the `Trigger` object. Gets or sets how often the task is run and how long the repetition pattern is repeated after the task is started.
StartBoundary	Inherited from the `Trigger` object. Gets or sets the date and time when the trigger is activated.
StateChange	Gets or sets the kind of Terminal Server session change that would trigger a task launch.
Type	Inherited from the `Trigger` object. Gets the type of the trigger.

ShowMessageAction

This scripting object represents an action that shows a message box when a task is activated.

Methods

The `ShowMessageAction` object does not define any methods.

Properties

The `ShowMessageAction` object has the following properties.

Properties	Description
Id	Inherited from the `Action` object. Gets or sets the identifier of the action.
MessageBody	Gets or sets the message text that is displayed in the body of the message box.
Title	Gets or sets the title of the message box.
Type	Gets the number of running tasks in the collection.
Item	Inherited from the `Action` object. Gets the type of the action.

TaskDefinition

This scripting object defines all the components of a task, such as the task settings, triggers, actions, and registration information.

Methods

The `TaskDefinition` object does not define any methods.

Properties

The `TaskDefinition` object has the following properties.

Properties	Description
Actions	Gets or sets a collection of actions that are performed by the task.
Data	Gets or sets the data that is associated with the task. This data is ignored by the Task Scheduler service, but is used by third parties who want to extend the task format.
Principal	Gets or sets the principal for the task that provides the security credentials.

(continued)

Properties	Description
RegistrationInfo	Gets or sets the registration information that is used to describe a task, such as the description of the task, the author of the task, and the date the task is registered.
Settings	Gets or sets the settings that define how the Task Scheduler service performs the task.
Triggers	Gets or sets a collection of triggers that are used to start a task.
XmlText	Gets or sets the XML-formatted definition of the task.

TaskFolder

This scripting object provides the methods that are used to register tasks in the folder, remove tasks from it, and create or remove subfolders from it.

Methods

The TaskFolder has the following methods.

Method	Description
CreateFolder	Creates a folder for related tasks.
DeleteFolder	Deletes a subfolder from the parent folder.
DeleteTask	Deletes a task from the folder.
GetFolder	Gets a folder that contains tasks at a specified location.
GetFolders	Gets all the subfolders in the folder.
GetSecurityDescriptor	Gets the security descriptor for the folder.
GetTask	Gets a task at a specified location in a folder.
GetTasks	Gets all the tasks in the folder.
RegisterTask	Registers a new task in the folder using XML to define the task.
RegisterTaskDefinition	Registers a task in a specified location using the ITaskDefinition interface to define a task.
SetSecurityDescriptor	Sets the security descriptor for the folder.

Properties

The TaskFolder object has the following properties.

Properties	Description
Name	Gets the name that is used to identify the folder that contains a task.
Path	Gets the path to where the folder is stored.

TaskFolderCollection

This scripting object provides information and control for a collection of folders that contain tasks.

Methods

The `TaskFolderCollection` object does not define any methods.

Properties

The `TaskFolderCollection` object has the following properties.

Properties	Description
Count	Gets the number of folders in the collection.
Item	Gets the specified folder from the collection.

TaskNamedValuePair

This scripting object is used to create a name-value pair in which the name is associated with the value.

Methods

The `TaskNamedValuePair` object does not define any methods.

Properties

The `TaskNamedValuePair` object has the following properties.

Properties	Description
Name	Gets or sets the name that is associated with a value in a name-value pair.
Value	Gets or sets the value that is associated with a name in a name-value pair.

TaskNamedValueCollection

This scripting object contains a collection of `TaskNamedValuePair` object name-value pairs.

Methods

The `TaskNamedValueCollection` has the following methods.

Method	Description
Clear	Clears the entire collection of name-value pairs.
Create	Creates a name-value pair in the collection.
Remove	Removes a selected name-value pair from the collection.

Properties

The `TaskNamedValueCollection` object has the following properties.

Properties	Description
Count	Gets the number of name-value pairs in the collection.
Item	Gets the specified name-value pair from the collection.

TaskService

This scripting object provides access to the Task Scheduler service for managing registered tasks.

Methods

The `TaskService` has the following methods.

Method	Description
GetFolder	Gets the path to a folder of registered tasks.
GetRunningTasks	Gets a collection of running tasks.
Connect	Connects to a remote machine and associates all subsequent calls on this interface with a remote session.
NewTask	Returns an empty task definition object to be filled in with settings and properties, and then registered using the `TaskFolder` `.RegisterTaskDefinition` method.

Properties

The `TaskService` object has the following properties.

Properties	Description
Connected	Gets a Boolean value that indicates if you are connected to the Task Scheduler service.
ConnectedDomain	Gets the name of the domain to which the TargetService computer is connected.
ConnectedUser	Gets the name of the user that is connected to the Task Scheduler service.
HighestVersion	Gets the highest version of Task Scheduler that a computer supports.
TargetServer	Gets the name of the computer that is running the Task Scheduler service that the user is connected to.

TaskSettings

This scripting object provides the settings that the Task Scheduler service uses to perform the task.

Methods

The TaskSettings object does not define any methods.

Properties

The TaskSettings object has the following properties.

Properties	Description
AllowDemandStart	Gets or sets a Boolean value that indicates that the task can be started by using either the Run command or the Context menu.
AllowHardTerminate	Gets or sets a Boolean value that indicates that the task may be terminated by using TerminateProcess.
Compatibility	Gets or sets an integer value that indicates which version of Task Scheduler a task is compatible with.
DeleteExpiredTaskAfter	Gets or sets the amount of time that the Task Scheduler will wait before deleting the task after it expires.
DisallowStartIfOnBatteries	Gets or sets a Boolean value that indicates that the task will not be started if the computer is running on battery power.
Enabled	Gets or sets a Boolean value that indicates that the task is enabled. The task can be performed only when this setting is True.

(continued)

Properties	Description
ExecutionTimeLimit	Gets or sets the amount of time allowed to complete the task.
Hidden	Gets or sets a Boolean value that indicates that the task will not be visible in the UI. However, administrators can override this setting through the use of a "master switch" that makes all tasks visible in the UI.
IdleSettings	Gets or sets the information that specifies how the Task Scheduler performs tasks when the computer is in an idle state.
MultipleInstances	Gets or sets the policy that defines how the Task Scheduler deals with multiple instances of the task.
NetworkSettings	Gets or sets the network settings object that contains a network profile identifier and name.
Priority	Gets or sets the priority level of the task.
RestartCount	Gets or sets the number of times that the Task Scheduler will attempt to restart the task.
RestartInterval	Gets or sets a value that specifies how long the Task Scheduler will attempt to restart the task.
RunOnlyIfIdle	Gets or sets a Boolean value that indicates that the Task Scheduler will run the task only if the computer is in an idle state.
RunOnlyIfNetworkAvailable	Gets or sets a Boolean value that indicates that the Task Scheduler will run the task only when a network is available.
StartWhenAvailable	Gets or sets a Boolean value that indicates that the Task Scheduler can start the task at any time after its scheduled time has passed.
StopIfGoingOnBatteries	Gets or sets a Boolean value that indicates that the task will be stopped if the computer begins to run on battery power.
WakeToRun	Gets or sets a Boolean value that indicates that the Task Scheduler will wake the computer when it is time to run the task.
XmlText	Gets or sets an XML-formatted definition of the task settings.

TaskVariables

This scripting object defines task variables that can be passed as parameters to task handlers and external executables that are launched by tasks.

Methods

The `TaskVariables` has the following methods.

Method	Description
GetInput	Gets the input variables for a task.
SetOutput	Sets the output variables for a task.
GetContext	Used to share the context between different steps and tasks that are in the same job instance.

Properties

The `TaskVariables` object does not define any properties.

TimeTrigger

This scripting object represents a trigger that starts a task at a specific date and time.

Methods

The `TimeTrigger` does not define any methods.

Properties

The `TimeTrigger` object has the following properties.

Properties	Description
Enabled	Inherited from the `Trigger` object. Gets or sets a Boolean value that indicates whether the trigger is enabled.
EndBoundary	Inherited from the `Trigger` object. Gets or sets the date and time when the trigger is deactivated. The trigger cannot start the task after it is deactivated.
ExecutionTimeLimit	Inherited from the `Trigger` object. Gets or sets the maximum amount of time that the task launched by the trigger is allowed to run.
Id	Inherited from the `Trigger` object. Gets or sets the identifier for the trigger.

(continued)

Properties	Description
RandomDelay	Gets or sets a delay time that is randomly added to the start time of the trigger.
Repetition	Inherited from the `Trigger` object. Gets or sets how often the task is run and how long the repetition pattern is repeated after the task is started.
StartBoundary	Inherited from the `Trigger` object. Gets or sets the date and time when the trigger is activated.
Type	Inherited from the `Trigger` object. Gets the type of the trigger.

Trigger

This scripting object provides the common properties that are inherited by all trigger objects.

Methods

The `Trigger` does not define any methods.

Properties

The `Trigger` object has the following properties.

Properties	Description
Enabled	Gets or sets a Boolean value that indicates whether the trigger is enabled.
EndBoundary	Gets or sets the date and time when the trigger is deactivated. The trigger cannot start the task after it is deactivated.
ExecutionTimeLimit	Gets or sets the maximum amount of time that the task launched by the trigger is allowed to run.
Id	Gets or sets the identifier for the trigger.
Repetition	Gets or sets how often the task is run and how long the repetition pattern is repeated after the task is started.
StartBoundary	Gets or sets the date and time when the trigger is activated.
Type	Inherited from the `Trigger` object. Gets the type of the trigger.

TriggerCollection

This scripting object is used to add to, remove from, and retrieve the triggers of a task.

Methods

The `TriggerCollection` has the following methods.

Method	Description
Clear	Clears all triggers from the collection.
Create	Creates a new trigger for the task.
Remove	Removes the specified trigger from the collection of triggers used by the task.

Properties

The `TriggerCollection` object has the following properties.

Properties	Description
Count	Gets the number of triggers in the collection.
Item	Gets the specified trigger from the collection.

WeeklyTrigger

This scripting object represents a trigger that starts a task based on a weekly schedule.

Methods

The `WeeklyTrigger` does not define any methods.

Properties

The `WeeklyTrigger` object has the following properties.

Properties	Description
DaysOfWeek	Gets or sets the days of the week on which the task runs.
Enabled	Inherited from the `Trigger` object. Gets or sets a Boolean value that indicates whether the trigger is enabled.
EndBoundary	Inherited from the `Trigger` object. Gets or sets the date and time when the trigger is deactivated. The trigger cannot start the task after it is deactivated.

(continued)

Properties	Description
ExecutionTimeLimit	Inherited from the `Trigger` object. Gets or sets the maximum amount of time that the task launched by the trigger is allowed to run.
Id	Inherited from the `Trigger` object. Gets or sets the identifier for the trigger.
RandomDelay	Gets or sets a delay time that is randomly added to the start time of the trigger.
Repetition	Inherited from the `Trigger` object. Gets or sets how often the task is run and how long the repetition pattern is repeated after the task is started.
StartBoundary	Inherited from the `Trigger` object. Gets or sets the date and time when the trigger is activated.
Type	Inherited from the `Trigger` object. Gets the type of the trigger.
WeeksInterval	Gets or sets the interval between the weeks in the schedule.

Sample Task Scheduler Script

Now, take a look at a completed Task Scheduler script. You will use this script to start the Disk Defragmenter shortly after a system is booted up.

```
const TriggerTypeTime = 1
const ActionTypeExec = 0


'*********************************************************
Set service = CreateObject("Schedule.Service")
call service.Connect()

'*********************************************************
Dim rootFolder
Set rootFolder = service.GetFolder("\")

Dim taskDefinition
Set taskDefinition = service.NewTask(0)

'*********************************************************
Dim regInfo
Set regInfo = taskDefinition.RegistrationInfo
regInfo.Description = "Start Disk Defragmenter"
regInfo.Author = "Administrator"

Dim settings
Set settings = taskDefinition.Settings
settings.Enabled = True
settings.StartWhenAvailable = True
settings.Hidden = False

'*********************************************************
```

```
Dim triggers
Set triggers = taskDefinition.Triggers

Dim trigger
Set trigger = triggers.Create(TriggerTypeTime)

Dim startTime, endTime

Dim time
time = DateAdd("s", 30, Now)
startTime = XmlTime(time)

time = DateAdd("n", 15, Now)
endTime = XmlTime(time)

WScript.Echo "startTime :" & startTime
WScript.Echo "endTime :" & endTime

trigger.StartBoundary = startTime
trigger.EndBoundary = endTime
trigger.ExecutionTimeLimit = "PT60M"
trigger.Id = "TimeTriggerId"
trigger.Enabled = True

'*************************************************************
Dim Action
Set Action = taskDefinition.Actions.Create( ActionTypeExec )
Action.Path = "C:\Windows\System32\dfrgui.exe"

WScript.Echo "Task definition created ... submitting task..."

'*************************************************************

call rootFolder.RegisterTaskDefinition( _
    "Test TimeTrigger", taskDefinition, 6, , , 3)

WScript.Echo "Task submitted."

Function XmlTime(t)
    Dim cSecond, cMinute, CHour, cDay, cMonth, cYear
    Dim tTime, tDate

    cSecond = "0" & Second(t)
    cMinute = "0" & Minute(t)
    cHour = "0" & Hour(t)
    cDay = "0" & Day(t)
    cMonth = "0" & Month(t)
    cYear = Year(t)

    tTime = Right(cHour, 2) & ":" & Right(cMinute, 2) & _
        ":" & Right(cSecond, 2)
    tDate = cYear & "-" & Right(cMonth, 2) & "-" & Right(cDay, 2)
    XmlTime = tDate & "T" & tTime
End Function
```

Let's walk through the code.

1. Define a constant for the time-based trigger and the executable action.

```
const TriggerTypeTime = 1
const ActionTypeExec = 0
```

2. Create the `TaskService` object.

```
Set service = CreateObject("Schedule.Service")
call service.Connect()
```

3. In the following code, you do several things:

   ❑ Set a folder for the task definition (C: drive).

   ❑ Set the `taskDefinition` variable to the object.

   ❑ Flag the `NewTask` parameter as `0` because it's not supported.

```
Dim rootFolder
Set rootFolder = service.GetFolder("\")

Dim taskDefinition
Set taskDefinition = service.NewTask(0)
```

4. In the next section of code, you create the registration information for the task by using the `RegistrationInfo` object:

```
Dim regInfo
Set regInfo = taskDefinition.RegistrationInfo
regInfo.Description = "Start Disk Defragmenter"
regInfo.Author = "Administrator"
```

5. In the following section of code, you create the `TaskSetting` object:

```
Dim settings
Set settings = taskDefinition.Settings
settings.Enabled = True
settings.StartWhenAvailable = True
settings.Hidden = False
```

6. Set the time-based triggers. Specifically:

   ❑ The start time is 30 seconds from when the task was set.

   ❑ The end time is 15 minutes from when the task was set.

   ❑ The execution limit is set to 60 minutes.

```
Dim triggers
Set triggers = taskDefinition.Triggers
```

```
Dim trigger
Set trigger = triggers.Create(TriggerTypeTime)

Dim startTime, endTime

Dim time
time = DateAdd("s", 30, Now)
startTime = XmlTime(time)

time = DateAdd("n", 15, Now)
endTime = XmlTime(time)

WScript.Echo "startTime :" & startTime
WScript.Echo "endTime :" & endTime

trigger.StartBoundary = startTime
trigger.EndBoundary = endTime
trigger.ExecutionTimeLimit = "PT60M"
trigger.Id = "TimeTriggerId"
trigger.Enabled = True
```

7. Set the action, which in this case is running the Windows Disk Defragmenter.

```
Dim Action
Set Action = taskDefinition.Actions.Create( ActionTypeExec )
Action.Path = "C:\Windows\System32\dfrgui.exe"

WScript.Echo "Task definition created ... submitting task..."
```

8. Register the task, as follows:

```
call rootFolder.RegisterTaskDefinition( _
    "Test TimeTrigger", taskDefinition, 6, , , 3)

WScript.Echo "Task submitted."
```

9. Use this function to get the time for the trigger `StartBoundary` and `EndBoundary`:

```
Function XmlTime(t)
    Dim cSecond, cMinute, CHour, cDay, cMonth, cYear
    Dim tTime, tDate

    cSecond = "0" & Second(t)
    cMinute = "0" & Minute(t)
    cHour = "0" & Hour(t)
    cDay = "0" & Day(t)
    cMonth = "0" & Month(t)
    cYear = Year(t)

    tTime = Right(cHour, 2) & ":" & Right(cMinute, 2) & _
        ":" & Right(cSecond, 2)
    tDate = cYear & "-" & Right(cMonth, 2) & "-" & Right(cDay, 2)
    XmlTime = tDate & "T" & tTime
End Function
```

Summary

This chapter gave you a detailed look at the new Task Scheduler that ships with Windows Vista and Windows Server 2008. In this chapter you examined:

❑ The new Task Scheduler features that are available

❑ How to interact with Task Scheduler

❑ How to define and create tasks

❑ What triggers are and how to use them

❑ What actions are and how to use them

You also looked at the new scripting objects for Task Scheduler 2.0 as well as an example script that made use of much of what was discussed in this chapter.

PowerShell

PowerShell (or Windows PowerShell) is the name that Microsoft gave its new extensible command-line interface shell and scripting language. PowerShell has gone under other names before being released — Microsoft Shell, MSH, and Monad. These terms are now obsolete and have been superseded by PowerShell.

This chapter introduces PowerShell and looks at how VBScript programmers can leverage the power offered by this new shell and scripting language.

Requirements

Microsoft PowerShell is based on object-oriented programming and version 2.0 of Microsoft's .NET Framework and is available for Windows XP SP2, Windows Server 2003 R2, Windows Vista, and Windows Server 2008. It doesn't ship as default with these operating systems but you can download it from Microsoft (`http://www.microsoft.com/windowsserver2003/technologies/management/powershell`).

> *It is expected that future versions of Windows will ship with PowerShell by default.*

PowerShell is supported on x86, x64, and IA64 architecture, requires the .NET Framework version 2.0, and is the basis for administrative tools for the following products:

- ❑ Exchange Server 2007
- ❑ System Center Virtual Machine Manager 2007
- ❑ System Center Operations Manager 2007

Features

Here are some of the features present in the initial release of PowerShell:

- ❏ PowerShell is free. Microsoft has no plans to charge for this feature.

- ❏ PowerShell is a C#-like scripting language. It has support for the following concepts:

  - ❏ Regular expressions

  - ❏ Switch statements

  - ❏ Array manipulation

  - ❏ Script blocks

  - ❏ Hash tables

  - ❏ Looping

  - ❏ Conditional statements

  - ❏ Variable scoping

- ❏ It has a suspend feature for help with debugging.

- ❏ Execution policies provide security and restrictions on PowerShell scripts. Four policies are supported:

  - ❏ `Restricted`

  - ❏ `AllSigned`

  - ❏ `RemoteSigned`

  - ❏ `Unrestricted`

- ❏ PowerShell scripts can interact with the Windows registry HKLM (`HKEY_LOCAL_MACHINE`) and HKCU (`HKEY_CURRENT_USER`) hives.

- ❏ It has support for script signing.

- ❏ The command-line options are usually whole words, but they can be specified using the minimum number of letters necessary to disambiguate.

Why a New Scripting Language?

Why does PowerShell need a brand new scripting language? What was wrong with leveraging VBScript or one of the other scripting languages? According to Microsoft, there were four overriding reasons why PowerShell needed a language of its own:

- ❏ PowerShell needed a scripting language capable of managing .NET objects.

- ❏ The scripting language needed to provide a consistent environment for using cmdlets (pronounced *command lets*), which are .NET classes designed to use the features of the environment.

❑ The scripting language needed to support complex tasks, but in an easy-to-use way.

❑ To make the scripting language more accessible to programmers, it needed to be consistent with higher-level .NET programming languages, such as C#.

Getting Started

The best way to familiarize yourself with PowerShell is to download it and start using it. PowerShell can be downloaded from the Microsoft web site (`http://www.microsoft.com/windowsserver2003/ technologies/management/powershell/download.mspx`) and the installation is quick, easy, and straightforward.

Once it's downloaded and installed you are then ready to fire it up:

1. In Windows, click Start ➪ All Programs ➪ Windows PowerShell 1.0 ➪ Windows PowerShell. Alternatively, Click Start ➪ Run (on Windows XP; on Vista the easiest way to bring up the Run dialog is to press Windows key + R).

2. Type **powershell,** and then press Enter.

3. To start PowerShell from the command prompt, type **powershell.**

4. To see the options for running PowerShell, type **powershell -?** Figure 13-1 shows Windows PowerShell in action.

Figure 13-1

5. When PowerShell is open, you can get more information by typing **get-help.** This fires up the PowerShell `get-help` cmdlet. The output displayed is shown in Figure 13-2.

Windows PowerShell commands are not case-sensitive.

```
Windows PowerShell

PS C:\Users\Adi> get-help
TOPIC
    Get-Help

SHORT DESCRIPTION
    Displays help about PowerShell cmdlets and concepts.

LONG DESCRIPTION

SYNTAX
    get-help {<CmdletName> | <TopicName>}
    help {<CmdletName> | <TopicName>}
    <CmdletName> -?

    "Get-help" and "-?" display help on one page.
    "Help" displays help on multiple pages.

    Examples:
        get-help get-process   : Displays help about the get-process cmdlet.
        get-help about-signing : Displays help about the signing concept.
        help where-object      : Displays help about the where-object cmdlet.
        help about_foreach     : Displays help about foreach loops in PowerShell.
        match-string -?        : Displays help about the match-string cmdlet.

    You can use wildcard characters in the help commands (not with -?).
    If multiple help topics match, PowerShell displays a list of matching
    topics. If only one help topic matches, PowerShell displays the topic.

    Examples:
        get-help *        : Displays all help topics.
        get-help get-*    : Displays topics that begin with get-.
        help *object*     : Displays topics with "object" in the name.
        get-help about*   : Displays all conceptual topics.
```

Figure 13-2

Using PowerShell

Now that you have PowerShell up and running and managed to fire up the `get-help` cmdlet, you're now ready to explore PowerShell in more detail.

The easiest way to begin exploring PowerShell is to take a look at other basic cmdlets that are installed with PowerShell. A few to get you started are:

❑ `get-command`

❑ `get-process`

❑ `get-service`

❑ `get-eventlog`

You can view the help for these cmdlets by typing `get-help` followed by the cmdlet name into the PowerShell console. For example:

```
get-help get-command
```

The output of this command is shown in Figure 13-3.

Figure 13-3

To display detailed help relating to the get-command cmdlet, type the following:

```
get-help get-command -detailed
```

The output of this command is shown in Figure 13-4.

Figure 13-4

To display all the available help for the `get-command` cmdlet, which will include technical information about the cmdlet and its parameters, type the following:

```
get-help get-command -full
```

The output of this command is shown in Figure 13-5.

Figure 13-5

To display only code examples for the `get-command` cmdlet, type the following:

```
get-help get-command -examples
```

The output of this command is shown in Figure 13-6.

To display all the parameters for the `get-command` cmdlet, type the following:

```
get-help get-command -parameter *
```

The output of this command is shown in Figure 13-7.

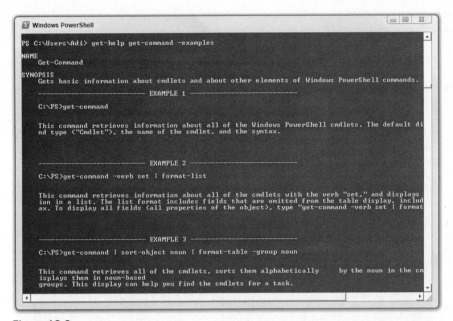

Figure 13-6

Figure 13-7

To display information on a particular parameter (for example, the `commandType` parameter) for the `get-command` cmdlet, type the same as before but replace the wildcard with the name of the parameter:

```
get-help get-command -parameter commandType
```

The output of this command is shown in Figure 13-8.

Figure 13-8

Deeper into PowerShell

You can do a lot with PowerShell, a lot more than we can cover in a single chapter (PowerShell is a topic that needs a book to cover it properly). However, before you learn how to create PowerShell scripts, take a closer look at PowerShell in action.

Using Aliases

Typing long cmdlet names can be a bit of a chore. This is where aliases come in because they allow you to assign a shorter name to a cmdlet. For example, if you wanted to type gd instead of `get-date`, you'd set this alias up as follows:

```
set-alias gd get-date
```

Now gd becomes shorthand for `get-date`, as shown in Figure 13-9.

Figure 13-9

Similarly, you can set aliases for commands, such as starting an application:

```
set-alias calc c:\windows\system32\calc.exe
```

Now typing `calc` into the PowerShell console will fire up the Windows Calculator program, as shown in Figure 13-10.

Figure 13-10

To delete the calc alias, type the following (also shown in Figure 13-11):

```
remove-item alias:calc
```

Figure 13-11

Using Functions

If you have log files in the root of C: drive that you want to read through PowerShell, you can open these in Windows Notepad through PowerShell using the following command:

```
notepad c:\logs.txt
```

You can turn this into a PowerShell function as follows:

```
function openlogs {notepad c:\logs.txt}
```

This function operates like an alias — to run the function you type openlogs (as shown in Figure 13-12).

Figure 13-12

Navigating the File System

You can navigate the Windows file system using PowerShell by using command-line commands that will be familiar to anyone who has used the command prompt. This is because commands such as cd, dir, and ls have been assigned as aliases to PowerShell cmdlets that carry out the same action (cd is an alias for the set-location cmdlet while dir and ls are aliases for the get-childitem cmdlet). Here are a few more tips that will help you get the most from your trip around the file system:

❑   The symbol for the current folder is the period .

❑   The symbol for the contents of a folder is the wildcard symbol *

❑   The following cmdlets can help you manipulate files and folders:

    ❑   `get-item`

    ❑   `get-childitem`

    ❑   `new-item`

    ❑   `remove-item`

    ❑   `set-item`

    ❑   `move-item`

    ❑   `copy-item`

Navigating the Windows Registry

You can use the Windows PowerShell to navigate through the Windows registry in much the same way that you navigate the file system. Under Windows PowerShell, the HKEY_LOCAL_MACHINE hive maps to the Windows PowerShell HKLM: drive while the HKEY_CURRENT_USER hive maps to the Windows PowerShell HKCU: drive. For example, Figure 13-13 shows the HKEY_LOCAL_MACHINE being accessed.

Figure 13-13

Can I Create My Own Cmdlets?

The term *cmdlet* seems to be used as a loose term that describes both cmdlet script files and the compiled cmdlets (such as the ones that ship with PowerShell). You'll learn in a moment how to create PowerShell script files, but what about compiled cmdlet files? Yes, you can create them, but not without Visual Studio. That said, the analysis of creating your own compiled cmdlets has to end there as far as this chapter is concerned.

Working with Scripts in PowerShell

OK, now take look at how to create script files that you can use within PowerShell. Before you start, there's one thing that you need to do. That is change the PowerShell execution policy so unsigned scripts will run.

Changing PowerShell Execution Policy

By default, Microsoft has blocked PowerShell's ability to run cmdlet scripts for security reasons. Therefore, if you want to create and run your own scripts, you'll need to change the execution policy from `Restricted` to `RemoteSigned`. There are two ways to do this.

❑ Editing the Registry: To check the setting launch Regedit and navigate to: `HKLM\SOFTWARE\ Microsoft\PowerShell\1\ShellIds\Microsoft.PowerShell`. Now change this registry key to: `REG_SZ ExecutionPolicy RemoteSigned`.

❑ Via PowerShell: At the PowerShell prompt type the following (see Figure 13-14):

```
get-executionpolicy
set-executionpolicy RemoteSigned
```

This setting is stored in the registry and will persist when PowerShell is closed or uninstalled.

To make this change, PowerShell needs to be run with administrator privileges.

Naming Scripts

A PowerShell cmdlet script is a text file that's given a specific filename and file extension. The filename can be anything that's valid but the file extension has to be `.ps1`. For example:

```
ExPolicyChange.ps1
```

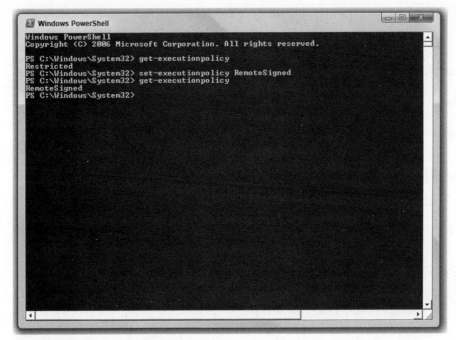

Figure 13-14

Creating and Calling
Your First PowerShell Cmdlet Script

Now, it's time to create a PowerShell cmdlet script and it's very easy to do. By way of example, create a script that displays the execution policy for the system following these steps:

1. Fire up Windows Notepad.

2. Type the following in the Notepad window (see Figure 13-15):

```
get-executionpolicy
```

Figure 13-15

3. Save the file with the following filename: **GetExPolicy.ps1**

That's it! You've created your first PowerShell cmdlet script.

Now that you have the cmdlet script, you can try running it. When you execute the cmdlet by calling the filename from the PowerShell command line, you don't need to worry about the `.ps1` extension; all you need to use is the filename. However, you need to be careful that you get the path right.

❑ If you store your scripts in a folder called scripts on the D: drive, to run `GetExPolicy.ps1` you would type the following into PowerShell (see Figure 13-16):

```
d:\scripts\GetExPolicy
```

Figure 13-16

Easy!

❑ You could make it even easier by assigning this to a function so that you have to type less into the console (see Figure 13-17):

```
function getpolicy {d:\scripts\GetExPolicy}
```

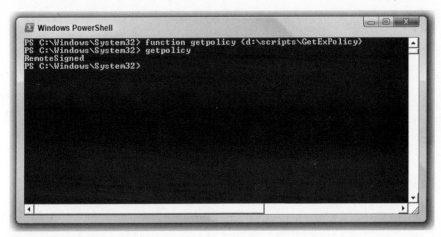

Figure 13-17

The Connection Between VBScript and PowerShell?

By now you're probably starting to wonder what the connection between VBScript and PowerShell cmdlet scripts is. The truth is, very little.

So why include PowerShell in a book on VBScript? Because Microsoft has anticipated that many VBScripters will want to leverage PowerShell, and have made it easier than it might have been to convert VBScripts to a format that works with PowerShell.

It's only fair to get it out in the open right from the start and make it clear that there's no "one-stop wonder-tool" that will take your VBScript code and translate it into PowerShell cmdlet scripts. In fact, the only way to convert scripts is to do it manually. However, what Microsoft has done is concentrate on creating a resource that allows VBScript programmers to translate VBScript commands (such as functions, statements, and operators) into PowerShell commands. This isn't an easy task and overall Microsoft has done a pretty good job.

Let's take a look at some common VBScript commands and examine the PowerShell analog.

Operators

Here are some of the most commonly used VBScript operators and their PowerShell analogs.

The VBScript operator will be placed in the title in parentheses.

Operator	Example

Addition (+)	```PS C:\> $sum = 5 + 5```
	```PS C:\> $sum```
	```10```
	```PS C:\>```

Subtraction (−)	```PS C:\> $sum = 5 - 5```
	```PS C:\> $sum```
	```0```
	```PS C:\>```

Multiplication (*)	```PS C:\> $sum = 5 * 5```
	```PS C:\> $sum```
	```25```
	```PS C:\>```

Division (/)	```PS C:\> $sum = 12 / 3```
	```PS C:\> $sum```
	```4```
	```PS C:\>```

Concatenation (&)	Under VBScript you're used to the concatenation being &, but under PowerShell it is +. Here's how you concatenate two text strings:
	```$string = "Hello, " + "World!"```
	Here it is in action:
	```PS C:\> $string = "Hello, " + "World!"```
	```PS C:\> $string```
	```Hello, World!```
	```PS C:\>```

And (AND)	For a change, this is a little different. Take this statement:
	```$sum = 34 -gt 62 -and 25 -gt 45```
	
	This statement reads:
	```If 32 is greater than 62 AND 25 greater than 45```
	The AND operator is used to evaluate two statements. If both statements are true, TRUE is returned; otherwise FALSE is returned.
	
	If you run this through the PowerShell console, here's what you get:
	```PS C:\> $sum = 34 -gt 62 -and 25 -gt 45```
	```PS C:\> $sum```
	```False```
	```PS C:\>```

Operator	Example

Or Operator (OR)	The OR operator is used to evaluate two statements. If one of the statements is true, TRUE is returned; otherwise FALSE is returned.
	
	`$sum = 34 -gt 62 -or 25 -gt 45`
	
	If you run this through the PowerShell console, here's what you get:
	
	`PS C:\> $sum = 34 -gt 62 -or 25 -gt 45`
	`PS C:\> $sum`
	`False`
	`PS C:\>`

Not Operator (NOT)	The NOT operator tests whether an expression is false. If an expression is false, then the NOT operator reports back TRUE. If an expression is true, then the NOT operator reports back FALSE.
	
	`PS C:\> $sum = 2not (5 + 5 2eq 10)`
	`PS C:\> $sum`
	`False`
	`PS C:\>`

Xor Operator (XOR)	XOR evaluates two expressions and returns TRUE if the two are different; that is, if one expression is true and the other expression is false. If both expressions are true (or false), then XOR returns FALSE.
	
	`PS C:\> $sum = 32 -gt 9 -xor 22 -lt 42`
	`PS C:\> $sum`
	`False`
	`PS C:\>`

Exponentiation operator (^)	This one is rather tricky because there's no exponential operation in PowerShell, so the `Pow` method of `System.Math` class is used instead.
	
	`PS C:\> $sum = [math]::pow(5,3)`
	`PS C:\> $sum`
	`125`
	`PS C:\>`

Mod operator (Mod)	The Mod operator is used to divide two numbers and return the remainder.
	
	`PS C:\> $sum = 5 % 2`
	`PS C:\> $sum`
	`1`
	`PS C:\>`

Functions

Let's now move on to look at VBScript functions and their PowerShell equivalents.

Function	Purpose	Example

Abs	In VBScript, Abs returns the absolute value of a number.	An example of an equivalent PowerShell command:
		`PS C:\> $sum = [math]::abs(-22)`
		`PS C:\> $sum`
		`22`
		`PS C:\>`

Array	Creating arrays are core to VBScript and all other programming languages, and Power-Shell is one of the easiest languages to create arrays with.	An example of an equivalent PowerShell command:
		`PS C:\> $favfruit = "banana","orange",`
		`"apple", "grapes","grapefruit","melon"`
		`PS C:\> $favfruit`
		`banana`
		`orange`
		`apple`
		`grapes`
		`grapefruit`
		`melon`
		`PS C:\>`

Asc	In VBScript, this returns the ANSI code of the first character in a string.	An example of an equivalent PowerShell command:
		`PS C:\> $string = [byte][char] "E"`
		`PS C:\> $string`
		`69`
		`PS C:\>`
		Entering a string longer than one character causes an error:
		`PS C:\> $string = [byte][char] "AEIOU"`
		`Cannot convert value "AEIOU" to type`
		`"System.Char". Error: "String must be`
		`exactly one character long."`
		`At line:1 char:23`
		`+ $string = [byte][char]  <<<< "AEIOU"`
		`PS C:\>`

CBool	In VBScript, this returns an expression that has been converted to a variant of the Boolean subtype. Zero is always converted to FALSE and everything else will convert to TRUE.	An example of an equivalent PowerShell command:
		`PS C:\> $x = 0`
		`PS C:\> $x = [bool] $x`
		`PS C:\> $x`
		`False`
		`PS C:\> $y = AEIOU`
		`PS C:\> $y = "AEIOU"`
		`PS C:\> $y = [bool] $y`
		`PS C:\> $y`
		`True`
		`PS C:\>`

Function	Purpose	Example
CDbl	In VBScript, this returns an expression that is converted to a variant of the Double subtype.	The double data type contains a double-precision, floating-point number in the range −1.79769313486232E308 to −4.94065645841247E-324 for negative values and 4.94065645841247E-324 to 1.79769313486232E308 for positive values.

		Here's an example of an equivalent PowerShell command:
		`PS C:\> $sum = "3.141592654"`
		`PS C:\> $sum = [double] $sum`
		`PS C:\> $sum.gettype()`
		
		`IsPublic IsSerial Name`
		`-------- -------- ----`
		`True     True     Double`

Chr	In VBScript, this returns the character associated with a specific ANSI code.	An example of an equivalent PowerShell command:
		`PS C:\> $char = [char]69`
		`PS C:\> $char`
		`E`
		`PS C:\>`

CInt	In VBScript, this returns an expression that has been converted to a variant of the Integer subtype.	An example of an equivalent PowerShell command:
		`PS C:\> $sum = "3.141592654"`
		`PS C:\> $sum = [int] $sum`
		`PS C:\> $sum`
		`3`
		`PS C:\>`

CLng	In VBScript, this returns an expression that has been converted to a variant of the Long subtype. Long values are integers in the range −2,147,483,648 to 2,147,483,647.	An example of an equivalent PowerShell command:
		`PS C:\> $sum = 321.123`
		`PS C:\> $sum = [long] $sum`
		`PS C:\> $sum`
		`321`
		`PS C:\>`

(continued)

Function	Purpose	Example

CStr	In VBScript, this returns an expression that has been converted to a variant of the String subtype.	An example of an equivalent PowerShell command:
		
		`PS C:\> $str = 69`
		`PS C:\> $str.gettype()`
		
		`IsPublic IsSerial Name`
		`-------- -------- ----`
		`True     True     Int32`
		
		`PS C:\> $str = [string] $str`
		`PS C:\> $str.gettype()`
		
		`IsPublic IsSerial Name`
		`-------- -------- ----`
		`True     True     String`
		`PS C:\>`

DateAdd	In VBScript, this returns a date to which a specified time interval has been added.	An example of an equivalent PowerShell command:
		
		`PS C:\> $a = (get-date).AddDays(123)`
		`PS C:\> $str = (get-date).AddDays(123)`
		`PS C:\> $str`
		
		`18 September 2007 10:44:52`
		
		`PS C:\>`
		
		You can do more than just add days:
		`(get-date).AddHours(25)`
		`(get-date).AddMilliseconds(25)`
		`(get-date).AddMinutes(25)`
		`(get-date).AddMonths(25)`
		`(get-date).AddSeconds(25)`
		`(get-date).AddTicks(25)`
		`(get-date).AddYears(25)`

Function	Purpose	Example
| Escape | In VBScript, this converts a string entirely to ASCII with non-ASCII characters replaced with `%xx` encoding, where xx is equivalent to the hexadecimal number representing the character. Unicode characters that have a value greater than 255 are stored using the `%uxxxx` format.<br><br>However, under PowerShell this useful feature is missing; you can obtain a similar result using the `Web.Utility` class from the `System.Web` class. Clumsy, yes, but at least it works. | ```
PS C:\> [Reflection.Assembly]::LoadWithPart
ialName("System.Web")

GAC     Version       Location
---     -------       --------
True    v2.0.50727    C:\Windows\assembly\
                      GAC_32\System.
                      Web\2.0.0.0_

PS C:\> $str = [web.httputility]::
urlencode("Funky//:;\\String!")
PS C:\> $str
Funky%2f%2f%3a%3b%5c%5cString!
PS C:\>
``` |
| Filter | In VBScript, this returns a zero-based array containing a subset of a string array based on specified criteria. | An example of an equivalent PowerShell command:<br>```
PS C:\> $str ="1","10","13","19","23","25","30
"
PS C:\> $filter = ($str | where-object {$_
-like "1*"})
PS C:\> $filter
1
10
13
19
PS C:\>
``` |

(continued)

365

Function	Purpose	Example

Format-Number	In VBScript, this returns an expression formatted as a number. This is particularly handy when you want to specify the number of decimal places to use.	An example of an equivalent PowerShell command:
		`PS C:\> $num = 7`
		`PS C:\> $num = "{0:N4}" -f $num`
		`PS C:\> $num`
		`7.0000`
		`PS C:\>`
		
		It can also be used for the automatic rounding of numbers:
		`PS C:\> $num = 7.1234567`
		`PS C:\> $num = "{0:N4}" -f $num`
		`PS C:\> $num`
		`7.1235`
		`PS C:\>`

GetLocale	In VBScript, this returns the current locale ID value, which can be useful when you want to determine things like keyboard layouts, currencies, date and time format, and so on.	An example of an equivalent PowerShell command:
		`PS C:\> $str = (get-culture).lcid`
		`PS C:\> $str`
		`1033`
		`PS C:\>`
		
		Alternatively, you can display the locale name:
		`PS C:\> $str = (get-culture).displayname`
		`PS C:\> $str`
		`English (United States)`
		`PS C:\>`

Hex	In VBScript, this is used to return a string representing the hexadecimal value of a number.	An example of an equivalent PowerShell command:
		`PS C:\> $num = 1066`
		`PS C:\> $num = "{0:X}" -f $num`
		`PS C:\> $num`
		`42A`
		`PS C:\>`

Hour	In VBScript, this returns a whole number between 0 and 23 inclusive, which represents the hour of the day.	An example of an equivalent PowerShell command:
		`PS C:\> $str = (get-date).hour`
		`PS C:\> $str`
		`13`
		`PS C:\>`

Function	Purpose	Example

InStr	In VBScript, this returns the position of the first occurrence of one string within another. This is to determine if a character is present in a string or where the position of the first occurrence is. Power-Shell can do both!	An example of an equivalent PowerShell command:
		`PS C:\> $str = "Hello, World!"`
		`PS C:\> $str2 = $str.contains("l")`
		`PS C:\> $str2`
		`True`
		`PS C:\> $str2 = $str.indexof("l")`
		`PS C:\> $str2`
		`2`
		`PS C:\>`

IsNull	In VBScript, this returns a Boolean value that indicates whether an expression contains no valid data (Null).	An example of an equivalent PowerShell command: PS C:\> $str1 = $strX -eq $null PS C:\> $str1 True PS C:\>

Join	In VBScript, this returns a string created by joining a number of substrings contained in an array. This is very handy when you want to concatenate the values held in an array.	An example of an equivalent PowerShell command:
		`PS C:\> $str2 = [string]::join("", $str)`
		`PS C:\> $str2`
		`aeiou`
		`PS C:\>`
		
		Here's a cool trick where you can put delimiters between the values:
		`PS C:\> $str = "a","e","i","o","u"`
		`PS C:\> $str2 = [string]::join("%", $str)`
		`PS C:\> $str2`
		`a%e%i%o%u`
		`PS C:\>`

LCase	In VBScript, this converts a string to lowercase.	An example of an equivalent PowerShell command:
		`PS C:\> $str = "AEIOU"`
		`PS C:\> $str = $str.ToLower()`
		`PS C:\> $str`
		`aeiou`
		`PS C:\>`

Left	In VBScript, this returns a specified number of characters from the left side of a string.	An example of an equivalent PowerShell command:
		`PS C:\> $str = $str.substring(0,3)`
		`PS C:\> $str`
		`AEI`
		`PS C:\>`

(continued)

Function	Purpose	Example
Len	In VBScript, this returns the number of characters in a string or the number of bytes needed to store a variable.	An example of an equivalent PowerShell command: PS C:\> $str = "AEIOU" PS C:\> $str = $str.length PS C:\> $str 5 PS C:\>
LTrim	In VBScript, this returns a copy of a string without leading spaces.	An example of an equivalent PowerShell command: PS C:\> $str = "AEIOU" PS C:\> $str = $str.TrimStart() PS C:\> $str AEIOU PS C:\>
RTrim	In VBScript, this returns a copy of a string without the trailing spaces.	An example of an equivalent PowerShell command: PS C:\> $str = "AEIOU" PS C:\> $str = $str.TrimEnd() PS C:\> $str AEIOU PS C:\>
Trim	In VBScript, this returns a copy of a string without the leading or trailing spaces.	An example of an equivalent PowerShell command: PS C:\> $str = $str.Trim() PS C:\> $str AEIOU PS C:\>
Mid	In VBScript, this returns a specified number of characters from a string.	An example of an equivalent PowerShell command: PS C:\> $str = "AEIOU" PS C:\> $str = $str.substring(2,3) PS C:\> $str IOU PS C:\>
Minute	In VBScript, this returns a whole number between 0 and 59 inclusive, which represents the minute of the hour.	An example of an equivalent PowerShell command: PS C:\> $str = (get-date).minute PS C:\> $str 41 PS C:\>
Month	In VBScript, this returns a whole number between 1 and 12 inclusive, which represents the month of the year. This can be done so that the leading zero is preserved or removed.	An example of an equivalent PowerShell command: PS C:\> $str = get-date -f "MM" PS C:\> $str 05 PS C:\> $str = [INT] (get-date -f "MM") PS C:\> $str 5 PS C:\>

Function	Purpose	Example

MonthName	In VBScript, this returns a string indicating the month.	An example of an equivalent PowerShell command:
		```PS C:\> $str = get-date -f "MMMM"```
		```PS C:\> $str```
		```May```
		```PS C:\>```

Now	In VBScript, this returns the current date and time (based on your system's settings).	An example of an equivalent PowerShell command:
		```PS C:\> $str = get-date```
		```PS C:\> $str```
		
		```18 May 2007 13:46:51```
		
		```PS C:\>```

Replace	In VBScript, this returns a string in which a specified substring has been replaced with another substring a specified number of times.	An example of an equivalent PowerShell command:
		```PS C:\> $str = "Hello%%there%%everybody!"```
		```PS C:\> $str = $str -replace("%%"," ")```
		```PS C:\> $str```
		```Hello there everybody!```
		```PS C:\>```

Right	In VBScript, this returns a specified number of characters from the right side of a string.	An example of an equivalent PowerShell command:
		```PS C:\> $str = "AEIOU"```
		```PS C:\> $str = $str.substring($str.length - 9, 9)```
		```PS C:\> $str = $str.substring($str.length - 2, 2)```
		```PS C:\> $str```
		```OU```
		```PS C:\>```

Rnd	In VBScript, this returns a pseudorandom number.	An example of an equivalent PowerShell command:
		```PS C:\> $str = new-object random```
		```PS C:\> $str2 = $str.next(1,100)```
		```PS C:\> $str2```
		```5```
		```PS C:\>```

Second	In VBScript, this returns a whole number between 0 and 59 inclusive, which represents the second of the minute.	An example of an equivalent PowerShell command:
		```PS C:\> $str = (get-date).second```
		```PS C:\> $str```
		```2```
		```PS C:\>```

(continued)

Function	Purpose	Example

Space	In VBScript, this returns a string made up of a specified number of spaces.	An example of an equivalent PowerShell command:
		`PS C:\> $str = " " * 10`
		`PS C:\> $str`
		
		`PS C:\>`

UCase	In VBScript, this returns a string that has been converted to uppercase.	An example of an equivalent PowerShell command:
		`PS C:\> $str = "aeiou"`
		`PS C:\> $str = $str.ToUpper()`
		`PS C:\> $str`
		`AEIOU`
		`PS C:\>`

Year	In VBScript, this returns a whole number representing the year.	Here's an example of an equivalent PowerShell command:
		`PS C:\> $str = (get-date).year`
		`PS C:\> $str`
		`2007`
		`PS C:\>`

Statements

Let's now move on to look at VBScript statements and their PowerShell equivalents.

Statement	Purpose	Example
Call Statement	In VBScript, this is used to transfer control to a Sub or Function procedure. In PowerShell there is no equivalent; you just specify the function along with the parameters.	
Dim Statement	In VBScript, this is used to declare variables and allocate appropriate storage space.	An example of an equivalent PowerShell command: `PS C:\> $str = [string]` This creates a new empty variable called `$str`.

Statement	Purpose	Example

`Do...Loop` `Statements`	In VBScript, this repeats a block of statements while a condition is TRUE or until a condition becomes TRUE.	An example of an equivalent Power-Shell command:
		`PS C:\> $num = 1`
		`PS C:\> do {$num; $num++}`
		`while ($num -lt 10)`
		`1`
		`2`
		`3`
		`4`
		`5`
		`6`
		`7`
		`8`
		`9`
		`PS C:\>`

`For...Next` `Statements`	In VBScript, this repeats a group of statements a specified number of times.	An example of an equivalent Power-Shell command:
		`PS C:\> for ($num = 1; $num -`
		`le 8; $num++) {$num}`
		`1`
		`2`
		`3`
		`4`
		`5`
		`6`
		`7`
		`8`
		`PS C:\>`

`If...Then...Else` `Statement`	In VBScript, this conditionally executes a group of statements, depending on the value of an expression.	An example of an equivalent Power-Shell command:
		`PS C:\> $num = "7"`
		`PS C:\> if ($num -eq "1")`
		`{"The number is 1."}`
		`    elseif ($num -eq "7")`
		`{"The number is 7."}`
		`    else {`
		`"The number is not 1 or 7."}`
		`The number is 7.`
		`PS C:\>`

(continued)

Statement	Purpose	Example

`On Error Statement`	In VBScript, this is used to enable or disable error handling.	An example of an equivalent PowerShell command:
		`PS C:\> $erroractionpreference = "SilentlyContinue"`
		
		You have to set the `$erroractionpreference` to one of the following four choices:
		`*SilentlyContinue`
		`*Continue` (default)
		`*Inquire`
		`*Stop`

`Randomize Statement`	In VBScript, this initializes the random-number generator.	An example of an equivalent PowerShell command:
		`PS C:\> $rnd = new-object random`
		`PS C:\> $rndnum = $rnd.next()`
		`PS C:\> $rndnum`
		`1536336435`
		`PS C:\>`

`Rem Statements`	In VBScript, this allows you to place comments inside the code. These comments are ignored by the interpreter.	An example of an equivalent PowerShell command:
		`PS C:\> $str = [string] #`
		`Creates a new empty variable`

`Select Case Statement`	In VBScript, this executes one of several groups of statements, depending on the value of an expression.	An example of an equivalent PowerShell command:
		`PS C:\> $num = 5`
		`PS C:\>`
		`PS C:\> switch ($num)`
		`>>       {`
		`>>            1 {"Number 1."}`
		`>>            2 {"Number 2."}`
		`>>            3 {"Number 3."}`
		`>>            4 {"Number 4."}`
		`>>            5 {"Number 5."}`
		`>>            6 {"Number 6."}`
		`>>            7 {"Number 7."}`
		`>>            8 {"Number 8."}`
		`>>            default {"Some other number was chosen ...."}`
		`>>       }`
		`>>`
		`Number 5.`
		`PS C:\>`

Statement	Purpose	Example

`While...Wend Statement`	In VBScript, this executes a series of statements as long as a given condition is TRUE.	An example of an equivalent Power-Shell command:
		`PS C:\> $num = 1`
		`PS C:\> while ($num -lt 10)`
		`{$num; $num++}`
		`1`
		`2`
		`3`
		`4`
		`5`
		`6`
		`7`
		`8`
		`9`
		`PS C:\>`

Summary

This chapter showed you a new command-line shell and interface scripting language from Microsoft called PowerShell. Although PowerShell doesn't ship with any current operating system (including Vista), it is available as a free download. PowerShell isn't directly linked to the VBScript language in any way but because PowerShell is based on .NET, it'll be familiar territory for the VBScript user. To help those familiar with VBScript get the most from PowerShell, this chapter discussed some of the most commonly used VBScript commands and introduced the PowerShell analog.

Super-Charged Client-Side Scripting

In this chapter, you continue to investigate client-side scripting, but you examine advanced technologies that give much needed functionality and extensibility to client-side pages. This includes:

❑   Scriptlets

❑   Behaviors

❑   HTML components

Each of these are subjects broad and deep enough to be books of their own, so this chapter focuses on small, well-tested examples that cover the major techniques required for you to begin using these technologies. In reality, to achieve maximum gain from these technologies, you'd have to read masses of documentation — a lot of which is very poorly written. This chapter shows you what is possible and how to go about doing it. The authors will have achieved what they've set out to do if, by the time you have finished this chapter, you can make any sense of the official documentation!

Microsoft's documentation is available as a free download at www.microsoft.com/scripting.

Requirements and Browser Security

Even though these are advanced applications and tools, the main thing you still need is a good text editor to manage these technologies. The following table lists the applications you need to make use of the technologies.

Technology	Requirements
Scriptlets	Internet Explorer 4 or later
Behaviors	Internet Explorer 5 or later
HTML Components	Internet Explorer 5 or later

The Internet Explorer browser is a *security-aware application*. Every component contained within the browser (flaws and bugs aside) is subject to the security settings defined for it. For detailed information about the security settings of your browser, refer to the documentation and help files. Typically, the *zone* containing the components-server should be `Medium` (`Medium-Low` in IE5, IE6, and IE7) or `Low`. If the security level is more restrictive, the components will not download on the client computer.

It is especially important to verify security settings when distributing an application that uses components. This is why these technologies are better suited for distribution in a corporate network setting than over the Internet to everyone. Asking a visitor to your site to change security settings in order to utilize something is, in today's security climate, absurd. For one thing, the security settings will be global. Second, how can they trust you?

Scriptlets — Ancestors of Behaviors

Introduced in IE4, the scriptlet mechanism was the first browser technology to permit the design of components using DHTML. While developing a Web or an intranet project, you usually produce a lot of HTML and scripting functionalities. Without a technology to implement components, you're limited to reusing your code by cutting it from a source file and pasting it into another file (or you can include external scripting files using the `src` attribute of the `<script>` tag: a useful facility, not a component-based technology). Also, cutting and pasting code usually requires lot of adaptations to make the code work in the new context, and there is enormous scope for things to go wrong and for errors to be introduced. On the other hand, the use of a component is straightforward. You include it in your context using its public interface made of properties, methods, and events — the usual stuff expected by an object-oriented programmer.

What Is a Scriptlet?

A *scriptlet* is a component developed using DHTML. What this actually means is that a scriptlet is an HTML file with a few extensions to allow the definition of properties, methods, and events that permit its use as a component.

To quickly show what a scriptlet is, we'll introduce the classic application "Hello, World!". The application's task is just to output the "Hello, World!" message using the technology under examination. To implement "Hello, World!" two files are required:

❑ The component file: `HELLOW.HTM`

❑ The client file: `CLIENT_HELLOW.HTM`

The following code shows the content of the `CLIENT_HELLOW.HTM` file.

```
<html>
<head>
<script language="VBScript">

Sub Hello()
    Document.All.myScriptlet.Hello
End Sub
```

```
</script>
</head>

<body onload="Hello()">

<OBJECT ID="myScriptlet"
    TYPE="text/x-scriptlet"
    DATA="hellow.htm"
    HEIGHT="0" WIDTH="0">
</OBJECT>

</body>
</html>
```

The scriptlet is identified by the name myScriptlet. This name is used as the ID of an <OBJECT> tag included in the HTML file. The details of this tag are as follows:

```
<OBJECT ID="myScriptlet"
    TYPE="text/x-scriptlet"
    DATA="hellow.htm"
    HEIGHT="0" WIDTH="0">
</OBJECT>
```

Note that the HEIGHT and WIDTH parameters of the <OBJECT> tag are set to zero. This is done to make the object invisible. There are certain cases where it might make sense to make the object visible (say if the scriptlet contains visible objects as well) but that is not the case here.

The following line calls the scriptlet code:

```
Document.All.myScriptlet.Hello
```

This line will require a scriptlet that exposes a Hello method. This very simple scriptlet is stored in the HELLOW.HTM file.

```
<script language="VBScript">

Sub public_Hello()
    MsgBox "Hello World!"
End Sub

</script>
```

So, what does the scriptlet comprise? It is an HTML file encapsulating the scripting code inside a <script> tag, which, in this case, contains just one VBScript function defined as public_Hello.

You can take note of several points from this example:

❑ The <OBJECT> tag lets you insert a scriptlet into an HTML document using a special object type defined as "text/x-scriptlet".

❑   The scriptlet code itself is contained in a separate HTML file specified in the DATA attribute of the <OBJECT> tag.

❑   The scriptlet is accessed for scripting through the ID specified for the <OBJECT> tag.

To run the scriptlet, you simply run the client file (the one that contains the <OBJECT> tag). Figure 14-1 shows the scriptlet in action!

Figure 14-1

The Prefix public_ Exposes Scriptlet Members

VBScript offers a very simple way to define which code is exposed by the scriptlet to the container: a simple to follow naming convention.

❑   The procedures and functions become public methods of the scriptlet if their names are prefixed with public_.

❑   The global variables in the code become properties of the scriptlet if their names are prefixed with public_ as well.

It is important for you to note (especially if you have used JScript) that JScript offers a mechanism called "Public Description Object" to further define the public interface of a scriptlet. JScript is outside the scope of this book and, anyway, you don't need it to implement scriptlets.

Additional naming conventions are shown in the following table.

Prefix	Used to Expose
public_	Variables as read/write properties and procedures or functions as methods
public_get	Functions as readable properties
public_put	Functions as writable properties

When a scriptlet member is exposed, its name in the host application does not have the prefix. Remember that the `Hello` function in the `HELLOW.HTM` scriptlet was defined as `public_Hello`:

```
Sub public_Hello()
```

While the `public_` prefix has been removed in the method call made by the host file `CLIENT_HELLOW.HTM`:

```
Document.All.myScriptlet.Hello ' and not
                            ' Document.All.myScriptlet.public_Hello
```

Scriptlets use prefixes to expose their public interface, but the host applications don't use the prefixes to access that interface. This is using quite an ambiguous syntax to simply declare a public interface.

Packaging Code in a Scriptlet for Reuse

Scriptlets are a good mechanism to package reusable code into one module. The next example shows you the beginnings of a more complex example that exposes a few methods and a property.

Using the Cookies Manager

The `Cookies Manager` is a scriptlet that exposes the following interface.

Member Type	Name	Description
Method	SetCookieKey (Key, Value)	Stores a value in a cookie and associates it with a specific key
Method	GetCookieKey (Key)	Returns the value of a specific key in a cookie
Method	RemoveCookieKey (Key)	Removes a specific key from a cookie
Property	KeyExists	True if the cookie key exists; usually checked after calling GetCookieKey or RemoveCookieKey

Using this interface, the client can store, read, or remove a specific key stored in a cookie.

An HTTP cookie is a small file stored on a client machine. By using cookies you can implement persistency among different sessions (so a user returning to the page will still find the values previously stored in the cookie). However, you cannot fully rely on this as many people do delete their cookies now on a regular basis.

Here is the code of the COOKIESMANAGER.HTM scriptlet.

```
<script language="VBScript">
<!--

Dim public_KeyExists
Sub public_SetCookieKey(sKey, sValue)
    Dim ck
    ck = sKey & "=" & sValue
    ck = ck & ";Expires=Thu 31-Dec-2020 12:00:00 GMT"
    Document.Cookie = ck
End Sub

Function public_GetCookieKey(sKey)

    public_KeyExists = True

    Dim iLoc
    iLoc = Instr(Document.Cookie, sKey)

    If iLoc = 0 Then
        public_GetCookieKey = ""
        public_KeyExists = False
    Else
        Dim sTemp
        sTemp = Right(Document.Cookie, Len(Document.Cookie) - iLoc + 1)

        Dim iKeyLen
        iKeyLen = Len(sKey)

        If Mid(sTemp, iKeyLen + 1, 1) <> "=" Then
            public_GetCookieKey = ""
            public_KeyExists = False
        Else
        Dim iNextSep
        iNextSep = Instr(sTemp, ";")

        If iNextSep = 0 Then iNextSep = Len(sTemp) + 1
        If iNextSep = (iKeyLen + 2) Then
            public_GetCookieKey = ""
        Else
            Dim iValLen
            iValLen = iNextSep - iKeyLen - 2
            public_GetCookieKey = Mid(sTemp, iKeyLen + 2, iValLen)
        End If
        End If
    End if

End Function

Sub public_RemoveCookieKey(sKey)
    Document.Cookie = sKey & "=NULL;Expires=Fri 31-Dec-1980 12:00:00 GMT"
End Sub

-->
</script>
```

You also need a new host application to display an example of using the Cookies Manager scriptlet. This is the code contained in the CLIENT_COOKIE.HTM.

```
<html>
<head>
<script language="VBScript">
<!--

  Sub btnGetName_onClick
    Dim sValue
    sValue = InputBox("Enter your name:")
    Document.All.myScriptlet.SetCookieKey "Name", sValue
    Document.All.Message.InnerHTML = "Please reload the page to see
the scriptlet in action ..."
  End Sub

-->
</script>

<script language="VBScript" for="window" event="onload">
<!--
  Dim sValue
  sValue = Document.All.myScriptlet.GetCookieKey("Name")

  If Document.All.myScriptlet.KeyExists Then
    Document.All.Main.InnerHTML = "Hello there " & sValue & "! Welcome back!"
  End If
-->
</script>

</head>
<body>

<OBJECT ID="myScriptlet"
    TYPE="text/x-scriptlet"
    DATA="cookiesManager.htm"
    HEIGHT="0" WIDTH="0">
</OBJECT>

<div id="Main">
<input TYPE="BUTTON" NAME="btnGetName" VALUE="Enter your name">
</div>

<br>

<div id="Message">
</div>

</body>
</html>
```

Here's a quick run-through of what this application does.

1. The first time you load the CLIENT_COOKIE.HTM file in the browser, you will just see a button, as shown in Figure 14-2.

2. Clicking the button results in a dialog box asking for your name, as shown in Figure 14-3.

3. After you enter your name (or at least a text string) into the dialog box, the text in the document window is updated and it asks you to reload the page, as shown in Figure 14-4.

4. After you reload the page, the text displayed demonstrates that you have added persistence to the page using the Cookies Manager by displaying the text you entered into the dialog box in the browser (see Figure 14-5).

Figure 14-2

Figure 14-3

Figure 14-4

Figure 14-5

How Does It Work?

The first time you load the page, the cookie storing your name doesn't exist. In this case, the following `<div>` tag is used to display a button:

```
<div id="Main">
<input TYPE="BUTTON" NAME="btnGetName" VALUE="Enter your name">
</div>
```

Once you've completed the process by entering a text string and then reloading the page, the same `<div>` is dynamically filled with new content by the VBScript code.

```
sValue = Document.All.myScriptlet.GetCookieKey("Name")

If Document.All.myScriptlet.KeyExists Then
    Document.All.Main.InnerHTML = "Hello there" & sValue & _
    "! Welcome back!"
End If
```

Using the `Cookies Manager`, your name has been stored in a cookie (very originally called `"Name"`).

The `Cookies Manager` script extends the `"Hello, World!"` example by showing the following:

❑ How to implement properties (`KeyExists`)

❑ How to pass variables to methods (`SetCookieKey`, `GetCookieKey`, `RemoveCookieKey`)

❑ How to retrieve values from methods (`GetCookieKey`)

Event Management

When the scriptlet is used in a host document, it is only logical that the host document can be notified about events raised from the scriptlet. A scriptlet can raise two types of events:

❑ Standard DHTML events

❑ Custom or nonstandard events (that is, events defined by the scriptlet)

Relationship to the Event Handler

Handlers have a one-to-one relationship with each other. This means that when one event handler is in the scriptlet and raises the event, another event handler is in the host document to capture the event raised by the scriptlet.

Standard DHTML Events

The standard DHTML events exposed by the scriptlet are:

❑ `onclick`

❑ `ondblclick`

- ❑ onkeydown
- ❑ onkeypress
- ❑ onkeyup
- ❑ onmousedown
- ❑ onmousemove
- ❑ onmouseup

The following example shows an HTML file that contains a simple implementation of an event handler in the scriptlet for the onclick event that is triggered when the user clicks the image that will be displayed on the page.

The following sample shows how to

- ❑ Access the object container through the External property of the Window object.
- ❑ Raise the event in the object container using the BubbleEvent method.

```
<html>

<head>
<title>Example</title>
</head>

<body>

<img src="myimage.gif" onclick="BubbleOnClick()">

<script language="VBScript">

Function BubbleOnClick()
' here you do something before raising the event in the container object
' usually, what you do is check the frozen property to be sure that
' the container object is ready to handle events
Window.External.BubbleEvent
' do something after raising the event, if required
End Function

</script>

</body>

</html>
```

What happens if the scriptlet does not implement an event handler for a standard event using the BubbleEvent method? In this case, the event is not passed to the host application and is not acted upon.

In a COM development environment the scriptlet container object exposes all standard events at design time, even if the scriptlet does not handle all of them.

In the preceding example, the scriptlet container object is the HTML document. The `Event` object is accessed via the `Window.Event` property. The `Event` object properties give additional information on the specific event.

Here is an example (for clarity and brevity we've omitted the HTML skeleton that surrounds this code) that shows how to access the additional event information using the `Window.Event` property.

```vbscript
<script language="VBScript" for="document" event="onkeydown">
    Window.Status = "Key code = " & Window.Event.KeyCode
    Window.Status = Window.Status & "Shift status = " & _
    Window.Event.ShiftKey
</script>
```

Custom Events

Custom events are used to:

❑ Expose more information about a standard DHTML event.

❑ Notify the host document about DHTML events that are not among the events handled by the `BubbleEvent` method.

❑ Notify the host document about changes in the internal state of the scriptlet.

The following sample (again, free from HTML) shows how to notify a change in the internal state of the scriptlet.

```vbscript
<script language="VBScript">

Function public_put_Title(sNewTitle)
    public_Title = sNewTitle
    Window.External.RaiseEvent ("event_ontitlechange", Window.Document)
End Function

</script>
```

This simple example demonstrates the following:

❑ How to raise an event from the scriptlet from which the `RaiseEvent` method is required

❑ That there is a naming convention; the exposed event name is prefixed with `event_`

❑ That the object involved is passed as an argument to the `RaiseEvent` method

A special event is captured in the host document to run the host event handler: `onscriptletevent`. The following example shows this technique in action.

```vbscript
<script language="VBScript" for="myScriptlet"
    event=onscriptletevent(EventName, EventData)>
    MsgBox "This scriptlet has just raised the following event: " & EventName
</script>
```

All the custom events are subsequently handled by the `onscriptletevent`. As a result, a `Select Case` structure is normally used in the `onscriptletevent` handler to customize the actions taken based on different events.

How Do You Know When a Scriptlet Is Ready?

To make sure everything works fine, the container object implements the property `ReadyState` and the event `onreadystatechange` that are used to ensure that specific code is executed only when the scriptlet has completely loaded into the container object.

The `onreadystatechange` event is fired multiple times while the scriptlet is loading. The final time it is fired indicates the point at which the scriptlet file has been fully loaded and its scripts can be called. The `ReadyState` property tests the current state. This property is read-only and it is available only at runtime. The `ReadyState` property returns an integer value indicating the loading state of the scriptlet.

Value	Description
1, 2	Scriptlet is still loading
3	Scriptlet has been loaded, but the page might not yet be fully functional
4	Scriptlet is completely loaded and functional

Scriptlet Model Extensions

Specific extensions have been introduced into the Dynamic HTML Object Model to help programmers design and implement scriptlets. All these extensions are available in the DHTML `Window.External` object.

Properties	Methods
Frozen	BubbleEvent
SelectableContent	RasieEvent
Version	SetContextMenu

Let's take a closer look at the properties and methods listed in the preceding table.

Frozen Property

Description	This property indicates whether the scriptlet container is ready to handle events.
Syntax	`aVariable = Window.External.Frozen`
Remarks	While this property is `True`, events are not received by the scriptlet container. When the container is ready to receive events the variable is set to `False`. This property is read-only.

SelectableContent Property

Description	This property specifies whether the user can select the contents of the scriptlet.
Syntax	`Window.External.SelectableContent = boolean`
Remarks	By default, the value of this property is set to `False`, and the user cannot select objects in the scriptlet. If it is set to `True`, then the user can select text or other objects contained in the scriptlet.

Version Property

Description	Returns the version and platform of the scriptlet container object. For example "6.0 Win32" is the value returned by the `Version` property when the scriptlet is hosted by IE7 for Windows 98/NT/2000/XP/Vista.
Syntax	`ver = Window.External.Version`
Remarks	`Version` is returned in the following format `N.nnnn platform`
	Where
	`N` is an integer representing the major version number
	`nnnn` is any number of characters (except a space) representing the minor version number
	`platform` is the platform (`win32`, `mac`, `alpha`, and so on)
	The `Version` property can be used to determine whether the page is being used as a scriptlet or as a stand-alone web page, as shown in the following code:
	`Mode = (TypeName(Window.External.Version) = "String")`
	If the value of `Mode` is `True`, the page is being used as a scriptlet; otherwise the page is being used as a stand-alone page

BubbleEvent Method

Description	This method sends event notification for a standard event to the host document.
Syntax	`Window.External.BubbleEvent`
Remarks	This method is used to pass a standard DHTML event from the scriptlet to the host document.

RaiseEvent Method

Description	This method is used to pass a custom event notification from the scriptlet to the host document.
Syntax	`Window.External.RaiseEvent EventName, EventObject`
Parameters	`EventName`: a string identifying the event that is being passed. `EventObject`: a variant type that typically includes a reference to the object on the scriptlet that triggered the event.
Remarks	This method is used to notify the host document about a nonstandard event. The `onscriptletevents` event is strictly related to this method.

SetContextMenu Method

Description	This method creates a context menu that is displayed when a user right-clicks a scriptlet in the scriptlet container object.
Syntax	`Window.External.SetContextMenu MenuDefinition`
Parameters	`MenuDefinition` defines the command text and commands contained in the context menu.
	A one-dimensional array in which the menu items are defined using sequences of two elements, n and n + 1.
	Element n is the command text. Shortcut keys are defined by preceding a letter with `"&"`.
	Element n + 1 is the method to be called when the command is chosen. You cannot pass parameters to the method.
	Example: The following script defines a context menu with two commands:

```
<script language="VBScript" for="Menu" event="onClick">
Dim MenuItems(4)
MenuItems(0) = "&Cut text"
MenuItems(1) = "CutText"
MenuItems(2) = "Co&py text"
MenuItems(3) = "CopyText"
Window.External.SetContextMenu MenuItems
</script>
```

Scriptlets Are Deprecated in IE5

This chapter shows examples of scriptlets that contain only code (no visible HTML tags). Originally scriptlets were introduced to contain HTML visible tags as well. You can actually use it by adopting the same techniques you've been looking at so far. The only thing to remember is not to set the WIDTH and HEIGHT parameters of the <OBJECT> tag to zero. If the scriptlet has visible parts, then it will occupy a visible place in the layout of the HTML page that contains the component. The examples display thinking in "behavior terms."

At the end of 1998, Microsoft deprecated the scriptlets technology. You can still use this technology but Microsoft suggests replacing it in your applications with HTCs (known as behaviors). As you'll see later in this chapter, behaviors have a strong influence during the design of an application, suggesting the separation of the code that defines the behavior of an HTML tag from the tag itself (that's the reason why they're called behaviors!). The authors have chosen to present scriptlets with the original approach because it was these that evolved into behaviors (or HTCs) and are still a widely used technology.

> *Behaviors are not supported in IE4.*

Behaviors

Introduced with the advent of Internet Explorer 5.0, behaviors are fascinating mechanisms that have the potential to bring a new programming paradigm in the DHTML world. The behaviors technology is based on a concept: the behavior. The previous sentence could appear to be a truism, but it introduces a major point. As you'll see, Microsoft overused the term behavior in different contexts (to indicate a concept, a technology label, and a keyword). We are now focusing on the first and most important occurrence: the behavior concept.

Unlike scriptlets that were created to group HTML elements and scripts together in an external HTML file, the behavior concept emphasizes the separation of script from HTML elements. The behavior concept is implemented as an encapsulated component that is associated to an HTML element or, more frequently, to a (CSS) class of HTML elements.

Which Technologies Implement Behaviors?

Currently two technologies allow us to implement behaviors:

❑   HTCs (HTML Components)

❑   Binary behaviors

HTML components are simply text files with an HTC extension containing code scripts (VBScript or JScript) while binary behaviors are built using compiled languages such as C++ or Visual Basic.

> *Binary behaviors do not fall within the scope of this book; they have been introduced to further clarify the relationship between the behavior concept and an HTML component.*

When the encapsulated component implementing a behavior is applied to an HTML element, that component then extends the behavior of the HTML element (that's where the term behavior comes from).

Applying a Behavior to an HTML Element

There are two approaches you can follow to apply a behavior to an HTML element: statically by using a CSS class, and dynamically by using scripting.

Applying a Behavior Statically

In IE5 and greater you can define a CSS class using a new property, behavior.

The following code defines a simple CSS class that will be used to apply a behavior to HTML elements:

```
<style>
.myClass {
    behavior: url(abehavior.htc);
}
</style>
```

After the declaration of such a CSS class, your HTML file could contain several different tags, for example:

```
<ul class="myClass">
    <li> an item </li>
    <li> an item </li>
</ul>

<div class="myClass">This is a div</div>
```

In the preceding example, a behavior has been applied to two different HTML elements: <ul> and <div>.

The behavior of both HTML elements will be extended by the code (either VBScript or JScript code) that is contained in the somebehavior.htc file.

The CSS property named behavior can be defined inline using the <style> attribute. In this case the programmer doesn't even need to declare a CSS class to apply the behavior. Also, if you wanted, a single specific element can be addressed. The following example demonstrates this technique:

```
<div style="behavior: url(somebehavior.htc)">another div</div>
```

Applying a Behavior Dynamically

A behavior can be applied through scripting in one of two ways: using the AddBehavior method or modifying the Behavior property of the Style object. The following code shows both ways in action:

```
<script language="VBScript">
    Sub ApplyOption1()
        Document.All.MyDiv.AddBehavior("somebehavior.htc");
    End Sub
    Sub ApplyOption2()
        Document.All.MyDiv.Style.Behavior = "url(somebehavior.htc)";
    End Sub
</script>

...

<div id="MyDiv">another div</div>
```

Note that the Behavior property still expects the syntax "url (somebehavior.htc)" while the AddBehavior method doesn't require this syntax.

Removing a Behavior Attached Dynamically

Think about the lifecycle of the relationship between an attached behavior and the HTML elements. Behaviors attached employing CSS classes are automatically detached from the elements as soon as the element or elements are removed from the document tree. This is not the case when using any other method. Under these circumstances, you will be required to use the `RemoveBehavior` method.

In all these cases it is not enough to just remove the elements themselves from the document tree. They will still maintain all the style sheet rules defined programmatically or by inline definitions (including the behavior rule itself).

So far, you have looked at what a behavior is as a concept and the ways that it can be used to augment and extend on HTML elements. As yet, you haven't examined any behavior implementation. You have already seen that behaviors could be implemented using VBScript through HTML components. It is time you looked at HTML components.

HTML Components (HTCs)

An HTML component is an encapsulated component, which implements a behavior. An actual HTC is simply a text file with an HTC extension. An HTC file contains VBScript code that is wrapped by HTML tags that define the public interface of the component.

Extending HTML Elements Behavior

It is not too difficult to confuse HTML components with scriptlets. Microsoft has recommended that programmers replace scriptlets with HTML components because they are the newer and better evolution of this technology. HTML components are evolving into something that is very different and far removed from scriptlets. The behavior concept (discussed earlier) is what makes the difference — and an enormous difference.

The main purpose of both scriptlets and HTML components is to make it easier for the programmer to reuse code. However, this produces the misconception that HTML components should replace scriptlets. Each one in fact captures different code aspects and both of them should be used together in large projects that are component-based.

In contrast to scriptlets, the goal of HTML components is to extend HTML elements' behavior. Take a look at a few techniques that are used to extend HTML elements using HTML components:

❑ Adding properties

❑ Adding methods

❑ Exposing component events

❑ Handling HTML element events

You can begin this journey by taking a look at a basic "Hello, World!" HTML component to get a feeling for how this technology actually works. The HTML component is stored in the HELLOW.HTC file.

```
<attach event="ondocumentready" ONEVENT="Hello()" />

<script language="VBScript">

Function Hello()
      MsgBox "Hello, World!"
End Function

</script>
```

The component has one line of code more than the analogue scriptlet sample. One thing that's important to note is that the prefix public_ is not required (the prefix naming conventions are only required for scriptlets).

In the case of this minimal sample, you will certainly find it more interesting to have a look at the HTML file that uses the component CLIENT_HTC_HELLOW.HTM.

```
<html>
<head>

<style>

.myClass   {
      behavior: url(hellow.htc);
}

</style>

</head>

<body class="myClass">}

</body>
</html>
```

As you can see, there is a total separation between scripting code (contained in one file) and HTML and CSS (contained in another).

If you think that we are exaggerating the minimalist nature of the actual HTML file, take a look at the following alternative for the client file (CLIENT_HTC_HELLOW2.HTM).

```
<html>
<body style="behavior: url(hellow.htc)">
</body>
</html>
```

This is an extremely minimalist file in terms of it being a complete HTML file. However, it can afford to be only four lines because the powerhouse is contained in the .htc file.

Enhancement 1: Adding Properties

An HTML component can expose properties to the containing document by using the `<property>` element. The following code is an example that implements an HTML component, which has a public interface made of only one property called `CryptedKey`. The example captures the essentials of the technique to expose properties. The HTML component is contained in a file named `CRYPTED.HTC`.

This sample shows you how to do the following:

❑ Declare the name of the property through the NAME attribute of the `<property>` tag.

❑ Declare a function to make the property writable using the PUT attribute.

❑ Declare a function to make the property readable using the GET attribute.

```
<property name="CryptedKey" put="PutCK" get="GetCK" />

<script language="VBScript">

Dim cKey

Function PutCK(ByVal newValue)
    cKey = newValue Xor 43960
End Function

Function GetCK()
    GetCK = cKey Xor 43960
End Function

</script>
```

The example uses the Xor function to crypt/decrypt the value of the property. Applying this crypt/decrypt transformation in the example shows how it is possible to use read/write property functions that actually do something more than simply give access to an internal variable.

A client example that uses the HTML component is shown next (`CLIENT_CRYPT.HTM`).

```
<html>
<head>

<style>

.myClass    {
    background: red;
    behavior: url(crypted.htc);
}

</style>

<script language="VBScript">

Sub WriteProp()
    Dim iKey
    iKey = CInt(InputBox("Enter the a number:"))
    Document.All.myDIV.CryptedKey = iKey
```

```
    End Sub

Sub ReadProp()
    MsgBox Document.All.myDiv.CryptedKey
End Sub

</script>

</head>
<body>

<div class="myClass" ID="myDIV">This div has been enhanced with the CryptEd
 property</div>

<input type="Button" onclick="VBScript:WriteProp" value="Change Property"></input>
<input type="Button" onclick="VBScript:ReadProp" value="Read Property"></input>

</body>
</html>
```

The example applies the behavior to a `<div>` element, identified by the `"myDIV"` ID. This is done using the following line of code:

```
MsgBox Document.All.myDiv.CryptedKey
```

The HTML component has actually enhanced the `<div>` adding to it the `CryptedKey` property that behaves as implemented. To check this you can generate an error by choice, changing a letter in the same line, as in:

```
MsgBox Document.All.myDiv.CryptKey
```

If you now click the button labeled `Read Property` you see the error message shown in Figure 14-6.

Figure 14-6

The error message is telling you that the `CryptKey` property it is not supported by the object. This is further evidence that you can actually extend HTML elements using behaviors.

❏ Overriding Standard Properties: It is possible to override the element's default behavior by specifying a name for the property that is the same as that of a property already defined for the element.

❏ Notifying the HTML Element that the Property Value has Changed: When the value of the property has changed, the HTML element can be notified by firing the `onpropertychange` event calling the `FireChange` method.

```
Function PutCK(ByVal newValue)
    cKey = newValue Xor 43960
    oCryptedKey.FireChange
End Function
```

❏ The `oCryptedKey` identifier indicates the `id` of the `<property>` element that has been specified.

```
<property name="CryptedKey" put="PutCK" get="GetCK" id="oCryptedKey" />
```

To verify that the event has fired effectively, modify the `<div>` definition in the client.

```
<div class="myClass" id="myDIV" onpropertychange="MsgBox('!')">
This div has been enhanced with a Crypted property
</div>
```

Enhancement 2: Adding Methods

Adding new methods to an HTML element using an HTML component is easier than adding properties. As an example, try modifying the `CRYPTED.HTC` component to expose a method named `isplayCryptedValue`, which displays the internal value of the `CryptedKey` property in a dialog. A further element named `method` is available to expose methods. The resulting `CRYPTED.HTC` code looks as follows:

```
<property name="CryptedKey" put="PutCK" get="GetCK" id="oCryptedKey" />
<method name="DisplayCryptedValue" />

<script language="VBScript">

Dim cKey

Function PutCK(ByVal newValue)
    cKey = newValue Xor 43960
    oCryptedKey.FireChange

End Function

Function GetCK()
    GetCK = cKey Xor 43960
End Function
```

```
Sub DisplayCryptedValue()
    MsgBox cKey
End Sub

</script>
```

For this new, modified code to work, the host application requires some modification to use the `DisplayCryptedValue` method. The following is the code for the modified host application (`CLIENT_CRYPT2.HTM`).

```
<html>
<head>

<style>

.myClass  {
      background: red;
      behavior: url(crypted.htc);
}

</style>

<script language="VBScript">

Sub WriteProp()
    Dim iKey
    iKey = CInt(InputBox("Enter a number:"))
    Document.All.myDIV.CryptedKey = iKey
End Sub

Sub ReadProp()
    MsgBox Document.All.myDiv.CryptedKey
End Sub

Sub DisplayCV()
    Document.All.myDIV.DisplayCryptedValue
End Sub

</script>

</head>
<body>

<div class="myClass" id="myDIV">This div has been enhanced with a Crypted
 property</div>

<input type="Button" onclick="VBScript:WriteProp" value="Change Property"></input>
<input type="Button" onclick="VBScript:ReadProp" value="Read Property"></input>
<input type="Button" onclick="VBScript:DisplayCV" value="Display Crypted
Value"></input>

</body>
</html>
```

Enhancement 3: Exposing Component Events

An HTML component is capable of defining its own events, and then exposing them through the <event> element. This method of exposing custom events is clearly more powerful than the one offered by script-lets (described earlier in this chapter). Actually, scriptlets are only capable of exposing one event — onscriptletevent. With HTML components you can expose any kind of event you want to the containing document. As an example, you will enhance your CRYPTED.HTC code with an OnReadWarning event, which informs the container that somebody has accessed the CryptedKey property.

```
<property name="CryptedKey" put="PutCK" get="GetCK" id="oCryptedKey" />
<method name="DisplayCryptedValue" />
<event name="OnReadWarning" id="orw" />

<script language="VBScript">

Dim cKey

Function PutCK(ByVal newValue)
    cKey = newValue Xor 43960
    oCryptedKey.FireChange
End Function

Function GetCK()
    Dim oEvent
    Set oEvent = CreateEventObject()
    orw.Fire(oEvent)
    GetCK = cKey Xor 43960
End Function

Sub DisplayCryptedValue()
    MsgBox cKey
End Sub

</script>
```

This code shows the technique to fire a component event in.

```
Dim oEvent
Set oEvent = CreateEventObject()
orw.Fire(oEvent)
```

The CreateEventObject function is required to create an event object and the event object becomes the parameter of the Fire method of the <event> element. The <event> element is identified by its id attribute (orw). The <event> element also defines the name of the exposed event.

```
<event name="OnReadWarning" id="orw" />
```

It is again necessary to modify the client, but this time only one line of code needs to be changed.

```
<div class="myClass" id="myDIV" onreadwarning="MsgBox('Someone is reading the
property')">This div has been enhanced with a Crypted property</div>
```

To generate the event, launch the client application, assign a value to the property, and then read that value. The `onreadwarning` event will be raised and the application will inform you with the message shown in Figure 14-7.

Figure 14-7

Enhancement 4: Handling HTML Element Events

HTML components offer a mechanism to further enhance HTML elements. They can attach handlers for the HTML element's events using the `<attach>` element. You can modify the `CRYPTED.HTC` example to handle the `onclick` event of the HTML elements to which the behavior is attached.

```
<property name="CryptedKey" put="PutCK" get="GetCK" id="oCryptedKey" />
<method name="DisplayCryptedValue" />
<event name="OnReadWarning" id="orw" />
<attach event="onclick" onevent="ClickHandler()" />

<script language="VBScript">

Dim cKey

Function PutCK(ByVal newValue)
    cKey = newValue Xor 43960
    oCryptedKey.FireChange
End Function

Function GetCK()
    Dim oEvent
    Set oEvent = CreateEventObject()
    orw.Fire(oEvent)
    GetCK = cKey Xor 43960
End Function

Sub DisplayCryptedValue()
    MsgBox cKey
End Sub

Function ClickHandler()
    MsgBox "You clicked on an element enhanced by the CRYPTED behavior"
End Function

</script>
```

The handler for the `onclick` event is declared in the following line:

```
<attach event="onclick" onevent="ClickHandler()" />
```

This time, no modifications are required in the code for the host application.

You can easily test the handler. Click the `<div>` element to run the handler. This produces a dialog box.

When the specified event fires on an element to which the behavior is attached, the behavior's handler is called after the element's event handler (if any).

Attach Event Handlers Through Scripting

Timing becomes a very critical issue when dealing with event handlers. Sometimes you need to attach an event handler that responds to specific events. It is possible to attach handlers through scripting using the `AttachEvent` method instead of the `<attach>` element.

The general technique to deal with dynamically attached event handlers is shown in the following lines of code:

```
<attach event="ondetach" onevent="DetachEvents()" />

<script language="VBScript">

Function DetachEvents()
    DetachEvent('onevent1', EvH1)
    DetachEvent('onevent2', EvH2)
End Function

Function EvH1()
    ' do something here
End Function

Function EvH2()
    ' do something here also
End Function

Function SomeTimeInTheBehavior()
    AttachEvent('onevent1', EvH1)
    AttachEvent('onevent2', EvH2)
    ' do something too
End Function

</script>
```

A `DetachEvent` method and an `ondetach` event have both been introduced in the preceding example. Event handlers that are attached using the `AttachEvent` method have to call the `DetachEvent` method to stop them from receiving any sent notifications. The HTML component will be notified with the `ondetach` event from the page to actually detach all the handlers attached through scripting.

Multiple Behaviors

It is possible to apply multiple behaviors to an element either by using the `AddBehavior` method multiple times or by using the syntax shown in the following example:

```
<style>

.myClass {
    behavior: url(b-one.htc), url(b-two.htc), url(b-three.htc);
}

</style>
```

But what about conflicts? Conflicts can happen when more than one behavior is applied to one element. For any conflicts resulting from applying multiple behaviors to an element, the following resolution rule is defined.

Each subsequent behavior takes precedence over the previous behavior in the order in which the behavior is applied to the element.

Name Clashing Resolution and the Component Element

A further element can actually be helpful in cases where there are multiple behaviors. This is the `<component>` element, which allows you to give a name to the HTML component that can be used to access properties and methods through scripting (solving name clashing issues whenever multiple behaviors are applied to the same element).

```
<component name="Crypted">

<property name="CryptedKey" put="PutCK" get="GetCK" id="oCryptedKey" />
<method name="DisplayCryptedValue" />
<event name="OnReadWarning" id="orw" />
<attach event="onclick" onevent="ClickHandler()" />

<script language="VBScript">

Dim cKey

Function PutCK(ByVal newValue)
    cKey = newValue Xor 43960
    oCryptedKey.FireChange
End Function

Function GetCK()
    Dim oEvent
    Set oEvent = CreateEventObject()
    orw.Fire(oEvent)
    GetCK = cKey Xor 43960
End Function

Sub DisplayCryptedValue()
    MsgBox cKey
End Sub
```

(continued)

```
Function ClickHandler()
    MsgBox "You clicked on an element enhanced by the CRYPTED behavior"
End Function

</script>

</component>
```

After you use the `<component>` element, it is possible to access the component properties and methods using the component name.

```
Sub ReadProp()
    MsgBox Document.All.myDiv.Crypted.CryptedKey
End Sub
```

This definitively solves the name clashing issue. Suppose you want to apply two behaviors (named, for example, bhone and bhtwo) both of which define a `Description` property to the same element (myDiv); it is possible to access both properties.

```
MsgBox Document.All.myDiv.bhone.Title & Document.All.myDiv.bhtwo.Title
```

The goal of this section was to introduce all the fundamental techniques to start you on your way using behaviors and HTML components. Experimenting with the preceding code and concepts can only help to further your understanding of these topics.

Summary

The goal of this chapter is to give you an understanding of how much further than a simple static web page VBScript can take you. You looked at sufficient code samples to make use of many and reuse or adapt them to suit your own needs. You discovered the evolution of scriptlets into behaviors and their use through HTML components. With regard to scriptlets, you saw how to:

- ❑ Implement properties
- ❑ Pass variables to methods
- ❑ Retrieve values from methods
- ❑ Manage events statically
- ❑ Manage events dynamically
- ❑ Use custom events

You also looked at behaviors and saw how to:

- ❑ Apply a behavior statically
- ❑ Apply a behavior dynamically
- ❑ Remove attached behaviors

This then led you to learn that the goal of HTML components is to extend HTML elements' behavior. And, with regard to HTML components, this chapter also covered:

- Adding properties
- Adding methods
- Exposing events
- Handling HTML element's events
- Enhancement techniques

Some enormous topics were covered here. Whole volumes can (and have!) been devoted to the these topics, so if you want to go deeper and do more, refer to more specialized sources to further your learning. However, what has been provided here will give you a good foundation on which to build!

15

Windows Script Host

Ask programmers if they use VBScript and most will answer "Yes, for ASP" or "Yes, on an intranet" or maybe even "Yes, for client-side scripting" (if their audience is made up entirely of people using Internet Explorer, unlikely nowadays). But you need to remember that these are nothing more than contexts where VBScript can be used to solve problems that are in need of scripting solutions. Because VBScript is designed as an ActiveX script engine, it can be used to provide scripting capability for any ActiveX scripting host environment.

Two of the most common hosts are:

❑   Active Server Pages (ASP)

❑   Internet Explorer

Both of these hosts provide the programmer with a lot of power but both also come with certain limitations. An example is that Internet Explorer does not provide a capability for script to interact with the local computer (such as file system access, registry access, and so on) unless the user explicitly sets permissions for this (and doing this can cause enormous security risks. For this reason, this is usually done only for trusted sites and intranets). So what's the point of having extended power within the VBScript language when you can't do anything with it? Well, this is where Windows Script Host (WSH) comes in. WSH is a totally scripting language–neutral host interface that will work with any ActiveX script engine. This means that programmers who want to use WSH can use VBScript, JScript, PerlScript, or any other scripting language that exposes the ActiveX scripting interfaces. The WSH host interface thus provides Windows platforms with a powerful, yet easy-to-use scripting platform that can be accessed from both the Windows GUI and the command prompt.

In this chapter, you examine the following aspects of WSH:

❑   The tools required for WSH development

❑   What WSH can be used for

❑   The two methods of execution for WSH scripts

❑   The use of .wsh files to customize script behavior

❑ The WSH object model

❑ The `.wsf` file format, used for creating more advanced scripts

❑ The use of WSH for disk and network administration

Tools of the Trade

To begin using WSH, you need the following:

❑ The WSH engine.

❑ A text editor, such as Notepad (although you are free to make use of one that is designed with programming in mind — there are plenty of alternatives).

❑ If you want to use a scripting language other than VBScript or JScript, you also need to download and install the proper ActiveX script engine (such as ActivePerl from ActiveState, `www.activestate.com`).

If your operating system is Windows 98, Windows Me, Windows NT 4.0 with Option Pack 4 installed, Windows 2000, Windows XP, or Windows Vista, then you probably already have Windows Script Host (WSH 1.0 is provided as an optional component for Win98 and WinNT). However, you may want to ensure that you have the latest version in order to run the scripts included in this chapter. You can download it from the Microsoft Scripting Technologies web site at `http://msdn.microsoft.com/library/en-us/script56/html/d78573b7-fc96-410b-8fd0-3e84bd7d470f.asp`. The authors suggest that you upgrade to the latest version, WSH 5.6 and Windows Script engine 5.6 for JScript and VBScript (if you are using Windows Vista, then you will be using version 5.7 script engines).

What Is WSH?

Windows Script Host (WSH) is a Windows administration tool. WSH creates an environment for hosting scripts so that when a script arrives at a computer, WSH plays the part of the host. WSH makes objects and services available for the script and provides a set of guidelines within which the script is executed. Among other things, WSH manages security and invokes the appropriate script engine.

Because WSH is script language independent, WSH also provides the facility to write scripts in JScript, Perl, Python, REXX, or any other ActiveX scripting language (only the VBScript and JScript languages are available from Microsoft — other ActiveX script engines are available from third parties). It provides network administrators with a handy toolkit to use for access to machines scattered across a network of computers running various flavors of the Windows operating system family. Much of this access comes through the use of Active Directory Service Interfaces (ADSI) and Windows Management Instrumentation (WMI). ADSI provides a single set of COM interfaces that can be used with multiple directory services, such as the Lightweight Directory Access Protocol (LDAP), the Windows NT directory service, and Novell's Netware and NDS services. WMI is Microsoft's implementation of Web-Based Enterprise Management (WBEM), a standard method of providing access to management information such as applications installed on a given client, system memory, and other client information.

By developing WSH scripts that take advantage of ADSI and WMI, administrators can develop scripts that make it very easy to perform the following tasks and much more:

❑   Access and manipulate servers.

❑   Add and remove users and change passwords.

❑   Add network file shares.

The current version of WSH, which is 5.7, was released with Windows Vista, and it brings with it significant changes over the previous version (2.0). The current release of WSH now includes a whole host of features that programmers will find appealing:

❑   Support for file inclusion

❑   Ability to use multiple languages within the same script

❑   Support for drag-and-drop functionality

❑   Argument handling

❑   Ability to run scripts remotely

❑   Enhanced access to external objects and type libraries

❑   Stronger debugging capability

❑   A mechanism for pausing script execution (useful for sinking events raised by controlled objects)

❑   Standard input/output and standard error support (only available via console-mode execution with `cscript.exe`)

❑   New processes that can be treated as objects

❑   Access to the current working directory

❑   New, improved security model

Version 5.7 that ships with Windows Vista comprises bug and security fixes for version 5.6.

WSH 1.0 operated by simply associating the file extensions for VBScript (`.vbs`) and JScript (`.js`) files with the actual script host. This meant that if you double-clicked on a script file, it would automatically execute. However, this had one major limitation — the association model did not allow for the use of code modules or for the integrating of multiple script languages in a single WSH script project. To appease programmers everywhere, Microsoft introduced a new type of script file (`.wsf`) in WSH 2.0, which utilized an XML syntax that provides much of the new functionality listed earlier.

This schema includes the tags `<script>`, `<object>`, and `<job>` among others. You'll see how this all works later on in this chapter.

> *The file extension .wsf is only available with final release of WSH 2.0 and later. Any developers still working with the beta releases of WSH 2.0 will have to use the .ws file extension. The authors suggest that you make use of the latest script engines and WSH.*

Types of Script Files

Stand-alone script files come in a few different formats, each having its own extension. The following table is a list of some common types. The script type that you choose ultimately depends on your needs. Most small projects only require the use of one file type while certain scenarios will mean that you could divide your overall problem into several smaller parts, writing a separate script for each part, with each script written in the most suitable scripting language.

Extension	Script Type	Description
.bat	MS-DOS batch file	MS-DOS operating system batch file.
.asp	ASP page	Active Server Page file.
.htm	HTML file	Web page.
.html	HTML file	Web page.
.js	JScript file	Windows script.
.vbs	VBScript file	Windows script.
.wsf	Windows Script Host file	Container or project file for a Windows script. This is supported by WSH 2.0 and later.
.wsh	Windows Script Host file	Property file for a script file. This is supported by WSH 1.0 and later.

This is where Windows Script Host files (WSF files) are useful. WSF files may include other script files as part of the script. This means that multiple WSF files can reference libraries of useful functions, which may be created and stored in a single place.

Running Scripts with the Windows Script Host

WSH provides two interfaces that allow you to execute scripts on the command line or from within the Windows environment. These two interfaces each use different host programs for the VBScript engine:

❑   cscript.exe: Used for running scripts via the command line

❑   wscript.exe: Used for running script through the Windows environment

The reason there are two host programs is that cscript.exe is designed for use from a console window (basically, an MS-DOS box within Windows) whereas wscript.exe is intended to interface directly with the Windows GUI. There is very little difference between them in terms of functionality.

Command-Line Execution

The console interface for executing script files, cscript.exe, is called as follows:

1. Open the Run dialog (press the Windows Key+R) or a command window (in Windows 9x, this is done via Start ➪ Programs ➪ DOS Prompt; in Windows NT via Start ➪ Programs ➪ Command Prompt; and in Vista/XP via Start ➪ All Programs ➪ Accessories ➪ Command Prompt).

Note that when using Windows Vista, you will need to open the Command Prompt with administrator privileges. The easiest way to do this is to right-click the Command Prompt entry in the Start Menu and choose Run as Administrator.

2. Execute your script as follows:

```
cscript c:\folderName\YourScriptName.vbs
```

If you run cscript.exe with no arguments directly from a command prompt, you will simply get the usage notes, as shown in Figure 15-1.

Figure 15-1

The usage syntax is as follows:

```
cscript scriptname.extension [option...] [arguments...]
```

The following command-line options are provided by `cscript.exe` to allow you to control various settings for the WSH environment.

`//B`	Batch mode.
	This mode suppresses script errors and prompts from being displayed.
`//D`	Enable active debugging.
`//E:engine`	Use engine for executing script.
`//H:Cscript`	Changes the default script host to `cscript.exe`.
`//H:Wscript`	Changes the default script host to `wscript.exe` (this is the default option).
`//I`	Interactive mode (this is the default option, and it is the opposite of `//B`).
`//Job:xxxx`	Execute a WSF job.
`//Logo`	Display logo (this is the default option).
`//Nologo`	Prevent logo from displaying. No banner will be shown at execution time.
`//S`	Save current command-line options for this user.
`//T:nn`	Time out in seconds. This sets the maximum time a script is permitted to run before being aborted.
`//X`	Execute script in debugger.
`//U`	Use Unicode for redirected I/O from the console.

To use these, add them as switches at the command line. The following example executes the script in the debugger.

```
cscript MyScript.vbs //X
```

Execution of WSH within the Windows Environment

The Windows GUI interface for script file execution, `wscript.exe`, allows you to execute files in several ways:

❑ If the file type is registered to execute within WSH, you can run the script by simply double-clicking its icon in any folder-view window or on the desktop.

❑ If you use the Run command dialog, simply type in the full path and name of the script.

From the Run dialog, you can invoke `wscript.exe`.

```
wscript c:\folderName\YourScriptName.vbs
```

If you run `wscript.exe` from a command prompt, you'll get no output in the command prompt. Instead you'll see the dialog box shown in Figure 15-2, which provides minimal customization options. This is the same dialog box displayed if `wscript.exe` is run from the Run command dialog.

Figure 15-2

When you click OK, nothing happens. The only way to customize script behavior on a system level is through the cscript options detailed earlier. This dialog is used for individual script customization through .wsh files, which is covered next.

So what's the difference between the two ways of running a script? The major difference between cscript and wscript really becomes apparent only when debugging a faulty script. This is because sending error messages to a console window is much quicker and easier to handle than perhaps endless error pop-ups produced by wscript. We recommend cscript for use when debugging scripts, and it is best to use the Echo method of the WScript object when printing debug output, as this can result in too many error messages being generated. In fact, it is possible that you get into loops where you can't exit from the error messages.

Using .WSH Files to Launch Scripts

Maybe you don't want or need to modify the settings for every script you execute, but you do need to be able to control individual files. You can do this by creating control files, which have the extension .wsh that allows you to control settings for individual scripts. A .wsh file is a small configuration file roughly following the .ini file format of past Windows versions (this isn't to say that some programmers don't still use configuration files like the .ini file). These files are good for customizing the way a script is started up — you can have several different .wsh files for the one script.

To create a .wsh file, right-click a file associated with WSH (a file with a .js, .vbs, or .wsf extension), select Properties, and then the Script tab from the dialog box as shown in Figure 15-3.

Figure 15-3

This dialog box allows you to change the time-out default setting, and whether or not logo information should be displayed when the script is executed on the command line. When you apply or accept any changes you have made, a new file is created, with the same name as the script in question, but containing the extension .wsh. This new file records these custom settings in a format that the host engines use to set runtime options. Here is a .wsh file created from a script named test.vbs.

```
[ScriptFile]
Path=C:\test.vbs

[Options]
Timeout=25
DisplayLogo=0
```

To execute the script with these options, you would run the test.wsh file.

Windows Script Host Intrinsic Objects

Every programming environment provides its own object model that developers can use to implement solutions, and WSH is no different. WSH contains a core set of objects, that in turn contains properties and methods, which can be used to access other computers on a network, import external scriptable objects for use within an application, or connect with Windows or the Windows shell.

The WScript Object

The root of the WSH object model is the WScript object. This object provides properties and methods that give the developer access to a variety of information, such as:

❏   Name and path information for the script file being executed

❏   Version of the Microsoft script engines

❏   Links to external objects

❏   User interaction

❏   Ability to delay or terminate script execution

WScript Properties

Following are the properties for the WScript object:

❏   Arguments

❏   FullName

❏   Interactive

❏   Name

❏   Path

❏   ScriptFullName

❏   ScriptName

❏   StdErr

❏   StdIn

❏   StdOut

❏   Version

Arguments

The Arguments property contains the WshArguments object (a collection of arguments). Use a zero-based index to retrieve individual arguments from this collection.

```
Set objArgs = WScript.Arguments
For x = 0 to objArgs.Count - 1
    WScript.Echo objArgs(x)
Next
```

FullName

The FullName property is a read-only string representing the fully qualified path of the host executable file (cscript.exe or wscript.exe). The following code uses the FullName property.

```
WScript.Echo WScript.FullName
```

This produces the output shown in Figure 15-4.

Figure 15-4

Interactive

The Interactive property sets the script mode, or identifies the script mode. When used, this property returns a Boolean value. Two possible modes are available for use: batch and interactive.

In interactive mode (the default), the script provides user interaction. Input to and output from the WSH is enabled and the script can echo information to dialog boxes and can wait for the user to provide feedback. In batch mode, this type of user interaction is not supported and all input and output to WSH is disabled.

Script mode can be set using the WSH command-line switches //I (for interactive) and //B (for batch).

Name

The Name property returns the name of the WScript object (the host executable file). This is a read-only string. The following code uses the Name property:

```
WScript.Echo WScript.Name
```

This produces the output shown in Figure 15-5.

Figure 15-5

Path

The `Path` property returns the name of the directory containing the host executable file (`cscript.exe` or `wscript.exe`). This returns a read-only string.

The following VBScript code echoes the directory where the executable file resides:

```
WScript.Echo WScript.Path
```

ScriptFullName

The `ScriptFullName` property returns the full path of the currently running script. This property returns a read-only string.

ScriptName

The `ScriptName` property returns the filename of the currently running script. This property returns a read-only string. The following code echoes the name of the script being run, as shown in Figure 15-6:

```
WScript.Echo WScript.ScriptName
```

Figure 15-6

StdErr

The `StdErr` property exposes the write-only error output stream for the current script. It returns an object representing the standard error stream. The `StdIn`, `StdOut`, and `StdErr` streams can be accessed while using `cscript.exe` only. Note that attempting to access these streams while using `wscript.exe` produces an error.

StdIn

The `StdIn` property exposes the read-only input stream for the current script. It returns an object representing the standard error stream. The `StdIn`, `StdOut`, and `StdErr` streams can be accessed while using `cscript.exe` only. Note that attempting to access these streams while using `wscript.exe` produces an error.

StdOut

The StdOut property exposes the write-only error output stream for the current script. It returns an object representing the standard error stream. The StdIn, StdOut, and StdErr streams can be accessed while using cscript.exe only. Note that attempting to access these streams while using wscript.exe produces an error.

The following example makes use of all three of the built-in stream types to print a list of all files matching a particular extension. This is implemented by piping the output from the DOS dir command into the filter script, with an extension string passed as an argument.

```
' Usage: dir | cscript filter.vbs ext
'           ext: file extension to match
'
Dim streamOut, streamIn, streamErr
Set streamOut = WScript.StdOut
Set streamIn = WScript.StdIn
Set streamErr = WScript.StdErr
Dim strExt, strLineIn
Dim intMatch
strExt = WScript.Arguments(0)
intMatch = 0

Do While Not streamIn.AtEndOfStream
  strLineIn = streamIn.ReadLine
  If 0 = StrComp(strExt, Right(strLineIn, Len(strExt)), _
                vbTextCompare) Then
    streamOut.WriteLine strLineIn
    intMatch = intMatch + 1
  End If
Loop

If 0 = intMatch Then
  streamErr.WriteLine "No files of type '" & strExt & "' found"
End If
```

Because this example uses StdIn, StdOut, and StdErr for all messaging, you could use it not only to print out matching files to the screen, but also to send output to a text file or another application with redirection or additional piping. For example, you could create a file containing all .vbs files in an entire directory tree, including all subdirectories, with the following command:

```
C:\wsh>dir /s | cscript filter.vbs vbs >> vbsfiles.txt
```

Version

This property returns the version of WSH. The following code echoes the current version of WSH, as shown in Figure 15-7:

```
WScript.Echo WScript.Version
```

Figure 15-7

WScript Methods

Following is a listing of the WScript methods:

- ❏ CreateObject
- ❏ ConnectObject
- ❏ DisconnectObject
- ❏ Echo
- ❏ GetObject
- ❏ Quit
- ❏ Sleep

CreateObject

This method of the WScript object is used to create a COM object.

```
object.CreateObject(strProgID[,strPrefix])
```

- ❏ object: WScript object.
- ❏ strProgID: String value indicating the programmatic identifier (ProgID) of the object you want to create.
- ❏ strPrefix: Optional. String value indicating the function prefix.

Objects created with the CreateObject method using the strPrefix argument are connected objects. The object's outgoing interface is connected to the script file after the object is created. Event functions are a combination of this prefix and the event name.

If you create an object and do not provide the strPrefix argument, you can still synchronize events on the object by using the ConnectObject method. When the object fires an event, WSH calls a subroutine with strPrefix attached to the beginning of the event name.

The following code uses the `CreateObject` method to create a `WshNetwork` object:

```
Set WshNetwork = WScript.CreateObject("WScript.Network")
```

ConnectObject

This method connects the object's event sources to functions with a given prefix.

```
object.ConnectObject(strObject, strPrefix)
```

❑   `object`: `WScript` object.

❑   `strObject`: Required. String value indicating the name of the object you want to connect.

❑   `strPrefix`: Required. String value indicating the function prefix.

Connected objects are useful when you want to synchronize an object's events. The `ConnectObject` method connects the object's outgoing interface to the script file after creating the object. Event functions are a combination of this prefix and the event name.

```
WScript.ConnectObject RemoteScript, "remote_"
```

DisconnectObject

This is used to disconnect a connected object's event sources.

```
object.DisconnectObject(obj)
```

❑   `object`: `WScript` object.

❑   `obj`: String value indicating the name of the object to disconnect.

Disconnecting an object means that WSH will no longer respond to its events. It is important to note, however, that the object is still capable of firing events. Note also that the `DisconnectObject` method does nothing if the specified object is not already connected.

```
WScript.DisconnectObject RemoteScript
```

Echo

This outputs text to either a message box or the command console window.

```
object.Echo [Arg1] [,Arg2] [,Arg3] ...
```

❑   `object`: `WScript` object.

❑   `Arg1, Arg2, Arg3, ...`: Optional. String value indicating the list of items to be displayed.

The `Echo` method gives a different type of output depending on which WSH engine you are using.

WSH Engine	Text Output
Wscript.exe	Graphical message box
Cscript.exe	Command console window

Figures 15-8 and 15-9 show an example of each output.

Figure 15-8

Figure 15-9

GetObject

The GetObject method retrieves an existing object with the specified ProgID, or creates a new one from a file.

```
object.GetObject(strPathname [,strProgID], [strPrefix])
```

- ❑ object: WScript object.
- ❑ strPathname: A fully qualified pathname of the file that contains the object persisted to disk.

❑   strProgID: Optional. The object's program identifier (ProgID).

❑   strPrefix: Optional. This is used when you want to synchronize the object's events. If you supply the strPrefix argument, WSH connects the object's outgoing interface to the script file after creating the object.

You use the GetObject method when an instance of the object exists in memory or when you want to create the object from a file. The GetObject method can be used with all COM classes, independent of the scripting language used to create the object.

If no current instance exists and you do not want the object created from a file, use the CreateObject method.

```
Dim MyObject As Object
Set MyObject = GetObject("C:\DRAWINGS\SCHEMA.DRW")
MyApp = MyObject.Application
```

Quit

This method forces the script execution to immediately stop at any time.

```
object.Quit([intErrorCode])
```

❑   object: WScript object.

❑   intErrorCode: Optional. An integer value is returned as the process's exit code. If you omit the intErrorCode parameter, no value will be returned.

The Quit method can be used to return an optional error code. If the Quit method is the final instruction in your script (and you have no need to return a non-zero value), you can leave it out and your script will terminate normally.

```
WScript.Quit 1

' This line of code is not executed.
MsgBox "This message will never be shown!"
```

Here is another example of the Quit method in action.

```
If Err.Number <> 0 Then
    WScript.Quit 1 ' some failure indicator Else
    WScript.Quit 0 ' success
End If
WScript.Quit 1
```

Sleep

This method suspends script execution for a specified length of time, and then continues execution.

```
object.Sleep(intTime)
```

- ❑ object: WScript object.
- ❑ intTime: This is an integer value indicating the interval (in milliseconds) that you want the script process to remain inactive for.

When using this method, the thread running the script is suspended and CPU utilization is released. Execution resumes when the interval expires. To be triggered by an event, a script must be continually active because a script that has finished executing will certainly not detect an event. Events handled by the script will still be executed during a sleep.

Passing the Sleep method a 0 or −1 will not cause a script to be suspended indefinitely.

```
<package>
    <job id="vbs">
        <script language="VBScript">
        set WshShell = WScript.CreateObject("WScript.Shell")
        WshShell.Run "calc"

        WScript.Sleep 100

        WshShell.AppActivate "Calculator"

        WScript.Sleep 100

        WshShell.SendKeys "1{+}"

        WScript.Sleep 500

        WshShell.SendKeys "2"

        WScript.Sleep 500

        WshShell.SendKeys "~"

        WScript.Sleep 500

        WshShell.SendKeys "*9"

        WScript.Sleep 500

        WshShell.SendKeys "~"

        WScript.Sleep 2500
        </script>
    </job>
</package>
```

The WshArguments Object

The use of arguments in programming tasks is a very useful mechanism for providing your script with input on which it can act. Think about working at a DOS prompt. Most command-line executable files use arguments to determine the right thing to do. For example, navigating within a directory structure:

```
c:\>cd wsh
```

In this instance, cd is the name of a DOS command (for change directory), while wsh is the name of the directory activated — it is an argument passed to cd.

Creating scripts that work with arguments is a good step toward writing reusable code. Developers creating scripts designed to execute on the command line may immediately see the benefits of working with the Arguments property. However, within WSH, there is another good reason to use this object, as this is how drag-and-drop functionality is implemented.

A final justification for the use of this object is that it allows developers to reuse script code within other scripts, by running the script in question as if it were executing on the command line, passing whatever arguments may be necessary at runtime.

Accessing the WshArguments Object

This is accessed by using WScript.Arguments property.

```
Set objArgs = WScript.Arguments
```

WshArguments Properties

The WshArguments object is a collection returned by the WScript object's Arguments property (WScript.Arguments).

There are three ways to access sets of command-line arguments:

❑ Access the entire set of arguments with the WshArguments object.

❑ Access the arguments that have names with the WshNamed object.

❑ Access the arguments that have no names with the WshUnnamed object.

The following example simply loops through the WshArguments collection, displaying each in turn:

```
Set objArgs = WScript. Arguments
For x = 0 to objArgs.Count - 1
    WScript.Echo objArgs(x)
Next
```

The interesting thing here is that this works in both cscript and wscript. You can try this out for yourself using the echoargs.vbs example. Execute on the command line, passing a few arguments:

```
c:\vbs\echoargs Hello, World!
```

Figure 15-10 shows the output from the command line.

Figure 15-10

Now try dragging a file or two, and then dropping them on `echoargs.vbs`. Figure 15-11 shows the output resulting from this.

Figure 15-11

The WshShell Object

Windows Script Host provides a convenient way to gain access to system environment variables, create shortcuts, access Windows special folders, such as the Windows Desktop, and add or remove entries from the registry. It is also possible to create more customized dialog boxes for user interaction by using features of the `Shell` object.

Accessing the WshShell Object

Programmers should create an instance of the object `WScript.Shell` in order to work with the properties listed in the next section. Further references to the `WshShell` object will refer to this created instance.

```
Set WshShell= WScript.CreateObject( "WScript.Shell" )
```

WshShell Properties

The WshShell object has three properties:

❑   CurrentDirectory

❑   Environment

❑   SpecialFolders

CurrentDirectory

This property retrieves or changes the current active directory.

```
object.CurrentDirectory
```

❑   object: WshShell object.

The CurrentDirectory property returns a string that contains the fully qualified path of the current working directory of the active process.

```
Dim WshShell
Set WshShell = WScript.CreateObject("WScript.Shell")
WScript.Echo WshShell.CurrentDirectory
```

Environment

This property returns the WshEnvironment object (a collection of environment variables).

```
object.Environment ([strType])
```

❑   object: WshShell object.

❑   strType: Optional. This specifies the location of the environment variable.

The Environment property contains the WshEnvironment object (a collection of environment variables). If strType is supplied, it specifies where the environment variable resides with possible values of:

❑   System

❑   User

❑   Volatile

❑   Process

If strType is not supplied, the Environment property returns different environment variable types depending on the operating system (see the following table).

Type of Environment Variable	Operating System
System	Microsoft Windows NT/2000/XP/Vista
Process	Windows 95/98/Me

For Windows 95/98/Me, only one `strType` is permitted: `Process`. None of the others can be used in scripts.

This table lists some of the variables that are provided with the Windows operating system.

Name	Description	System	User	Process (NT/2000/ XP/Vista)	Process (95/98/ Me)
NUMBER_OF _PROCESSORS	Number of processors running on the machine.	x	—	X	—
PROCESSOR _ARCHITECTURE	Processor type of the user's workstation.	x	—	X	—
PROCESSOR _IDENTIFIER	Processor ID of the user's workstation.	x	—	X	—
PROCESSOR _LEVEL	Processor level of the user's workstation.	x	—	X	—
PROCESSOR _REVISION	Processor version of the user's workstation.	x	—	X	—
OS	Operating system on the user's workstation.	x	—	X	—
COMSPEC	Operating system on the user's workstation.	—	—	X	x
HOMEDRIVE	Primary local drive (usually this is C drive).	—	—	X	—
HOMEPATH	Default directory for users.	—	—	X	—
PATH	Path environment variable.	x	x	X	x

(continued)

Name	Description	System	User	Process (NT/2000/ XP/Vista)	Process (95/98/ Me)
PATHEXT	Extensions for executable files (typically .com, .exe, .bat, or .cmd).	x	—	X	—
PROMPT	Command prompt (typically PG).	—	—	X	x
SYSTEMDRIVE	Local drive on which the system directory resides (typically c:\).	—	—	X	—
SYSTEMROOT	System directory (for example, c:\ winnt). This is the same as WINDIR.	—	—	X	—
WINDIR	System directory (for example, c:\). This is the same as SYSTEMROOT.	x	—	X	x
TEMP	Directory for storing temporary files (for example, c:\temp).	—	x	X	x
TMP	Directory for storing temporary files (for example, c:\temp).	—	x	X	x

Note that scripts can access environment variables that have been set by other applications and that none of the variables listed previously are available from the Volatile type.

Here is an example of how to use the variables listed in the table in your code. This returns the number of processors present on the system.

```
Set WshShell = WScript.CreateObject("WScript.Shell")
Set WshSysEnv = WshShell.Environment("SYSTEM")
WScript.Echo WshSysEnv("NUMBER_OF_PROCESSORS")
```

SpecialFolders

This property returns a `SpecialFolders` object (a collection of special folders).

```
object.SpecialFolders(objWshSpecialFolders)
```

❑ `object`: `WshShell` object.

❑ `objWshSpecialFolders`: The name of the special folder.

The `WshSpecialFolders` object is a collection. This contains the entire set of Windows special folders, which include the Desktop folder, the Start Menu folder, and the Documents/My Documents folder (note that the "my" prefix has been dropped under Windows Vista).

The special folder name is used to index into the collection to retrieve the special folder you want. The `SpecialFolders` property returns an empty string if the requested folder (`strFolderName`) is not available. For example, Windows 95 does not have an `AllUsersDesktop` folder and returns an empty string if `strFolderName` is `AllUsersDesktop`.

The following special folders are available:

❑ `AllUsersDesktop`

❑ `AllUsersStartMenu`

❑ `AllUsersPrograms`

❑ `AllUsersStartup`

❑ `Desktop`

❑ `Favorites`

❑ `Fonts`

❑ `MyDocuments`

❑ `NetHood`

❑ `PrintHood`

❑ `Programs`

❑ `Recent`

❑ `SendTo`

❑ `StartMenu`

❑ `Startup`

❑ `Templates`

The following code is used to retrieve the Start Menu folder and hold the path in the `strDesktop` variable for later use.

```
strDesktop = WshShell.SpecialFolders("StartMenu")
```

WshShell Methods

The `WshShell` object has 11 methods. All these methods relate to the operating system shell and allow you control over the Windows registry, as well as to create pop-ups and shortcuts and activate and control running applications:

- ❑ AppActivate
- ❑ CreateShortcut
- ❑ ExpandEnvironmentStrings
- ❑ LogEvent
- ❑ Popup
- ❑ RegDelete
- ❑ RegRead
- ❑ RegWrite
- ❑ Run
- ❑ SendKeys
- ❑ Exec

AppActivate

Here you have a method that allows you to activate a specific application window already open.

```
object.AppActivate title
```

- ❑ object: WshShell object.
- ❑ title: Specifies which application to activate. This can be a string that contains the title of the application (as it appears in the title bar) or the application's Process ID.

The `AppActivate` method returns a Boolean value that identifies whether the procedure call is successful. This method is used to change the focus to the named application or window. It does not affect whether it is maximized or minimized. Focus moves away from the activated application window when the user takes action to change the focus (or closes the window).

To determine which application to activate, the specified title is compared to the title string of each running application. If no exact match exists, any application whose title string begins with `title` is activated. If an application still cannot be found, any application whose title string ends with `title` is activated. If more than one instance of the application named by title exists, one instance is arbitrarily activated. You do not have control over which one is chosen.

```
<package>
    <job id="vbs">
        <script language="VBScript">
        set WshShell = WScript.CreateObject("WScript.Shell")
        WshShell.Run "calc"
        WScript.Sleep 100
        WshShell.AppActivate "Calculator"
        WScript.Sleep 100
        WshShell.SendKeys "1{+}"
        WScript.Sleep 500
        WshShell.SendKeys "2"
        WScript.Sleep 500
        WshShell.SendKeys "~"
        WScript.Sleep 500
        WshShell.SendKeys "*3"
        WScript.Sleep 500
        WshShell.SendKeys "~"
        WScript.Sleep 2500
        </script>
    </job>
</package>
```

CreateShortcut

This method can be used to either create a new shortcut or open an existing shortcut.

```
object.CreateShortcut(strPathname)
```

❑   object: WshShell object.

❑   strPathname: A string value indicating the pathname of the shortcut to create.

The CreateShortcut method returns either a WshShortcut object or a WshURLShortcut object. Calling the CreateShortcut method does not result in the creation of a shortcut. Instead, the shortcut object and changes you may have made to it are stored in memory until you save it to disk using the Save method. To create a shortcut, you must follow these steps:

❑   Create an instance of a WshShortcut object.

❑   Initialize its properties.

❑   Save it to disk with the Save method.

A common cause of problems is putting arguments in the TargetPath property of the shortcut object. This will not work. All arguments to the shortcut must be put in the Arguments property.

```
<package>
    <job id="vbs">
        <script language="VBScript">
        set WshShell = WScript.CreateObject("WScript.Shell")

        strDesktop = WshShell.SpecialFolders("Desktop")
        set oShellLink = WshShell.CreateShortcut(strDesktop & _
"\Shortcut Script.lnk")
        oShellLink.TargetPath = WScript.ScriptFullName
        oShellLink.WindowStyle = 1
        oShellLink.Hotkey = "CTRL+SHIFT+N"
        oShellLink.IconLocation = "notepad.exe, 0"
        oShellLink.Description = "Shortcut to Notepad"
        oShellLink.WorkingDirectory = strDesktop
        oShellLink.Save
        </script>
    </job>
</package>
```

ExpandEnvironmentStrings

This method returns an environment variable's expanded value.

```
object.ExpandEnvironmentStrings(strString)
```

❑   object: WshShell object.

❑   strString: A string value indicating the name of the environment variable you want
to expand.

This method expands environment variables defined in the PROCESS environment space only.
Environment variable names must be enclosed between "%" characters and are not case-sensitive.

```
set WshShell = WScript.CreateObject("WScript.Shell")
WScript.Echo "The path to WinDir is " _
& WshShell.ExpandEnvironmentStrings("%WinDir%")
```

LogEvent

The LogEvent method adds an event entry to a log file.

```
object.LogEvent(intType, strMessage [,strTarget])
```

❑   object: WshShell object.

❑   intType: Integer value representing the event type.

❑   strMessage: A string value that contains the log entry text.

❑   strTarget: Optional. A string value that indicates the name of the computer system where the
event log is stored (the default is the local computer system). Applies to Windows NT/2000/
XP/Vista only.

This method is used to return a Boolean value (`True` if an event is successfully logged, otherwise `False`). In Windows NT/2000/XP/Vista, events are logged in the Windows NT Event Log. In Windows 9x/Me, events are logged in `WSH.log` (which is located in the `Windows` directory).

There are six event types, as shown in the following table.

Type	Value
0	SUCCESS
1	ERROR
2	WARNING
4	INFORMATION
8	AUDIT_SUCCESS
16	AUDIT_FAILURE

The following code shows `LogEvent` in action, logging events based on their success of failure:

```
Set WshShell = WScript.CreateObject("WScript.Shell")

'assume that rS contains a return code
'from another part of the code

if rS then
    WshShell.LogEvent 0, "Script Completed Successfully"
else
    WshShell.LogEvent 1, "Script failed"
end if
```

Popup

This method is used to display text in a pop-up message box.

```
intButton = object.Popup(strText,[nSecondsToWait],[strTitle],[nType])
```

❑ `object`: `WshShell` object.

❑ `strText`: A string value that contains the text you want to appear in the pop-up message box.

❑ `nSecondsToWait`: Optional. A numeric value indicating the maximum length of time (in seconds) you want the pop-up message box displayed. If `nSecondsToWait` is equal to zero (the default), the pop-up message box remains visible until it is closed by the user. If `nSecondsToWait` is greater than zero, the pop-up message box closes after `nSecondsToWait` seconds.

❑ `strTitle`: Optional. A string value that contains the text you want to appear as the title of the pop-up message box. If you don't supply the argument `strTitle`, the title of the pop-up message box is set to the default string `"Windows Script Host"`.

❏ nType: Optional. A numeric value indicating the type of buttons and icons you want in the pop-up message box. These determine how the message box is used. The function of nType is the same as in the Microsoft Win32 application programming interface MessageBox function. The following tables show the values and their meanings. To get different results you can combine various values from these tables.

❏ IntButton: An integer value indicating the number of the button the user clicked to dismiss the message box. This is the value returned by the Popup method.

The Popup method is used to display a message box regardless of which host executable file is running the script (wscript.exe or cscript.exe).

To display text properly in RTL (Right-to-Left) languages such as Hebrew or Arabic, add hex & h00100000 (decimal 1048576) to the nType parameter.

Button Types

Value	Description
0	Show the OK button.
1	Show the OK and Cancel buttons.
2	Show the Abort, Retry, and Ignore buttons.
3	Show the Yes, No, and Cancel buttons.
4	Show the Yes and No buttons.
5	Show Retry and Cancel buttons.

Icon Types

Value	Description
16	Show the Stop Mark icon.
32	Show the Question Mark icon.
48	Show the Exclamation Mark icon.
64	Show the Information Mark icon.

The return value intButton denotes the number of the button that the user clicked on. If the user does not click a button before nSecondsToWait seconds, intButton is set to -1.

The following table shows a list of values indicating the number of the button the user clicked to dismiss the message box.

Value	Description
1	OK button
2	Cancel button
3	Abort button
4	Retry button
5	Ignore button
6	Yes button
7	No button

The following code shows an example of different message box buttons and icons in use:

```
Dim WshShell, BtnCode
Set WshShell = WScript.CreateObject("WScript.Shell")

BtnCode = WshShell.Popup("Do you like this code?", 7, "Quick survey:", 4 + 32)

Select Case BtnCode
    case 6      WScript.Echo "Glad to hear it - Thanks!"
    case 7      WScript.Echo "I'm sorry you didn't like it."
    case -1     WScript.Echo "Hellllooooooooo?"
End Select
```

RegDelete

This method deletes a key or one of its values from the registry.

```
object.RegDelete(strName)
```

❑   object: WshShell object.

❑   strName: A string value indicating the name of the registry key or key value to delete.

You can specify a key name by ending strName with a final backslash or leave it out to specify a value name.

Fully qualified key names and value names are prefixed with a root key. You can also use abbreviated versions of root key names with the RegDelete method.

The five possible root keys you can use are listed in the following table.

Root Key Name	Abbreviation
HKEY_CURRENT_USER	HKCU
HKEY_LOCAL_MACHINE	HKLM
HKEY_CLASSES_ROOT	HKCR
HKEY_USERS	HKEY_USERS
HKEY_CURRENT_CONFIG	HKEY_CURRENT_CONFIG

The script that follows creates, reads, and then deletes Windows registry keys. The highlighted part of the script does the key deleting.

```
Dim WshShell, bKey
Set WshShell = WScript.CreateObject("WScript.Shell")

WshShell.RegWrite "HKCU\Software\WROX\VBScript\", 1, "REG_BINARY"
WshShell.RegWrite "HKCU\Software\WROX\VBScript\ProgRef","VBS_is_great","REG_SZ"

bKey = WshShell.RegRead("HKCU\Software\WROX\VBScript\")
WScript.Echo WshShell.RegRead("HKCU\Software\WROX\VBScript\ProgRef")

WshShell.RegDelete "HKCU\Software\WROX\VBScript\ProgRef"
WshShell.RegDelete "HKCU\Software\WROX\VBScript\"
WshShell.RegDelete "HKCU\Software\WROX\"
```

> It is vitally important to take great care when modifying registry settings. Making incorrect changes to the registry can cause your system to become unstable or render it completely unusable. If you have any doubts about the inner workings of the registry, you are strongly advised to do some reading on the subject before beginning to experiment on your own.

RegRead

This method returns the value of a key or value name from the registry.

```
object.RegRead(strName)
```

❏ object: WshShell object.

❏ strName: A string value indicating the key or value name whose value you want.

The `RegRead` method returns values of the following five types.

Type	Description	In the Form of
REG_SZ	A string	A string
REG_DWORD	A number	An integer
REG_BINARY	A binary value	A VBArray of integers
REG_EXPAND_SZ	An expandable string (for example, %windir%\\notepad.exe)	A string
REG_MULTI_SZ	An array of strings	A VBArray of strings

You can specify a key name by ending `strName` with a final backslash or leave it off to specify a value name.

A value entry consists of three parts:

- ❑   Name
- ❑   Data type
- ❑   Value

When you specify a key name (as opposed to a value name) `RegRead` returns the default value. To read a key's default value, specify the name of the key.

Fully qualified key names and value names begin with a root key. You can also use abbreviated versions of root key names with the `RegRead` method. The five possible root keys are listed in the following table.

Root Key Name	Abbreviation
HKEY_CURRENT_USER	HKCU
HKEY_LOCAL_MACHINE	HKLM
HKEY_CLASSES_ROOT	HKCR
HKEY_USERS	HKEY_USERS
HKEY_CURRENT_CONFIG	HKEY_CURRENT_CONFIG

The script that follows creates, reads, and then deletes Windows registry keys. The highlighted part of the script does the key reading.

```
Dim WshShell, bKey
Set WshShell = WScript.CreateObject("WScript.Shell")
WshShell.RegWrite "HKCU\Software\WROX\VBScript\", 1, "REG_BINARY"
WshShell.RegWrite "HKCU\Software\WROX\VBScript\ProgRef","VBS_is_great","REG_SZ"

bKey = WshShell.RegRead("HKCU\Software\WROX\VBScript\")
WScript.Echo WshShell.RegRead("HKCU\Software\WROX\VBScript\ProgRef")

WshShell.RegDelete "HKCU\Software\WROX\VBScript\ProgRef"
WshShell.RegDelete "HKCU\Software\WROX\VBScript\"
WshShell.RegDelete "HKCU\Software\WROX\"
```

RegWrite

This method creates a new key, adds another value name to an existing key (and assigns it a value), or changes the value of an existing value name.

```
object.RegWrite(strName, anyValue [,strType])
```

❑   object: WshShell object.

❑   strName: A string value that indicates the key name, value name, or value you want to create, add, or change.

❑   anyValue: The name of the new key you want to create, the name of the value you want to add to an existing key, or the new value you want to assign to an existing value name.

❑   strType: Optional. A string value indicating the value's data type.

You can specify a key name by ending strName with a final backslash. Do not include the final backslash to specify a value name.

The RegWrite method automatically converts the parameter anyValue to either a string or an integer while the value of strType determines its data type (either a string or an integer). The following table lists the options available for the strType method.

Converted to	StrType
String	REG_SZ
String	REG_EXPAND_SZ
Integer	REG_DWORD
Integer	REG_BINARY

The REG_MULTI_SZ type is not supported for the RegWrite method.

RegWrite will write at most one DWORD to a REG_BINARY value. Larger values are not supported with this method. Fully qualified key names and value names are prefixed with a root key. You can use abbreviated versions of root key names with the RegWrite method. The five root keys of the Windows registry are listed in the following table.

Root Key Name	Abbreviation
HKEY_CURRENT_USER	HKCU
HKEY_LOCAL_MACHINE	HKLM
HKEY_CLASSES_ROOT	HKCR
HKEY_USERS	HKEY_USERS
HKEY_CURRENT_CONFIG	HKEY_CURRENT_CONFIG

The four possible data types you can specify with strType are listed in the following table.

Type	Description	In the Form of
REG_SZ	A string	A string
REG_DWORD	A number	An integer
REG_BINARY	A binary value	A VBArray of integers
REG_EXPAND_SZ	An expandable string (for example, %windir% \\notepad.exe)	A string

The following code shows how to access and modify the Windows registry:

```
Dim WshShell, bKey
Set WshShell = WScript.CreateObject("WScript.Shell")

WshShell.RegWrite "HKCU\Software\WROX\VBScript\", 1, "REG_BINARY"
WshShell.RegWrite "HKCU\Software\WROX\VBScript\ProgRef","VBS_is_great","REG_SZ"

bKey = WshShell.RegRead("HKCU\Software\WROX\VBScript\")
WScript.Echo WshShell.RegRead("HKCU\Software\WROX\VBScript\ProgRef")

WshShell.RegDelete "HKCU\Software\WROX\VBScript\ProgRef"
WshShell.RegDelete "HKCU\Software\WROX\VBScript\"
WshShell.RegDelete "HKCU\Software\WROX\"
```

> It is vitally important to take great care when modifying registry settings. Making incorrect changes to the registry can cause your system to become unstable or render it completely unusable. If you have any doubts about the inner workings of the registry, you are strongly advised to do some reading on the subject before beginning to experiment on your own.

Run

The Run method runs a program in a new process.

```
object.Run(strCommand, [intWindowStyle], [bWaitOnReturn])
```

❑ object: WshShell object.

❑ strCommand: A string value indicating the command line you want to run. You must include any parameters you want to pass to the executable file.

❑ intWindowStyle: Optional. An integer value indicating the appearance of the program's window. Not all programs make use of this information.

❑ bWaitOnReturn: Optional. A Boolean value indicating whether the script should wait for the program to finish executing before continuing to the next statement in your script. If set to True, script execution halts until the program finishes, and Run returns any error code returned by the program. If set to False (the default), the Run method returns immediately after starting the program, automatically returning 0 (this is not an error code).

The Run method returns an integer. The Run method starts a program running in a new Windows process. You can have your script wait for the program to finish executing before it continues, which allows you to run scripts and programs synchronously. If a file type has been properly registered to a particular program, calling Run on a file of that type executes the program. For example, calling Run on a *.txt file starts Notepad and loads the text file into it. The following table lists the available settings for intWindowStyle.

IntWindowStyle	Description
0	Hides the window and activates another window.
1	Activates and displays a window.
	If the window is minimized or maximized, the system restores it to its original size and position.
	An application should specify this flag when displaying the window for the first time.
2	Activates the window and displays it as a minimized window.
3	Activates the window and displays it as a maximized window.
4	Displays a window in its most recent size and position.
	The active window remains active.
5	Activates the window and displays it in its current size and position.
6	Minimizes the specified window and activates the next top-level window in the Z order.
7	Displays the window as a minimized window.
	The active window remains active.

IntWindowStyle	Description
8	Displays the window in its current state. The active window remains active.
9	Activates and displays the window. If the window is minimized or maximized, the system restores it to its original size and position. An application should specify this flag when restoring a minimized window.
10	Sets the show-state based on the state of the program that started the application.

The following code opens a command prompt window and displays the contents of C: drive.

```
Dim oShell
Set oShell = WScript.CreateObject ("WSCript.shell")
oShell.run "cmd /K CD C:\ & Dir"
Set oShell = Nothing
```

SendKeys

The SendKeys method sends one or more keystrokes to the active window (as if typed on the keyboard).

```
object.SendKeys(string)
```

❏   object: WshShell object.

❏   string: A string value indicating the keystroke or keystrokes that you want to send.

You use the SendKeys method to send keystrokes to applications that have no in-built automation interface. Most keyboard characters are represented by a single keystroke while some keyboard characters are made up of combinations of keystrokes (Alt + F4, for example).

To send a single keyboard character, you simply send the character itself as the string argument. For example, to send the letter v, send the string argument "v". To send a space, send the string " ".

You can also use the SendKeys method to send multiple keystrokes. You do this by creating a compound string argument that represents the sequence of keystrokes by appending each keystroke in the sequence to the one before it. For example, to send the keystrokes x, y, and z, you would send the string argument "xyz".

The SendKeys method uses some characters as modifiers of other characters. This set of special characters consists of parentheses, brackets, braces, and those shown in the following table.

Plus sign	"+"
Caret	"^"
Percent sign	"%"
Tilde	"~"

To send these characters, you enclose them inside curly braces "{}". So if you want to send the plus sign, send the string argument "{+}".

Square brackets "[]" have no special meaning when used with SendKeys, but you must enclose them within braces to accommodate applications that do give them a special meaning (Dynamic Data Exchange for example).

To send the square bracket characters, send the string argument "{[}" for the left bracket and "{]}" for the right one. To send curly brace characters, send the string argument "{{}" for the left brace and "{}}" for the right one.

Some keystrokes do not generate characters (such as Enter and Tab). Some keystrokes represent actions (such as Backspace and Break). To send these kinds of keystrokes, send the arguments shown in the following table.

Key	Argument
Backspace	{BACKSPACE}, {BS}, or {BKSP}
Break	{BREAK}
Caps Lock	{CAPSLOCK}
Del or Delete	{DELETE} or {DEL}
Down Arrow	{DOWN}
End	{END}
Enter	{ENTER} or ~
Esc	{ESC}
Help	{HELP}
Home	{HOME}
Ins or Insert	{INSERT} or {INS}
Left Arrow	{LEFT}
Num Lock	{NUMLOCK}
Page Down	{PGDN}
Page Up	{PGUP}
Print Screen	{PRTSC}
Right Arrow	{RIGHT}
Scroll Lock	{SCROLLLOCK}
Tab	{TAB}
Up Arrow	{UP}
F1	{F1}

Key	Argument
F2	{F2}
F3	{F3}
F4	{F4}
F5	{F5}
F6	{F6}
F7	{F7}
F8	{F8}
F9	{F9}
F10	{F10}
F11	{F11}
F12	{F12}
F13	{F13}
F14	{F14}
F15	{F15}
F16	{F16}

To send keyboard characters that are composed of a regular keystroke in combination with a Shift, Ctrl, or Alt, you will need to create a compound string argument to represent the keystroke combination. You do this by preceding the regular keystroke with one or more of the special characters shown in the following table.

Key	Special Character
Alt	%
Ctrl	^
Shift	+

When used for this purpose, these special characters are not enclosed within a set of braces.

To specify that a combination of Shift, Ctrl, and Alt should be held down while several other keys are pressed, you create a compound string argument with the modified keystrokes enclosed in parentheses. For example, to send the keystroke combination that specifies that the Shift key is held down while:

❑   V and B are pressed, send the string argument "+(VB)".

❑   V is pressed, followed by a lone B (with no Shift), send the string argument "+VB".

You can use the SendKeys method to send a pattern of keystrokes that consists of a single keystroke pressed multiple times. This is done by creating a compound string argument that specifies the keystroke you want to repeat, followed by the number of times you want the keystrokes repeated. You do this using a compound string argument of the form {keystroke number}. For example, to send the letter "V" ten times, you would send the string argument "{V 10}".

The only keystroke pattern you can send is the kind that is composed of a single keystroke pressed several times. For example, you can send "V" ten times, but you cannot do the same for "Ctrl+V". Note that you cannot send the Print Screen key {PRTSC} to an application.

```
<package>
    <job id="vbs">
        <script language="VBScript">
        set WshShell = WScript.CreateObject("WScript.Shell")
        WshShell.Run "calc"
        WScript.Sleep 100
        WshShell.AppActivate "Calculator"
        WScript.Sleep 100

WshShell.SendKeys "1{+}"
        WScript.Sleep 500
        WshShell.SendKeys "2"
        WScript.Sleep 500
        WshShell.SendKeys "~"

        WScript.Sleep 500

        WshShell.SendKeys "*9"

        WScript.Sleep 500

        WshShell.SendKeys "~"

        WScript.Sleep 2500
        </script>
    </job>
</package>
```

Exec

The Exec method runs an application in a child command shell, which provides access to the StdIn, StdOut, and StdErr streams.

```
object.Exec(strCommand)
```

❑   object: WshShell object.

❑   strCommand: A string value indicating the command line used to run the script.

The Exec method returns a WshScriptExec object, which provides status and error information about a script run with Exec along with access to the StdIn, StdOut, and StdErr channels. The Exec method allows the execution of command-line applications only and cannot be used to run remote scripts.

The WshNamed Object

The WshNamed object provides access to the named arguments from the command line.

The Named property of the WshArguments object returns the WshNamed object, which is a collection of arguments that have names. This collection uses the argument name as the index to retrieve individual argument values. There are three ways to access sets of command-line arguments:

❑ Access the entire set of arguments with the WshArguments object.

❑ Access the arguments that have names with the WshNamed object.

❑ Access the arguments that have no names with the WshUnnamed object.

Accessing the WshNamed Object

This is accessed by creating an instance of WScript.Named.

```
Set argsNamed = WScript.Arguments.Named
```

WshNamed Properties

The WshNamed object has two properties:

❑ Item

❑ Length

Item

The Item property provides access to the items in the WshNamed object.

```
Object.Item(key)
```

❑ Object: WshNamed object

❑ key: The name of the item you want to retrieve.

The Item property returns a string. For collections, it returns an item based on the specified key. When entering the arguments at the command line, you can use spaces in string arguments as long as you enclose the string in quotes. The following line is typed at the command prompt to run the script:

```
sample.vbs /a:arg1 /b:arg2
```

If the following code is executed inside the script

```
WScript.Echo WScript.Arguments.Named.Item("b")
WScript.Echo WScript.Arguments.Named.Item("a")
```

then the following output is produced.

```
arg2
arg1
```

Length

The `Length` property is a read-only integer that you use in scripts when you write in JScript. As such, this is beyond the scope of this book.

WshNamed Methods

The `WshNamed` object has two methods:

❑ `Count`

❑ `Exists`

Count

The `Count` method returns the number of switches in the `WshNamed` or `WshUnnamed` objects.

```
object.Count
```

❑ `object`: `Arguments` object.

The `Count` method is used to return an integer value. The `Count` method is intended for VBScript users, and JScript users should use the `length` property instead.

```
For x = 0 to WScript.Arguments.Count-1
    WScript.Echo WScript.Arguments.Named(x)
Next x
```

Exists

The `Exists` method indicates whether a specific key value exists in the `WshNamed` object.

```
object.Exists(key)
```

❑ `object`: `WshNamed` object.

❑ Key: String value indicating an argument of the `WshNamed` object.

This method returns a Boolean value. It returns `True` if the requested argument was specified on the command line (otherwise, it returns `False`). The following line is typed at the command prompt to run the script:

```
sample.vbs /a:arg1 /b:arg2
```

The following code could be used to discover whether the arguments `/a`, `/b`, and `/c` were used:

```
WScript.Echo WScript.Arguments.Named.Exists("a")
WScript.Echo WScript.Arguments.Named.Exists("b")
WScript.Echo WScript.Arguments.Named.Exists("c")
```

The WshUnnamed Object

The WshUnnamed object provides access to the unnamed arguments from the command line. It is a read-only collection that is returned by the Unnamed property of the WshArguments object. All individual argument values are retrieved from this collection using zero-based indexes.

There are three ways to access sets of command-line arguments:

❑ Access the entire set of arguments with the WshArguments object.

❑ Access the arguments that have names with the WshNamed object.

❑ Access the arguments that have no names with the WshUnnamed object.

Accessing the WshUnnamed Object

This is accessed by creating an instance of WScript.Arguments.Unnamed.

```
Set argsUnnamed = WScript.Arguments.Unnamed
```

WshUnnamed Properties

The WshUnnamed object has two properties:

❑ Item

❑ Length

Both these are similar to that of the WshNamed object and as such don't need to be covered again here.

WshUnnamed Methods

The WshUnnamed object has one method:

❑ Count

This method is similar to that of the WshNamed object and as such doesn't need to be covered again here.

The WshNetwork Object

The WshNetwork object provides access to the shared resources on the network to which the computer is connected. You will need to create a WshNetwork object when you want to connect to network shares and network printers, disconnect from network shares and network printers, map or remove network shares, or access information about a user on the network.

Accessing the WshNetwork Object

This is accessed by creating an instance of WScript.Network.

```
Set WshNetwork = WScript.CreateObject("WScript.Network")
```

WshNetwork Properties

The WshNetwork object has three properties:

❑ ComputerName

❑ UserDomain

❑ UserName

ComputerName

The ComputerName property returns the name of the computer system.

```
object.ComputerName
```

❑ object: WshNetwork object.

The ComputerName property contains a string value that indicates the name of the computer system.

```
<package>
    <job id="vbs">
        <script language="VBScript">
        Set WshNetwork = WScript.CreateObject("WScript.Network")
        WScript.Echo "Domain = " & WshNetwork.UserDomain

        WScript.Echo "Computer Name = " & WshNetwork.ComputerName

        WScript.Echo "User Name = " & WshNetwork.UserName
        </script>
    </job>
</package>
```

UserDomain

The UserDomain property returns a user's domain name.

```
object.UserDomain
```

❑ object: WshNetwork object.

The UserDomain property will not work on Windows 98 and Windows Me unless the USERDOMAIN environment variable is set. This variable is not set by default.

```
<package>
    <job id="vbs">
        <script language="VBScript">
        Set WshNetwork = WScript.CreateObject("WScript.Network")

        WScript.Echo "Domain = " & WshNetwork.UserDomain

        WScript.Echo "Computer Name = " & WshNetwork.ComputerName
        WScript.Echo "User Name = " & WshNetwork.UserName
        </script>
    </job>
</package>
```

UserName

The UserName property returns the name of a user.

```
object.UserName
```

❑ object: WshNetwork object.

The UserName property returns the name of a user as a string.

```
<package>
    <job id="vbs">
        <script language="VBScript">
        Set WshNetwork = WScript.CreateObject("WScript.Network")
        WScript.Echo "Domain = " & WshNetwork.UserDomain
        WScript.Echo "Computer Name = " & WshNetwork.ComputerName
        WScript.Echo "User Name = " & WshNetwork.UserName
        </script>
    </job>
</package>
```

WshNetwork Methods

The WshNetwork object makes available the following eight methods:

❑ AddWindowsPrinterConnection

❑ AddPrinterConnection

❑ EnumNetworkDrives

❑ EnumPrinterConnection

❑ MapNetworkDrive

❑ RemoveNetworkDrive

❑ RemovePrinterConnection

❑ SetDefaultPrinter

AddWindowsPrinterConnection

The AddWindowsPrinterConnection method adds a Windows printer connection to your computer system.

❑ Windows NT/2000/XP/Vista:

```
object.AddWindowsPrinterConnection(

    strPrinterPath

)
```

❑   Windows 9x/Me

```
object.AddWindowsPrinterConnection(
    strPrinterPath,
    strDriverName[,strPort]
)
```

- ❑   object: WshNetwork object.
- ❑   strPrinterPath: A string value indicating the path to the printer connection.
- ❑   strDriverName: A string value indicating the name of the driver (this is ignored on Windows NT/2000/XP).
- ❑   strPort: Optional. A string value that specifies a printer port for the printer connection (this is ignored on Windows NT/2000/XP/Vista systems).

❑   Using this method is very similar to using the Printer option on Control Panel to add a printer connection. This method allows you to create a printer connection without the inconvenience of having to direct it to a specific port.

❑   If the connection fails, an error is generated.

```
Set WshNetwork = WScript.CreateObject("WScript.Network")
PrinterPath = "\\printerserver\DefaultPrinter"
WshNetwork.AddWindowsPrinterConnection PrinterPath
```

AddPrinterConnection

The AddPrinterConnection method adds a remote printer connection to your computer system.

```
object.AddPrinterConnection(strLocalName,
strRemoteName[,bUpdateProfile][,strUser][,strPassword])
```

- ❑   object: WshNetwork object.
- ❑   strLocalName: A string value that indicates the local name to assign to the connected printer.
- ❑   strRemoteName: A string value that indicates the name of the remote printer.
- ❑   bUpdateProfile: Optional. A Boolean value that indicates whether the printer mapping is stored in the current user's profile. If bUpdateProfile is supplied and is True, the mapping is stored in the user profile. The default value is False.
- ❑   strUser: Optional. A string value that indicates the username. If you are mapping a remote printer using the profile of someone other than current user, you can specify strUser and strPassword.
- ❑   strPassword: Optional. A string value that indicates the user password. If you are mapping a remote printer using the profile of someone other than current user, you can also specify strUser and strPassword.

EnumNetworkDrives

The `EnumNetworkDrives` method returns the current network drive mapping information.

```
objDrives = object.EnumNetworkDrives
```

❑　`object`: `WshNetwork` object.

❑　`objDrives`: A variable that holds the network drive mapping information.

This method returns a collection, which is an array that associates pairs of items — network drive local names and their associated UNC (Universal Naming Convention) names. Even-numbered items in the collection represent local names of logical drives while odd-numbered items represent the associated UNC share names.

The first item in the collection is at index zero (`0`).

EnumPrinterConnection

The `EnumPrinterConnections` method returns the current network printer mapping information.

```
objPrinters = object.EnumPrinterConnections
```

❑　`object`: `WshNetwork` object.

❑　`objPrinters`: A variable that holds the network printer mapping information.

The `EnumPrinterConnections` method returns a collection that consists of an array that associates pairs of items — network printer local names and their associated UNC names. Even-numbered items in the collection represent printer ports while odd-numbered items represent the networked printer UNC names.

The first item in the collection is at index zero (`0`).

MapNetworkDrive

The `MapNetworkDrive` method adds a shared network drive to your computer system.

```
object.MapNetworkDrive(strLocalName, strRemoteName, [bUpdateProfile],
[strUser], [strPassword])
```

❑　`object`: `WshNetwork` object.

❑　`strLocalName`: A string value indicating the name by which the mapped drive will be known locally.

❑　`strRemoteName`: A string value indicating the share's UNC name (`\\xxx\yyy`).

❑　`bUpdateProfile`: Optional. A Boolean value indicating whether the mapping information is stored in the current user's profile. If `bUpdateProfile` is supplied and has a value of `True`, the mapping is stored in the user profile (the default is `False`).

❏ strUser: Optional. A string value indicating the username. You must supply this argument if you are mapping a network drive using the credentials of someone other than the current user.

❏ strPassword: Optional. A string value indicating the user password. You must supply this argument if you are mapping a network drive using the credentials of someone other than the current user.

An attempt to map a non-shared network drive will result in an error being generated.

RemoveNetworkDrive

The RemoveNetworkDrive method removes a shared network drive from your computer system.

```
object.RemoveNetworkDrive(strName, [bForce], [bUpdateProfile])
```

❏ object: WshNetwork object.

❏ strName: A string value indicating the name of the mapped drive you want to remove. The strName parameter can be either a local name or a remote name depending on how the drive is mapped.

❏ bForce: Optional. A Boolean value indicating whether to force the removal of the mapped drive. If bForce is supplied and its value is True, this method removes the connections whether the resource is used or not.

❏ bUpdateProfile: Optional. A string value indicating whether to remove the mapping from the user's profile. If bUpdateProfile is supplied and its value is True, this mapping is removed from the user profile. bUpdateProfile is False by default.

If the drive has a mapping between a local name (drive letter) and a remote name (UNC name), then strName must be set to the local name. If the network path does not have a local name mapping, then strName must be set to the remote name. The following script removes the network drive "G:".

```
Dim WshNetwork
Set WshNetwork = WScript.CreateObject("WScript.Network")
WshNetwork.RemoveNetworkDrive "G:"
```

RemovePrinterConnection

The RemovePrinterConnection method removes a shared network printer connection from a computer.

```
object.RemovePrinterConnection(strName, [bForce], [bUpdateProfile])
```

❏ object: WshNetwork object.

❏ strName: A string value indicating the name that identifies the printer. It can be a UNC name (in the form {\xxx\yyy}) or a local name (such as LPT1).

❑ bForce: Optional. A Boolean value indicating whether to force the removal of the mapped printer. If this is set to True (the default is False), the printer connection is removed whether or not a user is connected.

❑ bUpdateProfile: Optional. A Boolean value. If set to True (the default is False), the change is saved in the user's profile.

The RemovePrinterConnection method will remove both Windows- and MS-DOS-based printer connections.

If the printer was connected using the method AddPrinterConnection, strName must be the printer's local name.

If the printer was connected using the AddWindowsPrinterConnection method or was added manually, then strName must be the printer's UNC name.

SetDefaultPrinter

The SetDefaultPrinter method assigns a remote printer as the default printer.

```
object.SetDefaultPrinter(strPrinterName)
```

❑ object: WshNetwork object.

❑ strPrinterName: A string value that indicates the UNC name of the remote printer.

The SetDefaultPrinter method will fail when using a DOS-based printer connection. Also, you cannot use the SetDefaultPrinter method to determine the name of the currently installed default printer.

The WshEnvironment Object

The WshEnvironment object provides access to the collection of Windows environment variables.

This object is a collection of environment variables that are returned by the WshShell object's Environment property. This collection contains the entire set of environment variables (both those with names and those without).

To retrieve individual environment variables (and their values) from this collection, you would use the environment variable name as the index.

Accessing the WshEnvironment Object

This is accessed by creating an instance of WScript.Environment. The following script returns the number of processors installed on the system running the script:

```
Set WshShell = WScript.CreateObject("WScript.Shell")
Set WshSysEnv = WshShell.Environment("SYSTEM")
WScript.Echo WshSysEnv("NUMBER_OF_PROCESSORS")
```

WshEnvironment Properties

The `WshEnvironment` object has two properties:

❑ `Item`

❑ `Length`

Item

The `Item` property exposes a specified item from a collection.

```
Object.Item(natIndex)
```

❑ `Object`: The result of the `EnumNetworkDrive` or `EnumPrinterConnections` method, or the object returned by the `Environment` or `SpecialFolders` property.

❑ `natIndex`: Sets the item to retrieve.

`Item` is the default property for each collection. For `EnumNetworkDrive` and `EnumPrinterConnections` collections, index is an integer, while for the `Environment` and `SpecialFolders` collections, index is a string.

`WshShell.SpecialFolders.Item (strFolderName)` returns `"Empty"` in VBScript if the requested folder (`strFolderName`) is not available.

```
<package>
    <job id="vbs">
        <script language="VBScript">
        Set WshShell = WScript.CreateObject("WScript.Shell")
        Set WshSpecialFolders = WshShell.SpecialFolders
        For x = 0 To WshSpecialFolders.Count - 1
            WScript.Echo WshSpecialFolders.Item(x)
        Next
        </script>
    </job>
</package>
```

Length

The `Length` property is a read-only integer that you use in scripts when you write in JScript. As such, this is beyond the scope of this book.

WshEnvironment Methods

The `WshEnvironment` object has two methods:

❑ `Count`

❑ `Remove`

Count

The Count method returns a Long value, which is the number of items in the collection.

```
object.Count
```

❏   object: Arguments object.

The Count method returns an integer value. The Count method is intended for VBScript users and JScript users should use the Length property.

```
For x = 0 to WScript.Arguments.Count-1
    WScript.Echo WScript.Arguments.Named(x)
Next x
```

Remove

The Remove method removes an existing environment variable.

```
object.Remove(strName)
```

❏   object: WshEnvironment object.

❏   strName: A string value that indicates the name of the environment variable that you want to remove.

The Remove method removes environment variables from the following types of environments:

❏   PROCESS

❏   USER

❏   SYSTEM

❏   VOLATILE

Environment variables removed with the Remove method are restored at the end of the current session.

```
Dim WshShell, WshEnv
Set WshShell = WScript.CreateObject("WScript.Shell")
Set WshEnv = WshShell.Environment("PROCESS")
WshEnv("tVar") = "VBScript is Cool!"
WScript.Echo WshShell.ExpandEnvironmentStrings("The value of the test variable is:
'%tVar%'")
WshEnv.Remove "tVar"
WScript.Echo WshShell.ExpandEnvironmentStrings("The value of the test variable is:
'%tVar%'")
```

The WshSpecialFolders Object

The WshSpecialFolders object provides access to the collection of Windows special folders.

The WshShell object's SpecialFolders property returns the WshSpecialFolders object. This collection contains references to Windows special folders (for example, the Desktop folder and Start Menu folder).

This collection retrieves the paths to special folders using the special folder name as the index. The path of a special folder depends on the user environment. If several different users are on the same computer, several different sets of special folders will exist on the hard drive. The following special folders are available:

- ❑ AllUsersDesktop
- ❑ AllUsersPrograms
- ❑ AllUsersStartMenu
- ❑ AllUsersStartup
- ❑ Desktop
- ❑ Favorites
- ❑ Fonts
- ❑ MyDocuments
- ❑ NetHood
- ❑ PrintHood
- ❑ Programs
- ❑ Recent
- ❑ SendTo
- ❑ StartMenu
- ❑ Startup
- ❑ Templates

The following code demonstrates how to create a shortcut to Windows Notepad on the Windows desktop:

```
<package>
    <job id="vbs">
        <script language="VBScript">
        set WshShell = WScript.CreateObject("WScript.Shell")

        strDesktop = WshShell.SpecialFolders("Desktop")

            set oShellLink = WshShell.CreateShortcut(strDesktop & "\Shortcut
    Script.lnk")
```

```
            oShellLink.TargetPath = WScript.ScriptFullName
            oShellLink.WindowStyle = 1
            oShellLink.Hotkey = "CTRL+SHIFT+N"
            oShellLink.IconLocation = "notepad.exe, 0"
            oShellLink.Description = "A Script Generated Shortcut to Notepad"
            oShellLink.WorkingDirectory = strDesktop
            oShellLink.Save
            </script>
        </job>
    </package>
```

WshSpecialFolders Properties: Item

The WshSpecialFolders object has one property:

❑   Item

The Item property exposes a specified item from a collection.

```
Object.Item(natIndex)
```

❑   Object: The result of the EnumNetworkDrive or EnumPrinterConnections method, or the object returned by the Environment or SpecialFolders property.

❑   natIndex: Sets the item to retrieve.

Item is the default property for each collection. For EnumNetworkDrive and EnumPrinterConnections collections, index is an integer, while for the Environment and SpecialFolders collections, index is a string.

```
<package>
    <job id="vbs">
        <script language="VBScript">
        Set WshShell = WScript.CreateObject("WScript.Shell")
        Set WshSpecialFolders = WshShell.SpecialFolders
        For x = 0 To WshSpecialFolders.Count - 1
            WScript.Echo WshSpecialFolders.Item(x)
        Next
        </script>
    </job>
</package>
```

WshSpecialFolders Methods: Count

The WshSpecialFolders object has one method:

❑   Count

The Count method returns the number of switches in the WshNamed or WshUnnamed object.

```
object.Count
```

❑   object: Arguments object.

The Count method returns an integer value. The Count method is intended for VBScript users, and JScript users should use the Length property.

The WshShortcut Object

The WshShortcut object allows you to create shortcuts using script.

```
<package>
    <job id="vbs">
        <script language="VBScript">
        set WshShell = WScript.CreateObject("WScript.Shell")
        strDesktop = WshShell.SpecialFolders("Desktop")
            set oShellLink = WshShell.CreateShortcut(strDesktop & "\Shortcut
Script.lnk")
            oShellLink.TargetPath = WScript.ScriptFullName
            oShellLink.WindowStyle = 1
            oShellLink.Hotkey = "CTRL+SHIFT+N"
            oShellLink.IconLocation = "notepad.exe, 0"
            oShellLink.Description = "Shortcut Script"
            oShellLink.WorkingDirectory = strDesktop
            oShellLink.Save
        </script>
    </job>
</package>
```

WshShortcut Properties

The WshShortcut object has eight properties:

- ❑ Arguments
- ❑ Description
- ❑ FullName
- ❑ Hotkey
- ❑ IconLocation
- ❑ TargetPath
- ❑ WindowStyle
- ❑ WorkingDirectory

Arguments

The Arguments property contains the WshArguments object (a collection of arguments). Use a zero-based index to retrieve individual arguments from this collection.

```
Set objArgs = WScript.Arguments
For x = 0 to objArgs.Count - 1
    WScript.Echo objArgs(x)
Next
```

Description

The Description property returns a description of a shortcut.

```
object.Description
```

❏   object: WshShortcut object.

The Description property contains a string value describing a shortcut.

```
<package>
    <job id="vbs">
        <script language="VBScript">
        set WshShell = WScript.CreateObject("WScript.Shell")
        strDesktop = WshShell.SpecialFolders("Desktop")
        set oShellLink = WshShell.CreateShortcut(strDesktop & "\Shortcut
Script.lnk")
        oShellLink.TargetPath = WScript.ScriptFullName
        oShellLink.WindowStyle = 1
        oShellLink.Hotkey = "CTRL+SHIFT+N"
        oShellLink.IconLocation = "notepad.exe, 0"
```
```
        oShellLink.Description = "Script generated shortcut to Notepad"
```
```
        oShellLink.WorkingDirectory = strDesktop
        oShellLink.Save
        </script>
    </job>
</package>
```

FullName

The FullName property returns the fully qualified path of the shortcut object's target.

```
object.FullName
```

❏   object: WshShortcut object.

The FullName property contains a read-only string value that gives the fully qualified path to the shortcut's target.

```
<package>
    <job id="vbs">
        <script language="VBScript">
        set WshShell = WScript.CreateObject("WScript.Shell")
        strDesktop = WshShell.SpecialFolders("Desktop")
        set oShellLink = WshShell.CreateShortcut(strDesktop & "\Shortcut
Script.lnk")
        oShellLink.TargetPath = WScript.ScriptFullName
        oShellLink.WindowStyle = 1
        oShellLink.Hotkey = "CTRL+SHIFT+N"
        oShellLink.IconLocation = "notepad.exe, 0"
```

(continued)

```
        oShellLink.Description = "Shortcut Script"
        oShellLink.WorkingDirectory = strDesktop
        oShellLink.Save

        WScript.Echo oShellLink.FullName

    </script>
  </job>
</package>
```

Hotkey

The `Hotkey` property is used to assign a key combination to a shortcut, or identifies the key combination assigned to a shortcut. A *hotkey* is a combination of keys that starts a shortcut when all associated keys are held down at the same time.

```
object.Hotkey = strHotkey
```

❑   object: WshShortcut object.

❑   strHotkey: A string that represents the key combination to assign to the shortcut.

The following is the syntax of strHotkey:

```
[KeyModifier]KeyName
```

❑   KeyModifier: KeyModifier can be any one of the following: Alt+, Ctrl+, Shift+, Ext+.

Ext+ means "Extended key." This has been added in case a new type of Shift key is added to the character set in the future.

```
KeyName- a ... z,  0 ... 9,  F1 ... F12, ...
```

The KeyName is not case-sensitive.

Here you modify the previous code to add a hotkey.

```
<package>
    <job id="vbs">
        <script language="VBScript">
        set WshShell = WScript.CreateObject("WScript.Shell")
        strDesktop = WshShell.SpecialFolders("Desktop")
        set oShellLink = WshShell.CreateShortcut(strDesktop & "\Shortcut
Script.lnk")
        oShellLink.TargetPath = WScript.ScriptFullName
        oShellLink.WindowStyle = 1

        oShellLink.Hotkey = "CTRL+SHIFT+N"

        oShellLink.IconLocation = "notepad.exe, 0"
        oShellLink.Description = "Shortcut Script"
        oShellLink.WorkingDirectory = strDesktop
```

```
        oShellLink.Save
        WScript.Echo oShellLink.FullName
        </script>
    </job>
</package>
```

IconLocation

The `IconLocation` property is used to assign an icon to a shortcut, or identify the icon assigned to a shortcut.

```
object.IconLocation = strIconLocation
```

❑   object: `WshShortcut` object.

❑   `strIconLocation`: A string that specifies the icon to use. The string should contain a fully qualified path and an index associated with the icon. The index is used to select the appropriate icon when more than one exists. The index begins at zero (0).

Here you modify the code you had previously to add the standard Notepad icon to the shortcut.

```
<package>
    <job id="vbs">
        <script language="VBScript">
        set WshShell = WScript.CreateObject("WScript.Shell")
        strDesktop = WshShell.SpecialFolders("Desktop")
        set oShellLink = WshShell.CreateShortcut(strDesktop & "\Shortcut
Script.lnk")
        oShellLink.TargetPath = WScript.ScriptFullName
        oShellLink.WindowStyle = 1
        oShellLink.Hotkey = "CTRL+SHIFT+N"
        oShellLink.IconLocation = "notepad.exe, 0"
        oShellLink.Description = "Shortcut Script"
        oShellLink.WorkingDirectory = strDesktop
        oShellLink.Save
        WScript.Echo oShellLink.FullName
        </script>
    </job>
</package>
```

TargetPath

The `TargetPath` property gives the path to the shortcut's executable file.

```
object.TargetPath
```

❑   object: `WshShortcut` or `WshUrlShortcut` object.

This property is for the shortcut's target path only. Any arguments provided must be placed in the `Argument`'s property.

```
<package>
    <job id="vbs">
        <script language="VBScript">
        set WshShell = WScript.CreateObject("WScript.Shell")
        strDesktop = WshShell.SpecialFolders("Desktop")
        set oShellLink = WshShell.CreateShortcut(strDesktop & "\Shortcut
Script.lnk")
        oShellLink.TargetPath = WScript.ScriptFullName
        oShellLink.WindowStyle = 1
        oShellLink.Hotkey = "CTRL+SHIFT+N"
        oShellLink.IconLocation = "notepad.exe, 0"
        oShellLink.Description = "Shortcut Script"
        oShellLink.WorkingDirectory = strDesktop
        oShellLink.Save
        WScript.Echo oShellLink.FullName
        </script>
    </job>
</package>
```

WindowStyle

The `WindowStyle` property is used to either assign a window style to a shortcut or identify the type of window style used by a shortcut.

```
object.WindowStyle = intWindowStyle
```

❑   `object:` `WshShortcut` object.

❑   `intWindowStyle:` This sets the window style for the program being run.

The `WindowStyle` property returns an integer.

The following table lists the available settings for `intWindowStyle`.

InWindowStyle	Description
1	Activates and displays a window.
	If the window is minimized or maximized, the system restores it to its original size and position.
	An application should specify this flag when displaying the window for the first time.
3	Activates the window and displays it as a maximized window.
7	Displays the window as a minimized window.
	The active window remains active.

The modification made to the following code ensures that the Notepad window is active.

```
<package>
    <job id="vbs">
        <script language="VBScript">
        set WshShell = WScript.CreateObject("WScript.Shell")
        strDesktop = WshShell.SpecialFolders("Desktop")
        set oShellLink = WshShell.CreateShortcut(strDesktop & "\Shortcut
Script.lnk")
        oShellLink.TargetPath = WScript.ScriptFullName

        oShellLink.WindowStyle = 1

        oShellLink.Hotkey = "CTRL+SHIFT+N"
        oShellLink.IconLocation = "notepad.exe, 0"
        oShellLink.Description = "Shortcut Script"
        oShellLink.WorkingDirectory = strDesktop
        oShellLink.Save
        WScript.Echo oShellLink.FullName
        </script>
    </job>
</package>
```

WorkingDirectory

The WorkingDirectory property is used to assign a working directory to a shortcut, or to identify the working directory used by a shortcut.

```
object.WorkingDirectory = strWorkingDirectory
```

❏   object: WshShortcut object.

❏   strWorkingDirectory: A string. The directory in which the shortcut starts.

```
<package>
    <job id="vbs">
        <script language="VBScript">
        set WshShell = WScript.CreateObject("WScript.Shell")
        strDesktop = WshShell.SpecialFolders("Desktop")
        set oShellLink = WshShell.CreateShortcut(strDesktop & "\Shortcut
Script.lnk")
        oShellLink.TargetPath = WScript.ScriptFullName
        oShellLink.WindowStyle = 1
        oShellLink.Hotkey = "CTRL+SHIFT+N"
        oShellLink.IconLocation = "notepad.exe, 0"
        oShellLink.Description = "Shortcut Script"

        oShellLink.WorkingDirectory = strDesktop

        oShellLink.Save
        WScript.Echo oShellLink.FullName
        </script>
    </job>
</package>
```

WshShortcut Methods

The WshShortcut object has one method:

❏ Save

The Save method saves a shortcut object to disk.

```
object.Save
```

❏ object: WshShortcut or WshUrlShortcut object.

After you have used the CreateShortcut method to create a shortcut object and set the shortcut object's properties, you use the Save method to save the shortcut object to the hard drive. The Save method uses the information in the shortcut object's FullName property to determine where to place the shortcut object on a hard drive.

Shortcuts can only be created to system objects — files, directories, and drives. Shortcuts cannot be created to printer or scheduled tasks.

The WshUrlShortcut Object

The WshUrlShortcut object allows you to create shortcuts to Internet resource using script. It is a child object of the WshShell object. You must use the WshShell method's CreateShortcut to create a WshUrlShortcut object. This file would be saved as a .wsf Windows Script file.

```
WshShell.CreateShortcut(strDesktop & "\URLShortcut.lnk")

<package>
    <job id="vbs">
        <script language="VBScript">
        set WshShell = WScript.CreateObject("WScript.Shell")
        set oUrlLink = WshShell.CreateShortcut(strDesktop & "\Wrox Web Site.url")
        oUrlLink.TargetPath = "http://www.wrox.com"
        oUrlLink.Save
        </script>
    </job>
</package>
```

WshUrlShortcut Properties

The WshUrlShortcut object has two properties:

❏ FullName

❏ TargetPath

FullName

The FullName property returns the fully qualified path of the shortcut object's target.

```
object.FullName
```

❏ object: WshUrlShortcut object.

The `FullName` property contains a read-only string value that gives the fully qualified path to the shortcut's target. This file would be saved as a `.wsf` Windows Script file.

```
<package>
    <job id="vbs">
        <script language="VBScript">
        set WshShell = WScript.CreateObject("WScript.Shell")
        set oUrlLink = WshShell.CreateShortcut(strDesktop & "\Wrox Web Site.url")
        oUrlLink.TargetPath = "http://www.wrox.com"
        oUrlLink.Save

        WScript.Echo oUrlLink.FullName

        </script>
    </job>
</package>
```

TargetPath

The `TargetPath` property gives the path to the shortcut's executable file.

```
object.TargetPath
```

❑   object: `WshUrlShortcut` object.

This property is for the shortcut's target path only. Any arguments provided must be placed in the `Argument`'s property. This file would be saved as a `.wsf` Windows Script file.

```
<package>
    <job id="vbs">
        <script language="VBScript">
        set WshShell = WScript.CreateObject("WScript.Shell")
        set oUrlLink = WshShell.CreateShortcut(strDesktop & "\Wrox Web Site.url")

        oUrlLink.TargetPath = "http://www.wrox.com"

        oUrlLink.Save
        WScript.Echo oUrlLink.FullName
        </script>
    </job>
</package>
```

WshUrlShortcut Methods

The `WshUrlShortcut` object has one method:

❑   Save

The `Save` method saves a shortcut object to disk.

```
object.Save
```

❑   object: `WshUrlShortcut` object.

After you have used the CreateShortcut method to create a shortcut object and set the shortcut object's properties, you use the Save method to save the shortcut object to the hard drive. The Save method uses the information in the shortcut object's FullName property to determine where to place the shortcut object on a hard drive. This file would be saved as a .wsf Windows Script file.

```
<package>
    <job id="vbs">
        <script language="VBScript">
        set WshShell = WScript.CreateObject("WScript.Shell")
        set oUrlLink = WshShell.CreateShortcut(strDesktop & "\Wrox Web Site.url")
        oUrlLink.TargetPath = "http://www.wrox.com"
        oUrlLink.Save
        WScript.Echo oUrlLink.FullName
        </script>
    </job>
</package>
```

Summary

You covered a lot in this chapter. Here's a recap of the topics you looked at:

❑ The tools needed to get started writing scripts with Windows Script Host

❑ Ways in which WSH can be used, including the creation of custom solutions that integrate scripting with COM components

❑ The cscript.exe and wscript.exe execution environments and how they differ

❑ How to customize the behavior of individual scripts through the use of .wsh configuration files

❑ A detailed examination of the object model available to WSH developers

Windows Script Components

In this chapter, you examine Windows Script Components including their structure and how to create and register them. Later in the chapter, you'll see how to use classes in your components. If you are used to using XML, then the structure of the script here will be familiar to you and that will be a huge advantage. If not, work carefully through the examples and all will become clear!

What Are Windows Script Components?

Windows Script Components are interpreted COM components (they have to be interpreted because VBScript and all other scripting languages are interpreted). Structurally, they are XML-based files that contain script code. Within the files themselves you can use VBScript, JScript, Python, PScript, PERLScript, or any other scripting language. As always, the focus in this chapter is on using VBScript (for obvious reasons), but it is possible to use the scripting language of your choice.

The script components are interpreted by the Script Component Runtime, which exposes the internal properties and methods, fires the events, and makes the component look like a compiled COM component to the calling application. You'll look at the Script Component Runtime in more detail in the next section. Script components are full COM components, and have the ability to call others COM components. They also have some interfaces built into the Active Server Pages library and Internet Explorer DHTML behaviors that make it very easy to build these components for the Web.

One important point to note is that script components are not designed for use as early bound access objects. Early bound access gives you information about the object you are accessing while you are building your program, and it's normally faster when running your program to use early bound access. Late bound access means that there is no information available at compile time about the object being accessed, and everything is evaluated dynamically at runtime. If you reference a script component as an early bound component then your application will generate a runtime error. This is a common issue when using script components, which crops up all the time. Keep them late bound and you will have fewer problems implementing them.

You might be wondering, why you would want to use these when you could use Visual Basic to build a standard COM component instead. The main reason is that Windows Script Components don't require a compiler. The minimum that you will need to build script components is the good old Windows Notepad or another simple text editor. Script components are also a quick and easy way to encapsulate functions and routines that you write in VBScript. By doing this you can create a library of your source code. Finally, if you still need convincing, the ASP interfaces allow you to directly access the Active Server Pages library for quick and easy integration with your Internet or intranet sites.

What Tools Do You Need?

Before you move on, you need to get your toolkit in order. Here's a list of items that you must have to create script components.

- ❑ VBScript 5.0 libraries or later (use the 5.6 libraries if possible): You need to have the VBScript 5.0 libraries (preferably the latest 5.6 libraries) on your machine to run script components properly. Script components use the Windows Script Host when they run, so you'll also need that. Luckily, all this will be installed with the scripting libraries.

- ❑ Internet Explorer 5.0 or later (Internet Explorer 6.0 or 7.0 preferred)

- ❑ The Script Component Wizard (optional): You can create Windows Script Components with nothing more than Notepad and your imagination, but if you plan on doing a lot of scripting, you may find it a little tedious to do it all by hand. Microsoft provides the Script Component Wizard (which you can find at `www.microsoft.com/scripting/`— the precise URL for this varies but if you access the download section of the scripting area you will find it there. You are looking for a file called `wz10en.exe`) to help speed up the creation of the script component framework.

- ❑ A copy of the Script Component documentation (optional but might be useful, especially if you want to venture into more complex areas)

All these downloads are available free of charge from the Microsoft Web site.

The Script Component Runtime

Because Script Components are interpreted during runtime (as they are run), there is need for an interpreter to be installed on the client system. The Script Component Runtime (`scrobj.dll`) is the interpreter used to control calls between clients and script components. The runtime implements the basic COM interfaces for the component (`IUnknown`) and handles some of the basic COM methods (`QueryInterface`, `AddRef`) in the same way that the Visual Basic runtime handles the low-level COM routines of Visual Basic components.

Because you are running through an interpreter, your script components will look different from other COM components in the registry. Let's examine this in a little more detail. Assume that your object is called "`Math.WSC`" and that you're calling this object through script.

```
Set objMath = CreateObject("Math.WSC")
```

The first thing that happens is that the registry will be searched for the `Math.WSC` entry under `HKEY_CLASSES_ROOT`. If you look up the `GUID` (Globally Unique IDentifier) under `HKEY_CLASSES_ROOT\CLSID`, then it brings you to information for your COM component. Notice that the `InprocServer32` key is actually `scrobj.dll`, not the script component file itself. You're actually creating the `scrobj.dll` component when you call our `CreateObject` statement. The `scrobj.dll` file knows to look at the `ScriptletURL` key for the location of your component. It now knows that you need to look at that path for the actual object for the method calls.

Notice that the key is named `ScriptletURL`. This implies that these can be called over the Internet. Don't worry about this just yet, because this is covered later in the chapter. There is a bit more to know about script components first.

Script Component Files and Wizard

Now it's time to look at how to create the actual script component. As mentioned previously, you can build script files by hand, however, Microsoft makes a free wizard available for building a script component file, automating a lot of the laborious tasks when creating script components. The wizard simply builds the XML framework that defines your component. There's nothing at all to stop you creating this yourself if you know how it's done, however, XML is very strict and mistakes are easily made. Of course, the best way to find out how it's done is to use the wizard first, so let's do that.

Also, I placed your discussion below into steps.

1. Invoke the wizard under Vista/XP by clicking Start ➪ All Programs ➪ Microsoft Windows Script ➪ Windows Script Component Wizard (for other operating systems click Start ➪ Programs ➪ Microsoft Windows Script ➪ Windows Script Component Wizard shortcut). Step 1 of the Script Component Wizard is shown in Figure 16-1.

Figure 16-1

2.   Define the component. Tell the wizard the name of the component, along with its `ProgID`. One point to note is that script components use a special `ProgID` that defines the component. By default, the `ProgID` of the component will be `componentname.WSC`. Don't worry though, this can be changed in this step or after the component file has been created. Script components can also maintain version information just like any other COM component, as you can see in the `Version` field. This is very useful for keeping track of updates. Note that the `Location` in this dialog is simply the location of the source files that the wizard produces. The location of the source files will not be important to the actual Windows operating system until you register the component.

3.   Once you are satisfied with the settings that you have chosen for the various options (some you have huge scope over, such as version, others less so), select the `Next` button to go to the second step of the wizard. Step 2 of the Script Component Wizard is shown in Figure 16-2. When you have selected the options that you want, select the `Next` button to move to step 3 of the wizard. The options include the following:

Figure 16-2

❑   Language select: Windows Script Components can use VBScript or JScript natively, but other scripting platforms such as Python and PERL can be used as well if the proper interpreter is installed on the computer. Two options under the implements section need a little extra background information. These are DHTML behaviors and Active Server Pages.

❑   Special implementation support: DHTML behaviors are simple, lightweight components that interface with some of the DHTML objects and events of Internet Explorer. ASP support allows a script component to gain direct access to the ASP object model. The ASP object model exposes the vast `ASP Request`, `Response`, `Application`, `Session`, and `Server` objects.

DHTML components are beyond the scope of this chapter, but for more information you can refer to the Microsoft Scripting site and the MSDN Web Workshop (`http://msdn.microsoft.com/library`). Active Server Pages support will be covered in more detail in this chapter, and ASP itself will be covered later on in the book.

❑ Error checking and debugging can be selected as options. If you select debugging, you'll be allowed to use the script debugger. The script debugger can be found at `http://msdn.microsoft.com/scripting/`, and using it is the only way to debug a script component. It gives you the ability to check variables and view data, and works in a way very similar to the Visual Basic debugging tools.

4. In step 3 of the wizard, shown in Figure 16-3, define the properties of your object and then click the Next button. You can define the name, type, and default values for the component:

Figure 16-3

❑ The `Type` setting is not the data type but the property type, which can be either `Read/Write`, `Read-Only`, or `Write-Only`. The `Default` entry allows you to specify a default value for the property. The following code listing shows a read/write property with a default value of `5`.

```
Dim ReadWriteProperty
ReadWriteProperty = 5
```

❑ Note that this is how the wizard declares a variable that will be accessed by a property. This should be changed to read.

```
Private ReadWriteProperty
ReadWriteProperty = 5
```

❑ This ensures that the variable is private to the script component. If this isn't done the variable would be public, as would the property accessing it, which could in turn lead to problems and conflicts.

5. The fourth step of the wizard, shown in Figure 16-4, brings you to the methods of your component. Add a few methods here for your `Math` component. The Script Component Wizard will generate all methods as functions. If you want you can manually change these to subprocedures later if you don't need return values. It is an inconvenience that this can't be set in the wizard but again because there is nothing you can do about that, there's no point worrying about it here. Specify the name of the method as well as the parameter list and click the Next button. When adding parameters, be sure to separate them with a comma, so that the parameter list looks like the following:

```
param1, param2, param3, ...
```

Figure 16-4

Again, remember that VBScript uses only variants, so you don't need to specify a type. If you go as far as trying to specify a type you will get an error. For similar reasons, you also can't specify a return type. The use of variant data types does reduce overall performance somewhat because variants are the largest data type that can be used, and are designed to represent any other data type, so each time a variant is called the application must decide what format the variable should be in. But since there is nothing we can do about that, there's no point worrying about it.

6. The fifth step of the wizard (shown in Figure 16-5) allows you to specify the events for your component. This is one of the most exciting areas of script components. You'll see a little more on events in script components later in this section. The `Math` component won't actually use events as such. If you do want to have events in your objects, enter one event name per line.

A previous version of the Script Component Wizard had a bug that ignored any entries in this section. If you discover that you are affected by this, you must add events manually once the component has been created. This is discussed in more detail later in the chapter. If you are affected by this, we suggest that you upgrade to the latest release of the Script Component Wizard.

Figure 16-5

7. Once you are satisfied with the layout of the events, press the Next button to move to the final step of the wizard, shown in Figure 16-6. This final step gives you some information about your component and some of the settings that you have selected. If you find any errors or omissions at this point, then you can press the Back button to return to the previous steps and make the necessary changes. Click Finish to close the wizard.

Figure 16-6

Once you click `Finish`, the wizard will create a skeleton component like that in the following code example (note that the `classid` for your code will be different for this):

```xml
<?xml version="1.0"?>
<component>

<registration
 description="Math"
 progid="Math.WSC"
 version="1.00"
 classid="{585c5e81-addf-4006-993a-9701d7c4a41b}"
>
</registration>

<public>
 <property name="ReadOnlyProperty">
        <get/>
 </property>
 <property name="WriteOnlyProperty">
        <put/>
 </property>
 <property name="ReadWriteProperty">
        <get/>
        <put/>
 </property>
 <method name="Add">
        <PARAMETER name="X"/>
        <PARAMETER name="Y"/>
 </method>
 <method name="Subtract">
        <PARAMETER name="X"/>
        <PARAMETER name="Y"/>
 </method>
 <method name="Multiply">
        <PARAMETER name="X"/>
        <PARAMETER name="Y"/>
 </method>
 <method name="Divide">
        <PARAMETER name="X"/>
        <PARAMETER name="Y"/>
 </method>
 <event name="CalcError"/>
</public>

<implements type="Behavior" id="Behavior"/>

<script language="VBScript">
<![CDATA[

dim ReadOnlyProperty
dim WriteOnlyProperty
dim ReadWriteProperty
```

```
function get_ReadOnlyProperty()
 get_ReadOnlyProperty = ReadOnlyProperty
end function

function put_WriteOnlyProperty(newValue)
 WriteOnlyProperty = newValue
end function

function get_ReadWriteProperty()
 get_ReadWriteProperty = ReadWriteProperty
end function

function put_ReadWriteProperty(newValue)
 ReadWriteProperty = newValue
end function

function Add(X, Y)
 Add = "Temporary Value"
end function

function Subtract(X, Y)
 Subtract = "Temporary Value"
end function

function Multiply(X, Y)
 Multiply = "Temporary Value"
end function

function Divide(X, Y)
 Divide = "Temporary Value"
end function

]]>
</script>

</component>
```

If your code looks like the earlier listing, you have now created a Windows Script COM Component. Now let's take a look at it in a little more detail.

Exposing Properties, Methods, and Events

The next thing to do is to actually define the properties, methods, and events that your component needs to contain.

Properties

Properties within script components can be Read/Write, Read-Only, or Write-Only. They are implemented within the script file using `<property></property>` tags. Within these tags you set the get and put options for the property. The get options are used for reading the values and the put options are for writing to the properties. The following code example lists the structure that's created to first declare the three types of properties.

```
<property name="ReadOnlyProperty">
        <get/>
</property>
<property name="WriteOnlyProperty">
        <put/>
</property>
<property name="ReadWriteProperty">
        <get/>
```

The properties are then actually defined within script code later in the script file.

```
<script language="VBScript">
<![CDATA[


dim ReadOnlyProperty
dim WriteOnlyProperty
dim ReadWriteProperty

function get_ReadOnlyProperty()
 get_ReadOnlyProperty = ReadOnlyProperty
end function

function put_WriteOnlyProperty(newValue)
 WriteOnlyProperty = newValue
end function

function get_ReadWriteProperty()
 get_ReadWriteProperty = ReadWriteProperty
end function

function put_ReadWriteProperty(newValue)
 ReadWriteProperty = newValue
end function
function Add(X, Y)
 Add = "Temporary Value"
end function

function Subtract(X, Y)
 Subtract = "Temporary Value"
end function

function Multiply(X, Y)
 Multiply = "Temporary Value"
end function

function Divide(X, Y)
 Divide = "Temporary Value"
end function

]]>
</script>
```

You can script any additional logic within the get and put functions of the properties. This example hasn't included any real properties. Later on, when you look at classes, you'll actually see an example that does use properties.

Remember that script components can implement other COM objects, so you can create an ADO component, access LDAP (Lightweight Directory Access Protocol) and Exchange, or even call Microsoft Word and Excel. The sky is the limit with script components!

Methods

Methods in script components are defined within <method></method> tags in the object definition section of the script file. Parameters for a method use a <parameter> definition for the values, as you can see in the following code example.

```
<public>
    <method name="mNoParameters">
    </method>
    <method name="mWithParameters">
        <PARAMETER name="var1"/>
        <PARAMETER name="var2"/>
    </method>
</public>
```

The <parameter> tag simply defines the name of the input parameters. Remember that everything that comes from the Script Component Wizard is, by default, a function within the script components and no return type is specified because all variables are of the variant data type. However, you are free to use subprocedures as your methods in place of functions.

The actual method code is within the script tags of the script component.

```
<script language="VBScript">
<![CDATA[

Function mNoParameters()
    mNoParameters = "Temporary Value"
End Function
Function mWithParameters(var1, var2)
    mWithParameters = "Temporary Value"
End Function

]]>
</script>
```

Note that all methods that are created through the Windows Script Component Wizard return the value "Temporary Value". You need to change this (unless you really need a function that returns "Temporary Value"!). You also need to declare any temporary variables before the function definitions.

Let's add the real methods to your `Math` component.

```vbscript
<script language="VBScript">
<![CDATA[

Private ReadOnlyProperty
Private WriteOnlyProperty
Private ReadWriteProperty

function get_ReadOnlyProperty()
 get_ReadOnlyProperty = ReadOnlyProperty
end function

function put_WriteOnlyProperty(newValue)
 WriteOnlyProperty = newValue
end function

function get_ReadWriteProperty()
 get_ReadWriteProperty = ReadWriteProperty
end function

function put_ReadWriteProperty(newValue)
 ReadWriteProperty = newValue
end function

function Add(X, Y)

 Add = X + Y

end function


function Subtract(X, Y)

 Subtract = X - Y

end function


function Multiply(X, Y)

 Multiply = X * Y

end function


function Divide(X, Y)

 Divide = X / Y

end function

]]>
</script>
```

Something that is not in the WSC documentation (because it's specific to the scripting language you use) is that you can use the `byval` (by value) and `byref` (by reference) keywords within the parameter declaration of the method. By default in VBScript, all values are passed `byref`, so any changes to the variables in the method will change the underlying value in the calling function.

JScript variables are all passed `byval` *because JScript cannot pass a variable* `byref`*.*

Events

Events are defined within `<event></event>` tags in the object definition of the script file.

There was a bug in an older release (we can't call it a version because the Windows Script Component Wizard is still in version 1.0) of Windows Script Component Wizard, which meant that it did not create the events you specified. All event declarations had to be created manually within a script file. The latest release of the Windows Script Component Wizard behaves correctly.

```
<public>
    <method name="mNoParameters">
        </method>
    <event name="MethodCalled">
        </event>
</public>
```

The event is actually fired through the `FireEvent()` method. `FireEvent()` is called within the script of the script component. The event itself should also be described here, using the form `ComponentName_EventName`.

```
<script language="VBScript">
<![CDATA[

function mNoParameters()
  FireEvent("MethodCalled")
  mNoParameters = "Temporary Value"
end function

sub MyComponent_MethodCalled()
  'some event handling code
end sub

]]>
</script>
```

Script components can also handle events using an `<implements>` tag within the script definition. The syntax for capturing events in a script component is defined as follows:

```
<implements type="COMHandlerName" [id="internalName"] [default=fAssumed]>
    handler-specific information here
</implements>
```

The `COMHandlerName` is the name of the handler (ASP or behavior) or the COM object that is being handled. `InternalName` is an optional parameter that allows you to define a variable name for the COM handler. The `fAssumed` property is a Boolean flag (the default value is `True`) that indicates `InternalName` is assumed in scripts. If you set this to `False`, you would hide some members in the `<implements>` tag.

There are two built-in COM handlers: ASP and behaviors. The ASP COM handler is discussed later in this chapter.

Registration Information

To register a Windows Script Component, you need to have the Script Component Runtime (scrobj.dll) on your machine and have it properly registered. This file is automatically registered when you install the script engines for VBScript or JScript. Once you have the scripting runtime and a valid script component (.wsc) file, then you can register the component. Three methods are available for properly registering a WSC file:

❑ The easiest way to register and unregister a script component is to right-click the component file in Windows Explorer and select Register or Unregister from the pop-up menu. This is shown in Figure 16-7 and is both easy and convenient to use.

Figure 16-7

❑ In the event that you need to manually register and unregister a component, you can still use regsvr32.exe. If you are using an old version of regsvr32 that comes with Windows or Visual Studio, then you can use the following command.

```
regsvr32 scrobj.dll /n /i:Path/component_name.wsc
```

New versions of regsvr32 that ship with the script component packages can directly register the script component file.

```
regsvr32 path/component_name.wsc
```

❑ You can also add a registration entry into the script component that defines the registration behavior. You can add the <registration> tag to the component as defined in the following code:

```
<registration progid="progID" classid="GUID" description="description"
    version="version" [remotable=remoteFlag]>
<script>
    (registration and unregistration script)
</script>
</registration>
```

Within the <script> tags you can add a Register() and Unregister() event that will be fired whenever the component is registered or unregistered on the system. The progID attribute is optional, but you must have data for either the classid or progID in order for the component to register. If you leave either classid or progID out, then it will automatically be generated when the component is registered.

All of these methods will properly register a script component file on your system. This is nice, but what about remote components? Well, the short and simple (and sweet!) answer is that Windows Script Components can be registered remotely.

To make the components DCOM-ready, you need to follow these four simple steps:

1. Determine the `progid` and `clsid` of the component. Local components do not need an entry for a `clsid`. If it is absent, this tells the component to create a `clsid` entry at registration time.

2. On every local machine that needs to access the component, add an entry into the registry under `HKEY_CLASSES_ROOT\componentProgID`. Here `ComponentProgID` is the `ProgID` of the script component. This is a job ideally suited to Windows Script Host.

3. Beneath this entry, create a `CLSID` key and set the value to that of the `clsid` of the script component.

4. Set `remotable=true` within the `<registration>` tags of the component.

Another way to simplify this process would be to register the component on the server and export the registry key information using `regedit`. You can then copy the exported `.reg` file from `regedit` to each machine that needs the component. Once the file has been copied to the local machine, double-click the `.reg` file to merge the data into the registry. You now have a DCOM-ready script component that can be used throughout the enterprise.

You can quickly test the component with a short test script. Save the following code as a file called `testmathcomp.vbs`, and then run it after you've registered your `Math` component:

```
dim obj
set obj = wscript.createobject("math.wsc")
msgbox obj.add(15, 9)
msgbox obj.subtract(15, 9)
msgbox obj.multiply(15, 9)
msgbox obj.divide(28, 4)
set obj = nothing
```

Creating the Script Component Type Libraries

Script components are no different from any other COM component and can have type libraries generated. Type libraries are used in some environments (such as Visual Basic) for enabling events or for enabling the use of IntelliSense by programs such as Visual InterDev. Type libraries contain descriptions of the COM components and also help with early binding of objects or using tools such as OLE2VIEW to view the declarations and constants in a component.

To generate a type library for a script component, simply right-click the script component file and select the Generate Type Library option from the pop-up context menu, as shown in Figure 16-8.

Figure 16-8

Script components can also automatically generate a type library for themselves when the `Register` method is called. When this method is called, the component uses the information that exists within the `<registration>` tags. The syntax of the `<registration>` tag is as follows:

```
<registration progid="progID" classid="GUID" description="description"
    version="version" [remotable=remoteFlag]>
    <script>
    (registration and unregistration script)
    </script>
</registration>
```

Remember that both the `progID` and `classid` items are optional, but one of the two must be specified for the tags to be valid. The `progID` is the component name while the `classid` entry is for the `GUID` of the component. If the `classid` entry is left blank, then a `GUID` will be assigned to the component at registration time by the system.

Both description and version are optional as well. If you used a registration entry with your previous Math component, then you would add the following `<registration>` tags.

```
<registration
  description="My Simple Math Component"
  progid="Math.WSC"
  version="1.0"
  classid="{585C5E81-ADDF-4006-993A-9701D7C4A41B}">
  <script language="VBScript">
  <![CDATA[
    Function Register()
      Set oComponent = CreateObject("Scriptlet.GenerateTypeLib")
      oComponent.AddURL "C:\Program Files\Microsoft Windows Script\Math.wsc"
```

`AddURL` allows you to add other component files into the type library. If you used or exposed other components, then you would want to add them into one type library rather than using multiple files.

```
oComponent.Path = "C:\Program Files\Microsoft Windows Script\Math.tlb"
```

You add the path indicating where the component will be stored. If this is left blank, the type library is written to the current location of the script component.

```
oComponent.Doc = "Math component typelib" ' Documentation string.
oComponent.GUID = "{a1e1e3e0-a252-11d1-9fa1-00a0c90fffc0}"
oComponent.Name = "MathComponent" ' Internal name for tlb.
oComponent.MajorVersion = 1
oComponent.MinorVersion = 0
oComponent.Write
```

Here is the code that writes the type library to the hard drive.

```
    oComponent.Reset
 End Function
]]>
</script>
</registration>
```

Remember, if you plan to use this component through DCOM, then you also need to add this line.

```
remotable=true
```

This line of code tells the component that it needs to set itself up in the registry for DCOM.

How to Reference Other Components

A script component file can contain multiple components within itself. You can easily create a library of components just as you would in Visual Basic. However, you cannot use the Windows Script Component Wizard to do this, so you need to create one manually. The script components use a series of <package></package> tags to create script libraries. For example, you define a series of components within a file as follows:

```
<package>
    <component id="COMObj1">

    </component>

    <component id="COMObj2">

    </component>

    <component id="COMObj3">

    </component>
</package>
```

Within each script you add the appropriate properties, methods, and events for each component. You also need to add the necessary registration information.

You can reference another component within the package by using the CreateComponent function. To reference COMObj2 in the preceding code, you set a reference to an object using CreateComponent.

```
Set oComponent = CreateComponent("COMObj2")
```

This gives you a runtime reference of COMObj2. How does this help? It allows you to add components that implement ASP interfaces and DHTML behaviors, while at the same time exposing properties and methods to other client applications. Your ASP and DHTML components can access all of the properties and methods of the COM component and reduce the amount of redundant code.

While the Windows Script Component Wizard can't help you with all of it, it can build the individual objects for you. Once all of the objects have been created, you can then build a package and cut and paste the contents of the individual files into the one package.

Script Components for ASP

ASP script components include the functionality of the Active Server Pages library to allow for web-enabled script components. These script components are called from within ASP pages and can contribute greatly to code reuse of ASP components and business logic and also save time by separating functional code from the web page that displays it.

To ASP-enable a script component, you must add an <implements> tag with a reference to the ASP COM handler.

```
<implements type="ASP">
</implements>
```

Once the <implements> tag is set up, the script component will have a reference to ASP and can make use of the Response, Request, Session, Application, and Server ASP objects. For example, you can have a component that outputs the current date and time to an ASP page. The script component would look like the following:

```
<component id="ASPDateTimeObject">
<registration progid="ASPDateTimeObject"/>

<public>
  <method name="OutputDateTime"/>
</public>
<implements type="ASP"/>
<script language="VBScript">
<![CDATA[

Sub OutputDateTime()
  Response.Write("It is currently " & Time & " on " & Date)
End Sub

]]>
</script>
</component>
```

The code for the ASP page creates this object and calls the OutputDateTime method.

```
<html>
<head>
<title>ASP Script Objects</title>
</head>
<body>
<h1>ASP Script Objects</h1>
```

```
<%

Set objDateTime = CreateObject("ASPDateTimeObject")%>

objDateTime.OutputDateTime()

set objDateTime = nothing

%>
```

```
</body>
</html>
```

An ASP script component can also contain complex database functions, which can be reused for generic database output. Because script objects can call other COM components, you have access to all ADO functions, Office COM libraries, and third-party objects. That is a lot of power!

So, how do ASP script components operate? When the script object is called from an ASP page, the script object is run in the same namespace (or process space) as the calling page. This gives the script component direct access to the page, so it can use all of the intrinsic ASP objects, and all output to ASP is directed back to the page. The script component and the ASP page both see the exact same objects. This is similar to creating a Visual Basic COM component that implements the OnStartPage method. When a Visual Basic COM component has this method, ASP will call it automatically and send a reference to the ASP library, thus giving Visual Basic full control over ASP.

If you're familiar with using ASP, you might be wondering why this is better than using #include directives. Whenever you include a library into ASP files, the entire contents of the file is merged with the source file. As an example, say that you have a library that contains 50 relatively complicated functions. A library like this can easily run into several hundred, if not thousands, of lines of source code. If you wanted to use only one function out of the 50, you are still forced into a position where you must add all of the remaining lines of redundant code, code that will need processing. What if you don't happen to use any of the functions because of the way the page is processed? Too bad, because ASP must still merge all of the included files to process the page. This isn't an effective use of system resources that might be better needed elsewhere.

An ASP script component, on the other hand, can contain all of the library functions that you use, but it is only loaded when it is needed. If the page logic does not require a function, then the object is never loaded and the page contains less code and needs less processing which makes it smaller and faster. ASP script components are by far a better design choice for ASP pages because you can organize individual components with related functions. You're not required to add #include directives for every page that might need a function. You can also remotely execute complex scripts on middle-tier servers. Included files, on the other hand, run directly on the web server and cannot take advantage of n-tier architectures in intranet and Internet applications.

Compile-Time Error Checking

When you register your script component something else happens at the same time. The script syntax is also validated. You will receive error messages if there are scripting errors or if the XML cannot be validated. The error messages are not very verbose and give you little more than a position in the file and possibly a snippet of the affected code.

As an example, add a semicolon to your script (pretend you were converting the source from JScript).

```
function Add(X,Y)
   Add = X + Y;
end function
```

If you try to register this component, several dialog boxes pop up that show that there has been an error and that registration wasn't successful. The text shown in the error message gives the approximate location (expressed as line number followed by column number) of the error in the component. Unfortunately this is not usually completely accurate, but it's close. Also, it's not easy to count lines, let alone columns, in Notepad and this is where a text editor that gives line and column numbers comes in handy.

Compile-time error checking is far from perfect, but it will point you in the general direction of any errors that exist in your code.

Using VBScript Classes in Script Components

As you have seen previously, VBScript includes the ability to declare classes and class constructs. You can integrate a standard VBScript class into a Windows Script Component within the `<script></script>` tags in the data portion of the XML file. You still use the standard construct for classes.

```
class <classname>

    <internal class declaration>

end class
```

Limitations of VBScript Classes

There is one key limitation of using VBScript classes in Windows Script Components that you should be aware of: Class information is not exposed automatically. In essence, script components know nothing about the structure of an internal class. To expose the class to the outside world, you must wrap the class information around methods and properties declared in the script component file.

So, why use a class in a script component? Well, classes do not provide a lot of functionality for a small component, but a complex component can benefit from a class by helping a developer to organize the object structure in a more meaningful way. Large script components can get very complex because of the reliance on XML parsing, so your component may become harder to maintain over time. A well-defined class will always provide a more familiar structure to developers.

As you will see later in the chapter, you can include external source files. If you have defined many classes you can simply include the source file and provide a COM wrapper for the class definition. Remember that VBScript classes cannot be exposed automatically to COM, so you must provide a mechanism for other objects to access your class.

Using Internal Classes

In script components, you need a class construct and a series of methods and properties that wrap the internal class. You can take the Math component that you built earlier in the chapter and use it as a class wrapper. Initially your script component had the following form:

```
<?xml version="1.0"?>
<component>
<?component error="true" debug="true"?>

<registration
  description="Math"
  progid="Math.Scriptlet"
  version="1.00"
  classid="{b0a847a0-63c2-11d3-aa0e-00a0cc322d8b}"
>
</registration>
<public>
    <method name="Add">
        <PARAMETER name="X"/>
        <PARAMETER name="Y"/>
    </method>
    <method name="Subtract">
        <PARAMETER name="X"/>
        <PARAMETER name="Y"/>
    </method>
    <method name="Multiply">
        <PARAMETER name="X"/>
        <PARAMETER name="Y"/>
    </method>

    <method name="Divide">
        <PARAMETER name="X"/>
        <PARAMETER name="Y"/>
    </method>
</public>

<script language="VBScript">
<![CDATA[

function Add(X,Y)
    Add = X + Y
end function

function Subtract(X,Y)
    Subtract = X - Y
end function
```

(continued)

```
function Multiply(X,Y)
    Multiply = X * Y
end function

function Divide(X,Y)
    Divide = X / Y
end function

]]>
</script>

</component>
```

Within the `<script>` tags, you can build a class that handles the methods of the script component.

```
<script language="VBScript">
<![CDATA[

Class clsMath

  Public Function Add(X, Y)
      Add = X + Y
  End Function

  Public Function Subtract(X, Y)
      Subtract = X - Y
  End Function

  Public Function Multiply(X, Y)
      Multiply = X * Y
  End Function

  Public Function Divide(X, Y)
      Divide = X / Y
  End Function

End Class

Private oMath
set oMath = new clsMath

Function Add(X,Y)
    Add = oMath.Add(X,Y)
End Function

Function Subtract(X,Y)
    Subtract = oMath.Subtract(X,Y)
End Function

Function Multiply(X,Y)
    Multiply = oMath.Multiply(X,Y)
End Function
```

```
Function Divide(X,Y)
    Divide = oMath.Divide(X,Y)
End Function

]]>
</script>
```

You can see that you've built a VBScript class and you have wrapped the functionality into the script component. This can provide a new level of flexibility to a script component, as you will see next.

Including External Source Files

You are not required to have the class declarations (or your source for that matter) in the file itself. A declaration within the <script> tag allows you to include an external source file. The src= declaration acts as an include for another file. This gives you the ability to move the class declarations to a .vbs (or a .txt file for that matter) file for later use. You can then leverage your external source files across the Windows Script Host as well as within Active Server Pages and script components.

You can move the class declaration from your math sample to math.vbs. The text of math.vbs is simply the entire class declaration.

```
Class clsMath

  Public Function Add(X, Y)
     Add = X + Y
  End Function

  Public Function Subtract(X, Y)
     Subtract = X - Y
  End Function

  Public Function Multiply(X, Y)
     Multiply = X * Y
  End Function

  Public Function Divide(X, Y)
     Divide = X / Y
  End Function

End Class
```

You then change the text of the Math component to include the new source file.

```
<script language="VBScript" src="math.vbs">
<![CDATA[

private oMath set oMath = new clsMath
```

When the component is instantiated you parse the script file, add any included files into the <script> tag, and continue processing. As far as COM is concerned, both internal class declaration and the external class declaration are identical.

Summary

Windows Script Components provide added flexibility to web pages and can tightly integrate into your ASP code. You can use these objects as stand-alone COM components or you can have them interact directly with ASP. All you need is some scripting, a little bit of XML know-how, basic understanding of the Script Component Wizard, and a quick run through `regsvr32` and you have a perfectly formed and ready-to-run script component!

Script Encoding

One thing that becomes immediately obvious to those who write script coming from a programming background is that anything they create using script is easily and readily visible to anyone and everyone else. You have no compiler to turn the code into something that only a machine can make sense of. This easily visible code was a real worry, but on the whole it didn't stop people from writing and using scripts, who saw massive advantages in scripting. Just as the open, plain-text nature of HTML made learning web design easier than say learning C#, the same "open book" format for scripts encouraged a huge explosion of script use on the Web. Thinking back to those times, some of it was pretty bad and looked ugly, but we didn't care because it was scripting and it made pages look more exciting than the others out there. Because it was so easy to see how scripts worked (and to copy the code from one page and paste it into another), the future of scripting was guaranteed.

But now the future of script use is well established and a bit of privacy isn't a bad thing. Programmers who use script want to regain some of the mystique that they once had using C# or VB (using script to solve a problem is a bit like a magician in a see-through jacket). Things have moved on a little bit from the days of scripts being a total free-for-all and you can do a few things to make it harder for script snoopers to see your secrets! Protecting your scripts is much more than just protecting your intellectual property — although there's nothing wrong with doing that!

Although most people out there are honest and don't bother to look at plain-text scripts, taking precautions against accidental changes (such as those done with Windows Script Host) makes sense. Take the real-life example of a WSH script that searches folders for particular files, copies them, and then deletes the originals; you don't want someone to tamper with that script so that it just deletes files (this actually happened and it wasn't done maliciously, but rather a genuine accident caused by someone unfamiliar with the script). If you use the Microsoft Script Encoder, the advantage is that if someone changes an encoded script modify — just one character changed — it no longer works. Encoding scripts can help protect curious users from themselves as much as from malicious attack.

In this chapter, you see primarily how to encode VBScript code with the Microsoft Script Encoder, and then examine other things that you can do to discourage script snooping. These won't be as effective as the Microsoft Script Encoder but they are worth bearing in mind and can be quite effective in appropriate circumstances. But before you get into all that, the next two sections discuss the limitations of encoding as well as some dos and don'ts you should keep in mind.

Limitations of Script Encoding

It's only fair that you inject a bit of reality and caution here. None of the methods that discourage script snoopers reviewed in this chapter (or this section) are 100 percent guaranteed. In fact, the best of them, the Microsoft Script Encoder, isn't really all that robust. Why? Because ultimately the browser must still be able to execute the script. This means that the browser is still able to decrypt the script, and because it needs to do this fast, Microsoft has deliberately used weak encryption. Of course, if you want to protect a script from viewing you can take an encryption program, such as PGP, and run that on your script. Taking all the proper precautions, you could be pretty guaranteed that your script would be safe — the problem is that it's so safe the browser can't do anything with it anymore!

Fortunately, script snoopers come in a variety of forms:

❑   Someone who wants to take a look at how it works or someone who wants to learn how script works

❑   Someone who wants to use or modify the script for benign purposes

❑   Someone who wants to modify the script for malicious purposes

They also come in a variety of skill levels:

❑   The lower skilled "casual" snooper

❑   The skilled "interested" snooper

❑   The skilled "determined" snooper

It doesn't really matter why someone is trying to snoop on your script (although that might factor into why you might want to protect the script); the real factor here is how skilled they are and how determined. Taking simple precautions deters the casual snooper and sends them on their way but if someone is really determined to see your script, and they are skilled, nothing here will stop them. That's the plain truth and while it sounds harsh, it is much harsher to find out the hard way.

Encoded Scripts — Dos and Don'ts

Before and after encoding there are a few dos and don'ts you should follow to ensure trouble-free scripts after encoding:

❑   Do keep an unencoded backup of the script.

❑   Do take care over correctly specifying the script language used.

❑   Do remove comments before encoding — after encoding they are useless and add significant bulk to the script.

❑   Do test the script before and after it is encoded to make sure it works.

❑   Don't make any changes to the script once encoded.

❑   Don't leave testing and debugging until the script is encoded!

❑   Don't expect script encoding to offer 100 percent code security. There are ways that the "determined" script snooper can get around it.

Encoding with the Microsoft Script Encoder

The Microsoft Script Encoder is a simple, easy-to-use command-line tool for script programmers to encode their scripts so that others cannot view or modify the source. (This works with JScript too, although you'll only be looking at VBScript here.)

The application is a script encoder. It encodes the script, but doesn't encrypt it. Encryption is different from encoding, but the difference is subtle. With both, you take a file and change its format but with encryption, the file is unusable until it is decrypted. Encoding changes the file from the point of view of a human reader but the script engine can still understand what the file does.

Availability and Installation

The Microsoft Script Encoder installation file is available free from Microsoft as a small download (approximately 130KB) from `http://msdn2.microsoft.com/en-us/library/ms950396.aspx`, and is available in English, Chinese (traditional), German, and Korean.

Installing the Microsoft Script Encoder is easy:

1.   Locate the download (the English language version is called `sce10en.exe` while the Chinese version is called `sce10cht.exe`, the German version `sce10de.exe`, and the Korean version `sce10ko.exe`).

2.   Double-click it and follow the prompts. The default installation location for the command-line application and the help files is `C:\Program Files\Windows Script Encoder`.

In addition to installing the command-line application and the help file, the installation application also modifies the Windows registry so that the system recognizes `.vbe` and `.jse` files (VBScript Encoded files and JScript Encoded files).

You do not need to install the Microsoft Script Encoder to run encoded script files. Only the programmer needs to install the encoder. As far as the client goes, the browser handles the decoding.

Using the Microsoft Script Encoder

The Microsoft Script Encoder is, as mentioned earlier, a command-line utility and doesn't come with a Windows interface. This means that it's not as easy to use as a GUI application. But the command line also has advantages because you'll be able to make use of it through batch files.

The Microsoft Script Encoder doesn't do any encoding itself; it uses the scripting runtime module (scrrun.dll) to do the encoding for it. All the Script Encoder executable does is provide a command-line mechanism for calling the scripting.encoder object implemented in the scripting runtime. This is very handy because it provides the programmer with an extensible mechanism for using encoding in their applications or in third-party applications. Microsoft did this to ensure that the programmer could use script encoding wherever they wanted, rather than only in a few specific areas.

Because scripting.encoder is simply a COM object, you can use it wherever any other COM object would be. This means you can extend the functions that the Script Encoder provides in your own applications.

Because the installation program doesn't add the path to the encoder to the PATH system variable, it isn't available from every folder in a command prompt window. So that using the Microsoft Script Encoder is smooth and trouble-free, we recommend you do one of the following:

❑   Add the path to the Microsoft Script Encoder (the default path is C:\Program Files\Windows Script Encoder) to the PATH system variable.

❑   Copy the Microsoft Script Encoder executable (screnc.exe) to the folder you'll use for script encoding.

❑   Copy all of the scripts you want to encode to the folder that the Microsoft Script Encoder uses.

Syntax

The easiest way to familiarize yourself with the syntax of the Microsoft Script Encoder is to begin using it. Open a command prompt window and navigate to C:\Program Files\Windows Script Encoder. (You can also run the Microsoft Script Encoder from the Run dialog box in the Start Menu of Windows.) Once there, type the following:

```
screnc /?
```

This results in a Help list for the application. This is a very useful reference when you are in a hurry! The output is shown in Figure 17-1.

Figure 17-1

The syntax for the Microsoft Script Encoder is as follows:

```
screnc [/s] [/f] [/xl] [/l defLanguage ] [/e defExtension] source destination
```

Here is a run-through of the switches that the application supports.

Switch	Optional or Required	Description
/?	Optional	Lists the Help for the Script Encoder.
/s	Optional	Specifies that the Script Encoder is to work silently, that is, it produces no screen output. If omitted, the default is to provide verbose output.
/f	Optional	Specifies that the output file will overwrite the input file. Note that this option destroys your original input source file, and perhaps your only unencoded copy of the script! If omitted, the output file is not overwritten.
/xl	Optional	Specifies that the @language directive is not added at the top of .asp files. If omitted, the @language directive is added at the top of all .asp files.
/l defLanguage	Optional	Specifies the default scripting language (JScript or VBScript) to be used during encoding. Script blocks within the file being encoded that do not contain a language attribute are assumed to be of this specified language. If omitted, JScript is the default language for HTML pages and scriptlets, and VBScript is the default for Active Server Pages. For plain-text files, the file extension (either .js or .vbs) is used to determine the default scripting language.
/e defExtension	Optional	Associates the input file with a specific file type. You use this when the input file's extension doesn't make the file type clear, that is, when the input file extension is not one of the recognized extensions, but the file content does fall into one of the recognized types. There is no default for this option. If a file with an unrecognized extension is encountered and this option is not specified, the Script Encoder fails for that unrecognized file. Recognized file extensions are .asa, .asp, .cdx, .htm, .html, .js, .sct, and .vbs.
source	Required	Specifies the name of the input file to be encoded. It can include any necessary path information relative to the current directory.
destination	Required	Specifies the name of the output file to be produced. It can include any necessary path information relative to the current directory.

Now, you need to put the previous table together with some examples. What follows are a few examples of the use of the Microsoft Script Encoder, each accompanied by a brief explanation of the results.

To encode	Use
the input file `unencoded.htm` and produce an output file called `encoded.htm`	`screnc unencoded.html encoded.html`
the input file `test.htm` and overwrite the input file with the encoded output file	`screnc /f test.htm`
all files with the `.ASP` file extension in the current directory and place the encoded output files in `c:\output`	`screnc *.asp c:\output`
all files in the current directory as `.asp` files and place them in `c:\output`	`screnc /e asp *.* c:\output`
encode input file `unencoded.htm` and produce output file `encoded.htm`, while ensuring that all script blocks that don't have a specified language attribute are encoded as VBScript	`screnc /l vbscript unencoded.htm encoded.htm`
every scriptlet file (`.sct`) in the current directory and overwrite each of them with encoded files, while not displaying a message	`screnc /s /f *.sct`

What Files Can I Encode?

The Microsoft Script Encoder is designed to work with certain file types. The Script Encoder can process four kinds of files:

- ❏ HTML
- ❏ ASP
- ❏ Plain text
- ❏ Scriptlets

HTML Files

The Microsoft Script Encoder can process any HTML file, but remember that it only acts on the script in the page, so encoding an HTML page that doesn't contain any script won't have any effect on it but also won't generate any message to say that it doesn't contain script.

The following is the code of page you'll use:

```
<html>
<head>
<title>Simple VBScript Example</title>
<script language="vbscript">
    Sub ButtonClicked
        window.alert("You clicked on the button!")
    End Sub
</script>
</head>
<body>
  <button name="Button1" type=BUTTON onclick="ButtonClicked">
  Click Me If You Can!!!
  </button>
</body>
</html>
```

For clarity, the preceding file has been named unencoded.htm. Now, take a look at how to use to the Microsoft Script Encoder to encode this file:

1. Copy this file to the folder that contains the Microsoft Script Encoder.

2. Open a command prompt window and navigate to that folder.

3. Type in the following, and then press Enter.

```
screnc unencoded.htm encoded.htm
```

If everything has worked and there were no errors of faults, no error messages display and the command prompt returns as shown in Figure 17-2. Many people are surprised by this and expect some sort of confirmation that everything has worked out right.

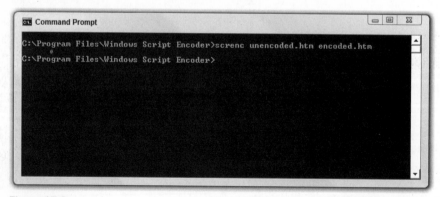

Figure 17-2

However, whereas in the beginning you had just the one HTML file (called unencoded.htm), you now have another new one — this one called encoded.htm. If you open a text editor and take a look at the source code for this new HTML page, you see some key differences as shown in (Figure 17-3).

```
<html>
<head>
<title>Simple VBScript Example</title>
<script
language="VBScript.Encode">#@ ~^YgAAAA==@#@&P ,PUE4,A!OYKx/VbmVn9@#@&, P,PP, Ak
 NKh lsnMYcJIGE,msr13+[ Kx Y4n,4;DYKx"r#@#@&P,P 2
N j!4@#@&DBoAAA==^#~@</script>
</head>
<body>
  <button name="Button1" type=BUTTON onclick="ButtonClicked">
  Click Me If You Can!!!
  </button>
</body>
</html>
```

Figure 17-3

In fact, two significant changes have been made: The script that previously was unencoded is now encoded (pretty obvious!) and the script language attribute value has been changed from VBScript to VBScript.Encode. Do not be alarmed by this as this is exactly as it should be and the browser will be able to run the script. To prove this, open the page in the browser and see if it still works. Click the button and a message box displays to show that indeed the VBScript code does still work (as shown in Figure 17-4)!

Figure 17-4

The great thing about the Microsoft Script Encoder is that you don't have to encode all the script on the page. You can choose where the encoding should start using the following encoding marker in your VBScript code:

```
'**Start Encode**
```

Note: For Jscript, the encoding marker would be `//**Start Encode**`.

Take a look at this modified example that follows. This example uses the encoding marker to begin encoding at the second subprocedure.

```
<html>
<head>
<title>Simple VBScript Example</title>
<script language="vbscript">
    Sub ButtonClicked
        window.alert("This is not encoded!")
    End Sub

'**Start Encode**
        Sub ButtonClicked2
        window.alert("This is encoded!")
    End Sub

</script>
</head>
<body>
  <button name="Button1" type=BUTTON onclick="ButtonClicked">
  Click Me If You Can!!!
  </button>

  <button name="Button2" type=BUTTON onclick="ButtonClicked2">
  Click On Me Too!!!
  </button>
</body>
</html>
```

Encoding the file alters any code that appears below the encoding marker. This results in the following output.

```
<html>
<head>
<title>Simple VBScript Example</title>
<script language="VBScript.Encode">
    Sub ButtonClicked
        window.alert("This is not encoded!")
    End Sub

'**Start Encode**#@~^YQAAAA==~,P~ @ # @&,PP,P, PUE8P EOOKxZ^rm0+Ny@ # @&P,P, _
P~P~Abx[WS1^+.OvJK4rkPr/,nmG9+9"J*@ # @ & P,P3x9Pj;(@ # @ &fhcAAA==^# @</script>

</head>
<body>
  <button name="Button1" type=BUTTON onclick="ButtonClicked">
  Click Me If You Can!!!
  </button>

  <button name="Button2" type=BUTTON onclick="ButtonClicked2">
  Click On Me Too!!!
  </button>
</body>
</html>
```

Both subprocedures work as exactly normal. There is no difference between the encoded code and the unencoded code when the page is loaded into Internet Explorer and the script run. The only difference is a visual one, that you can understand the unencoded script but not the encoded script.

Here's a great trick to prevent others from making changes to your copyright notices in scripts. Make your copyright notice part of the script! Place the copyright notice string into a variable and check to see if that variable is unaltered at runtime.

```
<html>
<head>
<title>Simple VBScript Example</title>
<script language="vbscript">

Dim strCopyright
strCopyright = "This script is copyright to me, 2007!"
'**Start Encode**
    Sub ButtonClicked
    If strCopyright = "This script is copyright to me, 2007!" Then
        MsgBox "Copyright notice is unaltered. Script cleared to continue ..."
        MsgBox "Script continues ..."
    Else
        MsgBox "Copyright notice is altered!!! Script halted!"
    End If
    End Sub
</script>
</head>
<body>
  <button name="Button1" type="BUTTON" onclick="ButtonClicked">
  Check copyright notice
  </button>
</body>
</html>
```

Encoding this script gives you the following:

```
<html>
<head>
<title>Simple VBScript Example</title>
<script language="VBScript.Encode">
Dim strCopyright
strCopyright = "This script is copyright to me, 2007!"
```

```
'**Start Encode**#@~ ^VAEAAA== ,P~@ # @&,PP,?!8P~EOYKx/sbm3□[@#@&PP,~ _
(0,/DD/W2zMkLtD ',JP4b/Pd^
Mk2Y,rkP^KwHDkTtD YKPh+BP+TZ&"r K4+x@ # @ & P,P,P P dTAG6,EZKwz.botO   WOk1n,kd,E _
    1VD+MnNcP ?1Dr2DPm^n1M+N,OGP1W         Yrx;n,R _
Rr~@ # @ & P ~~ ,PP~~,t/LAKa,Jj1DbwY,P1GxDkUE□/~
cRJ,@#@&,PP,3s/□@#@&P~ P~~,P~ HkLAK6~E;Wwz.bo4Y,UKYr1+,k/,1^O+M+ ["e"~~UmDb2Y,
t1^OnNeJ
,@#@&P  ,2UN,(0i@#@&~ ,PP3U9PjE(@#@&7V0AAA==^#~@</script>
```

```
</head>
<body>
  <button name="Button1" type="BUTTON" onclick="ButtonClicked">
  Check copyright notice
  </button>
</body>
</html>
```

Now, when you run the script with the unaltered copyright notice, the script proceeds normally. However, just making one small change to the copyright notice halts the script.

```
...
...Dim strCopyright
strCopyright = "This script is copyright to you instead, 2007!"
...
```

Figure 17-5 shows the result of such tampering! A message is shown indicating that the script has been tampered with. This message would be very hard to get rid of (certainly too hard for someone who wanted to borrow your code in the first place).

Figure 17-5

ASP Files

Because the ASP file format provides more information about script, encoding ASP files is a little more complex than encoding HTML. However, if you have a relatively simple ASP file that contains a single script element, you can run it through the Script Encoder and have it encoded without much trouble.

ASP lets you embed script code using the <%...%> notation and many ASP pages use this method rather than the alternate <SCRIPT runat="Server">. This presents a potential problem when encoding an ASP page because the <%...%> notation doesn't contain any language information, and the encoding mechanism needs that information to perform proper encoding. As it happens, the vast majority of ASP developers use VBScript as their programming language of choice. VBScript is also the default language for ASP. Based on these factors, the script encoder assumes that the default language is set to VBScript.

Here is a simple example so you can see the output you can expect. First, this is the unencoded page:

```
<html>
<head>
<title>Client/server Information</title>
</head>
<body>
<p>
<b>You are browsing this site with:</b>
<%Response.Write(Request.ServerVariables("http_user_agent"))%>
</p>
<p>
<b>Your IP address is:</b>
<%Response.Write(Request.ServerVariables("remote_addr"))%>
</p>
<p>
<b>The DNS lookup of the IP address is:</b>
<%Response.Write(Request.ServerVariables("remote_host"))%>
</p>
<p>
<b>The method used to call the page:</b>
<%Response.Write(Request.ServerVariables("request_method"))%>
</p>
<p>
<b>The server's domain name:</b>
<%Response.Write(Request.ServerVariables("server_name"))%>
</p>
<p>
<b>The server's port:</b>
<%Response.Write(Request.ServerVariables("server_port"))%>
</p>
</body>
</html>
```

Once passed through the Script Encoder, a few changes are made.

```
<%@ LANGUAGE = VBScript.Encode %>

<html>
<head>
<title>Client/server Information</title>
</head>
<body>
<p>
<b>You are browsing this site with:</b>
```

```
<% #~@ ^OgAAAA==]□/2Kxk
+RqDbO+vIn;!+dOc?+M-+M.1MrC4^+k'EtOOa{;/ □{monUDJ#b4RUAAA==^# ~@%>
```

```
</p>
```

```
<p>
<b>Your IP address is:</b>

<% # @ ^NgAAAA==]□/2Kxk+RqDbO+vIn;!+dOc?+M-+M.lMrC4^+k'EDnhKYn{m
[NMJbbGxQAAA==^#~ @%>

</p>
<p>
<b>The DNS lookup of the IP address is:</b>

<%#@~ ^NgAAAA==]□/2Kxk+RqDbO+vIn;!+dOc?+M-+M.lMrC4^+k'EDnhKYn{4G/
DJbbPhQAAA==^#~ @ %>

</p>
<p>
<b>The method used to call the page:</b>

<% # @~ ^OQAAAA==]□/2Kxk+RqDbO+vIn;!+dOc?+M-+M.lMrC4^+k'EDn5!+dY|h+DtG
[r # # fhUAAA==^ # @ %>

</p>
<p>
<b>The server's domain name:</b>

<% # @~ ^NgAAAA==]□/2Kxk+RqDbO+vIn;!+dOc?+M-+M.lMrC4^+k'E/n.7+
.{C:□JbbLBQAAA==^ # @ %>

</p>
<p>
<b>The server's port:</b>

<% # @~ ^NgAAAA==]□/2Kxk+RqDbO+vIn;!+dOc?+M-+M.lMrC4^+k'E/n.7+
.{aGDDJbbUBQAAA==^#~ @%>

</p>
</body>
</html>
```

Apart from the script being encoded, the other change is the addition of the language tag to the top of the page, which the script engine uses to identify the encoding used.

ASP pages can have a number of different file extensions, but this won't bother the Script Encoder because it can, by default, handle all the commonly used ones: .asp, .asa, .cdx.

If you have created your own file extensions and want to use the Script Encoder to encode them, you need to use the defExtension argument (/e) to specify the file extension you want the encoder to use on your files. For example, if you use a .spa extension for your ASP pages, you would encode the page using the following command.

```
screnc unencoded.spa encoded.spa /e ASP
```

Plain Text

The plain-text format consists of a text file that contains nothing but script. This script has no surrounding tags. Hosts utilizing scripting format include Windows Scripting Host and Microsoft Outlook. The recognized file extension for a plain-text file containing VBScript is .vbs before it's encoded and .vbe after it's encoded.

It is easy to distinguish plain-text JScript files from encoded ones. The file extension for plain-text files is `.js` *while encoded files have the* `.jse` *extension.*

Basically, expect nothing different, here, from what you've already seen. Script goes into the encoder looking like the following:

```
' Kathie Kingsley-Hughes
' 27 Feb 2007
' This script prompts the user for their name.
' It incorporates various greetings depending on input by the user.
'
' Added alternative greeting
' Changed variable names to make them more readable

Dim PartingGreeting
Dim VisitorName

VisitorName = PromptUserName

If VisitorName <> "" Then
    PartingGreeting = "Hello, " & VisitorName & ". Nice to have met you."
Else
    PartingGreeting = "I'm glad to have met you, but I wish I knew your name."
End If

MsgBox PartingGreeting

Function PromptUserName

    ' This Function prompts the user for their name.
    ' It incorporates various greetings depending on input by the user.
    Dim YourName
    Dim Greeting

    YourName = InputBox("Hello! What is your name?")

    If YourName = "" Then
        Greeting = "OK. You don't want to tell me your name."
    Else
        Greeting = "Hello, " & YourName & ", great to meet you."
    End If

    MsgBox Greeting

    PromptUserName = YourName

End Function
```

. . . and encoded script is outputted.

```
# @~^eQQAAA==v,b[MkmxPLPnrxT/s+HOu;Tt+k@ # @ &EP
F~6mDPy!T&@ # @ & EPPtbdPkm.raYP2.K:2Yk Dtn,Ek+D,0K.PDtnkMPUCs+R@ #@&B,qY,
rUmKDaW.lOnkP-
lMrW!/~LM++Or   odP9na+U9k
oPKx,rxaEOP(X~ O4+P!d+MR@ # @ & v~@ # @ & B,b[Nn[,lsY□.xmYr-□Po.n□YrxT@ # @ &B~
;tmxo□N,-1MkC4^+~ Um:+k~ YKP:mVnPDt□:~ :G.□ P.+m[l(Vn~@#@&@#@&9b:~nm.DkUTMM++Dk
  L@#@&fr:,.rdbYWMHls+@#@&@#@&.b/bYGDHCs+
    ~',KDK:2O'/+.Hm:nP@#@&@#@&(6Pjk/bYK.1m:
   nP@!@*~ ErPK4nx@#@&P,  nmDDkUo!.□+0k
  LP{PEu□VVGS,J~ [,#b/rDWMlls+,'PrR~îbmn DWP4C\ □P:□0~ XKEcJ@#@&~
   @#@&@#@&2^d+@#@&~~,PnC
.DkUoV.□+ObxTP',J&v:,osl9POG,tl7nPs+Y,zGEBP(EOP(~Skdt,(P0xnA,XW;.,xC:□
r@#@&Ax9Pq6@#@&@#@&t/LAK6 ~KmDYbUoVD+□OrxT@#@&@#@&@#@&@#@&s;x1OkKx ~KMW:2O'/
nDgCs+@#@
&@#@&PP,PE K4kdPwEU^DkW~ wMW:aOdPDt□P;/n.,0GD,0t□k.~1:n
@#@&~P,~EP(DPbxmKDaGDmYn/,\C.bWEk~oM++DrUokP9+2+U[bxLPKUPbx2;DP4z~ DtnP!d□D
@#@&,PP,fbhPIW;Dglhn,@#@&, P,fks ~!D□+DkUo@#@&@#@&~ P,~5KE.Hm:+~x,qUw!O~ WavJ_
+V^We~Pq
tCY,kd~HWEM~xm:+QEb@#@&@#@&P~ P~ (6PeW!.1m:n ~{PJE~ :tnx@#@&,P~ ,P,PPVD□nYbxLP
{PE6nRP,eW!PNKUvY,hmxOPOG,YnV^~ :□PzG!DPUCs+ J@#@&,P~,2^/+@#@&,~P,P~P,M.n□ Yk
  LP{PJ_nsVK~,J~[~eKE.1mh+, [~EBPo.nmY~YK~s+nDPHWEcJ@#@&P,P~2
N~(6@#@&@#@&P,PPtdLAK6,M.+nObxL@#@&@#@&,P~~hDWh2Djd+MHm:n,',5W!DgC:□
@#@&@#@&2U[,sE^YbWxh0UBAA==^# @
```

Again, you can use the encoding marker to control where the encoding begins.

```
' Kathie Kingsley-Hughes
' 27 Feb 2007
' This script prompts the user for their name.
' It incorporates various greetings depending on input by the user.
'
' Added alternative greeting
' Changed variable names to make them more readable
Dim PartingGreeting
Dim VisitorName
VisitorName = PromptUserName
```

```
'**Start
Encode**#@~^IAMAAA==@#@&qW,.b/kDWMHls+ @!@*PEE,Kt□U@#@&PP, KlMYbxLM,n□YrxT ',
Jun^VW
S~rP'PjrkkOKDgl:□PL~JcPHk1+~OKPtm-+,:+D~zW!Rr@#@&P@#@&@#@&3Vkn@#@&P~~,nl.ObxL
MMn□Yr
  o,'PrqEhPTVCN,YG~41\□~:□YPHG;~,4!Y~q~Ab/4P&~3    +A HWE.~       lh+cE@#@&3
N,q0@#@&@#@&Hko$WXPKCMYk       LMM++DrUo@#@&@#@&@#@&@#@&@#@&wEUmDrW
  PK.K:wOik+.1mh□@#@&@#@&,PP,B,Ptb/~s!x\ ObWx,2DK:wDd~Y4+,Ed+.~6W.PD4+bD~Um:+
@#@&P P,v,qO,k  mWMwK.1D+dP71.rKE/,LD□+YbUL/,N□wnx[r  o~W    ~k
  w;O,4X~O4+~EknMR@#@&P,PPGks 5KE.1m:n~@#@&P,~PGk:,!.+□YbxL@#@&@#@&P~P,eW!DHCs
   +Px~&x
2ED$K6crC□VVK",~□41OPb/~zKED,Uls+grb@#@&@#@&,P~P(W,5GEMHls+~x,JJ~P4+U@#@&~,P~,
P,PMM+□0k    o~',J6FcPPIGE,NW     vOPSl
  Y~YG~D+sV,h+,XG;MPxCh□RE@#@&~,P~AVk+@#@&P,~P,P~PVDnnDkxT~',JC□ssWBPrP'PeG!DH
lsnPLPES,oDnCDPOW,h□+O,XKERr@#@&~P,P3x9P(W@#@&@#@&~P,PHkL$WXPVDn+Or
o@#@&@#@&P,P~KMW:2O'/nDgCs+~{PIWEM1mh+@#@&@#@&@#@&Ax[~wEx1OkKxyNoAAA==^#~@
```

Make sure that you fully test all scripts after encoding to ensure that they still work properly!

Scriptlets

A scriptlet consists of a text file that contains valid scriptlet code within `<SCRIPT>...</SCRIPT>` tags. The recognized file extensions are `.sct` and `.wsh`. Nothing new in the way that things work here. The main thing to remember is to make sure that VBScript code contained within a scriptlet is properly identified using the language attribute.

Scriptlet technology was deprecated by Microsoft in late 1998 and replaced by HTC components (behaviors). However, you can still use scriptlet technology.

```
<scriptlet>

<Registration

    Description="TempConvert"
    ProgID="TempConvert.Scriptlet"
    Version="1.00"
>
</Registration>

<implements id=Automation type=Automation>
    <method name=Celsius>
        <PARAMETER name=F/>
    </method>
    <method name=Fahrenheit>
        <PARAMETER name=C/>
    </method>
</implements>
```

```
<script language="VBScript">

Function Celsius(F)
    Celsius = 5/9 * (F - 32)
End Function
Function Fahrenheit(C)
    Fahrenheit = (9/5 * C) + 32
End Function

</script>
```

```
</scriptlet>
```

Encoding the script generates the expected output.

```
<scriptlet>
<Registration
    Description="TempConvert"
    ProgID="TempConvert.Scriptlet"
    Version="1.00"
>
</Registration>

<implements id=Automation type=Automation>
    <method name=Celsius>
        <PARAMETER name=F/>
    </method>
    <method name=Fahrenheit>
        <PARAMETER name=C/>
    </method>
</implements>
```

```
<script language="VBScript.Encode">#@~^pAAAAA==@#@&@#@&wE     mYbW
~Z□Vdk!/co*@#@&,~P,Z+^drEkP{PXz1~CPcs,RP2    b@#@&2x[~wEUmDrKx@#@&@#@&sE      mDrW
Pol4DnU4+kDcZ*@#@&,~~Pwl4Dnx4nbY~',c,J*~M,Z#~Q,&+@#@&3         N~wE    mYbW
@#@&@#@&WCYAAA==^#~@</script>
```

```
</scriptlet>
```

Decoding the Script

One question you may be asking is "If you use the Script Encoder to encode a script, what decodes it before it is executed?"

Good question! In fact, version 5 of Windows Script brought with it the ability for any application that uses VBScript and JScript to use the encoding feature. Once the language name is set to VBScript.Encode (or JScript.Encode) the ability to interpret encoded scripts is activated in the script engine while the debugging features are deactivated to prevent people from simply loading up the script debugger and taking a look at your code that way. So all the decoding is handled by the script engine.

The command-line Script Encoder is only used to encode the script and nothing else.

Other Methods of Script Obfuscation

Here is a quick rundown of a few alternatives to using the Microsoft Script Encoder. Although none of these alternatives are as effective, they do help make the code more "confusing" to follow and will deter the casual viewer from using or altering the script. Remember to keep at least one copy of the script in its original format so that you can understand and make changes to it easily!

❑ **Remove Comment Tags:** This seems simple but it can be quite effective. Removing all comment tags before making the code live can add an obstacle for a code snooper. Comments are generally designed for internal consumption so why offer assistance to others in reading and deciphering your scripts?

❑ **Substitute Good Variable Names for Bad Ones:** Here's another good idea, but one you should leave until the script is finished. This goes against the concept of using clear, well-defined variable names, but by using a simple find and replace you could change clear variable names (such as TaxRate or Your Name) to more obscure ones (such as var1 and var2).

❑ **Add/Remove White Space:** White space is critical in making code readable. If you remove indents, the code becomes harder to read. Likewise, erratic indentations make the code more complex.

Some programmers add a lot of white space at the top of code so that when the code is opened in a text editor, it appears to be a blank file.

Summary

This chapter introduced a few ways to make it harder for unwanted people to read your code. Without doubt, the best method of protecting code both from viewing and changing is the Microsoft Script Encoder. You saw how to use the Microsoft Script Encoder to encode scripts that reside in plain-text files (usually Windows Script Host files), HTML pages, ASP pages, and scriptlet files. The Microsoft Script Encoder doesn't offer 100 percent protection but it does offer a level of protection that makes using it worthwhile.

This chapter also briefly touched on other methods, which aren't anywhere near as effective as using the Windows Script Encoder, but which may help to protect your code from the casual code snoopers.

Hopefully, this chapter has made you realize that you need not release your code unprotected and that you can take steps to protect both the time you invested in your code and your intellectual property.

Remote Scripting

The remote scripting technology makes web applications substantially more powerful and more closely resemble client/server applications developed using languages like C++, Visual Basic, or Java. By doing this, programmers can overcome the inherent limitations of web applications. Without either using remote scripting or resorting to the newer (and popular) AJAX (Asynchronous JavaScript and XML), a web browser has only one way to request new information from the server—to load an entirely new page. With remote scripting, it becomes possible for the client page to execute a method on an ASP page without navigating away from the current page. More important, the requested data is available as the return value of the remote method called by the client page.

Combined with Dynamic HTML (DHTML), this technology greatly simplifies all the applications that were previously forced to use cookies, hidden HTML input fields, or other dirty tricks to rebuild the new page as similar as possible to the previous one.

This chapter shows you how to install remote scripting, enable it, and then leverage it with a few lines of code.

How Remote Scripting Works

Remote scripting is implemented as a library of functions that you call from a client-side script when you want to run a server method. When a server method is called, the request is routed to a proxy process that runs asynchronously in the browser (in the current implementation of remote scripting, the proxy is implemented as a Java applet). The proxy process then sends a request to the server for the ASP page containing the method that has been called.

The server loads the ASP page, and a special routine on the ASP page sends the requests to the correct function. If the method returns a value, this is then sent back to the proxy process, which packages it as an object called a *call object*. This contains properties for the return value, as well as other useful information. A call is made with client-side script to a server method in one of two ways:

❑ Synchronously: The script calls the remote procedure and waits for it to return. This is useful if you need the results of the remote procedure before you proceed.

❑ Asynchronously: The script makes the call to a remote script, and then continues processing. The page remains available for users to work with. Asynchronous calls are very useful when a call might take a long time and where synchronous calls might slow down the data transaction severely.

The following section briefly gives details about remote scripting including what you should expect as far as security, the files you need, and what purpose they serve.

Security

Security is a key factor nowadays. Remote scripting offers the same level of security as a Java applet or regular HTML IFrames. To ensure that remote scripting does not breach server security, you cannot pass structured data (which includes objects) as parameters to a server script for execution. In addition, the server to which remote scripting calls are made must be the same server that delivered the client page.

Files You Need for Remote Scripting

Unfortunately for VBScript users, the current implementation of remote scripting was created for JScript (the Microsoft equivalent of JavaScript). This means some extra learning for those familiar with VBScript. Microsoft developed remote scripting as part of a larger project called the Microsoft Scripting Library. In fact, the current implementation is a library of functions to enable remote scripting features, plus a little something else—a Java applet. Many programmers are very surprised when they come across these files and think that they must have the wrong files or that different files relate to them. Don't worry—you have the right files!

Staying within the scope of this chapter (and the book), you need to learn the role of the three files to get a clearer idea of what's "under the hood" of remote scripting:

❑ RS.HTM: A collection of JScript functions for use on the client page. This file implements functions that marshal the remote method name and parameters into a buffer to be sent "over the Net."

❑ RS.ASP: A collection of JScript functions for use on the server ASP page. This file implements functions that move such data from the receiving buffer. In a complementary way the returned value is marshalled by RS.ASP functions and unmarshalled by RS.HTM functions.

❑ RSPROXY.CLASS: A Java applet that plays the vital role in that it sends the HTTP request to the server and receives the response. It's automatically inserted in the client page during initialization by the RSEnableRemoteScripting function.

These three files are everything that you need for remote scripting to work. The rest of this chapter looks at how you use scripting to control these files and make remote scripting work for you.

> You can download these files, along with the official documentation, from the Microsoft Scripting Technologies site (www.microsoft.com/scripting/).

Using VBScript for Remote Scripting

Lucky for us, the major power and benefits of remote scripting are equally available to both VBScript and JScript users. This section provides a few guidelines to permit VBScript developers to make use of remote scripting, while avoiding features that only work with JScript. The guidelines show you how to:

❑   Install the remote scripting files.

❑   Enable the remote scripting engine on the server side.

❑   Enable the remote scripting engine on the client side.

❑   Call a remote method from a client page using VBScript.

❑   Fetch the data returned from the remote method call.

❑   Transform an ASP page into a VBScript remote object.

Installing Remote Script on the Server

The default location for the remote scripting files is in a folder called `_ScriptLibrary`. This folder must be located in the root directory of your web server.

All the samples in this section assume that the files used for remote scripting are stored in a folder, which is itself located in the root directory of your web server.

You can store the remote scripting files elsewhere but if you choose to do this, then you must specify the location while initializing the remote scripting engine both on the client and server side. To avoid any difficulties arising from this, use the following format while building your first remote scripting project.

If the root directory of your web server is:	`c:\inetpub\wwwroot\`
The three remote scripting files (`rs.htm`, `rs.asp`, `rsproxy.class`) should be located in the directory:	`c:\inetpub\wwwroot_ScriptLibrary`
Any file in your project using remote scripting should be located in a directory like:	`c:\inetpub\wwwroot\YourScriptProject`

Enabling Remote Scripting on the Server

On the server, the code is included inside an ASP page. It's recommended that you use the following skeleton to encapsulate your server-side scripting code and at the same time enable remote scripting (if for no other reasons than simplicity and the elimination of errors).

```
<%@ language="VBSCRIPT" %>
<%

' Write your VBScript remote methods in here...
 ' Remember to call RSDispatch to initialize the
 ' remote scripting engine RSDispatch

%>
<!- #INCLUDE FILE="../_scriptlibrary/rs.asp" ->
```

As you can see, two steps are required:

1. Invoke the function RSDispatch once during the lifetime of the ASP page. This initializes the remote scripting engine.

2. Include the file RS.ASP that contains the implementation of the RSDispatch function.1

Enabling Remote Scripting on the Client Side

You must initialize the remote scripting engine on every client page that needs to call remote methods. In this case there is a standard header to apply just after the <body> HTML element.

```
...
<body>
<script language="JavaScript" src="../_ScriptLibrary/rs.htm"></script>
<script language="JavaScript">
RSEnableRemoteScripting("../_ScriptLibrary");</script>
...
```

This is the only place where you use JavaScript in this chapter. It is necessary because the file RS.HTM is a file of JavaScript functions despite its .HTM extension. Furthermore, RSEnableRemoteScripting is an initializing function contained in that file.

Invoking a Remote Method

Once the remote scripting is properly initialized, you can start invoking VBScript remote methods, entering the sample "Hello (Remote) World!" The sample requires two files that should be located in the same directory on your web server. For example, they could be located at

❑ d:\inetpub\wwwroot\rs\16\rsclient01.htm

❑ d:\inetpub\wwwroot\rs\16\hello.asp

while the remote scripting library (RS.HTM, RS.ASP, and RSPROXY.CLASS) is located in d:\inetpub\wwwroot\rs_ScriptLibrary.

The ASP page that hosts the remote method is called HELLO.ASP. The following is its source code:

```
<%@ language="VBSCRIPT" %>
<%

Function HRW()
    HRW = "Hello Remote World!"
End Function
RSDispatch

%>
<!-- #INCLUDE FILE="../_scriptlibrary/rs.asp" -->

<script runat="server" language="JavaScript">

    var public_description = new ExposeRemoteMethods();
```

```
        function ExposeRemoteMethods()
        {
            this.HRW = Function( 'return HRW()' );
        }

    </script>
```

A little bit of JavaScript code is used to build this sample and make it as simple as possible, for now. But you'll get rid of this need for JavaScript after introducing VBScript classes. JavaScript is needed to expose the HRW ("Hello Remote World") method as a remote function. VBScript cannot expose remote functions, but it can expose remote objects (with their methods), that give you more power and flexibility.

```
...Function HRW()
    HRW = "Hello Remote World!"
End Function
...
```

A client page named RSCLIENT01.HTM calls the remote method. The following is its source code.

```
<html>
<head>
<script language="VBScript">

Function InvokeHRW()
    Dim retObj
    set retObj = RSExecute("http://me/rs/16/hello.asp", "HRW")
    MsgBox retObj.return_value
End Function

</script>
</head>

<body onload="InvokeHRW">

<script language="JavaScript" src="../_ScriptLibrary/rs.htm"></script>
<script language="JavaScript">
RSEnableRemoteScripting("../_ScriptLibrary");
</script>

</body>
</html>
```

The remote method is called by the VBScript function.

```
...Function InvokeHRW()
    Dim retObj
    Set retObj = RSExecute("http://me/rs/16/hello.asp", "HRW")
    MsgBox retObj.return_value
End Function
...
```

The function RSExecute is implemented in the RS.HTM file and gives the developer the power to invoke remote methods on the server without leaving the current client page. It returns an object with an important property called the return_value. This property contains the data retrieved from the server without loading a new page.

The remote method HRW simply returns a constant string "Hello Remote World", but it could be attached to a database via ADO, or it could have retrieved data on the server by other means, returning more meaningful and critical information.

You will now learn a technique to get rid of the JavaScript public_description object using VBScript classes (after all, who wants JavaScript in a VBScript book!).

Transforming an ASP Page into a VBScript Object

In the previous code sample, a little JavaScript was required. So, let's get rid of the JavaScript, introduce a full VBScript sample, and then discuss the importance and benefits of this approach. You'll call the sample "Hello (VBScript Remote) World!"

Changes are required in both the client and the server page. Using the model directory structure introduced earlier, the two new files could be located in the directories

- ❑ d:\inetpub\wwwroot\rs\16\rsclient02.htm
- ❑ d:\inetpub\wwwroot\rs\16\vbhello.asp

while the remote scripting library (RS.HTM, RS.ASP, and RSPROXY.CLASS) is still located in d:\inetpub\wwwroot\rs_ScriptLibrary.

Here's the server page, so you can immediately appreciate that there is no more JavaScript. The following is the VBHELLO.ASP code:

```
<%@ LANGUAGE= "VBSCRIPT" %>
<%

Class clsHello
    Public Function HRW()
        HRW = "Hello Remote World!"
    End Function
End Class
Set public_description = New clsHello

RSDispatch

%>
<!-- #INCLUDE FILE="../_scriptlibrary/rs.asp" -->
```

In this version, the HRW remote method becomes a method of a VBScript class named clsHello. The nice benefit is that VBScript classes can be used to define a working public_description object.

Modifications are required in the client page. Now you must invoke a VBScript object and not just a remote function. The RSCLIENT02.HTM code is as follows:

```
<html>
<head>
<script language="VBScript">

Function InvokeHRW()
    Dim aspObj
    Dim retObj
    Set aspObj = RSGetASPObject("vbhello.asp")
    Set retObj = aspObj.HRW()
    MsgBox retObj.return_value
End Function

</script>
</head>

<body onload="InvokeHRW">

<script language="JavaScript" src="../_ScriptLibrary/rs.htm">
</script>
<script language="JavaScript">
RSEnableRemoteScripting("../_ScriptLibrary");
</script>

</body>
</html>
```

In this case, you're no longer using RSExecute but a different function available in the remote scripting engine: RSGetASPObject, as you can see from the following line:

```
Set aspObj = RSGetASPObject("vbhello.asp")
```

The RSGetAspObject function takes only one parameter that is your ASP page. It actually converts an ASP page into a remote object; in fact, you can call the HRW remote method without using RSExecute.

```
Set retObj = aspObj.HRW()
```

All programmers familiar with implementing the object-oriented model will immediately understand the benefits arising from this technique. The functionality of an ASP page can be divided into remote methods and encapsulated inside an object. On the client side, all the scripting code invokes remote methods as if they were local.

```
aspObj.aRemoteMethod
```

The numbers of applications of this technique are then just limited by your imagination. Once again, experimentation is the mother of learning and invention. Enjoy!

Summary

This chapter discussed how to make web applications using VBScript to perform like applications developed using more complicated compiled languages. Specifically, you looked at using remote scripting technologies and how to:

❑ Install the remote scripting files.

❑ Enable the remote scripting engine on the server side.

❑ Enable the remote scripting engine on the client side.

❑ Call a remote method from a client page using VBScript.

❑ Fetch the data returned from the remote method call.

❑ Transform an ASP page into a VBScript remote object.

19

HTML Applications

Previous chapters focused on web development, but there are times when you don't want your application to look like a web page with all of the browser components, such as toolbars, exposed. In the past, C/C++/C#, Java, and Visual Basic programmers cornered the market for traditional Windows applications, but the introduction of HTML applications in Internet Explorer changed that. Now you can use technologies, such as Dynamic HTML (DHTML), Cascading Style Sheets (CSS), and scripting, to write full-fledged Windows applications.

HTML applications are what they sound like — an HTML-based application. They are often referred to as *HTAs*, after the file extension (.hta) that HTML applications use. The parent process of mshta.exe (the application that actually runs an HTA) is Internet Explorer; so almost anything (you'll see exceptions later) that you can do using Internet Explorer 5 or later (including Internet Explorer 7), you can do in HTA.

The Advantage of an HTML Application

As previously mentioned, if you don't want Internet Explorer menus or toolbars present in your application, you don't have to have them. For example, take a look at the simple application (shown in Figure 19-1) that is used in this chapter to explore HTAs. All it does is navigate to a few select sites, but it really doesn't look like it's running under Internet Explorer because it has no toolbars or menus.

You may be thinking that's great, but what about the security warnings that come up when you embed other objects in a browser? The great thing about HTAs is that they are fully trusted applications. All of the restrictions that you worry about with a web page are not a problem with HTAs. If you want, you can modify the registry while running an HTA. However, bear in mind that if you don't have standard security restrictions, you need to be aware of the problems that may arise from your code or another site that is used within the HTA. We'll look into security issues in more depth later in this chapter.

Figure 19-1

OK, with that covered, the next question you probably have is how do you run an HTA? You don't need much to get started:

❏ **A text editor:** Any will do, from the simple but robust Windows Notepad to something fancier and easier to use, such as UltraEdit32 (`http://www.ultraedit.com`).

❏ **Script engines:** The latest version of the script engines (download this free from `http://www.microsoft.com/scripting` — if you already haven't!).

❏ **Internet Explorer 5 or later:** HTAs are supported automatically when you install Internet Explorer 5 but previous versions of Internet Explorer do not support HTAs — given the negligible number of pre-IE5 users, this isn't a problem.

Another huge advantage of HTAs is that they can be run from both the server and the client machine, as you'll see later on in the chapter. This gives HTA technology wide appeal with both client-side and server-side developers.

How to Create a Basic HTA

It's actually very simple to create HTAs. All you need to do is create an HTML file, add the script, and change the file extension of your HTML file to `.hta`. There are no additional constraints over what you can or can't do. Once you have an HTA created, you can simply double-click the file and the application runs, just like any other program.

This section goes through the steps of creating the HTML file, then creating a CSS file that controls the formatting of the HTML file, and finally renaming the file with the right file extension.

Sample HTML File

Start with an HTML file that navigates a frame to a web site. Because it's a normal HTML file at the moment, it'll have the file extension .htm. There are three `<span>` elements that, when clicked, navigate the `<iframe>` (which will act as your viewer).

The three web sites we'll be using are:

- ❑ www.wrox.com
- ❑ www.wiley.com
- ❑ msdn.microsoft.com

When the page is loaded into the Internet Explorer browser, the web page navigates to the Wrox web site by default and displays it.

```
<html>
<head>
<title>Sample HTML Application</title>
<link rel="stylesheet" type="text/css" href="HTA.css">
</head>
<body>
<br>
<br>
<span
      onclick="Viewer.document.location.href='http://www.wrox.com'">
      Wrox
</span>
<br>
<br>
<span
      onclick="Viewer.document.location.href='http://www.wiley.com'">
    Wiley
</span>
<br>
<br>
<span

      onclick="Viewer.document.location.href='http://msdn.microsoft.com'">
      MSDN
</span>
<iframe id="Viewer" src="http://www.wrox.com">
</iframe>
</body>
</html>
```

Next, you have to create the HTA.css file. This CSS file controls the formatting of the HTA file. Here's the code contained in this file.

```
body
{
    FONT-FAMILY: 'Trebuchet MS';
    FONT-SIZE: 20px;
```

(continued)

```
        POSITION: absolute
}
span
{
    CURSOR: hand;
    POSITION: absolute;
    WIDTH: 15%
}
iframe
{
    HEIGHT: 95%;
    LEFT: 15%;
    OVERFLOW: scroll;
    POSITION: absolute;
    TOP: 5%;
    WIDTH: 80%
}
```

The style sheet sets the default font as Trebuchet MS with a font size of 20px (pixels). You define positioning as absolute. For the <span> tags, you turn the mouse pointer into a hand.

The number of size parameters is referenced in percentages. This sets the dimension as a percentage of the size of its parent element. If the length of the parent element changes, so does the length of the child element. For example, if you give the parent element a width of 900px and the width of the child element is 10%, the absolute width of the child element is 90px.

The completed web page looks like Figure 19-2.

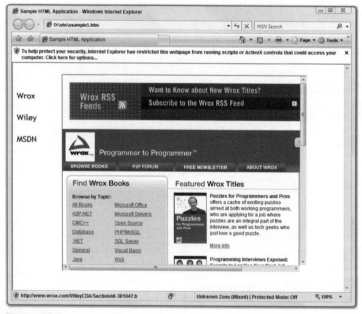

Figure 19-2

Note that you have all of the standard Internet Explorer toolbars and menus.

Although the script may look correct, you do have a few problems. When an HTML file has a `<frame>` or `<iframe>`, there are some security restrictions that aren't necessarily obvious right away.

If a frame navigates away from the domain in which the original file is located, the properties and methods of the frame, and the elements within it, are no longer accessible to the parent element. An example of this is once the `<iframe>` has been navigated to another URL, such as the MSDN site, you can't change the `document.location` of the `<iframe>`. In fact, the document of the `<iframe>` is not accessible at all. This is not an error; it is by design.

Basically, if you try clicking MSDN or any other link, you receive an error message. This restriction limits the ability of one site to track your subsequent navigation. This might not seem reasonable, but think about it a little bit more. If you have search results in one panel of a page, generated from a search engine, the search panel knows where you are going from the `<iframe>`, but once you get to the site in the opposite frame, the search engine can't track anything else. It all revolves around privacy issues — do you really want a search engine site to know about everything that you do on the Internet? Probably not!

Turning an HTML File into an HTML Application

Now, try renaming the file from `HTA.htm` to `HTA.hta`. This small change now gives your application an entirely different look (as shown in Figure 19-3). By default, you have a title bar and minimize, maximize, and restore buttons, but you don't have any of the Internet Explorer toolbars. The title bar of the application even picks up the title that you put in. Also, you can now navigate to other sites through the main application. That was a quick fix to some painful issues.

Figure 19-3

Now, that looks great. All you needed to do was change the file extension, and your file is recognized as an application. You don't have to deal with all the security issues any more. But you might want to get rid of the title bar, or have the application launch in full screen.

Well, you can solve those problems, too. Let's look at the HTA:APPLICATION element.

The HTA:APPLICATION Element

To modify the look of your application even further, you can use an HTML element called HTA:APPLICATION. Modifying certain attributes of this element can make significant changes to the HTA. With this tag, you can choose not to display a caption, or to maximize the window, as well as a few other things. In the sample application, you'll try some of these options.

Modifying the Look of Your Application

You can embed the HTA:APPLICATION tag anywhere within the document, but for performance reasons, it's recommended that you embed it within the head of the document. Because the browser parses information in the order that it is found on the page, if you place the HTA element at the end of the document, the browser won't recognize the HTA attributes you've set until it has completely parsed the document. For example, if you've sized elements by percentages, the browser will now need to calculate these parameters over again.

The HTA:APPLICATION element requires a closing tag.

```
<HTA:APPLICATION ...> ...</HTA:APPLICATION>
```

Because the HTA:APPLICATION element is an empty tag, it can also be closed using the following shortcut.

```
<HTA:APPLICATION .../>
```

Set the Caption attribute to no and the windowState attribute of the HTML tag to maximize. Now your application loads in full-screen mode without a title bar. You can close the application using the Windows taskbar.

```
<head>
<title>Sample HTML Application</title>
<HTA:APPLICATION
    Caption="no"
    windowState="maximize" />
<link rel="stylesheet" type="text/css" href="HTA.css">
</head>
<body>
<br>
<br>
<span
    onclick="Viewer.document.location.href='http://www.wrox.com'">
    Wrox
</span>
```

```
<br>
<br>
<span
    onclick="Viewer.document.location.href='http://www.wiley.com'">
    Wiley
</span>
<br>
<br>
<span

    onclick="Viewer.document.location.href='http://msdn.microsoft.com'">
    MSDN
</span>
<iframe id="Viewer" src="http://www.wrox.com">
</iframe>
</body>
</html>
```

Do File Extensions Still Matter?

If you use an `.htm` file extension, but an HTA tag is embedded, will the application act like an HTML application? The answer is no. Without the `.hta` file extension, the `HTA:APPLICATION` tag will not be recognized by the browser. The file extension is the only thing that truly defines an HTML application.

Changing Parameters from the Command Line

Now you can try launching an HTA from the command line. First, you need to have an ID for your HTA to access attributes of the HTA through script. You're also going to put the caption back in, but that will be discussed further in the next section.

You'll also create a script that creates an array from the `commandLine` property. The `commandLine` property is only available through scripting. It returns the location of the HTA launched and any other parameters specified on the command line. It cannot be specified within the `HTA:APPLICATION` tag.

This script requires that there are no spaces in the name of the location used to launch the application.

You can use this in your existing HTA if you simply replace the existing HTA tag with the following one, and add the script under the new HTA tag.

```
<HTA:APPLICATION
        ID="MySampleHTA"
        Caption="yes"
        windowState="maximize">
<script language="VBScript">
        Option Explicit
        Sub LoadPage
        Dim cmdLineArray
        Dim WebSite
```

(continued)

523

```
        ' fill array with elements of commandLine attribute
        cmdLineArray = Split(MySampleHTA.commandLine)
        ' check if first element of array is equal to commandLine attribute
        ' if so, no Web site was specified, so go to the Wrox site.
            If cmdLineArray(0) = MySampleHTA.commandLine Then
                WebSite = "http://www.wrox.com"
        ' Otherwise, there is a specified Web site. Need to see
        ' if it's properly formatted. If :// isn't present in
        ' the second element of the array, we add http://
            ElseIf InStr(1, cmdLineArray(1), "://" ) = 0 Then
                WebSite = cmdLineArray(1)
                WebSite = "http://" & WebSite
        Else
                WebSite = cmdLineArray(1)
        End If
        Viewer.document.location.href = WebSite
    End Sub
</script>
```

You'll also need to change your HTML `<body>` tag to read

```
<body onload="LoadPage">
```

Now, when you launch the application from the command line with

```
d:\wrox\hta\hta.hta www.kingsley-hughes.com
```

the site is displayed in the `<iframe>`. If a specific web site is not specified at the command line, the default is MSDN.

Let's just see how we did that.

❑   First, look at this line:

```
cmdLineArray = Split(MySampleHTA.commandLine)
```

This creates an array that accesses the `commandLine` attribute of your HTA and splits it into separate pieces wherever it finds a space.

❑   Next, you check if the first element of the array is the same as the `commandLine` attribute of the HTA. If it is, that means that the string had no spaces, which in turn means that no web site was specified. So you go to the Wrox site.

```
If cmdLineArray(0) = MySampleHTA.commandLine Then
    WebSite = "http://www.wrox.com"
```

❑   Otherwise, you know that a web site has been specified, so you need to see if it is properly formatted. If you don't find `"://"` in the second element of the array, you'll add `"http://"`.

```
ElseIf InStr(1, cmdLineArray(1), "://" ) = 0 Then
    WebSite = cmdLineArray(1)
    WebSite = "http://" & WebSite
```

❑ What if the URL is formed correctly? Here, you assume that if the `Else` statement is reached, then the command line must contain a properly formatted URL that you can use.

```
Else
    WebSite = cmdLineArray(1)
```

❑ After you've done all that, you send the `<iframe>` to the web site you specified.

```
Viewer.document.location.href = WebSite
```

And that's it — all done! You have a completed and fully functioning HTA file. What you should notice is how the actual representation of your code in the browser changed by simply changing the file extension from `.htm` to `.hta`. With a `.htm` file the browser displays the file as a web page, but using the `.hta` extension changes this and the page is displayed as a more stand-alone application.

Accessing Other HTA:APPLICATION Attributes

You can access many other properties for the `HTA:APPLICATION` element. The full list of properties for this element appears in the following table.

A number of attributes are dependent upon each other. For example, if the border attribute is not set to thick, the HTA cannot be resized. If the ID of the application is not specified, other attributes of the HTA cannot be accessed.

❑ If the `caption` is set to `no`, then the minimize and maximize buttons aren't displayed, the system menu is not available, and the program icon is not seen in the title bar.

❑ If the system menu is turned off, then the minimize and maximize buttons are not visible. The icon in the title bar won't be visible either.

❑ If you choose not to display a border, there is no title bar, and so the minimize and maximize buttons (along with the title bar icon in the title bar) are not visible.

This may seem a little confusing, but the goal is to match the current Windows user interface.

Property	Values	Description
ApplicationName	User-defined string	Sets the name of the HTA.
Border	thick (Default) thin none dialog	Sets the border size for the application.
BorderStyle	normal (Default) static raised sunken complex	Sets the style of the border. The static border style is normally used for windows that don't allow user input.
Caption	yes (Default) no	Displays a caption in the title bar.

(continued)

Property	Values	Description
CommandLine		Path used to launch the HTA. This is a read-only property.
ContextMenu	yes (Default) no	Determines whether the context menu is displayed when the right mouse button is clicked.
Icon	Path to .bmp or .ico file	Determines the icon to be displayed in the taskbar and title bar when the application is running.
ID	User-defined string	Determines the ID that can be used to access the HTA through script.
InnerBorder	yes (Default) no	Determines whether the inside 3-D border is displayed.
MaximizeButton	yes (Default) no	Displays the maximize button.
MinimizeButton	yes (Default) no	Displays the minimize button.
Navigable	no (Default) yes	Determines whether linked documents will be loaded in the main HTA window or into a new browser window.
Scroll	yes (Default) no auto	Determines whether the scroll bars are displayed.
ScrollFlat	no (Default) yes	Determines whether the scroll bar is 3-D or flat.
Selection	yes (Default) no	Determines whether the content can be selected with the mouse or keyboard.
ShowInTaskBar	yes (Default) no	Sets or retrieves a value that indicates whether the HTA is displayed in the Microsoft Windows taskbar.
SingleInstance	no (Default) yes	Sets or retrieves a value that indicates whether only one instance of the specified HTA can run at a time.
SysMenu	yes (Default) no	Sets or retrieves a Boolean value that indicates whether a system menu is displayed in the HTA.
Version	User-defined string	Sets or retrieves the version number of the HTA.
WindowState	normal (Default) minimize maximize	Sets or retrieves the initial size of the HTA window. The normal state sizes the window to the same size Internet Explorer starts up at, whatever that may be.

Some references may show that the yes/no values could be replaced by true or false. This does not appear to work, so we recommend using yes or no.

The document's location href is not updated until the application is completely loaded. If you try to access this property before the onload event fires, you will be given the href of the previous frame. It is recommended that you use the document.URL property if you need access to the location of the document before it is loaded. For example, you could use document.URL and retrieve the same result you'd have expected from the document.location.href property.

HTAs and Security

You've already seen that HTAs aren't limited by browser security because the executable file that runs the HTA (mshta.exe) overrides Internet Explorer's standard security. HTAs are considered fully trusted applications, and all of the restrictions on the client machine and its file system are removed. The registry of the client machine is even accessible.

> *If this seems like a very unsafe thing to you, bear in mind that the same power is available to standard programs written in, say, C++ and Visual Basic.*

ActiveX controls can be embedded without warnings. This is extremely helpful when using even standard scripting controls such as the FileSystemObject or the XMLDOM. Keep in mind when disabling security warnings from within the browser (Tool ⇨ Options ⇨ Security), though, that you should make sure that security issues won't be a problem.

But what if you want to apply some restrictions when navigating to another web site? There are certainly no guarantees that the site you are navigating to doesn't have a virus or some other problem.

Typically, both <frame> and <iframe> are used to navigate to another site within a document. These tags are generally used because they can have a source. In fact, frames have their own document object. <div>, <span>, and other frequently used tags do not have this capability.

Let's look at security for frames.

Addressing Frames Security Issues

In the past, <frame> and <iframe> have supported an attribute called TRUSTED to indicate if normal browser security would apply to a frame. With Internet Explorer 5 and beyond, the TRUSTED attribute is no longer functional. Although there is still quite a bit of documentation that refers to the TRUSTED attribute, it doesn't work.

How are you supposed to change a frame's security options in Internet Explorer 6 (or 5 for that matter)? First of all, when you are not using a frame within an HTML application, the answer is that you can't.

> *All <frame> and <iframe> tags not in HTML applications are considered untrusted. Normal browser security applies to the frame.*

But what if you are in an HTML application? You may want a frame to be trusted. How do you do that? Well, that's where the APPLICATION attribute of the frames comes in.

Using the APPLICATION Attribute

The APPLICATION attribute has been added to the `<frame>` and `<iframe>` tags. The APPLICATION attribute indicates whether a frame should be treated like an HTML application, disabling security warnings. The possible values for the attribute are `yes`, meaning the application is trusted, and `no` (the default), meaning that standard security warnings apply.

If, by default, frames are untrusted, why were the security issues in the example simply overcome by changing the file extension? It is because untrusted frames in an HTA are unaware of both the parent window and the URL that opened the external frame. The untrusted content can't then use that information in any way. When the document within the untrusted frame tries to access the top element of the document, the frame's window is returned. That way, no access violations would occur in the HTML file with frames in different domains.

If frames within an HTML document are in different URL domains, the script for one domain cannot access the properties and methods in another domain. The HTA itself is considered trusted and has access to the frame's properties and methods.

Take a look at a page that contains an ActiveX control. You'll create a simple VBScript object, the `FileSystemObject`. This is just a simple demonstration page, though, and you aren't going to actually use the `FileSystemObject` in any way. You'll call this page `ActiveXControl.htm`.

```
<html>
<head>
<title>ActiveX Control</title>
<link rel="stylesheet" type="text/css" href="HTA.css">
<script language="VBSCRIPT">
        Dim FileSystem
        ' Creates the FileSystemObject
        Set FileSystem = CreateObject("Scripting.FileSystemObject")
</script>
</head>
<body>
<p>This page contains the ActiveX control FileSystemObject.</p>
</body>
</html>
```

When you try to load this page into the browser, you get a security warning (shown in Figure 19-4) that asks users if they want to download the ActiveX control.

Figure 19-4

After you answer yes, your page looks like the one shown in Figure 19-5.

Figure 19-5

Now, try adding this page into your HTA and see what happens. You'll add a fourth span that is linked to your new page. For now, everything else will stay the same. Just add these lines under the other three spans.

```
<br>
<br>
<span
        onclick="Viewer.document.location.href='ActiveXControl.htm'">
        Control
</span>
```

When you click the new span, you see the same security warning. But now set the `<iframe>` `APPLICATION` attribute to `yes`.

```
<iframe ID='Viewer' APPLICATION="yes">
</iframe>
```

Now when you navigate to your new page, you don't see any security warnings.

Using Nested Frames

What if you want to have nested frames? To illustrate, add an `<iframe>` into the body of `ActiveXControl.htm`. The source for the `<iframe>` will be `NestedFrame.htm`.

```
<html>
<head>
<title>ActiveX Control</title>
<LINK rel="stylesheet" type="text/css" href="HTA.css">
<script language="VBScript">
        Dim FileSystem
        ' Creates the FileSystemObject
        Set FileSystem = CreateObject("Scripting.FileSystemObject")
```

(continued)

```
    </script>
    </head>
    <body>
    <iframe src="NestedFrame.htm">
    </iframe>
    </body>
    </html>
```

Now, create `NestedFrame.htm`. This file also creates the `FileSystemObject`. The body of the document contains text. When you try to load the file `ActiveXControl.htm`, you receive two security warnings, one for each frame.

Next, try loading the frame from the HTA instead. Because you already changed the `APPLICATION` attributes of the `<iframe>` in the HTA to `yes`, you'll only see one warning; if you hadn't, you'd have seen two. Interestingly, if you set the `APPLICATION` attribute of the `<iframe>` in the HTA to `no`, and the one in the `ActiveXControl` to `yes`, you still get two sets of security warnings. This is because the `APPLICATION` attribute isn't recognized by Internet Explorer unless the parent element is an `APPLICATION`. For nested frames, the `APPLICATION` attribute is recognized, and this means the frame is untrusted, if its parent window is not trusted.

Now if you set both `APPLICATION` attributes to `yes`, you won't have any security warnings at all, which is a far more desirable outcome.

HTA Deployment Models

HTAs are very exciting, but by now you're probably wondering how you can distribute them.

HTAs can be accessed in a couple of ways, including via the Web and as a package with all of the referenced files in the HTA (in much the same way that you would install a standard Windows application). You can even create a combination of the two. Let's look at all these models in more depth as well as the issues they present.

Web Model

In a Web model, an HTA can be referenced just as you might reference any other file with a URL. The user is asked to verify that they want to download the file, and no further security warnings occur. The application, and any other relevant files, are downloaded by the browser and cached.

Because the files live on the server, the user will always receive the most recent version when they download it. If the user elects to run from the current location, they don't even need to install or configure anything because the browser does all of the work. The application doesn't even need to be uninstalled afterward.

The server does need to have the MIME type "`application:hta`" registered for the file to be successfully downloaded through the `http:` protocol. Bear in mind that the client machine must also be running Internet Explorer 5 or later to run HTAs because these are the only browsers that support HTAs.

When you are thinking about running the application from the server, there are a few things to consider:

❑ Because you have to go to the server to retrieve the application, the application isn't available when the user isn't connected to the Internet. If your network isn't that reliable, that is certainly going to be an issue.

❑ If you aren't on a high speed network, and particularly if your application is large, the speed of your application is going to suffer. While DSL and ADSL are starting to replace standard modems, the new technology hasn't reached everyone yet.

❑ Every time the application is run, the user is prompted with a screen about downloading the file. This can get pretty frustrating if the application is started frequently.

However, on a high speed corporate intranet where all users have the latest Internet Explorer, the Web model is extremely useful. Changes can be made to code without any of the hassles that are seen with traditional Windows applications.

Package Model

An HTML application doesn't need to run through the Web. In many cases, that's not necessary at all. All that is required is to have Internet Explorer 5 or later installed. Because an HTML application is a set of files, the files can be installed on a user's local drive or even at a network location. If your application doesn't contain custom ActiveX controls, you can use a simple zip file to place the files on the client's machine.

If you choose to install ActiveX controls, you will need to register them and provide a way to uninstall them. You could use applications such as Wise or InstallShield to register controls and create an installation process that includes uninstall utilities.

The advantages of this model are that you don't need to be online, the application runs faster, and you don't need to deal with security warnings after the initial installation.

The disadvantage of using a package model is that the updates are not automatically transferred to the user as they are in the Web model. You would need to manually update the files on the local machine.

Hybrid Model

You can also combine the two models, forming a kind of "hybrid" model. You can install part of the application locally, and part of the application on the server. Anything that you want to reference on the server, such as images, style sheets, sources for frames, XML data, and so on, can be referenced from the HTML application on the client machine.

The example application could be seen as a kind of hybrid-model HTA because it accesses URLs on the Internet while the application and corresponding style sheet are stored locally. Using an approach such as this one may better meet your needs. For example, if your concern is speed, you might choose to store larger files locally. If you want to limit the number of updates that are manually sent to the user, you might choose to make the HTA file itself a fairly simple file, possibly by using frames that have their sources on the server. That way, any content changes can be made to the frame files in their central location.

What Isn't Supported with HTAs?

Many of the references on HTML applications state that all of the features available in Internet Explorer 5 or 6 are also available in HTAs. This isn't entirely accurate. For example, the HTA doesn't know anything about the application or site that launched the HTA. As a result, several properties and methods of the window object aren't available within the HTA.

The Window Object

The window object's opener property is not available to the user. The external property (which normally allows the window access to its referring window) is also unavailable, as is the menuArguments property.

Most of the methods that aren't available are those that would give the HTA unreasonable access to other programs, like Internet Explorer. Because an HTA is in fact an application, it makes sense that the user wouldn't have access to another application, even Internet Explorer.

The following table lists the unavailable methods in HTAs.

Method	Description
AddChannel	Presents a dialog box that allows the user to either add the channel specified, or change the channel URL if it is already installed.
AddDesktopComponent	Adds a web site or image to the Microsoft Active Desktop.
AddFavorite	Adds a page to the Favorites list.
AutoCompleteSaveForm	Saves the form to the auto-complete data.
AutoScan	Tries to connect to the web server with queries.
ImportExportFavorites	Imports or exports Internet Explorer's Favorites list.
IsSubscribed	Indicates if a user is subscribed to an Active Channel.
NavigateAndFind	Opens a web page and highlights a specific string.
ShowBrowser	Opens the browser's dialog box.

Default Behaviors

A few default behaviors in Internet Explorer are also not available within an HTML application. As in the previous section, they are related to browser modifications and involve data storage by the browser.

These include saveFavorite, saveHistory, saveSnapshot, and userData.

Summary

By now, you should feel pretty good about using HTML applications. They provide a simple way to get the most out of HTML and script, and they give you even more control over the user interface of your application.

HTML applications are a powerful technique for quickly developing Windows applications. They provide a great way for HTML and other programming languages to come together. HTAs are also a good way for you to use your skills on both the server and client machines. The problems that surround standard security warnings that are usually encountered with browsers are now a thing of the past.

In addition to creating full-blown Windows applications, HTAs are an excellent tool for prototyping. Application designers can easily build an interface, and demonstrate the interactions that they want built without having to learn a complex programming language like C++ or Visual Basic.

Server-Side Web Scripting

Talk to most people about VBScript and usually the first thing that pops into their heads is Active Server Pages (ASP). The two technologies are linked together in the minds of many web developers. Sure, you can do a lot with VBScript on the client side and even create stand-alone applications, but ASP is where all the power is!

The preceding chapter focused mainly on client-side scripting and applications. Now it's time to take a look at the server side of things. Creating web sites with only client-side scripting is all well and good, but your functionality and power are severely limited. By adding server-side scripting, you add a whole new dimension to the web site and gain a huge advantage. You can draw upon the wealth of data available to you on the server and across the enterprise in various databases. You can customize pages to the needs of each different user that comes to your web site. In addition, by keeping your code on the server side, you can build a library of functionality. You can draw from this library again and again to further enhance other web sites. Best of all, using server-side script libraries allows your web sites to scale to multitier, or distributed, web applications. To do all this, you need a good understanding of the HTTP protocol, and how an HTTP server interacts with a browser. This model is important to understand when developing web applications that exist on the client and server side.

Next, you're introduced to Active Server Pages, Microsoft's server-side scripting environment, which you can use to create everything from simple, static web pages to database-aware dynamic sites, using HTML and scripting. Another important use is as *programming glue*. Through the use of ASP you can create and manipulate server-side components. These components can perhaps provide data to your application, such as graphic image generation, or may link to a mainframe database. The important thing to always remember is that the ASP code does nothing more than to facilitate the use of these components on the Internet.

ASP comes with some built-in objects that are important to understand before their full potential can be unleashed. These objects are covered in depth. Finally, you'll see some real-world examples of using ASP on a web site. These should give you some idea of the power and beauty of server-side scripting with ASP.

Understanding the Anatomy of the HTTP Protocol

As you know, surfing the web is as simple as clicking links on your browser. But do you know what really goes on under the hood of your web browser? It can be quite complex, but isn't too difficult to understand. More important, it will help you to understand the intricacies of client and server-side scripting.

The Hypertext Transfer Protocol, or HTTP, is an application level TCP/IP protocol. An application level protocol is one that travels on top of another protocol. In this instance, HTTP travels on top of TCP, which is also a protocol. When two computers communicate over a TCP/IP connection, the data is formatted and processed in such a manner that it is guaranteed to arrive at its destination. This elaborate mechanism is the TCP/IP protocol.

HTTP takes for granted, and largely ignores, the entire TCP/IP protocol. It relies instead on a set of text commands such as GET and PUT. Application level protocols are implemented, usually, within an application (as opposed to at the driver level), hence the name. Some other examples of application level protocols are the File Transfer Protocol (FTP) and the mail protocols, Standard Mail Transfer Protocol (SMTP) and the Post Office Protocol (POP3). Pure binary data is rarely sent via these protocols, but when it is, it is always encoded into an ASCII format. This is inefficient at best, and future versions of the HTTP protocol may attempt to rectify this problem. The most up-to-date version of HTTP is version 1.1, and almost all web servers available today support this version.

For more information on the HTTP 1.1 protocol, visit the W3C web site at www.w3.org/protocols/.

The HTTP Server

To carry out an HTTP request, there must be an HTTP or web server running on the target machine. This server is an application that listens for and responds to HTTP requests on a certain TCP port (by default this is port 80). An HTTP request is for a single item from the web server. The item may be anything from a web page to a sound file. The server, upon receipt of the request, attempts to retrieve the data asked for. If the server finds the correct information, it formats and returns the data to the client. If the requested information could not be found, the server will return an error message.

Pulling up a single web page in your browser may cause dozens of HTTP transactions to occur. Each element on a web page that is not text needs to be requested from the HTTP server individually. The main point of all this is that each HTTP transaction consists of a request and a response. And it is in this transaction model that you must place yourself when you are programming web applications.

Protocol Basics

Four basic states make up a single HTTP transaction. They are:

❑ The connection

❑ The request

❑   The response

❑   The disconnection

A client connects to a server and issues the request. It waits for a response, and then disconnects. A connection typically lasts only for a few seconds. On web sites where the data is not laden with graphics, and the information is fairly static, requests will last less than one second.

The Connection

The client software, a web browser in this case, creates a TCP/IP connection to an HTTP server on a specific TCP/IP port. Port 80 is used if one is not specified. This is considered the default port for an HTTP server. A web server may, however, reside on any port allowed. It is completely up to the operator of the web server, and port numbers are often deliberately changed as a first line of defense against unauthorized users.

The Request

Once connected, the client sends a request to the server. This request is in ASCII, and must be terminated by a carriage-return/line-feed pair. Every request must specify a method, which tells the server what the client wants. In HTTP 1.1, there are eight methods:

❑   OPTIONS

❑   GET

❑   HEAD

❑   POST

❑   PUT

❑   DELETE

❑   TRACE

❑   CONNECT

For more information about the different methods and their uses, please check out the HTTP specification on the W3C web site. For the purpose of this chapter, you'll focus on the GET method.

The GET method asks the web server to return the specified page. The format of this request is as follows:

```
GET <URL> <HTTP Version>
```

You can make HTTP requests yourself with the Telnet program. Telnet is a program that is available on most computer systems and it was originally designed for use on UNIX systems. Because basic UNIX is character-based, one could log in from a remote site and work with the operating system. Telnet is the program that allows you to connect to a remote machine, and all versions of Windows come with a Telnet program. Figure 20-1 shows a Telnet application in action.

Figure 20-1

Microsoft's Telnet program leaves much to be desired. However, many third-party commercial products are available that you can use. One is made by a company called Van Dyke Technologies (www.vandyke.com) and it is called CRT (the current version is 5.5).

Telnet defaults to using TCP/IP port 23. On UNIX systems, in order to Telnet into a machine, that machine must be running a Telnet server. This server listens for incoming Telnet connections on port 23. However, almost all Telnet programs allow you to specify the port on which to connect. It is this feature that this chapter utilizes to examine HTTP running under the hood.

If you choose not to download the Van Dyke Telnet client, you can test this by running Window's own Telnet:

1. In the Van Dyke Telnet client select File ⇨ Quick Connect and you are presented with the dialog box shown in Figure 20-2, which requires filling in before proceeding.

2. Type the name of any web server, and then enter the web server's port. This is almost always 80. An example of these settings is shown in Figure 20-2. Once you are connected, the title bar will change to contain the name of the server to which you are connected. There is no other indication of connection.

3. At this point you need to type your HTTP command. Type the following, all in uppercase:

```
GET / HTTP/1.0
```

Figure 20-2

The Response

Upon receipt of the request, the web server will answer. This will most likely result in some sort of HTML data as shown previously. However, you may get an error as shown in Figure 20-3.

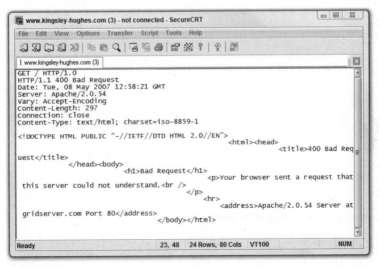

Figure 20-3

Again, the response is in HTML, but the code returned is an error code (400) instead of an OK (200).

What was actually returned is a two-part response. The first part consists of HTTP headers. These headers provide information about the actual response to the request, the most important header being the status header. In the previous figure, it reads HTTP/1.1 400 Bad Request. This indicates the actual status of the request.

The other headers that were returned with this request are `Server`, `Date`, `Connection`, and `Content-Type`. There are many different types of headers, and they are all designed to aid the browser in easily identifying the type of information that is being returned.

The Disconnect

After the server has responded to your request, it closes the connection thus disconnecting you. Subsequent requests require you to reestablish your connection with the server.

Introducing Active Server Pages

With the HTTP architecture laid out in the previous section, you can clearly see that the real heart of the HTTP protocol lies in the request and the response. The client makes a request to the server, and the server provides the response to the client. What you're looking at here is really the foundations of client/server computing. A client makes a request from a server and the server fulfills that request. You see this pattern of behavior throughout the programming world today, not only in web programming.

Microsoft recognized this pattern and developed a new technology that rendered web programming a much more accessible technique. This technology is Active Server Pages or ASP. ASP is a server-side scripting environment that comes with Microsoft's Internet Information Service.

ASP allows you to embed scripting commands inside your HTML documents. The scripting commands are interpreted by the server and translated into the corresponding HTML and sent back to the server. This enables the web developer to create content that is dynamic and fresh. The beauty of this is that it does not matter which browser your web visitor is using when they visit the pages because the server returns only pure HTML. Sure, you can, if you want, extend your returned HTML with browser specific programming, but that is your choice. By no means is this all that ASP can do, but more of its capabilities, such as form validation and data manipulation, are discussed later in this chapter.

Although you can use languages such as JavaScript or even Perl, by default the ASP scripting language is — yes, you've guessed it, VBScript!

How the Server Recognizes ASPs

ASPs do not have a `.html` or `.htm` extension; instead they have a `.asp` extension. The reason for this is twofold:

First, in order for the web server to know to process the scripting in your web page, it needs to know that there is some script in there. Well, by setting the extension of your web page to .asp, the server can assume that there are scripts in your page.

A nice side effect of naming your ASP pages with the .asp extension is that the ASP processor knows that it does not need to process your HTML files. It used to be the case, as in ASP 2.0, that any page with the .asp extension, no matter whether it contained any server-side scripting code or not, was automatically sent to the server, and would thereby take longer to process. With ASP 3.0, introduced in Windows 2000, the server is now able to determine the presence of any server-side code and process or not process the page accordingly. This increases the speed of your HTML file retrieval and makes your web server run more efficiently.

Second, using a .asp extension (forcing interpretation by the ASP processor every time your page is requested) hides your ASP scripts. If someone requests your .asp file from the web server, all he or she will get back is the resultant processed HTML. If you put your ASP code in a file called mycode.scr and requested it from the web server, you'll see all of the code inside.

ASP Basics

ASP files are just HTML files with scripting embedded within them. When a browser makes a request for an ASP file from the server, it is passed on to the ASP processing DLL for execution. After processing, the resulting file is then sent on to the requesting browser. Any scripting commands embedded from the original HTML file are executed, and then removed from the results. This is excellent because all of your scripting code is hidden from the person viewing your web pages with a browser. That is why it is so important that files containing ASP scripts have a .asp extension.

The Tags of ASP

To distinguish the ASP code from the HTML inside your files, ASP code is placed between <% and %> tags. This convention should be familiar to you if you have ever worked with any kind of server-side commands before in HTML. The tag combination implies to the ASP processor that the code within should be executed by the server and removed from the results. Depending on the default scripting language of your web site, this code could be VBScript, JScript, or any other language you've installed. Because this book is for the VBScript programmer, all of your ASP scripts will be in VBScript.

In the following snippet of HTML, you see an example of some ASP code between the <% and %> tags:

```
<table>
<tr>
<td>
<%
   x = x + 1
   y = y - 1
   ans = x * y
%>
</td>
</tr>
</table>
```

Using <SCRIPT> Blocks

You may also place your ASP code between `<script></script>` blocks. However, unless you direct the script to run at the server level, code placed between these tags will be executed at the client as normal client-side scripts. To direct your script block to execute on the server, use the `runat` command within your `<script>` block as follows:

```
<script language="VBScript" runat="Server">
' Your Script Goes Here
</script>
```

Specifying the Default Scripting Language

As stated previously, the default scripting language used by ASP is VBScript. However, you may change it for your entire site, or just a single web page. Placing a special scripting tag at the beginning of your web page does this. This tag specifies the scripting language to use for this page only.

```
<%@ language="ScriptingLanguage" %>
```

`"ScriptingLanguage"` can be any language for which you have the script engine installed. ASP comes with JScript, as well as VBScript.

Mixing HTML and ASP

You've probably guessed by now that you can easily mix HTML code with ASP scripts. The power of this feature is quite phenomenal! VBScript, as you know, has all of the control flow mechanisms such as `If...Then`, `For...Next`, and `Do...While` loops. But with ASP you can selectively include HTML code based on the results of these operators. For example, if you want to create a web page that greets the viewer with a "Good Morning," "Good Afternoon," or "Good Evening" depending on the time of day, you can easily do this as follows:

```
<html>

<head>
<title>Sample ASP Page</title>
</head>

<body>
<p>The time is now <%=Time()%></p>
<%
  Dim iHour

  iHour = Hour(Time())

  If (iHour >= 0 And iHour < 12 ) Then
%>
Good Morning!
<%
  ElseIf (iHour > 11 And iHour < 16 ) Then
%>
Good Afternoon!
```

```
<%
  Else
%>
Good Evening!
<%
End If
%>

</body>
</html>
```

First, you print out the current time. The <%= notation is shorthand to print out the value of an ASP variable or the result of a function call. You then move the hour of the current time into a variable called iHour. Based on the value of this variable, you write the normal HTML text.

Notice how the HTML code is outside of the ASP script tags. When the ASP processor executes this page, the HTML that lies between control flow blocks that aren't executed is discarded, leaving you with only the correct code. Here is the source of what is returned from our web server after processing this page.

```
<html>

<head>
<title>Sample ASP Page</title>
</head>

<body>
<p>The time is now 15:27:12 PM</p>

Good Afternoon!
</body>
</html>
```

As you can see, the scripting is completely removed leaving only the HTML and text.

The other way to output data to your web page viewer is using one of ASP's built-in objects called Response. This approach is covered in the next section, where you learn about the ASP object model.

Commenting Your ASP Code

As with any programming language, it is of utmost importance to comment your ASP code as much as possible. Try looking back at code you wrote a few days, weeks, or months ago and you'll then appreciate the comments! Do remember to make comments clear and concise — unclear comments are not worth putting in your code.

Comments in ASP are identical to comments in VBScript. When ASP comes across the single quote character it will graciously ignore the rest of the line.

```
<%
Dim iNumber

'Here is a comment
iNumber = iNumber + 1
%>
```

Using the Active Server Pages Object Model

ASP, like most Microsoft technologies, utilizes the Component Object Model, or COM, to expose functionality to consumer applications. ASP is actually an extension to your web server that allows server-side scripting. At the same time it also provides a compendium of objects and components, which manage interaction between the web server and the browser. These objects form the Active Server Pages Object Model. These "objects" can be manipulated by scripting languages.

ASP neatly divides up into six objects, which manage their own part of the interaction between client and server. At the heart of the interaction between client and server are the `Request` and `Response` objects, which deal with the HTTP request and response; but you'll be taking a quick tour through all of the different objects and components that are part of ASP.

Four of the six core objects of the object model (the `Request`, `Response`, `Application`, and `Session` objects) can use collections to store data. Before you look at each object in turn, you need to take a quick overview of collections.

Collections

Collections in ASP are very similar to their VBScript namesakes. They act as data containers that store their data in a manner close to that of an array. The information is stored in the form of name/value pairs. The `Application` and the `Session` objects have a collection property called `Contents`. This collection of variants can hold any information you wish to place in it. Using these collections allows you to share information between web pages.

To place a value into the collection, simply assign it a key, and then assign the value:

```
Application.Contents("Name") = "Homer Simpson"
```

Or you can follow this for numerical values:

```
Session.Contents("Age") = 39
```

Fortunately, Microsoft has made the `Contents` collection the default property for these two objects. Therefore, the following shorthand usage is perfectly acceptable:

```
Application("Name") = "Homer Simpson"
Session("Age") = 39
```

Having entered this data, you will want to retrieve it. To read values from the `Contents` collections just reverse the call:

```
sName = Application("Name")
sAge = Session("Age")
```

Iterating the Contents Collection

Because the `Contents` collections work like regular VBScript collections, they are easily iterated. You can use the collections `Count` property or use the `For Each` iteration method.

```
for x = 1 to Application.Contents.Count
   ...
next

for each item in Application.Contents
   ...
next
```

Note that the Contents *collections are 1 based. That is to say, the first element in the collection is at position 1, not 0.*

To illustrate this, the following ASP script dumps the current contents of the Application and Session objects' Contents collections.

```
<html>

<head>
<title>Sample ASP Page 2</title>
</head>

<body>
<p>The Application.Contents</p>
<%
   Dim Item

   For Each Item In Application.Contents
   Response.Write Item & " = [" & Application(Item) & "]<br>"
   Next
%>
<p>The Session.Contents</p>
<%
   For Each Item In Session.Contents
   Response.Write Item & " = [" & Session(Item) & "]<br>"
   Next
%>

</body>
</html>
```

Removing an Item from the Contents Collection

The Application object's Contents collection contains two methods, and these are Remove and RemoveAll. These allow you to remove one or all of the items stored in the Application.Contents collection.

In the following example, you add an item to the Application.Contents collection, and then remove it.

```
<%
   Application("MySign") = "Gemini"
   Application.Contents.Remove("MySign")
%>
```

(continued)

```
    Or we can just get rid of everything...

    <%
        Application.Contents.RemoveAll
    %>
```

Not all of the collections of each object work in this way, but the principles remain the same and you'll learn how each differs when each object is discussed.

The Request Object's Collection

When your web page is requested, along with the HTTP request, information such as the URL of the web page request and the format of the data requested is passed. It can also contain feedback from the user such as the input from a text box or drop-down list box. The `Request` object allows you to get at information passed along as part of the HTTP request. The corresponding output from the server is returned as part of the `Response`. The `Request` object has several collections to store information that warrant discussion.

The `Request` object has five collections. Interestingly, they all act as the default property for the object. That is to say, you may retrieve information from any of the five collections by using the abbreviated syntax:

```
    ClientIPAddress = Request("REMOTE_ADDR")
```

The `REMOTE_ADDR` value lies in the `ServerVariables` collection. However, through the use of the collection cascade, it can be retrieved with the previous notation. Please note that for ASP to dig through each collection, especially if they have many values, to retrieve a value from the last collection is extremely inefficient. It is always recommended that you use the fully qualified collection name in your code. Not only is this faster, but it improves your code in that it is more specific and less cryptic.

ASP searches through the collections in the following order:

- ❑   QueryString
- ❑   Form
- ❑   Cookies
- ❑   ClientCertificate
- ❑   ServerVariables

If there are variables with the same name, only the first is returned when you allow ASP to search. This is another good reason for you to fully qualify your collection.

QueryString

This contains a collection of all the information attached to the end of a URL. When you make a URL request, the additional information is passed along with the URL to the web page appended with a question mark. This information takes the following form:

```
    URL?item=data[&item=data][...]
```

The clue to the server is the question mark. When the server sees this, it knows that the URL has ended and variables are starting. So an example of a URL with a query string might look like this:

```
http://www.kingsley-hughes.com/book.asp?bookname=VBScriptProgrammersReference
```

It was mentioned earlier that the collections store information in name/value pairs. Despite this slightly unusual method of creating the name/value pair, the principle remains the same; bookname is the name and VBScriptProgrammersReference is the value. When ASP gets hold of this URL request, it breaks apart all of the name/value pairs and places them into this collection for easy access. This is another excellent feature of ASP. Query strings are built up using ampersands to delimit each name/value pair so if you wanted to pass the user information along with the book information, you could pass the following:

```
http://www.kingsley-
hughes.com/book.asp?bookname=VBScriptProgrammersReference&buyer=HSimpson
```

Query strings can be generated in one of three ways:

- ❑ The first is, as discussed, by a user typed URL.

- ❑ The second is as part of a URL specified in an Anchor tag.

```
<a href="book.asp?bookname=VBScriptProgrammersReference">Buy this book!</a>
```

So when you click the link, the name/value pair is passed along with the URL.

- ❑ The third and final method is via a form sent to the server with the GET method.

```
<form action="book.asp" method="GET">
Type your name: <input type="TEXT" name="buyer"><br>
Type your requested book: <input type="TEXT" name="bookname" SIZE=50><br>
<input type="SUBMIT" value="Submit">
</form>
```

This form that the last code generates is shown in Figure 20-4.

Type your name: [   ]
Type your requested book: [   ]
[Submit]

Figure 20-4

Next, you need to be able to retrieve information, and you use this technique to retrieve from each of the three methods used to generate a query string.

```
Request.QueryString("buyer")
Request.QueryString("bookname")
```

Please note that these lines won't display anything by themselves; you need to add either the shorthand notation (equality operator) to display functions in front of a single statement, or when a number of values need displaying then use `Response.Write` to separately display each value in the collection. For example:

```
<%=Request.QueryString("buyer")%> or Response.Write(Request.QueryString
("bookname"))
```

The first of the two `Request` object calls should return the name of `HSimpson` on the page and the second of the two should return `VBScript Programmers Reference`. Of course, you could always store this information in a variable for later access.

```
sBookName = Request.QueryString("bookname")
```

Form

This contains a collection of all the form variables posted to the HTTP request by an HTML form. Query strings aren't very private as they transmit information via a very visible method, the URL. If you want to transmit information from the form more privately, then you can use the form collection to do so which sends its information as part of the HTTP Request body. The easy access to form variables is one of ASP's best features.

If you go back to the previous example, the only alteration you need to make to the HTML form code is to change the `METHOD` attribute. Forms using this collection must be sent with the `POST` method and not the `GET` method. It is actually this attribute that determines how the information is sent by the form. So you change the method of the form as follows.

```
<form action="book.asp" method="POST">
Type your name: <input type="TEXT" name="buyer"><br>
Type your requested book: <input type="TEXT" name="bookname" size="40"><br>
<input type="SUBMIT" value="Submit">
</form>
```

Once the form has been submitted in this style, you can retrieve and display the information using the following:

```
=Request.Form("buyer")
```

Cookies

This contains a read-only collection of cookies sent by the client browser along with the request. Because the cookies were sent from the client, they cannot be changed here. You must change them using the `Response.Cookies` collection. A discussion of cookies can be found later in the chapter (see "The Response Object's Collection").

ClientCertificate

When a client makes a connection with a server requiring a high degree of security, either party can confirm who the sender/receiver is by inspecting their digital certificate. A digital certificate contains a number of items of information about the sender, such as the holder's name, address, and length of time the certificate is valid for. A third party, known as the Certificate Authority or CA, will have previously verified these details.

The `ClientCertificate` collection is used to access details held in a client-side digital certificate sent by the browser. This collection is only populated if you are running a secure server, and the request was via an `https://` call instead of an `http://` call. This is the preferred method to invoke a secure connection.

ServerVariables

When the client sends a request and information is passed across to the server, it's not just the page that is passed across, but also information such as who created the page, the server name, and the port that the request was sent to. The HTTP header that is sent across together with the HTTP request also contains information of this nature such as the type of browser and type of connection. This information is combined into a list of variables that are predefined by the server as environment variables. Most of them are static and never really change unless you change the configuration of your web server. The rest are based on the client browser.

These server variables can be accessed in the normal method. For example, the server variable `HTTP_USER_AGENT`, which returns information about the type of browser being used to view the page, can be displayed as follows:

```
<%=Request.ServerVariables("HTTP_USER_AGENT")%>
```

Alternatively you can print out the whole list of server variables and their values with the following ASP code:

```
For Each key in Request.ServerVariables
    Response.Write "<b>" & (Key) &"</b> "
    Response.Write (Request.ServerVariables(key)) & "<br>"
Next
```

Server variables are merely informative, but they do give you the ability to customize page content for specific browsers, or to avoid script errors that might be generated.

Request Object Properties and Methods

The `Request` object contains a single property and a single method. They are used together to transfer files from the client to the server. Uploading is accomplished using HTML forms.

TotalBytes Property

When the request is processed, this property will hold the total number of bytes in the client browser request. Most likely you'd use it to return the number of bytes in the file you wish to transfer. This information is important to the `BinaryRead` method.

BinaryRead Method

This method retrieves the information sent to the web server by the client browser in a POST operation. When the browser issues a POST, the data is encoded and sent to the server. When the browser issues a GET, there is no data other than the URL. The `BinaryRead` method takes one parameter, the number of bytes to read. So if you want it to read a whole file, you pass it the total number of bytes in the file, generated by the `TotalBytes` property.

It's very rarely applied because `Request.QueryString` and `Request.Form` are much easier to use. This is because `BinaryRead` wraps its answer in a safe array of bytes. For a scripting language that essentially only handles variants, this makes life a little complicated. However, this format is essential for file uploading.

You can find full details on how to upload files, and then decode a safe array of bytes in an excellent article at 15seconds.com (`www.15seconds.com/Issue/981121.htm`).

The Response Object's Collection

After you've processed the request information from the client browser, you'll need to be able to send information back. The `Response` object is just the ticket. It provides you with the tools necessary to send anything you need back to the client. The `Response` object contains only one collection: `Cookies`. This is the version of the `Request` object's `Cookies` collection that can be written to.

If you haven't come across them before, cookies are small (limited to 4KB of data) text files stored on the hard drive of the client that contain information about the users, such as whether they have visited the site before and on what date they last visited the site. There are lots of misapprehensions about cookies being intrusive as they allow servers to store information on the user's drive. However, you need to remember that first, the user has to voluntarily accept cookies or activate an Accept Cookies mechanism on the browser for them to work; second, this information is completely benign and cannot be used to determine the user's email address or the like. They are used to personalize pages that the user might have visited before.

Examples of things to store in cookies are unique user IDs or usernames; then, when the user returns to your web site, a quick check of cookies will let you know if this is a return visitor or not.

You can create a cookie on the user's machine as follows:

```
Response.Cookies("BookBought") = "VBScript Programmers Reference"
```

You can also store multiple values in one cookie using an index value key. The cookie effectively contains a VBScript Dictionary object and using the key can retrieve individual items. Its functioning is very close to that of an array.

```
Response.Cookies("BookBought")("1") = "VBScript Programmers Reference"
Response.Cookies("BookBought")("2") = "XSLT Programmers Reference"
```

A cookie will automatically expire — disappear from the user's machine — the moment a user ends a session. To extend the cookie beyond this natural lifetime, you can specify a date with the `Expires` property. The date takes the following format WEEKDAY DD-MON-YY HH:MM:SS.

```
Response.Cookies("BookBought").Expires = #31-Dec-04#
```

The # sign can be used to delimit dates in ASP (as in VBScript).

Other properties that can be used in conjunction with this collection are:

- ❑   `Domain`: A cookie is only sent to page requested within the domain from which it was created.
- ❑   `Path`: A cookie is only sent to pages requested within this path.
- ❑   `HasKeys`: Specifies whether the cookie uses an index/dictionary object or not.

❑   Secure: Specifies whether the cookie is secure. A cookie is only deemed secure if sent via the HTTPS protocol.

You can retrieve the cookie's information using the Request object cookies collection, mentioned earlier. To do this, you could use the following code:

```
You purchased <%=Request.Cookies("BookBought")%> last time you visited the site.
```

If several cookies were in the collection, you could iterate through each cookie and display the contents as in the following ASP code:

```
For Each cookie in Request.Cookies
    Response.Write (Request.Cookies(cookie))
Next
```

The Response Object's Methods

To understand what the Response object's methods and properties do, you need to examine the workings of how ASP sends a response in more detail. When an ASP script is run, an HTML output stream is created. This stream is a receptacle for the web server to store details and create the dynamic/interactive web page. As mentioned before, the page has to be created entirely in HTML for the browser to understand it (excluding client-side scripting, which is ignored by the server).

The stream is initially empty when created. New information is added to the end. If any custom HTML headers are required, then they have to be added at the beginning. Then the HTML contained in the ASP page is added next to the script, so anything not encompassed by <%%> tags is added. The Response object provides two ways of writing directly to the output stream, either using the Write method or its shorthand technique.

Method	Description/Example

Write	Probably the most used method of all the built-in objects, Write allows you to send information back to the client browser. You can write text directly to a web page by encasing the text in quotation marks.
	`Response.Write "Hello World!"`
	
	Or to display the contents of a variant you just drop the quotation marks.
	`sText = "Hello World!`
	`"Response.Write sText`
	
	For single portions of dynamic information that only require adding into large portions of HTML, you can use the equality sign as shorthand for this method, as specified earlier. For example:
	`My message is <% =sText %>`
	
	This technique reduces the amount of code needed, but at the expense of readability. There is nothing to choose between these techniques in terms of performance.

AddHeader	This method allows you to add custom headers to the HTTP response. For example, if you were to write a custom browser application that examined the headers of your HTTP requests for a certain value, you'd use this method to set that value.

(continued)

Method	Description/Example

	Usage is as follows:
	`Response.AddHeader "CustomServerApp",`
	`"CustomApp/1.2"`
	
	This would add the header `CustomServerApp` to the response with the value of `CustomApp/1.2`. There are no restrictions regarding headers and header value.

AppendToLog	Calling this method allows you to append a string to the web server log file entry for this particular request. This allows you to add custom log messages to the log file.
BinaryWrite	This method allows you to bypass the normal character conversion that takes place when data is sent back to the client. Usually, only text is returned, so the web server cleans it up. By calling `BinaryWrite` to send your data, the actual binary data is sent back, bypassing that cleaning process.
Clear	This method allows you to delete any data that has been buffered for this page so far. See discussion of the `Buffer` property for more details.
End	This method stops processing the ASP file and returns any currently buffered data to the client browser.
Flush	This method returns any currently buffered data to the client browser, and then clears the buffer. See discussion of the `Buffer` property for more details.

Redirect	This method allows you to relinquish control of the current page to a different web page.
	
	For example, you can use this method to redirect users to a login page if they have not yet logged on to your web site.
	`<%`
	`If (Not Session("LoggedOn") ) Then`
	`    Response.Redirect "login.asp"`
	`End If`
	`%>`

The Response Object's Properties

Now take a look at the properties of the `Response` object.

Buffer

You may optionally have ASP buffer your output for you. This property tells ASP whether or not to buffer output. Usually, output is sent to the client as it is generated. If you turn buffering on (by setting this property to `True`), output will not be sent until all scripts have been executed for the current page, or the `Flush` or `End` methods are called.

`Response.Buffer` has to be inserted after the language declaration, but before any HTML is used. If you insert it outside this scope you will most likely generate an error. A correct use of this method would look like:

```
<@ language="VBScript">
<% Response.Buffer = True %>
<html>
...
```

The `Flush` method is used in conjunction with the `Buffer` property. To use it correctly you must set the `Buffer` property first, and then at places within the script you can flush the buffer to the output stream, while continuing processing. This is useful for long queries, which might otherwise worry the user that nothing was being returned.

The `Clear` method erases everything in the buffer that has been added since the last `Response.Flush` call. It erases only the response body however, and leaves intact the response header.

CacheControl

Generally when a proxy server retrieves an ASP web page, it does not place a copy of it into its cache. That is because by their very nature ASP pages are dynamic and, most likely, a page will be stale the next time it is requested. You may override this feature by changing the value of this property to `Public`.

Charset

This property will append its contents to the HTTP content-type header that is sent back to the browser. Every HTTP response has a content-type header that defines the content of the response. Usually the content-type is `"text/html"`. Setting this property will modify the type sent back to the browser.

ContentType

This property allows you to set the value of the content-type that is sent back to the client browser.

Expires

Most web browsers keep web pages in a local cache. The cache is usually good as long as you keep your browser running. Setting this property allows you to limit the time the page stays in the local cache. The value of the `Expires` property specifies the length of time in minutes before the page will expire from the local cache. If you set this to zero, the page will not be cached.

ExpiresAbsolute

Just like the `Expires` property, this property allows you to specify the exact time and date on which the page will expire.

IsClientConnected

This read-only property indicates whether or not the client is still connected to the server. Remember that the client browser makes a request, and then waits for a response. Well, imagine you're running a lengthy script and during the middle of processing, the client disconnects because he was waiting too long. Reading this property will tell you if the client is still connected or not.

Status

This property allows you to set the value returned on the status header with the HTTP response.

Understanding the Application and Session Objects

The `Application` and `Session` objects, like `Request` and `Response`, work together very closely. `Application` is used to tie all of the pages together into one consistent application, while the `Session` object is used to track and present a user's series of requests to the web site as a continuous action, rather than an arbitrary set of requests.

Scope

Normally, you will declare a variable for use within your web page. You'll use it, manipulate it, and then perhaps print out its value or whatever. But when your page is reloaded or the viewer moves to another page, the variable and its value are gone forever. By placing your variable within the `Contents` collection of the `Application` or `Session` objects, you can extend the life span of your variable!

Any variable or object that you declare has two potential scopes: procedure and page. When you declare a variable within a procedure, its life span is limited to that procedure. Once the procedure is executed, your variable is gone. You may also declare a variable at the web page level but like the procedure-defined variable, once the page is reloaded the value is reset.

The `Contents` collections of these two objects allow you to extend the scope of your variables to session-wide and application-wide. If you place a value in the `Session` object, it will be available to all web pages in your site for the life span of the current session (more on sessions later). Good session scope variables are user IDs, usernames, login time, and other data items that pertain only to the session. Likewise, if you place your value into the `Application` object, it will exist until the web site is restarted. This allows you to place application-wide settings into a conveniently accessible place. Good application scope variables are font names and sizes, table colors, system constants, and other data that pertains to the application as a whole.

The global.asa File

Every ASP application may utilize a special script file. This file is named `global.asa` and it must reside in the root directory of your web application. It can contain script code that pertains to the application as a whole or each session. You may also create ActiveX objects for later use in this scripting file.

The Application Object

ASP works on the concept that an entire web site is a single web application. Therefore, there is only one instance of the `Application` object available for use in your scripting at all times.

Please note that it is possible to divide your web site into separate applications, but for the purposes of this discussion it's assumed there is only one application per web site.

Collections

The `Application` object contains two collections: `Contents` and `StaticObjects`. The `Contents` collection was discussed earlier in this chapter. The `StaticObjects` collection is similar to `Contents`, but only contains the objects that were created with the <object> tag in the scope of your application. This collection can be iterated just like the Contents collection.

You cannot store references to ASP's built-in objects in the Application collections.

Methods

The Application object contains two methods as detailed in the following table.

Method	Description
Lock	The Lock method is used to "lock down" the Contents collection so that it cannot be modified by other clients.
	This is useful if you are updating a counter, or perhaps grabbing a transaction number stored in the Application's Contents collection.
Unlock	The Unlock method "unlocks" the Application object, thus allowing others to modify the Contents collection.

Events

The Application object generates two events: Application_OnStart and Application_OnEnd:

❑ Application_OnStart: Is fired when the first view of your web page occurs.

❑ Application_OnEnd: Is fired when the web server is shut down. If you choose to write scripts for these events, they must be placed in your global.asa file.

The most common use of these events is to initialize application-wide variables. These would include items such as font names, table colors, and database connection strings. This could also include writing information to a system log file. The following is an example of global.asa file with script for these events:

```
<script language="VBScript" runat="Server">
Sub Application_OnStart
    'Globals...
    Application("ErrorPage") = "handleError.asp"
    Application("SiteBanAttemptLimit") = 10
    Application("AccessErrorPage") = "handleError.asp"
    Application("RestrictAccess") = False

    'Keep track of visitors…
    Application("NumVisits") = Application("NumVisits") + 1
End Sub
</script>
```

The Session Object

Each time a visitor comes to your web site, a Session object is created for the visitor if the visitor does not already have one. Therefore, an instance of the Session object is available to you in your scripting as well. The Session object is similar to the Application object in that it can contain values. However, the Session object's values are lost when your visitor leaves the site. The Session object is most useful for transferring information from web page to web page. Using the Session object, there is no need to pass information in the URL.

The most common use of the Session object is to store information in its Contents collection. This information would be session-specific in that it would pertain only to the current user.

Many web sites today offer a "user personalization" service, that is, to customize a web page to their preference. This is easily done with ASP and the Session object. The user variables are stored in the client browser for retrieval by the server later. Simply load the user's preferences at the start of the session, and then as the user browses your site, utilize the information regarding the user's preferences to display information.

Suppose your web site displays stock quotes for users. You could allow users to customize the start page to display their favorite stock quotes when they visit the site. By storing the stock symbols in your Session object, you can easily display the correct quotes when you render your web page.

This session management system relies on the use of browser cookies. The cookies allow the user information to be persisted even after a client leaves the site. Unfortunately, if a visitor to your web site does not allow cookies to be stored, you will be unable to pass information between web pages within the Session object.

Collections

The Session object contains two collections, Contents and StaticObjects.

The Contents collection was discussed earlier in this chapter. The StaticObjects collection is similar to Contents, but only contains the objects that were created with the <object> tag in your HTML page. This collection can be iterated just like the Contents collection.

Properties

Following are the properties that the Session object exposes for your use.

Property	Description
CodePage	Setting this property allows you to change the character set used by ASP when it is creating output. This property could be used if you were creating a multinational web site.
LCID	This property sets the internal locale value for the entire web application. By default, your application's locale is your server's locale.
	If your server is in the United States, then your application will default to the United States. Much of the formatting functionality of ASP utilizes this locale setting to display information correctly for the country in question. For example, the date is displayed differently in Europe versus the United States. So based on the locale setting, the date formatting functions will output the date in the correct format.
	You can also change this property temporarily to output data in a different format. A good example is currency. Suppose your web site had a shopping cart and you wanted to display totals in U.S. dollars for U.S. customers, and pounds sterling for U.K. customers. To do this, you'd change the LCID property to the British locale setting, and then call the currency formatting routine.

Property	Description
SessionID	Every session created by ASP has a unique identifier. This identifier is called the SessionID and is accessible through this property. It can be used for debugging ASP scripts.
Timeout	By default, an ASP session will time-out after 20 minutes of inactivity. Every time a web page is requested or refreshed by a user, this internal ASP time clock starts ticking. When the time clock reaches the value set in this property, the session is automatically destroyed. You can set this property to reduce the time-out period if you wish.

Methods

The Session object contains a single method, Abandon. This instructs ASP to destroy the current Session object for this user. This method is what you would call when a user logs off your web site.

Events

The Session object generates two events, Session_OnStart and Session_OnEnd. The Session_OnStart event is fired when the first view of your web page occurs. The Session_OnEnd event is fired when the web server is shut down. If you choose to write scripts for these events, they must be placed in your global.asa file. The most common use of these events is to initialize session-wide variables, items such as usage counts, login names, real names, user preferences, and so on.

The following is an example global.asa file with script for these events:

```
<script language="VBScript" runat="Server">

Sub Session_OnStart
    Session("LoginAttempts") = 0
    Session("LoggedOn") = False
End Sub

Sub Session_OnEnd
    Session("LoggedOn") = False
End Sub
</script>
```

The Server Object

The next object in the ASP object model is the Server object. The Server object enables you to create and work with ActiveX controls in your web pages. In addition, the Server object exposes methods that help in the encoding of URLs and HTML text. The following sections look at the properties and methods associated with it.

ScriptTimeout

This property sets the time, in seconds, which a script will be allowed to run. The default value for all scripts on the system is 90 seconds. That is to say, if a script has run for more than 90 seconds, the web server will intervene and let the client browser know something is wrong. If you expect your scripts to run for a long time, you will want to use this property.

CreateObject

This method is the equivalent to VBScript's `CreateObject`, or using the `New` keyword — it instantiates a new instance of an object. The result can be placed into the `Application` or `SessionContents` collection to lengthen its life span.

Generally you'll create an object at the time the session is created and place it into the `Session.Contents` collection. For example, suppose you've created an ActiveX DLL with a class that converts Fahrenheit to Celsius and vice versa. You could create an instance of this class with the `CreateObject` method and store it in the `Session.Contents` collection like the following:

```
Set Session("MyConverter") = Server.CreateObject("MyDLL.CDegreeConverter")
```

This object will be around as long as the session is and will be available for you to call. As you've seen in other chapters, this method is invaluable when working with database connections.

ASP comes with its own built-in set of components that you can create instances of using the `CreateObject` method. These are:

❑ **Ad Rotator:** This displays a random graphic and link every time a user connects to the page.

❑ **Browser Capabilities:** This manipulates a file `browscap.ini` contained on the server computer to determine the capabilities of a particular client's browser.

❑ **Content Linker:** This provides a central repository file from where you manage a series of links and their URLs, and provides appropriate descriptions about them.

❑ **Content Rotator:** This is a cut-down version of the Ad Rotator that provides the same function but without optional redirection.

❑ **Page Counter:** This counts the number of times a page has been hit.

❑ **Permission Checker:** This checks to see if a user has the permission before allowing them to access a given page.

❑ **Counters:** This counts any value on an ASP page from anywhere within an ASP application.

❑ **MyInfo:** This can be used to store personal information about a user within an XML file.

❑ **Status:** This collects server profile information.

❑ **Tools:** This is a set of miscellaneous methods grouped under the generic heading of Tools.

❑ **IIS Log:** This allows you to create an object that permits your applications to write to and otherwise access the IIS log.

Execute

This method executes an ASP file and inserts the results into the response. You can use this call to include snippets of ASP code, such as subroutines.

GetLastError

This method returns an `ASPError` object that contains all of the information about the last error that has occurred.

HTMLEncode

This method encodes a string for proper HTML usage. This is useful if you want to actually display HTML code on your web pages.

MapPath

This method returns a string that contains the actual physical path to the file in question. Subdirectories of your web site can be virtual. That is to say, they don't physically exist in the hierarchy of your web site. To find out the true whereabouts of a file, you can call this method.

Transfer

The `Transfer` method allows you to immediately transfer control of the executing page to another page. This is similar to the `Response.Redirect` method except for the fact that the `Transfer` method makes all variables and the `Request` collections available to the called page.

URLEncode

This method, as the title says, encodes a URL for transmission. This encoding includes replacing spaces with a plus sign (+) and replacing unprintable characters with hexadecimal values. You should always run your URLs through this method when redirecting.

The ObjectContext Object

The final object to consider is `ObjectContext`, which comes into play when you use transactions in your web page. When an ASP script has initiated a transaction, it can be either committed or aborted by this object. It has two methods to do this.

SetAbort

`SetAbort` is called when the transaction has not been completed and you don't want resources updated.

SetComplete

`SetComplete` is called when there is no reason for the transaction to fail. If all of the components that form part of the transaction call `SetComplete`, then the transaction will complete.

Using Active Server Pages Effectively

Is it true that a little bit of knowledge is a bad thing? In the realm of ASP, I think not. A little bit of knowledge is probably just enough to get you interested in learning more!

For the final part of this chapter you build a web site to demonstrate some of the features of ASP. This sample site demonstrates many of the ASP features and principles described earlier in this chapter.

Designing the Site

Before you start creating the new web site, you should think about design. For your first ASP application, we'll keep it quite simple. What you want to create is an HTML form that accepts for input the following information:

- First name
- Last name
- Email address

After the user submits the form, your ASP page will reformat the first and last name and check the email address for proper syntax.

Creating the global.asa File

The first step in creating a new ASP application is to create your global.asa file. This is the file that houses your event handlers for the Application and Session objects. In addition, in this file you may set application and session-wide variables to their default values. In the root of your web server directory, create a file called global.asa. Following is the content of your sample global.asa:

```
<script language="VBScript" runat="Server">
Sub Application_OnStart
    Application("AllowedErrorsBeforeWarning") = 3
End Sub

Sub Session_OnStart
    Session("ErrorCount") = 0
End Sub

Sub Session_OnEnd
 'Nothing to do here...
End Sub

Sub Application_OnEnd
 'Nothing to do here...
End Sub
</script>
```

The file has handlers defined for Application_OnStart, Application_OnEnd, Session_OnStart, and Session_OnEnd. The Application_OnEnd and Session_OnEnd events are shown earlier for completeness but are not used in this example.

You want to set a limit on the number of submissions the user gets before a warning message is shown. Because this is a feature of the application and affects all users, you will store this constant in the Application.Contents collection. This is done in the Application_OnStart event. You add to the collection an item named AllowedErrorsBeforeWarning and set its value to 3.

Now that you know how many times a user can try to get it right, you need a place to store the number of times the user has tried to get it right. Because this counter is different for each user, you'll place this into the Session.Contents collection. You initialize your variable to 0. This is done in the Session_OnStart event. You add to the collection an item named, appropriately, ErrorCount, with a value of 0.

Creating the Main Page

Now that you've laid the groundwork for the ASP application, it's time to build the main page. Because this is a simple example, you will only utilize a single web page. Begin by creating this single page.

Create a new web page on your site and name it `default.asp`. This is the filename used by IIS as the default web page. The default web page is the one that is returned by a web server when no web page is specified. For example, when you call up `www.wrox.com/`, you aren't specifying a web page. The server looks through its list of default filenames and finds the first match in the web site's root directory.

The following shows the contents of your `default.asp` page:

```
<%@ language="VBScript" %>
<%
Dim txtFirstName, txtLastName, txtEmailAddr
Dim sMessage

'*******************************************************************
'* Main
'*
'* The main subroutine for this page...
'*******************************************************************

Sub Main()
 'Was this page submitted?
 if ( Request("cmdSubmit") = "Submit" ) Then
   'Reformat the data into a more readable format...
   txtFirstName = InitCap(Request("txtFirstName"))
   txtLastName = InitCap(Request("txtLastName"))
   txtEmailAddr = LCase(Request("txtEmailAddr"))

   'Check the email address for the correct components...
   if (Instr(1, txtEmailAddr, "@") = 0 _
       or Instr(1, txtEmailAddr, ".") = 0 ) Then
     sMessage = "The email address you entered does not " _
       & "appear to be valid."
   Else
     'Make sure there is something after the period..
     if ( Instr(1, txtEmailAddr, ".") = Len(txtEmailAddr) _
     or Instr(1, txtEmailAddr, "@") = 1 or _
     (Instr(1, txtEmailAddr, ".") = Instr(1, txtEmailAddr, "@") + 1) ) Then
       sMessage = "You must enter a complete email address."
     end if
   End If
   'We passed our validation, show that all is good...
   if ( sMessage = "" ) Then
     sMessage = "Thank you for your input. All data has " _
       & "passed verification."
   else
   Session("ErrorCount") = Session("ErrorCount") + 1
```

(continued)

```
      if ( Session("ErrorCount") > _
          Application("AllowedErrorsBeforeWarning") ) then
        sMessage = sMessage & "<P><Font Size=1>You have exceeded " _
          & "the normal number of times it takes to get this right!</Font>"
      end if
   End If
 Else
   'First time in here? Set some default values...
   txtFirstName = "Enter Your First Name"
   txtLastName = "Enter Your Last Name"
   txtEmailAddr = "Enter Your Email Address"
 End If
End Sub


'**********************************************************************
'* InitCap
'*
'* Capitalizes the first letter of the string
'**********************************************************************

Function InitCap(sStr)
 InitCap = UCase(Left(sStr, 1)) & LCase(Right(sStr, Len(sStr) - 1))
End Function


'**********************************************************************
'* Call our main subroutine
'**********************************************************************

Call Main()
%>

<html>
<head>
   <title>My First ASP Application</title>
</head>

<body>

<table border="0" cellPadding="0" cellSpacing="0" width="600">
<tbody>
   <tr>
     <td width="100"><a href="http://www.wrox.com" target="_blank" border=0
alt><img border=0 title="Check out the Wrox Press web Site!"
src="images/wroxlogo.gif" WIDTH="56" HEIGHT="56"></a></td>
     <td width="500"><center><font size="5" face="Trebuchet MS">My First ASP
     Application</font></center></td>
   </tr>
```

```
    <tr>
      <td width="100"> </td>
      <td width="500" align="left"><font face="Trebuchet MS"><br>
      Please fill out the following form and press the [Submit] button.
      The information you enter will be reformatted and the email address will be
      verified.</font><form action="default.asp" id="FORM1" method="post"
      name="frmMain">
       <table border="0" cellPadding="1" cellSpacing="5" width="100%">
        <tr>
          <td width="100" nowrap align="right"><font size="2" face="Trebuchet MS">
          First Name:</font></td>
          <td width="350"><font size="2" face="Trebuchet MS">
            <input title="Enter your first name here" name="txtFirstName"
            size="30" value="<%=txtFirstName%>" tabindex="1"></font></td>
            <td width="50"><div align="right"><font size="2" face="Trebuchet MS">
            <input type="submit" title="Submit this data for processing..."
             value="Submit" name="cmdSubmit" tabindex="4"></font></td>
        </tr>

        <tr>
          <td width="100" nowrap align="right">
            <font size="2" face="Trebuchet MS">Last Name:</font></td>
          <td width="400" colspan="2">
            <font size="2" face="Trebuchet MS">
            <input title="Enter your last name here" name="txtLastName"
             size="30" value="<%=txtLastName%>" tabindex="2"></font></td>
        </tr>

        <tr>
          <td width="100" nowrap align="right"><font size="2" face="Trebuchet MS">
          Email Address:</font></td>
          <td width="400" colspan="2"><font size="2" face="Trebuchet MS">
          <input title="Enter your valid email address here" name="txtEmailAddr"
          size="40" value="<%=txtEmailAddr%>" tabindex="3"></font></td>
        </tr>
        <tr>
          <td nowrap width=500 colspan="3" align="center"><font face="Trebuchet
          MS"><br>
         <strong><%=sMessage%></strong> </font></td>
        </tr>
      </table>
    </form>
    <p> </td>
  </tr>
</tbody>
</table>
</body>
</html>
```

As you can see, the page is quite long. But it breaks logically into two distinct sections: the ASP/VBScript portion and the HTML portion. Let's examine each section individually.

The ASP/VBScript Section

The top half of your file is where the ASP code lives. This code is executed by the server before the page is returned to the browser that requested it. As you've seen, any code that is to be executed on the server before returning is enclosed in the special <% and %> tags.

For clarity (and sanity!) the ASP code has been divided into subroutines. This not only makes the code more readable, but also will aid in its reuse. The code has two routines: `Main` and `InitCap`. Before you do anything however, you declare some variables.

```
Dim txtFirstName, txtLastName, txtEmailAddr
Dim sMessage
```

When variables are declared outside of a subroutine in an ASP page, the variables retain their data until the page is completely processed. This allows you to pass information from your ASP code to your HTML code as you'll see.

After your variables have been declared, you have the `Main` routine. This is called by the ASP code every time a browser retrieves the page. The `Main` subroutine is not called automatically: You must explicitly call it.

```
'*****************************************************************
'* Main
'*
'* The main subroutine for this page...
'*****************************************************************

Sub Main()
 '  Was this page submitted?
  if ( Request("cmdSubmit") = "Submit" ) Then
 ' Reformat the data into a more readable format...
    txtFirstName = InitCap(Request("txtFirstName"))
    txtLastName = InitCap(Request("txtLastName"))
    txtEmailAddr = LCase(Request("txtEmailAddr"))

    '  Check the email address for the correct components...
    if ( Instr(1, txtEmailAddr, "@") = 0 or Instr(1, txtEmailAddr, ".") _
      = 0 ) Then
     sMessage = "The email address you entered does not appear to be valid."
    Else
      '  Make sure there is something after the period..
     if ( Instr(1, txtEmailAddr, ".") = Len(txtEmailAddr) _
         or Instr(1, txtEmailAddr, "@") = 1 or & _
         (Instr(1, txtEmailAddr, ".") = Instr(1, txtEmailAddr, "@") + 1) ) _
         Then
       sMessage = "You must enter a complete email address."
     end if
    End If
```

```
    ' We passed our validation, show that all is good...
        if ( sMessage = "" ) Then
          sMessage = "Thank you for your input. All data has " _
            & "passed verification."
        else
          Session("ErrorCount") = Session("ErrorCount") + 1

          if ( Session("ErrorCount") > _
            Application("AllowedErrorsBeforeWarning") ) then
            sMessage = sMessage & "<P><Font Size=1>You have exceeded " _
              & "the normal number of times it takes to get this right!</Font>"
          end if
        End If
      Else
        '    First time in here? Set some default values...
        txtFirstName = "Enter Your First Name"
        txtLastName = "Enter Your Last Name"
        txtEmailAddr = "Enter Your Email Address"
      End If
End Sub
```

First, you see if the form was actually submitted by the user; otherwise you initialize your variables. To determine if the page has been submitted, you check the value of the cmdSubmit Request variable. This is the button on your form. When pressed, the form calls this page and sets the value of the cmdSubmit button to Submit. If a user just loads the page without pressing the button, the value of cmdSubmit is blank (" "). There are other ways to determine if a web page was submitted, but this method is the simplest.

After you determine that the page is in fact submitted, run the names through the second function on this page: InitCap. InitCap is a quick little function that will format a word to proper case, that is, the first letter will be capitalized and the rest of the word will be lowercase. Following is the function:

```
'*******************************************************************
'* InitCap
'*
'* Capitalizes the first letter of the string
'*******************************************************************

Function InitCap(sStr)
    InitCap = UCase(Left(sStr, 1)) & LCase(Right(sStr, Len(sStr) - 1))
End Function
```

Now that you've cleaned up the names, you need to check the email address for validity. To do this you ensure that it contains an "@" sign and a period (.). Once past this check, you make sure that there is data after the period and before the "@" sign. This is "quick and dirty" email validity checking.

If either of these checks fails, you place a failure message into the string sMessage. This will be displayed in the HTML section after the page processing is complete.

Now, if your email address has passed the test, you set the message (sMessage) to display a thank you note. If you failed the test, you increment the error counter that you set up in the global.asa file. Here you also check to see if you have exceeded your limit on errors. If you have, a sterner message is set for display.

Finally, the last thing in the ASP section is your call to `Main`. This is what is called when the page is loaded.

```
'**********************************************************************
'* Call our main subroutine
'**********************************************************************

Call Main()
```

The HTML Section

This section is a regular HTML form with a smattering of ASP thrown in for good measure. The ASP that you've embedded in the HTML sets default values for the input fields and displays any messages that your server-side code has generated.

The most important part of the HTML is where the ASP code is embedded. The following example illustrates this:

```
<input title="Enter your first name here" name="txtFirstName" size="30"
  value="<%=txtFirstName%>" tabindex="1">
```

Here you see a normal text input box. However, to set the value of the text box you use the `Response.Write` shortcut (`<%=`) to insert the value of the variable `txtFirstName`. Remember that you dimensioned this outside of your ASP functions so that it would have page scope. Now you utilize its value by inserting it into the HTML.

You do exactly the same thing with the Last Name and Email Address text boxes:

```
<input title="Enter your last name here" name="txtLastName" size="30"
  value="<%=txtLastName%>" tabindex="2">
<input title="Enter your valid email address here" name="txtEmailAddr"
  size="40" value="<%=txtEmailAddr%>" tabindex="3">
</tr>
```

The last trick in the HTML section is the display of the failure or success message. This message is stored in the variable called `sMessage`. At the bottom of the form, you display the contents of this variable.

```
<td nowrap width=500 colspan="3" align="center">
   <font face="Trebuchet MS">
   <br>
   <strong>
   <%=sMessage%>
   </strong>
   </font>
</td>
```

The beauty of this code is that if `sMessage` is blank, then nothing is shown; otherwise the message is displayed.

Summary

You learned much in this chapter! You first covered how HTTP is the transaction system that sends web pages to requesting clients. It is a very important piece of the puzzle. Next, you learned about Active Server Pages or ASP, how to create them, and what special HTML tags you need to include in your files to use ASP.

You looked through the ASP object model and saw that the Request and Response objects are used to manage details of the HTTP request and responses. You saw that the Application object is used to group pages together into one application and that the Session is used to create the illusion that the interaction between user and site is one continuous action. Finally, you created a small application that demonstrates two uses for ASP: form validation and data manipulation.

21

Adding VBScript to Your VB and .NET Applications

By now, it should be clear that VBScript is useful in many contexts within Windows. Not surprisingly, along with a variety of different technologies, Microsoft provides yet another component capable of supporting VBScript — the Script Control. This *ActiveX control* provides a simple way for your application written in Visual Basic (or any other language that supports ActiveX controls) to host its own scripting environment, allowing you, or your users, to customize the application. Thanks to Microsoft's attention to backward compatibility in the .NET framework, the Script Control, and by extension VBScript, can also be used to automate and extend .NET applications.

In the past, programmers had to struggle to provide customizability to their projects, or pay license fees for other products such as Microsoft's portable VB variant, Visual Basic for Applications (VBA). In 1997, Microsoft released Windows Script Interfaces (WSI) as an interface to script engines, and eventually followed up with Script Control. WSI was intended for C++ programmers, and the Script Control was tailor-made for use in a Visual Basic (VB) application — and as noted, it works great with .NET, too.

At the time of the writing of the third edition of this *VBScript Programmer's Reference*, Visual Basic 6 is considered "legacy" technology, and most new applications for the Windows platform are being written using the .NET framework. One may wonder why the Script Control is still relevant, almost ten years after its initial release, and why the authors are including this chapter in this edition of the book. In short, there are two reasons:

❑   Millions of lines of VB 6 code are still in use in enterprises around the world. It may be some time yet before those applications are ported to .NET. The Script Control and VBScript actually offer an excellent opportunity to extend and modify existing VB 6 applications without adding or changing actual VB 6 code.

❑   While Microsoft does offer the Microsoft.Vsa namespace for .NET and Visual Studio for Applications as viable .NET scripting options, the Script Control is so simple and easy to adopt, you might be tempted to use it instead.

Why Add Scripting to Your Application?

Allowing customization of your application through scripting can open many opportunities — not only to you, the programmer (allowing you to change or customize your application's behavior without having to recompile and redistribute), but also to your end users, who will be able to do more with your application. The possibilities of scripting are almost endless but, as usual, adding this capability to your application will require additional time and effort for design, coding, testing.

Adding scripting support to your application is most appropriate when you want to allow customization of the application "from within" — as opposed to "from without." Adding customization "from without" (allowing external applications to utilize your code) is often what you really want, but scripting is not necessarily the best way to achieve it; exposing your functionality through a well-defined API in a component library (DLL) is generally the best option for exposing your code's functionality to other applications and libraries. However, when you want to extend your VB 6 or .NET application's native functionality from within, scripting is a great option.

For example, consider Microsoft Excel, which offers customization through scripting both "from within" and "from without." Customization of Excel from without comes from the fact that Excel exposes a public, COM-based programming interface that programmers in any other COM-enabled language (like Visual Basic, VBScript, or VB.NET) can code against, all without even starting the Excel graphical interface. However, you can also add macros and VBA code to customize the behavior of Excel from *within* Excel itself.

In your VB 6 or .NET application, you can accomplish customization "from without" simply by creating COM or .NET libraries that expose published interfaces. This technique does not necessarily require any additional coding or testing time, though you do need to design your program and segregate your code in a particular way in order to do it right. For many applications, this level of customization is all that is needed.

However, you can also, like Excel, offer customization "from within" by using the Script Control. There are different approaches to this, and you have to design the internals of your program (at least the parts you want to expose to scripting) a little differently than you are used to. This chapter discusses these techniques and introduces freely downloadable sample applications in both Visual Basic 6 and .NET that implement the Script Control.

Macro and Scripting Concepts

Before you dig into the details of the Script Control, it is helpful to conceptualize how the Script Control can be used inside an application. There are two approaches:

❑   Using "scriptlets" (perhaps stored in text files or a database table) that are executed at certain times for very targeted purposes.

❑   Exposing whole sections of an application to customization and automation through scripting. In both approaches, you have the option of sharing some or all of your application's internal object model with your application's hosted scripts.

Both approaches are similar in that your application gives up control over some portion of its logic or functionality to scripts that are loaded at runtime (as opposed to being compiled into your application). The approaches are different primarily in terms of scope. Let's look at two examples.

Using Scriptlets

As an example of the smaller scope approach, imagine an application that has a complex algorithm coded as a series of steps spread across several procedures and/or classes. Suppose this complex algorithm is part of an accounting system and computes the amounts for a series of invoices; each invoice is calculated based on a series of subformulas that have different inputs and outputs depending on the portion of the total invoice amount being computed. Suppose there are 10 subformulas required to compute the amount of one invoice. Imagine that nine of these formulas are static, meaning that they are the same in all cases and can therefore be hard-coded.

However, imagine that one of the 10 formulas is different based on the type of invoice. Sometimes the formula must work one way, sometimes another. Also, the company paying for this application adds new types of invoices all the time, each with unique requirements for this tenth formula. The company wants to be able to add new invoice types without having to add unique, hard-coded versions of this formula for each invoice type. They don't want to have to redeploy or recompile the application each time a new invoice type is added.

The application designers decide to use the Script Control to solve this quandary. They add a column called `ForumlaScript` to the `InvoiceType` table in the database. In this column they store scriptlets, written in VBScript, that compute the result for this tenth subformula in a unique way for each invoice type. Each scriptlet is different based on the requirements for each invoice type. When the invoice amount calculation algorithm reaches the step for the tenth subformula it loads the appropriate scriptlet from the `InvoiceType` table and uses the Script Control to dynamically execute the scriptlet.

Using Scripts

As you can see, in this first example, the application uses scripting capability for a very targeted purpose, adding just the necessary amount of customizability. In a larger scope example, a whole section of the application might be opened up for scripting and automation. The scripts used by the application might be more complex, such as the Windows Script Host (WSH) and ASP scripts you've been looking at in this book. The scripts could have access to the entire object model of the hosting application, much in the way that the WSH and ASP engines expose objects such as `WScript` and `Request` to the scripts they host.

This larger scope approach might be used to allow users to write their own macros to control the user interface of the application (imagine exposing menu items, toolbar buttons, textboxes, and other form controls to your users' scripts). Or the application might expose an object model that allows users to write and plug in their own scripts to generate reports.

Which Scope Is the Best?

Whether large scope or small scope, the possibilities are endless. If you are trying to add customizability for your end users, then the Script Control may indeed be the best thing because you probably want to allow your users to create and edit scripts from within your application, and you have no control over how or which users to choose to add scripting to the application. Or maybe your application is deployed at the customer's site, and your deployment consultants (who may not be expert programmers) need the flexibility to customize the application on the spot, right when they are in the customer's office installing the application.

However, if you are trying to achieve a design that simply allows for "plug-in" components to ease deployment of bug fixes and new features into your production environment, upon further consideration of your design options, and perhaps a little research, you may decide that an object-oriented polymorphic design that utilizes binary interfaces and the Class Factory design pattern might be a better, more stable, and more predictable alternative.

That's a mouthful. Unfortunately, there is no room here to explain what we exactly mean by "an object-oriented polymorphic design that utilizes interfaces and the Class Factory design pattern." The point is that the Script Control is not the solution to every design problem. Consider carefully *why* you are thinking of using the Script Control. What requirements exactly are you trying to implement? You may find that another solution that achieves the same thing without some of the downsides of the Script Control, namely the fact that script code will almost always run slower than your application's native compiled code and that you do not have any control over syntax errors and poor programming practices that people might insert into the scripts.

Adding the Script Control to a VB 6 or .NET Application

If you have not already downloaded the Script Control, you can download it from the Microsoft web site. The installation program automatically adds the control to your machine and registers it. You may find that the Script Control is already installed on your machine. Somewhere along the way, Microsoft started including the Script Control with the default installation of Windows. Search your machine for the file msscript.ocx to see if you already have it (it's most likely in C:\Windows\System32).

When you are ready to use the Script Control in your application (you might want to read ahead first, and perhaps take some time to go through this chapter's downloadable sample projects), the Script Control can be easily added to a VB 6 or .NET Windows Forms project as an ActiveX control (attached to a form) or as a normal COM object that you declare and instantiate in code. In the comments and code of the sample projects, you can observe the differences between adding the Script Control to a form as a component versus simply instantiating a ScriptControl object and using it directly. Either option works well in both .NET and VB 6.

Generally speaking, using the Script Control as a form-attached component is the easier option because you don't need to worry about controlling the lifetime of the object (it's always there as a member of the form, just like a button or timer control would be). However, there is no strict rule that you have to use a form at all — in which case, you can just instantiate the ScriptControl object inline in your code.

In theVB 6 IDE, you add the Script Control to a form from the Component Toolbox just as you would other form controls, such as CommandButton or Timer control. If you prefer to instantiate an object directly in your code, of if your solution does not use a form, you can add a reference to the Script Control using the Project ⇨ References menu. The reference is called "Microsoft Script Control 1.0."

Similarly, in .NET you can add the Script Control to the Component Toolbox in the Visual Studio IDE (use the "Add Items" right-click menu) or add a normal reference using the Add Reference dialog box; the Script Control will be found on the COM tab and will be called "Microsoft Script Control 1.0."

In the case of .NET, the .NET framework pretty much renders invisible the fact that the Script Control is a COM object, including the sharing of your .NET objects as COM objects to your scripts, though you may run into situations where a general knowledge of the topic of .NET-COM interop is helpful.

One area where interop could be potentially complex is the sharing of your assembly's .NET objects with VBScript code hosted by the Script Control. Even this, though, is rendered very simple in most situations by checking the Assembly Information dialog box (available from the Application tab in the project properties in Visual Studio) to ensure that the "Make Assemble COM-Visible" check box is checked.

Script Control Reference

This middle part of the chapter is a complete reference for the Script Control, including the objects, collections, properties, methods, method syntax, and examples. After the reference, the chapter continues with some additional explanation, followed by information about the downloadable sample Visual Basic 6 and VB.NET applications that make use of the Script Control. The code and syntax examples are based on VB 6; please consult the documentation of your .NET language (such as VB.NET or C#) for the equivalent syntax. The sample VB.NET project that comes with this chapter is a good place to seek .NET-specific guidance.

Object Model

The Script Control object model is illustrated in Figure 21-1. The details of these objects and their properties and methods are documented in the upcoming sections.

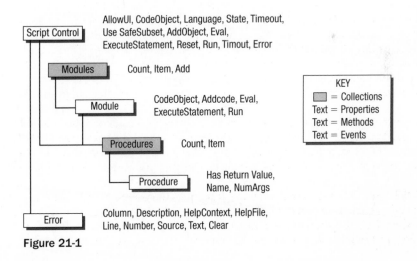

Figure 21-1

Objects and Collections

The Script Control component has several objects and collections (which are a special kind of multivalued object) that work together to provide a wide range of capabilities for adding scripts to a Visual Basic application. For each object and collection, this section describes the object in general; documents its properties, methods, and events; and, where appropriate, provides example code.

ScriptControl Object

`ScriptControl` is the main element that enables scripting in an application. It provides a simple interface for hosting script engines, such as VBScript or JScript. All the other available objects that depend on an instance of `ScriptControl`. `ScriptControl` can be instantiated in three different ways:

❑   Early bound, on a form (add it through the Components dialog)

❑   Early bound, through code (add it through the References dialog)

❑   Late bound (at any time)

Declaration Syntax

This is the VB 6 syntax to declare an early bound variable for the `ScriptControl` object (this is generally preferred over the late bound syntax).

```
Dim|Private|Public [WithEvents] objSC As [MSScriptControl.]ScriptControl
```

This is the syntax to declare a late bound variable for the `ScriptControl` object. A late bound variable cannot handle events. If you use a late bound variable, the Script Control does not need to be referenced in the project.

```
Dim|Private|Public objSC [As Object|Variant]
```

Properties

The properties of the `ScriptControl` object are described in the following table.

Name	Accepts/Returns	Access	Description
AllowUI	Boolean	Read/Write	Sets or returns the value indicating whether or not visual elements such as MsgBox or InputBox can be displayed. When this is set to False, the only way to communicate visually with the user is directly through the hosting application.

Name	Accepts/Returns	Access	Description
Error	Error object	Read-only	Returns a reference to the Error object for a ScriptControl instance.
Language	String	Read/Write	Sets or returns the name of the scripting language used by the ScriptControl object. "VBScript" and "JScript" are natively supported. If other compatible scripting languages are installed, the name of other scripting languages can be used as well. Setting this property resets all other members of the ScriptControl and its child objects.
Modules	Modules object	Read-only	Returns a reference to the Modules collection of the ScriptControl object.
Name	String	Read-only	If the ScriptControl object is attached to a form, this property returns the name assigned to the control on its properties page.
Procedures	Procedures object	Read-only	Returns a reference to the Procedures collection of the default "Global" module. To access the Procedures collection of other modules, access the module directly through the Modules collection and use the Module.Procedures property.

(continued)

Name	Accepts/Returns	Access	Description
SitehWnd	Long	Read/Write	Sets or returns the "handle" to the parent window used by the executing code. When the Script Control is used as an ActiveX Control, placed on a form, the default value of SitehWnd is the hWnd property of the container of the control. Otherwise, when the Script Control is used as an object (not attached to a form), SitehWnd is always 0, which corresponds to the Desktop. This property may impact which window (or control) has UI control over the scripted UI elements. You may change this property to make the Script Control dependent upon a specific window rather than, in some cases, the Desktop (for example, you might want the Script Control to freeze a part of your application and not the Desktop). Circumstances under which you would need to change this property should be rare.
State	Long (States)	Read/Write	Sets or returns the mode of the ScriptControl object; uses the States enumerated constant. When this value is set to Connected (1), the ScriptControl will be able to sink events generated by objects added using the AddObject method. Thus, changing the state gives you some control over the handling of events.

Name	Accepts/Returns	Access	Description
TimeOut	Long	Read/Write	Sets or returns a number representing time in milliseconds, indicating how long the ScriptControl object will wait before aborting a script that is taking a long time. This property can be set to a constant NoTimeout (-1), which removes time restrictions placed on the execution of script code; turning off the timeout can be dangerous, however, because someone might, for example, create a script that contains an endless loop. The default value is 10,000 milliseconds (10 seconds). When the timeout expires, a Timeout event may occur (depending on whether or not the ScriptControl can handle events) and at that time, if the ScriptControl has the AllowUI property enabled, the user is alerted with a dialog box, permitting the user to continue execution of the script. Otherwise, the script is terminated and an error is raised. When this property is set to 0 (not recommended), a Timeout event occurs as soon as the script stops Windows messaging for slightly more than 100 milliseconds.

(continued)

Name	Accepts/Returns	Access	Description
UseSafeSubset	Boolean	Read/Write	Sets or returns a `Boolean` value indicating whether or not the Script Control may run components that are not marked as "Safe for Scripting." For example, a script may try to use the scripting runtime `FileSystemObject,` which is not "Safe for Scripting" because it allows access to the file system. You may set this property to `True` when you are concerned about the ability of the script to create damage on the client computer. When the Script Control is used in a host that requires that components are "Safe for Scripting" (such as Internet Explorer), this property defaults to `True` and is read-only.

Methods

The methods of the `ScriptControl` object are described in the following table.

Name	Arguments	Returns	Description
AddCode	*code:* `String` value representing a valid script	N/A	This is the primary method of adding script to the Script Control. When called on the `ScriptControl` object, automatically adds the new code to the default `"Global"` module. Calls on an individual `Module` object to add code to a particular module. When adding code for entire procedures and blocks of code, the code must be added in a single call to the `AddCode` method. Each statement in the block can be separated by colons (:) or the line break characters `vbNewLine` (preferred), `vbCr`, `vbLf`, and `vbCrLf`.

Name	Arguments	Returns	Description
AddObject	*Name:* Unique `String` name for the object being added *object:* Any object within the scope of your application *addmembers:* Optional Boolean value indicating whether or not the object's public members should be accessible to the `ScriptControl` object and its scripts	N/A	Allows the script to access the host's runtime object model as exposed by the object(s) added through this method. Objects added to the `ScriptControl` are available globally within the `ScriptControl` object. The optional `addmembers` parameter indicates whether or not the members of the added object are also available to the scripts within.
Eval	*Expression:* A `String` value representing a valid "expression," meaning any script fragment that can be compiled and executed	The output of the expression, if any	Evaluates an expression. Similar to `Eval` function in VBScript. This is one of the best ways to evaluate dynamic expressions provided by the user. When comparing `Eval` to the `ExecuteStatement` method, be aware that the `"="` operator is treated as a comparison operator when used with `Eval`, but as an assignment operator when used with `ExecuteStatement`. Hence, x = y will evaluate to a `Boolean` subtype when used with `Eval`, but when used with `ExecuteStatement`, the value of y will be assigned to variable x, and nothing will be returned. The expression evaluated can take advantage of any members within scope of the `Module` or `ScriptControl` object.

(continued)

Name	Arguments	Returns	Description
Execute Statement	*statement:* String value representing the statement to be executed	N/A	Unlike the Eval method, ExecuteStatement only executes a statement and does not return any value. When comparing Eval to the ExecuteStatement method, be aware that the "=" operator will be treated as a comparison operator when used with Eval, but as an assignment operator when used with ExecuteStatement. Hence, x = y will evaluate to a Boolean subtype when used with Eval, but when used with ExecuteStatement, the value of y will be assigned to variable x, and nothing will be returned. The statement executed can take advantage of any members within scope of the Module or ScriptControl object. To obtain a return value from a procedure, you should use either the Eval or Run methods.
Reset	None	N/A	Discards all the members and child objects of the ScriptControl object and initializes them to their default state. When the Reset method is called, the State property is reset to Initialized(0).
Run	*procedurename:* String name of the procedure or function to run *paramarray():* optional array of parameter values, as accepted by the procedure or function	If a function is called, returns the value of that function	When you call Run() on the ScriptControl object, the method attempts to run the named procedure or function in the default "Global" module. When you call Run() on a Module object, it attempts to run the named procedure or function within that module. Alternatively, you can use the CodeObject property to call procedures and functions directly.

Events

The events of the `ScriptControl` object are described in the following table.

Name	Arguments	Description
Error	None	Occurs when the `ScriptObject` encounters an error while running a script. To receive notification of this event, you must declare the `ScriptControl` object variable "early bound" and using the `WithEvents` keyword.
Timeout	None	Occurs when script execution exceeds the time allotted in the `Timeout` property, and the user decides to stop the execution of the script. When several `ScriptControl` objects are present, a `Timeout` event will occur only for the first `ScriptControl` object to timeout.

Examples

This line of code shows how to instantiate a new early bound Script Control object.

```
Set objSC = New [MSScriptControl.]ScriptControl
```

This line of code shows how to instantiate a new late bound Script Control object.

```
Set objSC = CreateObject("[MSScriptControl.]ScriptControl")
```

This script fragment shows how variables and procedures that are outside the scope of a procedure or function can be added in separate steps using the `AddCode` method. Entire procedures and functions should be added in one call.

```
strCode = "Option Explicit" & vbNewLine & vbNewLine
objSC.AddCode strCode

strCode = "Dim x, y" & vbNewLine & vbNewLine
objSC.AddCode strCode

strCode = "x = 15" & vbNewLine & "y = 2"
objSC.AddCode strCode

strCode = "Function MultiplyXY(): MultiplyXY = x * y : End Function"
objSC.AddCode strCode
```

The `Eval` function allows you to execute code fragments at runtime. `Eval` is simple but effective, capable of achieving tasks nearly impossible in VB.

```
MsgBox objSC.Eval(InputBox$( _
    "Enter Numeric Expression", _
    "Eval Example", "5 * 3 - 1"))
```

Based on the type of a procedure, you may call the `Run` method in several different ways, depending on return values and parameters.

```
strCode = "Sub TwoArg(a,b): MsgBox CInt(a + b)" & " : End Sub"
objSC.AddCode strCode
objSC.Run "TwoArg", 1, 2
strCode = "Function ManyArg(a,b,c,d): ManyArg = a * b + c - d"
strCode = strCode & ": End Function"
objSC.AddCode strCode
lngResult = objSC.Run("ManyArg", 1, 2, 3, 4)
```

The following script fragment illustrates the use of the `Error` event:

```
Private WithEvents objSC As ScriptControl

Private Sub Main()
    Set objSC = New ScriptControl
    ...
    objSC.Run "MyProc"
End Sub

Private Sub objSC_Error
    MsgBox "Script error occurred:" & vbNewLine & _
        "Number: " & objSC.Error.Number & vbNewLine & _
        "Description: " & objSC.Error.Description & vbNewLine & _
        "Line: " & objSC.Error.Line & vbNewLine & _
        "Column: " & objSC.Error.Column & vbNewLine & _
        "Script Text: " & objSC.Error.Text
End Sub
```

The script following fragment illustrates the use of the `Timeout` event:

```
Private WithEvents objSC As ScriptControl

Private Sub Main()
    Set objSC = New ScriptControl
    ...
    objSC.Timeout = 10000
    objSC.Run "MyProc"
End Sub

Private Sub objSC_TimeOut
    MsgBox "The script has timed out."
End Sub
```

Module Object

The `Module` object, a member of the `Modules` collection (covered later in this chapter), contains procedure, type, and data declarations used in a script. The Script Control has a default `Global` module, which is automatically used unless specific member calls are made to other modules that have been added. You can add code to a Module object using the `AddCode` method. Individual `Module` objects, on the other hand, are added by using the `Add` method of the `Modules` collection. Because the code in each module is private in scope to its module, you can repeat variable and procedure names across modules. This is useful when you have several similar scripts that are only partially different from each other.

Declaration Syntax

This is the syntax to declare a variable for a `Module` object.

```
Dim|Private|Public objModule [As [MSScriptControl.]Module|Object]
```

Properties

The properties of the `Module` object are described in the following table.

Name	Returns	Access	Description
CodeObject	Object	Read-only	Returns an object that can be used to call the public procedures and functions in a `Module` object. This is a late bound object, but it is useful in that it allows direct calls to procedures in the script without using the `Run` method. Procedures and functions in the module will appear as public methods of the object returned by this property.
Name	String	Read/Write	The logical name of a `Module` object. Also used as its `Modules` collection key, so must be unique within the `Modules` collection. If you add another `Module` object of the same name to the collection, the new object will overwrite the original object.
Procedures	Procedures object	Read-only	Returns a reference to the `Procedures` collection of a `Module` object.

Methods

The methods of the `Module` object are described in the following table.

Name	Arguments	Returns	Description
Eval	*it expression:* A `String` value representing a valid "expression," meaning any script fragment that can be compiled and executed	The output of the expression, if any	Evaluates an expression. Similar to `Eval` function in VBScript. This is one of the best ways to evaluate dynamic expressions provided by the user. When comparing `Eval` to the `ExecuteStatement` method, you should be aware that the `"="` will be treated as a comparison operator when used with `Eval`, but as an assignment operator when used with `ExecuteStatement`. Hence, `x = y` will evaluate to a `Boolean` subtype when used with `Eval`, but when used with `ExecuteStatement`, the value of `y` will be assigned to variable `x`, and nothing will be returned. The `Eval` method may be used against the `ScriptControl` or `Module` object, and take advantage of its members.
AddCode	*code:* `String` value representing a valid script	N/A	This is the primary method of adding script to the Script Control. When you call `AddCode()` on the `ScriptControl` object, the method automatically adds the new code to the default `"Global"` module. Call on an individual `Module` object to add code to a particular module. When adding code for entire procedures and blocks of code, the code must be added in a single call to the `AddCode` method. Each statement in the block can be separated by colons (:) or the line break characters `vbNewLine` (preferred), `vbCr`, `vbLf`, and `vbCrLf`.

Name	Arguments	Returns	Description
Execute Statement	*Statement:* `String` value representing the statement to be executed	N/A	Unlike the `Eval` method, `ExecuteStatement` only executes a statement and does not return any value. When comparing `Eval` to the `ExecuteStatement` method, be aware that the `"="` operator will be treated as a comparison operator when used with `Eval`, but as an assignment operator when used with `ExecuteStatement`. Hence, $x = y$ will evaluate to a `Boolean` subtype when used with `Eval`, but when used with `ExecuteStatement`, the value of y will be assigned to variable x, and nothing will be returned. The statement executed can take advantage of any members within scope of the `Module` or `ScriptControl` object. In order to obtain a return value from a procedure, you should use either the `Eval` or `Run` methods.
Run	*procedurename:* `String` name of the procedure or function to run *paramarray():* optional array of parameter values, as accepted by the procedure or function	If a function is called, returns the return value of that function	When you call `Run()` on the `ScriptControl` object, the method attempts to run the named procedure or function in the default `"Global"` module. When called on a `Module` object, it attempts to run the named procedure or function within that module. Alternatively, you can use the `CodeObject` property call procedures and functions directly.

Examples

The script following fragment illustrates the use of the `Module.Run` method to call a procedure contained in a module.

```
Set objModule = objSC.Modules.Add("NewModule")
objModule.AddCode "Sub Test(): " & _
    vbNewLine & vbTab & "MsgBox ""Hello, world.""" & _
    vbNewLine & "End Sub"
objModule.Run "Test"
```

The following script fragment illustrates the use of the `Module.CodeObject` to call code within the module. You may find that calling procedures this way is more natural, and perhaps more readable than using the `ScriptControl.Run` method because procedures are exposed as methods of the `CodeObject` object.

```
Set objModule = objSC.Modules.Add("TestMod")

objModule.AddCode "Sub TestProc(): " & _
    vbNewLine & vbTab & "MsgBox ""Hello, world.""" & _
    vbNewLine & "End Sub"
objModule.AddCode "Function TestFunction(a) : & _
    vbNewLine & vbTab & "TestFunction = a * a " & _
    vbNewLine & "End Function"

Set objCodeObject = objModule.CodeObject
objCodeObject.TestProc
lngVal = objCodeObject.TestFunction(2)
```

This script fragment shows how variables and procedures that are outside the scope of a procedure or function can be added in separate steps. Entire procedures and functions should be added in one call.

```
strCode = "Option Explicit" & vbNewLine & vbNewLine
objModule.AddCode strCode

strCode = "Dim x, y" & vbNewLine & vbNewLine
objModule.AddCode strCode

strCode = "x = 15" & vbNewLine & "y = 2"
objModule.AddCode strCode

strCode = "Function MultiplyXY(): MultiplyXY = x * y : End Function"
objModule.AddCode strCode
```

The `Eval` function allows you to execute code fragments at runtime. `Eval` is simple but effective, capable of achieving tasks nearly impossible in VB.

```
MsgBox objSC.Eval(InputBox$( _
        "Enter Numeric Expression", _
        "Eval Example", "5 * 3 - 1"))
```

Based on the type of a procedure, you may call the `Run` method in several different ways, depending on return values and parameters.

```
strCode = "Sub TwoArg(a,b): MsgBox CInt(a + b)" & " : End Sub"
objSC.AddCode strCode
objSC.Run "TwoArg", 1, 2

strCode = "Function ManyArg(a,b,c,d): ManyArg = a * b + c - d"
strCode = strCode & ": End Function"
objSC.AddCode strCode
lngResult = objSC.Run("ManyArg", 1, 2, 3, 4)
```

Modules Collection

The `Modules` collection contains all the `Module` objects for a `ScriptControl` object, including the default `Global` module. Calls to the members of the `Global` module can be made directly through the `ScriptControl` object without iterating through the `Modules` collection. It also has an index matching the value of the constant `GlobalModule`.

`Module` objects can be added to the `Modules` collection using the `Add` method. Specific `Module` objects can be accessed through the default `Modules.Item` method. The `Count` property provides the number of `Module` objects in the collection. The entire collection can be iterated in various ways, most commonly using the `For Each...Next` loop. Because there is no way of deleting individual modules, you must use the `Reset` method of the `ScriptControl` object to delete unwanted modules, which clears the entire collection.

Properties

The single property of the `Modules` collection object is described in the following table.

Name	Returns	Access	Description
Count	Long	Read-only	Returns the number of `Module` objects in the `Modules` collection

Methods

The methods of the `Modules` collection object are described in the following table.

Name	Arguments	Returns	Description
Add	*name:* `String` value representing the name of the `Module` object being added; will be used as the `Modules` collection key *module:* optional `Module` object to be added to the collection	If *module* argument omitted, returns new `Module` object	Use this method to add a new `Module` object to the collection of `Modules`; if your project has a relatively small set of scripts, you may want to just use the default `"Global"` module, but if you have a larger set of scripts, you may find it beneficial to break them up into separate modules — especially if you need to repeat procedures and functions with the same name in different modules.
Item	*index:* A `Long` or `String` value, representing an index or key, respectively	Returns a `Module` object from the collection if one matching the *index* exists	This is the default property of the collection, so many programmers omit the actual name of the item method: `Set objModule = objSC.Modules("MyModule").`

Examples

The following line of code shows how to access the `Global` module directly. The same syntax, using different module names, can be used with other named modules.

```
Set objModule = sc.Modules("Global")
```

The following script fragment illustrates how to iterate through the `Modules` collection:

```
For Each objModule In objSC.Modules
    strModuleList = strModuleList & vbNewLine & objModule.Name
Next
```

Modules allow the use of separate scripts and provide separate namespaces. The following script fragment shows how two different modules can contain scripts with the same name:

```
' Add code to separate modules, using same sub names.

Set objModule = objSC.Modules.Add("Maine")
objModule.AddCode "Sub ShowState" & _
    vbNewLine & vbTab & "MsgBox ""In Maine""" & _
    vbNewLine & "End Sub"
Set objModule = Nothing

Set objModule = objSC.Modules.Add("Ohio")
objModule.AddCode "Sub ShowState" & _
    vbNewLine & vbTab & "MsgBox ""In Ohio""" & _
    vbNewLine & "End Sub"
```

Procedure Object

The `Procedure` object defines a logical unit of code, which in the case of VBScript can be either a `Sub` or a `Function`. The `Procedure` object contains a number of useful properties that allow you to inspect a procedure's name, the number of arguments, and whether or not the procedure returns any values. Entry to the script code is also provided via the `Procedure` object.

Declaration Syntax

This is the syntax to declare a variable for a `Procedure` object.

```
Dim|Private|Public objProc [As [MSScriptControl.]Procedure|Object]
```

Properties

The properties of the `Procedure` object are described in the following table.

Name	Returns	Access	Description
HasReturnValue	Boolean	Read-only	Returns whether or not a procedure returns a value (in other words, whether it is a procedure or a function).

Name	Returns	Access	Description
Name	String	Read-only	The name of a `Procedure` object, which will match the actual name of the procedure or function contained in the object. Also used as the `Procedures` collection key, so must be unique within the `Procedures` collection. If you use the AddCode method to add another procedure of the same name to a module, the new procedure will overwrite the original procedure in that module.
NumArgs	Long	Read-only	Returns the number of arguments accepted by a procedure or function in a `Procedure` object.

Methods

The methods of the `Procedure` object are described in the following table.

Name	Arguments	Returns	Description
Item	*index:* A Long or String value, representing an index or key, respectively	Returns a `Procedure` object from the collection if one matching the *index* exists	This is the default property of the collection, so many programmers omit the actual name of the item method: `Set objProc = objMod.Procedures("MyProc")`.

Note that the `Procedures` collection does not have an Add method. New procedures are added to a module using the `AddCode` method; `Procedure` objects are created and added to the collection behind the scenes.

Procedures Collection

The `Procedures` collection holds all of the procedures in a given `Module` object. It provides a convenient way to iterate through all of the procedures in a module and access the code therein. Individual procedures are added through the `Module` object's `AddCode` method, not through the `Procedures` collection directly. Also, you can't remove an individual procedure once it has been added, as there is no Remove method on the `Procedures` collection.

Properties

The single property of the `Procedures` collection object is described in the following table.

Name	Returns	Access	Description
Count	Long	Read-only	Returns the number of `Procedure` objects in the `Procedures` collection.

Methods

The `Procedures` collection object does not have any methods.

Examples

The following script fragment iterates through the `Procedures` collection using the `For Each...Next` loop syntax:

```
For Each objProcedure In objModule.Procedures
    strList = strList & "Name: " & objProcedure.Name
    strList = strList & vbNewLine & vbTab

    strList = strList & "Argument Count: " & objProcedure.NumArgs
    strList = strList & vbNewLine & vbTab

    strList = strList & "Has Return: " & objProcedure.HasReturnValue
    strList = strList & vbNewLine & vbNewLine
Next
```

Error Object

The `Error` object provides information about syntax and runtime errors associated with the Script Control. Although information provided by the `Error` object is similar to that of the `Err` object in VB and VBScript, there are additional properties (`Column`, `Text`, `Line`) that are invaluable when diagnosing problems associated with the script. Although it is possible to declare and initialize the `Error` object in VB, it is common to access members of the `Error` object directly through the `ScriptControl` object.

Unlike the `Err` object, the `Error` object is not global in scope and only handles errors associated with a single instance of a `ScriptControl` object. The `Error` object is reset each time you change the `ScriptControl.Language` property, or when you call the `Reset`, `AddCode`, `Eval`, `ExecuteStatement`, or `Clear` methods of the `ScriptControl` object. Use the `Clear` method to explicitly reset the `Error` object properties. Runtime errors handled internally by the script will not be raised to the application level.

> *The section called "Error Handling with the Script Control" provides additional information about error handling strategies. Chapter 6, "Error Handling and Debugging," is also a good reference if you need a primer on VBScript error handling.*

Properties

The properties of the `Error` object are described in the following table.

Name	Returns	Access	Description
Column	Long	Read-only	Returns the column number indicating the place where a syntax error occurred while adding script code.
Description	String	Read-only	Returns a description of a script error.

Name	Returns	Access	Description
HelpContext	Long	Read-only	If the error raised from a script has a help file available (which is highly unlikely), this property returns the identifier for the section within the help file that has information about the error.
HelpFile	String	Read-only	If the error raised from a script has a help file available (which is highly unlikely), this property returns the pathname to the help file.
Line	Long	Read-only	Returns the line number indicating the place where a syntax error occurred while adding script code.
Number	Long	Read-only	Returns the error number of a script error.
Source	String	Read-only	Returns the name of the source where a script error occurred.
Text	String	Read-only	Returns a string containing a snippet of code where a script syntax error has occurred. If you allow your users to add or edit scripts from within your application, you can use this property along with Description, Line, and Column to help the user understand how to fix the syntax error. Also useful for debugging scripts.

Methods

The single method of the Error object is described in the following table.

Name	Arguments	Returns	Description
Clear	None	N/A	Resets all of the properties of the Error object. This method is called implicitly when the ScriptControl.Language property is changed or when the Reset, AddCode, Eval, or ExecuteStatement methods are called.

Constants

The following named constants and enumerated constants are available to projects with a reference to the Script Control. These constants are globally available within any Visual Basic application that has a reference to the Script Control. For each of the constants, this section explains the type, value(s), and where the constant is used.

GlobalModule Named Constant

Type: String

Value: "Global"

When using the Script Control with script engines (like VBScript or Jscript) that support more than one module, use the GlobalModule constant to access the default Global module in the ScriptControl.Modules collection.

NoTimeout Named Constant

Type: Long

Value: -1

This constant can be used to set the Timeout property of the ScriptControl object, and prevent the execution from timing out. Please refer to the ScriptControl.Timeout property reference (earlier in this chapter) for more specifics.

ScriptControlState Enumerated Constant

This enumerated constant is intended for use with the ScriptControl.State property. The purpose of the State property is to control how events raised by objects are added to the ScriptControl through the AddObject method. The default value, Initialized (0), means that the ScriptControl will *not* respond to events raised by these objects. The other possible value, Connected (1) means that the ScriptControl *will* respond to raised events.

Error Handling with the Script Control

Error handling can never be underestimated, especially when dealing with several sources of code. This is especially true for dynamically generated scripts, and user-entered expressions. To handle the errors, you may have to work with both VB's Err object and the Script Control's Error object. If you are working with several instances of the Script Control, each will have a separate Error object. When an error occurs, if you have a proper strategy to handle the error, you may always clear the error and continue execution of the program. You should use all possible script error-handling techniques in your scripts (especially the scripts you load from files), and handle them internally as much as possible.

> *Depending on VB's settings, your error handlers may not work properly in debug mode (check Break on Unhandled Errors in IDEs General Options tab). In addition, error handlers in script will depend on the Disable Script Debugging option set in Internet Explorer, and on the availability of the debugger. Script errors may automatically invoke the debugger, bypassing your error handling code. Consult Chapter 6 for more information on script debugging.*

In .NET, unhandled errors will propagate up to the .NET layer as Exceptions, which can be caught and handled using standard .NET error handling mechanisms such as Try...Catch blocks.

The Script Control may raise several types of errors when setting global properties.

Error	Description
Can't execute; script is running	An attempt has been made to modify one of `ScriptControl` object's members while the script is running.
Can't set `UseSafeSubset` property	The application hosting the Script Control may force it into safe mode.
Executing script has timed out	Script execution has ended because it went over the time allotted in the `Timeout` property.
Language property not set	Certain properties can only be set after the `Language` property is set.
Member is not supported by selected script engine	When working with languages other than VBScript or JScript, not all of the properties and methods may be supported.
Object is no longer valid	When the Script Control is reset (caused by call to the `Reset` method or change to `Language` property), objects that have been set previously are released.

These errors can most probably be avoided by careful programming, and should not be a big factor of your error handling strategy. The two cases when errors will be a major nuisance are when adding the scripting code to the Script Control (syntax errors in the script), and when executing it (runtime errors in the script). When an error occurs, you may inspect both the `Err` and `Error` objects; however, the Script Control's `Error` object provides additional information about the nature of the error. The following example shows hypothetical error handling through VB:

```
Dim strCode As String
Dim strValue As String
sc.Reset

On Error GoTo SyntaxErrorHandler
strCode = InputBox("Enter Function (name it Test(a))", _
 "Syntax Error Testing", _
 "Sub Test(a): MsgBox ""Result: "" & CStr(a*a): End Sub")

sc.AddCode strCode

On Error GoTo RuntimeErrorHandler
strValue = InputBox("Enter a Value for Test function", _
 "Runtime Error Testing", _
 "test")
sc.Run "Test", strValue

Exit Sub

SyntaxErrorHandler:
    MsgBox "Error # " & Err.Number & ": " & _
        Err.Description, vbCritical, "Syntax Error in Script"
```

(continued)

```
        Exit Sub

RuntimeErrorHandler:
    MsgBox "Error # " & Err.Number & ": " & _
        Err.Description, vbCritical, "Runtime Error in Script"
```

VB can handle errors in several different ways: through use of `On Error GoTo [Label]` and, as in VBScript, through `On Error Resume Next` and immediate testing of `Err.Number`. The following example illustrates the use of `On Error Resume Next`, combined with an inspection of the `Err` object as well as Script Control's `Error` object, which provides you with more information:

```
On Error Resume Next
    sc.AddCode strCode
    If Err Then
        With sc.Error
            MsgBox "Error # " & .Number & ": " _
                & .Description & vbCrLf _
                & "At Line: " & .Line & " Column: " & .Column _
                & " : " & .Text, vbCritical, "Syntax Error"
        End With
    Else
        MsgBox "No Error, result: " & CStr(sc.Run("Test", _
            strValue))
        If Err Then
            With sc.Error
                MsgBox "Error # " & .Number & ": " _
                    & .Description & vbCrLf _
                    & "At Line: " & .Line _
                        {}, vbCritical, "Runtime Error"
            End With
        End If
    End If
```

You may also use two of the events exposed by the `ScriptControl` object/control, `Event` and `Timeout`, to handle some of the errors; however, in some circumstances it may be a nuisance, and the use of the `On Error...` statement may be preferred because:

❑ The `Timeout` event will only occur for the initial `ScriptControl` object if more than one is in use.

❑ The Script Control either has to be attached to a form, or has to be initialized using the `WithEvents` keyword, which may not always be desirable.

❑ You may lose the granularity required when executing certain scripts that are likely to cause errors.

You should use the `Error` event when you do not plan on adding any other error-handling script code to your application, as the following example code shows:

```
Private Sub sc_Error()
    Dim strMsg As String

    With sc.Error
        strMsg = "Script error has occurred:" & vbCrLf & vbCrLf
        strMsg = strMsg & .Description & vbCrLf
        strMsg = strMsg & "Line # " & .Line
        ' Syntax errors have additional properties
        If InStr(.Source, "compilation") > 0 Then
            strMsg = strMsg & ", Column# " & .Column
            strMsg = strMsg & ", Text: " & .Text
        End If
        strMsg = strMsg & vbCrLf
    End With

    MsgBox strMsg, vbCritical, "Script Error"
    sc.Error.Clear
End Sub
```

Note that when you use the `ScriptControl Error` event, the event handler is invoked *before* any `On Error...` code. Hence, use of both error handling techniques may produce double error messages and disable any effective error handling.

Debugging

A quick note on debugging scripts hosted by your application using the Script Control: You can debug your native Visual Basic code in the VB IDE. However, to debug the code inside of a script, you have to use the freely downloadable Microsoft Script Debugger. When the debugger is installed, any unhandled errors or `Stop` statements inside of a script will invoke the debugger, just as with any other script.

See Chapter 6, "Error Handling and Debugging," for more information on the Script Debugger and script debugging techniques.

Also, keep in mind that if the debugger is invoked during script execution, the script execution time as it relates to the `Timeout` property continues to accumulate. In other words, if your `Timeout` is set to 10,000 milliseconds (10 seconds) and the debugger comes up and the script pauses for more than 10 seconds, the Script Control will bring up the timeout dialog box.

For this reason, while you are debugging, you might want to set the `Timeout` property to `NoTimeout` (−1) and then set it to another value when you release to production. A good way to do this is to use a named constant for setting the Timeout value, but control the value of this constant using a conditional compilation flag and the `#IFDEF` statement, such as the following:

```
#IFDEF blnDebugging
        Const TIMEOUT_VAL = -1
#ELSE
        Const TIMEOUT_VAL = 15000
#ENDIF
...objSC.Timeout = TIMEOUT_VAL
...
```

Using Encoded Scripts

The Script Control does support encoded scripts (see Chapter 14). There are two things to keep in mind.

First, when setting the Language property for an encoded script, set the property to "VBScript.Encode" instead of the normal "VBScript."

Second, if you are loading an encoded script from a file or database, you may have to use alternative techniques to account for the fact that an encoded script will have a lot of special characters. For loading from a file, you might want to use the scripting runtime `TextStream` object with the `FileSystemObject.OpenTextFile` method (see Chapter 7) rather than using native Visual Basic functions to open the file. For storing in and loading from a database, your best bet is to store the script as binary data rather than in a normal `Char` or `VarChar` column.

Sample .NET Project

The sample project, `ScriptControlDemo`, demonstrates the basics of the Script Control in a .NET environment, including how an application can share its objects with the script and various other techniques. This VB.NET demo project does not represent a realistic application scenario, but rather simply exercises various features of the Script Control to demonstrate that they work pretty much the same way with the .NET runtime as they do in Visual Basic 6 and other COM-aware languages.

> *You can download this sample project, and all of the other code in this book, from* www.wrox.com. *The* ComplexSC *project is contained in a file called* VisualBasic6Demo.zip.

You can read the code in the `ScriptControlDemo` project in any text editor (the file `frmMain.vb` contains all of the actual Script Control code), or you can load the project in Visual Studio .NET 2005. The project was actually created in the free Visual Basic 2005 Express Edition, which, if you do not have access to the full version of Visual Studio .NET 2005, is available for download from Microsoft at this URL:

```
http://msdn.microsoft.com/vstudio/express/vb/
```

Even if you are not familiar with VB.NET, if you are familiar with Visual Basic, VBA, or VBScript, the syntax should be relatively familiar to you. Here is one code example from the project, which demonstrates adding a simple script to the control and running it:

```vbnet
Dim scriptCtl As MSScriptControl.ScriptControl = _
    New MSScriptControl.ScriptControl()
scriptCtl.Language = "VBScript"

Dim stringBldr As System.Text.StringBuilder = New System.Text.StringBuilder()
stringBldr.Append("Sub ShowMyName(ByVal firstName, ByVal lastName)")
stringBldr.Append(vbNewLine)
stringBldr.Append(" MsgBox(""My name is "" & firstName & "" "" & lastName)")
stringBldr.Append(vbNewLine)
stringBldr.Append("End Sub")
scriptCtl.AddCode(stringBldr.ToString())
```

```
Dim parms() As Object = {"Super", "Fly"}
scriptCtl.AllowUI = True
scriptCtl.Run("ShowMyName", parms)
```

Sample Visual Basic 6 Project

The sample project, ComplexSC, demonstrates the basics of the Script Control, including how an application can share its objects with the script and pass static events — because of this requirement, the project is an ActiveX EXE type.

> *You can download this sample project, and all of the other code in this book, from* www.wrox.com. *The* ComplexSC *project is contained in a file called* Chapter 21 downloads.VisualBasic6Demo.zip.

When building database applications that depend on an outside database, you always encounter the problem of feeding the application with the connection string associated with the appropriate database and the appropriate server. Often, this information is retrieved from the system registry, identifying the software author and the application, and then by a custom key:

```
Sample Registry Path: SOFTWARE\Company Name\App Name\
Sample Key Name: MyAppConnection
```

The sample project provides a way to create, store, and edit registry settings for application settings such as connection strings. The Visual Basic form and code in the ComplexSC project are designed to be generic and customized through a script. This means that you can distribute a new script without having to recompile or redistribute the VB application.

Figure 21-2 shows the main form of the ComplexSC project.

Figure 21-2

The possibilities here are almost endless: By exposing the objects in the application, and passing some of the events to the script, the script can act as a macro and adapt to your needs. There are some idiosyncrasies, especially when it comes to passing events between the form and the script. To make this possible, all of the controls are placed on the form at design time, some of them in control arrays. The script can easily control all of the properties and methods of all controls, but when the control arrays (optional connection string tags and their values) are used, dynamic modification of the form members is simplified. Here, depending on the choice of connection (OLE DB, ODBC, and DSN), you can display different labels and editable values associated with the connection type.

Sharing of the form members is easily achieved through the `CShared` class, which allows you to share the main form and all of its members with a script (shown in the following example). Although you could expose individual elements as opposed to the entire form, and prevent the script from manipulating any of the elements you want protected, in the case of this application it is simply not necessary.

```
Option Explicit

Private m_Form As Form

Public Property Get Form() As Object
    Set Form = m_Form
End Property

Friend Property Set Form(ByVal newValue As Object)
    Set m_Form = newValue
End Property
```

Here you are wrapping the form in the `CShared` class. With the `CShared` class in place, you need to use the `AddObject` method of the Script Control to share the form with the script. This is done via the `InitScriptControl` procedure, which is executed when the form is loaded (called from the `Form_Load` event handler). You're passing the reference to the VB form, exposed through the `CShared.Form` property.

```
Private Sub Form_Load()
    Set objScript = InitScriptControl(Me)
    objScript.Run "init"
End Sub
```

The `InitScriptControl` instantiates the `ScriptControl` object, loads the script, instantiates the `CShared` object, and exposes it to the Script Control. Because you set the third parameter of the `AddObject` method to true, all of the members of the form are shared, too.

```
Function InitScriptControl(frmForm As Form) As ScriptControl
    Dim objSC As ScriptControl
    Dim fileName As String, intFnum As Integer
    Dim objShare As New CShared

    ' create a new instance of the control
    Set objSC = New ScriptControl
    objSC.Language = "VBScript"
    objSC.AllowUI = True
    Set objShare.Form = frmForm
    objSC.AddObject "share", objShare, True
```

```
        ' load the code into the script control
        fileName = App.Path & "regeditor.scp"
        intFnum = FreeFile
        Open fileName For Input As #intFnum

        objSC.AddCode Input$(LOF(intFnum), intFnum)
        Close #intFnum

        ' return to the caller
        Set InitScriptControl = objSC

    End Function
```

After the Script Control is initialized, the Form_Load code calls the Init procedure in the script, which sets up all of the necessary controls on the form. In actuality, some of the controls are preset with certain properties (such as background color, enabled, and so on), while others are initialized by the script by accessing the members of the form exposed by CShared.Form.

```
    Sub Init()
        Dim i, strTmp

        Form.Caption = "Connection Registration Manager"
        strTmp = "This application saves the database connection"
        strTmp = strTMP & " string in the registry. " & vbCrLf
        Form.lblExplanation = strTmp
        Form.lblRegistry.Caption = ""

        ' this information should be reflected in your application
        ' the standard is to store the registry keys in subhives
        ' for different companies and projects
        Form.txtSubpath.Text = "SOFTWARE Company Name App Name "

        ' finally the name of the key
        ' you could similarly extend this application so it would
        ' work like a wizard, and register several keys
        Form.txtKey.Text = "MyAppConnection"
        Form.lblRegistry.Caption = ""
        Form.cmdRegister.Enabled = False
        Form.cmdProcess.Enabled = True
        For i = 0 To 5
            Form.lblLabel(i).Visible = False
            Form.txtText(i).Visible = False
        Next

        Form.cboCombo.Clear
        Form.cboCombo.AddItem "OLE DB"
        Form.cboCombo.AddItem "ODBC"
        Form.cboCombo.AddItem "DSN"
    End Sub
```

Next, you need to respond to events generated by the application. In this simple case, you simply pass the events as intercepted by the application directly to the script. Hence, your application may have the following events passed to the script:

```
Private Sub cboCombo_Click()
    objScript.Run "cboCombo_Click"
End Sub

Private Sub txtText_KeyPress(Index As Integer, KeyAscii As Integer)
    KeyAscii = objScript.Run("txtText_KeyPress",Index, KeyAscii)
End Sub
```

As the example shows, you pass the events directly to the script, optionally passing along the parameters generated by the event. Because in certain cases, you might want to modify one of the parameters, you should treat the event-handling procedure as a function, which would return the modified value. This is probably the simplest mechanism for modifying such parameters. Although this functionality is not required by your application, the following function inside the script would capitalize each character entered into one of the text boxes.

```
Function txtText_KeyPress(Index , KeyAscii)
   txtText_KeyPress = Asc(Ucase(Chr(KeyAscii)))
End Function
```

This approach is a little different from what you'd expect in VB code, because even if you pass the value of KeyAscii by reference (normal VB code would be KeyAscii = Asc(Ucase(Chr(KeyAscii)))), the script will not update this value back in VB. Hence, you employ a simple work-around by turning the event handler from a procedure into a function.

It is also possible to override the default event handling, or to provide optional event handling in the script. When the script does not have the member procedure, an error is generated, which provides you with a possibility of either ignoring events or providing default events, in case the script does not have an appropriately named procedure. The following example shows the simplest error trapping, which allows you to create a default event handler. Moreover, when the error handler is disabled (with On Error Resume Next), the script must contain an appropriately named procedure with the correct number of parameters.

```
Private Sub cboCombo_Click()
    On Error Resume Next
        objScript.Run "cboCombo_Click"
    If Err = 0 Then Exit Sub
    ' default event handler goes here
...End Sub
```

Details of the application lie in the script itself, so rather than copying the entire code listing, the following example only shows partial implementation of the cboCombo_Click procedure within the script.

After the key controls are reset, you set up values of the labels and the associated text that would correspond to an OLE DB type connection string.

```
Sub cboCombo_Click()
    Dim strComboSelection, strTmp

    ' Clean Up in case this was pressed already
    Form.cmdRegister.Enabled = False
    Form.cmdProcess.Enabled = True
    Form.lblRegistry.Caption = ""
    For i = 0 To 5
        Form.lblLabel(i).Visible = False
        Form.txtText(i).Visible = False
    Next

    strComboSelection = _
            Trim(Form.cboCombo.List(Form.cboCombo.ListIndex))
    Select Case strComboSelection
        Case "OLE DB"
            For i = 0 To 4
                Form.lblLabel(i).Visible = True
                Form.txtText(i).Visible = True
            Next
            Form.lblLabel(0).Caption = "Provider="
            Form.lblLabel(1).Caption = "Data Source="
            Form.lblLabel(2).Caption = "Initial Catalog="
            Form.lblLabel(3).Caption = "User ID="
            Form.lblLabel(4).Caption = "Password="
            Form.txtText(0).Text = "SQLOLEDB"
            Form.txtText(1).Text = "DATABOX"
            Form.txtText(2).Text = "MyAppDB"
            Form.txtText(3).Text = "Student"
            Form.txtText(4).Text = "teacher"

    [...]

    End Select
    strTmp = "Please Fill In Remaining Values in the available"
    strTmp = strTmp & " text boxes. " & vbCrLf
    strTmp = strTmp & "You may press ""Proceed"" button, or"
    strTmp = strTmp & " change the connection method again. "
    strTmp = strTmp & "Leaving User ID empty will leave out"
    strTmp = strTmp & " user infromation from registry"
    Form.lblExplanation = strTmp
End Sub
```

The remainder of the application responds to the end-user events, and builds the connection string as required by the core application, enabling and disabling controls, and modifying values on the form, depending on the stage. The last action is actually carried out directly by the application itself; a value is written to the registry based on the string that is stored in one of the labels on the form.

This little application can be further extended to take advantage of several scripts, and provide wizard-like functionality that can easily be scripted.

Summary

The Script Control is a free control provided by Microsoft that enables your VB 6, .NET, or other COM-aware application to host a script engine. Uses of the Script Control can range from simple dynamic evaluation of expressions, to a full-fledged macro language add-on capable of automating your applications.

This chapter covered the following topics:

- ❑ What the Script Control is
- ❑ How the Script Control can be a useful addition to your Visual Basic 6 and .NET applications
- ❑ Why you would want to consider using the Script Control (or why not)
- ❑ The Script Control object model, including its properties, methods, and events
- ❑ Error handling and debugging
- ❑ Two sample projects demonstrating the use of the Script Control in VB.NET and VB 6

VBScript Functions and Keywords

This appendix contains a complete reference of functions and keywords in VBScript 5.6. You will also find a list of the VB/VBA functions and keywords that are not supported in VBScript. Where appropriate, an alternative to an unsupported function or keyword is shown.

Operators

An operator acts on one or more operands when comparing, assigning, concatenating, calculating, and performing logical operations.

Assignment Operator

The assignment operator is simply used for assigning a value to a variable or property.

See the `Set` keyword for an explanation of how to reference and assign objects.

=	Name	Assignment
	Description	Assigns the result of an expression, the value of a constant, or the value of another variable to a variable or property
	Syntax	`Variable = value`

Arithmetic Operators

The arithmetic operators are all used to calculate a numeric value, and are normally used in conjunction with the assignment operator and/or one of the comparison operators; they are listed in order of operator precedence.

^	**Name**	Exponentiation
	Description	Raises a number to the power of an exponent.
	Syntax	`Result = number ^ exponent` `number` and `exponent` is any valid numeric expression.
	Example	`MsgBox 5 ^ 5` `MsgBox` displays 3125, which is the result of raising the number 5 to the exponent 5.

*	**Name**	Multiplication
	Description	Multiplies two numbers.
	Syntax	`Result = number1 * number2` `number1` and `number2` is any valid numeric expression.
	Example	`MsgBox 5 * 5` `MsgBox` displays 25, which is the result of multiplying the number 5 by 5.

/	**Name**	Floating-point division
	Description	Returns a floating-point result when dividing two numbers.
	Syntax	`Result = number1/number2` `number1` and `number2` is any valid numeric expression.
	Example	`MsgBox 5 / 4` `MsgBox` displays 1.25, which is the result of dividing the number 5 by 4.

\	**Name**	Integer division
	Description	Returns the integer part of the result when dividing two numbers.
	Syntax	`Result = number1\ number2` `number1` and `number2` is any valid numeric expression.
	Example	`MsgBox 5 \ 4` `MsgBox` displays 1, which is the integer part of the result, when dividing the number 5 by 4.
	Notes	The numeric expressions are rounded to `Byte`, `Integer`, or `Long` subtype expressions, before the integer division is performed. Outputs are rounded to the smallest possible subtype; that is, a value of 255 is rounded to a `Byte`, 256 is rounded to an `Integer`, and so on.

Mod	**Name**	Modulus division
	Description	Returns the remainder when dividing two numbers.
	Syntax	`Result = number1 Mod number2` `number1` and `number2` is any valid numeric expression.
	Example	`MsgBox 5 Mod 4` `MsgBox` displays 1, which is the remainder part of the result, when dividing the number 5 by 4.
	Notes	The numeric expressions are rounded to `Byte`, `Integer`, or `Long` subtype expressions, before the modulus division is performed.
		Outputs are rounded to the smallest possible subtype; that is, a value of 255 is rounded to a `Byte`, 256 is rounded to an `Integer`, and so on.

+	**Name**	Addition
	Description	Sums two expressions.
	Syntax	`Result = expression1 + expression2` `expression1` and `expression2` is any valid numeric expression.
	Example	`MsgBox 5 + 5`
		`MsgBox` displays 10, which is the result of adding the expression 5 to 5.
	Notes	If one or both expressions are numeric, the expressions will be summed, but if both expressions are strings, they will be concatenated. This is important to understand, especially if you have a Java background, in order to avoid runtime errors.
		In general, use the `&` operator (see "Concatenation Operators") when concatenating, and the + operator when dealing with numbers.

–	**Name**	Subtraction
	Description	Subtracts one number from another or indicates the negative value of an expression.
	Syntax (1)	`Result = number1 - number2` `number1` and `number2` is any valid numeric expression.
	Example (1)	`MsgBox 5 - 4`
		`MsgBox` displays 1, which is the result of subtracting the number 4 from 5.
	Syntax (2)	`-number` `number` is any valid numeric expression.
	Example (2)	`MsgBox -(5 - 4)`
		`MsgBox` displays -1, which is the result of subtracting the number 4 from 5 and using the unary negation operator ($-$) to indicate a negative value.

Concatenation Operators

Concatenation operators are used for concatenating expressions; they are listed in order of operator precedence.

&	Name	Ampersand
	Description	Concatenates two expressions.
	Syntax	Returns the concatenated expressions.
		`Result = expression1 & expression2.`
	Example	If `expression1` is `"WROX"` and `expression2` is `"Press"`, then the result is `"WROX Press"`.
	Notes	The expressions are converted to a `String` subtype, if they are not already of this subtype.

+	Name	+ Operator
	Description	Does the same as the & operator if both expressions are strings.
	Syntax	Returns the concatenated or summed expressions.
		`Result = expression1 + expression2`
	Example	`1 + "1" = 2`
		`"1" + "1" = "11"`
	Notes	If one or both expressions are numeric, the + operator will work as an arithmetic + operator and sum the expressions.
		A runtime error occurs if one expression is numeric and the other a string containing no numbers.
		It is highly recommended that + should be used only for numeric addition and never for concatenation purposes (to carry out this operation, use & instead).

Comparison Operators

The comparison operators are used for comparing variables and expressions against other variables, constants, or expressions; they are listed in order of operator precedence.

=	**Name**	Equal to
	Description	Returns True if expression1 is equal to expression2; False otherwise.
	Syntax	Result = expression1 = expression2

<>	**Name**	Not equal to
	Description	Returns True if expression1 is not equal to expression2; False otherwise.
	Syntax	Result = expression1 <> expression2

<	**Name**	Less than
	Description	Returns True if expression1 is less than expression2; False otherwise.
	Syntax	Result = expression1 < expression2

>	**Name**	Greater than
	Description	Returns True if expression1 is greater than expression2; False otherwise.
	Syntax	Result = expression1 > expression2

<=	**Name**	Less than or equal to
	Description	Returns True if expression1 is less than or equal to expression2; False otherwise.
	Syntax	Result = expression1 <= expression2

>=	**Name**	Greater than or equal to
	Description	Returns True if expression1 is greater than or equal to expression2; False otherwise.
	Syntax	Result = expression1 >= expression2

Is	Name	Compare objects
	Description	Returns `True` if `object1` and `object2` refer to the same memory location (if they are in fact the same object).
	Syntax	`Result = object1 Is object2`
	Note	Use the `Not` operator (see "Logical Operators") with the `Is` operator to get the opposite effect.

`Result = object1 Not Is object2`

Use the `Nothing` keyword with the `Is` operator to check if an object reference is valid. Returns `True` if object has been destroyed (`Set object = Nothing`).

`Result = object Is Nothing`

Be careful, `Nothing` is *not* the same as `Empty`. `Nothing` references an invalid object reference, whereas `Empty` is used for any variable, which has been assigned the value of `Empty`, or has not yet been assigned a value.

Logical Operators

The logical operators are used for performing logical operations on expressions; they are listed in order of operator precedence. All logical operators can also be used as bitwise operators (see "Bitwise Operators").

Not	**Used to**	Negate the expression.
	Returns	Returns the logical negation of an expression.
	Syntax	`Result = Not expression`
	Note	Result will be `True` if expression is `False`; and `False` if expression is `True`. `Null` will be returned if expression is `Null`.

And	**Used to**	Check if both expressions are true.
	Returns	Returns `True` if both expressions evaluate to `True`; otherwise, `False` is returned.
	Syntax	`Result = expression1 And expression2`

Or	**Used to**	Check if one or both expressions are true.
	Returns	Returns `True` if one or both expressions evaluate to `True`; otherwise `False` is returned.
	Syntax	`Result = expression1 Or expression2`

Xor	Used to	Check if one and only one expression is true.
	Returns	`Null` will be returned if either expression is `Null`.
	Syntax	`Result = expression1 Xor expression2`
	Note	Returns `True` if only one of the expressions evaluates to `True`; otherwise `False` is returned.

Eqv	Used to	Check if both expressions evaluate to the same value.
	Returns	Returns `True` if both expressions evaluate to the same value (`True` or `False`).
	Syntax	`Result = expression1 Eqv expression2`
	Note	`Null` will be returned if either expression is `Null`.

Imp	Used to	Perform a logical implication.

	Returns	Returns these values:
		`true Imp true = true`
		`false Imp true = true`
		`false Imp false = true`
		`false Imp Null = true`
		`Null Imp true = true`
		`true Imp false = false`
		`true Imp Null = Null`
		`Null Imp false = Null`
		`Null Imp Null = Null`

	Syntax	`Result = expression1 Imp expression2`

Bitwise Operators

Bitwise operators are used for comparing binary values bit-by-bit; they are listed in order of operator precedence. All bitwise operators can also be used as logical operators (see "Logical Operators").

Not	Used to	Invert the bit values.
	Returns	Returns 1 if bit is 0 and vice versa.
	Syntax	`Result = Not expression` If expression is 101, then result is 010.

Appendix A: VBScript Functions and Keywords

And	**Used to**	Check if both bits are set to 1.
	Returns	Returns 1 if both bits are 1; otherwise 0 is returned.
	Syntax	`Result = expression1 And expression2`
		If `expression1` is `101` and `expression2` is `100`, then result is `100`.

Or	**Used to**	Check if one of the bits is set to 1.
	Returns	Returns 1 if one or both bits are 1; otherwise 0 is returned.
	Syntax	`Result = expression1 or expression2`
		If `expression1` is `101` and `expression2` is `100`, then result is `101`.

Xor	**Used to**	Check if one and only one of the bits is set to 1.
	Returns	Returns 1 if only one of the bits is 1; otherwise 0 is returned.
	Syntax	`Result = expression1 Xor expression2`
		If `expression1` is `101` and `expression2` is `100`, then result is `001`.

Eqv	**Used to**	Check if both bits evaluate to the same value.
	Returns	Returns 1 if both the bits have the same value; otherwise 0 is returned.
	Syntax	`Result = expression1 Eqv expression2`
		If `expression1` is `101` and `expression2` is `100`, then result is `110`.

Imp	**Used to**	Perform a logical implication on 2 bits.

	Returns	Returns these values:
		`0 Imp 0 = 1`
		`0 Imp 1 = 1`
		`1 Imp 1 = 1`
		`1 Imp 0 = 0`

	Syntax	`Result = expression1 Imp expression2`
		If `expression1` is `101` and `expression2` is `100`, then result is `110`.

Operator Precedence

When more than one operation occurs in an expression they are normally performed from left to right. However, there are several rules. Operators from the arithmetic group are evaluated first, and then concatenation, comparison, and logical operators.

This is the complete order in which operations occur.

Arithmetic	^
	-
	*
	/
	Mod
	+
	-
Concatenation	&
	+
Comparison	=
	<>
	<
	>
	<=
	>=
	Is
Bitwise	Not
	And
	Or
	Xor
	Eqv
	Imp

This order can be overridden by using parentheses. Operations in parentheses are evaluated before operations outside the parentheses, but inside the parentheses, the normal precedence rules apply.

Unsupported Operators

The following VB/VBA operator is not supported in VBScript:

❑ Like

Math Functions

The following listing is in alphabetical order.

Abs	Returns the absolute value of a number, that is, its unsigned magnitude.
Syntax	Abs(number)
	number is any valid numeric expression.
Note	Null will be returned if number contains Null.
Example	Abs(-50) ' 50 Abs(50) ' 50
See also	Sgn

Atn	Returns the arc tangent of a number as Variant subtype Double(5).
Syntax	Atn(number)
	number is any valid numeric expression.
Note	This function takes the ratio of two sides of a right-angled triangle (number) and returns the corresponding angle in radians.
	The ratio is the length of the side opposite the angle divided by the length of the side adjacent to the angle.
	The range of the result is $-\pi/2$ to $\pi/2$ radians.
Example	Dim dblPi ' Calculate the ' value of Pi dblPi = 4 * Atn(1)
See also	Cos, Sin, and Tan

Cos	Returns the cosine of an angle as `Variant` subtype `Double(5)`.
Syntax	`Cos(number)`
	`number` is any valid numeric expression that expresses an angle in radians.
Note	This function takes an angle and returns the ratio of two sides of a right-angled triangle.
	The ratio is the length of the side adjacent to the angle divided by the length of the hypotenuse (`dblSecant`).
	The result is within the range –1 to 1, both inclusive.

Example	`Dim dblLength`
	`dblLength = 10`
	`    ' Convert 30° to radians`
	`    dblAngle = (30 * 3.14 / 180)`
	`    dblSecant = dblLength /`
	`Cos(dblAngle)`

See also	`Atn`, `Sin`, and `Tan`

Exp	Returns a `Variant` subtype `Double(5)` specifying e (the base of natural logarithms) raised to a power.
Syntax	`Exp(number)`
	`number` is any valid numeric expression.
Note	A runtime error occurs if `number` is larger than 709.782712893. e is approximately 2.718282.
	Sometimes this function is referred to as the antilogarithm, and complements the action of the `Log` function.

Example	`Dim dblAngle, dblHSin`
	`    dblAngle = 1.3`
	`    dblHSin = (Exp( dblAngle) - Exp(`
	`    -1 * dblAngle)) / 2`

	Here the `Exp` function is used to return e raised to a power.
See also	`Log`

Fix	Returns the integer part of a number.
Syntax	`Fix(number)`
Note	`Fix` is internationally aware, which means that the return value is based on the locale settings on the machine.
	`Null` is returned if number contains `Null`. The data type returned will be decided from the size of the integer part. Possible return data types in ascending order:

	`Integer`
	`Long`
	`Double`

	If number is negative, the first negative integer equal to or greater than `number` is returned.

Example	`Dim vntPosValue`
	`Dim vntNegValue`
	`    vntPosValue = Fix(5579.56)`
	`    vntNegValue = Fix(-5579.56)`

	`vntPosValue` now holds the value 5579, and `vntNegValue` the value −5579.
	`Fix` is the equivalent of `Int` when dealing with nonnegative numbers.
	When you handle negative numbers, `Fix` returns the first negative integer, greater than, or equal to the number supplied.
See also	`Int`, `Round`, and the conversion functions `CInt` and `CLng`

Int	Returns the integer part of a number.
Syntax	`Int(number)`
	`number` is any valid numeric expression.
Note	`Int` is internationally aware, which means that the return value is based on the locale settings on the machine.
	`Null` is returned if number contains `Null`. The data type returned will be decided from the size of the integer part. Possible return data types in ascending order:

	`Integer`
	`Long`
	`Double`

	If number is negative, the first negative integer equal to or less than number is returned.

Example	```Dim vntPosValue```
	```Dim vntNegValue```
	``` vntPosValue = Int(5579.56)```
	``` vntNegValue = Int(-5579.56)```

`vntPosValue` now holds the value 5579, and `vntNegValue` the value -5580.

`Int` is the equivalent of `Fix` when dealing with nonnegative numbers.

When you handle negative numbers, `Int` returns the first negative integer, less than or equal to the number supplied.

See also	`Fix`, `Round`, and the conversion functions `CInt` and `CLng`

Log	Returns the natural logarithm of a number.
Syntax	`Log(number)` `number` is any valid numeric expression greater than zero.

Example	```Dim vntValueBase10```
	``` vntValueBase10 = Log(5) / Log(10)```
	
	This sample code calculates the base-10 logarithm of the number 5, which is 0.698970004336019.

See also	`Exp`

Randomize	Initializes the random number generator, by giving it a new seed-value. A *seed-value* is an initial value used for generating random numbers.
Syntax	`Randomize[number]` `number` is any valid numeric expression.
Note	You can repeat a sequence of random numbers, by calling the `Rnd` function with a negative number, before using the `Randomize` statement with a numeric argument.

(continued)

| **Example** | ```
Const LNG_UPPER_BOUND = 20
Const LNG_LOWER_BOUND = 1
Dim intValue
Dim lngCounterIn
Dim lngCounterOut
    For lngCounterOut = 1 To 3
       Rnd -1
    Randomize 3
    For lngCounterIn = 1 To 3
       intValue =
Int((LNG_UPPER_BOUND -
LNG_LOWER_BOUND + 1) * _
          Rnd + LNG_LOWER_BOUND)
       MsgBox intValue
    Next
  Next
``` |

This sample has an inner loop that generates three random numbers and an outer loop that calls the Rnd function with a negative number, immediately before calling Randomize with an argument. This makes sure that the random numbers generated in the inner loop will be the same for every loop the outer loop performs.

See also	Rnd

Rnd	Returns a random number, less than 1 but greater than or equal to 0.
Syntax	Rnd[(number)]

number (Optional) is any valid numeric expression that determines how the random number is generated; if number is:

< 0: uses same number every time
> 0 or missing: uses next random number in sequence
= 0: uses most recently generated number

Note	Use the Randomize statement, with no argument, to initialize the random-number generator with a seed based on the system timer, before calling Rnd.

The same number sequence is generated for any given initial seed, because each successive call to Rnd uses the previous number as the seed for the next number in the sequence.

Call Rnd with a negative argument immediately before using Randomize with a numeric argument in order to repeat sequences of random numbers.
```

| **Example** | ```
Const LNG_UPPER_BOUND = 20
Const LNG_LOWER_BOUND = 1
Dim intValue
Dim lngCounter
    For lngCounter = 1 To 10
        intValue = Int( _
                        (LNG_UPPER_BOUND
- -
            LNG_LOWER_BOUND + 1) * _
            Rnd + LNG_LOWER_BOUND)
        MsgBox intValue
    Next
``` |
| | This code produces 10 random integers in the range 1–20. |
| **See also** | `Randomize` |

`Round`	Returns a number rounded to a specified number of decimal places as a `Variant` subtype `Double(5)`.
Syntax	`Round(number, [numdecimalplaces])`
	`number` is any valid numeric expression.
	`numdecimalplaces` (Optional) indicates how many places to the right of the decimal separator should be included in the rounding.
Note	An integer is returned if `numdecimalplaces` is missing.
| **Example** | ```
Round(10.4)
' Returns 10
Round(10.456)
' Returns 10
Round(-10.456)
' Returns -10
Round(10.4, 1)
' Returns 10.4
Round(10.456, 2)
' Returns 10.46
Round(-10.456, 2)
' Returns -10.46
``` |
| **See also** | `Int` and `Fix` |

617

Sgn	Returns an integer indicating the sign of a number.
Syntax	Sgn(number)
	number is any valid numeric expression.
Note	Sgn returns the following when number is:
	< 0: -1
	= 0: 0
	> 0: 1
| **Examples** | ```
Sgn(10.4)
' Returns 1
Sgn(0)
' Returns 0
Sgn(-2)
' Returns -1
``` |
| **See also** | Abs |

Sin	Returns a Variant subtype Double(5) specifying the sine of an angle.
Syntax	Sin(number)
	number is any valid numeric expression that expresses an angle in radians.
Note	This function takes an angle and returns the ratio of two sides of a right-angled triangle. The ratio is the length of the side opposite the angle (dblCosecant) divided by the length of the hypotenuse (dblSecant).
	The result is within the range −1 to 1, both inclusive.
| **Example** | ```
Dim dblAngle, dblCosecant
Dim dblSecant
   dblSecant = 11.545
             ' Convert 30  to radians
   dblAngle = (30 * 3.14 / 180)
   dblCosecant = dblSecant *
Sin(dblAngle)
``` |
| | Here the Sin function is used to return the sine of an angle. |
| **See also** | Atn, Cos, and Tan |

Sqr	Returns the square root of a number.
Syntax	Sqr(number) number is any valid numeric expression greater than or equal to zero.
Example	Sqr(16) ' Returns 4

Tan	Returns a Variant subtype Double(5) specifying the tangent of an angle.
Syntax	Tan(number) number is any valid numeric expression that expresses an angle in radians.
Note	This function takes an angle and returns the ratio of two sides of a right-angled triangle. The ratio is the length of the side opposite the angle (dblCosecant) divided by the length of the side adjacent to the angle (dblLength). The result is within the range –1 to 1, both inclusive.
Examples	Tan(10.4) ' Returns 1.47566791425166 Tan(0) * ' Returns 0 Tan(--2) ' Returns 2.18503986326152
See also	Atn, Cos, and Tan

Date and Time Functions and Statements

There are many ways to display and represent dates and times. This includes date literals, which are valid date expressions, enclosed in number signs (#).

You need to be careful when using date literals because VBScript lets you use only the U.S. date format, mm/dd/yyyy. This is true even if a different locale is being used on the machine. This might lead to problems when you try to use date literals in other formats, because in most cases the date will be accepted, although converted to a different date. For example, #10/12/2008# will be interpreted as October 12, 2008, but you might in fact want December 10, 2008, because your locale settings interpret dates as dd/mm/yyyy.

Date literals accept only the forward slash (/) as the date separator.

Appendix A: VBScript Functions and Keywords

The data range for a date is January 1, 100 to December 31, 9999, both inclusive. Internally, dates are stored as part of real numbers or, to be more specific, as a `Variant` subtype `Double(5)`. The digits to the left of the decimal separator represent the date and the digits to the right of the decimal separator represent the time. Negative numbers are used internally for representing dates prior to December 30, 1899.

The following is a list of functions used for converting and formatting dates and times.

`Cdate`	Returns an expression converted to `Variant` subtype `Date(7)`.
Syntax	`CDate(date)` `date` is any valid date expression.
Note	`CDate` is internationally aware, which means that the return value is based on the locale settings on the machine. Dates and times are formatted with the appropriate time and date separators, and for dates the correct order of year, month, and day are applied. Date and time literals are recognized.

Example	`Dim dtmValue`
	`    dtmValue = CDate( #12/10/2003#)`
	
	`dtmValue` now holds the value `10-12-03`, if your locale settings use the dash (−) as the date separator and the short date format is dd/mm/yy.

See also	`IsDate`

`Date`	Returns a `Variant` subtype `Date(7)` indicating the current system date.
Syntax	`Date`
Example	`MsgBox Date` Assuming that today is February 28, 2008, the `MsgBox` now displays 28-02-08, if your locale settings use the dash (−) as the date separator and the short date format is dd/mm/yy.
See also	`Now` and `Time`

DateAdd	Adds or subtracts a time interval to a specified date and returns the new date.
Syntax	`DateAdd(interval, number, date)`
	Interval can have these values:

d	Day
h	Hour
m	Month
n	Minute
q	Quarter
s	Second
w	Weekday
ww	Week of year
y	Day of year
yyyy	Year

number is a numeric expression that must be positive if you want to add or negative if you want to subtract.

number is rounded to the nearest whole number if it's not a `Long` value.

date must be a `Variant` or `Date` literal to which interval is added.

Note	`DateAdd` is internationally aware, which means that the return value is based on the locale settings on the machine.
	Dates and times are formatted with the appropriate time and date separators and for dates the correct order of year, month, and day are applied. An error occurs if the date returned is less than the year 100.
Example	`MsgBox DateAdd("m", 3, "1-Jan-08")`
	This adds three months to January 1, 2008, and the `MsgBox` now displays 01-04-08, if your locale settings use the dash (−) as the date separator and the short date format is dd/mm/yy.
See also	`DateDiff` and `DatePart`

DateDiff	Returns the interval between two dates.
	`DateDiff(interval, date1, date2, [firstdayofweek], [firstweekofyear])`
Syntax	Interval can have these values:

d	Day
h	Hour
m	Month
n	Minute
q	Quarter
s	Second
w	Weekday
ww	Week of year
y	Day of year
yyyy	Year

date1 and date2 are date expressions.

firstdayofweek (Optional) specifies the first day of the week. Use one of the following constants:

vbUseSystemDayOfWeek 0 (National Language Support (NLS) API setting. NLS functions help Win32-based applications support the differing language- and location-specific needs of users around the world.)

vbSunday	1 (Default)
vbMonday	2
vbTuesday	3
vbWednesday	4
vbThursday	5
vbFriday	6
vbSaturday	7

firstweekofyear (Optional) specifies the first week of the year. Use one of the following constants:

vbUseSystem 0 (Use NLS API setting)

vbFirstJan1 1 (Default)

(Week in which January 1 occurs)

vbFirstFourDays 2 (First week in the new year with at least four days)

vbFirstFullWeek 3 (First full week of the new year)

Note	A negative number is returned if date1 is later in time than date2.
Example	`MsgBox DateDiff("yyyy", #06-12-1972#, Now)`
	This calculates the number of years between 06/12/1972 and now. In 2008, the MsgBox displays 36.
See also	DateAdd and DatePart

DatePart	Returns a specified part of a date.
Syntax	`DatePart(interval, date, [firstdayofweek], [firstweekofyear])`

Interval can have these values:

d	Day
h	Hour
m	Month
n	Minute
q	Quarter
s	Second
w	Weekday
ww	Week of year
y	Day of year
yyyy	Year

date is a date expression.

firstdayofweek (Optional) specifies the first day of the week. Use one of the following constants:

vbUseSystemDayOfWeek	0 (NLS API setting)
vbSunday	1 (Default)
vbMonday	2
vbTuesday	3
vbWednesday	4
vbThursday	5
vbFriday	6
vbSaturday	7

firstweekofyear (Optional) specifies the first week of the year. Use one of the following constants:

vbUseSystem	0 (Use NLS API setting)
vbFirstJan1	1 (default) (Week in which January 1 occurs)
vbFirstFourDays	2 (First week in the new year with at least four days)
vbFirstFullWeek	3 (First full week of the new year)

Example	`MsgBox DatePart("ww", Now, vbMonday, vbFirstFourDays)` This will extract the week number from the current system date. On July 29, 2008, the `MsgBox` will display 31.
See also	DateAdd and DateDiff

DateSerial	Returns a `Variant` subtype `Date(7)` for the specified year, month, and day.
Syntax	`DateSerial(year, month, day)`
	`year` is an expression that evaluates to a number between 0 and 9999. Values between 0 and 99, both inclusive, are interpreted as the years 1900–1999.
	`month` is an expression that must evaluate to a number between 1 and 12.
	`day` is an expression that must evaluate to a number between 1 and 31.
Note	If an argument is outside the acceptable range for that argument, it increments the next larger unit.
	Specifying 13 as the month will automatically increment year by 1 and subtract 12 from month leaving a value of 1.
	The same is true for negative values and a value of 0.
	However, instead of incrementing, the next larger unit is decremented.
	An error occurs if any of the arguments is outside the `Variant` subtype `Integer` range, which is -32768 to $+32767$.
	The same is true if the result is later than December 31, 9999. If you specify the year as 0, and the month and day as 0 or a negative value, the function wrongly assumes that the year is 100 and decrements this value.
	So `DateSerial(0, 0, 0)` returns 11/30/99.
Example	`MsgBox DateSerial( 2008, 07, 29)`
	The `MsgBox` displays 29-07-08, if your locale settings use the dash ($-$) as the date separator and the short date format is dd/mm/yy.
See also	`Date`, `DateValue`, `Day`, `Month`, `Now`, `TimeSerial`, `TimeValue`, `Weekday`, and `Year`

DateValue	Returns a `Variant` subtype `Date(7)`.
Syntax	`DateValue(date)`
	`date` is an expression representing a date, a time, or both, in the range January 1, 100 to December 31, 9999.
Note	Time information in date is not returned, but invalid time information will result in a runtime error. `DateValue` is internationally aware and uses the locale settings on the machine when recognizing the order of a date with only numbers and separators.
	If the year is omitted from date, it is obtained from the current system date.

Example	`DateValue("06/12/2008")`
	`DateValue("June 12, 2008")`
	`DateValue("Jun 12, 2008")`
	`DateValue("Jun 12")`

	All of these return the same valid date of 06/12/08.
See also	`Date`, `DateSerial`, `Day`, `Month`, `Now`, `TimeSerial`, `TimeValue`, `Weekday`, and `Year`

Day	Returns a number between 1 and 31 representing the day of the month.
Syntax	`Day(date)`
	`date` is any valid date expression.
Note	A runtime error occurs if date is not a valid date expression. `Null` is returned if date contains `Null`.
Example	`MsgBox Day("June 12, 2008")`
	The `MsgBox` will display 12.
See also	`Date`, `Hour`, `Minute`, `Month`, `Now`, `Second`, `Weekday`, and `Year`

Hour	Returns an integer between 0 and 23, representing the hour of the day.
Syntax	`Hour(time)` `time` is any valid time expression.
Note	A runtime error occurs if time is not a valid time expression. `Null` will be returned if time contains `Null`.
Example	`MsgBox Hour("12:05:12")`
	The `MsgBox` will display 12.
See also	`Date`, `Day`, `Minute`, `Month`, `Now`, `Second`, `Weekday`, and `Year`

IsDate	Returns a `Variant` subtype `Boolean(11)` indicating whether an expression can be converted to a valid date.
Syntax	`IsDate(expression)` `expression` is any expression you want to evaluate as a date or time.

Example	`MsgBox IsDate(Now)        ' true`
	`MsgBox IsDate(" ")        ' false`
	`MsgBox IsDate(#6/12/2008#) ' true`

See also	`CDate`, `IsArray`, `IsEmpty`, `IsNull`, `IsNumeric`, `IsObject`, and `VarType`

Minute	Returns a number between 0 and 59, both inclusive, indicating the minute of the hour.
Syntax	`Minute(time)`
	`time` is any valid time expression.
Note	A runtime error occurs if time is not a valid time expression. `Null` is returned if time contains `Null`.
Example	`MsgBox Minute("12:45")`
	The `MsgBox` will display 45.
See also	`Date`, `Day`, `Hour`, `Month`, `Now`, `Second`, `Weekday`, and `Year`

Month	Returns a number between 1 and 12, both inclusive, indicating the month of the year.
Syntax	`Month(date)` `date` is any valid date expression.
Note	A runtime error occurs if date is not a valid date expression. `Null` is returned if date contains `Null`.
Example	`MsgBox Month(#7/29/2008#)` The `MsgBox` will display 7.
See also	`Date`, `Day`, `Hour`, `Minute`, `Now`, `Second`, `Weekday`, and `Year`

MonthName	Returns a `Variant` subtype `String(8)` for the specified month.
Syntax	`MonthName(month, [abbreviate])` `month` is a number between 1 and 12 for each month of the year beginning with January. `abbreviate` (Optional) is a `Boolean` value indicating if the month name should be abbreviated or spelled out (default).
Note	A runtime error occurs if month is outside the valid range (1–12). `MonthName` is internationally aware, which means that the returned strings are localized into the language specified as part of your locale settings.
Example	`MsgBox MonthName(2)  ' February` `MsgBox MonthName(2, true)  ' Feb`
See also	`WeekDayName`

Now	Returns the system's current date and time.
Syntax	`Now`

Example	`Dim dtmValue`
	`        dtmValue = Now`
	
	`dtmValue` now holds the current system date and time.

See also	`Date`, `Day`, `Hour`, `Month`, `Minute`, `Second`, `Weekday`, and `Year`

Second	Returns a `Variant` subtype `Date(7)` indicating the number of seconds (0–59) in the specified time.
Syntax	`Second(time)` `time` is any valid time expression.
Note	A runtime error occurs if time is not a valid time expression. `Null` is returned if time contains `Null`.
Example	`MsgBox Second("12:45:56")` The `MsgBox` will display 56.
See also	`Date`, `Day`, `Hour`, `Minute`, `Month`, `Now`, `Weekday`, and `Year`

Time	Returns a `Variant` subtype `Date(7)` indicating the current system time.
Syntax	`Time`

Example	`    Dim dtmValue`
	`            dtmValue = Time`
	
	`dtmValue` now holds the current system time.

See also	`Date` and `Now`

Timer	Returns a `Variant` subtype `Single(5)` indicating the number of seconds that have elapsed since midnight. This means that it is "reset" every 24 hours.
Syntax	`Timer`

Example	`    Dim dtmStart, dtmStop`
	`            dtmStart = Timer`
	`            ' Do processing here`
	`            dtmStop = Timer`
	`            ' Display how many`
	`            ' seconds the operation`
	`            ' took`
	`            MsgBox dtmStop - dtmStart`

TimeSerial	Returns a `Variant` subtype `Date(7)` for the specified hour, minute, and second.
Syntax	`TimeSerial(hour, minute, second)` `hour` is an expression that evaluates to a number between 0 and 23. `minute` is an expression that must evaluate to a number between 0 and 59. `second` is an expression that must evaluate to a number between 0 and 59.
Note	If an argument is outside the acceptable range for that argument, it increments the next larger unit. Specifying 61 as minute automatically increments hour by 1 and subtracts 60 from minute leaving a value of 1. The same is true for negative values and a value of 0. However, instead of incrementing, the next larger unit is decremented. An error occurs if any of the arguments is outside the `Variant` subtype `Integer` range, which is −32768 to +32767.
Example	`    MsgBox TimeSerial(23, 07, 29)` The `MsgBox` will display 23:07:29.
See also	`Date`, `DateSerial`, `DateValue`, `Day`, `Month`, `Now`, `TimeValue`, `Weekday`, and `Year`

TimeValue	Returns a Variant subtype Date(7) containing the time.
Syntax	TimeValue(time) time is an expression in the range 0:00:00 to 23:59:59.
Note	Date information in time is not returned, but invalid date information will result in a runtime error. Null is returned if time contains Null. You can use both 24- and 12-hour representations for the time argument.
Example	TimeValue("23:59") TimeValue("11:59 PM") Both will return the same valid time.
See also	Date, DateSerial, DateValue, Day, Month, Now, TimeSerial, Weekday, and Year

Weekday	Returns a number indicating the day of the week.
Syntax	Weekday(date, [firstdayofweek]) date is any valid date expression. firstdayofweek (Optional) specifies the first day of the week. Use one of the following constants: vbUseSystemDayOfWeek0 (Use NLS API setting) vbSunday 1 (Default) vbMonday 2 vbTuesday 3 vbWednesday 4 vbThursday 5 vbFriday 6 vbSaturday 7
Note	Null is returned if date contains Null. A runtime occurs if date is invalid. Possible return values are: vbSunday 1 vbMonday 2 vbTuesday 3 vbWednesday 4 vbThursday 5 vbFriday 6 vbSaturday 7
Example	Weekday(#July 29, 2008#) Returns 5 for Thursday.
See also	Date, Day, Month, Now, and Year

WeekdayName	Returns a Variant subtype String(8) for the specified weekday.
Syntax	WeekdayName(weekday, [abbreviate], [firstdayofweek])
	weekday is a number between 1 and 7 for each day of the week. This value depends on the firstdayofweek setting.
	abbreviate (Optional) is a Boolean value indicating if the weekday name should be abbreviated or spelled out (default).
	firstdayofweek (Optional) is a numeric value indicating the first day of the week. Use one of the following constants:
	vbUseSystemDayOfWeek0 (Use NLS API setting)
	vbSunday 1 (Default) vbMonday 2 vbTuesday 3 vbWednesday 4 vbThursday 5 vbFriday 6 vbSaturday 7
Note	A runtime error occurs if weekday is outside the valid range (1–7). WeekdayName is internationally aware, which means that the returned strings are localized into the language specified as part of your locale settings.
Example	WeekdayName(2, , vbSunday) ' Monday WeekdayName(1, , vbMonday) ' Monday
See also	MonthName

Year	Returns a number indicating the year.
Syntax	Year(date) date is any valid date expression.
Note	A runtime error occurs if date is not a valid date expression. Null is returned if date contains Null.
Example	MsgBox Year(#6/12/2008#) The MsgBox will display 2008.
See also	Date, Day, Month, Now, and Weekday

Unsupported Date Functions and Statements

The following VB/VBA statements are not supported in VBScript.

Function/ Statement Name	Alternatives
Date statement	Sets the system date, which is not possible in VBScript.
Time statement	Sets the system time, which is not possible in VBScript.

Array Functions and Statements

One major difference between VB/VBA and VBScript is the way you can declare your arrays. VBScript does not support the Option Base statement and you cannot declare arrays that are not zero-based.

The following is a list of functions and statements that you can use for array manipulation in VBScript.

Array	Returns a comma-delimited list of values as a Variant subtype Array (8192).
Syntax	Array(arglist)
	arglist is a comma-delimited list of values that is inserted into the one-dimensional array in the order they appear in the list.
Note	An array of zero length is created if arglist contains no arguments.
	All arrays in VBScript are zero-based, which means that the first element in the list will be element 0 in the returned array.
| **Example** | ```
Dim arrstrTest
    ' Create an array with three elements
        arrstrTest = Array( _
                125pt"Bart", "Lisa",
"Maggie")
        ' Show the first list element
        ' now in the array
MsgBox arrstrTest(0)
``` |
| | MsgBox displays Bart. |
| **See also** | Dim |
```

Erase	Reinitializes the elements if it is a fixed-size array and deallocates the memory used if it is a dynamic array.
Syntax	`Erase array` `array` is the array to be reinitialized or erased.

Note	You must know if you are using a fixed-size or a dynamic array, because this statement behaves differently depending on the array type.
	
	Because the memory is deallocated when using `Erase` with dynamic arrays, you must redeclare the array structure with the `ReDim` statement, before you use it again.
	
	Fixed-size arrays are reinitialized differently depending on the contents of the elements:
	
	`Numeric    Set to 0`
	`Strings    Set to " "`
	`Objects    Set to Nothing`

Example	`Dim arrstrDynamic()`
	`Dim arrstrFixed(3)`
	`            ' Allocate space for the`
	`            ' dynamic array`
	`            ReDim arrstrDynamic(3)`
	`            ' Free the memory used by`
	`            ' the dynamic array`
	`            Erase arrstrDynamic`
	`            ' Reinitialize the elements`
	`            ' in the fixed-size array`
	`            Erase arrstrFixed`

See also	`Dim` and `ReDim`

For Each	Performs a group of statements repeatedly for each element in a collection or an array.

Syntax	`For Each element In group`
	`[statements]`
	`[Exit For]`
	`Next [element]`
	
	`element` is a variable used for iterating through the elements in a collection or an array.
	
	`group` is the name of the object or array.
	
	`statements` is one or more statements you want to execute on each item in the group.

(continued)

Note	The For Each loop is only entered if there is at least one element in the collection or array. All the statements in the loop are executed for all the elements in the group. You can control this by executing the Exit For statement if a certain condition is met. This will exit the loop and start executing on the first line after the Next statement. The For Each loops can be nested, but you must make sure that each loop element is unique.

Example	```
	Dim arrstrLoop
	Dim strElement
	    ' Create the array
	    arrstrLoop = Array _
	("Bart", "Lisa", "Maggie")
	    ' Loop through the array
	    For Each strElement In _
	arrstrLoop
	        ' Display element content
	        MsgBox strElement
	    Next
	``

IsArray	Returns a Variant subtype Boolean(11) indicating if a variable is an array.
Syntax	IsArray(varname) varname is a variable you want to check is an array.
Note	Only returns True if varname is an array.

Example	```
	Dim strName
	Dim arrstrFixed(3)
	    strName = "Wrox is Great!"
	    MsgBox IsArray(strName)
	            ' false
	    MsgBox IsArray(arrstrFixed)
	            ' true
	``

See also	IsDate, IsEmpty, IsNull, IsNumeric, IsObject, and VarType

Lbound	Returns the smallest possible subscript for the dimension indicated.
Syntax	LBound(arrayname[,dimension]) arrayname is the name of the array variable. dimension is an integer indicating the dimension you want to know the smallest possible subscript for. The dimension starts with 1, which is also the default that will be used if this argument is omitted.

Note	The smallest possible subscript for any array is always 0 in VBScript.
	`LBound` will raise a runtime error if the array has not been initialized.
Example	`Dim arrstrFixed(3)` `    MsgBox LBound(arrstrFixed)`
	`MsgBox` displays 0.
See also	`Dim`, `ReDim`, and `UBound`

`ReDim`	This statement is used to size or resize a dynamic array.
Syntax	`ReDim [Preserve] varname(subscripts[, varname(subscripts)]...)`
	`Preserve` (Optional) is used to preserve the data in an existing array, when you resize it. The overhead of using this functionality is quite high and should only be used when necessary.
	`varname` is the name of the array variable. `subscripts` is the dimension of the array variable `varname`. You can declare up to 60 multiple dimensions.
	The syntax is: `upper[, upper]...` where you indicate the upper bounds of the `subscript`. The lower bound is always 0.
Note	A dynamic array must already have been declared without dimension subscripts, when you size or resize it.
	If you use the `Preserve` keyword, only the last array dimension can be resized and the number of dimensions will remain unchanged.
	Because an array can be made smaller when resizing, you should take care that you don't lose any data already in the array.

Example	`Dim arrstrDynamic()`
	`    ' Size the dimension to`
	`    ' contain one dimension`
	`    ' with 3 elements`
	`    ReDim arrstrDynamic(2)`
	`    ' Put data in the array`
	`    arrstrDynamic(0) = "1"`
	`    arrstrDynamic(1) = "2"`
	`    arrstrDynamic(2) = "3"`
	`    ' Resize the array, but`
	`    ' keep the existing data`
	`    ReDim Preserve arrstrDynamic(5)`
	`    ' Display the 3rd element`
	`    MsgBox arrstrDynamic(2)`

	`MsgBox` displays 3.
See also	`Dim` and `Set`

Ubound	Returns the largest possible subscript for the dimension indicated.
Syntax	UBound(arrayname[, dimension])
	arrayname is the name of the array variable.
	dimension is an integer indicating the dimension you want to know the largest possible subscript for.
	The dimension starts with 1, which is also the default that will be used if this argument is omitted.
Note	UBound will raise a runtime error if the array has not been initialized.
	If the array is empty, −1 is returned.
Example	Dim arrstrFixed(3) MsgBox UBound(arrstrFixed)
	MsgBox displays 3.
See also	Dim, Ubound, and ReDim

String Functions and Statements

FormatCurrency	Formats an expression as a currency value with the current currency symbol.
	The currency symbol is defined in Regional Settings in Windows Control Panel.
Syntax	FormatCurrency(expression [,numdigitsafterdecimal [,includeleadingdigit [,useparensfornegativenumbers [,groupdigits]]]])
	expression is the expression that you want formatted.
	numdigitsafterdecimal (Optional) is a numeric value that indicates how many places to the right of the decimal separator should be displayed. If you omit this argument, the default value (−1) is assumed and the settings from Control Panel is used.
	includeleadingdigit (Optional) indicates if a leading zero is displayed for fractional values. Use one of the following constants: vbUseDefault 2 (Uses the settings from the Number tab in Control Panel) vbtrue −1 vbfalse 0
	useparensfornegativenumbers (Optional) indicates if negative numbers are enclosed in parentheses. Use one of the following constants: vbUseDefault 2 (Uses the settings from the Regional Settings tab in Control Panel) vbTrue −1 vbFalse 0

groupdigits (Optional) indicates if numbers are grouped using the thousand separator specified in Control Panel. Use one of the following constants:

vbUseDefault 2 (Uses the settings from the Regional Settings tab in Control Panel)

vbtrue -1
vbfalse 0

Note	The way the currency symbol is placed in relation to the currency value is determined by the settings in the Regional Settings tab in Control Panel — Is the currency symbol placed before the number or after the number, is there a space between the symbol and the number, and so on.

Example	`MsgBox FormatCurrency(7500000)`
	`MsgBox FormatCurrency(7500000, , vbtrue)`
	`MsgBox FormatCurrency(7500000, 2, vbtrue)`
	
	If the currency symbol is a dollar sign ($), the thousand separator a comma (,), and the currency symbol placed in front of the number with no spaces between, then `MsgBox` displays $7,500,000.00 in all these statements.

See also	`FormatDateTime`, `FormatNumber`, and `FormatPercent`

`FormatDateTime`	Returns a string formatted as a date and/or time.
Syntax	`FormatDateTime(date, [namedformat])` date is any valid date expression. namedformat (Optional) is a numeric value that indicates the date/time format used. Use one of the following constants: vbGeneralDate 0 (Format date (if present) and time (if present) using the short date and long time format from the machine's locale settings) vbLongDate 1 (Format date using the long date format from the machine's locale settings) vbShortDate 2 (Format date using the short date format from the machine's locale settings) vbLongTime 3 (Format time using the long time format from the machine's locale settings) vbShortTime 4 (Format time using the short time format from the machine's locale settings)
Note	A runtime error occurs if date is not a valid date expression. Null is returned if date contains Null.
Example	`MsgBox FormatDateTime(Now, vbShortDate)` On June 12, 2004, the MsgBox displays 06/12/04, if the locale settings use mm/dd/yy as the short date order and the forward slash (/) as the date separator.
See also	`FormatCurrency`, `FormatNumber`, and `FormatPercent`

FormatNumber	Returns a string formatted as a number.
Syntax	FormatNumber (expression, [, numdigitsafterdecimal [, includeleadingdigit [, useparensfornegativenumbers [, groupDigits]]]]) expression is the expression that you want formatted. numdigitsafterdecimal (Optional) is a numeric value that indicates how many places to the right of the decimal separator should be displayed. If you omit this argument, the default value (−1) is assumed and the settings from Control Panel is used. includeleadingdigit (Optional) indicates if a leading zero is displayed for fractional values. Use one of the following constants: TristateUseDefault −2 (Uses the settings from the Number tab in Control Panel) TristateTrue −1 TristateFalse 0 useparensfornegativenumbers (Optional) indicates if negative numbers are enclosed in parentheses. Use one of the following constants: TristateUseDefault −2 (Uses the settings from the Number tab in Control Panel) TristateTrue −1 TristateFalse 0 groupdigits (Optional) indicates if numbers are grouped using the thousand separator specified in Control Panel. Use one of the following constants: TristateUseDefault −2 (Uses the settings from the Number tab in Control Panel) TristateTrue −1 TristateFalse 0
Note	The Number tab in Regional Settings in Control Panel supplies all the information used for formatting.
Example	MsgBox FormatNumber("50000", 2, vbtrue, vbfalse, vbtrue) MsgBox FormatNumber("50000") The MsgBox will display 50,000.00, if the locale settings use a comma (,) as the thousand separator and a period (.) as the decimal separator.
See also	FormatCurrency, FormatDateTime, and FormatPercent

`FormatPercent`	Returns a string formatted as a percentage, such as 45%.

Syntax	`FormatPercent(expression,`
	`[, numdigitsafterdecimal`
	`[, includeleadingdigit`
	`[, useparensfornegativenumbers [, groupDigits]]]])`
	
	`expression` is any valid expression that you want formatted.
	
	`numdigitsafterdecimal` (Optional) is a numeric value that indicates how many places to the right of the decimal separator should be displayed. If you omit this argument, the default value (-1) is assumed and the settings from Control Panel is used.
	
	`includeleadingdigit` (Optional) indicates if a leading zero is displayed for fractional values. Use one of the following constants:
	
	`TristateUseDefault` -2 (Uses the settings from the Number tab in Control Panel)
	`TristateTrue` -1
	`TristateFalse` 0
	
	`useparensfornegativenumbers` (Optional) indicates if negative numbers are enclosed in parentheses. Use one of the following constants:
	
	`TristateUseDefault` -2 (Uses the settings from the Number tab in Control Panel)
	`TristateTrue` -1
	`TristateFalse` 0
	
	`groupdigits` (Optional) indicates if numbers are grouped using the thousand separator specified in Control Panel. Use one of the following constants:
	
	`TristateUseDefault` -2 (Uses the settings from the Number tab in Control Panel)
	`TristateTrue` -1
	`TristateFalse` 0

Note	The Number tab in Regional Settings in Control Panel supplies all the information used for formatting.

Example	`MsgBox FormatPercent(4 / 45)`
	`MsgBox FormatPercent(4 / 45, 2,`
	`vbtrue, vbtrue, vbtrue)`
	
	The `MsgBox` displays 8.89%, if the locale settings use a period (.) as the decimal separator.

See also	`FormatCurrency`, `FormatDateTime`, and `FormatNumber`

InStr	Returns an integer indicating the position for the first occurrence of a substring within a string.
Syntax	`InStr([start,] string1, string2[, compare])`

Syntax (continued)

`start` (Optional) is any valid nonnegative expression indicating the starting position for the search within `string1`. Noninteger values are rounded. This argument is required if the compare argument is specified.

`string1` is the string you want to search within.
`string2` is the substring you want to search for.

`compare` (Optional) indicates the comparison method used when evaluating. Use one of the following constants:

`vbBinaryCompare` 0 (Default) (Performs a binary comparison, that is, a case-sensitive comparison)

`vbTextCompare` 1 (Performs a textual comparison, that is, a case-insensitive comparison)

Note

A runtime error will occur, if `start` contains `Null`. If `start` is larger than the length of `string2` (> `Len(string2)`) 0 is returned.

Possible return values for different `stringx` settings:

```
string1    Zero-length    0
string1    Null           Null
string2    Zero-length    start
string2    Null           Null
string2    Not found      0
string2    Found          Position
```

Example

```
Dim lngStartPos
Dim lngFoundPos
Dim strSearchWithin
Dim strSearchFor
    ' Set the start pos
    lngStartPos = 1
    ' Initialize the strings
    strSearchWithin = _
    "This is a test string"
    strSearchFor = "t"
    ' Find the first occurrence
    lngFoundPos = InStr( _
        lngStartPos, _
        strSearchWithin, _
        strSearchFor)
    ' Loop through the string
    Do While lngFoundPos > 0
        ' Display the found position
        MsgBox lngFoundPos
```

```
' Set the new start pos to
' the char after the found
' position
lngStartPos = lngFoundPos + 1
' Find the next occurrence
lngFoundPos = InStr( _
    lngStartPos, _
    strSearchWithin, _
    strSearchFor)
Loop
```

This code finds all occurrences of the letter t in string1, at position 11, 14, and 17. Please note that we use binary comparison here, which means that the uppercase T will not be "found."

If you want to perform a case-insensitive search, you will need to specify the compare argument as vbTextCompare.

See also	InStrB and InStrRev

InStrB	Returns an integer indicating the byte position for the first occurrence of a sub-string within a string containing byte data.
Syntax	InStrB([start,] string1, string2[, compare])

start (Optional) is any valid nonnegative expression indicating the starting position for the search within string1. Noninteger values are rounded. This argument is required, if the compare argument is specified.

string1 is the string containing byte data you want to search within. string2 is the substring you want to search for.

compare (Optional) indicates the comparison method used when evaluating. Use one of the following constants:

vbBinaryCompare -0 (Default) (Performs a binary comparison, that is, a case-sensitive comparison)

vbTextCompare -1 (Performs a textual comparison, that is, a case-insensitive comparison)

Note	A runtime error will occur, if start contains Null. If start is larger than the length of string2 (> Len(string2)), 0 will be returned.

Possible return values for different stringx settings:

string1	Zero-length	0
string1	Null	Null
string2	Zero-length	start
string2	Null	Null
string2	Not found	0
string2	Found	Position

(continued)

Example

```
Dim lngStartPos
Dim lngFoundPos
Dim strSearchWithin
Dim strSearchFor
    ' Set the start pos
    lngStartPos = 1
    ' Initialize the strings
    strSearchWithin = _
    "This is a test string"
    strSearchFor = ChrB(0)
    ' Find the first occurrence
    lngFoundPos = InStrB( _
        lngStartPos, _
        strSearchWithin, _
        strSearchFor)
    ' Loop through the string
Do While lngFoundPos > 0
    ' Display the found position
MsgBox lngFoundPos
    ' Set the new start pos to
    ' the char after the
    ' found position
lngStartPos = lngFoundPos + 1
    ' Find the next occurrence
lngFoundPos = InStrB( _
        lngStartPos, _
        strSearchWithin, _
        strSearchFor)
Loop
```

This code finds all occurrences of the byte value 0 in string1, at position 2, 4, 6, . . ., 40, and 42. This is because only the first byte of the Unicode character is used for the character.

If you use a double-byte character set like the Japanese, the second byte will also contain a nonzero value.

See also

InStr and InStrRev

InStrRev	Returns an integer indicating the position of the first occurrence of a substring within a string starting from the end of the string. This is the reverse functionality of InStr.
Syntax	InStrRev(string1, string2[, start[, compare]]) string1 is the string you want to search within. string2 is the substring you want to search for. start (Optional) is any valid nonnegative expression indicating the starting position for the search within string1; −1 is the default and it will be used if this argument is omitted. compare (Optional) indicates the comparison method used when evaluating. Use one of the following constants: vbBinaryCompare -0 (Default) (Performs a binary comparison, that is, a case-sensitive comparison) vbTextCompare -1 (Performs a textual comparison, that is, a case-insensitive comparison).
Note	A runtime error will occur, if start contains Null. If start is larger than the length of string2 (> Len(string2)), will be returned. Possible return values for different stringx settings:

string1	Zero-length	0
string1	Null	Null
string2	Zero-length	start
string2	Null	Null
string2	Not found	0
string2	Found	Position

InStrRev and InStr do not share the same syntax.

| **Example** | ```
Dim lngStartPos
Dim lngFoundPos
Dim strSearchWithin
Dim strSearchFor
    ' Set the start pos
    lngStartPos = -1
    ' Initialize the strings
    strSearchWithin = _
      "This is a test string"
    strSearchFor = "t"
    ' Find the first occurrence
    lngFoundPos = InStrB( _
    lngStartPos, _
    47.8ptstrSearchWithin, _
    47.8ptstrSearchFor, lngStartPos)
    ' Loop through the string
    Do While lngFoundPos > 0
``` |

(continued)
```

```
                        ' Display the found
                        ' position
                        MsgBox lngFoundPos
                        ' Set the new start pos to
                        ' the char before the
                        ' found position
                        lngStartPos = lngFoundPos -1
                        ' Find the next occurrence
                        lngFoundPos = InStrB( _
                            strSearchWithin, _
                            strSearchFor, _
                            lngStartPos)
                    Loop
```

This code finds all occurrences of the letter t in string1, at position 17, 14, and 11. Please note that you use binary comparison here, which means that the uppercase T are not "found."

If you want to perform a case-insensitive search, you must specify the compare argument as vbTextCompare.

See also	InStr and InStrB

Join	Joins a number of substrings in an array to form the returned string.
Syntax	Join(list[, delimiter])
	list is a one-dimensional array that contains all the substrings that you want to join.
	delimiter (Optional) is the character(s) used to separate the substrings. A space character " " is used as the delimiter if this argument is omitted.
Note	All the substrings are concatenated with no delimiter if a zero-length string is used as delimiter.
	If any element in the array is empty, a zero-length string will be used as the value.
| **Example** | ```
Dim strLights
Dim arrstrColors(3)
    ' Fill the array
    arrstrColors(0) = "Red"
    arrstrColors(1) = "Yellow"
    arrstrColors(2) = "Green"
    ' Join the array into a string
    strLights = Join( arrstrColors, ",")
``` |
| | strLights contains "Red,Yellow,Green". |
| **See also** | Split |
```

Lcase	Converts all alpha characters in a string to lowercase.
Syntax	`LCase(string)`
	`string` is the string you want convert to lowercase.
Note	`Null` is returned if string contains `Null`.
	Only uppercase letters are converted.
Example	`MsgBox LCase("ThisIsLowerCase")`
	`MsgBox` displays thisislowercase.
See also	`Ucase`

Left	Returns length number of leftmost characters from string.
Syntax	`Left(string, length)`
	`string` is the string you want to extract a number of characters from.
	`length` is the number of characters you want to extract starting from the left. The entire string is returned if length is equal to or greater than the total number of characters in string.
Note	`Null` is returned if string contains `Null`.

Example	`Dim strExtract`
	`    strExtract = "LeftRight"`
	`    MsgBox Left(strExtract, 4)`
	`    MsgBox` displays Left.

See also	`Len`, `LenB`, `Mid`, `MidB`, and `Right`

Len	Returns the number of characters in a string.
Syntax	`Len(string)`
	`string` is any valid string expression you want the length of.
Note	`Null` is returned if string contains `Null`.

Example	`Dim strLength`
	`    strLength = "1 2 3 4 5 6 7 8 9"`
	`    MsgBox Len(strLength)`
	`MsgBox` displays 17.

See also	`Left`, `LenB`, `Mid`, `MidB`, and `Right`

LenB	Returns the number of bytes used to represent a string.
Syntax	`LenB(string)`
	`string` is any valid string expression you want the number of bytes for.
Note	`Null` is returned if string contains `Null`.
Example	```
Dim strLength
    strLength = "123456789"
    MsgBox LenB(strLength)
```
`MsgBox` displays 18. |
| **See also** | `Left`, `Len`, `Mid`, `MidB`, and `Right` |

| Ltrim | Trims a string of leading spaces; " " or `Chr(32)`. |
|---|---|
| **Syntax** | `LTrim(string)` |
| | `string` is any valid string expression you want to trim leading (leftmost) spaces from. |
| **Note** | `Null` is returned if string contains `Null`. |
| **Example** | ```
Dim strSpaces
    strSpaces = " Hello again *"
    MsgBox LTrim(strSpaces)
```
`MsgBox` displays Hello again *. |
| **See also** | `Left`, `Mid`, `Right`, `Rtrim`, and `Trim` |

Mid	Returns a specified number of characters from any position in a string.
Syntax	`Mid(string, start[, length])`
	`String` is any valid string expression you want to extract characters from.
	`start` is the starting position for extracting the characters. A zero-length string is returned if it is greater than the number of characters in string.
	`length` (Optional) is the number of characters you want to extract.
	All characters from start to the end of the string are returned if this argument is omitted or if length is greater than the number of characters counting from start.
Note	`Null` is returned if string contains `Null`.
Example	```
Dim strExtract
    strExtract = "Find ME in here"
    MsgBox Mid(strExtract, 6, 2)
```
`MsgBox` displays ME. |
| **See also** | `Left`, `Len`, `LenB`, `LTrim`, `MidB`, `Right`, `Rtrim`, and `Trim` |
```

MidB	Returns a specified number of bytes from any position in a string containing byte data.
Syntax	`MidB(string, start[, length])`
	`string` is a string expression containing byte data you want to extract characters from.
	`start` is the starting position for extracting the bytes. A zero-length string is returned if it is greater than the number of bytes in string.
	`length` (Optional) is the number of bytes you want to extract. All bytes from start to the end of the string are returned if this argument is omitted or if length is greater than the number of bytes counting from start.
Note	`Null` is returned if string contains `Null`.

Example	`Dim strExtract`
	`    strExtract = "Find ME in here"`
	`    MsgBox MidB(strExtract, 11, 4)`

	`MsgBox` displays ME because VBScript uses 2 bytes to represent a character. The first byte contains the ANSI character code when dealing with "normal" ANSI characters like M, and the next byte is 0. So byte 11 in the string is the first byte for the letter M, and then you extract 4 bytes/2 characters.
See also	`Left`, `Len`, `LTrim`, `Mid`, `Right`, `Rtrim`, and `Trim`

Replace	Replaces a substring within a string with another substring a specified number of times.
Syntax	`Replace(expression, find, replacewith[, start[, count[, compare]]])`
	`expression` is a string expression that contains the substring you want to replace.
	`find` is the substring you want to replace.
	`replacewith` is the substring you want to replace with.
	`start` (Optional) is the starting position within expression for replacing the substring. 1 (default), the first position, is used if this argument is omitted. You must also specify the `count` argument if you want to use start.
	`count` (Optional) is the number of times you want to replace `find`. −1 (default) is used if this argument is omitted, which means all find in the expression. You must also specify the `start` argument if you want to use `count`.

(continued)

`compare` (Optional) indicates the comparison method used when evaluating. Use one of the following constants:

`vbBinaryCompare` `-0` (Default) (Performs a binary comparison, that is, a case-sensitive comparison).

`vbTextCompare` `-1` (Performs a textual comparison, that is, a case-insensitive comparison).

Note

If `start` and `count` are specified, the return value becomes the original expression, with `find` replaced `count` times with `replacewith`, from start to the end of the expression, and not the complete string. A zero-length string is returned if `start` is greater than the length of expression (`start>Len(expression)`). All occurrences of `find` are removed if `replacewith` is a zero-length string ("").

Possible return values for different argument settings:

Expression	Zero-length	zero-length
Expression	Null	Error
Find	Zero-length	expression
Count	0	expression

Example

```
Dim strReplace
    strReplace = Replace( _
    "****I use binary", _
    "I", "You", 5, 1, _
    vbBinaryCompare)
    ' You use binary
    strReplace = Replace( _
    "****I use text", "i", _
    "You", , , _
    vbTextCompare)
    ' ****You use text
```

See also

`Left`, `Len`, `LTrim`, `Mid`, `Right`, `Rtrim`, and `Trim`

`Right`

Returns length number of rightmost characters from string.

Syntax

`Right(string, length)`

`string` is the string you want to extract a number of characters from.

`length` is the number of characters you want to extract starting from the right. The entire string is returned if length is equal to or greater than the total number of characters in string.

Note

`Null` is returned if string contains `Null`.

Example

```
Dim strExtract
    strExtract = "LeftRight"
        MsgBox Right(strExtract, 5)
```

`MsgBox` displays Right.

See also

`Left`, `Len`, `LenB`, `Mid`, and `MidB`

RTrim	Trims a string of trailing spaces; " " or `Chr(32)`.
Syntax	`RTrim(string)`
	`string` is any valid string expression you want to trim trailing (rightmost) spaces from.
Note	—

Example	```
	Dim strSpaces
	    strSpaces = "* Hello again "
	    MsgBox RTrim(strSpaces)
	``
	`MsgBox` displays * Hello again.

See also	`Left`, `LTrim`, `Mid`, `Right`, and `Trim`

Space	Returns a string made up of a specified number of spaces (" ").
Syntax	`Space(number)`
	`number` is the number of spaces you want returned.

Example	```
	Dim strSpaces
	    strSpaces = "Hello again"
	``
	`MsgBox "*"& Space(5) & strSpaces`
	
	`MsgBox` displays ^* Hello again.

See also	`String`

Split	Returns a zero-based one-dimensional array "extracted" from the supplied string expression.
Syntax	`Split(expression[,delimiter[,count[,compare]]])`
	`expression` is the string containing substrings and delimiters that you want to split up and put into a zero-based one-dimensional array.
	`delimiter` (Optional) is the character that separates the substrings. A space character is used if this argument is omitted.
	`count` (Optional) indicates the number of substrings to return. –1 (default) means all substrings are returned.
	`compare` (Optional) indicates the comparison method used when evaluating. Use one of the following constants:
	`vbBinaryCompare` –0 (Default) (Performs a binary comparison, that is, a case-sensitive comparison).
	`vbTextCompare` –1 (Performs a textual comparison, that is, a case-insensitive comparison).
Note	An empty array is returned if expression is a zero-length string. The result of the `Split` function cannot be assigned to a variable of `Variant` subtype `Array` (8192). A runtime error occurs if you try to do so.

(continued)

| **Example** | ```
Dim arrstrSplit
Dim strSplit
  ' Initialize the string
  strSplit = _
  "1,2,3,4,5,6,7,8,9,0"
  ' Split the string using _
  ' comma as the delimiter
  arrstrSplit = Split( _
    strSplit, ",")
``` |

The array `arrstrSplit` now holds 10 elements, 1, 2, …, 0.

See also	`Join`

`StrComp`	Performs a string comparison and returns the result.
Syntax	`StrComp(string1, string2[, compare])`

`string1` is a valid string expression.
`string2` is a valid string expression.

`compare` (Optional) indicates the comparison method used when evaluating. Use one of the following constants:

`vbBinaryCompare` -0 (Default) (Performs a binary comparison, that is, a case-sensitive comparison).

`vbTextCompare` -1 (Performs a textual comparison, that is, a case-insensitive comparison).

Note	Possible return values for different `stringx` settings
| | ```
string1 < string2   -1
string1 = string2    0
string1 > string2    1
``` |

`Null` is returned if `string1` or `string2` is `Null`.

| **Example** | ```
Dim intResult
    intResult = StrComp(
        "abc", "ABC",_
        vbTextCompare)
            ' 0
    intResult = StrComp(
        "ABC", "abc",
        vbBinaryCompare)
            ' -1
    intResult = StrComp( _
        "abc", "ABC")
            ' 1
``` |
|---|---|
| **See also** | `String` |
```

String	Returns a string with a substring repeated a specified number of times.
Syntax	`String(number, character)`
	`number` indicates the length of the returned string.
	`character` is the character code or string expression for the character used to build the returned string. Only the first character of a string expression is used.
Note	`Null` is returned if number or character contains `Null`. The character code is automatically converted to a valid character code if it is greater than 255. The formula is `character Mod 256`.
Example	```
Dim strChars
    strChars = "Hello again"
    MsgBox "*" & Space(5)&Starspace
```
|
| | `MsgBox` displays *Hello again. |
| **See also** | `Space` |

| StrReverse | Returns a string with the character order reversed. |
|---|---|
| **Syntax** | `StrReverse(string)` |
| | `string` is the string expression you want reversed. |
| **Note** | A runtime error occurs if string is `Null`. If string is a zero-length string, a zero-length string is returned. |
| | The case of the characters is not changed. |
| **Example** | `MsgBox StrReverse("Hello again")` |
| | `MsgBox` displays niaga olleH. |

| Trim | This trims a string of leading and trailing spaces; " " or `Chr(32)`. |
|---|---|
| **Syntax** | `Trim(string)` |
| | `string` is any valid string expression you want to trim leading (leftmost) and trailing (rightmost) spaces from. |
| **Note** | `Null` is returned if string contains `Null`. |
| **Example** | ```
Dim strSpaces
    strSpaces = " *Hello again* "
    MsgBox Trim(strSpaces)
```
|
| | `MsgBox` displays *Hello again*. |
| **See also** | `Left`, `Ltrim`, `Mid`, `Right`, and `RTrim` |

UCase	Converts all alpha characters in a string to uppercase and returns the result.
Syntax	UCase(string)
	string is the string you want converted to uppercase.
Note	Null is returned if string contains Null. Only lowercase letters are converted.
Example	MsgBox UCase("ThisIsUpperCase")
	MsgBox displays THISISUPPERCASE.
See also	Lcase

Unsupported String Functions, Statements, and Constructs

The following VB/VBA string functions/statements and constructs are not supported in VBScript.

Function/ Statement Name	Alternative
Format	FormatCurrency, FormatDateTime, FormatNumber, and FormatPercent
Mid (statement)	Left, Mid, and InStr functions, or the Replace function.
	Here is how to replace a substring identified by characters using the Replace function.

```
Dim strText
Dim strFind
Dim strSubstitute
    strText = "This is the text I want
to replace a substring in"
    strFind = "want to replace"
    strSubstitute = "have replaced"
    strText = Replace(strText, _
    strFind, strSubstitute)
```

strText now holds "This is the text I have replaced a substring in".

Function/ Statement Name	Alternative
	Here is how to replace a substring identified by position and length using the `InStr`, `Left`, and `Mid` functions.
	``` Dim strText Dim strSubstitute strText = "This is the text + _ I want to replace a + _ substring in" strSubstitute = "have replaced" strText = Left(strText, 19) & strSubstitute & Mid$(strText, _ 35, Len(strText) - 34) ```
	`strText` now holds "This is the text I have replaced a substring in".
StrConv	It is very unlikely that this will be needed as all variables are `Variant` and this will be done implicitly.

Note that fixed length strings (`Dim strMessage As String * 50`) *are not supported.*

String Constants

Constant	Value	Description
vbCr	Chr(13)	Carriage Return.
vbCrLf	Chr(13) & Chr(10)	A combination of Carriage Return and line feed.
vbFormFeed	Chr(12)	Form Feed*.
vbLf	Chr(10)	Line Feed.
vbNewLine	Chr(13) & Chr(10) or Chr(10)	New-line character. This is platform-specific, meaning whatever is appropriate for the current platform.
vbNullChar	Chr(0)	Character with the value of 0.
vbNullString	String with the value of 0	This is not the same as a zero-length string (""). Mainly used for calling external procedures.
vbTab	Chr(9)	Tab (horizontal).
VbVerticalTab	Chr(11)	Tab (vertical)*.

*Not useful within the Microsoft Windows environment.

Conversion Functions

Asc	Returns the ANSI character code for the first character in a string.
Syntax	`Asc(string)` `string` is any valid string expression.
Note	A runtime error occurs if string doesn't contain any characters. `string` is converted to a `String` subtype if it's a numeric subtype.
Example	`intCharCode = Asc("WROX")` `intCharCode` now holds the value 87, which is the ANSI character code for "W."
See also	`AscB`, `AscW`, `Chr`, `ChrB`, and `ChrW`

AscB	Returns the ANSI character code for the first byte in a string containing byte data.
Syntax	`AscB(string)` `string` is any valid string expression.
Note	A runtime error occurs if string doesn't contain any characters. For normal ANSI strings this function will return the same as the `Asc` function. Only if the string is in Unicode format will it be different from `Asc`. Unicode characters are represented by 2 bytes as opposed to ANSI characters that only need 1.
Example	`intCharCode = AscB("WROX")` `intCharCode` now holds the value 87, which is the ANSI character code for "W."
See also	`Asc`, `AscW`, `Chr`, `ChrB`, and `ChrW`

AscW	Returns the Unicode character code for the first character in a string.
Syntax	`AscW(string)` `string` is any valid string expression.
Note	A runtime error occurs if string doesn't contain any characters. `string` is converted to a `String` subtype if it's a numeric subtype. For use on 32-bit Unicode enabled platforms only, to avoid conversion from Unicode to ANSI.
Example	`intCharCode = AscW("WROX")` `intCharCode` now holds the value 87, which is the Unicode character code for "W."
See also	`Asc`, `AscB`, `Chr`, `ChrB`, and `ChrW`

Cbool	Returns a `Boolean` value (`Variant Subtype 11`) corresponding to the value of an expression.
Syntax	`CBool(expression)` `expression` is any valid expression.
Note	A runtime error occurs if expression can't be evaluated to a numeric value. If expression evaluates to zero, then `False` is returned; otherwise, `True` is returned.
| **Example** | ```
Dim intCounter, blnValue
    intCounter = 5
    blnValue = CBool(intCounter)
```<br><br>`blnValue` now holds the value `True`, because `intCounter` holds a nonzero value. |
| **See also** | `CByte`, `CCur`, `CDbl`, `CInt`, `CLng`, `CSng`, and `CStr` |

Cbyte	Returns an expression converted to `Variant` subtype `Byte(17)`.
Syntax	`CByte(expression)` `expression` is any valid numeric expression.
Note	A runtime error occurs if expression can't be evaluated to a numeric value or if expression evaluates to a value outside the acceptable range for a byte (0–255). Fractional values are rounded.
| **Example** | ```
Dim dblValue, bytValue
    dblValue = 5.456
    bytValue = CByte(dblValue)
```<br><br>`bytValue` now holds the value 5, because `dblValue` is rounded. |
| **See also** | `CBool`, `CCur`, `CDbl`, `CInt`, `CLng`, `CSng`, and `CStr` |

Ccur	Returns an expression converted to `Variant` subtype `Currency (6)`.
Syntax	`CCur(expression)` `expression` is any valid expression.
Note	CCur is internationally aware, which means that the return value is based on the locale settings on the machine. Numbers are formatted with the appropriate decimal separator and the fourth digit to the right of the separator is rounded up if the fifth digit is 5 or higher.
| **Example** | ```
Dim dblValue, curValue
    dblValue = 724.555789
    curValue = CCur(dblValue)
```<br><br>`curValue` now holds the value 724.5558 or 724,5558, depending on the separator. |
| **See also** | `CBool`, `CByte`, `CDbl`, `CInt`, `CLng`, `CSng`, and `CStr` |
```

Cdate	See "Date and Time Functions and Statements."

CDbl	Returns an expression converted to Variant subtype Double (5).
Syntax	CDbl(expression) expression is any valid expression.
Note	CDbl is internationally aware, which means that the return value is based on the locale settings on the machine. Numbers are formatted with the appropriate decimal separator. A runtime error occurs if expression lies outside the range ($-1.79769313486232E308$ to $-4.94065645841247E{-}324$ for negative values, and $4.94065645841247E{-}324$ to $1.79769313486232E308$ for positive values) applicable to a Double.
| **Example** | ```
Dim dblValue
    dblValue = CDbl("5,579.56")
```<br><br>dblValue now holds the value 5579.56 or 5,57956, depending on the thousand and decimal separators in use. |
| **See also** | CBool, CByte, CCur, CInt, CLng, CSng, and CStr |

Chr	Returns the ANSI character corresponding to character code.
Syntax	Chr(charactercode) charactercode is a numeric value that indicates the character you want.
Note	Supplying a charactercode from 0 to 31 returns a standard nonprintable ASCII character.
| **Example** | ```
Dim strChar
    strChar = Chr(89)
```<br><br>strChar now holds the character Y, which is number 89 in the ANSI character table. |
| **See also** | Asc, AscB, AscW, ChrB, and ChrW |

ChrB	Returns the ANSI character corresponding to charactercode.
Syntax	ChrB(charactercode) charactercode is a numeric value that indicates the character you want.
Note	Supplying a charactercode from 0 to 31 returns a standard nonprintable ASCII character. This function is used instead of the Chr (returns a 2-byte character) function when you want only the first byte of the character returned.
Example	Dim strChar strChar = ChrB(89) strChar now holds the character Y, which is number 89 in the ANSI character table.
See also	Asc, AscB, AscW, Chr, and ChrW

ChrW	Returns the Unicode character corresponding to charactercode.
Syntax	ChrW(charactercode) charactercode is a numeric value that indicates the character you want.
Note	Supplying a charactercode from 0 to 31 returns a standard nonprintable ASCII character. This function is used instead of the Chr function when you want to return a 2-byte character. It is for use on 32-bit Unicode enabled platforms only, to avoid conversion from Unicode to ANSI.
Example	Dim strChar strChar = ChrW(89) strChar now holds the character Y, which is number 89 in the Unicode character table.
See also	Asc, AscB, AscW, Chr, and ChrB

Cint	Returns an expression converted to Variant subtype Integer (2).
Syntax	CInt(expression) expression is any valid expression.
Note	CInt is internationally aware, which means that the return value is based on the locale settings on the machine. Note that decimal values are rounded, before the fractional part is discarded. A runtime error occurs if expression lies outside the range (−32,768 to 32,767) applicable to an Integer.
Example	``` Dim intValue intValue = CInt("5,579.56") ``` intValue now holds the value 5580, 6, 56, 558, or more, depending on the thousand and decimal separators in use.
See also	CBool, CByte, CCur, CDbl, CLng, CSng, CStr, and the math functions Fix and Int

CLng	Returns an expression converted to Variant subtype Long (3).
Syntax	CLng(expression) expression is any valid expression.
Note	CLng is internationally aware, which means that the return value is based on the locale settings on the machine. Note that decimal values are rounded, before the fractional part is discarded. A runtime error occurs if expression lies outside the range (−2,147,483,648 to 2,147,483,647) applicable to a Long.
Example	``` Dim lngValue lngValue = CLng("5,579.56") ``` lngValue now holds the value 5580, 6, 56, 558, or more, depending on the thousand and decimal separators in use.
See also	CBool, CByte, CCur, CDbl, CInt, CSng, CStr, and the math functions Fix and Int

CSng	Returns an expression converted to Variant subtype Single (4).
Syntax	CSng(expression)
	expression is any valid expression.
Note	CSng is internationally aware, which means that the return value is based on the locale settings on the machine.
	A runtime error occurs if expression lies outside the range ($-3.402823E38$ to $-1.401298E{-}45$ for negative values, and $1.401298E{-}45$ to $3.402823E38$ for positive values) applicable to a Single.
| **Example** | ```
Dim sngValue
    sngValue = CSng("5,579.56")
``` |
| | sngValue now holds the value 5579.56 or 5,57956, depending on the thousand and decimal separators in use. |
| **See also** | CBool, CByte, CCur, CDbl, CInt, CLng, CStr, and the math functions Fix and Int |

CStr	Returns an expression converted to Variant subtype String(8).
Syntax	CStr(expression)
	expression is any valid expression.
Note	CStr is internationally aware, which means that the return value is based on the locale settings on the machine.
	A runtime error occurs if expression is Null. Numeric and Err values are returned as numbers, Boolean values as True or False, and Date values as a short date.
| **Example** | ```
Dim strValue
    strValue = CStr("5,579.56")
``` |
| | strValue now holds the value 5,579.56. |
| **See also** | CBool, CByte, CCur, CDbl, CInt, CLng, CSng, and the math functions Fix and Int |

Fix	See "Math Functions."
Hex	Returns the hexadecimal representation (up to 8 characters) of a number as a `Variant` subtype `String(8)`.
Syntax	`Hex(number)` `number` is any valid expression.
Note	`number` is rounded to nearest even number before it is evaluated. `Null` will be returned if number is `Null`.

Example	`Dim strValue`
	`    strValue = Hex(5579.56)`
	
	`strValue` now holds the value 15CC.

See also	`Oct`

Int	See "Math Functions."
Oct	Returns the octal representation (up to 11 characters) of a number as a `Variant` subtype `String(8)`.
Syntax	`Oct(number)` `expression` is any valid expression.
Note	`number` is rounded to nearest whole number before it is evaluated. `Null` will be returned if number is `Null`.

Example	`Dim strValue`
	`    strValue = Oct(5579.56)`
	
	`strValue` now holds the value 12714.

See also	`Hex`

Unsupported Conversion Functions

The following VB/VBA conversion functions are not supported in VBScript.

Function Name	Alternative
Cvar	Not needed since conversion to a `Variant` is implicit
CVDate	`CDate`, `Date`
Str	`CStr`
Val	`CDbl`, `CInt`, `CLng`, and `CSng`

Miscellaneous Functions, Statements, and Keywords

Some functionalities do not fit under any of the other categories, and so they have been gathered here. In the following table you will find descriptions of various functions for handling objects, user input, variable checks, output on screen, and so on.

`CreateObject`	Returns a reference to an Automation/COM/ActiveX object. The object is created using COM object creation services.
Syntax	`CreateObject(servername.typename[, location])`
	`servername` is the name of the application that provides the object.
	`typename` is the object's type or class that you want to create.
	`location` (Optional) is the name of the network server you want the object created on. If this is missing, the object is created on the local machine.
Note	An Automation/COM/ActiveX object always contains at least one type or class, but usually several types or classes are contained within. `servername` and `typename` are often referred to as `progid`.
	Note that a `progid` is not always a two part one, like `servername.typename`. It can have several parts, like `servername.typename.version`.
| **Example** | ```
Dim objRemote
Dim objLocal
    ' Create an object from class
    ' MyClass contained in the
    ' COM object MyApp on a
    ' remote server named FileSrv
Set objRemote = CreateObject( _
    "MyApp.MyClass", "FileSrv")
    ' Create an object from class
    ' LocalClass contained in the
    ' COM object LocalApp on the
    ' local macine
Set objLocal = CreateObject( _
    "LocalApp.LocalClass")
``` |
| **See also** | `GetObject` |
```

Dim	Declares a variable of type Variant and allocates storage space.
Syntax	Dim varname[([subscripts])][,varname[([subscripts])]]...
	varname is the name of the variable.
	subscripts (Optional) indicates the dimensions when you declare an array variable. You can declare up to 60 multiple dimensions using the following syntax: upperbound[, upperbound] ...
	upperbound specifies the upper bounds of the array. Because the lower bound of an array in VBScript is always zero, upperbound is one less than the number of elements in the array.
	If you declare an array with empty subscripts, you can later resize it with ReDim; this is called a dynamic array.
Note	This statement is scope specific; that is, you need to consider when and where you want to declare your variables. Variables that are used only in a specific procedure should be declared in this procedure. This makes the variable invisible and inaccessible outside the procedure.
	You can also declare your variables with script scope. This means that the variables are accessible to all procedures within the script. This is one way of sharing data between different procedures.
	Dim statements should be put at the top of a procedure to make the procedure easier to read.
Example	```' Declare a dynamic array
Dim arrstrDynamic()
' Declare a fixed size array
' with 5 elements
Dim arrstrFixed(4)
' Declare a non-array variable
Dim vntTest```
See also	ReDim and Set

Eval	Evaluates and returns the result of an expression.
Syntax	result = Eval(expression)
	result (Optional) is the variable you want to assign the result of the evaluation to. Although result is optional, you should consider using the Execute statement, if you don't want to specify it.
	expression is a string containing a valid VBScript expression.
Note	Because the assignment operator and the comparison operator are the same in VBScript, you need to be careful when using them with Eval. Eval always uses the equal sign (=) as a comparison operator; so if you need to use it as an assignment operator, you should use the Execute statement instead.

| **Example** | ```
Dim blnResult
Dim lngX, lngY
    ' Initialize the variables
    lngX = 15: lngY = 10
    ' Evaluate the expression
    blnResult = Eval( _
    "lngX = lngY")
``` |

`blnResult` holds the value `False`, because 15 is not equal to 10.

See also	`Execute`

`Execute`	Executes one or more statements in the local namespace.
Syntax	`Execute statement`

`statement` is a string containing the statement(s) you want executed. If you include more than one statement, you must separate them using colons or embedded line breaks.

Note	Because the assignment operator and the comparison operator are the same in VBScript, you need to be careful when using them with `Execute`. `Execute` always uses the equal sign (=) as an assignment operator; so if you need to use it as a comparison operator, you should use the `Eval` function instead.

All in-scope variables and objects are available to the statement(s) being executed, but you need to be aware of the special case when your statements create a procedure.

```
Execute "Sub ExecProc: MsgBox ""In
here""": End Sub"
```

The scope of `ExecProc` is global and, thus, everything from the global scope is inherited. The context of the procedure is only available within the scope it is created. This means that if you execute the aforementioned `Execute` statement in a procedure, the `ExecProc` procedure is only accessible within the procedure where the `Execute` statement is called. You can bypass this by simply moving the `Execute` statement to the script level or using the `ExecuteGlobal` statement.

| **Example** | ```
Dim blnResult
Dim lngX, lngY
    ' Initialize the variables
    lngX = 15: lngY = 10
    ' Execute the statement
    Execute("lngResult = + _
    lngX + lngY")
``` |

`lngResult` holds the value 25.

See also	`Eval` and `ExecuteGlobal`

ExecuteGlobal	Executes one or more statements in the global namespace.
Syntax	`ExecuteGlobal statement`
	`statement` is a string containing the statement(s) you want executed. If you include more than one statement, they need to be separated using colons or embedded line breaks.
Note	Because the assignment operator and the comparison operator are the same in VBScript, you need to be careful when using them with `ExecuteGlobal`. `ExecuteGlobal` always uses the equal sign (=) as an assignment operator; so if you need to use it as a comparison operator, you should use the `Eval` function instead.
	All variables and objects are available to the statement(s) being executed.
| **Example** | ```
Dim lngResult
Dim lngX, lngY
    ' Initialize the variables
    lngX = 15: lngY = 10
    ' Execute the statement
    ExecuteGlobal("lngResult = + _
    lngX + lngY")
``` |
| | `lngResult` holds the value 25. |
| **See also** | `Eval` and `Execute` |

Filter	Returns an array that contains a subset of an array of strings. The array is zero-based as are all arrays in VBScript and it holds as many elements as are found in the filtering process. The subset is determined by specifying a criterion.
Syntax	`Filter(inputstrings, value[, include[, compare]])`
	`inputstrings` is a one-dimensional string array that you want to search.
	`value` is the string you want to search for.
	`include` (Optional) is a `Boolean` value indicating if you want to include (`True`) or exclude (`False`) elements in `inputstrings` that contain value.
	`compare` (Optional) indicates the comparison method used when evaluating. Use one of the following constants:
	`vbBinaryCompare` -0 (Default) (Performs a binary comparison, that is, a case-sensitive comparison).
	`vbTextCompare` -1 (Performs a textual comparison, that is, a case-insensitive comparison).
Note	An empty array is returned if no matches are found. A runtime error occurs if `inputstrings` is not a one-dimensional array or if it is `Null`.
```

| **Example** | ```
Dim arrstrColors(3)
Dim arrstrFilteredColors
    ' Fill the array
    arrstrColors(0) = "Red"
    arrstrColors(1) = "Green"
    arrstrColors(2) = "Blue"
    ' Filter the array
    arrstrFilteredColors = _
Filter(arrstrColors, "Red")
``` |

arrstrFilteredColors now holds one element (0) which has the value Red.

See also	See the string function Replace

GetObject	Returns a reference to an Automation object.
Syntax	GetObject([pathname] [, class]])

pathname (Optional) is a string specifying the full path and name of the file that contains the object you want to retrieve. You need to specify class if you omit this argument.

class (Optional) is a string that indicates the class of the object. You need to specify pathname if you omit this argument. The following syntax is used for class:

appname.objecttype

appname is a string indicating the application that provides the object.

objecttype is a string specifying the object's type or class that you want created.

Note	You can use this function to start the application associated with pathname and activate/return the object specified in the pathname.

A new object is returned if pathname is a zero-length string ("") and the currently active object of the specified type is returned if pathname is omitted.

Note that if the object you want returned has been compiled with Visual Basic, you cannot obtain a reference to an existing object by omitting the pathname argument. A new object is returned instead.

The opposite is true for objects that are registered as single-instance objects; the same instance will always be returned. However, you should note the aforementioned problems with ActiveX DLLs compiled using Visual Basic.

Some applications allow you to activate part of a file and you can do this by suffixing the pathname with an exclamation mark (!) and a string that identifies the part of the object you want.

You should only use this function when there is a current instance of the object you want to create, or when you want the object to open up a specific document. Use CreateObject to create a new instance of an object. |

(continued)
```

| **Example** | ```
Dim myobj
Set myobj =
CreateObject("Excel.Application")
Dim objAutomation
    ' Create a reference to an
    ' existing instance of an
    ' Excel application (this
    ' call will raise an error
    ' if no Excel.Application
    ' objects already exists)
    Set objAutomation = _
GetObject(, "Excel.Application")
    ' Create a reference to a
    ' specific workbook in a new
    ' instance of an Excel
    ' application
    Set objAutomation = _
        GetObject( "C:\Test.xls ")
``` |
| **See also** | `CreateObject` |

GetRef	Returns a reference to a procedure. This reference can be bound to an object event. This will let you bind a VBScript procedure to a DHTML event.
Syntax	`Set object.eventname = GetRef(procname)` `object` is the name of the object in which `eventname` is placed. `eventname` is the name of the event to which the procedure is to be bound. `procname` is the name of the procedure you want to bind to `eventname`.
| **Example** | ```
Sub NewOnFocus()
    ' Do your stuff here
End Sub
    ' Bind the NewOnFocus
    ' procedure to the
    ' Window. OnFocus event
    Set Window.OnFocus = _
        GetRef("NewOnFocus ")
``` |

InputBox	Displays a dialog box with a custom prompt and a text box. The content of the text box is returned when the user clicks OK.
Syntax	InputBox(prompt[, title][, default][, xpos][, ypos], [helpfile, context])
	prompt is the message you want displayed in the dialog box. The string can contain up to 1024 characters, depending on the width of the characters you use. You can separate the lines using one of these VBScript constants.
	vbCr, vbCrLf, vbLf, or vbNewLine
	title (Optional) is the text you want displayed in the dialog box title bar. The application name is displayed, if this argument is omitted.
	default is the default text that is returned, if the user doesn't type in any data. The text box is empty if you omit this argument.
	xpos (Optional) is a numeric expression that indicates the horizontal distance of the left edge of the dialog box measured in TWIPs (1/20 of a printer's point, which is 1/72 of an inch) from the left edge of the screen. The dialog box is centered horizontally if you omit this argument.
	ypos (Optional) is a numeric expression that indicates the vertical distance of the upper edge of the dialog box measured in TWIPs from the upper edge of the screen. The dialog box is vertically positioned approximately one third of the way down the screen, if you omit this argument.
	helpfile (Optional) is a string expression that indicates the help file to use when providing context-sensitive help for the dialog box. This argument must be used in conjunction with context. This is not available on 16-bit platforms.
	context (Optional) is a numeric expression that indicates the help context number that makes sure that the right help topic is displayed. This argument must be used in conjunction with helpfile. This is not available on 16-bit platforms.
Note	A zero-length string will be returned if the user clicks Cancel or presses Esc.
| **Example** | ```
Dim strInput
    strInput = InputBox( _
        "Enter User Name:", "Test")
    MsgBox strInput
``` |
| | The MsgBox displays either an empty string or whatever the user entered into the text box. |
| **See also** | MsgBox |
```

IsEmpty	Returns a `Boolean` value indicating if a variable has been initialized.
Syntax	`IsEmpty(expression)`
	`expression` is the variable you want to check has been initialized.
Note	You can use more than one variable as expression. If, for example, you concatenate two `Variants` and one of them is empty, the `IsEmpty` function will return `False`, because the expression is not empty.

Example	`Dim strTest`
	`Dim strInput`
	`    strInput = "Test"`
	`    MsgBox IsEmpty(strTest)      ' true`
	`    MsgBox IsEmpty(strInput & _`
	`    strTest)                    ' false`

See also	`IsArray`, `IsDate`, `IsNull`, `IsNumeric`, `IsObject`, and `VarType`

IsNull	Returns a `Boolean` value indicating if a variable contains `Null` or valid data.
Syntax	`IsNull(expression)`
	`expression` is any expression.
Note	This function returns `True` if the whole of expression evaluates to `Null`. If you have more than one variable in expression, all of them must be `Null` for the function to return `True`. Please be aware that `Null` is not the same as `Empty` (a variable that hasn't been initialized) or a zero-length string (`""`). `Null` means no valid value. You should always use the `IsNull` function when checking for `Null` values, because using the normal operators will return `False` even if one variable is `Null`.

Example	`Dim strInput`
	`    strInput = "Test"`
	`    MsgBox IsNull( strInput _`
	`    & Null) 'false`
	`    MsgBox IsNull(Null) ' true`

See also	`IsArray`, `IsDate`, `IsEmpty`, `IsNumeric`, `IsObject`, and `VarType`

IsNumeric	Returns a `Boolean` value indicating if an expression can be evaluated as a number.
Syntax	`IsNumeric(expression)` `expression` is any expression.
Note	This function returns `True` if the whole expression evaluates to a number. A `Date` expression is not considered a numeric expression.

Example	```MsgBox IsNumeric(55.55)```
	`    ' true`
	`MsgBox IsNumeric("55.55")`
	`    ' true`
	`MsgBox IsNumeric("55.55aaa")`
	`    ' false`
	`MsgBox IsNumeric( "March 1, 1999")`
	`    ' false`
	`MsgBox IsNumeric(vbNullChar)`
	`    ' false`

See also	`IsArray`, `IsDate`, `IsEmpty`, `IsNull`, `IsObject`, and `VarType`

IsObject	Returns a `Boolean` value indicating if an expression is a reference to a valid `Automation` object.
Syntax	`IsObject(expression)` `expression` is any expression.
Note	This function returns `True` only if expression is in fact a variable of `Variant` subtype `Object (9)` or a user-defined object.

Example	`Dim objTest`
	`    MsgBox IsObject(objTest)`
	`        ' false`
	`    Set objTest = CreateObject( _`
	`        "Excel.Application")`
	`    MsgBox IsObject(objTest)`
	`        ' true`

See also	`IsArray`, `IsDate`, `IsEmpty`, `IsNull`, `IsNumeric`, `Set`, and `VarType`

`LoadPicture`	Returns a picture object.

Syntax

`LoadPicture(picturename)`

`picturename` is a string expression that indicates the filename of the picture you want loaded.

Note

This function is available only on 32-bit platforms.

The following graphic formats are supported:

```
Bitmap - .bmp
Icon - .ico
Run-length encoded - .rle
Windows metafile - .wmf
Enhanced metafile - .emf
GIF - .gif
JPEG - .jpg
```

A runtime error occurs if `picturename` doesn't exist or if it is not a valid picture file. Use `LoadPicture("")` to return an "empty" picture object in order to clear a particular picture.

Example

```
Dim objPicture
    ' Load a picture into
    ' objPicture
    objPicture = LoadPicture( _
        "C:\Test.bmp")
    ' Clear objPicture
    objPicture = LoadPicture("")
```

`MsgBox`	Displays a dialog box with a custom message and a custom set of command buttons. The value of the button the user clicks is returned as the result of this function.

Syntax

`MsgBox(prompt[, buttons][, title [, helpfile, context])`

`prompt` is the message you want displayed in the dialog box. The string can contain up to 1024 characters, depending on the width of the characters you use.

You can separate the lines using one of these VBScript constants.

`vbCr`, `vbCrLf`, `vbLf`, or `vbNewLine`

`buttons` (Optional) is the sum of values indicating the number and type of button(s) to display, which icon style to use, which button is the default, and if the `MsgBox` is modal.

The settings for this argument are:

`vbOKOnly` -0 (Displays OK button)

`vbOKCancel` -1 (Displays OK and Cancel buttons)

`vbAbortRetryIgnore` -2 (Displays Abort, Retry, and Ignore buttons)

`vbYesNoCancel` -3 (Displays Yes, No, and Cancel buttons)

vbYesNo -4 (Displays Yes and No buttons)

vbRetryCancel -5 (Displays Retry and Cancel buttons)

vbCritical -16 (Displays critical icon)

vbQuestion -32 (Displays query icon)

vbExclamation -48 (Displays warning icon)

vbInformation -64 (Displays information icon)

vbDefaultButton1 -0 (Makes the first button the default one)

vbDefaultButton2 -256 (Makes the second button the default one)

vbDefaultButton3 -512 (Makes the third button the default one)

vbDefaultButton4 -768 –(Makes the fourth button the default one)

vbApplicationModal -0 (When the MsgBox is application modal, the user must respond to the message box, before he or she can continue)

vbSystemModal -4096 (The same effect as vbApplicationModal)

Buttons (values 0–5)

Icon (values 16, 32, 48, and 64)

Default button (values 0, 256, 512, and 768)

Modal (values 0 and 4096)

You should only pick one value from each group when creating your MsgBox.

title (Optional) is the text you want displayed in the dialog box title bar. The application name is displayed if this argument is omitted.

helpfile (Optional) is a string expression that indicates the help file to use when providing context-sensitive help for the dialog box. This argument must be used in conjunction with context. This is not available on 16-bit platforms.

context (Optional) is a numeric expression that indicates the help context number that makes sure that the right help topic is displayed. This argument must be used in conjunction with helpfile.

Note

The following values can be returned:

vbOK (1)

vbCancel(2)

vbAbort (3)

vbRetry (4)

vbIgnore (5)

vbYes (6)

vbNo (7)

The Esc key has the same effect as the Cancel button. Clicking the Help or pressing F1 will not close the MsgBox.

(continued)

Example	
| | ```
Dim intReturn
    intReturn = MsgBox( "Exit the _
    application?", vbYesNoCancel + _
                vbQuestion)
``` |

The `MsgBox` will display the message `"Exit the application?"`, the buttons `Yes`, `No`, and `Cancel`, and the question mark icon. This `MsgBox` will be application modal.

See also	`InputBox`

RGB	Returns an integer that represents an RGB color value.
	The RGB color value specifies the relative intensity of red, green, and blue to cause a specific color to be displayed.
Syntax	`RGB(red, green, blue)`
	`red` is the red part of the color. Must be in the range 0–255.
	`green` is the green part of the color. Must be in the range 0–255.
	`blue` is the blue part of the color. Must be in the range 0–255.
Note	255 will be used, if the value for any of the arguments is larger than 255. A runtime error occurs if any of the arguments cannot be evaluated to a numeric value.
| **Example** | ```
' Returns the RGB number for white
RGB(255, 255, 255)
``` |

ScriptEngine	Returns a string indicating the scripting language being used.
Syntax	`ScriptEngine`
Note	The following scripting engine values can be returned:
| | ```
VBScript MS VBScript
Jscript  MS  JScript
VBA      MS Visual Basic for Applications
``` |
	Other third-party ActiveX Scripting engines can also be returned, if you have installed one.
See also	`ScriptEngineBuildVersion`,
	`ScriptEngineMajorVersion`, and
	`ScriptEngineMinorVersion`
```

ScriptEngineBuildVersion	Returns the build version of the script engine being used.
Syntax	`ScriptEngineBuildVersion`
Note	This function gets the information from the DLL for the current scripting language.
See also	`ScriptEngine`, `ScriptEngineMajorVersion`, and `ScriptEngineMinorVersion`

ScriptEngineMajorVersion	Returns the major version number of the script engine being used. The major version number is the part before the decimal separator, for example 5 if the version is 5.6.
Syntax	`ScriptEngineMajorVersion`
Note	This function gets the information from the DLL for the current scripting language.
See also	`ScriptEngine`, `ScriptEngineBuildVersion`, and `ScriptEngineMinorVersion`

ScriptEngineMinorVersion	Returns the minor version number of the script engine being used. The minor version number is the part after the decimal separator, for example 6 if the version is 5.6.
Syntax	`ScriptEngineMinorVersion`
Note	This function gets the information from the DLL for the current scripting language.
See also	`ScriptEngine`, `ScriptEngineBuildVersion`, and `ScriptEngineMajorVersion`

Set	Returns an object reference, which must be assigned to a variable or property, or returns a procedure reference that must be associated with an event.
Syntax	`Set objectvar = objectexpression	New classname	Nothing`  `objectvar` is the name of a variable or property.  `objectexpression` (Optional) is the name of an existing object or another variable of the same object type. It can also be a method or function that returns either.  `classname` (Optional) is the name of the class you want to create.  `Set object.eventname = GetRef(procname)`  `object` is the name of the object that `eventname` is associated with.  `eventname` is the name of the event you want to bind `procname` to.  `procname` is the name of the procedure you want to associate with `eventname`.

(continued)

Note	objectvar must be an empty variable or an object type consistent with objectexpression being assigned.
	Set is used to create a reference to an object and not a copy of it. This means that if you use the Set statement more than once on the same object, you will have more than one reference to the same object. Any changes made to the object will be "visible" to all references. New is used only in conjunction with classname, when you want to create a new instance of a class.
	If you use the Nothing keyword, you release the reference to an object, but if you have more than one reference to an object, the system resources are released only when all references have been destroyed (by setting them to Nothing) or they go out of scope.
| **Example** | ```
Dim objTest1
  Dim objTest2
  Dim objNewClass
    ' Create a new dictionary object
    Set objTest1 = CreateObject( _
    "Scripting.Dictionary")
    ' Create a reference to the
    ' newly created dictionary
    ' object
    Set objTest2 = objTest1

    ' Destroy the object reference
    Set objTest1 = Nothing
    ' Although objTest2 was set
    ' to refer to objTest1, you can
    ' still refer to objTest2,
    ' because the system resources
    ' will not be released before
    ' all references have been
    ' destroyed. So let's add a key
    ' and an item
      objTest2.Add "TestKey", "Test"
      ' Destroy the object reference
    Set objTest2 = Nothing

      ' Create an instance of the
      ' class clsTest (created with
      ' the Class keyword)
    Set objNewClass = New clsTest
      ' ...
      ' Destroy the class instance
    Set objNewClass = Nothing
``` |
| **See also** | Class and GetRef |
```

TypeName	Returns the Variant subtype information for an expression as a Variant subtype String(8).
Syntax	TypeName(expression)
	expression is the variable or constant you want subtype information for.
Note	This function has the following return values (strings):
	Byte : Byte
	Integer: Integer
	Long: Long integer
	Single: Single-precision floating-point number
	Double: Double-precision floating-point number
	Currency: Currency
	Decimal: Decimal
	Date: Date and/or time
	String: Character string
	Boolean: True or False
	Empty: Unitialized
	Null: No valid data
	<object type>: Actual type name of an object
	Object: Generic object
	Unknown: Unknown object type
	Nothing: Object variable that doesn't refer to an object instance
	Error: Error
Example	``` Dim arrstrTest(10) MsgBox TypeName(10) ' Integer MsgBox TypeName("Test") ' String MsgBox TypeName(arrstrTest) ' Variant() MsgBox TypeName(Null) ' Null ```
See also	IsArray, IsDate, IsEmpty, IsNull, IsNumeric, IsObject, and VarType

VarType	Returns an integer indicating the subtype of a variable or constant.
Syntax	`VarType(expression)`
	`expression` is the variable or constant you want subtype information for.
Note	This function has the following return values:

`vbEmpty` 0 (Uninitialized)

`vbNull` -1 (No valid data)

`vbInteger` -2 (Integer)

`vbLong` -3 (Long integer)

`vbSingle` -4 (Single-precision floating-point number)

`vbDouble` -5 (Double-precision floating-point number)

`vbCurrency` -6 (Currency)

`vbDate` -7 (Date)

`vbString` -8 (String)

`vbObject` -9 (`Automation` object)

`vbError` -10 (Error)

`vbBoolean` -11 (Boolean)

`vbVariant` -12 (Variant (only used only with arrays of Variants))

`vbDataObject` -13 (A data-access object)

`vbByte` -17 (Byte)

`vbArray` -8192 (Array)

Example	

```
Dim arrstrTest(10)
    MsgBox VarType(10)
        ' 2
    MsgBox VarType("Test")
        ' 8
    MsgBox VarType(arrstrTest)
        ' 8204
    MsgBox VarType(Null)
        ' 1
```

See also	`IsArray`, `IsDate`, `IsEmpty`, `IsNull`, `IsNumeric`, `IsObject`, and `TypeName`

Variable Naming Convention

Because variables are used to hold values, it makes sense to choose names for them that describe their purpose or what they contain. The bigger the project you are working on is, the more important it is to keep track of its variables. This appendix offers some things to keep in mind, including standards:

❑ You'll want to keep your naming consistent. For example if you use Cnt as a variable in one part of the script and Count in another when you are in fact dealing with the same data, you're very likely to introduce runtime errors by confusing the variables.

❑ It is useful to include the scope of a variable by prefixing it with g for global, or l for local (to a subprocedure), such as gstrCompanyName and lstrDepartmentName.

❑ One of the best ways to organize variable names is to prefix all variable names you use with a shorthand representation of the data type that the variable will hold. The standard prefixes used to accomplish this are called Hungarian notation.

Following is a listing of data types and their associated Hungarian prefixes, complete with examples of use.

Data Type	Hungarian Prefix	Example	VarType()
Boolean	bln (or bool)	BlnValid	11
Byte	Byt	bytColor	17
Currency	Cur	CurTotal	6
Date or Time	Dtm	dtmMember	7
Double	Dbl	DblTotal	5
Error	Err	errInvalidEmailAddress	10
Integer	Int	intCount	2
Long	Lng	lngHeight	3
Object	Obj	ObjWS	9 or 13

(continued)

Appendix B: Variable Naming Convention

Data Type	Hungarian Prefix	Example	VarType()
Single	Sng	sngWidth	4
String	Str	strName	8
Variant	Var	varNumber	12

Following is a listing of control types and their associated Hungarian prefixes, complete with examples of use.

Control Type	Hungarian Prefix	Example
Animated button	Ani	AniButton
Check box	Chk	ChkNo
Combo list box	Cbo	CboOS
Command button	Cmd	CmdSend
Common dialog	Dlg	DlgOpen
Frame	Fra	FraOptions
Horizontal scroll bar	Hsb	HsbContrast
Image control	Img	ImgHeading
Label	Lbl	LblText
Line	Lin	LinDivide
List box	Lst	LstDueBy
3D panel	Pnl	PnlMain
Pop-up menu	Mnu	MnuContextSelect
Radio/Option button	Opt	OptIncludeFreeGift
Slider	Sld	SldSetVolume
Spin button	Spn	SpnCounter
Tab strip	Tab	TabOptions
Text box	Txt	TxtComment
Vertical scroll bar	Vsb	VsbSetVolume

Coding Conventions

This appendix covers coding conventions and, like the previous appendix covering variable naming, will help you to produce code that is easily readable and understandable, minimizing errors and speeding up the inevitable debugging process.

Constants

Constants should be clearly identifiable in any code that you write by using either capitals or a `con` prefix. This is done to avoid confusion with variables in the code. For example:

- ❑   `TAX_RATE`
- ❑   `conTaxRate`

Arrays

Arrays should be prefixed with the letter `a` or letters `arr`, depending on your preference or company policy, as well as adhering to the conventions already detailed in earlier chapters. By doing this all arrays in your code will be easier to find later. For example:

- ❑   `astrName`
- ❑   `arrstrName`

Procedure Naming

Another key to writing easy-to-read, easy-to-debug, and easy-to-reuse code is to give your procedures descriptive names. This makes them easier to find in the code and also allows you to keep sections of code for later use—because the descriptive name makes their purpose easier to understand. One trick to this is to start your procedure names with a verb:

- ❑   `InitValues`
- ❑   `ReadData`
- ❑   `CloseWindow`

Mixed case (that is, the capitalization of the first letter of each word) and consistency (using similar verbs) of use between different routines should also be used.

Indentation

The single most valuable thing that you can do to make your code more readable and easy to follow is proper indentation. This is the greatest way to enhance clarity and add a visual cue to the hierarchy of the script.

After a procedure declaration, opening loop statement, or conditional test, you indent by two (or four) spaces, or use tabs. Similarly, closing statements follow the reverse indentation.

By doing this, you can easily follow the flow of your program, as the following example demonstrates. The structure of the code contained within the `For...Next` loop and the `If...End If` statements are clear and easy to follow.

```
Sub ShowIndentation()
    Dim intCount
    Dim strMessage
    For intCount = 1 to 5
        strMessage = strMessage & " " & intCount
        If strMessage = " 1 2" then
            strMessage = strMessage & " -"
        End If
    Next
    MsgBox(strMessage)
End Sub
```

Commenting

Comments are a must, especially when more than one person is working on a project, with functions that other team members will use. Even if you're in a position to write code that only you will ever see, we can guarantee you that after a few months of not dealing with it (or even just certain parts of it), you will forget what it does or how exactly it does it. This is where commenting comes in handy.

You can comment all sorts of aspects of the code and add different comments to your procedures. Here are a few suggestions:

❑   Describe what the procedures do.

❑   Explain pre- and post-conditions.

❑   Indicate return values.

You can also comment things such as important variables (ones that are changed in the procedure or passed by reference) and other parts of your code. Not only will you then be able to remember what it does six months down the line, but another programmer can easily follow your logic when they take over the maintenance of your code after your promotion.

Remember to also make use of the two different types of comments in your code:

❑ **Tombstone:** Comments that appear at the beginning of the code and are used to describe the code as a whole.

❑ **Inline:** Comments that are specific to particular lines that appear within the code.

Following is an example of well-commented code using both inline and tombstone comments:

```
' These comments here describe what the
' function does and what it is for.
' It can also contain information such as
' copyright notices and author name
Sub ShowIndentation()
    Dim intCount

Dim strMessage ' comment specific to this line

    For intCount = 1 to 5
        strMessage = strMessage & " " & intCount

If strMessage = " 1 2" then ' another specific comment

            strMessage = strMessage & " -"
        End If
    Next
    MsgBox(strMessage)
End Sub
```

Visual Basic Constants Supported in VBScript

This appendix is primarily aimed at the Visual Basic programmer who wants to make the jump to VBScript. It covers all of the Visual Basic constants that are supported in VBScript. Constants are useful in script because they allow you to use a specific value without explicitly writing it.

Color Constants

These constants are used within script code to specify particular colors.

Constant	Value	Description
VbBlack	&h00	Black
VbRed	&Hff	Red
VbGreen	&hFF00	Green
VbYellow	&hFFFF	Yellow
VbBlue	&hFF0000	Blue
VbMagenta	&hFF00FF	Magenta
VbCyan	&hFFFF00	Cyan
VbWhite	&hFFFFFF	White

Comparison Constants

These constants are used to switch between binary or textual comparisons.

Constant	Value	Description
VbBinaryCompare	0	Perform a binary comparison.
VbTextCompare	1	Perform a textual comparison.
vbUseSystemDayOfWeek	0	Use the day of the week specified for your computer as the first day of the week.
vbFirstJan1	1	Use the week in which January 1 occurs as the first week of the year (this is the default).
VbFirstFourDays	2	Use the week that has at least four days in the new year.
VbFirstFullWeek	3	Use the first full week of the year.

Date Format Constants

These constants determine how a date is displayed.

Constant	Value	Description
VbGeneralDate	0	Displays a date and/or time. The format is determined by your system settings.
VbLongDate	1	Display a date using your system's long date format.
VbShortDate	2	Display a date using your system's short date format.
VbLongTime	3	Display a time using your system's long time format.
VbShortTime	4	Display a time using your system's short time format.

Miscellaneous Constants

Constant	Value	Description
VbObjectError	2147221504	Used as the base for user-defined error numbers.

MsgBox Constants

These constants specify which buttons and icons appear on the message box, and which button is the default. Some of the constants are also used to determine the modality of the MsgBox.

Constant	Value	Description
VbOKOnly	0	Display the OK button only.
VbOKCancel	1	Display the OK and Cancel buttons.
VbAbortRetryIgnore	2	Display the Abort, Retry, and Ignore buttons.
VbYesNoCancel	3	Display the Yes, No, and Cancel buttons
VbYesNo	4	Display the Yes and No buttons.
VbRetryCancel	5	Display the Retry and Cancel buttons.
VbCritical	16	Display the Critical Message icon.
VbQuestion	32	Display the Warning Query icon.
VbExclamation	48	Display the Warning Message icon.
VbInformation	64	Display the Information Message icon.
VbDefaultButton1	0	The first displayed button is the default.
VbDefaultButton2	256	The second displayed button is the default.
VbDefaultButton3	512	The third displayed button is the default.
VbDefaultButton4	768	The fourth displayed button is the default.
VbApplicationModal	0	The user must respond to the message box.
VbSystemModal	4096	The user must respond to the message box. The message box is always on top in all other windows.

The following determine which MsgBox button the user has selected. These constants must be explicitly declared in your code before they can be used.

Constant	Value	Description
VbOK	1	The OK button was clicked.
VbCancel	2	The Cancel button was clicked.
VbAbort	3	The Abort button was clicked.
VbRetry	4	The Retry button was clicked.
VbIgnore	5	The Ignore button was clicked.
VbYes	6	The Yes button was clicked.
VbNo	7	The No button was clicked.

String Constants

These constants allow for the convenient insertion of nonvisible characters into strings.

Constant	Value	Description
VbCr	Chr(13)	Carriage return.
VbCrLf	Chr(13) & Chr(10)	Carriage return and line feed combination.
VbFormFeed	Chr(12)	Form feed. This is not useful within Windows applications.
VbLf	Chr(10)	Line feed.
VbNewLine	Chr(13) Chr(10) or Chr(10)	Platform-specific newline character.
VbNullChar	Chr(0)	Character having the value 0.
VbNullString	String having value 0	Not the same as a zero-length string ("---"). This is used for calling external procedures.
VbTab	Chr(9)	Horizontal tab.
VbVerticalTab	Chr(11)	Vertical tab. This is not useful within Windows applications.

Tristate Constants

These constants are used to switch arguments on or off, or to use the default setting.

Constant	Value	Description
TristateUseDefault	-2	Use default from computer's regional settings
TristateTrue	-1	True
TristateFalse	0	False

VarType Constants

The VarType constants are used to determine the subtype of a Variant. These constants must be explicitly declared in your code before they can be used.

Constant	Value	Description
VbEmpty	0	Uninitialized (this is the default)
VbNull	1	Contains no valid data
VbInteger	2	Integer subtype
VbLong	3	Long subtype
VbSingle	4	Single subtype
VbDouble	5	Double subtype
VbCurrency	6	Currency subtype
VbDate	7	Date subtype
VbString	8	String subtype
VbObject	9	Object
VbError	10	Error subtype
VbBoolean	11	Boolean subtype
VbVariant	12	Variant (used only for arrays of Variants)
VbDataObject	13	Data access object
vbDecimal	14	Decimal subtype
vbByte	17	Byte subtype
vbArray	8192	Array

VBScript Error Codes and the Err Object

Here you'll find all the error codes associated with VBScript along with the Err object.

Runtime Errors

Runtime errors occur wherever your script attempts to perform an invalid action. The vast majority of these errors should be caught during the debugging and testing stage. VBScript contains 43 runtime errors, which are listed in the following table with their decimal and hexadecimal representations.

Decimal	Hexadecimal	Description
5	800A0005	Invalid procedure call or argument
6	800A0006	Overflow
7	800A0007	Out of memory
9	800A0009	Subscript out of range
10	800A000A	This array is fixed or temporarily locked
11	800A000B	Division by zero
13	800A000D	Type mismatch
14	800A000E	Out of string space
17	800A0011	Can't perform requested operation
28	800A001C	Out of stack space
35	800A0023	Sub or Function not defined
48	800A0030	Err in loading DLL
51	800A0033	Internal error
91	800A005B	Object variable not set
92	800A005C	For loop not initialized

(continued)

Decimal	Hexadecimal	Description
94	800A005E	Invalid use of Null
424	800A01A8	Object required
429	800A01AD	ActiveX component can't create object
430	800A01AE	Class doesn't support Automation
432	800A01B0	Filename or class name not found during Automation operation
438	800A01B6	Object doesn't support this property or method
445	800A01BD	Object doesn't support this action
447	800A01BF	Object doesn't support current locale setting
448	800A01C0	Named argument not found
449	800A01C1	Argument not optional
450	800A01C2	Wrong number of arguments or invalid property assignment
451	800A01C3	Object not a collection
458	800A01CA	Variable uses an Automation type not supported in VBScript
462	800A01CE	Remote server machine does not exist or is unavailable
481	800A01E1	Invalid picture
500	800A01F4	Variable is undefined
502	800A01F6	Object not safe for scripting
503	800A01F7	Object not safe for initializing
504	800A01F8	Object not safe for creating
505	800A01F9	Invalid or unqualified reference
506	800A01FA	Class not defined
507	800A01FB	An exception occurred
5008	800A1390	Illegal assignment
5017	800A1399	Syntax error in regular expression
5018	800A139A	Unexpected quantifier
5019	800A139B	Expected ']' in regular expression
5020	800A139C	Expected ')' in regular expression
5021	800A139D	Invalid range in character set

Syntax Errors

Syntax errors occur wherever your script contains statements that do not follow the predefined rules for that language. This type of error should be caught during development. VBScript contains 49 syntax errors, listed in the following table with their decimal and hexadecimal representations.

Decimal	Hexadecimal	Description
1001	800A03E9	Out of memory
1002	800A03EA	Syntax error
1005	800A03ED	Expected '('
1006	800A03EE	Expected ')'
1010	800A03F2	Expected identifier
1011	800A03F3	Expected '='
1012	800A03F4	Expected 'If'
1013	800A03F5	Expected 'To'
1014	800A03F6	Expected 'End'
1015	800A03F7	Expected 'Function'
1016	800A03F8	Expected 'Sub'
1017	800A03F9	Expected 'Then'
1018	800A03FA	Expected 'Wend'
1019	800A03FB	Expected 'Loop'
1020	800A03FC	Expected 'Next'
1021	800A03FD	Expected 'Case'
1022	800A03FE	Expected 'Select'
1023	800A03FF	Expected expression
1024	800A0400	Expected statement
1025	800A0401	Expected end of statement
1026	800A0402	Expected integer constant
1027	800A0403	Expected 'While' or 'Until'
1028	800A0404	Expected 'While', 'Until', or end of statement
1029	800A0405	Expected 'With'
1030	800A0406	Identifier too long

(continued)

Decimal	Hexadecimal	Description
1013	800A0407	Invalid number
1014	800A0408	Invalid character
1015	800A0409	Unterminated string constant
1034	800A040A	Unterminated comment
1037	800A040D	Invalid use of 'Me' keyword
1038	800A040E	'loop' without 'do'
1039	800A040F	Invalid 'exit' statement
1040	800A0410	Invalid 'for' loop control variable
1041	800A0411	Name redefined
1042	800A0412	Must be first statement on the line
1044	800A0414	Cannot use parentheses when calling a Sub
1045	800A0415	Expected literal constant
1046	800A0416	Expected 'In'
1047	800A0417	Expected 'Class'
1048	800A0418	Must be defined inside a Class
1049	800A0419	Expected Let, Set, or Get in property declaration
1050	800A041A	Expected 'Property'
1051	800A041B	Number of arguments must be consistent across properties specification
1052	800A041C	Cannot have multiple default property/method in a Class
1053	800A041D	Class initialize or terminate do not have arguments
1054	800A041E	Property Set or Let must have at least one argument
1055	800A041F	Unexpected 'Next'
1057	800A0421	'Default' specification must also specify 'Public'
1058	800A0422	'Default' specification can only be on property Get

Understanding the Err Object

Errors usually make their way into code and it's important to spot and remove them. At the core of this is error handling using the Err object, which is the heart and soul of error handling in VBScript, and exposes information about runtime errors through its properties. Unlike other objects in VBScript, it is an intrinsic object with global scope; hence, there is no need to declare and initialize the Err object. The sections that follow take a quick tour of the Err object and the On Err statement and look at ways to make use of them in VBScript code.

Initially the Err properties are either zero-length strings or 0, and when a runtime error occurs the properties of the Err object get populated by the generator of the error (e.g. VBScript, an Automation object, or by the programmer). Err.Number contains an integer, and Number is the default property of the Err object. It is easy to test whether the error actually occurred with an If Err Then statement because of automatic conversion between integer and Boolean subtypes: The integer 0 (no error) converts to Boolean False, and all other numbers evaluate to True.

The following example illustrates a partial IE VBScript (although it could just as easily be from a .wsc, or .hta file) in which the programmer raises one of the predefined VBScript errors. Note that the Err object is not declared and it cannot be created as a separate object.

```
<script language="VBScript">
On Error Resume Next
Err.Raise 11 ' Division by Zero MsgBox ("Error # " & CStr(Err.Number) & " " &
Err.Description)
</script>
```

Err Object Properties

The Description property returns or sets a descriptive string associated with an error. By default this is a zero-length string until the property is set by the programmer or by the generator of an error. The description is useful when displaying or logging errors and when raising custom errors. If the programmer raises one of the default runtime errors, the Description property contains the string associated with the error.

Syntax

```
Err.Description [= stringexpression]
```

Name	Subtype	Description
Err	Err Object	This is always the Err Object
Stringexpression	String	A string expression containing a description of the error

Example Usage

The following sample script produces `Variable` as undefined inside a message box.

```
<script language="VBScript">
Option Explicit
On Error Resume Next

IntTest = 5
MsgBox ("Error Description: " & Err.Description)
</script>
```

HelpContext

The `HelpContext` property is used to automatically display the Help topic specified in the `HelpFile` property. This property either sets or retrieves the value of the help context. If both `HelpFile` and `HelpContext` are empty, the value of `Number` is checked. The following summarizes the use of `HelpContext`:

❑   If `Number` corresponds to a VBScript runtime error value, then the VBScript help context `ID` for the error is used.

❑   This property is rarely used, and requires coordination between the person authoring the Help system and the scripter.

❑   Use of the `HelpFile` and `HelpContext` only make sense in a non-IE setting with the older `.hlp` system. Newer HTML help simply uses HTML documents, which may be displayed under most circumstances using techniques discussed in HTML Help manuals.

The following sample illustrates the use of the traditional `.hlp` files with the Windows Script Host.

Syntax

```
Err.HelpContext [= contextID]
```

Name	Subtype	Description
Err	Err Object	This always is the `Err` Object.
ContextID	Integer	Optional. A valid identifier for a Help topic within the Help file.

Example Usage

```
On Error Resume Next
Dim Msg
Err.Clear
Err.Raise 6 ' Generate "Overflow" error.
Err.Helpfile = "c: \ windows\ help\ yourHelp.hlp"
Err.HelpContext = 21
If Err.Number <> 0 Then
    Msg = "Press Help to see " & Err.Helpfile & " topic for" & _
```

```
      " the following HelpContext: " & Err.HelpContext
      MsgBox Msg, , "error: " & Err.Description, Err.Helpfile, Err.HelpContext
   End If
```

HelpFile

The `HelpFile` property is used to set and retrieve a fully qualified path to a programmer-authored Help File. Often it is used in conjunction with the `HelpContext` property — see the notes and the earlier example. The most common way of setting the value is through the `Err.Raise` method.

Syntax

```
Err.HelpFile [= filepath]
```

Name	Subtype	Description
Err	Err Object	This always is the Err Object.
Filepath	String	Optional. Fully qualified path to the Help File.

Number

This is the default property of the `Err` object, and returns or sets a numeric value specifying an error. Custom error handling functions utilize the `Number` property to diagnose the runtime error.

When setting or retrieving a custom error, the `vbObjectErr` constant is used to ensure that custom errors do not conflict with VBScript and common Automation `Errs`.

Syntax

```
Err.Number [= errornumber]
```

Name	Subtype	Description
Err	Err Object	This is always the Err Object.
Errornumber	Integer	An integer representing a VBScript error number or an SCODE error value. SCODE is a long integer value that is used to pass detailed information to the caller of an interface member or API function.

Example Usage

The following sample code sets a custom error number in `Err.Number` through the `Err.Raise` method, and then displays the return value through a Message Box (`MsgBox`).

```
On Error Resume Next
Err.Raise vbObjectError + 16, ,"CustomObject Error" ' Raise Custom Error #16.
If Err.Number <> 0 Then        ' (If Err Then) can be used too
    MsgBox ("Error # " & CStr(Err.Number) & " " & Err.Description)
End If
```

Source

The Source property sets or returns the name of the object or application that reported the error. Most commonly the source is the class name or ProgID of the object generating the error.

Most of the time the Source property will show "Microsoft VBScript," but in cases where the error occurs while accessing a property or method of an Automation object, the source property will show the component's class name. This is useful not only because it allows for a greater degree of granularity (or visibility) in error handling, but it also allows for better error display and logging possibilities. This property can be set through the Err.Raise method in both VBScript and in custom COM components.

Syntax

```
Err.Source [= stringexpression]
```

Name	Subtype	Description
Err	Err Object	This always is the Err Object.
Stringexpression	Integer	A string expression representing the application that generated the error.

Example Usage

```
On Error Resume Next
Err.Raise vbObjectError + 1, "cTestClass", "CustomObject Error"
If Err.Number <> 0 Then          " (If Err Then) can be used too
    MsgBox ("Error # " & CStr(Err.Number) & " " & Err.Description & " Source: " &
    Err.Source)
End If
```

Err Object Methods

Now take a look at the Err object methods.

Clear

The Clear method resets all of the properties of the Err object to either 0 or a zero-length string. The Err object should ideally be reset after an error has been handled because of the deferred nature of error handling in VBScript, to avoid the potential mistake of handling the same error twice.

The Err object is additionally cleared by any of the following statements:

- ❑   On Error Resume Next
- ❑   On Error Goto 0
- ❑   Exit Sub
- ❑   Exit Function

Therefore, error-handling functions must be called before any of the preceding statements are executed.

Syntax

```
Err.Clear
```

Name	Subtype	Description
Err	Err Object	This always is the Err Object.

Example Usage

```
On Error Resume Next       ' The Err Object is Reset
Err.Raise 5
Err.Clear
If Err.Number = 0 Then     ' (If Err Then) can be used too
    MsgBox ("Error has been reset: Err.Number - " & CStr(Err.Number))
End If
```

Raise

The `Raise` method generates a runtime error. All of the parameters of the `Raise` method, except for its number, are optional. When optional parameters are not specified, and the `Err` object has not been cleared, old values may appear.

The best practice is to use `Err.Clear` after error handling, and to inspect the `Err` object before using `Err.Raise` (in case an error has occurred in the meantime). When raising custom error numbers, the `vbObjectErr` constant should be added.

The `HelpFile` and `HelpContext` parameters are used with the traditional `.hlp` help, and not with the HTML help systems.

Raising errors is a popular technique to stop the execution of a procedure, and handle it via some error handling function. You may raise errors when data is invalid, and when you want to pass an error up the call stack. This is a popular technique when you want to change one error into another so that it can be handled properly.

Syntax

```
Err.Raise (number, source, description, helpfile, helpcontext)
```

Name	Subtype	Description
Err	Err Object	This is always the Err Object.
Number	Long	This identifies the nature of the error. All VBScript (predefined and user-defined) error numbers are in the range 0-65535.

(continued)

Name	Subtype	Description
Source	String	This identifies the name of the object or application that generates the error. When setting this property for Windows Script Components, use the ProgID form.
		If nothing is specified, the current ID of the project is used; often, it just defaults to 'Microsoft VBScript'.
Description	String	This is the description of the error. If unspecified, the value in number is examined. If it can be mapped to a VBScript runtime error code, a string provided by VBScript is used as the description. If there is no VBScript error corresponding to number, a generic error message is used.
Helpfile	String	This is the fully qualified path to a customized help file in which help on this error can be found. If unspecified, VBScript uses the fully qualified drive, path, and filename of the VBScript help file.
Helpcontext	Integer	This is the context ID identifying a topic within helpfile that provides help for the error. If omitted, the VBScript help file context ID for the error corresponding to the number property is used, if it exists.

Example Usage

The following example shows a common way of raising an error in Windows Script Host, where the help file is readily available:

```
Dim strMsg
On Error Resume Next
Err.Raise vbObjectError + 1, "prjProject.clsClass", "Custom Error",
"c: windowsYourHelpfile.hlp", 1
If Err.Number <> 0 Then
    strMsg = "Error Number: " & CStr(Err.Number) & vbCrLf
    strMsg = strMsg & "Description: " & Err.Description & vbCrLf
    strMsg = strMsg & "Source: " & Err.Source
    If Err.HelpFile <> "" Then
        strMsg = strMsg & vbCrLf & "Press Help to see the help file"
        MsgBox strMsg, , "Error: " & Err.Description, Err.Helpfile, Err
.HelpContext
    End If
    MsgBox strMsg    ' No Help file available here
    Err.Clear
End If
```

vbObjectError Constant

This is a built-in constant that can be used in conjunction with programmer-defined errors and `Err`
`.Raise`. It does not have to be declared or initialized; its decimal value is –2147221504 (or –0 × 8004000
in hexadecimal). Whereas previous examples have shown how to use the `vbObjectError` constant
with the `Err.Raise` method, the following example shows a skeleton of a centralized error handler that
combines `Select Case` with custom errors.

Example Usage

```
If Err.Number <> 0 Then                ' this should call separate subs
    Select Case Err.Number
        Case vbObjectError + 1
        ' call sub handling error 1
        Case vbObjectError + 3
        ' call sub handling error 3
        Case Else
        ' call reporting sub to display errors
    End Select
End If
```

On Error Resume Next

This statement enables error handling within the scope of a script or a procedure. Without the `On Error`
`Resume Next` statement, the default runtime error handler displays the error and stops the execution of
the script.

`On Error Resume Next` continues the execution of the script on the next line following the error. The
error handling routine has to exist within the same scope as this statement. The statement becomes inactive with a call to another procedure or when an `On Error Goto 0` statement is used.

Syntax

```
On Error Resume Next
```

*When Internet Explorer's advanced option Disable Script Debugging is not selected and the Script
Debugger is installed on the same system,* `On Error Resume Next` *does not go into effect; instead,
the browser automatically goes into the "debug" mode. So, when testing the effectiveness of your error
handler through Internet Explorer, make sure that this option is selected.*

On Error Goto 0

The `On Error Goto 0` statement disables the error handling that was enabled by `On Error Resume Next`.
This statement is especially useful in the testing stage, when there is a need to identify certain errors and yet
handle others. `On Error Goto 0` can be placed immediately after the error handling procedure is called.

Like `On Error Resume Next`, this statement is also scope dependent.

Syntax

```
On Error Goto 0
```

Scope of On Error Statement and How VBScript's and VBs (or VBAs) Error Handling Differ

It is important to understand the scope of the On Error statement; otherwise your error handling procedures may never execute. VBScript — unlike its parent language — does not support labels, and it does not support the VB On Error Goto label. Thus, VBScript provides support only for in-line error handlers that can cause understandable grief. Basically, to mimic a block of code in VB that would respond to an On Error Goto label statement, you might be inclined to use several If Err Then statements to check for an error with each single line of execution. However, with a little bit of programming, you can easily achieve this by enabling an error handler around a given procedure. Should one of the lines in the procedure fail, the error can be thrown up the calling stack. Of course, there is no Resume statement, which complicates some of the scripting. This can only be circumvented by trying to correct the problem that generated the error and attempting to call the procedure again.

Before you see some error handling techniques, let's examine the scope of error handling. The following script illustrates an important concept behind the scope of the error-enabling and error-disabling statements, as well as showing the differences in scope and the importance in clearing of errors:

```
Sub TestError()
    On Error Resume Next
    Err.Raise 6                    ' Execution will continue
    MsgBox ("TestError: Error # " & CStr(Err.Number) & " " & Err.Description)
Err.Clear
End Sub

Sub TestError2()
    Err.Clear                 ' Execution stops, moves up in scope
    MsgBox ("TestError2: This will never Show Up")
End Sub

' Main body of the script
' TestError() has local Error Handler no need for global Handler
On Error Resume Next
Call TestError()
If Err.Number <> 0 Then
    MsgBox ("Global: Error # " & CStr(Err.Number) & " " & Err.Description)
    Err Clear
Else
   MsgBox ("Global: No Error, It was handled locally and cleared")
End If

' TestError2 has no local error handler
Call TestError2()
If Err.Number <> 0 Then
    MsgBox ("Global: Error # " & CStr(Err.Number) & " " & Err.Description)
    Err.Clear
End If
' Global script Error handling is turned off, cause crash
On Error goto 0
Call TestError2()
```

Upon execution, the error is first handled locally, and after it is cleared, it is ignored. Next, the calls to the `Test Error2()` subroutine are first handled by the global error handler and, after it is disabled on the second-last line, a runtime error appears.

Now, to consider the importance of clearing errors and the scope of `On Error Resume Next`, the following example makes two adjustments, commenting out certain code:

```
Sub TestError()
    On Error Resume Next
    Err.Raise 6                 ' Execution will continue
    MsgBox ("TestError: Error # " & CStr(Err.Number) & " " & Err.Description)
    REM Err.Clear
End Sub

Sub TestError2()
    Err.Clear               ' Execution stops, moves up in scope
    MsgBox ("TestError2: This will never Show Up")
End Sub

' Main body of the script
' TestError() has local Error Handler no need for global Handler
REM On Error Resume Next
```

With these changes, an error message is still displayed after the call to `TestError()`, but the first call to the `TestError2()` subprocedure results in an invocation of the default error handler, and stoppage of the script immediately after the call, that is, the `On Error Resume Next` statement was local in scope to the `TestError()` subprocedure.

The following code illustrates the possibility of mimicking the `On Error Goto` label statement by encompassing a block of code in a procedure, rather than trapping errors inline, as in VB. Here the scripter can invoke an error handler at a higher level rather than at the level where the error occurred (in this case, a procedure without a local error handler).

```
Option Explicit
Dim intZero, intNonZero, intResult
intZero = 0
intNonZero = 1

Sub TestError()
    ' Statements that will execute
    MsgBox ("This will always execute")
    ' now cause an error
    intResult = intNonZero / intZero        ' causes error 11
    ' Statements that will not execute if error occurs
    MsgBox ("Finally executed, Result = " & CStr(intResult) )
End Sub

' simulate On Error Goto Label by having a block of code in a sub
On Error Resume Next
Call TestError()
If Err.Number = 11 Then
    MsgBox "Division By Zero - may still continue" & vbCrLf & Err.Description
    Err.Clear
```

(continued)

```
        intZero = 1
        TestError()
   End If
   On Error Goto 0                          'kill other error handling
```

Error Handling in Internet Explorer

Besides VBScript itself, some Web authors might also turn to DHTML events. Internet Explorer's DHTML object model supports a variety of events, including events occurring as a result of an error. Essentially, this allows for a different degree of control when authoring scripts for IE. Thanks to the GetRef() function, which returns a pointer to a function, it is now possible to bind VBScript procedures to an event.

For example, the following line executes the RunMySub procedure in response to the Window.Onload event in IE:

```
Set Window.Onload = GetRef("RunMySub")
```

Similarly, you can write procedures that will execute when the OnError event is fired, either for an element or for the window object.

There are two additional techniques for error handling in IE:

❏   Centralized, through the use of the window.onerror event

❏   Decentralized, through the use of the element.onerror event

The code example that follows illustrates the old and the new syntax for handling DHTML errors.

Old Syntax

```
Function element_onerror (message, url, line)
```

element is the name of the element or window.

```
<script language="VBScript">
Function window_onerror ( message, url, line )
    ' handle error here
    window_onerror = true
End Function
</script>
```

New Syntax

```
Set element.onerror = GetRef("functionName")
```

The new syntax allows you to bind functions to events, just like in JScript. Again, element is the name of the element or window, and functionName is an actual function or a sub.

```
<script language="VBScript">
Function onErrorHandler ( message, url, line )
    ' handle error here
    onErrorHandler = True
End Function
set window.onerror = GetRef("onErrorHandler")
</script>
```

There are a few important differences between the VBScript's error handling and the use of the `onerror` event in IE. Following is a summary of the `onerror` IE handlers:

❏   Execution does not resume on the next line. The script may resume with the next user action or handled event — for example, the user "clicks" on another element. If you want greater error-handling control in individual procedures executed in the browser, the `On Error Resume Next` statement should be used.

❏   All errors pertaining to the element (or window) are handled by the event unless handled via VBScript's `On Error Resume Next` technique.

❏   Errors can be passed to a higher-level element via event bubbling.

❏   Custom errors cannot be created; there is no `Err.Raise` counterpart in the DHTML object model.

The Scripting Runtime Library Object Reference

The default scripting languages installed with Microsoft Windows Vista and XP, Office 2007 and XP, ASP 3.0, and many other applications provide a scripting runtime library in the file `scrrun.dll`, which implements a series of objects that can be used in ASP on the server and in client-side code running on the client.

❑ **The Dictionary object:** This provides a useful storage object that can be used to store values, accessed and referenced by their name rather than by index as would be the case in a normal array — it's ideal for storing the name/value pairs that you retrieve from the ASP `Request` object, for example.

❑ **The FileSystemObject object:** This provides you with access to the underlying file system on the server (or on the client in Internet Explorer 5/6 when used in conjunction with a special type of page named HTML Application or HTA) — you can use the `FileSystemObject` object to iterate through the machine's local and networked drives, folders, and files.

❑ **The TextStream object:** This provides access to files stored on disk, and is used in conjunction with the `FileSystemObject` object — it can read from or write to text (sequential) files.

The Scripting.Dictionary Object

The `Dictionary` object provides a useful storage object that you can use to store values, accessed and referenced by their name rather than by index, as would be the case in a normal array. The properties and methods exposed by the `Dictionary` object are as follows.

Properties

Property	Description
Count	Returns the number of key/item pairs in the Dictionary (read-only)
Item (key)	Sets or returns the value of the item for the specified key
Key (key)	Sets or returns the value of a key

Methods

Method	Description
Add (key, item)	Adds the key/item pair to the Dictionary. You can also add items with a simple assignment, and in fact, you must use this syntax in order to store object references in a dictionary: `Set objDict("keyname") = objMyObject`
Exists (key)	Returns true if the specified key exists or false if not.
Items ()	Returns an array containing all the items in a Dictionary object.
Keys ()	Returns an array containing all the keys in a Dictionary object.
Remove (key)	Removes a single key/item pair specified by key.
RemoveAll ()	Removes all the key/item pairs.

> An error will occur if you try to add a key/item pair when that key already exists, remove a key/item pair that doesn't exist, or change the CompareMode of a Dictionary object that already contains data.

The Scripting.FileSystemObject Object

The FileSystemObject object provides you with access to the underlying file system on the server (or on the client in Internet Explorer 5/6 when used in conjunction with a special type of page named an HTML Application or HTA).

The FileSystemObject object exposes a series of properties and methods of its own, some of which return other objects that are specific to objects within the file system. These subsidiary objects are as follows:

❑ The Drive object provides access to all the drives available on the machine.

❑ The Folder object provides access to the folders on a drive.

❑ The File object provides access to the files within each folder.

While these three objects form a neat hierarchy, the FileSystemObject object also provides methods that can bridge the hierarchy by creating instances of the subsidiary objects directly.

The FileSystemObject Object

The FileSystemObject object provides overall access to the underlying file system and is used as a starting point when navigating the file system.

Property

Property	Description
Drives	Returns a collection of Drive objects that are available from the local machine. This includes network drives that are mapped from this machine.

Method

Method	Description
BuildPath (path, name)	Adds the file or folder specified in a name to the existing path, adding a path separator character ('\') if required. This does not check for a valid or existing path.
CopyFile (source, destination, overwrite)	Copies the file or files specified in source (wildcards can be included) to the folder specified in destination. If source contains wildcards or destination ends with a path separator character ('\') then destination is assumed to be a folder; otherwise, it is assumed to be a full path and name for the new file. Note that leaving off the last '\' when the source doesn't contain wildcards throws a "Permission denied" error because the name (assumed to be a filename without an extension) exists as a folder name. An error will occur if the destination file already exists and the optional overwrite parameter is set to False. The default for overwrite is True.
CopyFolder (source, destination, overwrite)	Copies the folder or folders specified in source (wildcards can be included) to the folder specified in destination, including all the files contained in the source folder(s). If source contains wildcards or destination ends with a path separator character ('\') then destination is assumed to be a folder into which the copied folder(s) will be placed; otherwise, it is assumed to be a full path and name for a new folder to be created. An error will occur if the destination folder already exists and the optional overwrite parameter is set to False. The default for overwrite is True.

(continued)

705

Method	Description
CreateFolder (foldername)	Creates and returns a reference to a new folder, which has the path and name specified in foldername. Only the last folder in the path is created — all parent folders must exist. An error occurs if the specified folder already exists.
CreateTextFile (filename, overwrite, unicode)	Creates a new text file on disk with the specified filename and returns a TextStream object that refers to it.
	If the optional overwrite parameter is set to True, any existing file with the same path and name will be overwritten. The default for overwrite is False. If the optional unicode parameter is set to True, the content of the file will be stored as Unicode text.
	The default for unicode is False for an ASCII file.
DeleteFile (filespec, force)	Deletes the file or files specified in filespec (wildcards can be included).
	If the optional force parameter is set to True the file(s) will be deleted even if the read-only attribute is set.
	The default for force is False.
DeleteFolder (folderspec, force)	Deletes the folder or folders specified in folderspec (wildcards can be included in the final component of the path) together with all their contents.
	If the optional force parameter is set to True the file(s) will be deleted even if the read-only attribute is set.
	The default for force is False.
DriveExists (drivespec)	Returns True if the drive specified in drivespec exists, or False if not.
	The drivespec parameter can be a drive letter as a string or a full absolute path for a folder or file.
FileExists (filespec)	Returns True if the file specified in filespec exists, or False if not.
	The filespec parameter can contain an absolute or relative path for the file, or just the filename to look in the current folder.
FolderExists (folderspec)	Returns True if the folder specified in folderspec exists, or False if not.
	The folderspec parameter can contain an absolute or relative path for the folder, or just the folder name to look in the current folder.

Method	Description
GetAbsolutePathName (pathspec)	Takes a `path` that unambiguously identifies a folder and, taking into account the current folder's path, returns a full unambiguous path specification for the `pathspec` folder.
	For example, if the current folder is "c:\docs\sales" and `pathspec` is "jan" the returned value is "c:\docs\sales\jan". Wildcards and the ".", "..", and "\\" path operators are accepted.
GetBaseName (filespec)	Returns just the name of a file or folder specified in `filespec`, that is, with the path and file extension removed.
GetDrive (drivespec)	Returns a `Drive` object corresponding to the drive specified in `drivespec`.
	The format for `drivespec` can include the colon, path separator or be a network share, that is, "c," "c:", "c:\", or "\\machine\sharename."
GetDriveName (drivespec)	Returns the name of the drive specified in `drivespec` as a string.
	The `drivespec` parameter must be an absolute path to a file or folder, or just the drive letter such as "c:" or just "c"
GetExtensionName (filespec)	Returns just the extension of a file or folder specified in `filespec`, that is, with the path and filename removed.
GetFile (filespec)	Returns a `File` object corresponding to the file specified in `filespec` or the last folder name if there is no file.
	This can be a relative or absolute path to the required file.
GetFileName (pathspec)	Returns the name part (that is, without the path or file extension) of the path and filename specified in `pathspec`, or the last folder name of which there is no filename.
	This does not check for existence of the file or folder.
GetFileVersion (filespec)	Returns the version information from a file in Windows 2000, XP, Vista and Windows Script Host 2.0 and 5.6
GetFolder (folderspec)	Returns a `Folder` object corresponding to the folder specified in `folderspec`.
	This can be a relative or absolute path to the required folder.
GetParentFolderName (pathspec)	Returns the name of the parent folder of the file or folder specified in `pathspec`.
	This does not check for existence of the folder.

(continued)

Method	Description
`GetSpecialFolder (folderspec)`	Returns a `Folder` object corresponding to one of the special Windows folders.
	The permissible values for `folderspec` are: `WindowsFolder (0)` `SystemFolder (1)` `TemporaryFolder (2)`
`GetTempName ()`	Returns a randomly generated filename that can be used for performing operations that require a temporary file or folder.
`MoveFile (source, destination)`	Moves the file or files specified in `source` to the folder specified in `destination`. Wildcards can be included in `source` but not in `destination`. If `source` contains wildcards or `destination` ends with a path separator character (`'\'`) then destination is assumed to be a folder; otherwise, it is assumed to be a full path and name for the new file. Note that leaving off the last `'\'` when the source doesn't contain wildcards throws a "Permission denied" error because the name (assumed to be a filename without an extension) exists as a folder name.
	An error will occur if the destination file already exists.
`MoveFolder (source, destination)`	Moves the folder or folders specified in `source` to the folder specified in `destination`. Wildcards can be included in `source` but not in `destination`. If `source` contains wildcards or `destination` ends with a path separator character (`'\'`), then `destination` is assumed to be the folder in which to place the moved folders; otherwise, it is assumed to be a full path and name for a new folder.
	An error will occur if the `destination` folder already exists.
`OpenTextFile (filename, iomode, create, format)`	Creates a filenamed `filename`, or opens an existing filenamed `filename`, and returns a `TextStream` object that refers to it.
	The `filename` parameter can contain an absolute or relative path.
	The `iomode` parameter specifies the type of access required.
	The permissible values are `ForReading (1)` (the default), `ForWriting (2)`, and `ForAppending (8)`.
	If the `create` parameter is set to `True` when writing or appending to a file that does not exist, a new file will be created.
	The default for `create` is `False`. The `format` parameter specifies the format of the data to be read from or written to the file.

Method	Description
	Permissible values are `TristateFalse` (0) (the default) to open it as ASCII, `TristateTrue` (-) to open it as Unicode, and `TristateUseDefault` (-2) to open it using the system default format.

The Drive Object

The `Drive` object provides access to all the drives available on the machine. The properties (note that it has no methods) exposed by the `Drive` object are shown in the following table.

Properties	Description
`AvailableSpace`	Returns the amount of space in bytes available to this user on the drive, taking into account quotas and/or other restrictions
`DriveLetter`	Returns the drive letter of the drive

`DriveType`	Returns the type of the drive. The values are:
	`Unknown (0)`
	`Removable (1)`
	`Fixed (2)`
	`Network (3)`
	`CDRom (4)`
	`RamDisk (5)`

`FileSystem`	Returns the type of file system for the drive. The values include:
	`"FAT"`
	`"NTFS"`
	`"CDFS"`

`FreeSpace`	Returns the actual amount of free space in bytes available on the drive
`IsReady`	Returns a Boolean value indicating if the drive is ready (`True`) or not (`False`)
`Path`	Returns the path for the drive as a drive letter and colon, that is, "`C:`"
`RootFolder`	Returns a `Folder` object representing the root folder of the drive
`SerialNumber`	Returns a decimal serial number used to uniquely identify a disk volume
`ShareName`	Returns the network share name for the drive if it is a networked drive
`TotalSize`	Returns the total size in bytes of the drive
`VolumeName`	Sets or returns the volume name of the drive if it is a local drive

The Folder Object

The Folder object provides access to the folders on a drive.

Properties

Property	Description
Attributes	Returns the attributes of the folder
	Can be a combination of any of the values: Normal (0) ReadOnly (1) Hidden (2) System (4) Volume (name) (8) Directory (folder) (16) Archive (32) Alias (1024) Compressed (2048)
	Can also be used to set the following file attributes: ReadOnly Hidden System Archive
DateCreated	Returns the date and time that the folder was created where available
DateLastAccessed	Returns the date and time that the folder was last accessed
DateLastModified	Returns the date and time that the folder was last modified
Drive	Returns the drive letter of the drive on which the folder resides
Files	Returns a Files collection containing File objects representing all the files within this folder
IsRootFolder	Returns a Boolean value indicating if the folder is the root folder of the current drive
Name	Sets or returns the name of the folder
ParentFolder	Returns the Folder object for the parent folder of this folder
Path	Returns the absolute path of the folder using long filenames where appropriate
ShortName	Returns the DOS-style 8.3 version of the folder name
ShortPath	Returns the DOS-style 8.3 version of the absolute path of this folder
Size	Returns the total combined size of all files and subfolders contained in the folder

Property	Description
SubFolders	Returns a `Folders` collection consisting of all folders contained in the folder, including hidden and system folders
Type	Returns a string that is a description of the folder type (such as "Recycle Bin"), if available
DateCreated	Returns the date and time that the folder was created where available

Methods

Method	Description
Copy (destination, overwrite)	Copies this folder and all its contents to the folder specified in `destination`, including all the files contained in this folder.
	If `destination` ends with a path separator character (' \ ') then destination is assumed to be a folder into which the copied folder will be placed; otherwise, it is assumed to be a full path and name for a new folder to be created.
	An error will occur if the `destination` folder already exists and the optional `overwrite` parameter is set to `False`. The default for `overwrite` is `True`.
Delete (force)	Deletes this folder and all its contents.
	If the optional `force` parameter is set to `True` the folder will be deleted even if the read-only attribute is set on it or on any contained files.
	The default for `force` is `False`.
Move (destination)	Moves this folder and all its contents to the folder specified in `destination`.
	If `destination` ends with a path separator character (' \ ') then `destination` is assumed to be the folder in which to place the moved folder; otherwise, it is assumed to be a full path and name for a new folder.
	An error will occur if the destination folder already exists.
CreateTextFile (filename, overwrite, unicode)	Creates a new text file within this folder with the specified `filename` and returns a `TextStream` object that refers to it. If the optional `overwrite` parameter is set to `True` any existing file with the same name will be overwritten.
	The default for `overwrite` is `False`.
	If the optional `unicode` parameter is set to `True`, the content of the file will be stored as Unicode text.
	The default for `unicode` is `False`.

The File Object

The `File` object provides access to the files within each folder.

Properties

Property	Description

Attributes	Sets or returns the attributes of the file. Can be a combination of any of the values:
	`Normal (0)`
	`ReadOnly (1)`
	`Hidden (2)`
	`System (4)`
	`Volume (name) (8)`
	`Directory (folder) (16)`
	`Archive (32)`
	`Alias (1024)`
	`Compressed (2048)`
	
	Can also be used to set the following attributes:
	`ReadOnly`
	`Hidden`
	`System`
	`Archive`

DateCreated	Returns the date and time that the file was created where available
DateLastAccessed	Returns the date and time that the file was last accessed
DateLastModified	Returns the date and time that the file was last modified
Drive	Returns the drive letter of the drive on which the file resides
Name	Sets or returns the name of the file
ParentFolder	Returns the `Folder` object for the parent folder of this file
Path	Returns the absolute path of the file using long filenames where appropriate
ShortName	Returns the DOS-style 8.3 version of the filename
ShortPath	Returns the DOS-style 8.3 version of the absolute path of this file
Size	Returns the size of the file in bytes
Type	Returns a string that is a description of the file type (such as "Text Document" for a `.txt` file) if available

Methods

Method	Description
Copy (destination, overwrite)	Copies this file to the folder specified in `destination`.
	If `destination` ends with a path separator character (`''`), then `destination` is assumed to be a folder into which the copied file will be placed; otherwise, it is assumed to be a full path and name for a new file to be created.
	Note that leaving off the last `'\'` when the source doesn't contain wildcards throws a "Permission denied" error because the name (assumed to be a filename without an extension) exists as a folder name.
	An error will occur if the destination file already exists and the optional `overwrite` parameter is set to `False`.
	The default for `overwrite` is `True`.
Delete (force)	Deletes this file.
	If the optional `force` parameter is set to `True`, the file will be deleted even if the read-only attribute is set.
	The default for `force` is `False`.
Move (destination)	Moves this file to the folder specified in `destination`.
	If `destination` ends with a path separator character (`'\'`) then `destination` is assumed to be the folder in which to place the moved file; otherwise, it is assumed to be a full path and name for a new file.
	An error will occur if the destination file already exists.
OpenAsTextStream (iomode, format)	Opens a specified file and returns a `TextStream` object that can be used to read from, write to, or append to the file.
	The `iomode` parameter specifies the type of access required.
	The permissible values are: ForReading (1) (the default) ForWriting (2) ForAppending (8)
	If the `create` parameter is set to `True` when writing or appending to a file that does not exist, a new file will be created. The default for `create` is `False`. The `format` parameter specifies the format of the data to be read from or written to the file. Permissible values are `TristateFalse` (0) (the default) to open it as ASCII, `TristateTrue` (-1) to open it as Unicode, and `TristateUseDefault` (-2) to open it using the system default format.

The TextStream Object

The `TextStream` object provides access to files stored on disk, and is used in conjunction with the `FileSystemObject` object.

Properties

Property	Description
AtEndOfLine	Returns `True` if the file pointer is at the end of a line in the file
AtEndOfStream	Returns `True` if the file pointer is at the end of the file
Column	Returns the column number of the current character in the file starting from 1
Line	Returns the current line number in the file starting from 1

The `AtEndOfLine` and `AtEndOfStream` properties are only available for a file that is opened with the `iomode` parameter set with the value `ForReading`. Referring to them otherwise causes an error to occur.

Methods

Method	Description
Close ()	Closes an open file
Read (numchars)	Reads `numchars` characters from the file
ReadAll ()	Reads the entire file as a single string
ReadLine ()	Reads a line from the file as a string
Skip (numchars)	Skips and discards `numchars` characters when reading from the file
SkipLine ()	Skips and discards the next line when reading from the file
Write (string)	Writes string to the file
WriteLine (string)	Writes `string` (optional) and a new-line character to the file
WriteBlankLines (n)	Writes n new-line characters to the file

The Windows Script Host Object Model

This appendix gives details about the Windows Script Host objects. You can find further details and examples in Chapter 12.

Windows Script Host has fifteen objects outlined.

Object	Description
Scripting.Signer	Allows a script to be digitally signed so that the recipient can verify authenticity and trust.
WScript	Provides access to most of the objects, methods, and properties contained in the WSH object model.
WshArguments	Gives the programmer access to the entire collection of command-line parameters in the order in which they were originally entered.
WshController	Exposes the method CreateScript() that creates a remote script process.
WshEnvironment	Gives the programmer access to the collection of Microsoft Windows system environment variables.
WshNamed	Provides access to the named command-line script arguments contained within the WshArguments object.
WshNetwork	Gives the programmer access to the shared resources on the network to which the host computer is connected.
WshRemote	Provides access to the remote script process.
WshRemoteError	Used to expose the error information available when a remote script terminates as a result of a script error.
WshScriptExec	Provides status and error information about a script.

(continued)

Object	Description
WshShell	Use to give the programmer access to the native Windows shell functionality.
WshShortcut	Allows the programmer to create shortcuts.
WshSpecialFolders	Used to access Windows Special Folders.
WshUnnamed	Provides access to unnamed command-line script arguments within the WshArguments object.
WshUrlShortcut	Allows the programmer to create a shortcut to an Internet resource.

The Scripting.Signer Object

This object allows the author of a script to digitally sign it so that the recipient can verify the authenticity of the script. This object has no properties and four methods:

❑ Sign

❑ SignFile

❑ Verify

❑ VerifyFile

The WScript Object

The root of the WSH object model is the WScript object. This object provides properties and methods that give the developer access to a variety of information, such as:

❑ Name and path information for the script file being executed

❑ Version of the Microsoft Scripting engines

❑ Links to external objects

❑ User interaction

❑ The ability to delay or terminate script execution

The WScript object has twelve properties and seven methods, as shown in the following table.

Properties	Methods
Arguments	CreateObject
BuildVersion	ConnectObject
FullName	DisconnectObject
Interactive	Echo
Name	GetObject
Path	Quit
ScriptFullName	Sleep
ScriptName	
StdErr	
StdIn	
StdOut	
Version	

The WshArguments Object

This object gives the programmer access to the entire collection of command-line parameters. This object has four properties and two methods as shown in the following table.

Properties	Methods
Item	Count
Length	ShowUsage
Named	
Unnamed	

WshController Object

This object is used to expose the method CreateScript() that creates a remote script process. This object has no properties and one method: CreateScript.

WshEnvironment Object

This object provides access to the collection of Windows environment variables. The WshEnvironment object has two properties and two methods, as shown in the following table.

Properties	Methods
Item	Count
Length	Remove

WshNamed Object

This object is used to provide access to named arguments from the command line. This object has two properties and two methods as shown in the following table.

Properties	Methods
Item	Count
Length	Exists

The WshNetwork Object

The WshNetwork object provides access to the shared resources on the network to which the computer is connected. This object has three properties and eight methods, as shown in the following table.

Properties	Methods
ComputerName	AddWindowsPrinterConnection
UserDomain	AddPrinterConnection
UserName	EnumNetworkDrives
	EnumPrinterConnection
	MapNetworkDrive
	RemoveNetworkDrive
	RemovePrinterConnection
	SetDefaultPrinter

WshRemote Object

This object is used to provide access to the remote script process. This object has two properties and two methods as shown in the following table.

Properties	Methods
Status	Execute
Error	Terminate

WshRemoteError Object

This object provides access to the error information available when a remote script terminates because of a script error. It has one method: WshRemote. It also has six properties:

❑ Description

❑ Line

❑ Character

❑ SourceText

❑ Source

❑ Number

WshScriptExec Object

The WshScriptExec object provides status information about a script run with Exec when used in conjunction with the StdIn, StdOut, and StdErr streams. The WshScriptExec object has one method: Terminate. It also has six properties:

❑ ExitCode

❑ ProcessID

❑ Status

❑ StdOut

❑ StdIn

❑ StdErr

The WshShell Object

Windows Script Host provides a convenient way to gain access to system environment variables, create shortcuts, access Windows special folders such as the Windows Desktop, and add or remove entries from the registry. It is also possible to create more customized dialogs for user interaction by using features of the Shell object. The WshShell object has three properties and eleven methods, as shown in the following table.

Properties	Methods
CurrentDirectory	AppActivate
Environment	CreateShortcut
SpecialFolders	ExpandEnvironmentStrings
	LogEvent
	Popup
	RegDelete
	RegRead
	RegWrite
	Run
	SendKeys
	Exec

The WshShortcut Object

The WshShortcut object allows you to create shortcuts using script. The object has one method, Save, and nine properties:

- ❑ Arguments
- ❑ Description
- ❑ FullName
- ❑ Hotkey
- ❑ IconLocation
- ❑ RelativePath
- ❑ TargetPath
- ❑ WindowStyle
- ❑ WorkingDirectory

The WshSpecialFolders Object

The WshSpecialFolders object provides access to the collection of Windows special folders. The special folders shown in the following list are available.

- ❏ AllUsersDesktop
- ❏ AllUsersPrograms
- ❏ AllUsersStartMenu
- ❏ AllUsersStartup
- ❏ Desktop
- ❏ Favorites
- ❏ Fonts
- ❏ MyDocuments
- ❏ NetHood
- ❏ PrintHood
- ❏ Programs
- ❏ Recent
- ❏ SendTo
- ❏ StartMenu
- ❏ Startup
- ❏ Templates

The WshSpecialFolders object has one method, Count, and two properties: Item and Length.

The WshUnnamed Object

The WshUnnamed object provides access to the unnamed arguments from the command line.
The WshUnnamed object is a read-only collection that is returned by the Unnamed property of the
WshArguments object. All individual argument values are retrieved from this collection using zero-based
indexes.

There are three ways to access sets of command-line arguments:

- ❏ Access the entire set of arguments with the WshArguments object.
- ❏ Access the arguments that have names with the WshNamed object.
- ❏ Access the arguments that have no names with the WshUnnamed object.

The WshUnnamed object has one method, Count, and two properties: Item and Length.

The WshUrlShortcut Object

The WshUrlShortcut object allows you to create shortcuts to Internet resources using script. The WshUrlShortcut object is a child object of the WshShell object. You must use the WshShell method CreateShortcut to create a WshUrlShortcut object. The WshUrlShortcut object has one method, Save, and two properties: FullName and TargetPath.

Regular Expressions

A regular expression is a pattern of text that consists of ordinary characters (such as letters a through z) and special characters that are known as *metacharacters*. The pattern is used to describe one or more strings to match when searching a body of text. The regular expression acts as a template for matching a character pattern to the string that is being searched for.

The following table contains the complete list of metacharacters and their behavior in the context of a regular expression.

Character	Description
\	Marks the next character as either a special character or a literal
^	Matches the beginning of input
$	Matches the end of input
*	Matches the preceding character zero or more times
+	Matches the preceding character one or more times
?	Matches the preceding character zero or one time
.	Matches any single character except a new-line character
(pattern)	Matches pattern and remembers the match. The matched substring can be retrieved from the resulting Matches collection, using Item [0]...[n]. To match the parentheses characters themselves, precede with slash — use "\" or "(\")".
(?:pattern)	Matches pattern but does not capture the match, that is, it is a noncapturing match that is not stored for possible later use. This is useful for combining parts of a pattern with the "or" character (!). For example, "anomal (?:y ! ies)" is a more economical expression than "anomaly ! anomalies".

(continued)

Character	Description
`(?=pattern)`	Positive lookahead matches the search string at any point where a string matching pattern begins. This is a noncapturing match, that is, the match is not captured for possible later use. For example `"Windows (?= 95 | 98 | NT | 2000 | XP | Vista)"` matches "Windows" in "Windows Vista" but not "Windows" in "Windows 3.1".
`(?!pattern)`	Negative lookahead matches the search string at any point where a string not matching pattern begins. This is a noncapturing match, that is, the match is not captured for possible later use. For example, `"Windows ( ?! 95 | 98 | NT | 2000 | XP | Vista)"` matches "Windows" in "Windows 3.1" but does not match "Windows" in "Windows Vista".
`x|y`	Matches either `x` or `y`
`{n}`	Matches exactly n times (n must always be a nonnegative integer)
`{n, }`	Matches at least n times (n must always be a nonnegative integer — note the terminating comma)
`{n,m}`	Matches at least n and at most m times (m and n must always be nonnegative integers)
`[xyz]`	Matches any one of the enclosed characters (`xyz` represents a character set)
`[^xyz]`	Matches any character not enclosed (`^xyz` represents a negative character set)
`[a-z]`	Matches any character in the specified range (`a-z` represents a range of characters)
`[^m-z]`	Matches any character not in the specified range (`^m-z` represents a negative range of characters)
`\b`	Matches a word boundary, that is, the position between a word and a space
`\B`	Matches a nonword boundary
`\d`	Matches a digit character. Equivalent to `[0 - 9]`
`\D`	Matches a nondigit character. Equivalent to `[^ 0-9]`
`\f`	Matches a form-feed character
`\n`	Matches a new-line character
`\r`	Matches a carriage return character
`\s`	Matches any white space including space, tab, form-feed, and so on. Equivalent to `"[\f\n\r\t\v\]"`
`\t`	Matches a tab character `"[^\f\n\r\t\v\]"`
`\v`	Matches a vertical tab character

Character	Description
\w	Matches any word character including underscore. Equivalent to "[A-Za-z0-9_]"
\W	Matches any nonword character. Equivalent to "[^A-Za-z0-9_]"
\.	Matches .
\ |	Matches |
\{	Matches {
\}	Matches }
\\	Matches \
\ [	Matches [
\ ]	Matches]
\ (	Matches (
\ )	Matches)
$ num	Matches num, where num is a positive integer. A reference back to remembered matches (note the $ symbol — differs from some Microsoft documentation)
\n	Matches n, where n is an octal escape value. Octal escape values must be 1, 2, or 3 digits long
\uxxxx	Matches the ASCII character expressed by the UNICODE xxxx
\xn	Matches n, where n is a hexadecimal escape value. Hexadecimal escape values must be exactly two digits long

The Variant Subtypes

The reference material in this appendix is a companion to the detailed explanation in Chapter 3 of *data types*, in particular the VBScript `Variant` data type. However, a brief description of these concepts follows.

VBScript is what is known as a *weakly typed* programming language, which is the opposite of a *strongly typed* language. A weakly typed language does not allow you to declare variables with specific data types such as `String`, `Date`, or `Boolean`. Instead, in VBScript, all variables are automatically and implicitly assigned a special data type called `Variant`. The `Variant` data type is actually many data types in one. VBScript still has the concept of data types such as `String`, `Date`, and `Boolean`, but they are embedded within the "container" of the `Variant` type. The more specific type inside of the `Variant` type is called a *subtype*. A `Variant` variable can have one of many different subtypes — but only one subtype at a time.

The subtype of a `Variant` variable can change in one of two ways: implicitly and explicitly.

❑ An implicit change in subtype occurs when a new value is assigned to a `Variant` variable. Before the new value being assigned to the variable is committed, the VBScript engine uses its own logic to examine the new value and automatically decide what the subtype should be. If the new value fits within the bounds of the already assigned subtype, VBScript does not change it. This automatic subtype change process is called *implicit type coercion*. As a VBScript programmer, it is very important to understand how implicit type coercion works and when and how it occurs.

❑ The other method of initiating a change in a variable's subtype is called explicit coercion. This means that the VBScript programmer is taking specific measures to deliberately control the subtype of a variable. This can be done using certain syntax techniques (see Chapter 3) and also VBScript's *conversion functions*. As an example of the latter, the `CLng()` function will change the subtype to `Long`. Similarly, the `CStr()` function will change it to `String`. Sometimes it is necessary to use a conversion function to force a subtype change so that a particular operation or function call will work properly.

The `Variant` data type, the subtypes, and the ins and outs of implicit and explicit type coercion are covered in great detail in Chapter 3. Even an experienced programmer coming from another language would do well to read this chapter. Management of the `Variant` subtypes in your scripts is a key to your success as a VBScript programmer. The following two sections discuss the `Variant` subtypes as well as the Visual Basic data types.

The Variant Subtypes

The following table lays out the particulars of all of the `Variant` subtypes. This is intended as a reference for those times when you're not sure which subtype you might need or when you're not sure if a particular value is too big for a certain subtype.

Subtype	Visual Basic Data Type Equivalent	Conversion Function to Force TheSubtype	Test Function (Other than VarType and TypeName)	VarType() Function Return Value (with Named Constant Equivalent)	TypeName() Function Return Value
Empty	N/A	N/A	IsEmpty()	0 (vbEmpty)	Empty
Null	N/A	N/A	IsNull()	1 (vbNull)	Null
Integer	Integer	CInt()	IsNumeric()	2 (vbInteger)	Integer
Long	Long	CLng()	IsNumeric()	3 (vbLong)	Long
Single	Single	CSng()	IsNumeric()	4 (vbSingle)	Single
Double	Double	CDbl()	IsNumeric()	5 (vbDouble)	Double
Currency	Currency	CCur()	IsNumeric()	6 (vbCurrency)	Currency
Date	Date	CDate()	IsDate()	7 (vbDate)	Date
String	String	CStr()	None	8 (vbString)	String
Object	Object	N/A	IsObject()	9 (vbObject)	Object
Error	N/A	[a]	None	10 (vbError)	Error
Boolean	Boolean	CBool()	None	11 (vbBoolean)	Boolean
Variant	Variant	CVar()	None	12 (vbVariant)	Variant
Decimal	N/A	[a]	IsNumeric()	14 (vbDecimal)	Decimal[b]
Byte	Byte	CByte()	IsNumeric()	17 (vbByte)	Byte
Array	N/A	N/A	IsArray()	8192 (vbArray)[c]	Array

[a]Visual Basic supports conversion functions for the `Error` and `Decimal` subtypes called `CVErr()` and `CDec()`, respectively. VBScript, however, does not support these conversion functions.

[b]Because of a bug in VBScript, the `TypeName()` function does not support the `Decimal 1` subtype (although `VarType()` does).

[c]This value is actually returned from the `VarType()` function in combination with the value for `Variant (12)`.

The Visual Basic Data Types

The following table shows the Visual Basic data types. Visual Basic is a strongly typed language. Visual Basic also supports the `Variant` data type, but many others besides. The list of Visual Basic data types lines up pretty closely with the list of `Variant` subtypes. The VBScript and legacy Visual Basic subtypes and data types also map pretty closely to the common .NET and COM data types. When communicating with external components that expose these common data types, it is a good idea to use your knowledge of how type coercion works to make sure that your `Variant` subtype corresponds to the Visual Basic data type required by the external component.

Data	Storage Required	Range of Allowable Values	Comments
Byte	1 byte	0 to 255	Often used to store binary data in the form of a "Byte array."
Integer	2 bytes	−32,768 to 32,767	None.
Long	4 bytes	−2,147,483,648 to 2,147,483,647	The most commonly used numeric data type.
Single	4 bytes	Negative values: −3.402823 E38 to −1.401298E-45 Positive values: 1.401298E-45 to 3.402823E38	For storing IEEE 32-bit single precision floating point numbers (in other words, numbers with decimals).
Double	8 bytes	Negative values: −1.79769313486232 E308 to 4.94065645841247E-324 Positive values: 4.94065645841247E-324 to 1.79769313486232E308	For storing IEEE 64-bit double precision floating point numbers; offers greater precision than the `Single`.
Currency	8 bytes	−922,337,203,685,477.5808 to 922,337,203,685,477.5807	Automatically rounds to four decimal places.
Decimal	14 bytes	With no decimal point:+/−79,228,162,514,264,337,593,543,950,335 With 28 decimal places:+/−7.9228162514264337593543950335 Smallest non-zero number: +/−0.0000000000000000000000000001	Can only be stored in a variant; use when maximum floating point accuracy is needed.
Boolean	2 bytes	`True` or `False`	Only has two possible values; `False` can also be represented as zero (0), and `True` can also be represented as −1 (or, really, any non-zero value); this is often used as a success/failure return value for functions; also very common for procedure arguments.

(continued)

Appendix I: The Variant Subtypes

Data	Storage Required	Range of Allowable Values	Comments
String	10 bytes + string length	0 to approximately 2 billion characters	Can be used to store any kind of text characters, numbers, or symbols.
Date	8 bytes	January 1, 100 to December 31, 9999	When displayed, by default uses the Windows "Short Date" format setting.
Object	4 bytes	Any object reference	A generic data type that can hold a "late bound" reference to any COM object.
Variant	16 or 22 bytes	Any data within the range of the above data types	Takes up 16 bytes when storing numeric data, 22 bytes when storing string data; can have a different "subtype" depending on the type of value stored within it; also takes up a little more space when storing an array; equivalent to the VBScript Variant type.

ActiveX Data Objects

ActiveX Data Objects (ADO) is a data access component from Microsoft that you can use by VBScript running under a variety of hosts, including Active Server Pages and the Windows Script Host. ADO was the primary data access component used by VBScript, Visual Basic, and Visual C++ developers in the years before Microsoft introduced the .NET platform. While ADO is no longer in the spotlight, it is a very mature data access component that is still supported by Microsoft. Better yet, it's a safe bet that ADO is available by default on most installations of Windows. You can use ADO in your VBScript programs to write to and read from structure data sources such as databases like Access, Oracle, and SQL Server as well as spreadsheets and flat files.

ADO is too large a subject to cover thoroughly in one appendix. Therefore, the purpose here is not to discuss the details and powerful features of ADO, but rather, because ADO is so often used in combination with VBScript, to give a brief overview and reference. This overview assumes that you are familiar with basic relational database concepts such as tables, columns, queries, stored procedures, and so on. If you make significant use of ADO in your scripts, you may want to purchase a book dedicated to ADO. This guide to ADO covers ADO 2.8, the latest version of ADO at press time.

The appendix discussion includes the ADO objects shown in the following table.

Object	Purpose
Connection	Connects to a data source and manages transactions.
Command	Executes commands such as queries and stored procedures against a data source.
Parameters and Parameter	Parameter objects are stored in the Command object's Parameters collection. Together, Parameter and Parameters specify parameters for a stored procedure being called through a Command object.

(continued)

Object	Purpose
Recordset	Stores a series of structured data — usually data returned from a query or stored procedure — represented as a series of rows and columns. You can also use the Recordset object to manually construct a data set that you want to submit to a database.
Error	If one or more errors occur while using any of the ADO objects, the Connection object's Errors collection will contain one or more Error objects. An Error object has information about an error such as the number, description, and source.

This appendix either does not cover or limits discussion on the following:

❑ Because VBScript is a pre-.NET technology, the appendix doesn't discuss ADO.NET, which is the latest version of ADO. ADO.NET is intended for use by .NET languages such as C# and VB.NET. It is not natively compatible with VBScript. To ensure that you have the latest version of ADO, you can download the latest release of Microsoft Data Access Components (MDAC) from msdn.microsoft.com/data.

❑ The appendix does not cover the Record or Stream objects because these are more advanced than the basic ADO overview.

❑ This appendix does not have separate sections for the Fields and Field objects, but the basic usage of these are covered in the section on the Recordset object. The example code in this appendix is based on the Northwind sample database that ships with Microsoft Access.

❑ The downloadable script files are designed for running under the Windows Script Host (see Chapter 15), but the code is easily transferable to other hosts. The discussion focuses on using ADO for relational database access, because that is the most common use for ADO, but because ADO is part of Microsoft's "Universal Database" strategy, it can be used to access other structured data formats such as spreadsheets, email systems, text files, and so on.

❑ Certain advanced or seldom used properties and methods may be excluded for some objects.

The Connection Object

The Connection object is almost always required in order to do anything interesting with the other ADO objects. The Connection object represents the primary access point to a data source. If you want to read from or write to a data source, you need to use the Connection object to establish a connection with that data source. The following example script (ADO_CONNECTION.VBS) illustrates the basic technique for opening a connection:

```
Option Explicit

Const adStateOpen = 1

Dim cnNorthwind
Dim strStatus

Set cnNorthwind = CreateObject("ADODB.Connection")

cnNorthwind.ConnectionString = _
    "Provider=Microsoft.Jet.OLEDB.4.0;" & _
    "User ID=Admin;Password=;Data Source=" & _
    "C:\Program Files\Microsoft Office\Office\Samples\" & _
    "Northwind.mdb"

cnNorthwind.Open

If cnNorthwind.State = adStateOpen Then
    MsgBox "Connection is open."
Else
    MsgBox "Connection is not open."
End If

cnNorthwind.Close
Set cnNorthwind = Nothing
```

After instantiating the Connection object, this code sets the ConnectionString property. The connection string is how you tell the Connection object what kind of data source to connect to (Provider=), how to locate that data source (Data Source=), and what security information to use for logging into the data source (UserID and Password). To get this connection string to work on your machine, you may have to change the path to the Northwind.mdb file (it's also possible that you may not have the Northwind.mdb file on your machine).

> There are many different "provider" types for different data source types and many different versions of these providers. There are also different styles of connection strings that different providers may or may not support. Unfortunately, there is not enough space here to include information on the dozens of providers and connection string formats. Please consult the documentation for the type of database you are using. There is also an excellent comprehensive connection string reference available online at www.connectionstrings.com.

Getting back to the script: After setting the connection string, you call the Open method, which tells the Connection object to attempt to connect to the data source. Finally, just to prove that your connection was successful, you check the State property to find out the status of the connection. Notice also that you call the Close method when you are done with the connection. It is always a good idea to close any database connections as soon as you are done with them.

The following two tables describe in detail the important Connection object properties and methods.

Connection Object Properties

Name	Accepts/Returns	Access	Description
CommandTimeout	Long	Read/Write	Sets or obtains the number of seconds a Connection object will wait when executing a command (see Execute method) before giving up; has no effect on the Command-Timeout property of the Command object.
ConnectionString	String	Read/Write	Sets or obtains the connection details for a data source, including provider type, data source location, username, and password.
ConnectionTimeout	Long	Read/Write	Sets or obtains the number of seconds a Connection object will wait when connecting to a data source (see Open method) before giving up.
CursorLocation	Long (Cursor-LocationEnum)	Read/Write	Sets or obtains the location of the "cursor" of any Record-set objects opened with a Connection object; a cursor can be "client-side" or "server-side."
Errors	Collection	Read-Only	If an error occurs during usage of a Connection object, this collection contains one or more Error objects, which have properties exposing error number, description, source, and so on.
State	Long (Object-StateEnum)	Read-Only	Returns information about the status of a connection to a data source. Most often, the status is either "open" or "closed"; other statuses apply when using asynchronous methods on ADO objects using the connection.

Connection Object Methods

Name	Arguments	Returns	Description
`BeginTrans`	None	Long	Begins a transaction at the data source; must be followed, eventually, by a call to either `Commit-Trans` or `Rollback-Trans`; the `Long` return value (seldom used) indicates the "nesting level" of the new transaction.
`CommitTrans`	None	N/A	"Commits" a transaction that was started with a call to `BeginTrans`.
`Rollback-Trans`	None	N/A	Aborts a transaction that was started with a call to `BeginTrans`.
`Cancel`	None	N/A	Aborts a method call (such as `Connection.Execute` or `Recordset.Open`) that was executed asynchronously.
`Close`	None	N/A	Closes an open connection; important to call this when done using a `Connection` object, before setting it to `Nothing`.
`Execute`	`CommandText`: `String` value containing an SQL query, stored procedure call, or URL to execute at the data source `RecordsAffected`: Optional `Long` in/out argument that will contain the number of records returned by the data source `Options`: Optional `Long` value indicating the type of command in the `Command-Text` argument; can be any combination of values from `CommandTypeEnum` and `ExecuteOptionEnum`	Recordset object	To execute a command on a data source, you can use either the `Execute` method of the `connection` object or the `Command` object; use a `Command` object when you need to pass parameters to a stored procedure; otherwise `Connection.Execute` is a convenient shortcut; for an SQL query, use `adCmdText` (1) in the `Options` argument; for a stored procedure, use `adCmdStoredProc` (4).

(continued)

Name	Arguments	Returns	Description
Open	`ConnectionString`: Optional `String` value that can be used in place of, or to override, the `ConnectionString` property `UserID`: Optional `String` value that can be used in place of specifying a user ID in the connection string `Password`: Optional `String` value that can be used in place of specifying a password in the connection string `Options`: Optional `Long` (`ConnectOptionEnum`) value; default value of `adConnectUnspecified` causes normal, synchronous connection; `adAsyncConnect` will cause asynchronous connection	N/A	Opens a connection object; traditionally, most programmers set the `ConnectionString` property before calling `Open` instead of using the arguments of the `Open` method.

The Command Object

The `Command` object is an optional alternative to using the `Execute` and `Open` methods of the `Connection` object. Some programmers prefer the explicitness of using a `Command` object instead of `Connection` `.Execute` and `Connection.Open`. Other programmers prefer the brevity of using the `Connection` object. The choice is up to you. Note, however, that if you are calling a stored procedure that uses parameters, you pretty much have to use the `Command` object instead of `Connection.Execute` or `Connection.Open`.

The following script (`ADO_COMMAND.VBS`) demonstrates the basic technique of using a SQL query to open a `Recordset` object from the Northwind database's `Suppliers` table. This script example borrows from the `Connection` object example in the previous section and is continued in the `Recordset` object section, later.

```
Option Explicit

Const adCmdText = 1
Const adStateOpen = 1

Dim cnNorthwind
Dim cmdQuery
Dim rsSuppliers
```

```
Set cnNorthwind = CreateObject("ADODB.Connection")

cnNorthwind.ConnectionString = _
    "Provider=Microsoft.Jet.OLEDB.4.0;" & _
    "User ID=Admin;Password=;Data Source=" & _
    "C:\Program Files\Microsoft Office\Office\Samples\" & _
    "Northwind.mdb"

cnNorthwind.Open

Set cmdQuery = CreateObject("ADODB.Command")
With cmdQuery
    Set .ActiveConnection = cnNorthwind
    .CommandText = "SELECT [SupplierID], [CompanyName] " & _
                    "FROM Suppliers " & _
                    "WHERE [Country] = 'Australia'"
    .CommandType = adCmdText
    Set rsSuppliers = .Execute
End With

If rsSuppliers.State = adStateOpen Then
    MsgBox "Recordset opened successfully."
    rsSuppliers.Close
End If

Set rsSuppliers = Nothing
Set cmdQuery = Nothing
cnNorthwind.Close
Set cnNorthwind = Nothing
```

Notice that once you have an open Connection object, you instantiate a Command object and set the ActiveConnection property of the Command to the Connection object. This gives the Command object its link to the data source. Next, you set the CommandText property to a SQL query and set the CommandType to 1, which is the value for the adCmdText enumerated constant (see "ADO Enumerated Constants" at the end of this appendix). Then you use the Execute method to run the query and return a Recordset object.

The Execute method may or may not return a Recordset depending on the type of command sent through CommandText. For example, a SQL UPDATE statement would not return a Recordset. In that case, you would just call the Execute method as a procedure instead of as a function.

Another common use of the Command object is calling a stored procedure (which may or may not return a Recordset). In this case, most programmers use the Parameters collection to specify any parameters accepted by the stored procedure. The Parameter object section later includes an example of this syntax. (You can also pass parameters to a stored procedure in two other ways: one, as part of the CommandText or CommandStream property; and two, using the Parameters argument of the Execute method (which is not the same as the Parameters collection). Keep in mind that these alternative methods only support input-only parameters.

The following two tables describe in detail the important Command object properties and methods.

Command Object Properties

Name	Accepts/ Returns	Access	Description
Active-Connection	Connection object (in a Variant)	Read/Write	Sets or obtains a reference to a Connection object used by the Command; all ADO objects must go through a Connection object to get to the data source; this is usually the first property you set after instantiating a Command object.
Command-Stream	Stream object	Read/Write	A mutually exclusive alternative to the CommandText property; whereas CommandText accepts/returns a String value and CommandStream accepts/returns a Stream object.
Command-Text	String	Read/Write	Sets or obtains the string representing the "command" that you want the Command object to execute. Can be a SQL query, stored procedure call, or URL. You should also set the CommandType property to the type value corresponding to the type of command.
Command-Timeout	Long	Read/Write	Sets or obtains the number of seconds a Command object will wait before giving up on a call to the Execute method.
Command-Type	Long (Command-TypeEnum)	Read/Write	Must be set to match the type of command value placed into the CommandText or CommandStream property; use 1 (adCmdText) for SQL queries and 4 (adCmdStoredProc) for stored procedure calls.
Named-Parameters	Boolean	Read/Write	If the Command object is using the Parameters collection to pass parameters to a stored procedure, this property controls how those parameters are interpreted; True means that the parameters will be matched up by Parameter.Name with the parameter names defined in the stored procedure; False (the default) means that Parameter.Name is ignored and the parameters will be sent to the stored procedure in the order in which they are added to the Parameters collection.

Name	Accepts/ Returns	Access	Description
Parameters	Collection of `Parameter` objects	Read/ Write	Holds a collection of `Parameter` objects; used when calling stored procedures that accept parameters; initially the collection is empty; `Parameter` objects must be added manually or can be auto-populated using the `Parameters.Refresh` method.
Prepared	Boolean	Read/ Write	Sets or obtains whether the `Execute` method should tell the data source to cache a compiled version of the command, which can increase performance when repeatedly executing the same command.

Command Object Methods

Name	Arguments	Returns	Description
Cancel	None	N/A	If the `Execute` method was called asynchronously, a call to this method aborts the pending or in-progress command.
Create-Parameter	`Name`: Optional `String` value representing the parameter name `Type`: Optional `Long` value (`DataTypeEnum`) representing the data type of the parameter `Direction`: Optional `Long` value (`ParameterDirectionEnum`) indicating whether the parameter is input, output, or both. `Size`: Optional `Long` value indicating the maximum parameter value length in bytes or characters `Value` — Optional `Variant` representing the value for the parameter (must correspond to the `Type` argument)	Parameter object	When calling a stored procedure and manually creating `Parameter` objects to add to the `Parameters` collection, use this method to create a new `Parameter` object; note that this method returns only a `Parameter` object — it does not add it to the `Parameters` collection; you can either use the arguments to initialize the `Parameter` object or omit the arguments and manually set the properties on the returned `Parameter` object; if you use the arguments, the returned `Parameter` object will already have its properties set.

(continued)

Name	Arguments	Returns	Description
Execute	RecordsAffected: Optional Long in/out argument that ADO will use to return the number of records affected by the command Parameters: Optional Variant array of parameters to pass to a stored procedure; does not support in/out parameters Options—Optional Long value indicating the type of command in the CommandText argument; can be any combination of values from CommandTypeEnum and ExecuteOptionEnum	Either returns a Recordset object, a Stream object, or Nothing, depending on the command sent to the data source	When you have prepared a Command object with properties such as CommandText, CommandType, and the Parameters collection, the Execute method will actually issue the command to the data source; depending on the content of the command, the data source may or may not return data, which influences the return type of the Execute method.

The Parameters and Parameter Objects

The Parameter object is used in conjunction with the Command object and its Parameters collection. *Parameter* in this context refers to parameters/arguments expected by a stored procedure that is being called with a Command object. There are actually a few ways to pass parameters to a stored procedure:

❑ Embed the parameters in the text of CommandText or CommandStream.

❑ Pass them in a Variant array to the Execute method's Parameters argument.

❑ Explicitly create Parameter objects and add them to the Command object's Parameters collection.

Only the third technique actually involves the use of the Parameter object. Using the third technique has two advantages:

❑ The code is more explicit and a little more readable.

❑ It supports in/out parameters, which the other two methods do not.

On the downside, using the third method is a little slower because you have to instantiate (potentially) several Parameter objects for a single call to a stored procedure.

Using `Parameter` objects for passing parameters to a stored procedure involves these steps:

1. Create a new `Parameter` object using `Command.CreateParameter` (using the arguments of the `CreateParameter` method to set the properties of the `Parameter` object).

2. Add the `Parameter` object to the `Parameters` collection using the `Parameters.Append` method.

3. Repeat the first two steps for as many times as the stored procedure's parameter list requires.

All this must be done before calling the `Execute` method and, ideally, after setting the `CommandText` or `CommandStream` property of the `Command` object. Also, many programmers prefer to expedite the process by performing the first and second steps simultaneously. The following code snippet illustrates this technique (please note that this code is not included in the downloadable code for this chapter because the authors are using Access for examples and Access does not support stored procedures).

```
Const adCmdStoredProc = 4
Const adVarChar = 200
Const adParamInput = 1

Set cmdStoredProc = CreateObject("ADODB.Command")

With cmdStoredProc
    Set .ActiveConnection = cnConnection
    .CommandText = "GetSuppliersByCountry"
    .CommandType = adCmdStoredProc

    .Parameters.Append .CreateParameter("strCountry", _
        adVarChar, adParamInput, 15, "Australia")

    Set rsSuppliers = .Execute
End With
```

The benefit of the shortcut used here is that you do not have to explicitly declare or instantiate any `Parameter` objects. The `CreateParameter` method returns a `Parameter` object that is immediately passed to the `Parameters.Append` method.

Another technique is to call the `Command.Parameters.Refresh` method after setting the stored procedure name in `CommandText` or `CommandStream`. The `Refresh` method will retrieve the parameter list from the data source and automatically populate the `Parameters` collection. Then you can loop back through the `Parameters` collection to set all of the `Value` properties. However, while this is a cool technique, it is usually avoided because of the extra round trip to the database.

The following four tables describe in detail the important `Parameter` and `Parameters` object properties and methods.

Parameter Object Properties

Name	Accepts/Returns	Access	Description
Direction	Long (Parameter-DirectionEnum)	Read/Write	Sets or obtains the "direction" for a stored procedure parameter; parameters can be input only (adParamInput), output only (adParamOutput), both input and output (adParamInputOutput), or return values (adParamReturn).
Name	String	Read/Write before appended to Parameters, Read-Only after appended	Depending on the value of Command .NamedParameters, the Name of a Parameter object may or may not be used in the execution of the stored procedure; if NamedParameters is True, Parameter.Name must match exactly the name of one of the stored procedure's parameters.
NumericScale	Byte	Read/Write	Sets or obtains the number of decimal places to which numeric parameter values are resolved.
Precision	Byte	Read/Write	Sets or obtains the precision for numeric parameters.
Size	Long	Read/Write	Sets or obtains the maximum size, in characters or bytes (depending on the Type), for a parameter.
Type	Long (DataTypeEnum)	Read/Write	Sets or obtains the data type of a parameter.
Value	Variant	Read/Write	Sets or obtains the value of a parameter; for output or input/output parameters, the value is set by the stored procedure.

Parameter Object Methods

Name	Arguments	Returns	Description
AppendChunk	Data—Variant value to be appended to the Value property of the Parameter	N/A	In situations in which you are sending large amounts of text or binary data in a Parameter object, use the AppendChunk method to gradually build up the Value property rather than setting the Value property directly; for example, if you have 10,000 bytes of data you might call AppendChunk 10 times in a loop, appending 1000 bytes each time; can only be used when Type is adFldLong.

Parameters Object Properties

Name	Accepts/Returns	Access	Description
Count	Long	Read-Only	Obtains the number of Parameter objects in the Parameters collection.
Item	Parameter	Read-Only	Obtains a reference to a certain Parameter object based on its index in the Parameters collection.

Parameters Object Methods

Name	Arguments	Returns	Description
Append	Parameter: A Parameter object that has already been initialized with Name, Type, Value, and so on	N/A	Adds a new Parameter object to the Parameters collection; the Parameter object should have been created with Command .Create Parameter; its Type and Name properties must be set, but the Value can optionally be set or changed after appending.

(continued)

Name	Arguments	Returns	Description
Delete	Index: The numeric collection index of the Parameter object you want to remove from the Parameters collection	N/A	Removes a Parameter object from the Parameters collection.
Refresh	None	N/A	If the Command .CommandText or CommandStream property have already been set with the name of a stored procedure, the Parameters.Refresh method will make a trip to the database to obtain the parameter list for the stored procedure and automatically populate the Parameters collection, after which you can loop through the collection to set the Value properties, if necessary.

The Recordset Object

In general, setting aside the Stream object for a moment, the Recordset is where a programmer can work with actual data. The typical scenario for the use of the Recordset object is that a programmer creates Connection and Command objects in order to execute a query or stored procedure in a database. The query or stored procedure returns a set of data, formatted as rows and columns, which is stored in a Recordset object. Then the programmer can use the Recordset object to read, update, add, or delete the data.

The Recordset object is also quite versatile beyond this typical scenario. It has a long list of properties and methods, and the authors could go on explaining all the cool things you can do with a Recordset. For example, you can programmatically create a Recordset object from scratch, create fields for it, and fill it up with data — all without using a data source at all. You can also save a Recordset to disk and re-create it later without having to connect to the original source of the Recordset. Recordset objects can even be nested inside of other Recordset objects. However, the focus here is on the primary properties and methods used to work with Recordset objects that are returned by queries and stored procedures.

The rest of this section shows two example scripts: one that opens a Recordset from a query and loops through the data one time; and another that opens a Recordset, changes some of the data it contains, and updates the database with the changes. The following example script (ADO_RECORDSET_READ.VBS) illustrates the open and read technique.

```
Option Explicit

Const adCmdText = 1
Const adStateOpen = 1
Const adOpenForwardOnly = 0
Const adUseClient = 3
Const adLockReadOnly = 1

Dim cnNorthwind
Dim cmdQuery
Dim rsSuppliers
Dim strMsg
Set cnNorthwind = CreateObject("ADODB.Connection")

cnNorthwind.ConnectionString = "Provider=Microsoft.Jet.OLEDB.4.0;" & _
    "User ID=Admin;Password=;Data Source=" & _
    "C:\Program Files\Microsoft Office\Office\Samples\" & _
    "Northwind.mdb"

cnNorthwind.Open

Set cmdQuery = CreateObject("ADODB.Command")
With cmdQuery
    Set .ActiveConnection = cnNorthwind
    .CommandText = "SELECT [SupplierID], [CompanyName] " & _
                   "FROM Suppliers " & _
                   "WHERE [Country] = 'Australia'"
    .CommandType = adCmdText
End With

Set rsSuppliers = CreateObject("ADODB.Recordset")
Set rsSuppliers.Source = cmdQuery
rsSuppliers.CursorType = adOpenForwardOnly
rsSuppliers.CursorLocation = adUseClient
rsSuppliers.LockType = adLockReadOnly
rsSuppliers.Open

If rsSuppliers.State = adStateOpen Then
    Do While Not rsSuppliers.EOF
        strMsg = strMsg & rsSuppliers.Fields("SupplierID").Name
        strMsg = strMsg & ":" & vbTab
        strMsg = strMsg & rsSuppliers.Fields("SupplierID").Value
        strMsg = strMsg & vbNewLine

        strMsg = strMsg & rsSuppliers.Fields("CompanyName").Name
        strMsg = strMsg & ":" & vbTab
        strMsg = strMsg & rsSuppliers.Fields("CompanyName").Value
        strMsg = strMsg & vbNewLine & vbNewLine

        rsSuppliers.MoveNext
```

(continued)

```
        Loop
        rsSuppliers.Close

        MsgBox strMsg
    Else
        MsgBox "Recordset not opened."
    End If

    Set rsSuppliers = Nothing
    Set cmdQuery = Nothing
    cnNorthwind.Close
    Set cnNorthwind = Nothing
```

If you've been following along, you'll see that this is an extension of the example script from the previous Command object section. However, notice that you've changed the way you open the Recordset. Instead of using Command.Execute, you use CreateObject to instantiate an empty Recordset, and then set the Command object to the Recordset.Source. A few lines later, when you call Recordset.Open, the Command object you put in the Source property (and its Connection object) is used to communicate with the database. This alternative method is necessary if you want to have control over some important properties of the Recordset *before* opening it.

In this example, you set the CursorType property to adOpenForwardOnly, the CursorLocation to adUseClient, and the LockType to adLockReadOnly. What this means is that you'll only loop through this Recordset one time and you'll do this as fast as possible while using the least amount of resources. Other cursor types, such as adOpenDynamic and adOpenKeyset, are more flexible in that they allow you to move back and forth between records and to loop through the Recordset more than once, but these cursor types incur more overhead and are therefore slower.

As far as CursorLocation, server-side cursors can enable certain Recordset features, such as the ability to receive dynamic updates to the data in the Recordset as it changes in the data source, but use more resources on the server. In this case you're not using those features, so you use a client-side cursor because it puts less of a tax on the database.

Finally, you set the LockType to adLockReadOnly because you do not intend to make any updates to the data. This is not strictly necessary because adLockReadOnly happens automatically when using adOpenForwardOnly, but it illustrates the point that CursorType, CursorLocation, and LockType have primary influence over what you can and can't do with a Recordset, how fast you'll be able to do it, and how much resource overhead you'll incur.

When working with the Recordset object, it is important to have in mind how you plan to use the Recordset and then to set properties such as CursorType, CursorLocation, and LockType so that the Recordset will have the features you need while using the least amount of resources and offering the best performance. If you want to experiment to find out which capabilities are supported by which cursor types and locations (and this is different depending on the "Provider" specified in the connection string), you can use the Recordset.Supports method with CursorOptionEnum to find out if a feature you want (such as "move previous" support or the ability to update the Recordset) is supported by a certain cursor type and location.

After you open the Recordset, you use a Do loop to move through each of the records. One key to making this work is using the EOF property to make sure that you stop looping when you've reached the end (and that you don't *start* looping if the Recordset is empty). Another key to the loop is the call to

Recordset.MoveNext right before the Loop statement. MoveNext moves the cursor to the next record. This call is essential or you will create an endless loop that reads the first record in the Recordset over and over again.

Inside the loop, you use the Fields collection, which returns a Field object based on the Name of the field, to read the data out of each record. The two important Field properties here are Name and Value. The Name is the same as the column name you used in the SQL query. The Value is the value that came back from the data source for that column on that row.

The second example (ADO_RECORDSET_WRITE.VBS) uses a Recordset object to update data.

```
Option Explicit

Const adCmdText = 1
Const adStateOpen = 1
Const adOpenKeyset = 1
Const adUseServer = 2
Const adLockOptimistic = 3

Dim cnNorthwind
Dim cmdQuery
Dim rsOrders
Dim datOrder

Set cnNorthwind = CreateObject("ADODB.Connection")

cnNorthwind.ConnectionString = "Provider=Microsoft.Jet.OLEDB.4.0;" & _
    "User ID=Admin;Password=;Data Source=" & _
    "C:\Program Files\Microsoft Office\Samples\" & _
    "Northwind.mdb"

cnNorthwind.Open

Set cmdQuery = CreateObject("ADODB.Command")
With cmdQuery
    Set .ActiveConnection = cnNorthwind
    .CommandText = "SELECT [OrderDate] " & _
                    "FROM Orders " & _
                    "WHERE [ShipCountry] = 'Italy'"
    .CommandType = adCmdText
End With

Set rsOrders = CreateObject("ADODB.Recordset")
Set rsOrders.Source = cmdQuery
rsOrders.CursorType = adOpenKeyset
rsOrders.CursorLocation = adUseServer
rsOrders.LockType = adLockOptimistic
rsOrders.Open
```

(continued)

747

```
If rsOrders.State = adStateOpen Then
    Do While Not rsOrders.EOF
        datOrder = rsOrders("OrderDate")
        If Not IsNull(datOrder) Then
            'Add one second to the OrderDate
            datOrder = DateAdd("s", 1, datOrder)
            rsOrders("OrderDate") = datOrder
            rsOrders.Update
        End If

        rsOrders.MoveNext
    Loop
    rsOrders.Close

    MsgBox "Finished updating recordset."
Else
    MsgBox "Recordset not opened."
End If
Set rsOrders = Nothing
Set cmdQuery = Nothing
cnNorthwind.Close
Set cnNorthwind = Nothing
```

First, notice that you've changed your query to return a list of order dates that are to be shipped to Italy. This was done to demonstrate an update operation without messing up your Northwind database if you decide to run this script on your machine. As will be explained in a minute, and as you can see from reading the code, to keep the update as harmless as possible, you are adding one second to the OrderDate value.

Second, you've changed the values you're using for the CursorType, CursorLocation, and LockType properties to a combination that will open an updateable Recordset. The adOpenKeyset cursor type gives you an updateable cursor that detects any new records that are added while you have the Recordset open, but that does not use as many resources as adOpenDynamic. You changed the cursor location to adUseServer to support the adOpenKeyset cursor, which needs to run on the server in order to detect new records. Finally, you changed the lock type to adLockOptimistic to indicate that you want to update records but that you don't care if other users update the same records while you have the Recordset open. (If you did care, you would use adLockPessimistic.)

Inside of the loop, you retrieve the value of the OrderDate field, add one second to the date, and then write the new date value back to the field. You call the Update method to save to the database to change to the current record. Notice that you have altered the syntax you use to access the Recordset.Fields collection. This new syntax is a shorthand that takes advantage of the fact that the Fields property is the default property of the Recordset object and that the Value property is the default property of the Field object. Typing rsOrders.Fields("OrderDate") is equivalent to just typing rsOrders("OrderDate").

The following two tables describe in detail the important Recordset object properties and methods.

Recordset Object Properties

Name	Accepts/Returns	Access	Description
BOF and EOF	Boolean	Read-Only	Indicates whether the cursor is at the beginning of the Recordset or at the end; if the cursor is one position before the first record, BOF will be True; if one after the last record, EOF will be True; if directly on one of the records, both BOF and EOF will be False.
Cursor-Location	Long (Cursor-LocationEnum)	Read/Write before open; Read-Only after open	As explained in the "Recordset Object" section, CursorLocation is one of the essential properties for controlling cursor behavior and feature support; value can be either adUseClient or adUseServer.
CursorType	Long (Cursor-TypeEnum)	Read/Write before open; Read-Only after open	As explained in the "Recordset Object" section, CursorType is one of the essential properties for controlling cursor behavior and feature support; different cursor types support different features; set the CursorType based on the features you need.
Fields	Fields collection holding Field objects	Read-Only	A Recordset is a matrix of columns and rows; the Fields property exposes the collection of columns, represented as Field objects; when reading a Recordset returned by a data source, you do not add or remove Field objects from the collection, but this can be done when working with a Recordset that is not associated with a data source.

(continued)

Name	Accepts/Returns	Access	Description
LockType	Long (LockTypeEnum)	Read/Write before open; Read-Only after open	As explained in the previous section, Overview, CursorType is one of the essential properties for controlling cursor behavior and feature support; if you do not need to update the data in the Recordset, use adLockReadOnly; for updates use either adLockOptimistic or adLockPessimistic, depending whether you need to protect against other processes changing data at the same time.
RecordCount	Long	Read-Only	Returns the number of records in the Recordset; will return -1 if the CursorType and CursorLocation do not support this feature; count may not be reliable if the cursor does not support "approximate positioning" or "bookmarks" (see Supports method); you must use the exactly correct combination of CursorType and CursorLocation in order to depend on this property based on the underlying provider.

Name	Accepts/Returns	Access	Description
Source	`String` or `Command` object	Read/Write before open; Read-Only after open	If you want to set properties such as `CursorType` and `CursorLocation` before opening the `Recordset`, create a `Command` object and set it into this property; you can also put a SQL query or stored procedure call string in this property if you also set the `ActiveConnection` property to a `Connection` object, but using a `Command` object that already has a `Connection` is more explicit.
State	`Long` (`Object-StateEnum`)	Read-Only	Indicates the status of the `Recordset`; for example, `adStateOpen` or `adStateClosed`.

Recordset Object Methods

Name	Arguments	Returns	Description
AddNew	`FieldList`: Optional `String` or array of names or ordinal positions that must correspond to the fields in the `Recordset`. `Fields` collection `Values` — Optional `String` or array of values for the fields; elements must line up with the `FieldList`	N/A	If you are working with an updateable `Recordset`, use this to add a new record; you can either pass the fields and values as arguments to this method or omit the arguments and then set the value of each field as separate calls.
Close	None	N/A	Closes an open `Recordset`; it's a good idea to always close a `Recordset` when you're done with it; will return an error if the `Recordset` is not open, so check the `State` property before calling `Close`.

(continued)

Name	Arguments	Returns	Description
Delete	AffectRecords: Optional Long (AffectEnum) value indicating which records to include in the delete operation	N/A	Use this method to delete records from an update-able Recordset; most often, you would call this method while the cursor is positioned on the record you wish to delete — in which case you can omit the AffectRecords argument because the default is adAffectCurrent.
MoveFirst MoveLast MoveNext Move- Previous	None	N/A	These four methods are used to move the cursor from its current position to another position; Move-Next is most often used because normally you start at the beginning of the Recordset and move through it one row at a time; if the CursorType and CursorLocation settings support it, you can use MoveFirst and Move-Previous to move the cursor backward.
Open	Source: Optional Variant that can contain a Command object, SQL string, or stored procedure call string; can be omitted if Source property is set ActiveConnection — Optional Variant that can contain an open Connection object or a connection string; can be omitted if ActiveConnection property is set or if the Command object has an open connection	N/A	As demonstrated in the "Recordset Object" section, Open() is used to open a Recordset using a certain source with certain options; you can either set the properties you want first and call Open with the arguments omitted, or you can pass the arguments to Open, which will set the corresponding properties automatically.

Name	Arguments	Returns	Description
	CursorType: Optional Long (CursorTypeEnum) indicating desired cursor type; can be omitted if CursorType property is set LockType — Optional Long (LockTypeEnum) indicating desired locking behavior; can be omitted if LockType property is set Options — Optional Long value indicating how to treat Source argument if other than a Command object; can be any combination of values from CommandTypeEnum and ExecuteOptionEnum		
Supports	CursorOptions — Long (CursorOptionEnum) value indicating which feature/behavior you wish to test	Boolean	Because the various features and behaviors of a Recordset object may or may not be available depending on CursorType and CursorLocation, this method is helpful in determining whether a given operation is supported.
Update	Fields — Optional Variant containing a single field name or an array of field names or ordinal positions that must correspond to the fields in the Recordset .Fields collection Values — Optional Variant containing a single value or an array of values; elements must line up with Fields	N/A	Call this method after performing any edits of Field.Value or after a call to AddNew and before moving the cursor; data will not be saved until Update is called.

ADO Enumerated Constants

A note regarding enumerated constants: enumerated constants are not directly supported by VBScript. This is because they are an easy way to keep your code readable. For example, instead of setting Command.CommandType with the value of 1, you can set it to the value of adCmdText, making it a lot easier to understand what's going on in your code. However, there are two workarounds that can help you achieve that same code readability.

First, if you are writing an ASP (Active Server Pages) application, you can add this line to each of your pages that are going to include ADO code.

```
<!--#include File="adovbs.inc"-->
```

This include file is provided by Microsoft and should already be installed on your machine. This include file contains constant declarations equivalent to the ADO enumerated constants so that you can use them in your code just as if VBScript supported enumerated constants.

Second, if you are using another host, such as the Windows Script Host, you can declare named constants of your own as you need. We have used this technique with the example Windows Script Host scripts included with this appendix. Manually declaring your constants is a little tedious, but worth the trouble. Besides, you have to only declare the few that you will need in any given script. Take a look at these two equivalent lines of code and decide which one is more readable.

```
.Parameters.Append .CreateParameter("strCountry", _
    200, 4, 15, "Germany")
```

```
.Parameters.Append .CreateParameter("strCountry", _
    adVarChar, adParamInput, 15, "Germany")
```

If you're not using ASP, all that's required to achieve the improved readability of the second line is to add these two lines to your script.

```
Const adVarChar = 200
Const adParamInput = 1
```

Here are the ADO enumerated constants referred to in this ADO object reference.

Name	Values
AffectEnum	adAffectAll − 3
	adAffectAllChapters − 4
	adAffectCurrent − 1
	adAffectGroup − 2
CommandTypeEnum	adCmdUnspecified − 1
	adCmdText − 1
	adCmdTable − 2
	adCmdStoredProc − 4
	adCmdUnknown − 8 (Default)
	adCmdFile − 256
	adCmdTableDirect − 512
ConnectOptionEnum	adAsyncConnect − 16
	adConnectUnspecified − 1

Name	Values
`CursorLocationEnum`	`adUseClient – 3`
	`adUseNone – 1 (obsolete—do not use)`
	`adUseServer – 2`
`CursorOptionEnum`	`adAddNew – 16778240`
	`adApproxPosition – 16384`
	`adBookmark – 8192`
	`adDelete – 16779264adFind – 524288`
	`adHoldRecords – 256 adIndex – 1048576`
	`adMovePrevious – 512`
	`adNotify – 262144`
	`adResync – 131072`
	`adSeek – 2097152`
	`adUpdate – 16809984`
	`adUpdateBatch – 65536`
`CursorTypeEnum`	`adOpenDynamic – 2`
	`adOenForwardOnly – 0`
	`adOenKeyset – 1`
	`adOpenStatic – 3`
	`adOpenUnspecified – 1`
`DataTypeEnum`	`adArray – 8192`
	`adBigInt – 20`
	`adBinary – 128`
	`adBoolean – 11`
	`adBSTR – 8`
	`adChapter – 136`
	`adChar – 129`
	`adCurrency – 6`
	`adDate – 7adDBDate – 133`
	`adDBTime – 134`
	`adDBTimeStamp – 135`
	`adDecimal – 14`

(continued)

Name	Values
	adDouble – 5
	adEmpty – 0
	adError – 10
	adFileTime – 64
	adGUID – 72
	adInteger – 3
	adLongVarBinary – 205
	adLongVarChar – 201
	adLongVarWChar – 203
	adNumeric – 131
	adPropVariant – 138
	adSingle – 4
	adSmallInt – 2
	adTinyInt – 16
	adUnsignedBigInt – 21
	adUnsignedInt – 19
	adUnsignedSmallInt – 18
	adUnsignedTinyInt – 17adUserDefined – 132
	adVarBinary – 204adVarChar – 200
	adVarNumeric – 139
	adVarWChar – 202
	adWChar – 130
ExecuteOptionEnum	adAsyncExecute – 16
	adAsyncFetch – 32
	adAsyncFetchNonBlocking – 64
	adExecuteNoRecords – 128
	adExecuteStream – 1024
	adOptionUnspecified – 1

Name	Values
LockTypeEnum	adLockBatchOptimistic – 4
	adLockOptimistic – 3
	adLockPessimistic – 2
	adLockReadOnly – 1
	adLockUnspecified – 1
ObjectStateEnum	adStateClosed – 0
	adStateOpen – 1
	adStateConnecting – 2
	adStateExecuting – 4
	adStateFetching – 8
ParameterDirectionEnum	adParamInput – 1
	adParamInputOutput – 3
	adParamOutput – 2
	adParamReturnValue – 4
	adParamUnknown – 0

Index

E

ECMAScript, 264–265
editors
  automatic code completion, 262
  built-in event scripting support, 262
  syntax highlighting, 262
  WYSIWYG, 262
Empty subtype, 65–69
encoded scripts, Script Control, 596
End method, Response object, 552
Eqv operator, 609
Erase function, 631
erasing, arrays, 78–80
Err object, 139–140
  error handling, Internet Explorer and, 700
  On Error statement, 698–699
  methods, 694–697
  properties, 691–694
error handling, 129
  Err object, 139–140
  Script Control, 592–595
Error subtype, 71–72
errors
  client-side, Internet Explorer and, 137–138
  compilation, 130
  custom
    Err.Raise, 152–154
    generating, 154–157
  error control, 140–141
  On Error statements, 140–145
  hot spots, 143
  logging, 145–147
  logic, 135–136
  presenting, 145–147
  runtime, 131–132, 687–688
    native, 132–134
    non-VBScript, 134
    Option Explicit related, 134–135
  server-side ASP, 137
    displaying, 147–151
  syntax, 130–131, 689–690
  traps for, 143–145
  WSH (Windows Script Host), 137
Err.Raise, 152–154

event-driven programming, 24
event handlers
  adding, 266–267
  parameter passing and, 267–268
event scripting, built-in support, 262
events. *See also* class events
  cancelling, 268–269
  order, 269–273
  script components, 477
exception handling, 129. *See also* error
    handling
Exists method, Dictionary object, 195
exiting
  functions, 94–95
  procedures, 94–95
Exp function, 613

F

files
  copying, FileSystemObject library,
    200–201
  gadgets, 290
  remote scripting, 510
FileSystemObject library, 196–198
  collections, 198
  files, copying, 200–201
  folders
    copying, 201–202
    creating, 200
  objects, 198–199
  text files
    reading, 202–205
    writing to, 205–207
Fix function, 614, 658
floating-point numbers, 2
flow control, 109
  branching, 9–13, 109–110
    If branch, 110–112
    Select Case branch, 112–114
  looping
    Do, 121–127
    do . . . loop while loop, 14–16
    For Each . . . Next, 119–120
    For . . . Next, 114–118